COMPARING REGULATION IN 175 ECONOMIES

Doing Business 2007

How to reform

A copublication of the World Bank and the International Finance Corporation

This volume is a product of the staff of the World Bank Group. The findings, interpretations, and conclusions expressed in this volume do not necessarily reflect the views of the Executive Directors of The World Bank or the governments they represent. The World Bank Group does not guarantee the accuracy of the data included in this work.

Additional copies of *Doing Business 2007: How to Reform, Doing Business in 2006: Creating Jobs, Doing Business in 2005: Removing Obstacles to Growth,* and *Doing Business in 2004: Understanding Regulation* may be purchased at www.doingbusiness.org.

ISBN-10: 0-8213-6488-X
ISBN-13: 978-0-8213-6488-8
E-ISBN: 0-8213-6489-8
DOI: 10.1596/978-0-8213-6488-8
ISSN: 1729-2638

Library of Congress Cataloging-in-Publication data has been applied for.

Contents

Doing Business 2007: How to Reform is the fourth in a series of annual reports investigating the regulations that enhance business activity and those that constrain it. *Doing Business* presents quantitative indicators on business regulations and the protection of property rights that can be compared across 175 economies—from Afghanistan to Zimbabwe—and over time.

Regulations affecting 10 areas of everyday business are measured: starting a business, dealing with licenses, employing workers, registering property, getting credit, protecting investors, paying taxes, trading across borders, enforcing contracts and closing a business. The indicators are used to analyze economic outcomes and identify what reforms have worked, where and why.

The methodology has limitations. Other areas important to business—such as a country's proximity to large markets, quality of infrastructure services (other than services related to trading across borders), the security of property from theft and looting, the transparency of government procurement, macroeconomic conditions or the underlying strength of institutions—are not studied directly by *Doing Business*. To make the data comparable across countries, the indicators refer to a specific type of business—generally a limited liability company operating in the largest business city.

The methodology for 4 of the *Doing Business* topics changed in this edition. For paying taxes, the total tax rate now includes all labor contributions paid by the employer and excludes consumption taxes. For enforcing contracts, the case study was revised to reflect a typical contractual dispute over the quality of goods rather than a simple debt default. For trading across borders, *Doing Business* now reports the cost associated with exporting and importing cargo in addition to the time and number of documents required. And for employing workers, nonwage labor costs are no longer included in the calculation of the ease of employing workers. For these reasons—as well as the addition of 20 new economies—last year's rankings on the ease of doing business are recalculated using the new methodology and reported in the Overview.

Overview

In Bolivia 400,000 workers have formal jobs in the private sector—out of a population of 8.8 million. In India 30 million workers have such jobs—in a country of 1.1 billion people. In Malawi, 50,000 out of a population of 12 million. In Mozambique, 350,000 in a country of 20 million.

Reform can change this, by making it easier for formal businesses to create more jobs. Women and young workers benefit the most. Both groups account for a large share of the unemployed (figure 1.1). Reform also expands the reach of regulation by bringing businesses and workers into the formal sector. There, workers can have health insurance and pension benefits. Businesses pay some taxes. Products are subject to quality standards. And businesses can more easily obtain bank credit or use courts to resolve disputes.

FIGURE 1.1
High unemployment among youth, especially females

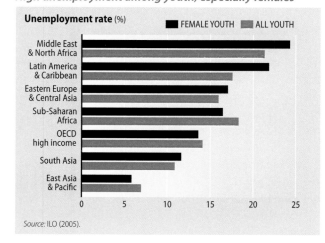

Source: ILO (2005).

Many governments are taking action. Two hundred and thirteen reforms—in 112 economies—were introduced between January 2005 and April 2006. Reformers simplified business regulations, strengthened property rights, eased tax burdens, increased access to credit and reduced the cost of exporting and importing.

Georgia is the top reformer, improving in 6 of the 10 areas studied by *Doing Business* (table 1.1). It reduced the minimum capital required to start a new business from 2,000 lari to 200 ($85). Business registrations rose by 20% between 2005 and 2006. Reforms in customs and the border police simplified border procedures. It took 54 days to meet all the administrative requirements to export in 2004—it now takes 13. Georgia also amended its procedural code for the courts, introducing specialized commercial sections of the courts and reforming the appeals process. The time to resolve simple commercial disputes fell from 375 days to 285.

Georgia's new labor regulations help workers move to better jobs. The social security contributions paid by businesses decreased from 31% of wages to 20%, making it easier for employers to hire new workers. Better collection of corporate taxes, which shot up by 300%, more than made up for the loss in revenues. And unemployment has fallen by 2 percentage points.

Romania is the runner-up, also with reforms in 6 of the 10 areas of *Doing Business*. It simplified the procedures for obtaining building permits and set up a single office to process applications. Before, entrepreneurs had to run around to 5 different agencies. The time required for obtaining construction documents fell by 49 days. To encourage businesses to hire first-time workers,

TABLE 1.1
The top 10 reformers in 2005/06

Economy	Starting a business	Dealing with licenses	Employing workers	Registering property	Getting credit	Protecting investors	Paying taxes	Trading across borders	Enforcing contracts	Closing a business
Georgia	✓	✓	✓		✓			✓	✓	
Romania		✓	✓		✓	✓		✓		✓
Mexico	✓					✓	✓			
China	✓				✓	✓		✓		
Peru	✓				✓	✓			✓	✗
France		✓			✓				✓	✓
Croatia	✓			✓					✓	
Guatemala	✓	✓		✓						
Ghana				✓			✓	✓		
Tanzania	✓			✓			✓	✓		

Note: Economies are ranked on the number and impact of reforms. First, *Doing Business* selects the economies that reformed in 3 or more of the *Doing Business* topics. Second, it ranks these economies on the increase in rank in the ease of doing business from the previous year. The larger the improvement, the higher the ranking as a reformer. "X" indicates a negative reform.
Source: Doing Business database.

Romania adopted new labor regulation allowing term contracts to extend up to 6 years. It also eased trading across borders. After-clearance audits now enable customs to quickly release cargo to importers, with the container contents verified after it reaches the warehouse. The time that traders need to satisfy all regulatory requirements was cut in half, to 14 days. And the number of export documents fell to 4, matching the EU average.

Mexico is third, with reforms in business entry, protecting investors and paying taxes. A new securities law defines for the first time the duties of company directors, combining an obligation to "take care of the business as if it were your own" with a list of activities that violate that duty. The law also increases scrutiny of related-party transactions. It requires full disclosure before any deal benefiting a company insider can take place. Other reforms cut the time to start a business in Mexico City from 58 days to 27, by allowing notaries to issue a tax registration number on the spot and streamlining company registration. And the corporate income tax rate was cut from 33% in 2004 to 30% in 2005 and 29% in 2006.

Africa is reforming

Last year and the year before, Africa lagged behind all other regions in the pace of reform. This year it ranks third, behind only Eastern Europe and Central Asia and the OECD high-income countries (figure 1.2). Two-thirds of African countries made at least one reform, and Tanzania and Ghana rank among the top 10 reformers.

In Côte d'Ivoire registering property took 397 days in 2005. Reforms eliminated a requirement to obtain the urban minister's consent to transfer property. Now it takes 32 days. Burkina Faso cut the procedures for starting a business from 12 to 8 and the time from 45 days to 34. Madagascar reduced the minimum capital for start-ups from 10 million francs to 2 million. Tanzania introduced electronic data interchange and risk-based inspections at customs. The time to clear imports fell by 12 days. Gambia, Nigeria and Tanzania reduced delays in the courts.

More improvements are under way, and these will be reflected in the *Doing Business* indicators next year. Benin, Burkina Faso, Cameroon, Gambia, Madagascar, Malawi, Mali, Mozambique, Niger, Nigeria and Zambia have all started to simplify business regulation. The easy reforms—what can be done by the stroke of a minister's pen—are coming first. Small as these initial reforms may be, they can attract investors who seek the growth opportunities that will follow. India's economic boom may have started with just such reforms in the 1980s.[1]

Several African countries are more ambitious. Mauritius set a goal of reaching the top 10 on the ease of

FIGURE 1.2
Africa ranks third in reforms

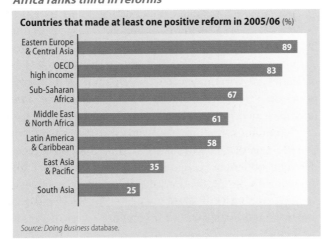

Countries that made at least one positive reform in 2005/06 (%)

Eastern Europe & Central Asia	89
OECD high income	83
Sub-Saharan Africa	67
Middle East & North Africa	61
Latin America & Caribbean	58
East Asia & Pacific	35
South Asia	25

Source: Doing Business database.

doing business by 2009. It has targeted several areas of reform: making labor regulation more flexible, reducing the burden of paying taxes and speeding business entry and property registration. One reform: starting in 2007 every business will receive a unique business registration number, and entrepreneurs will no longer have to register in person for the income tax, value added tax, customs and social security numbers. The aim is to have data move around inside the government, not to have entrepreneurs run around from one office to another.

China, Eastern Europe—fast reformers

Watch out, rest of the world: China is a top-10 reformer. The government sped business entry, increased investor protections and reduced red tape in trading across borders. China also established a credit information registry for consumer loans. Now 340 million citizens have credit histories.

Eastern Europe improved the most in the ease of doing business. The desire to join the European Union inspired reformers in Croatia and Romania. And Bulgaria and Latvia are among the runner-up reformers—economies that rank 11–15 on the list of top reformers—along with El Salvador, India and Nicaragua. Regulatory competition in the enlarged union added to the impetus for reform.

The 3 boldest reforms, driving the biggest improvements in the *Doing Business* indicators:

- Mexico's increase in investor protections, in its new securities law.
- Georgia's flexible labor rules, in its new labor code.
- Serbia's easing of exporting and importing procedures, in its new customs code.

The most popular reform in 2005/06 was easing the regulations on starting a business. Forty-three countries simplified procedures, reducing costs and delays (figure 1.3). The second most popular was reducing tax rates and the administrative hassle that businesses endure when paying taxes. It is easy to understand why these reforms top the list: elections can be won on the "more jobs, lower taxes" platform.

Several countries—including Bolivia, Eritrea, Hungary, Timor-Leste, Uzbekistan, Venezuela and Zimbabwe—went backward. Venezuela made it more difficult for businesses to register property, get credit and trade across borders. The worst reform of the year took place in Eritrea: in November 2005 the government suspended all construction licenses and prohibited any private businesses from entering the construction sector.

Singapore—where doing business is easiest

Singapore became the most business-friendly economy in the world in 2005/06, as measured by the *Doing Business* indicators (table 1.2). New Zealand is the runner-up. The United States is third.

Some countries climbed far in the rankings on the ease of doing business. Georgia ranked 112 in 2004. This year it ranks 37. Mexico jumped 19 ranks, to 43. These big changes show the gains possible when countries press on with reform every year.

But rankings on the ease of doing business do not tell the whole story. The indicator is limited in scope: it covers only business regulations. It does not account for a country's proximity to large markets, the quality of its infrastructure services (other than those related to trading across borders), the security of property from theft and looting, the transparency of government procurement, macroeconomic conditions or the underlying strength of institutions.[2] So while Namibia ranks close to Portugal on the ease of doing business, this does not mean that businesses are just as eager to operate in Windhoek as they are in Lisbon. Distance from large markets and poor infrastructure—2 issues not directly studied in *Doing Business*—make Namibia a less attractive destination for investors.

Still, a high ranking on the ease of doing business does mean that the government has created a regulatory environment conducive to operating a business. Improvements on the *Doing Business* indicators often proxy for broader reforms to laws and institutions—whose effects go beyond the administrative procedures and the time and cost to comply with business regulations.

What gets measured gets done

In 2003 the donors to the International Development Association set targets for reducing the time and cost to start a business as conditions for obtaining additional grant money. Sixteen countries reformed business entry, reducing the time by 9% on average, and the cost by 13%.[3] In 2004 the United States' Millennium Challenge Account also introduced conditions for grant eligibility based on performance in the time and cost of business start-up. Since then 13 countries have started reforms aimed at meeting the criteria. Burkina Faso, El Salvador, Georgia and Madagascar have already met them. The lesson: what gets measured gets done.

Publishing comparative data on the ease of doing business inspires governments to reform. Since its start in October 2003, the *Doing Business* project has inspired

FIGURE 1.3
213 reforms made business easier—25 made it more difficult

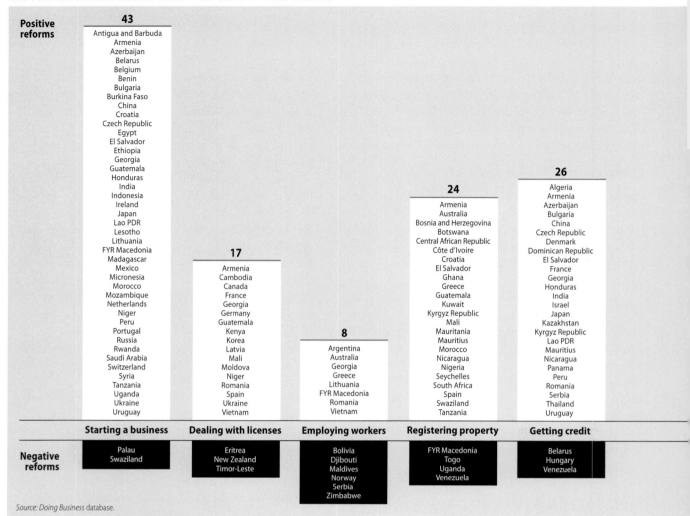

Positive reforms	Starting a business	Dealing with licenses	Employing workers	Registering property	Getting credit
	43	**17**	**8**	**24**	**26**
	Antigua and Barbuda	Armenia	Argentina	Armenia	Algeria
	Armenia	Cambodia	Australia	Australia	Armenia
	Azerbaijan	Canada	Georgia	Bosnia and Herzegovina	Azerbaijan
	Belarus	France	Greece	Botswana	Bulgaria
	Belgium	Georgia	Lithuania	Central African Republic	China
	Benin	Germany	FYR Macedonia	Côte d'Ivoire	Czech Republic
	Bulgaria	Guatemala	Romania	Croatia	Denmark
	Burkina Faso	Kenya	Vietnam	El Salvador	Dominican Republic
	China	Korea		Ghana	El Salvador
	Croatia	Latvia		Greece	France
	Czech Republic	Mali		Guatemala	Georgia
	Egypt	Moldova		Kuwait	Honduras
	El Salvador	Niger		Kyrgyz Republic	India
	Ethiopia	Romania		Mali	Israel
	Georgia	Spain		Mauritania	Japan
	Guatemala	Ukraine		Mauritius	Kazakhstan
	Honduras	Vietnam		Morocco	Kyrgyz Republic
	India			Nicaragua	Lao PDR
	Indonesia			Nigeria	Mauritius
	Ireland			Seychelles	Nicaragua
	Japan			South Africa	Panama
	Lao PDR			Spain	Peru
	Lesotho			Swaziland	Romania
	Lithuania			Tanzania	Serbia
	FYR Macedonia				Thailand
	Madagascar				Uruguay
	Mexico				
	Micronesia				
	Morocco				
	Mozambique				
	Netherlands				
	Niger				
	Peru				
	Portugal				
	Russia				
	Rwanda				
	Saudi Arabia				
	Switzerland				
	Syria				
	Tanzania				
	Uganda				
	Ukraine				
	Uruguay				

Negative reforms	Starting a business	Dealing with licenses	Employing workers	Registering property	Getting credit
	Palau	Eritrea	Bolivia	FYR Macedonia	Belarus
	Swaziland	New Zealand	Djibouti	Togo	Hungary
		Timor-Leste	Maldives	Uganda	Venezuela
			Norway	Venezuela	
			Serbia		
			Zimbabwe		

Source: Doing Business database.

or informed 48 reforms around the world. Mozambique is reforming several aspects of its business environment, with the goal of reaching the top rank on the ease of doing business in southern Africa. Burkina Faso, Mali and Niger are competing for the top rank in West Africa. Georgia has targeted the top 25 list and uses *Doing Business* indicators as benchmarks of its progress. Mauritius and Saudi Arabia have targeted the top 10.

Comparisons among states or cities within a country are even stronger drivers of reform. Recent studies across 13 cities in Brazil and 12 in Mexico have created fierce competition to build the best business environment.[4] The reason is simple: with identical federal regulations, mayors have difficulty explaining why it

takes longer or costs more to start a business or register property in their city. There are no excuses.

To be useful for reformers, indicators need to be simple, easy to replicate and linked to specific policy changes. Only then will they motivate reform and be useful in evaluating its success. Few such measures exist. But this is changing. In several countries, such as Mali and Mozambique, private businesses now participate in identifying the most needed reforms. Used to bottom lines, they bring a renewed focus on measurement. The culture of bureaucrats telling bureaucrats what's good for business is disappearing. Going with it is the aversion to measuring the results of regulatory reforms.

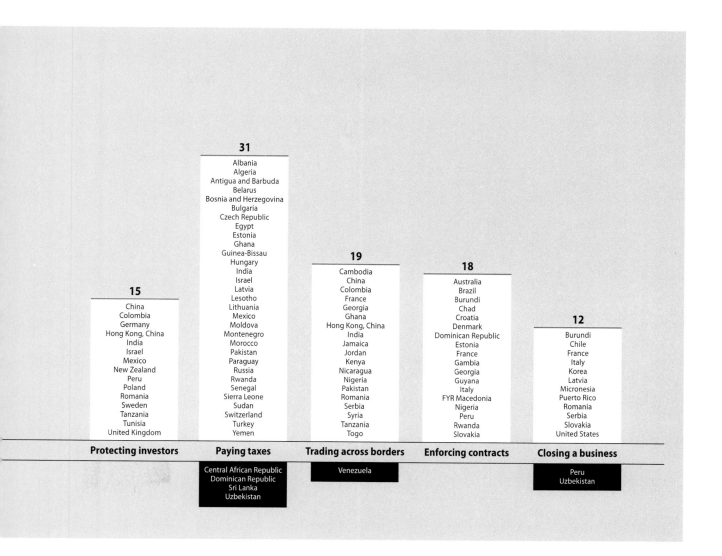

How to reform

In the top reforming economies in the past 3 years, nearly 85% of reforms took place in the first 15 months of a new government. The message: for a government recently elected (as in Benin) or reelected (as in Colombia and Mexico), the time to push through ambitious reforms is at the start of its term. In the words of one reformer: "Reform is like repairing a car with the engine running—there is no time to strategize."

When the government succeeds in these early reforms, citizens start seeing benefits—more jobs, more resources for health and education. The appetite for further reforms grows. In Georgia and Romania—the countries that have moved up fastest in the *Doing Business* rankings—reformers took on simultaneous reforms in several areas at the start of their mandate.

But few countries have the opportunity (or feel the pressure) for a reform blitz. Instead, reformers must decide which reforms to tackle first. The 4 steps to successful reform:

- Start simple and consider administrative reforms that don't need legislative changes.
- Cut unnecessary procedures, reducing the number of bureaucrats entrepreneurs interact with.
- Introduce standard application forms and publish as much regulatory information as possible.
- And remember: many of the frustrations for businesses come from how regulations are administered. The internet alleviates these frustrations without changing the spirit of the regulation.

TABLE 1.2
Rankings on the ease of doing business

2007 rank	2006 rank	Economy	2007 rank	2006 rank	Economy	2007 rank	2006 rank	Economy
1	2	Singapore	60	58	Kiribati	119	113	Iran
2	1	New Zealand	61	56	Slovenia	120	115	Albania
3	3	United States	62	57	Palau	121	122	Brazil
4	4	Canada	63	82	Kazakhstan	122	119	Suriname
5	6	Hong Kong, China	64	70	Uruguay	123	120	Ecuador
6	5	United Kingdom	65	78	Peru	124	134	Croatia
7	7	Denmark	66	60	Hungary	125	125	Cape Verde
8	9	Australia	67	72	Nicaragua	126	121	Philippines
9	8	Norway	68	95	Serbia	127	127	West Bank and Gaza
10	10	Ireland	69	61	Solomon Islands	128	132	Ukraine
11	12	Japan	70	64	Montenegro	129	124	Belarus
12	11	Iceland	71	75	El Salvador	130	135	Syria
13	14	Sweden	72	65	Dominica	131	126	Bolivia
14	13	Finland	73	63	Grenada	132	129	Gabon
15	16	Switzerland	74	66	Pakistan	133	130	Tajikistan
16	15	Lithuania	75	74	Poland	134	138	India
17	17	Estonia	76	67	Swaziland	135	131	Indonesia
18	19	Thailand	77	68	United Arab Emirates	136	133	Guyana
19	18	Puerto Rico	78	73	Jordan	137	139	Benin
20	20	Belgium	79	76	Colombia	138	143	Bhutan
21	21	Germany	80	77	Tunisia	139	136	Haiti
22	22	Netherlands	81	79	Panama	140	137	Mozambique
23	23	Korea	82	69	Italy	141	156	Côte d'Ivoire
24	31	Latvia	83	80	Kenya	142	150	Tanzania
25	25	Malaysia	84	83	Seychelles	143	142	Cambodia
26	26	Israel	85	85	St. Kitts and Nevis	144	141	Comoros
27	27	St. Lucia	86	87	Lebanon	145	140	Iraq
28	24	Chile	87	86	Marshall Islands	146	152	Senegal
29	28	South Africa	88	81	Bangladesh	147	151	Uzbekistan
30	30	Austria	89	89	Sri Lanka	148	146	Mauritania
31	29	Fiji	90	104	Kyrgyz Republic	149	148	Madagascar
32	32	Mauritius	91	84	Turkey	150	157	Equatorial Guinea
33	33	Antigua and Barbuda	92	94	FYR Macedonia	151	154	Togo
34	37	Armenia	93	108	China	152	147	Cameroon
35	47	France	94	102	Ghana	153	145	Zimbabwe
36	34	Slovakia	95	91	Bosnia and Herzegovina	154	161	Sudan
37	112	Georgia	96	97	Russia	155	166	Mali
38	35	Saudi Arabia	97	96	Ethiopia	156	155	Angola
39	38	Spain	98	101	Yemen	157	149	Guinea
40	45	Portugal	99	100	Azerbaijan	158	158	Rwanda
41	36	Samoa	100	90	Nepal	159	164	Lao PDR
42	39	Namibia	101	93	Argentina	160	170	Niger
43	62	Mexico	102	92	Zambia	161	153	Djibouti
44	42	St. Vincent and the Grenadines	103	88	Moldova	162	159	Afghanistan
45	41	Mongolia	104	98	Vietnam	163	171	Burkina Faso
46	40	Kuwait	105	99	Costa Rica	164	144	Venezuela
47	43	Taiwan, China	106	105	Micronesia	165	165	Egypt
48	44	Botswana	107	103	Uganda	166	160	Burundi
49	71	Romania	108	109	Nigeria	167	162	Central African Republic
50	48	Jamaica	109	111	Greece	168	163	Sierra Leone
51	46	Tonga	110	106	Malawi	169	167	São Tomé and Principe
52	50	Czech Republic	111	107	Honduras	170	168	Eritrea
53	49	Maldives	112	110	Paraguay	171	169	Congo, Rep.
54	59	Bulgaria	113	118	Gambia	172	172	Chad
55	52	Oman	114	116	Lesotho	173	173	Guinea-Bissau
56	51	Belize	115	117	Morocco	174	174	Timor-Leste
57	53	Papua New Guinea	116	123	Algeria	175	175	Congo, Dem. Rep.
58	54	Vanuatu	117	114	Dominican Republic			
59	55	Trinidad and Tobago	118	128	Guatemala			

Note: The rankings for all economies are benchmarked to April 2006 and reported in the Country tables. Rankings on the ease of doing business are the average of the country rankings on the 10 topics covered in Doing Business 2007. Last year's rankings are presented in italics. These are adjusted for changes in the methodology, data corrections and the addition of 20 new economies. See the Data notes for details.
Source: Doing Business database.

FIGURE 1.4
How El Salvador reformed business start-up

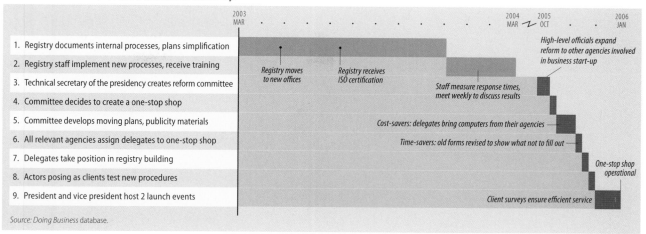

Source: Doing Business database.

El Salvador did all these things. In 2 years it reduced the time to start a business from 115 days to 26—with no changes to the law (figure 1.4). The reform started in 2003 in the company registry, which had set the goal of becoming the first registry in Latin America to earn an ISO certification. The staff developed time-and-motion studies of all transactions and cut unnecessary steps. Customer surveys ensured timely feedback. In 18 months start-up time dropped to 40 days, and the share of satisfied customers rose from 32% to 87%. In a second round of reforms staff from the Ministries of Finance and Labor and the social security institute were transferred to the company registry. Entrepreneurs can now register with all 4 agencies in a single visit.

Pakistan followed a similar track. It introduced a new customs clearance process that allows importers to file cargo declarations before goods arrive at the port. Now it takes 19 days to import goods—from the conclusion of a sales contract to the arrival of the goods at the warehouse. In 2004 it took 39 days. Jamaica introduced software that detects whether a cargo document is incomplete and calculates the customs duties to be paid. In Ghana new technology links customs with several commercial banks so that customs officers can confirm the payment of duties without any additional paperwork.

New technologies can also simplify interactions between entrepreneurs and the tax authority. Madagascar computerized tax declarations in October 2005. Now if there is no change in information submitted previously, a business can file the same declaration again—with the click of a button. The benefit: the time to comply with tax regulations fell by 17 days. Croatia simplified its tax forms, cutting out 8 pages of tax returns in the process. The time to comply with tax regulations fell by 5 days.

Make it easier for all businesses

Whatever reformers do, they should always ask the question, "Who will benefit the most?" If reforms are seen to benefit only foreign investors, or large investors, or bureaucrats-turned-investors, they reduce the legitimacy of the government. Reforms should ease the burden on all businesses: small and large, domestic and foreign, rural and urban. This way there is no need to guess where the next boom in jobs will come from. Any business will have the opportunity to thrive—whether it's making movies in Lagos, writing software programs in Bangalore or transcribing doctors' notes in Belize City.

Notes

1. Rodrik and Subramanian (2005).
2. Next year's *Doing Business* will expand the scope of indicators to cover the quality of business infrastructure and possibly transparency in government procurement.
3. These targets were replaced with soft targets in the following round of grants. An opportunity to inspire further reforms was missed.
4. FIAS (2006a, 2006b).

Starting a business

Portugal was the top reformer in business entry in 2005/06. While a year ago starting up took 54 days, today a business can begin operating in 8. "I spent weeks going from one bureaucrat to another, begging for a stamp here and a signature there. Just to get the company name approved took 15 days. And then there was the notary, the company registry, tax agency, social security and others," recalls José, an entrepreneur in Lisbon. No longer.

Forty-three countries made it easier to start a business in the past year. More reforms took place in Africa than ever before. Ten African countries reformed, led by Burkina Faso and Madagascar. In contrast, in 2004 only Côte d'Ivoire and Nigeria made entry easier. The upswing is sorely needed—6 of the 10 most difficult places to start a business are in Africa (table 2.1).

The recent pick-up in reform shows that what gets measured gets done. The United States' Millennium Challenge Account sets explicit targets on the time and cost to start a business: to qualify for its grants, countries must do better on both measures than the median eligible country. Reforms in Burkina Faso, El Salvador, Georgia and Madagascar all met the targets.

Reforms also broke some long-standing taboos. Seven countries (China, Georgia, Japan, Lao PDR, Madagascar, Micronesia and Morocco) reduced or eliminated the minimum capital requirement—more than in the previous 5 years combined. Other countries still justify capital requirements as protecting creditors. But this makes little sense. For capital requirements to reduce the risks for creditors, shouldn't they differ by a company's size and industry? And with capital requirements as high as $58,422

in Syria and $124,464 in Saudi Arabia, few entrepreneurs can afford to register. Many turn to informality.

If it is easy to set up a business, more businesses register. Five times as many businesses register annually in El Salvador since its reforms. New entry jumped by 78% after reforms in FYR Macedonia, 55% in Georgia, 25% in Lithuania and 16% in Uganda.

Enticing enterprises into the formal economy has 2 benefits. First, formally registered businesses grow larger. In a recent study on informality in São Paulo entrepreneurs said they could double operations after registering.[1] The reason? They would be able to supply larger customers and export directly. And they would have no fear of harassment by government inspectors or the police—and no need to pay them bribes. Second, formally registered enterprises pay taxes, adding to government revenues.[2]

TABLE 2.1
Where is it easy to start a business—and where not?

Easiest	Rank	Most difficult	Rank
Canada	1	Tajikistan	166
Australia	2	Haiti	167
New Zealand	3	Eritrea	168
United States	4	Togo	169
Hong Kong, China	5	Angola	170
Ireland	6	Yemen	171
Romania	7	Congo, Dem. Rep.	172
Puerto Rico	8	West Bank and Gaza	173
United Kingdom	9	Chad	174
Jamaica	10	Guinea-Bissau	175

Note: Rankings are the average of the country rankings on the procedures, time, cost and paid-up minimum capital for starting a business. See the Data notes for details.
Source: Doing Business database.

Who is reforming?

In Portugal, now one of the fastest economies for start-up (table 2.2), an entrepreneur using the new fast-track service simply chooses a preapproved name from the registry's website, then goes to the one-stop shop to register the company. The registry deals with tax, social security and labor registration and publishes the incorporation notice on the Ministry of Justice website. Standard articles of association make the application fast and error-free—with no need for a notary. More and more businesses are taking advantage of the new service. Within a year the number of companies using it rose from 12 a day to 75.

Reforms picked up more in Africa than in any other region in 2005/06. Madagascar reduced the minimum capital requirement by 80% and sped registration by relocating a legal clerk to the one-stop shop. The improvements placed Madagascar among the top 10 reformers (figure 2.1). Burkina Faso combined the professional license, company, tax and social security registrations at a single access point—cutting the time to start a business by a fourth. Ethiopia and Uganda sped company registration. Benin and Niger lifted the requirement for entrepreneurs to prepay taxes before starting operations. Mozambique and Tanzania simplified their business licensing regimes. Nigeria now allows entrepreneurs to verify the availability of company names online. Lesotho cut time by introducing a single form for value added and income tax registration. And Rwanda scrapped a law, originally adopted by King Leopold of Belgium during colonial times, that allowed only 1 notary in the entire country. Now 33 notaries are working throughout the country, reducing start-up delays.

FIGURE 2.1
Top 10 reformers in business start-up

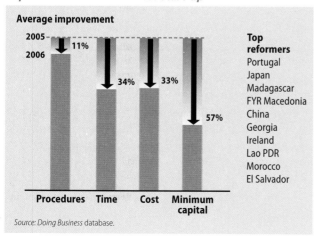

Source: Doing Business database.

TABLE 2.2
Who regulates business start-up the most—and who the least?

Procedures (number)

Fewest		Most	
Australia	2	Azerbaijan	15
Canada	2	Bolivia	15
New Zealand	2	Belarus	16
Afghanistan	3	Venezuela	16
Denmark	3	Brazil	17
Finland	3	Guinea-Bissau	17
Sweden	3	Paraguay	17
Belgium	4	Uganda	17
Ireland	4	Chad	19
Norway	4	Equatorial Guinea	20

Time (days)

Least		Most	
Australia	2	Angola	124
Canada	3	Equatorial Guinea	136
Denmark	5	Venezuela	141
Iceland	5	São Tomé and Principe	144
United States	5	Brazil	152
Singapore	6	Congo, Dem. Rep.	155
Puerto Rico	7	Lao PDR	163
France	8	Haiti	203
Jamaica	8	Guinea-Bissau	233
Portugal	8	Suriname	694

Cost (% of income per capita)

Least		Most	
Denmark	0.0	Yemen	228.0
New Zealand	0.2	Cambodia	236.4
Ireland	0.3	Togo	252.7
United States	0.7	Guinea-Bissau	261.2
Sweden	0.7	Gambia	292.1
United Kingdom	0.7	West Bank and Gaza	324.7
Puerto Rico	0.8	Niger	416.8
Singapore	0.8	Congo, Dem. Rep.	481.1
Canada	0.9	Angola	486.7
Finland	1.1	Sierra Leone	1,194.5

Paid-in minimum capital

Most	% of income per capita	US$
Timor-Leste	667	5,000
Egypt	695	8,683
Niger	778	1,867
Jordan	864	21,610
Guinea-Bissau	1,029	1,852
Saudi Arabia	1,057	124,464
Ethiopia	1,084	1,734
West Bank and Gaza	1,890	18,008
Yemen	2,566	15,394
Syria	4,233	58,422

Note: Sixty-four countries have no minimum capital requirement.
Source: Doing Business database.

FIGURE 2.2
Big improvements in China and India

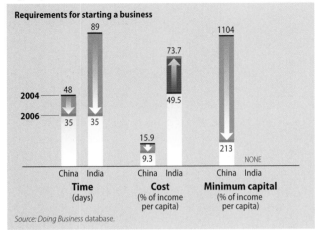

Source: Doing Business database.

TABLE 2.3
Single access points—a popular reform in 2005/06

Created single access point
Burkina Faso, Croatia, El Salvador, Guatemala, Lithuania, FYR Macedonia, Portugal, Ukraine

Simplified tax registration
Armenia, Benin, Bulgaria, India, Lesotho, Lithuania, Tanzania, Uruguay

Abolished or reduced minimum capital requirement
China, Georgia, Japan, Lao PDR, Madagascar, Micronesia, Morocco

Sped registration through institutional reforms
Belarus, Ethiopia, Honduras, Mexico, Russia, Rwanda, Saudi Arabia

Cut stamp duty or capital tax
Belgium, Ireland, Netherlands, Switzerland, Syria

Simplified document requirements at registry
Azerbaijan, Egypt, Indonesia, Lao PDR, Niger

Streamlined licensing procedures
Mozambique, Peru, Tanzania

Made registration administrative
Antigua and Barbuda, Czech Republic, FYR Macedonia, Uganda

Source: Doing Business database.

China and India both cut business start-up to 35 days (figure 2.2). India simplified a complex tax registration system, more than halving start-up time. China amended its company law, reducing the minimum capital requirement by 70% and eliminating substantive review at the registry. Elsewhere in East Asia, Indonesia continued to speed the approval process at the Ministry of Justice, cutting weeks from the time for start-up.

Countries in Europe focused on cutting costs or simplifying registration. Ireland and the Netherlands abolished capital taxes. Switzerland eliminated stamp duties for the first €1,000,000 of start-up capital. Belgium halved start-up cost by abolishing the registration fee—and also piloted online registration. Georgia reduced its minimum capital requirement by 90%. FYR Macedonia, another top 10 reformer, made registration administrative rather than judicial and combined company, tax and social security registration. Time dropped from 48 days to 18. Ukraine introduced a one-stop shop for new business registration. Lithuania created a virtual one (table 2.3).

El Salvador led the reforms in Latin America for the second year in a row. It reduced the number of procedures from 12 to 10, the time from 40 days to 26. Honduras cut 18 days from the process by delegating company registration to private chambers of commerce. Guatemala linked commercial, tax and social security registration. Mexico allows entrepreneurs to obtain the tax registration number through the notary at the time of incorporation—saving 3 weeks. The municipality of Lima, in Peru, now grants a municipal license in a week rather than a month. Uruguay merged tax and social security registration.

Four reforms took place in the Middle East and North Africa. Morocco lowered the minimum capital requirement to 67% of income per capita. Syria reduced the stamp duty from 1.5% of start-up capital to 0.5%. Egypt cut cost by 30% by lowering registration fees and publishing the incorporation notice at the registry rather than in the government gazette. Saudi Arabia simplified procedures at the Ministry of Commerce and cut time from 64 days to 39.

How to reform

For a government that has just come to power on a reform platform, here's how to start: change the company law. Eliminate the minimum capital requirement, make business registration administrative rather than judicial and allow registration notices to be published online or at the registry.

Business start-up takes 20 days more on average where judges have to approve the applications. Serbia and Uganda avoided these delays by creating a new ad-ministrative registry. Bulgaria did the same in April 2006, despite fierce opposition from the judiciary. Honduras and Italy transferred registration from judges to private chambers of commerce. Bosnia and Herzegovina, the Czech Republic, Romania and Slovakia left registration in the courts but shifted responsibility for it from judges to legal clerks.

Here is how Serbia did it. The government decided that radical reform was better than wrestling with the existing system. The reform took nearly 2 years to complete, starting in January 2003 with a seminar on business registration in countries of the European Union (figure 2.3). It faced fierce opposition from the judiciary, an 8-month hiatus after the assassination of Prime Minister Zoran Djindjic and technical difficulties just before the new administrative registry opened. But it succeeded.

In May 2004 parliament passed a law to create the new registry. Registration was simplified, and agencies linked through a central electronic database. The registry no longer has the authority to check the authenticity of data or to refuse registration if the application is complete. A "silence is consent" rule ensures automatic registration within 5 days.

As soon as the law came into force, the focus shifted to training and publicity. The registry's director, named in July 2004, became the spokesperson in the publicity campaign. By January 2005, when the registry opened, everyone knew about it. New registrations increased by 43% in the first year.

Slovakia took a different approach, reforming in steps. In October 2003—in time for its entry into the European Union the following year—Slovakia passed the Act on the Commercial Register, transferring registration from judges to court clerks. Standard documents and clear filing procedures replaced substantive review by judges. And Slovakia did not stop there. In July 2004 it cut the statutory time limit for issuing a trade license from 15 days to 7. In October 2004 it amended the commercial code to clarify grounds for rejecting registration applications. And in January 2005, by amending its tax administration and value added tax acts, it simplified tax registration. Three years after the commercial register act was adopted, opening a business takes 25 days rather than 103.

Reformers who want to start simple could consider administrative reforms first: cut unnecessary procedures, create a one-stop shop for business registration, introduce standard application forms and a single business identification number and move any tax payments to after the business has started operations.

Portugal followed this track and reformed in 5 months. As soon as the new government came into power in March 2005, it formed a working group in the Ministry of Justice. The aim was to reduce the number of approvals and government visits in business start-up as much as possible. A new law was drafted in 3 months and approved by the government on June 30, 2005. No parliamentary approval was needed because the law concerned only company matters, not the courts. A week later the law was signed by the president and published in the gazette. On July 13 it became effective. The registry's software was upgraded while the law was being drafted. And because the system is now simpler, staff needed little training. By August the fast-track system was operational. The cost of the reform was $350,000.

Creating one-stop shops for company registration was the most popular reform in 2005/06. Eight countries—Burkina Faso, Croatia, El Salvador, Guatemala, Lithuania, FYR Macedonia, Portugal and Ukraine—combined company, tax and social security registration in one building. Another 15 had created one-stop shops between 2003 and 2005.

But one-stop shops are not enough. Many other procedures may be required before a business can legally operate—such as obtaining documents and having them notarized, depositing initial capital or registering for social security. Even in Portugal an entrepreneur needs to complete 5 procedures on top of visiting the one-stop shop. In Burkina Faso it is 7, in FYR Macedonia 9. One-

FIGURE 2.3

How Serbia reformed company registration

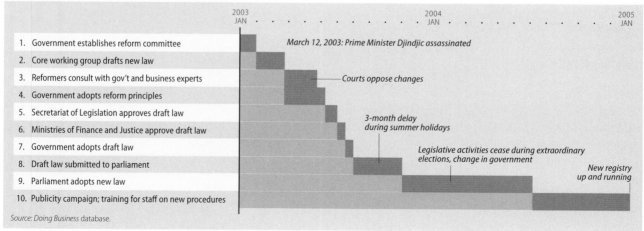

Source: Doing Business database.

FIGURE 2.4
Easier start-up—more new firms, less corruption

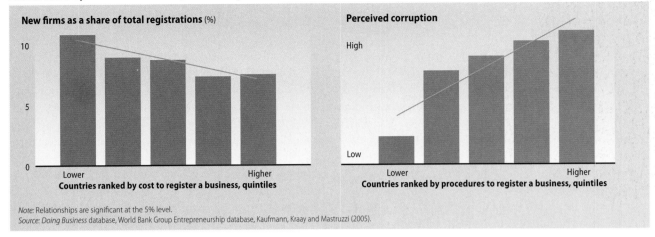

Note: Relationships are significant at the 5% level.
Source: Doing Business database, World Bank Group Entrepreneurship database, Kaufmann, Kraay and Mastruzzi (2005).

stop shops work best when other start-up procedures are cut or simplified.

El Salvador cut the time to start a business—with no changes to the law. The reform started in 2003 in the company registry with a single goal: to become the first registry in Latin America to earn an ISO certification. The staff developed time-and-motion studies of all transactions and cut unnecessary steps. Customer surveys ensured timely feedback. In 18 months start-up time dropped to 40 days and the share of satisfied customers rose to 87%.

But reformers went even further, transferring staff from the Ministries of Finance and Labor and the social security institute to the company registry. Entrepreneurs now register with all 4 agencies in a single visit and can open their business in 26 days—down from 115 before the reform.

Whatever reforms are made, reformers should ad-vertise the changes and monitor their effect on new registrations. Most reformers are bad marketers. So, few entrepreneurs know how much easier registration has become. El Salvador first established a one-stop shop in 1999, but local entrepreneurs thought it was only for foreigners. A lesson was learned. The second time around reformers staged 2 "ribbon cutting" events with President Antonio Saca and Vice President Ana Escobar. The media coverage ensured that everyone knew about the new system when it opened in January 2006.

Finally, reformers best stick to one principle—simplify. Cumbersome entry procedures mean more hassle for entrepreneurs and more corruption, particularly in developing countries (figure 2.4).[3] Each procedure is a point of contact—an opportunity to extract a bribe. The cost of such systems is the forgone jobs that new firms would have created.[4]

Notes

1. Bertrand and others (2006).
2. Djankov and others (2002).
3. Svensson (2005).
4. Klapper (2006).

Dealing with licenses

Inspecting the quality of construction is necessary to protect those who will live or work in a building. Governments have been concerned with such protection for centuries. Records of Socrates' house, built in the 4th century BC, show the inspection requirements of his day: "The builder shall set the joints against each other, fitting, and before inserting the dowels he shall show the architect all the stones to be fitting, and shall set them true and sound and dowel them with iron dowels, two dowels to each stone…"[1]

There is a tradeoff between the safety that licenses create and their cost—both to entrepreneurs and to the government. In 70 countries obtaining a construction permit takes longer than the actual construction. Many of these are in Africa, which accounts for 5 of the 10 countries where it is most difficult to build legally (table 3.1).

Where procedures are complicated and the time and cost to get licenses are great, few formal projects get

started. Consider the daunting task of obtaining a construction permit in Mozambique, where building regulations date to the 1880s: it takes 13 procedures involving 9 agencies and 5 separate inspections.

Doing Business looks at licensing in the construction industry, since it is among the largest sectors in every economy and there is a clear rationale for regulating it. But the same problems occur in other sectors too. In Kenya the government is evaluating licenses in all business sectors. In 2005 it initiated a review of 1,347 business licenses and permit requirements. So far, 118 licenses are proposed for elimination. By the end of 2007 another 700 are to be simplified and 320 abolished. Problems remain. Some ministries did not submit lists of all the licenses they regulate and the related fees. And the new business regulation bill is awaiting parliamentary approval.

Persistence will pay off. Consider what a study of permits in France suggests about the potential gains from reducing burdensome licensing regulation.[2] In 1974 the Ministry of Industry issued a regulation to protect small shopkeepers against competition from chain stores. Zoning permits were issued at the discretion of municipal councils. Few such permits were given. Had this regulation not been introduced, employment in the formal retail sector could be 10% higher today.

Besides creating more jobs, cutting red tape can provide the resources to improve public services. Sweden spends 8% of its budget on regulating business, the United Kingdom 10% and the Netherlands 11%. Cutting red tape by 15% would free resources equal to around half the public health budget in these countries.[3] It would also reduce the costs to businesses of complying with regulation.

TABLE 3.1
Where is building a warehouse easy—and where not?

Easiest	Rank	Most difficult	Rank
St. Vincent and the Grenadines	1	Guatemala	165
Japan	2	Guinea	166
Thailand	3	Iran	167
Belize	4	Burkina Faso	168
Marshall Islands	5	Egypt	169
Denmark	6	Croatia	170
St. Kitts and Nevis	7	Zimbabwe	171
Singapore	8	Tanzania	172
Maldives	9	Eritrea	173
St. Lucia	10	Timor-Leste	174

Note: Rankings are the average of the country rankings on the procedures, time and cost to build a warehouse. One country (Afghanistan) is missing data. See the Data notes for details.
Source: Doing Business database.

Who is reforming?

In 2005/06, 17 countries made it easier to comply with building requirements or simplified their business licensing regimes. Most reforms took place in rich countries—in Canada, France, Germany, Korea and Spain—and in Eastern Europe and Central Asia—in Armenia, Georgia, Latvia, Moldova, Romania and Ukraine.

Georgia made the most extensive reforms, ranking as the top reformer for the second year in a row. Building permits are now issued at a single office, which consolidates approvals of construction projects by the Ministry of Culture, the Ministry of Environment and the water, electricity and telecommunications authorities. Shorter time limits were imposed for issuing permits. Several procedures were abolished, including approval from the sanitary inspector before construction starts and permission from the archaeology bureau. As a result the number of procedures to fulfill all requirements to construct a warehouse fell from 29 to 17, and the time from 285 days to 137 (figure 3.1). It is now as easy to comply with building regulations in Tbilisi as it is in Hong Kong (China).

One of the most popular reforms in 2005/06 was to introduce statutory time limits for issuing licenses (table 3.2). This makes it easier for builders to plan their projects—hiring workers, contracting with suppliers, arranging for credit lines with a bank. And it puts pressure on bureaucrats to be efficient. In Canada, for example, the province of Ontario revised its building code to mandate a 15-day limit for the review of building permits. The time to complete all the paperwork for building a warehouse fell from 87 days to 77.

Cambodia also introduced deadlines, imposing a 30-day limit for issuing construction permits for smaller projects and a 45-day limit for larger ones. The building design still needs approval from 5 separate agencies: the municipal, district governor, local land management, urban planning and construction offices. The old rules allowed these departments up to 60 days to issue approvals. The new regulation cuts this to 14 days.

Nine countries reduced the number of licenses. In Germany simpler construction no longer requires a permit. Instead, the builder only notifies the municipality when construction starts. Inspectors show up at the site once the project has begun. Time to comply with licensing and permit requirements fell from 165 days to 133. In France the number of licenses required for construction projects was reduced from 11 to 3. And a month of delay was cut by requiring the building inspectorate to visit and issue a declaration of work completion within 3 months. Elsewhere in Europe, Spain no longer requires an installation license on top of the building license, cutting 1 procedure. It also adopted a "silence is consent" rule, setting the maximum time for approval at 90 days.

Countries in Eastern Europe and Central Asia also simplified the permitting process. Romania cut the number of forms required for building permits and simplified the filing of technical documents. It also set up a single office for processing applications for building permits. The time required to obtain permits fell by 49 days. Armenia simplified approval procedures. Before, builders needed approvals from both the mayor and the municipality to start construction. Now they need only a permit from the mayor. The process can be completed within 112 days, more than 2 months faster than in 2005. Costs dropped by 15%, from $730 to $633.

Mali, where costs are among the highest in the world

FIGURE 3.1
Big improvements in Georgia

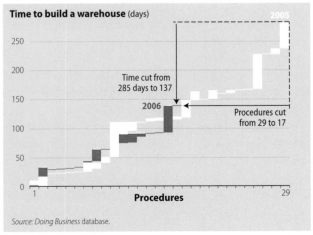

Source: *Doing Business* database.

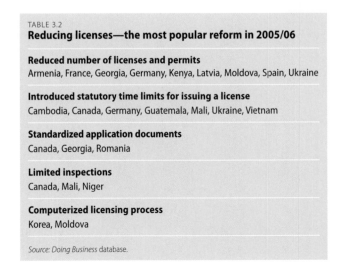

TABLE 3.2
Reducing licenses—the most popular reform in 2005/06

Reduced number of licenses and permits
Armenia, France, Georgia, Germany, Kenya, Latvia, Moldova, Spain, Ukraine

Introduced statutory time limits for issuing a license
Cambodia, Canada, Germany, Guatemala, Mali, Ukraine, Vietnam

Standardized application documents
Canada, Georgia, Romania

Limited inspections
Canada, Mali, Niger

Computerized licensing process
Korea, Moldova

Source: *Doing Business* database.

TABLE 3.3
Who regulates licensing the least—and who the most?

Procedures (number)

Fewest		Most	
Denmark	7	China	29
New Zealand	7	Guinea	29
Vanuatu	7	Egypt	30
Grenada	8	Czech Republic	31
Sweden	8	Burkina Faso	32
Marshall Islands	9	Kazakhstan	32
St. Lucia	9	Taiwan, China	32
Thailand	9	Turkey	32
France	10	Moldova	34
Ireland	10	Sierra Leone	48

Time (days)

Least		Most	
Korea	52	Nepal	424
Finland	56	Suriname	431
Belize	66	Cameroon	444
United States	69	Brazil	460
Denmark	70	Nigeria	465
St. Kitts and Nevis	72	Bosnia and Herzegovina	467
Micronesia	73	Zimbabwe	481
Solomon Islands	74	Russia	531
St. Vincent and the Grenadines	74	Côte d'Ivoire	569
Canada	77	Iran	668

Cost (% of income per capita)

Least		Most	
Palau	6.8	Zambia	1,766
Trinidad and Tobago	9.9	Mali	1,813
St. Vincent and the Grenadines	10.6	Serbia	1,947
Thailand	11.1	Congo, Dem. Rep.	2,282
Mauritius	13.7	Bosnia and Herzegovina	2,423
Australia	13.8	Guinea-Bissau	2,665
Czech Republic	14.5	Niger	2,987
St. Kitts and Nevis	15.2	Tanzania	3,797
Iceland	15.7	Montenegro	5,869
United States	16.0	Burundi	8,808

Source: Doing Business database.

FIGURE 3.2
Longest delays in South Asia

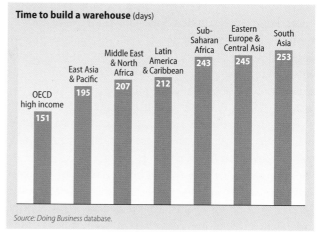

Source: Doing Business database.

(table 3.3), was the main African reformer in construction licensing. A new decree capped the time for issuing building permits to 20 days from the application. Inspections now take place after construction is complete. Previously, 2 separate "certificates of compliance" were required for inspection and fire safety before construction had even started. The reforms cut delays by 41 days.

No reforms took place in South Asia, the region with the longest delays (figure 3.2). And in 2 countries, Timor-Leste and Eritrea, construction licenses are no longer issued. Since January 2006 the government of Timor-Leste has refused to grant any new licenses for construction firms. The reason given: too many businesses already operate in the construction sector. In September 2005 the Eritrean government imposed price and profit controls on construction businesses, because "most of the houses that have been built during the past few years have inflated prices based on speculation."[4] Soon after, the Department of Infrastructural Services suspended all construction licenses and prohibited any private businesses from entering the construction sector. The decree was signed "Victory for the masses."

How to reform

It is easier to create new regulations than to remove old ones. Most countries, particularly developing ones, have amassed too many license and permit requirements. Many of them are contradictory. Some are pointless. For example, why does Kenya require permits to purchase onion seeds or licenses to rent out bicycles? Even for a simple commercial or industrial business, 72 countries always require a business license on top of regular company registration (figure 3.3).

Countries may do well to review all their business licensing regulations every decade, to discard obsolete ones and simplify others. Australia has the best such system in place. Another approach, pioneered in Sweden in the 1980s, is to conduct a one-time review of all licenses. The default action: eliminate a license unless it can be justified before a set deadline. Last year Moldova reviewed 1,130 ministerial decrees, amending about 400 and eliminating another 150. Ukraine reviewed almost 1,000 licenses and eliminated half. Georgia cut licenses from 909 to 144 (figure 3.4).

Reducing licensing requirements demands action by many ministries. Here are 2 ways to make this happen. First, make an agency with direct authority over all ministries responsible for the reform. The best choice is the ministry of finance or the prime minister's office, since ministries respond best when their budgets depend on it. Second, commit to a target reduction in the administrative costs of issuing and regulating licenses, and set up a measuring system to ensure that it is achieved. This captures the attention of businesses and bureaucrats alike and holds regulators accountable.

The Netherlands, with the best such reform yet, did both. The government set a target to reduce the administrative burden 25% by the end of 2006. The minister of finance is responsible for achieving the target and reports to parliament every 6 months. Uncooperative ministries may see their budget cut. An independent agency, the Advisory Board on Administrative Burden (ACTAL), was established to monitor progress and publicize its findings. The estimated savings from streamlining tax requirements alone are $600 million. ACTAL also vets new regulatory proposals before they reach parliament—to stop creeping reregulation, a common problem.[5]

Whatever reformers do, they should involve the private sector. Businesses know which licensing regimes are most onerous, with the biggest costs and bureaucratic hassle. These would be a good place to start.

To ease the work of construction businesses, reformers can introduce "silence is consent" rules for issuing building licenses. Once the deadline for reviewing a license application has passed, the business can automatically start operations. Spain introduced a silent consent rule for construction licenses in 2005. And 7 of the top 10 countries on the ease of licensing have such rules.

Another reform that can smooth the licensing of construction projects: adjusting licenses and inspections to the size and nature of the project. Smaller projects could receive less scrutiny, lowering compliance costs and allowing regulators to focus their energy on more complex projects. Korea and Lao PDR implemented such reforms in 2006. Korea exempted small construction projects from the requirement to apply for an advance building permit. Lao PDR transferred the authority for issuing building permits for small projects to district construction management offices.

FIGURE 3.3
Unnecessary licensing requirements in poor countries

Source: Doing Business database.

FIGURE 3.4
Big cuts in licensing requirements

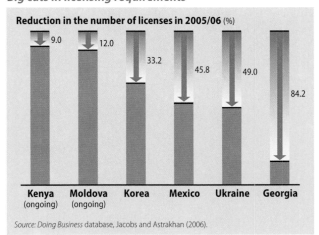

Source: Doing Business database, Jacobs and Astrakhan (2006).

For governments that want to reduce corruption in construction licensing and inspections, here are several tips. First, allow for some rotation of inspectors so that businesses don't get cozy with a regular visitor to their premises. Second, require annual disclosure of income and assets for all employees of the inspectorate. Inspectors whose finances reveal unofficial sources of income can be charged with fraud. Third, set up a hotline to hear complaints about the work of the inspectorate. Follow up on the complaints and report back, including on any actions taken. Cambodia set up such a service in 2006. Finally, have the national inspectorate conduct random checks of the work of local inspectors. This would provide more incentive to work by the rules.

There is one hitch: what if the managers of the licensing agency and the inspectorate are also corrupt? In this case penalties for taking bribes need to come from the top of the government. One recent success occurred in Georgia in 2004: perceptions of corruption in the road police fell drastically after the new government fired the entire management team and all the heads of local units and instituted examinations for new police.

Something that does not work: increasing inspectors' salaries in the hope that this will curb bribe taking. In OECD countries inspectors receive between 125% and 150% of the average manufacturing wage. This ratio can be taken as a guide in developing countries too. If salaries are lower, inspectors and licensing officials may not have enough to provide for their families. Taking bribes would come naturally. But paying more than 150% of the average manufacturing wage is unlikely to reduce bribes. Businesses that knowingly disregard safety rules can offer bribes that far exceed an official's salary.

This is the case in rich countries too. In the United States the average salary of inspectors at the Occupational Safety and Health Administration is $60,000. Surely a business could cover up shoddy construction by paying a bribe larger than that. Sometimes this does happen—but rarely. What businesses fear are criminal investigations and prison time. Hotlines, random checks and disclosure of financial information are ways to keep this fear high and prevent bad behavior.

Notes

1. Emporia, Department of Inspections (2006).
2. Bertrand and Kramarz (2002).
3. Data for Sweden are from NNR (2005); those for the United Kingdom, from British Chambers of Commerce (2005); and those for the Netherlands, from the Danish Commerce and Companies Agency.
4. Eritrea, Department of Infrastructural Services (2005).
5. Ladegaard (2005).

Employing workers

In Venezuela workers fear promotion. A recent law prohibits businesses from firing anyone who earns less than 1.5 times the minimum wage. Creative employers have found a way around this—they promote workers, give them higher wages and then fire them.

But many small businesses cannot afford this tactic. Ignacia runs a dairy business in Caracas with 20 workers. A shift in demand toward organic products means that she needs only 15. "If I could release 5 workers now, within a year I could purchase new machines and start selling organic food. Then I could expand to serve other customers and hire a dozen new workers. But the current law doesn't allow any of this. I am not hiring anyone." Unemployment in the country is rising.

Bolivia is among the countries with the most rigid labor regulations. Yet in 2006 it made hiring and firing even more difficult. A new decree requires employers to get the permission of workers before firing them. No workers are being fired as a result, but few new workers are hired either.

FIGURE 4.1
Rigid employment regulation, more informality

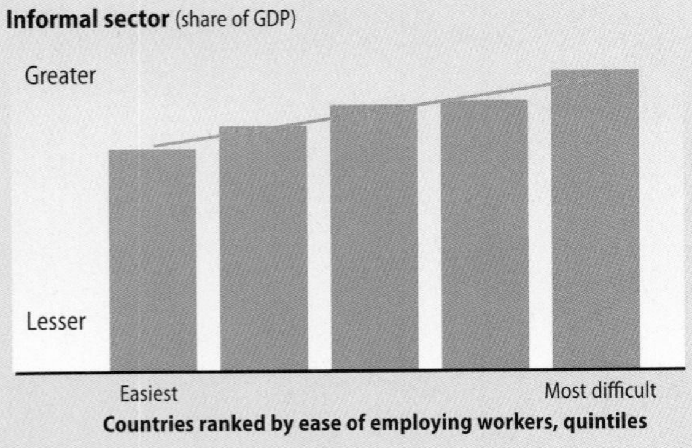

Note: Relationships are significant at the 1% level and remain significant when controlling for income per capita.
Source: Doing Business database, Schneider and Klinglmair (2004).

Employment regulations are designed to protect workers from arbitrary, unfair or discriminatory actions by their employers. These regulations—from mandatory minimum wage, to premiums for overtime work, to grounds for dismissal, to severance pay—have been introduced to remedy apparent market failures. In addition, the International Labour Organization has established a set of fundamental principles and rights at work, including the freedom of association, the right to collective bargaining, the elimination of forced labor, the abolition of child labor and the elimination of discrimination in hiring and work practices.

Beyond these regulations and principles, governments struggle to reach the right balance between labor market flexibility and job stability. Most developing countries err on the side of excessive rigidity, to the detriment of businesses and workers alike. But businesses find ways around rigid employment regulations. The less flexible the regulations, the more businesses hire workers informally, pay them lower wages and avoid providing health insurance and social benefits (figure 4.1).[1] Those whom employment regulation is supposed to protect are hurt the most. Women are 3 times as likely as men to be hired informally. And where parents fail to find decent employment, children often turn up in the workplace.

Who is reforming?

Eight countries made their labor laws more flexible in 2005/06. Eastern Europe and Central Asia reformed the most—4 countries enacted new labor codes and a fifth introduced amendments to the current law.

With unemployment around 15% and many jobs in the informal sector, Georgia undertook the most far-reaching reform of labor regulation. A new law eases restrictions on the duration of term contracts and the number of overtime hours and discards the premium required for overtime work. It also eliminates the requirement to notify and get permission from the labor union to fire a redundant worker. The new law provides for 1 month's severance pay, replacing complex rules under which required notice periods depended on seniority and the manager had to write long explanations to labor unions and the Ministry of Labor. Together, these changes brought Georgia into the top 10 economies on the ease of employing workers (table 4.1).

FYR Macedonia followed a similar path. A new labor code extends the maximum duration of term contracts from 36 months to 48 and reduces both the notice period and the severance pay for dismissal due to economic downturns. The law also allows businesses to use 150 hours of overtime in a year, at normal wages. And it scraps earlier regulations offering numerous perks to trade union leaders, including longer vacations and guaranteed wages during strikes.

Other Eastern European and Central Asian countries also made regulations more flexible. Romania permitted term contracts to extend up to 6 years. Lithuania increased the number of overtime hours

allowed in a year. The Kyrgyz Republic shortened notice periods. Armenia eliminated the priority rules for dismissal and reduced severance payments. But it also restricted term contracts to fixed term tasks, reducing the flexibility of hiring.

Labor laws in rich economies, already among the most flexible, continue to evolve (table 4.2). In 2005 Australia eliminated restrictions on night and weekend work and strengthened workers' ability to negotiate their own wages with employers. The Australian Industrial Relations Commission lost its wage setting powers. Greece loosened restrictions on overtime. Introduced 5

TABLE 4.1
Where is it easy to employ workers—and where not?

Easiest	Rank	Most difficult	Rank
Marshall Islands	1	Greece	166
United States	2	Angola	167
Singapore	3	Niger	168
Tonga	4	Paraguay	169
Maldives	5	Congo, Dem. Rep.	170
Georgia	6	Sierra Leone	171
Palau	7	Equatorial Guinea	172
Uganda	8	Guinea-Bissau	173
Australia	9	Bolivia	174
New Zealand	10	São Tomé and Principe	175

Note: Rankings are the average of the country rankings on the difficulty of hiring, rigidity of hours, difficulty of firing and cost of firing indices. See the Data notes for details.
Source: Doing Business database.

TABLE 4.2
Who regulates employment the least—and who the most?

Rigidity of employment index (0–100)

Least		Most	
Hong Kong, China	0	Equatorial Guinea	66
Maldives	0	São Tomé and Principe	67
Marshall Islands	0	Tanzania	67
Singapore	0	Congo, Rep.	69
United States	0	Central African Republic	73
Australia	3	Bolivia	74
Canada	4	Venezuela	76
Jamaica	4	Guinea-Bissau	77
Palau	4	Niger	77
New Zealand	7	Congo, Dem. Rep.	78

Firing cost (weeks of salary)

Least		Most	
Marshall Islands	0	Equatorial Guinea	133
Micronesia	0	Ecuador	135
New Zealand	0	Argentina	139
Palau	0	Mozambique	143
Puerto Rico	0	Ghana	178
Tonga	0	Sri Lanka	178
United States	0	Zambia	178
Italy	2	Egypt	186
Romania	3	Sierra Leone	329
Australia	4	Zimbabwe	446

Nonwage labor cost (% of salary)

Least		Most	
12, including:		Czech Republic	35
Bangladesh	0	Hungary	35
Botswana	0	Slovakia	35
Cambodia	0	Brazil	37
Comoros	0	Belarus	39
Ethiopia	0	Ukraine	39
Lesotho	0	Italy	42
Maldives	0	China	44
Suriname	0	France	47
Tonga	0	Belgium	55

Source: Doing Business database.

years earlier, these restrictions had aimed at encouraging employers to hire new workers rather than extend the hours of existing ones. But this backfired: some companies—especially those in the apparel industry, where demand fluctuates with seasonal fashions—promptly moved their factories to Bulgaria and FYR Macedonia. The change was reversed.

Not a single African country reformed (table 4.3). This is despite Africa's having the most rigid labor regulations and more than 90% of its workers in informal employment. Zimbabwe is one example. Although the labor law provides for 4 months' severance pay, newly created retrenchment boards, given authority by recent regulation, have introduced higher payments—up to 3–6 months' salary for each year of service. This means that Tawanda, a restaurant owner who needs to dismiss 3 workers because of a drop in demand, must pay each

of them a lump sum equal to 4–10 years' salary. Instead, Tawanda abandons the business and flees to Malawi, leaving the workers with no severance at all.

TABLE 4.3
Easier dismissal rules—the most popular reform in 2005/06
Decreased mandatory notice period or severance pay
Argentina, Georgia, FYR Macedonia
Reduced work hour restrictions or overtime cost
Australia, Georgia, Greece, Lithuania
Made fixed term contracts more flexible
Romania, Vietnam
Removed procedural requirements for redundancy
Georgia

Source: Doing Business database.

How to reform

On paper Malawi and Mozambique appear to have stricter worker protections than Sweden and Switzerland (figure 4.2). Yet labor regulation in Africa and in many other developing countries applies to only a select minority, since few workers have formal jobs. In Malawi 50,000 workers have formal jobs in the private sector —out of a population of 12 million. In Mozambique 350,000 workers are in the formal private sector—in a country of 20 million people. Others are unemployed or work informally. They have no legal protections.

"Labor reforms are among the easiest to introduce… when they go backwards," says Alberto, an entrepreneur from Peru. "Making laws more flexible is the hard part." More flexible labor rules expand the reach of regulation, by bringing more jobs into the formal economy. But few countries make such reforms. Colombia and several OECD countries adopted reforms early in the term of new governments. And countries in Eastern Europe and Central Asia simplified labor regulations the most in the past 4 years. Slovakia was the top reformer in the world in 2003, Serbia in 2004, FYR Macedonia and Romania in 2005. In this period 15 countries in the region carried out reforms that made labor laws more flexible.

It wasn't always smooth. Reforms took place in the face of rapidly rising unemployment, and they sometimes went awry. In 2001 Slovakia adopted a labor code that made it nearly impossible to fire workers. The aim was to protect existing jobs in formerly state-owned enterprises. But employers responded by moving opera-

FIGURE 4.2
Africa makes it hard to employ workers

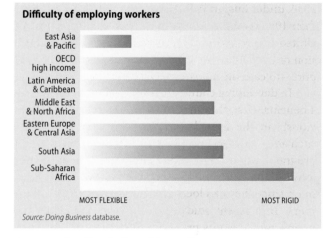

Difficulty of employing workers

Source: Doing Business database.

tions to the Czech Republic. When a new government came into power in November 2002, it introduced more flexibility. Paradoxically, it was the rigidity of the previous code that made large reform possible.

In 2001 FYR Macedonia had the highest officially recorded unemployment rate in the world, at 37%. Youth unemployment stood at 66%. Strict regulations made any dismissals subject to approval by the labor unions. When a new government came into power the following year, labor market regulation was its main priority for reform. The reform was driven by the labor minister. An entrepreneur himself, he reckoned that creating new jobs was possible only if regulations were made more flexible. He was right—and 25,000 new jobs were created.

But in developing countries reform is stalled. Half-hearted attempts often lead to more confusion. Take Malawi. Its Labor Act of 2000 requires employers to pay both severance and a full pension to every dismissed employee. In February 2004 the labor minister issued an amendment allowing employers to pay either severance or the pension, whichever is higher. The aim was to reduce the cost for businesses and encourage job creation. But the amendment was revoked a year later. The result: courts overflowing with cases of employees suing for back severance or pension payments. Other countries are not even contemplating reforms because critics denounce them as reducing worker protections. This disregards reality—most people work informally, beyond the reach of labor laws.

One way to make labor reform in poor countries more palatable: combine it with temporary public works programs that can provide employment for those without jobs. These can involve building roads, schools, hospitals—but also constructing irrigation canals for farmers or planting trees for soil conservation. The first such program was introduced nearly 200 years ago, in 1834, under England's Poor Law Amendment Act.[2] More than 100 countries have used them since, including the United States and much of Europe during the Depression of the 1930s. This is where donors can provide support—to ease the adjustment after reforms.

In developing countries public works programs have 4 benefits. First, they may reach everyone—whether previously in the formal or informal sector. Alternatives such as unemployment insurance or active labor market programs extend only to workers who have lost formal jobs.[3] Second, the programs are good at targeting the poor, since they can locate in areas of higher unemployment. In a recent study of 122 poverty reducing programs, public works programs like Argentina's Trabajar and India's Maharashtra Employment Guarantee Scheme rank highest in reaching the needy.[4] In Trabajar, a program started in Argentina in 1996, 82% of the recipients of jobs had fallen under the poverty line before enrolling.[5] Third, such programs require little administrative capacity, because candidates self-select. And finally, they can provide much-needed infrastructure.

Reformers who resort to public works programs should be aware of their main weakness: Public money can easily be wasted because of corrupt or inefficient management. This is likely even if the program is run by local communities. A recent study of 600 road projects in Indonesia estimates 28% waste when central auditing is not present.[6] For this reason many countries introduce such programs in the private sector—for example, by

FIGURE 4.3
Flexible labor laws, low unemployment in Denmark

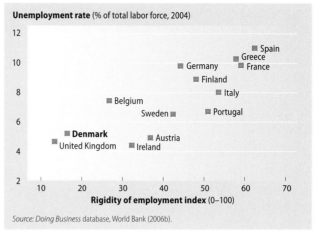

Source: *Doing Business* database, World Bank (2006b).

temporarily subsidizing workers who find employment in private enterprises. Monitoring is then the task of the employer, who also provides training and the possibility of a permanent job.

In middle-income countries reformers might introduce unemployment insurance in place of rigid dismissal rules. This shifts the focus of regulation from protecting jobs to protecting workers—by helping them deal with moving to new jobs. Reform could start with modest benefits and simple rules. Jordan and Lebanon limit their severance requirements to 1 month's wages per year of service. The Chilean reform of 2002 introduced savings accounts: the employee pays 0.6% of gross wages and the employer pays 2.4%, with two-thirds going to an individual account and a third to a common fund. Severance pay was cut from 30 days to 24 for each year worked. Unemployed Chilean workers receive benefits for 5 months. The payments are progressively reduced each month, to encourage searching for another job.

Among rich countries Denmark has the best example of flexible labor regulations, a generous system of unemployment benefits and active labor market programs. Since its reforms in the mid-1990s Denmark has enjoyed one of the lowest unemployment rates in the OECD, at 4.7%, along with one of the shortest average spells in unemployment in Europe (figure 4.3). This is the Rolls-Royce of social security programs, requiring enormous monitoring capacity. If you have dirt roads, don't try it.

A lesson for all reformers—market your goals. Making labor regulations more flexible is about creating jobs, but the message is often lost in bad marketing. Opponents of flexible employment laws pit business against workers. It is a simple trick to stall reforms. Rigid regulation indeed benefits a select group of incumbent workers, but it shuts out others from a job in the formal sector altogether. And when someone loses a job, it is harder to find a new one. The best protection for workers is to make labor rules flexible so that the economy will have more jobs in the formal sector—and transitions from one job to another are easy.

Notes

1. Botero and others (2004).
2. Himmelfarb (1984).
3. Vodopivec (2006).
4. Coady, Grosh and Hoddinott (2004).
5. Subbarao (2003). See also Haddad and Adato (2001).
6. Olken (2005).

Registering property

Only 1 in 10 properties is officially registered in Tanzania. Rashid, a local entrepreneur, explains why: "The Lands Registry has archaic files and cannot cope with the mass of records and transactions. Property titles are not located in good time, and the whole transfer process gets inordinately delayed . . . and in many instances the registrars are not available to execute documents." On average, it takes 10 procedures and 123 days to register property in Dar es Salaam. The good news is that the process got cheaper in 2005, with the stamp duty lowered from 4% of the property value to 1%.

Reform is gaining momentum in other countries too. Twenty-four countries made it easier to register property in 2005/06—up 50% from the year before. Most reforms made the process cheaper. Six countries sped procedures at the registry. On average, the top 10 reformers cut registration time by 23% and cost by 38%. Three of the most difficult countries in which to register property in 2004—Côte d'Ivoire, Nigeria and Tanzania —were among the top reformers (figure 5.1).

Still, registering property is much harder than it need be in many countries. In Uzbekistan an entrepreneur must complete 12 procedures, wait 97 days and pay 10.5% of the property value to transfer title. The Maldives does not allow companies to transfer property at all. In Timor-Leste property cannot be officially transferred. In the Marshall Islands only one property has been registered—and that took 2 years and numerous disputes. It is one of the world's most difficult countries in which to register property (table 5.1).

The more difficult property registration is, the more assets stay in the informal sector. But informal titles

FIGURE 5.1
Top 10 reformers in registering property

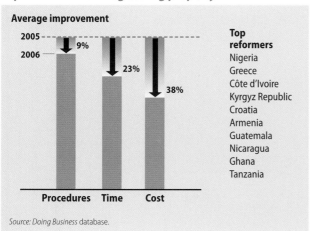

Source: *Doing Business* database.

TABLE 5.1
Where is registering property easy—and where not?

Easiest	Rank	Most difficult	Rank
New Zealand	1	Uganda	166
Armenia	2	Bangladesh	167
Lithuania	3	Sierra Leone	168
Saudi Arabia	4	Afghanistan	169
Slovakia	5	Nigeria	170
Norway	6	Guinea-Bissau	171
Sweden	7	Maldives	172
Iceland	8	Marshall Islands	173
United Arab Emirates	9	Micronesia	174
United States	10	Timor-Leste	175

Note: Rankings are the average of the country rankings on the procedures, time and cost to register property. See the Data notes for details.
Source: *Doing Business* database.

cannot be used as security in obtaining loans. And without formal title, property values are lower and property owners invest less.[1] A recent study in Argentina found up to 47% higher investment when properties are formally registered.[2] Research in Peru documented a 60% increase.[3]

Who is reforming?

In 2004 transferring title in Nigeria required 21 procedures, 274 days and 27% of the property value in fees. The biggest bottleneck was the requirement to obtain consent from the governor of Lagos for any property transfer, a relic from military rule that cost 6 months and 10% of the property value. Bribery was rampant and many transactions occurred informally.

Reforms began after a new governor was elected. It took 3 years to see results. The registry digitized most of its records, trained staff and started periodic evaluations of the speed of registrations. Five fees were consolidated into one, and requirements to obtain tax clearances and inspections were eliminated. Fee schedules and documentation requirements were published in the media. The time to register property fell from 274 days to 80 (figure 5.2). Registrations jumped by 90%, though from a small base. The next step is to eliminate the requirement for the governor's consent.

Eleven other African countries also improved property registration in 2005/06, making Africa the fastest-reforming region (figure 5.3). The Central African Republic, Ghana, Mauritania, Mauritius, Seychelles and Tanzania lowered taxes and fees, cutting overall costs by a third on average. Administrative improvements at registries reduced the time to obtain titles in Botswana and Mali. As a result Mali saw monthly revenue on land sales triple—from 67,000 francs in August 2005, just after the reform, to 182,000 francs in May 2006.

Still, much remains to be done in Africa. With the share of properties formally registered across the continent estimated at only 2%, few people benefit from administrative improvements. Expanding the coverage of registration requires properties to be included in the land cadastre in the first place.

In Latin America, El Salvador digitized and restructured its registry—reducing delays by 19 days. Guatemala cut time in half after simplifying registration procedures and hiring more staff. Brazilian entrepreneurs can now obtain online clearance from the workers fund and the tax authority to sell property. Nicaragua cut the transfer tax to 1% of the property value.

Eastern Europe and Central Asia continued to reform. Croatia reduced delays by 18 months and the backlog of unissued titles by 36% by computerizing the registry and making the process administrative (previously a judge was also involved). Romania gave notaries electronic access to the registry, reducing time by 20 days. Bosnia and Herzegovina lowered the transfer tax by 1% of the property value. And in Armenia new regulation allows entrepreneurs to pay the stamp duty directly to the notary, rather than making an extra trip to the bank.

Rich countries expanded their use of the Internet in property registrations. Germany now allows online applications for titles. In Portugal entrepreneurs can obtain tax clearances online. And a new law in Spain requires

FIGURE 5.2
Registering property in Nigeria—faster

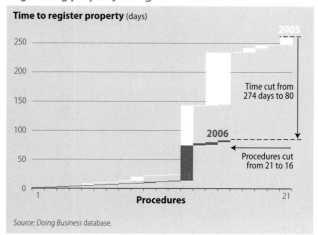

Source: Doing Business database.

FIGURE 5.3
African countries made registering property easier

notaries to use online procedures; as a result delays have dropped by more than 30%. Some countries cut costs. Greece slashed the transfer tax from 10% of the property value to 1%, while Australia abolished its 2.25% vendor duty (table 5.2).

In the Middle East and North Africa, Kuwait and the United Arab Emirates introduced new technologies in their registries and trained staff in managing workflow, cutting delays by 33% and 27%, respectively. Morocco halved its transfer fee.

Four countries made registering property more difficult. Venezuela introduced additional clearances, adding procedures and delays. Togo now requires documentation to prove nationality, adding a month to an already grueling 7-month process. To reduce corruption at the registry, Uganda requires all payments to be made at a bank instead—and is now among the 10 countries with the largest number of procedures (table 5.3). In

TABLE 5.2

Lower cost to register—the most popular reform in 2005/06

Decreased taxes or fees
Australia, Bosnia and Herzegovina, Central African Republic, Ghana, Greece, Kyrgyz Republic, Mauritania, Mauritius, Morocco, Nicaragua, Nigeria, Seychelles, South Africa, Tanzania

Sped procedures in the registry
Botswana, Croatia, El Salvador, Kuwait, Mali, Nigeria

Computerized the registry, made online procedures possible
Croatia, El Salvador, Guatemala, Spain

Combined and eliminated procedures
Armenia, Côte d'Ivoire, Nigeria

Source: Doing Business database.

FYR Macedonia property owners must now pay taxes at the municipality rather than the revenue office, adding 30 days of delay.

How to reform

It is easier to register property in New Zealand than anywhere else in the world. The entire process can be completed in 2 online procedures at a cost of 0.1% of the property value. Lawyers certify land transfer documents for their clients and submit them electronically for registration. Confirmation is returned within minutes.

It wasn't always that way. In 1995 the registry's paper records required 30 kilometers of shelving and were growing by 1 kilometer a year. The reform started shortly after with the merger of the land titling office and the Department of Lands and Survey Information. Title certificates were digitized between 1997 and 2002, at a cost of $90 million. In 2002 the Land Transfer Act, then 50 years old, was amended to allow online titling. Use is still not universal: by the end of 2005 about half of formal land transactions were fully electronic. A new law mandates that all transactions be handled electronically by July 2008.[4]

The easiest way to follow New Zealand's lead—even without the large and time-consuming investment in technology—is to cut unnecessary procedures. Côte d'Ivoire is one example. A requirement to obtain the urban minister's consent for every property transaction resulted in year-long delays. In 2005 a reformist minister eliminated the requirement, slashing the time required to obtain title from 397 days to 32. Several other countries have similar consent requirements (figure 5.4). They serve no purpose other than delaying registration and

fueling corruption. "My title came back with 18 signatures of approval on it, and I had to pay almost as many people to make sure I got it," said a Gambian entrepreneur.

Another simple reform is to cut costs. Reform opponents argue that high fees and transfer taxes are needed to meet government revenue targets. Yet cutting costs often increases revenues, as shown by reforms in India and Mali.[5] High costs encourage informal transactions and underreporting of property values. Governments lose revenue, and property owners lose security of title. With costs amounting to more than 10% of the property value in 42 poor countries, titling programs have little chance of success. As soon as a newly titled property changes hands, it quickly slips back to informal status.

The desire to formalize land titles is what motivated Georgia to reform. Like other former Soviet Union states, Georgia struggled in the transition from government ownership of land. The post-Soviet government created a department of land management, tasked with reforming the land cadastre and property registration. It took 6 years to produce a proposal. Several study visits to the best-functioning property registries around Europe provided ideas. But the proposal was promptly shelved by (then) President Eduard Shevardnadze, on grounds that state interests were insufficiently protected.

Enter a new government—with reform of land administration as part of its election platform. In just 4 months, between February and June 2004, a new land law was passed and a new registry established. Both were based on the previously shelved proposal. Procedures

TABLE 5.3
Who regulates property registration the least—and who the most?

Procedures (number)				Time (days)				Cost (% of property value)			
Fewest		**Most**		**Least**		**Most**		**Least**		**Most**	
Norway	1	Afghanistan	11	Norway	1	Bosnia & Herzegovina	331	Bhutan	0.0	Burundi	17.9
Sweden	1	Swaziland	11	New Zealand	2	Angola	334	Saudi Arabia	0.0	Senegal	18.1
Netherlands	2	Eritrea	12	Sweden	2	Gambia	371	Kiribati	0.1	Cameroon	18.7
New Zealand	2	Greece	12	Thailand	2	Rwanda	371	Slovakia	0.1	Mali	20.7
Oman	2	Uzbekistan	12	Lithuania	3	Ghana	382	New Zealand	0.1	Comoros	20.8
Thailand	2	Ethiopia	13	Armenia	4	Slovenia	391	Belarus	0.1	Nigeria	21.2
United Kingdom	2	Uganda	13	Iceland	4	Croatia	399	Azerbaijan	0.3	Chad	21.2
Vanuatu	2	Brazil	14	Saudi Arabia	4	Bangladesh	425	Russia	0.3	Zimbabwe	24.0
Iceland	3	Algeria	15	Netherlands	5	Kiribati	513	Switzerland	0.4	Congo, Rep.	27.2
Singapore	3	Nigeria	16	Taiwan, China	5	Haiti	683	Palau	0.4	Syria	27.9

Source: Doing Business database.

were simplified and the transfer tax eliminated. The time to register fell from 39 days to 9.

Reducing corruption was also a priority in the Georgian reforms. To attract capable staff, salaries were increased 20-fold. A bonus scheme was introduced, enabling staff to double their pay if their unit outperformed others on growth in registrations and customer satisfaction. An extensive recruitment campaign ensured that qualified candidates came forward. By the end of 2004 the registry was operational. The registry and the Ministry of Justice then led a public information campaign to encourage owners to register their property (figure 5.5). In January 2005, just after the new registry was established, 519 properties were registered in Tbilisi. By December registrations topped 11,000. The fees allow the registry to be self-financed and to invest in new technology.

Peru's reform was motivated by the government's determination to give equal opportunity to women and poor people to own land. The reforms ran from 1999 to 2004—based on earlier pilots in 1992–93—with the goal of increasing access to formal titles among the urban poor. A new registry was established, along with a new cadastre. The new agency replaced 14 others that had previously dealt with registration. The time to formalize a title went from 6 years to 1 month. More than 1.3 million titles were issued, two-thirds of them to women. Most people who received formal title now also found jobs outside the home. Before, an adult had to stay at home and guard the property against intruders. Children often ended up with informal jobs to help their family.[6]

Disputes over landownership often end up in revolts. Many people know about Thomas Muentzer's peasant uprising in 1525 and its bloody end. But few know about the 60 peasant uprisings in the preceding 2 centuries—in Germany alone. These days, fights between landowners (including the state) and informal squatters continue to dominate the news in some African and Latin American countries.

Honduras is one example of reform motivated by the many land disputes that arose because of lack of formal titles. Before the reforms an estimated 70% of the 2.6 million properties were not legally registered. In 2003 the government presented its plans to transform the system. In 2004 a new property law created an administrative registry outside the judiciary, which was considered corrupt and inefficient. Once the agency started work, cadastral data were integrated with property information. Between 2004 and 2005 the number of new titles increased by 160%.

Whatever the motivation for reform, the social problem it addresses is clear: without the ability to

FIGURE 5.4
Obtaining government consent—a big bottleneck

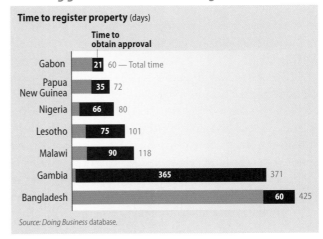

Time to register property (days)

Source: Doing Business database.

FIGURE 5.5

How Georgia reformed property registration

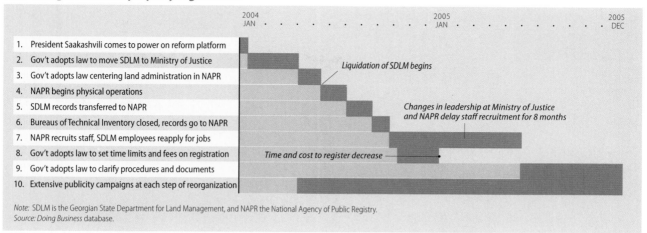

Note: SDLM is the Georgian State Department for Land Management, and NAPR the National Agency of Public Registry.
Source: Doing Business database.

legally own land, some people are denied opportunities that others have. This is not based on their ability or willingness to work, but on antiquated and often corrupt government policies. Reforming land laws and related registration requirements goes a long way toward reducing inequality in economic opportunities. It is what many urban and rural poor people need. Governments would be wise to oblige.

Notes

1.   Deininger (2003).
2.   Galiani and Schargrodsky (2006).
3.   Field (2005).
4.   Burns (2005).
5.   Data for India are from the Maharashtra Ministry of Finance; those for Mali, from Direction Nationale des Domeines et du Cadastre in Bamako.
6.   Field (2003).

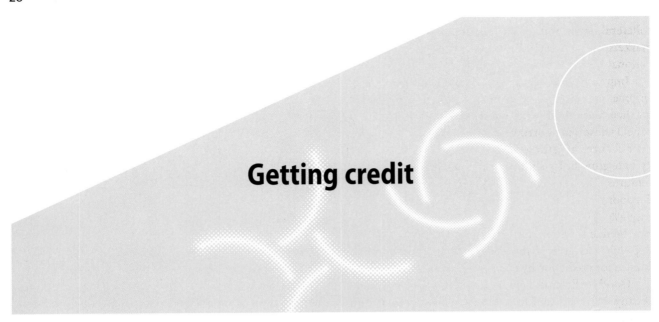

Getting credit

Governments often come up with strange ways to increase access to finance for small businesses. "In my country access-to-credit programs only improve access for those who run them," says a businesswoman from Cambodia. Regulations in Benin, India and Syria cap the interest rates that banks can charge. And laws in Bolivia, Mali and the United Arab Emirates exempt real estate and business equipment from seizure as collateral to cover a bad debt, giving bankers few incentives to lend.

The rationale for such arrangements is that borrowers need protection. But high-risk borrowers—most start-ups and small firms—will not get loans when interest rates are capped or collateral enforcement is restricted. If borrower protections are too strong, banks will invest their money in government securities or lend to large businesses with which they do repeat business.

A more effective way to improve access to credit is to increase information about potential borrowers' creditworthiness and make it easy to create and enforce collateral agreements. Twenty-six countries made such reforms in 2005/06. Sixteen established or upgraded credit registries to give lenders better information on borrower risk. Nine reformed collateral laws, allowing businesses to use more types of assets as collateral and creditors to enforce claims faster and cheaper—often without resorting to the courts. France introduced both types of reforms.

Lenders look at the borrower's credit history and collateral when extending loans. Where credit registries and effective collateral laws are lacking—as in most poor countries—banks make fewer loans (figure 6.1). Credit to the private sector averages 14% of national income in the 10 economies ranking at the bottom on how well

FIGURE 6.1
Stronger legal rights, more information sharing—more credit

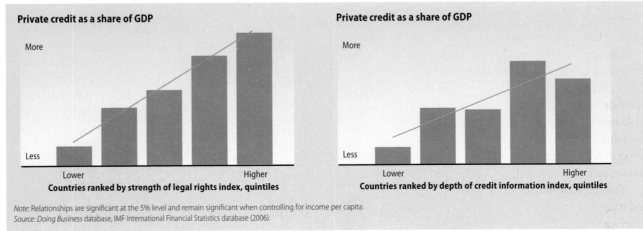

Note: Relationships are significant at the 5% level and remain significant when controlling for income per capita.
Source: *Doing Business* database, IMF International Financial Statistics database (2006).

collateral laws and credit registries facilitate credit markets (table 6.1). In the top 10, credit tops 120% of national income.

Improving credit information and laws to create and enforce collateral—both in and out of bankruptcy—is not just about strengthening the rights of creditors. It benefits deserving borrowers just as much, by increasing their chances of getting credit.[1] And it boosts productivity and growth, by shifting capital to the best business ventures. The gains are large. In Bangladesh nearly half the poor people who received credit escaped poverty, but only 4% of those without credit did.[2] Some of the effect may be due to differences in education and landownership, but a large role remains for improving access to finance for creditworthy entrepreneurs.

Good collateral laws also keep bank portfolios healthy. In countries where few types of assets can be used as collateral or the cost of creating collateral is high, entrepreneurs resort to consumer loans. In Mexico, for example, consumer loans are now growing 8 times as fast as business loans. The stock of consumer lending exceeds $25 billion. In Peru consumer credit is now larger than business credit, at $2 billion. The advantage of consumer loans is that borrowers do not have to pledge assets to get the money. The problem with these loans is that if the economy slows, many will turn bad and banks will have nothing to cover their losses.

TABLE 6.1
Where is getting credit easy—and where not?

Easiest	Rank	Most difficult	Rank
United Kingdom	1	Comoros	166
Hong Kong, China	2	Congo, Dem. Rep.	167
Australia	3	Egypt	168
Germany	4	Eritrea	169
Malaysia	5	Guyana	170
New Zealand	6	Rwanda	171
Ireland	7	Timor-Leste	172
Canada	8	Lao PDR	173
Singapore	9	Afghanistan	174
United States	10	Cambodia	175

Note: Rankings are based on the sum of the strength of legal rights index and the depth of credit information index. See the Data notes for details.
Source: Doing Business database.

Who is reforming?

France was the top reformer in 2005/06, with improvements in both collateral laws and credit information. A new collateral law unified regulations, allowed enforcement of collateral out of court and set up a unified registry of movable property, to open in 2007. Businesses can now pledge all types of assets as collateral—present and future. Reforms in the public registry expanded coverage to 1 million new businesses by lowering the minimum loan cutoff from €76,000 to €25,000.

Another 16 countries reformed their credit information systems in 2005/06. New private credit bureaus launched in Bulgaria, Georgia, Kazakhstan and Nicaragua. Mauritius—the sole reformer in Africa—set up a public credit registry. New consumer credit bureaus opened in China and Israel, with Israel's among the top 10 in coverage (table 6.2). The Czech Republic established a private credit bureau for nonbank institutions (such as trade creditors and utility companies) and linked it with the bank bureau. Thailand's 2 national credit bureaus merged. And competition in Mexico's credit information market intensified as a third bureau opened.

The biggest trend in credit-related reforms was updating credit information laws, especially in Latin America (figure 6.2). The Dominican Republic abolished consumer consent for giving data to credit bureaus and implemented a new data verification procedure so that borrowers can check their credit histories. El Salvador's new consumer protection law also guarantees consumers access to their credit data (figure 6.3). Financial institutions in Costa Rica are now required to consult the credit bureau before granting loans. A new law in Honduras makes credit data available for 5 years. The credit bureau law in Ecuador makes data available for 6

TABLE 6.2
Who has the most credit information—and who the least?
Borrowers covered as a share of adults

Most	(%)	Least	(%)
Argentina	100	Chad	0.18
Australia	100	Algeria	0.15
Canada	100	Ethiopia	0.15
Iceland	100	Nepal	0.14
Ireland	100	Kenya	0.14
Israel	100	Burundi	0.12
New Zealand	100	Yemen	0.08
Norway	100	Nigeria	0.05
Sweden	100	Georgia	0.02
United States	100	Guinea	0.02

Note: The rankings reflected in the table include only countries with public or private credit registries (122 in total). Another 53 countries have no credit registry and therefore no coverage.
Source: Doing Business database.

FIGURE 6.2

Most reforms were in Eastern Europe and Latin America

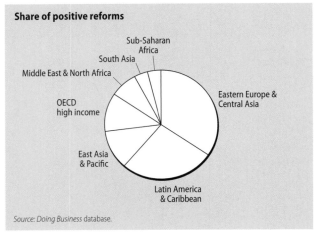

Share of positive reforms

Source: *Doing Business* database.

FIGURE 6.3

Expanding credit information

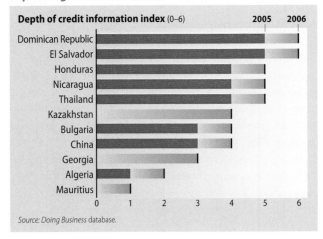

Depth of credit information index (0–6)   2005 2006

Source: *Doing Business* database.

years; in Lithuania, for 7 years; in Poland, for 5.

Governments in the Middle East and North Africa increased their support for the establishment of private credit bureaus. Egypt's central bank revised the banking secrecy law to allow the opening of the country's first private bureau. Kuwait's central bank stopped circulating to large banks the list of loans in default, doubling the number of inquiries to the private bureau. Algeria created a registry on unpaid debt that can be accessed by private businesses.

Several economies broadened the scope of credit reports (table 6.3). The Dominican Republic, Hong Kong (China) and Romania now offer more information on outstanding loans and on-time payments. Australia, the Dominican Republic, Honduras and Portugal allowed bureaus to use public sources of credit information, such as court files. Public credit registries in Austria, Belgium,

France, Germany, Italy and Portugal also expanded the amount of data available in credit reports. Hungary and Italy moved in the other direction, restricting the range of data providers to the registry.

Indonesia and Pakistan now record all loans in their credit registries, expanding coverage of borrowers by 5 and 18 times, respectively. Previously, both had a high minimum loan threshold for coverage. Uruguay also reduced its minimum loan threshold, increasing coverage of borrowers by 5%.

Ten countries made it easier to create and enforce collateral. Peru went the furthest, allowing businesses to use more types of assets as collateral and to enforce such collateral outside the courts. This reform faced opposition from notaries, but the government persevered. As a result the time and cost to enforce a collateral agreement are expected to fall by three-quarters.

Several other countries also expanded the range of assets that can be used as collateral. Denmark introduced a floating charge, allowing businesses to use a changing pool of assets as collateral. Now there is no need to amend the agreement every time assets enter or leave the pool. Under the old rules businesses had to continually revise collateral agreements to reflect the day's inventory. The reforms moved Denmark into the top 10 on strength of legal rights.

Making out-of-court enforcement possible was the most popular reform to collateral laws, as in the Kyrgyz Republic and Serbia. Armenia encouraged enforcement out of court by removing the requirement that agreements to use this procedure be made only after debtors default. India's supreme court upheld the right of banks to take possession of collateral without court involvement. A simple notice to the debtor is now sufficient to

TABLE 6.3

More credit information—the most popular reform in 2005/06

Introduced or revised law for credit bureaus
Algeria, Dominican Republic, El Salvador, Honduras, Nicaragua, Panama, Romania, Thailand, Uruguay

Established new credit registry
Bulgaria, China, Czech Republic, Georgia, Israel, Kazakhstan, Mauritius, Nicaragua

Made enforcement of collateral out of court possible
Armenia, France, India, Kyrgyz Republic, Peru, Serbia

Expanded set of information collected in the credit registry
Algeria, France, Romania, Thailand, Uruguay

Established collateral registry
Azerbaijan, France, Japan, Lao PDR, Peru

Expanded the range of assets that can be used as collateral
Denmark, France, Lao PDR, Peru

Source: *Doing Business* database.

obtain payment in at least half of defaults. The reform also introduced time limits on initial judgments and appeals in collateral enforcement cases.

Three countries made getting credit more difficult. In 2004 Belarus allowed creditors to enforce collateral agreements out of court. But a new law passed in 2005 makes such enforcement impossible and also restricts who can pledge collateral—placing Belarus among the bottom 10 countries on legal rights for borrowers and lenders (table 6.4). Burundi stopped giving out information on outstanding loans, though a new database on loan defaults is still running. And Venezuela halted the sharing of credit data altogether.

TABLE 6.4

Who has the most legal rights for borrowers and lenders—and who the least?

Strength of legal rights index (0–10)

Most		Least	
Hong Kong, China	10	Belarus	2
United Kingdom	10	Burundi	2
Albania	9	China	2
Australia	9	Equatorial Guinea	2
New Zealand	9	Lao PDR	2
Singapore	9	Madagascar	2
Slovakia	9	Egypt	1
Denmark	8	Rwanda	1
Ireland	8	Afghanistan	0
Malaysia	8	Cambodia	0

Note: See the Data notes for details on the index.
Source: Doing Business database.

How to reform

An ambitious reformer would allow a broad range of assets to be used as collateral and a broad range of loans and types of information to be provided to the credit registry. That may sound like a lot to ask, but Slovakia did it. As part of its reform in 2002, Slovakia permitted borrowers to use all movable assets as collateral—present and future, tangible and intangible. Since then more than 70% of new business credit has been secured by movables and receivables. And the Banking Act is now being amended to make rules on submitting data to the credit registry more flexible.

Some countries go halfway and get little out of it. In 1997 Panama introduced a floating charge over an entire business, but only for assets located outside the country. And enforcement remains a long and costly court process. Paraguay allows borrowers to pledge inventory, but only if it consists of mining or industrial products—and each item must be listed individually. Micronesia introduced a new collateral law last year—but it still lacks a functioning collateral registry, so the law has no effect on lending. Brazil's laws on credit information give borrowers the right to inspect their data, but they still restrict the sharing of positive information on repayments and outstanding loans.

Legal reforms work best when lenders contribute to the drafting. Lawyers may miss what matters to business. In Mexico, for example, the 2000 reforms introduced two new types of collateral, but banks didn't use them because recovery was limited to the value of the collateral (and not the value of the loan). Banks successfully lobbied to remove the legal constraint, and

the new instruments are now widely used. In Panama initial proposals to reform the credit information law included a requirement to erase a record of defaults as soon as the debts are repaid. Later consultations with lenders, the private credit bureau and consumer groups eliminated that requirement and led to a law that permits broad sharing of information and strong consumer rights (figure 6.4).

For those with no appetite for pushing laws through parliament, much can be done with administrative reforms. A place to start is to unify credit registries across types of loans and unify collateral registries geographically and across types of assets. France is doing just that. Until 2005 France operated local collateral registries that specialized in pledges over shares, bank accounts, receivables or equipment. If a creditor in Paris needed to check information on a borrower from Lyon, a trip was required. With recent reforms, this is changing.

Other rich countries also need reform: Austria, Germany and Switzerland lack unified collateral registries. Another 32 countries require multiple registrations, including Cameroon, Colombia and Ecuador. The solution: create a unified registry of movable property charges indexed by the names of the debtors. In 2005 Peru passed legislation that will result in a unified registry of movable property, while Azerbaijan introduced a unified registry of charges over immovable property. Spain unified its registries in 1998. Eastern European countries— Bulgaria, Hungary, Moldova, Romania—have led the way in such reforms. The most efficient registries do not require legal review or authentication of filings, which stalls the registration process.

FIGURE 6.4
How Panama reformed the credit information law

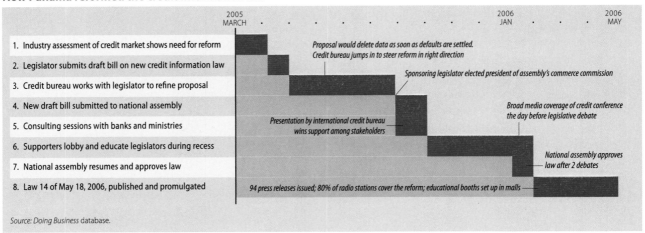

Source: *Doing Business* database.

Unifying credit information registries across types of loans is a similar task. This is easily done in public credit registries running separate databases for outstanding loans, loan defaults and checks, as in Algeria, Burundi and the West African Monetary Union. Morocco is a recent reformer: its banking law allows the merger of databases and even the outsourcing of their management to private contractors. Lebanon is in the process of merging separate databases.

And a warning: don't think that subsidies will increase access to credit. There are enough failed subsidy schemes around to show otherwise. Before being closed in 2005, Mexico's Banrural, which subsidized loans for farmers, lost $20 million a month. Every dollar of loans cost 30 cents to process, and more than 45% of loans were nonperforming. Worse, the continued subsidies kept out sound lending from private banks.

Problems with access to credit usually lie in a lack of credit information and weak collateral laws. Reformers may address those first.

Notes

1. Djankov, McLiesh and Shleifer (forthcoming).
2. Grameen Bank (2004).

Protecting investors

Aisha Al Hamra is the owner of a food processing business in Dar es Salaam, Tanzania. She needs $8 million to buy trucks and warehouse equipment. A bank loan would charge 20% annual interest and require $15 million in collateral—which Aisha doesn't have. A better choice would be to sell shares in her company to local investors, eliminating the need for collateral and giving her cash to buy the trucks. But first she must convince those investors that she won't run off with their money.

Regulations can help Aisha by requiring companies to report on their operations and allowing investors to vet managers' decisions that involve large amounts of money. Tanzania revised its Companies Act in 2005—for the first time since 1929—to give investors greater protections. The new law requires better disclosure of company activities and codifies directors' duties toward small shareholders. As a result local investors are more likely to hand over their money.

Financial markets can prosper where laws regulate self-dealing—the use of corporate assets for personal gain—and punish looting by corporate insiders. Both extensive disclosure requirements and court access for investors are associated with larger stock markets (figure 7.1).[1] Where laws fail to stop self-dealing, ownership concentration is higher because having a majority stake is the only way to prevent being cheated.

New Zealand tops the *Doing Business* investor protection ranking again this year, scoring 29 of 30 possible points (table 7.1). Singapore comes in second. Protecting investors against self-dealing is just one corporate governance issue, but it is the most important one in developing countries. Most other issues in investor protection—such

FIGURE 7.1
Better investor protection—more listed firms and higher market capitalization

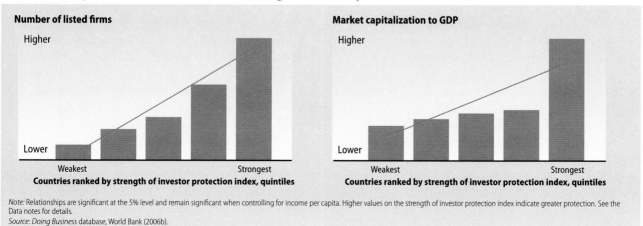

Note: Relationships are significant at the 5% level and remain significant when controlling for income per capita. Higher values on the strength of investor protection index indicate greater protection. See the Data notes for details.
Source: *Doing Business* database, World Bank (2006b).

TABLE 7.1
Where are investors protected, and where not?

Most protected	Rank	Least protected	Rank
New Zealand	1	Albania	164
Singapore	2	Gambia	165
Hong Kong, China	3	Rwanda	166
Malaysia	4	Venezuela	167
Canada	5	Djibouti	168
Ireland	6	Swaziland	169
Israel	7	Lao PDR	170
United States	8	Vietnam	171
United Kingdom	9	Tajikistan	172
South Africa	10	Afghanistan	173

Note: Rankings are on the strength of investor protection index. Two countries are missing data. See the Data notes for details.
Source: Doing Business database.

FIGURE 7.2
Rich countries protect investors the most

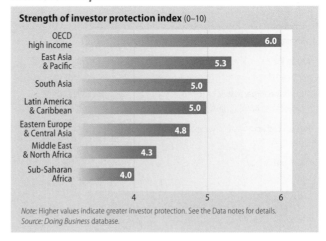

Note: Higher values indicate greater investor protection. See the Data notes for details.
Source: Doing Business database.

as writing management contracts that provide incentives for optimal investment decisions—arise in rich countries. Management of state-owned enterprises, another problem not discussed here, arises mostly in developing countries.

Across the sample, rich countries provide more protection against self-dealing (figure 7.2). They have stronger disclosure requirements for related-party transactions—those between a director or controlling shareholder and the company, like the example considered by *Doing Business*. And investors can rely on private enforcement—hiring lawyers and going to court—to protect their money.

Developing countries rely more on public regulators than private lawsuits to enforce investor rights. This is because court rules are often lacking and investors don't bother using them. For example, Cambodia's laws offer investors multiple avenues of redress against company directors, but no access to company documents to help prove their cases. Public enforcement is also deficient, though investors may have at least some chance to protect their money. Often government inspectors can obtain files—from tax offices, banks or business partners—that private lawyers cannot.

Who is reforming?

Fifteen economies reformed their investor protections in 2005/06 (table 7.2). Both rich and poor economies reformed, benefiting investors in every region.

Mexico was the top reformer in investor protections in 2005/06. "We had a saying: rich businessmen, poor companies," says one investor. Indeed, corporate insiders could—and did—run companies as they pleased. A new securities law changed that. The law defines for the first time the duties of company directors, combining an obligation to "take care of the business as if it were your own" with a specific list of activities that violate that duty. This approach eliminates loopholes in the previous regulations and gives a guide for judges with its specific bans on corporate misbehavior.

The Mexican law also increases scrutiny of related-party transactions. It requires full disclosure before any deal benefiting a company insider can occur. In addition, management must obtain a fairness opinion from external experts. And in case greater disclosure fails to prevent abuse, the law increases criminal penalties against directors. Mexico's ranking on the *Doing Business* strength of investor protection index leapt 92 places after the reform, from 125 to 33.

Other reformers made company finances more transparent. Tunisian lawmakers required companies to open their books to shareholders, providing access to financial statements and prohibiting company loans to directors, managers and their families. New amendments also require auditors to immediately inform the stock exchange regulator about any transaction that may hurt the interests of investors. Tunisia passed these provisions as part of its bid to complete an association agreement with the European Union.

China also improved investor protections against related-party transactions. Amendments to the Company Act obligate companies with multiple owners to get approval for such transactions from the various sharehold-

TABLE 7.2
Greater disclosure—the most popular reform in 2005/06

Increased disclosure requirements
Mexico, Peru, Poland, Romania, Sweden, United Kingdom

Made it easier to sue directors
Germany, India, Mexico, Tanzania

Opened company books for shareholder inspection
China, Hong Kong (China), Tunisia

Regulated approval of related-party transactions
Israel, New Zealand

Centralized financial market regulation in one agency
Colombia

Source: Doing Business database.

ers. (Stock exchange rules already required this for listed companies.) Yet more remains to be done: investors who vote against a transaction cannot later sue for the damage it may cause. As a result China has a perfect score on the extent of disclosure index, but scores only 1 of 10 points on the extent of director liability index. This imbalance unnerves investors—especially foreign ones, who are used to challenging improper behavior in the courts.

Several countries in Europe aligned their regulations with EU directives. Poland, for example, replaced its securities law with 4 new acts that more closely track EU regulations. Among other things, shareholders holding 5% of a company's shares can now ask external auditors to investigate suspicious business activities. Poland also simplified its stock market listing requirements. In response, 27 new companies listed in 2005, infusing more than $1.5 billion in new capital into the Polish market.[2] In comparison, only 3 new companies listed in 2004—for $212 million. Germany dropped its shareholding requirement for bringing derivative suits from 10% to 1%. And the Czech Republic—adopting the EU takeover directive—introduced regulatory review of share offers where majority owners buy out small investors at preset prices (otherwise known as "squeeze-outs").

How to reform

Financial crises allow governments to address regulatory problems ignored in good times. After the stock market crash of 1929, investors rewarded reforms of U.S. securities markets with years of growth. "There was a consensus that for the economy to recover, the public's faith in the capital markets needed to be restored," states the country's Securities and Exchange Commission.[3] Reform increased the potential liability of company directors, which is still among the highest in the world (table 7.3).

Thailand responded to the 1997 financial crisis with several regulatory and institutional reforms, starting with its enforcement agencies. Reformers transferred supervision of listed companies from the Ministry of Commerce to an independent Securities and Exchange Commission. Specialized bankruptcy courts were established to expedite the resolution of financial distress. That was followed by new company and securities regulations.[4] An institute of directors was created to train company directors on their role and responsibilities. The market rebounded quickly.

Thailand didn't stop there. Reform continues with stronger incentives—including tax breaks and favorable publicity—for companies with better investor protections.[5]

TABLE 7.3
Who protects investors the most—and who the least?

Extent of disclosure		Extent of director liability		Ease of shareholder suits	
Most	**Least**	**Most**	**Least**	**Easiest**	**Most difficult**
Bulgaria	Afghanistan	Cambodia	Swaziland	Kenya	Afghanistan
China	Albania	Canada	Timor-Leste	New Zealand	Cambodia
France	Guinea-Bissau	Israel	Zimbabwe	Colombia	Croatia
Hong Kong, China	Lao PDR	Malaysia	Afghanistan	Hong Kong, China	Syria
Ireland	Maldives	New Zealand	Dominican Republic	Ireland	Guyana
Malaysia	Micronesia	Singapore	Marshall Islands	Israel	Morocco
New Zealand	Palau	Trinidad and Tobago	Micronesia	Mauritius	Rwanda
Singapore	Sudan	United States	Palau	Poland	Saudi Arabia
Thailand	Switzerland	Hong Kong, China	Tajikistan	Singapore	Djibouti
United Kingdom	Tajikistan	South Africa	Vietnam	United States	Iran

Source: Doing Business database.

FIGURE 7.3
How Mexico reformed investor protections

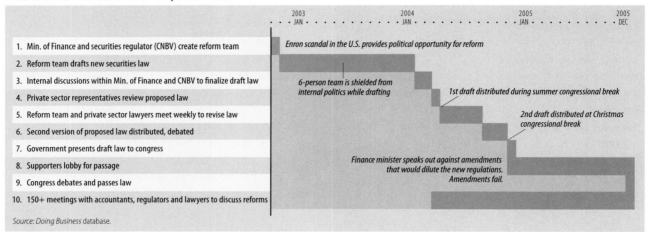

Source: *Doing Business* database.

Not every country uses such opportunities well. Lack of enforcement powers was the main weakness that surfaced in Malaysia after the 1997 crisis. Yet 5 government agencies still regulate the capital market: the securities commission, central bank, companies commission, foreign investment committee and the Ministry of Trade and Industry. This setup creates confusion about who is supposed to do what. The result? Regulators aren't aggressive about addressing potential violations, and a perception lingers that they aren't enforcing the law.[6]

It shouldn't take a financial crisis to improve investor protections. Governments lacking corporate scandals in their countries can draw on problems elsewhere to catalyze reform. The Enron and Parmalat scandals triggered regulatory activity around the world because they exposed weaknesses in markets previously considered examples of sound regulations. Canada, India and Japan passed reforms inspired by the U.S. Sarbanes-Oxley Act.

Top reformer Mexico also used the U.S. experience to push through regulatory reforms. In 2004 its Ministry of Finance introduced a new securities law rather than revise the existing company law. That approach limited opponents of reforms to those fearing broader ownership and increased financial disclosure. In contrast, revising the company law would have galvanized opposition from notaries and other legal professionals who benefit from the restrictions that the law imposes on who can certify company documents.

The new securities law passed, helped by 2 factors. The first was the inclusion of the private sector in its drafting. Private lawyers and government officials formed a working group to reconcile their differences over the proposed changes. "We met every Thursday evening for 5 months," said one reformer. "The lawyers helped us write a law that met our goals and was workable for the private sector. By the end, the lawyers were using 'we' when discussing the law: 'we intended this,' or 'we used this language because….'"

A second factor for success was giving legislators time to get familiar with the likely benefits of the new law. Reformers educated legislators during congressional holidays, giving them months to debate the new ideas (figure 7.3).

Colombia provides another example of learning from others. Reformers there recently consolidated regulatory powers into a single and more powerful agency, inspired by reforms in Japan and the United Kingdom. The securities regulator was merged with the banking and insurance regulators to form a financial market authority. The motivation was an increased number of rules without the associated capacity to enforce them. "Only regulate that which you can supervise," advises one Colombian reformer.

There is a lot to learn from reform initiatives in other countries—including about what doesn't work. Reforms to increase investor protections became a global phenomenon after the East Asian financial crisis and the recent corporate scandals in Europe and the United States. But some reforms are more popular than they deserve to be. One is the adoption of a "comply or disclose" policy for companies to meet a stock exchange's corporate governance standards. Companies that do not adopt all the standards must declare so, and why, to investors. The idea is to prevent problems by raising accountability without significantly increasing the cost of compliance. But that hardly ever works. Typically, companies file disclosures that say "too costly to comply" or "not sufficient information." These disclosures are rarely reviewed, even in advanced markets like the United Kingdom's. While costs are low, so are benefits.

Vibrant stock markets are not the only reason to introduce stronger investor protections. Tanzania started reforms of investor protections as part of a larger initiative to reduce corruption and create an "integrity environment" that inspires the trust needed to do business.[7] Such an approach bolsters investor confidence in local business and government alike.

Notes

1. La Porta, López-de-Silanes and Shleifer (2005) and Djankov, La Porta, López-de-Silanes and Shleifer (2005).
2. Ernst & Young (2005) and World Bank (2005b).
3. SEC (2006).
4. Thailand Investment Service Center (2004).
5. Strong market incentives to depress disclosure and governance are cited as contributing factors to the country's financial collapse in 1997 (Alba, Claessens and Djankov 1998).
6. World Bank (2005a).
7. Sitta (2005).

Paying taxes

No one likes paying taxes, but some like it less than others. "Tax evasion is a national sport in Bolivia. People avoid paying taxes because rates are high, the administration is complex and their tax money is wasted," says José, a businessman in La Paz—where a company must pay 80% of its profits, spend 189 days and make 41 payments a year to comply with tax regulation, making it one of the world's most burdensome tax systems (table 8.1). One would think large revenues are collected and used for public projects. Yet Bolivia is among the bottom 10 economies in global rankings of education and infrastructure quality.[1]

Other countries have similar shortcomings. In Mauritania a company has to pay 104% of its profits, spend 122 days and make 61 payments a year to comply with tax regulation. In Belarus 186% of profits are to be paid as taxes, 125 payments should be made and 208 days spent preparing, filing and paying taxes—if businesses comply. Most companies can't afford to declare all their output, and 42% of business activity is unrecorded.

To comply with tax regulation, businesses in the 175 economies covered by *Doing Business* submit, on average, 35 pages of tax returns a year—equivalent to 100,000 trees a year, even after accounting for the few countries where business taxes can be filed electronically.[2] In Cameroon the average annual tax return for businesses is 172 pages. In Ukraine, 92. In the United States, 64.

Governments impose taxes to finance public services. But taxes must first be collected, and high tax rates do not always lead to high tax revenues. Between 1982 and 1999 the average profit tax rate worldwide fell from 46% to 33%, while profit tax collection rose from 2.1% to 2.4% of national income.[3] This outcome was achieved because more businesses entered the formal economy and because tax exemptions and other tax incentives were reduced or eliminated.

Reducing tax rates has been a trend in Eastern Europe and Central Asia. Most reformers—Armenia, Bulgaria, Estonia, Kazakhstan, Slovakia, Russia—have seen tax revenues rise. The larger is the share of informal business activity before reform, the higher is the revenue growth after.

There is more to collecting taxes than higher or lower rates. Complicated tax systems lead to high evasion even when rates are low. Although taxes in Peru are low by Latin American standards, evasion is a problem because it takes 74 days and 53 payments to fulfill tax requirements. In Brazil the average business spends 455

TABLE 8.1
Where is it easy to pay taxes—and where not?

Easiest	Rank	Most difficult	Rank
Maldives	1	Bolivia	166
Ireland	2	Venezuela	167
Oman	3	China	168
United Arab Emirates	4	Algeria	169
Hong Kong, China	5	Congo, Rep.	170
Saudi Arabia	6	Central African Republic	171
Switzerland	7	Colombia	172
Singapore	8	Mauritania	173
St. Lucia	9	Ukraine	174
New Zealand	10	Belarus	175

Note: Rankings are the average of the country rankings on the number of payments, time and total tax rate. See the Data notes for details.
Source: Doing Business database.

FIGURE 8.1
Burdensome taxes, and still poor public services

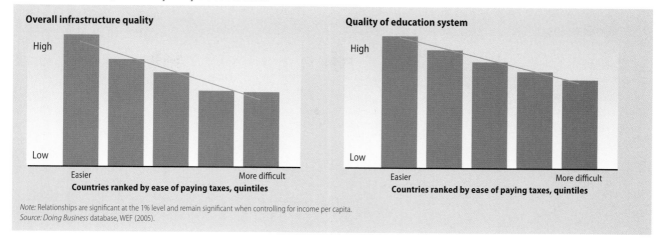

Note: Relationships are significant at the 1% level and remain significant when controlling for income per capita.
Source: Doing Business database, WEF (2005).

days a year to comply with taxes—because there are, on average, 55 changes to tax rules a day.[4] Being up to date on tax law isn't easy.

Businesses are more willing to pay taxes if they see that the money is used to improve public services. Yet many developing countries with high tax rates fail to improve business infrastructure or education and training —two things that employers care about (figure 8.1). Instead, a lot of money goes into sustaining inefficient state-owned enterprises or simply disappears into personal bank accounts.

In Comoros the government recently arrested the former finance and justice ministers and charged them with embezzling $350,000. In Ethiopia a former prime minister is serving an 18-year sentence for embezzling

$16 million. Few cases of kleptocracy match that of former Indonesian President Suharto, who is accused of siphoning off $400 million from the country's accounts.

Simplifying the tax regime by reducing tax rates and eliminating exemptions is the main way to reduce corruption in tax administration. Georgia—the top reformer in paying taxes in last year's report—has seen a drastic fall in perceived corruption of tax officials. In 2005 only 11% of surveyed businesses reported that bribery was frequent, down from 44% in 2002. That was the sharpest drop in perceived corruption among the 27 transition economies.[5] Romania, the other large reformer in 2004, and Slovakia, the main reformer in 2003, also saw falls in perceived corruption: from 14% to 8% of surveyed businesses and from 11% to 5%, respectively.

Who is reforming?

Thirty-five countries reformed their corporate tax systems in 2005/06. Thirty-one reduced the tax burden on businesses by cutting tax rates or reducing administrative hassles. Four increased it.

Reducing the profit tax was by far the most popular change, with 23 reformers (table 8.2). Albania, Egypt, Mexico and Morocco adopted new tax codes. Bosnia and Herzegovina and India shifted from sales to value added taxes, which are harder to evade. Egypt, Ghana and Lithuania cut the number of taxes.

The Central African Republic, the Dominican Republic, Sri Lanka and Uzbekistan introduced new and higher taxes. The Central African Republic raised its minimum corporate income tax from 2% of turnover to 10%. The

Dominican Republic increased its profit tax and introduced a new asset tax. Sri Lanka reintroduced a stamp duty, raised its profit tax and levied a new tax on profits. And Uzbekistan introduced a 1% tax on turnover, which outweighed reductions in corporate and labor taxes.

Yemen was the top reformer in 2005/06: after it eliminated its production tax, the total tax that businesses would pay fell from 170% to 48% of profits. Before the reforms, businesses paid a 10% production tax on their sales. When they sold products to other businesses, another 10% was paid. So every time products changed hands, tax was paid on tax. By the time products reached consumers, the hidden turnover taxes could reach 151% of profits. The reforms replaced the production tax with a 5% sales tax, levied on final consumers.

Senegal, the runner-up in reforms, consolidated taxes

TABLE 8.2
Reducing tax rates—the most popular reform in 2005/06

Reduced profit tax rates
Albania, Algeria, Antigua and Barbuda, Czech Republic, Egypt, Estonia, Ghana, Guinea-Bissau, Hungary, India, Israel, Lesotho, Mexico, Moldova, Montenegro, Pakistan, Paraguay, Rwanda, Senegal, Sierra Leone, Sudan, Switzerland, Turkey

Reduced number of taxes
Belarus, Egypt, Ghana, Lithuania, Russia, Yemen

Revised tax code
Albania, Egypt, Mexico, Morocco

Introduced value added tax
Bosnia and Herzegovina, India

Introduced electronic filing
Bulgaria, Latvia

Source: Doing Business database.

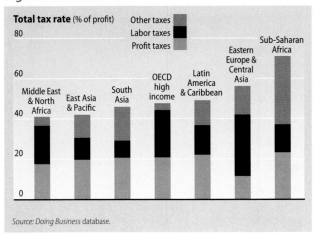

FIGURE 8.2
Highest taxes in Africa

Source: Doing Business database.

for small businesses, eliminated exemptions for large ones and cut the profit tax from 33% to 25%. Elsewhere in Africa, Ghana reduced its corporate income tax rate from 32.5% to 28% in 2005 and to 25% in 2006. It also phased out its reconstruction levy. Guinea-Bissau cut its profit tax from 39% to 25%. Four other African countries also lowered their profit taxes. These are much-needed reforms, as Africa is the region with the highest tax rates (figure 8.2).

The most reforms happened in Eastern Europe and Central Asia, where 13 countries had tax reforms. The main motivation was competition among neighboring countries to attract investors. Albania introduced a new tax code, reducing its corporate income tax from 23% to 20%. Belarus cut its turnover tax from 3.9% to 3.0%, and

its transport tax from 4% to 3%. Georgia and Lithuania abolished road taxes altogether.

Two reforms occurred in Latin America. Paraguay lowered its corporate tax by 10 percentage points. Mexico went beyond changing tax rates and simplified its tax code, eliminating some exemptions and reducing required paperwork.

Business taxes are traditionally low in the Middle East and North Africa because many governments collect large revenues from oil. Still, Egypt and Morocco consolidated their tax regulations and simplified filings. Algeria cut its corporate income tax from 30% to 25%, and Israel started a gradual reduction from 34% to 25% by 2010.

How to reform

The boldest reform is to simplify tax law so that every business faces the same tax burden—with no exemptions, tax holidays or special treatment for large or foreign businesses. Many tax laws start that way. But when hard times come and governments need revenue, tax rates are often raised. This is unpopular, and large or well-connected businesses usually obtain special treatment. Soon the tax law becomes riddled with exceptions, generally at the expense of small businesses, which have the least ability to lobby. Often they are pushed into the informal sector.

Few reformers dare eliminate exemptions. Egypt is an exception: since 2005 all businesses have paid a 20% profit tax—rather than 32% or 40%, depending on the sector. All sector-, location- or business-specific tax holidays and exemptions were eliminated, about

3,000 in all. Businesses can file and pay taxes electronically. As a result 2 million Egyptians filed taxes in 2005, double the number in 2004 (figure 8.3).

If radical changes are not feasible, reforms can be phased in. In 2005 Estonia, Ghana, Israel, Mexico and Paraguay introduced gradual reforms. For example, Ghana cut its corporate tax rate by 4.5 percentage points in 2005 and by another 3 points in 2006. This way the government can defuse lobbying. This was learned the hard way: Ghana tried to introduce a value added tax in 1995, only to withdraw it 2 months later after public demonstrations scared reformers. It took 4 more years for its eventual introduction.

Good reforms go beyond reducing corporate taxes.[6] Argentina's profit tax is 9% of total taxes, while social security contributions paid by employers account for 26% and turnover and financial transaction taxes for almost 62%. And the profit tax is just 1 of 34 required pay-

FIGURE 8.3
How Egypt created a flat profit tax

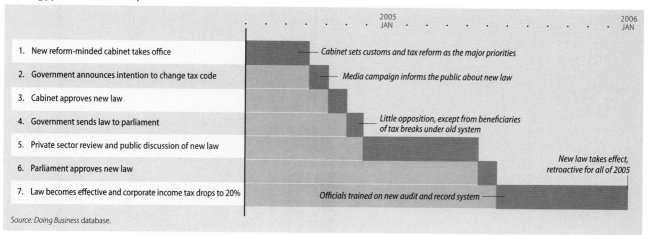

Source: *Doing Business* database.

ments. Simplifying the other 33 payments spread over 11 separate taxes would go a long way toward reducing the tax burden on businesses. Latvia is another example: social security and other labor contributions account for 66% of the tax burden, profit taxes for 21%. Around the world, profit taxes account for an average of 36% of the tax burden on businesses.[7] Profit taxes account for only 4 of 35 business tax payments (figure 8.4).

Good reforms also go beyond reducing tax rates (figure 8.5). Making electronic filing and payment available to businesses is a start. In Madagascar tax declarations were computerized in October 2005. If there is no change in the information submitted previously, a business can file the same declaration again with the click of a mouse. This innovation is especially important for compliance with labor taxes, where the information submitted by small businesses changes less often. As a result the time needed to comply with taxes fell by 17

days. Croatia simplified its tax forms, cutting 8 pages of tax returns and shortening the time required to comply with tax regulations by 5 days.

Consolidating taxes is also a worthwhile reform. For example, most countries have more than one labor tax, yet such taxes are typically based on gross salaries. Why not unify them? Tax offices can then distribute the revenues among government agencies. Slovakia did just that: its single social contribution tax funds health insurance, sickness insurance, old age pensions, disability insurance, unemployment benefits, injury insurance, guarantee insurance and reserve fund contributions. In many countries social security agencies would be reluctant to part with their powers—especially if there is a chance that tax offices won't give them their share of revenues. To gain their trust, an automatic separation of revenues can be introduced so that there is no room for discretion.

Small businesses have a particularly hard time dealing

FIGURE 8.4
Profit taxes—less than half the tax burden worldwide

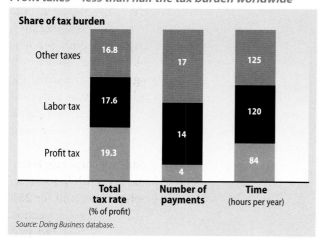

Source: *Doing Business* database.

FIGURE 8.5
Paying taxes takes longest in Latin America

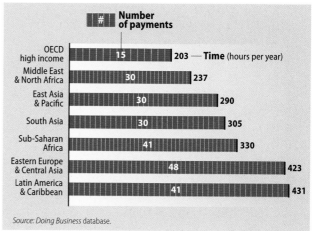

Source: *Doing Business* database.

TABLE 8.3
Who makes paying taxes easy—and who does not?

Payments (number per year)				**Time** (hours per year)				**Total tax rate** (% of profit)			
Fewest		**Most**		**Least**		**Most**		**Lowest**		**Highest**	
Maldives	1	Jamaica	72	Maldives	0	Azerbaijan	1,000	Maldives	9.3	Tajikistan	87.0
Afghanistan	2	Bosnia and Herzegovina	73	United Arab Emirates	12	Vietnam	1,050	Vanuatu	14.4	Mauritania	104.3
Norway	3	Montenegro	75	Singapore	30	Bolivia	1,080	Saudi Arabia	14.9	Argentina	116.8
Hong Kong, China	4	Dominican Republic	87	St. Lucia	41	Taiwan, China	1,104	United Arab Emirates	15.0	Uzbekistan	122.3
Sweden	5	Kyrgyz Republic	89	Oman	52	Armenia	1,120	Oman	20.2	Belarus	186.1
Mauritius	7	Romania	89	Dominica	65	Nigeria	1,120	Samoa	22.1	Central African Rep.	209.5
Portugal	7	Congo, Rep.	94	Switzerland	68	Belarus	1,188	Zambia	22.2	Congo, Dem. Rep.	235.4
Spain	7	Ukraine	98	New Zealand	70	Cameroon	1,300	Cambodia	22.3	Sierra Leone	277.0
United Kingdom	7	Belarus	125	Saudi Arabia	75	Ukraine	2,185	Mauritius	24.8	Burundi	286.7
Ireland	8	Uzbekistan	130	Ireland	76	Brazil	2,600	Switzerland	24.9	Gambia	291.4

Source: *Doing Business* database.

with multiple tax payments. Why not help them by making their business forms shorter? This is what Brazil did. In 2001 it introduced the Simples system, which allows for 1 monthly tax payment for businesses with annual revenues below $1.1 million. The payment covers 8 taxes, including 4 federal and state consumption taxes, 2 profit taxes, 1 labor tax and 1 municipal tax. Opinion surveys have found that nearly 90% of businesses think highly of this reform—emboldening the government to plan more ambitious reforms to collect taxes electronically. These are needed—it takes larger businesses 455 days to comply with taxes, the longest in the world (table 8.3).

Notes

1. WEF (2005).
2. A grown tree produces, on average, 80,500 sheets of paper. There are about 250 million formal businesses in the world.
3. Hines (2005).
4. *Folha de São Paulo,* "País edita 55 normas tributaries por dia," May 7, 2006.
5. World Bank (2006a).
6. Desai, Foley and Hines (2004).
7. See also PricewaterhouseCoopers (2005).

Trading across borders

Trade costs—delays, documents and administrative fees—continue to slow business in many developing countries. "My cargo of copper wire was held up in Durban, South Africa, for a week," says Michele, a Zambian trader. "The port authorities required proof that the wooden pallets on which the wire was loaded were free of pests. After some days the Ministry of Agriculture's inspector checked that the wood was fumigated, for a $100 fee."

The good news: as more products move internationally, so do new technologies that reduce trade costs. Electronic filing of cargo documents has reduced delays in many ports. Software that works in Hamburg or Sydney can also be used in Baku and Colombo. Regional trade agreements have brought with them simpler customs and transit forms, uniform across several countries. The speed of trading is now greater than ever: between

January 2005 and April 2006 the time needed to comply with export-related requirements fell by nearly 1.5 days worldwide (figure 9.1). The largest drop—by 3 days on average—occurred in Eastern Europe and Central Asia. This despite more detailed inspections and additional paperwork required by new security regulations.

Yet progress is uneven. Trading across Europe is becoming seamless, thanks to the European Union and related free trade agreements. Many of the top 10 economies on the ease of trading are European (table 9.1). Colombia, Nicaragua and other Central American countries are reforming fast too, energized by free trade pacts with the United States. Several African countries have also made big improvements. Still, businesses in some African and South Asian economies are hampered by long delays in complying with trade-related regulations (figure 9.2).

FIGURE 9.1
Export delays drop worldwide

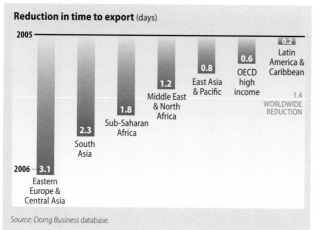

Source: Doing Business database.

TABLE 9.1
Where is trading easy—and where not?

Easiest	Rank	Most difficult	Rank
Hong Kong, China	1	Congo, Rep.	166
Finland	2	Mali	167
Denmark	3	Zimbabwe	168
Singapore	4	Uzbekistan	169
Norway	5	Zambia	170
Estonia	6	Burundi	171
Germany	7	Kazakhstan	172
Canada	8	Kyrgyz Republic	173
Sweden	9	Niger	174
United Arab Emirates	10	Rwanda	175

Note: Rankings are the average of the country rankings on the documents, time and cost required to import and export. See the Data notes for details.
Source: Doing Business database.

Trade costs increase domestic prices and restrict businesses from exporting abroad. One recent study estimates that each day a product is delayed in transit reduces trade by at least 1%.[1] Another shows that reducing trade costs by 50% could increase global trade in manufacturing by up to $377 billion a year and triple the benefits for consumers from tariff reductions.[2] A third study estimates that Bangladesh's garment exports could earn 30% more if inefficiencies at the port of Chittagong were resolved.[3]

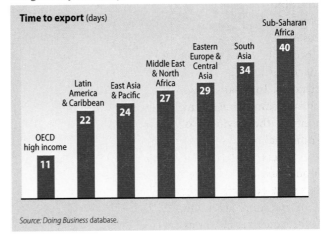

FIGURE 9.2
Longest export delays in Africa and South Asia

Source: Doing Business database.

Who is reforming?

In 2005/06, 19 economies made it easier to trade across borders. Serbia was the top reformer, reducing the time to fulfill all administrative requirements for exporters by 21 days and for importers by 32 days (figure 9.3). A new customs code was adopted, allowing electronic filing of cargo declarations. Risk management software was introduced for customs inspection. Physical inspection of cargo dropped from 100% of shipments to 8%. And a border cooperation agreement, signed with Albania, Croatia and Hungary, introduced uniform customs forms.

Pakistan is the runner-up in reform. It now takes 19 days to import—from the conclusion of a sales contract to the arrival of goods at the warehouse. In 2004 it took 39 days. The improvement comes from a new customs clearance process that allows traders to file cargo decla-

rations before shipments arrive and to pay tariff and port fees electronically. Risk management techniques are now used for choosing which containers to inspect. A pilot run between April 2005 and January 2006 trained staff and the main traders. The Karachi container terminal has since moved fully to the new system.

Reforms have also allowed traders in Colombia, Kenya, Syria and Tanzania to submit customs declarations before the goods arrive at the border (table 9.2). Clearances have sped up by 12 days in Tanzania, 3 days in Kenya, 2 days in Colombia and a day in Syria. "Before you were at the mercy of customs officials, but now I don't see them face-to-face so I don't pay bribes," says a Kenyan trader.

The benefits of electronic filing depend on how many related procedures are automated. Jamaica introduced software that detects whether a cargo document is

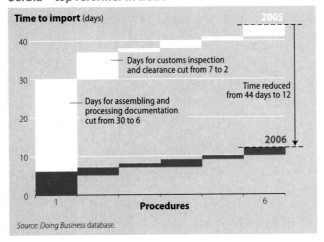

FIGURE 9.3
Serbia—top reformer in trade

Source: Doing Business database.

TABLE 9.2
Risk-based inspections—the most popular reform in 2005/06

Applied risk management techniques
China, Colombia, Ghana, Hong Kong (China), India, Jamaica, Kenya, Nigeria, Pakistan, Romania, Serbia, Syria, Tanzania

Introduced or improved electronic data interchange systems
China, Colombia, France, Ghana, Hong Kong (China), Jamaica, Kenya, Nigeria, Pakistan, Serbia, Syria, Tanzania

Introduced customs administration reforms
Cambodia, Georgia, Hong Kong (China), Jordan, Kenya, Nigeria, Pakistan, Romania, Syria

Implemented border cooperation agreements
China, Hong Kong (China), Kenya, Nicaragua, Romania, Serbia, Tanzania

Improved infrastructure and interagency cooperation at the ports
China, Colombia, Jordan, Kenya, Nigeria, Togo

Source: Doing Business database.

incomplete and calculates the customs duties to be paid. In China new software permits the release of cargo from bonded warehouses before payments are transferred, based on the importer's past payment record. India, Korea, Serbia and Taiwan (China) are all introducing mechanisms that expedite the release of cargo from customs. In Ghana new technology links customs with several commercial banks so that customs officers can confirm the payment of duties without the need for additional paperwork.

Several reformers adopted risk management techniques and after-clearance audits. These allow countries to target customs inspections to higher-risk cargo. In Tanzania more than 90% of cargo is now risk-assessed before it arrives at Dar es Salaam. In Nicaragua new risk management techniques have reduced physical inspections to less than 10% of shipments. After-clearance audits introduced in Egypt, Jordan and Romania have allowed customs to quickly release cargo to importers, with the container contents verified after it reaches the warehouse.

Many other countries reduced port congestion, a common reason for delays at the border. Take the port of Pointe-Noire, in the Republic of Congo: arriving ships wait 8 days before entering a berth, unloading the cargo takes 2 days, and terminal handling another 7. In Gambia these activities take 5 days; in Singapore, half a day. To reduce delays, Kenya installed new cranes at the port of Mombasa. Nigeria introduced competition at its container terminals by signing concession agreements with 3 private businesses. Brazil, China and Colombia made large investments in port infrastructure.

Congestion at ports increases costs as well as delays. In 2006 port congestion surcharges ranging between $60 and $500 per 20-foot container are imposed on traders in Ashdod (Israel), Chittagong (Bangladesh), Cotonou (Benin), Dakar (Senegal), Lagos (Nigeria), Latakia (Syria) and Luanda (Angola). Traders used to face a similar burden at the Jordanian port of Aqaba. No longer: new investment in port infrastructure made it possible to abolish the $150 congestion surcharge.

Cooperation between economies in simplifying and then unifying border requirements has also reduced delays. In 2005 Honduras and Nicaragua cut the waiting time at their shared border in half. Before, traders had to go through inspections on both sides of the border; now the mutual recognition of inspections ensures that a single inspection suffices. A harmonized document for trade between China and Hong Kong (China) reduced paperwork by 60%.

How to reform

If a country wants to become a favored destination for trade, it could start by reducing the number of its tariff bands. This is what Estonia did in 1996, 1 of 3 economies in the world to abolish all tariffs (the others are Singapore and Hong Kong, China). Estonia also ranks in the top 10 on the speed of trading across borders. Similar reforms took place in Egypt in 2004. Customs established a single window for trade documentation and merged 26 approvals into 5. The number of tariff bands was cut from 27 to 6. In Georgia a draft customs code awaiting approval by parliament suggests only 2 tariff bands (down from the current 32): 0% on manufactured goods and 8% on agricultural imports.

Cutting the number of tariff bands is one of the best ways to reduce corruption in customs. An estimated 70% of the bribes paid to customs officials exchange hands when a trader wants to get a lower tariff band.[4] There is no corruption at customs in Hong Kong (China) because there is no such "arbitrage." With fewer tariff bands, it also takes less time for customs officials to complete inspections and paperwork. If Georgia adopted its proposed customs code, a customs officer would no longer have to distinguish containers of cocoa from those of chocolate, but only to identify the products as agricultural or not.

But tariff reforms are difficult. Lobbying groups get involved, to argue for reducing their own tariffs or

FIGURE 9.4
Too many tariff bands in some developing countries

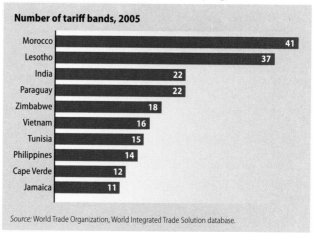

Number of tariff bands, 2005

Morocco	41
Lesotho	37
India	22
Paraguay	22
Zimbabwe	18
Vietnam	16
Tunisia	15
Philippines	14
Cape Verde	12
Jamaica	11

Source: World Trade Organization, World Integrated Trade Solution database.

for keeping those on their foreign competitors high. And governments often claim that reform would lead to a loss of revenues. The first thing a reformer needs to check is the amount of revenues under the existing rules. In Georgia this is a small amount—in 2005, less than 3.5% of the budget. In Egypt before the 2004 reform, it was about 5%. The reason: many goods came into the 2 countries as contraband, to avoid the high tariffs.

In other countries, such as in Africa, this share is larger. There, moving to fewer tariff bands—while keeping the same average tariff rate—would still be a big improvement. There is no reason why Lesotho should have 37 tariff bands and Cape Verde 12 (figure 9.4).

The second thing a reformer can do is establish a set of performance indicators for how rapidly goods are processed at the border. The Tanzanian tax authority started an annual exercise of random checks across border points. In August 2005 the average time to process documents for imports, from arrival to entry into the country, was 8 days, 23 hours across seaports; 6 days, 15 hours across airports; and 3 days, 9 hours across land crossings.[5] In August 2006 the exercise was repeated to monitor the pace of improvements. Thailand recently set a target of 1 day for clearance at customs.

Measuring the time it takes for customs to clear goods is not enough. Other agencies are also involved in inspecting goods or approving documents as cargo crosses borders. For example, the police usually check drivers' identification, the phytosanitary authority inspects all goods, and ministry of agriculture officials check goods for pest control and contagious diseases. The time a trader spends with all these agencies needs to be monitored too. Once this is taken into account, exporters spend 3 days dealing with administrative requirements in

Estonia and 105 days in Iraq (table 9.3).

Such indicators identify bottlenecks and help address them. They also can serve as a basis for bonuses, with border officials receiving extra pay based on the speed of clearing goods. A word of caution: several countries have introduced a measurement scheme only to find strong resistance (and subversion) from staff. Customs officials do not like to have their performance measured, especially if they don't work hard.

Reforms shouldn't stop at the border crossing. "Our road was rendered impassable by rain 3 times, causing

FIGURE 9.5
Better roads, more trade

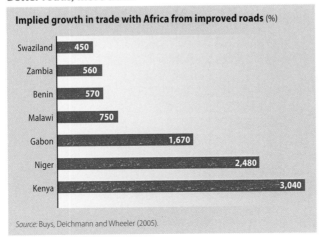

Implied growth in trade with Africa from improved roads (%)

Swaziland	450
Zambia	560
Benin	570
Malawi	750
Gabon	1,670
Niger	2,480
Kenya	3,040

Source: Buys, Deichmann and Wheeler (2005).

TABLE 9.3
Who makes exporting easy—and who does not?

Time (days)

Least		Most	
Estonia	3	Lao PDR	66
Denmark	5	Azerbaijan	69
Germany	6	Burkina Faso	69
Hong Kong, China	6	Eritrea	69
Lithuania	6	Tajikistan	72
Singapore	6	Angola	74
Sweden	6	Burundi	80
Canada	7	Chad	87
Finland	7	Kazakhstan	93
Norway	7	Iraq	105

Documents (number)

Fewest		Most	
Hong Kong, China	2	Congo, Rep.	12
Canada	3	Ecuador	12
Denmark	3	Lao PDR	12
Kiribati	3	Sudan	12
Tanzania	3	Uganda	12
Austria	4	Kazakhstan	14
Finland	4	Rwanda	14
France	4	Tajikistan	14
Germany	4	Djibouti	15
Norway	4	Zambia	16

Cost (US$ per container)

Least		Most	
Tonga	265	Kazakhstan	2,780
China	335	Mongolia	3,007
Israel	340	Congo, Dem. Rep.	3,120
New Zealand	355	Zimbabwe	3,175
Singapore	382	Guyana	3,606
United Arab Emirates	392	Burundi	3,625
Fiji	418	Mauritania	3,733
Finland	420	Rwanda	3,840
Gambia	422	Gabon	4,000
Hong Kong, China	425	Tajikistan	4,300

Source: Doing Business database.

delays of up to 4 hours. The Cameroonian government has grappled with the problem by erecting a series of barriers that stop heavy trucks from passing while it is pouring. Early on the second evening we met a locked barrier in the middle of the forest. It was dark and the man with the keys wasn't there. He returned shortly before midnight. It didn't matter anyway: early the next morning a driver coming in the opposite direction told us that the bridge ahead had collapsed," says a beer distributor in Douala.[6] A recent study estimates that trade among West African countries could expand by up to 400% on average if the road network was upgraded.[7] Similar investment could increase trade in southern Africa by up to 300%, and several times more for some countries (figure 9.5).

But better roads cost money—money that many developing countries don't have. Upgrading roads (from gravel or dirt to asphalt) takes an estimated $125,000 per kilometer in Africa. Maintaining existing roads requires another $5,000 per kilometer.[8]

In some cases there are private firms willing to make these investments. Where investment is risky, donors can provide the needed finance. Projects can be designed as output-based aid, where a private investor builds the road according to specifications (quality of road surface, length of route) and then gets paid. In this way risk is shared: production risks are borne by the private investor, while country risk and expropriation risk are taken by the donor.

Who makes importing easy—and who does not?

Time (days)

Least		Most	
Singapore	3	Kazakhstan	87
Denmark	5	Afghanistan	88
Estonia	5	Niger	89
Hong Kong, China	5	Congo, Dem. Rep.	92
Germany	6	Rwanda	95
Sweden	6	Chad	111
Finland	7	Burundi	124
Norway	7	Kyrgyz Republic	127
Kiribati	8	Iraq	135
Netherlands	8	Uzbekistan	139

Documents (number)

Fewest		Most	
Hong Kong, China	2	Kazakhstan	18
Kiribati	2	Kyrgyz Republic	18
Denmark	3	Uzbekistan	18
Finland	3	Central African Republic	19
Sweden	3	Côte d'Ivoire	19
Canada	4	Iraq	19
Ireland	4	Niger	19
Netherlands	4	Uganda	19
Norway	4	Zambia	19
United Kingdom	4	Rwanda	20

Cost (US$ per container)

Least		Most	
Singapore	333	Niger	3,266
Tonga	360	Congo, Dem. Rep.	3,308
China	375	Tajikistan	3,550
United Arab Emirates	398	Guyana	3,656
Finland	420	Burundi	3,705
Hong Kong, China	425	Mauritania	3,733
Malaysia	428	Uzbekistan	3,970
Iceland	443	Gabon	4,031
Norway	468	Rwanda	4,080
Gambia	494	Zimbabwe	4,565

Notes

1. Djankov, Freund and Pham (2006).
2. Dennis (2006).
3. Asian Development Bank (2003).
4. See also Fisman and Wei (2004) for a study of tariff evasion in trade between China and Hong Kong (China). They find that a 1-percentage-point increase in the tariff rate in China is associated with a 3% increase in tariff evasion. This evasion takes place through misclassification of imports to lower-taxed categories.
5. Tanzania Revenue Authority (2005).
6. *The Economist,* "The Road to Hell Is Unpaved," December 19, 2002.
7. Buys, Deichmann and Wheeler (2005).
8. Buys, Deichmann and Wheeler (2005) and Heggie and Vickers (1998).

48

Enforcing contracts

Enforcing a simple commercial contract in India takes 56 procedures and almost 4 years. "We do not have any lawsuits pending—we simply avoid the courts. By the time the judge decides the case, the defendant's assets have disappeared. In the end the only ones gaining from lawsuits are the lawyers," says Sriram, a beverage manufacturer in Mumbai. Foreign investors share this view: fewer of them set up shop in India than in any other large emerging economy (figure 10.1).

Sriram is not alone. Enforcing a commercial contract in Djibouti takes 59 procedures and almost 3.5 years. In Mozambique it takes nearly 3 years—and for disputes under $600, costs more than the value of the claim. Both countries are among the most difficult in which to enforce contracts (table 10.1).

Without efficient courts, less wealth is created. Fewer

transactions take place, and those that do generally involve a small group of people who are linked through kinship, ethnic origin or previous dealings. Businesses that have little or no access to courts must rely on social networks to decide whom to do business with. In some countries industry associations provide mediation services. But these are not binding, so nothing prevents one party from pretending to go along, then refusing to comply. Credit bureaus help too—but many small countries like Lesotho and Suriname don't have one.

Efficiency and fairness need to be balanced. Achieving that kind of balance was the intention of a recent reform in Russia. Under the old rules a strict 2-month deadline applied to all cases in the Russian *arbitrazh* courts, which deal with commercial cases. But many judges were uncomfortable with the emphasis on speed

FIGURE 10.1
Foreign investors avoid countries with inefficient courts

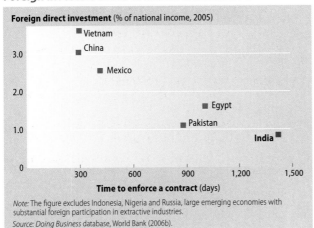

Note: The figure excludes Indonesia, Nigeria and Russia, large emerging economies with substantial foreign participation in extractive industries.
Source: Doing Business database, World Bank (2006b).

TABLE 10.1
Where is enforcing contracts easy—and where not?

Easiest	Rank	Most difficult	Rank
Denmark	1	Sierra Leone	166
Sweden	2	Comoros	167
Norway	3	Mozambique	168
Lithuania	4	Djibouti	169
Japan	5	Cameroon	170
United States	6	Congo, Dem. Rep.	171
Australia	7	Chad	172
Iceland	8	India	173
Switzerland	9	Bangladesh	174
Hong Kong, China	10	Timor-Leste	175

Note: Rankings are the average of the country rankings on the procedures, time and cost to resolve a commercial dispute through the courts. See the Data notes for details.
Source: Doing Business database.

over quality of rulings. As a result the court rules were amended in 2002 to distinguish among different types of cases. Now only cases that are undisputed or involve small amounts can be heard using an accelerated procedure.

Last year, only 1 in 4 attempted reforms succeeded in reducing costs and delays. This low success rate suggests that reformers have little knowledge of what has worked and what has not in other countries. Romania, for example, allowed attorneys to handle the exchange of evidence out of court. Witnesses can be heard at locations such as the office of an attorney. The idea was to shorten delays. It didn't work, because by law both the plaintiff and the defendant must agree to this—and de-

fendants usually try to delay the case. A rule empowering the judge to impose this simplified process on both parties would have done the trick.

Studies on the effects of reforms find that when contracts can be enforced quickly and cheaply, small businesses get better financial terms on loans.[1] Other research finds that new technologies are adopted faster when courts are efficient.[2] The reason is that most innovations take place in new businesses—which unlike large firms do not have the clout to resolve disputes outside the courts. And when contracts can be efficiently enforced, businesses expand their trade networks and employ more workers.[3]

Who is reforming?

In 2005/06, 18 countries reformed contract enforcement —and their reforms are reducing delays and the cost of going through court proceedings. Most reforms took place in Eastern Europe—in Croatia, Estonia, FYR Macedonia and Slovakia—and in Africa—in Burundi, Chad, Gambia, Nigeria and Rwanda. No reforms took place in South Asia, the region with the longest court delays (figure 10.2).

A popular reform was to speed up enforcement once the judge has ruled (table 10.2). Five countries adopted new rules to make enforcement both faster and cheaper. In another country, Thailand, the costs to enforce a claim through public auction were reduced from 5% of the sale's proceeds to 3%. Three countries moved enforcement to the private sector. Slovakia required that commercial cases be enforced by private bailiffs. Bulgaria and FYR Macedonia also introduced private

bailiffs but restricted their operations to a certain location. This is likely to hurt. When territorial restrictions for bailiffs are reduced, as was recently done in Algeria, private enforcement works better. Bailiffs can compete on their fees and the quality of their services.

Georgia—the top reformer in 2005/06—established specialized commercial sections in the courts. The supreme court can now decide which cases to review. Before, it dealt with every case sent by the lower courts. As a result of the new rules, its caseload dropped by 35% from 2004. There is also a proposal to establish 2 specialized bankruptcy courts so as to pool expertise.

Five African countries reformed their courts. In Nigeria, Lagos State introduced a specialized commercial division in the high court. Pretrial conferences between the disputing parties are now required, to dismiss cases without serious opposition and to reduce the points of dispute in others. Nearly a third of all cases don't go

FIGURE 10.2
Long court delays in South Asia

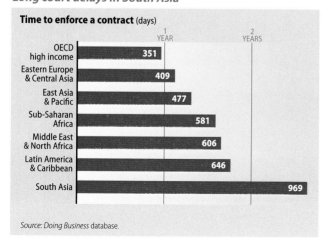

Source: *Doing Business* database.

TABLE 10.2
Specialized courts—a popular reform in 2005/06

Introduced or expanded scope of specialized courts
Australia, Burundi, Chad, Gambia, Georgia, Guyana, Nigeria, Peru, Rwanda

Modified procedural rules or adopted new ones
Brazil, Burundi, Estonia, France, Gambia, Georgia, Italy, FYR Macedonia, Nigeria

Made enforcement of judgments more efficient
Brazil, France, Gambia, FYR Macedonia, Slovakia

Introduced out-of-court enforcement of small or uncontested claims
Croatia, Denmark

Reduced backlog in lower courts
Dominican Republic, FYR Macedonia

Source: *Doing Business* database.

beyond this stage. In addition, new procedural rules require that evidence be exchanged at the beginning of the proceedings. The time to enforce contracts has fallen from 730 days to 457.

Burundi raised its size limit on cases for the small claims court from $300 to $1,000. In October 2005 the Chadian commercial court in N'Djamena held its first hearing. And Gambia established a commercial division in its high court.

Peru also separated the resolution of simple commercial cases from more complex civil and criminal cases. In early 2005, 7 commercial courts and 1 commercial appeals court began functioning in Lima. Of the 8,805 cases filed in the courts between April 5, 2005, and June 30, 2006, 85% were resolved within a year. For certain types of simple debt collection, the time to enforce contracts fell from an average of 285 days in 2004 to 150 days in 2005/06. While an early success, the courts started with no caseload. As more businesses learn about them, filings are increasing and delays are starting to grow. To keep ahead, in July 2006 the president of the court asked for 5 more judges.

European reformers focused on reducing court delays. Italy, the country with the second longest delays in 2004, reduced time by 6 months—from 1,390 days to 1,210 (table 10.3). The reforms eliminated 1 and sometimes 2 mandatory hearings. Parties are now required to raise objections at the outset of the court proceedings.

In FYR Macedonia a program to reduce delays cut the number of cases pending for more than 3 years by 46%. Litigants in long-standing disputes were contacted and asked to appear in court. If neither party showed up, the case was dismissed. Statistics on court backlogs were circulated monthly to track progress. The reforms cut the time to enforce contracts from 509 days to 385.

One way to ease court delays is to take all undisputed claims out of court and bring them before enforcement courts or bailiffs. There is no need for a judge to intervene when claims are uncontested or supported by indisputable evidence. Three countries undertook such reform in 2005/06. Norway, which introduced direct enforcement of claims in 1992, expanded it to cover "any written notification, with mention of the basis for the claim and the amount due." Invoices, most often used in simple commercial transactions, fall into this category. In Denmark debt claims of less than DKr 50,000 ($8,600) now go directly to the bailiff's court. Copenhagen's general courts have received 38% fewer cases since the reform. And 53% of the cases that went straight to

the bailiff's court were resolved within 4 months. Croatia adopted a similar reform in 2005, allowing creditors to bring uncontested claims directly before a notary public and request an enforcement order.

In Eastern Europe and Central Asia 3 countries—Armenia, Estonia and Ukraine—introduced accelerated "payment order procedures" for small, undisputed cases in 2005/06. The effects may be limited. As soon as a claim is opposed, the case is referred back to the normal court procedure. Still, courts can dispose of some cases without spending significant resources.

TABLE 10.3
Where is enforcing contracts the most efficient—and where the least?
Procedures (number)

Fewest		Most	
Iceland	14	India	56
Norway	14	Cameroon	58
Denmark	15	Lesotho	58
Hong Kong, China	16	Sierra Leone	58
Canada	17	Djibouti	59
United States	17	Comoros	60
Ireland	18	Iraq	65
Jamaica	18	São Tomé and Principe	67
Australia	19	Sudan	67
United Kingdom	19	Timor-Leste	69

Time (days)

Fastest		Slowest	
New Zealand	109	Italy	1,210
Singapore	120	Djibouti	1,225
Kyrgyz Republic	140	Suriname	1,290
Lithuania	166	Trinidad and Tobago	1,340
Russia	178	Colombia	1,346
Australia	181	Slovenia	1,350
Kazakhstan	183	India	1,420
Ukraine	183	Bangladesh	1,442
Armenia	185	Guatemala	1,459
Denmark	190	Afghanistan	1,642

Cost (% of claim)

Least		Most	
Korea	5.5	Micronesia	77.0
Finland	5.9	Burkina Faso	95.4
Sweden	5.9	Papua New Guinea	110.3
Iceland	5.9	Cambodia	121.3
Denmark	6.5	Indonesia	126.5
United States	7.7	Mozambique	132.1
Lithuania	8.6	Malawi	136.5
Norway	9.0	Congo, Dem. Rep.	156.8
Austria	9.0	Timor-Leste	183.1
Japan	9.5	Sierra Leone	227.3

Source: Doing Business database.

How to reform

Courts serve businesses best when they are fast, fair and affordable. But in countries where judges are considered corrupt and incompetent, businesses lack confidence that the government can transform the courts. It may be best to rebuild the judiciary from scratch. Rwanda did just that.

In May 2001 President Paul Kagame created the Rwanda Law Reform Commission and gave its 10 members a mandate to review all existing laws and court rules and recommend reforms to improve the delivery of justice. The commission produced a list of suggestions in 4 months, among them to adopt a new procedural code, establish commercial sections in the courts and introduce competitive hiring and pay for court employees. Opposition soon began to form. Many old judges protested proposals that would make all judicial appointments competitive and subject to exams. Indeed, when the new supreme court was staffed, only 3 of the 27 judges were reappointed.

The commission was able to overcome the opposition thanks to the support of President Kagame. He met with the commission regularly and, when necessary, called meetings with all judicial employees—often the site of heated debates—to consider opposing views.

Parliament adopted a slew of new laws for the judicial system in 2003/04. In September 2005 a second set of reforms targeted revisions in the commercial law. Six months later specialized commercial chambers began operating in the higher instance courts. And in May 2006 draft legislation was introduced to set up separate commercial appeals courts (figure 10.3).

The reform hasn't been easy. It faced several obstacles. First, the genocide in the 1990s had left few qualified

people. It took 18 months for the commercial sections to consider their first cases, because candidates for judicial appointments sometimes failed the exam. Second, some ideas didn't work out. For example, the new procedural code calls for 2 lay judges—businesspeople—to review commercial disputes. But it also mandated that the work be voluntary and unpaid. For a long time no one volunteered. Third, foreign experts were uneasy about the magnitude of personnel changes. Wouldn't this endanger the independence of the judiciary? It may, if changes are based on favoritism, not ability. Independence is worth pursuing only if judges are honest and competent. The worst combination is independence and corruption.

Many countries have attempted to reduce corruption in the courts. Few have achieved results. One country that may succeed is Georgia. The latest opinion survey of businesses, in 2005, showed that the share perceiving the judiciary as corrupt had fallen to half its 2002 level.[4] Among transition economies, only Slovakia recorded a larger drop.

How did Georgia do it? Since 2004, when the new government came in, 7 judges have been detained for taking bribes and 15 brought before the criminal courts. In 2005 alone the judicial disciplinary council reviewed cases against 99 judges, about 40% of the judiciary, and 12 judges were dismissed. At the same time judges' salaries were increased fourfold, to reduce dependence on bribe money. As in many other countries undergoing economic transition, in Georgia judges' salaries had fallen to a level that made it difficult to support their families.

Salary increases alone do not solve the problem of judicial corruption. Several other measures help. First, randomly assigning cases to judges, by using case man-

FIGURE 10.3
How Rwanda reformed contract enforcement

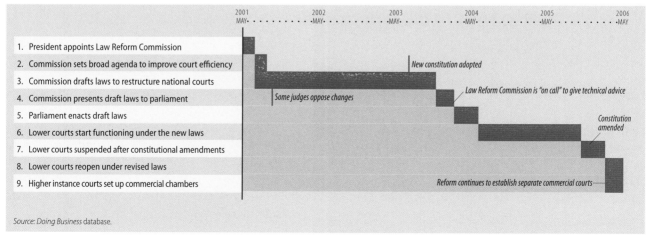

Source: *Doing Business* database.

agement software, can prevent shopping for the judge most willing to accept bribes. Second, requiring judges to disclose their assets annually can deter them from accepting large bribes. If caught, they would face prison time. Third, introducing transparent and objective processes for selecting judges can help attract the best and brightest to the judiciary as well as give judges the moral authority to enforce court rules. Fourth, publicizing cases of corrupt judges being caught and punished convinces citizens that a government is serious about reducing corruption. In October 2003 Kenya's newspapers published the names and photographs of 23 judges who had been charged with corruption and temporarily suspended. Five of the judges resigned, and a tribunal was set up to review the allegations against the others. Opinion polls showed that the public approved.

If the appetite for judicial changes is weak, reformers can start small. Pilot reforms require fewer resources and are unlikely to face as much opposition. Last year Bangladesh and Korea launched pilots to speed contract enforcement in their capital cities. If the pilots prove beneficial, they can be expanded throughout the country.

Introducing specialized courts or specialized commercial sections in the general court is one of the most successful pilot reforms. These simplify procedures to allow "mass production." Small claims courts, with simpler procedural rules, have substantially reduced delays and are typically much cheaper than regular courts. Last year the small claims courts in Melbourne, Australia, raised their threshold to cover cases worth up to $100,000. These changes ensure that claims for small

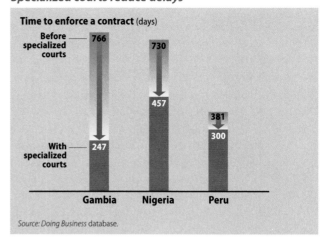

FIGURE 10.4
Specialized courts reduce delays

Source: *Doing Business* database.

amounts go through a simpler process and get quick resolution.

One reason for the greater efficiency of specialized courts is that judges become expert in handling commercial disputes. Another is that these courts often have less formal procedures—for example, they permit oral arguments even in countries where the general courts require written procedures. Countries that have specialized courts or specialized commercial sections in the general courts resolve commercial disputes about 40% faster than countries that don't. Gambia, Nigeria and Peru show the big gains to be had from specialization (figure 10.4). If reforms in the specialized courts yield satisfied users, they embolden governments to try broader reforms.[5]

Notes

1. Qian and Strahan (2006).
2. Cooley, Marimon and Quadrini (2004).
3. Desai, Gompers and Lerner (2004) and Laeven and Woodruff (2004).
4. World Bank (2006a).
5. Ogoola (2006).

Closing a business

In medieval Italy moneylenders conducted their trade from benches set up in town squares. When a moneylender became insolvent, his bench was broken—sometimes over his head. This custom became so associated with insolvency that *banca rotta*, Italian for "broken bench," eventually became *bankrott* in German, *banqueroute* in French and *bankrupt* in English.

Today bankruptcy in most countries does not involve the threat of serious head injury. But the procedure is often more painful than it needs to be. In Chad and India bankruptcy takes 10 years on average. Creditors recover almost nothing (table 11.1). Even in the Czech Republic a company can spend 9 years in bankruptcy. And in Mauritania, where only one company was officially liquidated in the past decade, that liquidation took 11 years.

It doesn't have to be this way. A new bankruptcy law drafted in the Czech Republic may drastically improve the efficiency of resolving financial distress. Brazil introduced sweeping changes in 2004. It now has a re-organization procedure that helps viable enterprises stay alive and gives secured creditors more influence over the process. The time to go through bankruptcy has fallen from 10 years to 4. The reform faced its first test in June 2005, when the Brazilian airline carrier Varig filed for bankruptcy. In little more than a year the airline's assets were sold to a new owner and bankruptcy is nearly complete.

Serbia also introduced reforms in 2004, setting strict time limits and strengthening accountability standards for bankruptcy administrators. The average time for bankruptcy fell from 7 years to less than 3. And the recovery rate for creditors jumped by 45%.

Such reforms make it easier for small firms to get credit, because better bankruptcy laws reassure creditors that they will not lose their money if their debtor's business goes sour. Recent research shows that in countries with long and costly bankruptcy procedures, small firms get only 9% of their new investment in bank credit while large firms get 34%, a difference of 25 percentage points.[1] In countries with efficient bankruptcy the difference is only 4 percentage points.

More important, good bankruptcy laws close unviable businesses and reorganize viable ones.[2] One example of successful reform is Mexico, where the 2000 reform of reorganization proceedings cut delays by 4 years. As a result only 44% of businesses that file for reorganization end up in liquidation. Under the old law more than half did.[3]

TABLE 11.1
Where is it easy to close a business—and where not?

Easiest	Recovery rate	Most difficult	Recovery rate
Japan	92.7	Congo, Dem. Rep.	4.9
Singapore	91.3	Haiti	4.0
Norway	91.1	Philippines	4.0
Taiwan, China	89.5	Micronesia	3.1
Canada	89.3	Angola	2.0
Finland	89.1	Zimbabwe	0.1
Ireland	87.9	Central African Republic	0.0
Belgium	86.4	Chad	0.0
Netherlands	86.3	Eritrea	0.0
United Kingdom	85.2	Lao PDR	0.0

Note: Rankings are based on the recovery rate: how many cents on the dollar claimants (creditors, tax authorities and employees) recover from the insolvent firm. See the Data notes for details.
Source: Doing Business database.

Who is reforming?

Twelve economies made bankruptcy more efficient in 2005/06 (table 11.2). France and Italy adopted reforms that increase the chance of success in reorganization. Chile, Latvia and Serbia improved the regulation of bankruptcy administrators. Creditors got more say in Puerto Rico, Romania, Slovakia and the United States.

Slovakia was the top reformer in 2005/06. Its old law gave creditors only a limited role in the bankruptcy process. Businesses often didn't enter bankruptcy until it was too late and their financial problems were severe. And once begun, bankruptcy could take 5 years or more. The reform changed all that. A company that is in financial difficulty but whose business is still viable can apply for reorganization before it is insolvent. An independent expert evaluates the business and assesses whether reorganization is likely to succeed. Creditors can form a committee to represent their interests. The law also shortens time limits, speeding bankruptcy by at least 9 months. Expected recovery rates increased by 5 percentage points, to 48 cents on the dollar.

Korea, the runner-up in reform, condensed 4 bankruptcy acts into 1. The new act encourages reorganization by simplifying rules for keeping the business running. And it gives creditors more power during bankruptcy by allowing them to establish creditors' committees.

OECD countries have the highest recovery rates in bankruptcy (figure 11.1). Several are getting even better. The United States and France, 2 countries whose bankruptcy regulations are widely emulated around the world, reformed. The United States made it more difficult for debtors in reorganization to cause delays. Debtors have 120 days to propose a reorganization plan. While the previous law allowed bankruptcy judges to extend this period at their discretion, the new law allows only 1 extension of up to 18 months. As a result creditors can now push earlier for liquidation of unviable businesses. The expected time in bankruptcy fell from 2 years to 1.5. The new U.S. law also applies to Puerto Rico.

France made reorganization more accessible to troubled companies, increasing the likelihood that viable businesses will continue operating. A new procedure allows companies in financial difficulty to apply for bankruptcy protection before they are insolvent. The idea is to start reorganizing before it is too late. In addition, creditors that lend money to businesses that are in the preinsolvency procedures will receive priority in the payment of claims, making it more likely that distressed businesses will get new loans. France also increased the

TABLE 11.2
Greater creditors' powers—a popular reform in 2005/06

Strengthened creditors' powers
France, Korea, Romania, Slovakia

Allowed preinsolvency proceedings and made reorganization more attractive
France, Italy, Korea, Slovakia

Improved supervision of administrators
Chile, Latvia, Serbia, Slovakia

Shortened time limits
Puerto Rico, Slovakia, United States

Introduced first bankruptcy law
Burundi, Micronesia

Source: Doing Business database.

involvement of creditors in reorganizations: creditors' committees vote on the proposed reorganization plan. Previously, creditors had little say.

Elsewhere in Europe, Italy allowed financially distressed businesses to seek a deal with creditors before entering formal bankruptcy, a practice widely used in Germany and the United States. The new Italian law also loosens the conditions for coming to terms with creditors: while before an Italian business needed to satisfy 40% of unsecured creditors and 100% of secured creditors to start reorganization, now it needs to satisfy only secured creditors.

Burundi and Micronesia both enacted their first bankruptcy law. Burundi's law gives jurisdiction in bankruptcy to the recently established commercial courts, sets time limits and introduces creditors' committees. Micronesia introduced a single procedure that can result in either liquidation or reorganization. Still, bankruptcy

FIGURE 11.1
Highest recovery rate in OECD countries

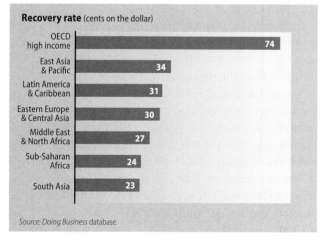

Source: Doing Business database.

there is an expensive undertaking (table 11.3).

Several countries upgraded standards for bankruptcy administrators. Serbia created a new agency to supervise administrators, established ethical standards for the profession and required administrators to pass an examination. Chile changed its law to require exams of administrators. It also imposed new rules on administrators' pay that reduce the incentive for administrators to let cases drag on. Latvia introduced random selection of administrators for every bankruptcy case, to reduce corruption.

The benefits of some reforms may become apparent in 2007. FYR Macedonia passed a new bankruptcy law that introduces strict deadlines—some appeals must now be resolved in as little as 8 days. Creditors will have more influence over the bankruptcy procedure. And the claims in a bankruptcy case can now be consolidated, which will reduce delays and improve secured creditors' ability to enforce their claims. Nepal introduced its first bankruptcy law. But the commercial court designated to administer bankruptcy cases has yet to be established.

Peru and Uzbekistan changed their bankruptcy laws for the worse. In Peru it is no longer possible to amend a reorganization plan once it has been approved. In effect, the new law forces debtors and creditors to draft an entirely new plan if it becomes necessary to adjust the old one. Uzbekistan downgraded secured creditors' claims, placing them behind court fees, utility providers' claims, damages claims and employee compensation. This is easily the worst bankruptcy reform of the year.

TABLE 11.3

Where is bankruptcy the most efficient—and where the least?

Time (years)

Least		Most	
Ireland	0.4	Haiti	5.7
Japan	0.6	Belarus	5.8
Canada	0.8	Turkey	5.9
Singapore	0.8	Angola	6.2
Taiwan, China	0.8	Maldives	6.7
Belgium	0.9	Ecuador	8.0
Finland	0.9	Mauritania	8.0
Norway	0.9	Czech Republic	9.2
Australia	1.0	Chad	10.0
Belize	1.0	India	10.0

Cost (% of estate)

Least		Most	
Antigua and Barbuda	1.0	Albania	38
Colombia	1.0	Dominican Republic	38
Kuwait	1.0	Fiji	38
Netherlands	1.0	Micronesia	38
Norway	1.0	Guyana	42
Singapore	1.0	Sierra Leone	42
Belgium	3.5	Ukraine	42
Canada	3.5	Chad	63
Finland	3.5	Central African Republic	76
Georgia	3.5	Lao PDR	76

Source: Doing Business database.

How to reform

A country that wants efficient bankruptcy should regulate only what it can enforce. Sophisticated reorganization procedures work only in rich countries, with experienced judges and lawyers and a liquid market for the assets of reorganizing firms. In middle-income countries a simpler procedure—liquidation—brings the most benefits to all parties, including employees and suppliers.

In poor countries the highest return comes in debt enforcement procedures—not in reorganization. The differences in outcome are significant (figure 11.2). And the likelihood of saving a viable firm is higher in a simple foreclosure or liquidation than in a reorganization proceeding. Efforts to introduce complex reorganization procedures—for example, in the Organization for the Harmonization of Commercial Law in Africa—only make matters worse.

FIGURE 11.2

Foreclosure works best in poor countries

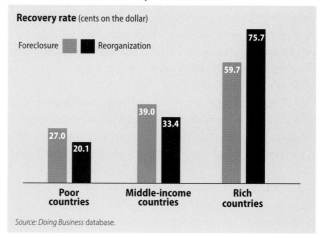

Recovery rate (cents on the dollar)

Source: Doing Business database.

FIGURE 11.3
Creditor involvement increases the recovery rate

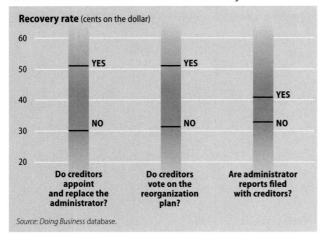

Source: Doing Business database.

FIGURE 11.4
Floating charges improve results in bankruptcy

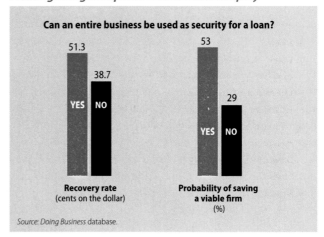

Source: Doing Business database.

The lesson: recognize limitations and introduce bankruptcy regulations that the courts can handle.

A country that wants to improve an existing law would give creditors a greater role—both in the reforms and in the bankruptcy process. This speeds the resolution of insolvency and increases the possibility of saving viable firms.[4] Creditors have an interest in rescuing viable companies and closing unviable ones. Countries that let creditors decide what happens to a distressed business have a higher recovery rate for all parties in the bankruptcy process—including employees and suppliers—than those that do not (figure 11.3). France, Korea and Slovakia, 3 of the reformers in 2005/06, have done just that: allowed the formation of creditors' committees or increased creditors' say in the bankruptcy process.

Another reform trend is to limit appeals. Fast resolution of bankruptcy is crucial, as the deterioration of a company's value over time can rob creditors of any chance of getting their money back and rob employees of their jobs. But many countries unnecessarily introduce delays by allowing multiple appeals on wide grounds. Any good lawyer will use all possibilities to delay the bankruptcy process—if that's what the client wants. In Guatemala appeals delay bankruptcies for months on as little as a spelling error in documents.

Not all appeals need to halt the proceedings: an initial bankruptcy order can go forward with appointing a trustee, forming creditors' committees and so on. If an appeal is successful, the court can suspend the pro-

ceedings. Reducing delay makes the difference between rescuing a viable business and seeing it close. In India an appeal on the initiation of enforcement proceedings can delay the process for up to a year. In this time a creditor's recovery rate will fall by at least 15 cents on the dollar. (Recognizing this, the government is preparing a revision of the bankruptcy act.)

Reformers can also implement simple administrative changes. In Romania reformers amended the bankruptcy law with one goal—to speed the process. Analysis showed that one of the big bottlenecks was notifying all creditors of the bankruptcy. Each creditor had to be tracked down and sent a direct notice by registered mail. Invariably some notices were served improperly or not delivered. Now notices are published only in a central register, which individual creditors can read.

But reformers shouldn't focus on bankruptcy law alone. One reform outside bankruptcy law with a big impact: allow creditors to take security over an entire business (a "floating charge"). This increases the likelihood that a viable business can be sold as a going concern in liquidation and foreclosure proceedings, since it prevents creditors from laying claim to different assets of the company. Countries that allow floating charges have a higher recovery rate than countries that don't (figure 11.4). Denmark introduced a floating charge in 2006, as have many Eastern European countries in the past decade.

FIGURE 11.5

How Serbia reformed bankruptcy law

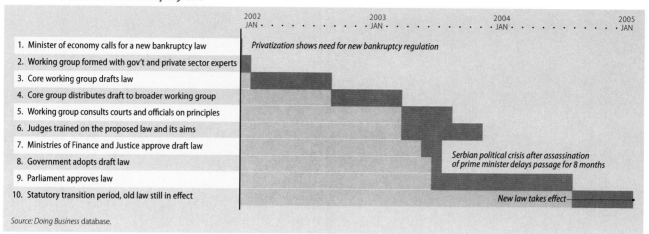

Source: Doing Business database.

And a warning to reformers: judges and justice ministry officials are usually the last to recognize the need for reform. The reason is that in many countries legal training is based on enforcing the rule of law, not on asking whether the rules are outdated and need change. The push for reform comes mostly from banks and other creditors and from governments that want to expand access to finance to households and smaller firms.

Still, the cooperation of the judiciary is essential to any bankruptcy reform. The drafters of Serbia's bankruptcy law recognized that the reform's success depended on judges' ability to carry it out. They invited commercial court judges to comment on the draft (figure 11.5). They also held conferences to inform judges about the new law and organized trips for judges to observe how similar procedures work in other countries. These efforts greatly eased the transition from the old law to the new.

Notes

1. Galindo and Micco (2005).
2. Djankov and others (2006).
3. Gamboa-Cavazos and Schneider (2006).
4. Djankov and others (2006).

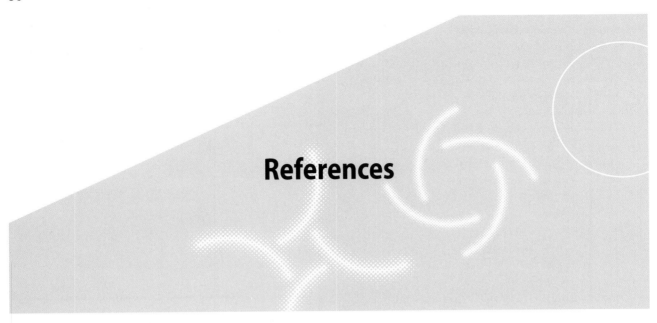

58

References

Alba, Pedro, Stijn Claessens and Simeon Djankov. 1998. "Thailand's Corporate Financing and Governance Structures." Policy Research Working Paper 2003. World Bank, Washington, D.C.

Asian Development Bank. 2003. "Technical Assistance to the People's Republic of Bangladesh for Preparing the Chittagong Port Trade Facilitation Project." Project 36105. Manila.

Bertrand, Marianne, and Francis Kramarz. 2002. "Does Entry Regulation Hinder Job Creation? Evidence from the French Retail Industry." Quarterly Journal of Economics 117 (4): 1369–413.

Bertrand, Marianne, Simeon Djankov, Sendhil Mullainathan and Phillip Schnabl. 2006. "Who Runs Informal Businesses in São Paulo." Harvard University, Department of Economics, Cambridge, Mass.

Booz Allen Hamilton. 2006. "Investor Protection Reforms in Vietnam." Working paper prepared for Doing Business project. World Bank, Investment Climate Department, Washington, D.C.

Botero, Juan C., Simeon Djankov, Rafael La Porta, Florencio López-de-Silanes and Andrei Shleifer. 2004. "The Regulation of Labor." Quarterly Journal of Economics 119 (4): 1339–82.

British Chambers of Commerce. 2005. "Burdens Barometer." London. http://www.chamberonline.co.uk/czP1NeJohOhB8A.html.

Burns, Tony. 2005. "Registering Property: Country Case Studies of Reform in Armenia, Ghana, New Zealand, Peru and Thailand." Working paper. World Bank, Private Sector Development Vice Presidency, Washington, D.C.

Buys, Piet, Uwe Deichmann and David Wheeler. 2005. "Road Network Upgrading and Overland Trade Expansion in Sub-Saharan Africa." World Bank, Development Research Group, Washington, D.C.

Coady, David, Margaret Grosh and John Hoddinott. 2004. "Targeting Outcomes Redux." World Bank Research Observer 19 (1): 61–85.

Cooley, Thomas, Ramon Marimon and Vincenzo Quadrini. 2004. "Aggregate Consequences of Limited Contract Enforceability." Journal of Political Economy 112 (4): 817–47.

Deininger, Klaus. 2003. Land Policies for Growth and Poverty Reduction. World Bank Policy Research Report. New York: Oxford University Press.

De Lara, Yadira. 2006. "The Secret of Venetian Success: The Role of the State in Financial Markets." University of Alicante, Department of Economics, Alicante, Spain.

Dennis, Allen. 2006. "The Impact of Regional Trade Agreements and Trade Facilitation in the Middle East and North Africa Region." Policy Research Working Paper 3837. World Bank, Washington, D.C.

Desai, Mihir, C. Fritz Foley and James R. Hines Jr. 2004. "Foreign Direct Investment in a World of Multiple Taxes." Journal of Public Economics 88: 2727–44.

Desai, Mihir, Paul Gompers and Josh Lerner. 2004. "Institutions, Capital Constraints and Entrepreneurial Firm Dynamics: Evidence from Europe." Harvard Business School, Cambridge, Mass.

Devereux, Michael, Rachel Griffith and Alexander Klemm. 2002. "Corporate Income Tax Reforms and Tax Competition." Economic Policy 35: 451–95.

Djankov, Simeon, Caroline Freund and Cong Pham. 2006. "Trading on Time." Policy Research Working Paper 3909. World Bank, Washington, D.C.

Djankov, Simeon, Caralee McLiesh and Rita Ramalho. Forthcoming. "Regulation and Growth." Economics Letters.

Djankov, Simeon, Caralee McLiesh and Andrei Shleifer. Forthcoming. "Private Credit in 129 Countries." Journal of Financial Economics.

Djankov, Simeon, Oliver Hart, Caralee McLiesh and Andrei Shleifer. 2006. "Efficiency in Bankruptcy." Harvard University, Department of Economics, Cambridge, Mass.

Djankov, Simeon, Rafael La Porta, Florencio López-de-Silanes and Andrei Shleifer. 2002. "The Regulation of Entry." Quarterly Journal of Economics 117 (1): 1–37.

———. 2003. "Courts." Quarterly Journal of Economics 118 (2): 453–517.

———. 2005. "The Law and Economics of Self-Dealing." Harvard University, Department of Economics, Cambridge, Mass.

Emporia, Department of Inspections. 2006. "Building Licenses and Permits." City of Emporia, Va. http://www. ci.emporia.va.us/New_Folder/code%20history.htm.

Eritrea, Department of Infrastructural Services. 2005. "Proclamation 147: A Proclamation to Regulate Construction Activities." Asmara.

Ernst & Young. 2005. "Accelerating Growth: Global IPO Trends in 2005." New York.

FIAS (Foreign Investment Advisory Service). 2006a. "Doing Business in Brazil." World Bank, Washington, D.C. http://www.worldbank.org/brazil.

———. 2006b. "Doing Business in Mexico." World Bank, Washington, D.C. http://www.doingbusiness.org/Main/ Mexico.aspx.

Field, Erica. 2003. "Entitled to Work: Urban Property Rights and Labor Supply in Peru." Working Paper 220. Princeton University, Research Program in Development Studies, Princeton, N.J.

———. 2005. "Property Rights and Investment in Urban Slums." Journal of the European Economic Association 3 (2–3): 279–90.

Fisman, Raymond, and Shang-Jin Wei. 2004. "Tax Rates and Tax Evasion: Evidence from 'Missing Imports' in China." Journal of Political Economy 112 (2): 471–96.

Galiani, Sebastian, and Ernesto Schargrodsky. 2006. "Property Rights for the Poor: Effects of Land Titling." Working paper. Universidad de San Andres and Universidad Torcuato Di Tella, Buenos Aires.

Galindo, Arturo, and Alejandro Micco. 2005. "Bank Credit to Small and Medium-Sized Enterprises: The Role of Creditor Protection." Working Paper 347. Central Bank of Chile, Santiago.

Gamboa-Cavazos, Mario, and Frank Schneider. 2006. "Reforms in Mexican Bankruptcy and Their Effects." Harvard University, Department of Economics, Cambridge, Mass.

Grameen Bank. 2004. "Grameen Bank at a Glance." Dhaka. http://www.grameen-info.org/bank/GBGlance.htm.

Haddad, Lawrence, and Michelle Adato. 2001. "How Efficiently Do Public Works Programs Transfer Benefits to the Poor? Evidence from South Africa." Discussion Paper 108. International Food Policy Research Institute, Washington, D.C.

Heggie, Ian, and Piers Vickers. 1998. Commercial Management and Financing of Roads. World Bank Technical Paper 409. Washington, D.C.

Himmelfarb, George. 1984. The Idea of Poverty. London: Faber.

Hines, James R., Jr. 2005. "Corporate Taxation and International Competition." University of Michigan, Ross School of Business, Department of Accounting, Ann Arbor.

ILO (International Labour Organization). 2005. "Global Employment Trends Brief." February. Geneva. http:// www.ilo.org/public/english/employment/strat/download/ get05en.pdf.

Jacobs, Scott, and Irina Astrakhan. 2006. "Effective and Sustainable Regulatory Reform: The Regulatory Guillotine in Three Transition and Developing Countries." Jacobs and Associates, Washington, D.C.

Kaufmann, Daniel, Aart Kraay and Massimo Mastruzzi. 2005. "Governance Matters IV: Governance Indicators for 1996–2004." Policy Research Working Paper 3630. World Bank, Washington, D.C.

Klapper, Leora. 2006. "Measuring Entrepreneurship: World Bank Group Questionnaire on Entrepreneurship." World Bank Group, Small and Medium Enterprise Department, Washington, D.C. http://www.ifc.org/ifcext/sme.nsf/ Content/Resources.

Ladegaard, Peter. 2005. "Improving Business Environments through Regulatory Impact Analysis: Opportunities and Challenges for Developing Countries." Paper presented at the "International Conference on Reforming the Business Environment," Cairo, November 29–December 1. World Bank, FIAS (Foreign Investment Advisory Service), Washington, D.C.

Laeven, Luc, and Christopher Woodruff. 2004. "The Quality of the Legal System, Firm Ownership and Firm Size." Policy Research Working Paper 3246. World Bank, Washington, D.C.

La Porta, Rafael, Florencio López-de-Silanes and Andrei Shleifer. 2005. "What Works in Securities Laws?" Journal of Finance 61 (1): 1–32.

La Porta, Rafael, Florencio López-de-Silanes, Andrei Shleifer and Robert Vishny. 1998. "Law and Finance." Journal of Political Economy 106 (6): 1113–55.

NNR (Board of Swedish Industry and Commerce for Better Regulation). 2005. "The NNR Regulation Indicator for 2005." Stockholm. http://www.nnr.se/pdf/Regulation_ Indicator_2005_eng.pdf.

Ogoola, James. 2006. "The Current State of Affairs in the High Court and the Role of Division Heads and Registrars." Paper presented at Judges' Conference, Kampala, Uganda, February 6. http://www.judicature.go.ug/uploaded_files/1141051083PJ-presentation.pdf.

Olken, Ben. 2005. Monitoring Corruption: Evidence from a Field Experiment in Indonesia. NBER Working Paper 11753. Cambridge, Mass.: National Bureau of Economic Research.

Osei, Robert, and Peter Quartey. 2005. "Tax Reforms in Ghana." Research Paper 2005/66. United Nations University–World Institute for Development Economics Research, Helsinki.

PricewaterhouseCoopers. 2005. "What Is Your Company's Overall Tax Contribution?" http://www.pwc.com/Extweb/insights.nsf/docid/75D58AF8B3774A3C80256F8800586AC6.

Qian, Jun, and Philip Strahan. 2006. "How Laws and Institutions Shape Financial Contracts." Wharton Financial Institutions Center, Philadelphia.

Rodrik, Dani, and Arvind Subramanian. 2005. "From 'Hindu Growth' to Productivity Surge: The Mystery of the Indian Growth Transition." IMF Staff Papers 52 (2): 193–228.

Schneider, Friedrich, and Robert Klinglmair. 2004. "Shadow Economies around the World: What Do We Know?" CESifo Working Paper 0403. Center for Economic Studies and Ifo Institute for Economic Research (CESifo), Munich.

SEC (U.S. Securities and Exchange Commission). 2006. "The Investor's Advocate: How the SEC Protects Investors, Maintains Market Integrity, and Facilitates Capital Formation." Washington, D.C. http://www.sec.gov/about/whatwedo.shtml#create.

Sitta, S. J. 2005. "Integrity Environment and Investment Promotion: The Case of Tanzania." Paper presented at the Organisation for Economic Co-operation and Development, New Partnership for Africa's Development and Transparency International conference "Alliance for Integrity—Government & Business Roles in Enhancing African Standards of Living," Addis Ababa, March 7–8. Tanzania Investment Center, Dar es Salaam.

Standard & Poor's. 2004. Global Stock Market Factbook. New York.

Subbarao, Kalanidhi. 2003. "Systemic Shocks and Social Protection: Role and Effectiveness of Public Works Programs." World Bank, Human Development Network, Social Protection Unit, Washington, D.C.

Svensson, Jakob. 2005. "Eight Questions about Corruption." Journal of Economic Perspectives 19 (3): 19–42.

Tanzania Revenue Authority. 2005. Time Release Study. Dar es Salaam.

Thailand Investment Service Center. 2004. "Capital Market: Corporate Governance." Bangkok. http://www.thailandoutlook.com.

Vodopivec, Milan. 2006. "Choosing a System of Unemployment Income Support: Guidelines for Developing and Transition Countries." World Bank Research Observer 21 (1): 49–89.

WEF (World Economic Forum). 2005. Global Competitiveness Report 2006. Geneva.

World Bank. 2005a. "Malaysia: Report on Observance of Standards and Codes." Washington, D.C. http://www.worldbank.org/ifa/rosc_cg_malaysia.html.

———. 2005b. "Poland: Corporate Governance Country Assessment." Washington, D.C. http://www.worldbank.org/ifa/rosc_cg_pol_05.pdf.

———. 2006a. Anticorruption in Transition 3: Who Is Succeeding and Why. Washington, D.C.

———. 2006b. World Development Indicators 2006. Washington, D.C.

Data notes

The indicators presented and analyzed in *Doing Business* measure business regulation and the protection of property rights—and their effect on businesses, especially small and medium-size domestic firms. First, the indicators document the degree of regulation, such as the number of procedures to start a business or register commercial property. Second, they gauge regulatory outcomes, such as the time and cost to enforce a contract, go through bankruptcy or trade across borders. Third, they measure the extent of legal protections of property, for example, the protections of investors against looting by company directors or the scope of assets that can be used as collateral according to secured transactions laws. Fourth, they measure the flexibility of employment regulation. Finally, a set of indicators documents the tax burden on businesses. The data for all sets of indicators in *Doing Business 2007* are for April 2006.

The *Doing Business* data are collected in a standardized way. To start, the *Doing Business* team, with academic advisers, designs a survey. The survey uses a simple business case to ensure comparability across countries and over time—with assumptions about the legal form of the business, its size, its location and the nature of its operations. Surveys are administered through more than 5,000 local experts, including lawyers, business consultants, accountants, government officials and other professionals routinely administering or advising on legal and regulatory requirements. These experts have several (typically 4) rounds of interaction with the *Doing Business* team, involving conference calls, written correspondence and country visits. For *Doing Business 2007* team members visited 65 countries to verify data and expand the pool of respondents. The data from surveys are subjected to numerous tests for robustness, which lead to revisions or expansions of the information collected.

The *Doing Business* methodology offers several advantages. It is transparent, using factual information about what laws and regulations say and allowing multiple interactions with local respondents to clarify potential misinterpretations of questions. Having representative samples of respondents is not an issue, as the texts of the relevant laws and regulations are collected and answers checked for accuracy. The methodology is inexpensive and easily replicable, so data can be collected in a large sample of economies—175 published in *Doing Business 2007*. Because standard assumptions are used in the data collection, comparisons and benchmarks are valid across countries. And the data not only highlight the extent of obstacles to doing business but also help identify their source, supporting policymakers in designing reform.

The *Doing Business* methodology has 5 limitations that should be considered when interpreting the data. First, the collected data refer to businesses in the country's most populous city and may not be representative of regulatory practices in other parts of the country. Second, the data often focus on a specific business form—a limited liability company of a specified size—and may not be representative of the regulation on other businesses, for example, sole proprietorships. Third, transactions described in a standardized case study refer to a specific set of issues and may not represent the full set of issues a business encounters. Fourth, the measures of time involve an element of judgment by the expert respondents. When sources indicate different estimates, the time indicators reported in *Doing Business* represent the median values of several responses given under the assumptions of the case study. Fifth, the methodology assumes that a business has full information on what is required and does not waste time when completing procedures. In practice, completing a procedure may take longer if the business lacks information or is unable to follow up promptly.

The methodology for 4 of the *Doing Business* topics changed for *Doing Business 2007*. For paying taxes, the total tax rate measure now includes all labor contributions paid by the employer (such as social security contributions) and excludes consumption taxes (such as sales tax or value added tax). And the measure is now expressed as a percentage of commercial profits rather than gross profits. This change reflects the total tax burden borne by businesses. For enforcing contracts, the case study was revised to reflect a typical contractual dispute over the quality of goods rather than a simple debt default. For trading across borders, *Doing Business* now reports the cost associated with exporting and importing cargo in addition to the time and number of documents required. And for employing workers, hiring costs are no longer included in the calculation of the ease of employing workers.

Doing Business now publishes more than 8,750 data points. Since the publication of *Doing Business* in 2006, 19 challenges to last year's data have been received. In 6 cases—Algeria, France, Hong Kong (China), Jordan, Morocco and the United Kingdom—every data point was reviewed by government experts. The challenges resulted in 12 corrections to the data.

In other cases complaints were resolved without a need for corrections, through explanations of the assumptions underlying the methodology and the date as of which data are collected. In addition, the *Doing Business* team has corrected 37 data points as a result of new information obtained during its travel and the recruitment of additional respondents. The ease of doing business index reflects these changes. For these reasons—as well as the addition of 20 new economies—this year's rankings on the ease of doing business are not comparable with the rankings reported in *Doing Business in 2006*. To make comparisons across time, table 1.2 reports recalculated rankings for last year.

The laws and regulations underlying the *Doing Business* data are now available on the *Doing Business* website at http://www.doingbusiness.org. All the sample surveys and the details underlying the indicators are also published on the website. Questions on the methodology and challenges to data may be submitted through the "Ask a Question" function on the *Doing Business* home page. Updated indicators, as well as any revisions of or corrections to the printed data, are posted continuously on the website.

Economy characteristics

Region and income group

Doing Business uses the World Bank regional and income group classifications, available at http://www.worldbank.org/data/countryclass/countryclass.html. Throughout the report the term *rich economies* refers to the high-income group, *middle-income economies* to the upper-middle-income group and *poor economies* to the lower-middle-income and low-income groups.

Population

Doing Business 2007 reports midyear 2005 population statistics as published in *World Development Indicators 2006*.

Gross national income (GNI) per capita

Doing Business 2007 reports 2005 income per capita as published in the World Bank's *World Development Indicators 2006*. Income is calculated using the Atlas method (current US$). For cost indicators expressed as a percentage of income per capita, 2005 GNI in local currency units is used as the denominator. GNI data were not available from the World Bank for Equatorial Guinea, Puerto Rico and West Bank and Gaza. In these cases GDP or GNP per capita data from the Economist Intelligence Unit 2005 country profiles were used.

Starting a business

Doing Business records all procedures that are officially required for an entrepreneur to start up and formally operate an industrial or commercial business. These include obtaining all necessary licenses and permits and completing any required notifications, verifications or inscriptions for the company and employees with relevant authorities.

After a study of laws, regulations and publicly available information on business entry, a detailed list of procedures is developed, along with the time and cost of complying with each procedure under normal circumstances and the paid-in minimum capital requirements. Subsequently, local incorporation lawyers and government officials complete and verify the data. On average 4 law firms participate in each country.

Information is also collected on the sequence in which procedures are to be completed and whether procedures may be carried out simultaneously. It is assumed that any required information is readily available and that all agencies involved in the start-up process function efficiently and without corruption. If answers by local experts differ, inquiries continue until the data are reconciled.

To make the data comparable across countries, several assumptions about the business and the procedures are used.

Assumptions about the business

The business:

- Is a limited liability company. If there is more than one type of limited liability company in the country, the limited liability form most popular among domestic firms is chosen. Information on the most popular form is obtained from incorporation lawyers or the statistical office.
- Operates in the country's most populous city.
- Is 100% domestically owned and has 5 owners, none of whom is a legal entity.
- Has start-up capital of 10 times income per capita at the end of 2005, paid in cash.

- Performs general industrial or commercial activities, such as the production or sale of products or services to the public. It does not perform foreign trade activities and does not handle products subject to a special tax regime, for example, liquor or tobacco. The business is not using heavily polluting production processes.
- Leases the commercial plant and offices and is not a proprietor of real estate.
- Does not qualify for investment incentives or any special benefits.
- Has up to 50 employees 1 month after the commencement of operations, all of them nationals.
- Has a turnover of at least 100 times income per capita.
- Has a company deed 10 pages long.

Procedures

A procedure is defined as any interaction of the company founder with external parties (government agencies, lawyers, auditors, notaries). Interactions between company founders or company officers and employees are not counted as procedures. Procedures that must be completed in the same building but in different offices are counted as separate procedures. The founders are assumed to complete all procedures themselves, without middlemen, facilitators, accountants or lawyers, unless the use of such a third party is mandated by law.

Both pre- and post-incorporation procedures that are officially required for an entrepreneur to formally operate a business are recorded. Procedures that are not required to start and formally operate a business are ignored. For example, obtaining exclusive rights over the company name is not counted in a country where businesses may use a number as identification.

Procedures required for official correspondence or transactions with public agencies are included. For example, if a company seal or stamp is required on official documents, such as tax declarations, obtaining it is counted. Similarly, if a company must open a bank account before registering for sales tax or value added tax, this transaction is included as a procedure. Shortcuts are counted only if they fulfill 3 criteria: they are legal, they are available to the general public, and avoiding them causes substantial delays.

Only procedures required of all businesses are covered. Industry-specific procedures are excluded. For example, procedures to comply with environmental regulations are included only when they apply to all businesses conducting general commercial or industrial activities. Procedures that the company undergoes to connect to electricity, water, gas and waste disposal services are not included.

Time

Time is recorded in calendar days. The measure captures the median duration that incorporation lawyers indicate is necessary to complete a procedure. It is assumed that the minimum time required for each procedure is 1 day. Although procedures may take place simultaneously, they cannot start on the same day. A procedure is considered completed once the company has received the final document, such as the company registration certificate or tax number. If a procedure can be accelerated for an additional cost, the fastest procedure is chosen. It is assumed that the entrepreneur does not waste time and commits to completing each remaining procedure without delay. The time that the entrepreneur spends on gathering information is ignored. It is assumed that the entrepreneur is aware of all entry regulations and their sequence from the beginning but has had no prior contact with any of the officials.

Cost

Cost is recorded as a percentage of the country's income per capita. Only official costs are recorded. The company law, the commercial code and specific regulations and fee schedules are used as sources for calculating costs. In the absence of fee schedules, a government officer's estimate is taken as an official source. In the absence of a government officer's estimate, estimates of incorporation lawyers are used. If several incorporation lawyers provide different estimates, the median reported value is applied. In all cases the cost excludes bribes.

Paid-in minimum capital

The paid-in minimum capital requirement reflects the amount that the entrepreneur needs to deposit in a bank before registration starts and is recorded as a percentage of the country's income per capita. The amount is typically specified in the commercial code or the company law. Many countries have a minimum capital requirement but allow businesses to pay only a part of it before registration, with the rest to be paid after the first year of operation. In Mozambique in March 2006, for example, the minimum capital requirement for limited liability companies was 1,500,000 meticais, of which half was payable before registration. The paid-in minimum capital recorded for Mozambique is therefore 750,000 meticais, or 10% of income per capita. In the Philippines the minimum capital requirement was 5,000 pesos, but only a quarter needed to be paid before registration. The paid-in minimum capital recorded for the Philippines is therefore 1,250 pesos, or 2% of income per capita.

This methodology was developed in Djankov and others (2002) and is adopted here with minor changes.

Dealing with licenses

Doing Business records all procedures required for a business in the construction industry to build a standardized warehouse as an example of dealing with licenses. These procedures include obtaining all necessary licenses and permits, receiving all required inspections and completing all required notifications and submitting the relevant documents (for example, building plans and site maps) to the authorities. *Doing Business* also records procedures for obtaining utility connections, such as electricity, telephone, water and sewerage. Procedures necessary to be able to use the property as collateral or transfer it to another business are also counted. The survey divides the process of building a warehouse into distinct procedures and calculates the time and cost of completing each procedure under normal circumstances.

Information is collected from construction lawyers, construction firms, utility service providers and public officials who deal with building regulations. To make the data comparable across countries, several assumptions about the business, the warehouse project and the procedures are used.

Assumptions about the construction company

The business (BuildCo):
- Is a limited liability company.
- Operates in the country's most populous city.
- Is 100% domestically owned and has 5 owners, none of whom is a legal entity.
- Carries out construction projects, such as building a warehouse.
- Has up to 20 builders and other employees, all of them nationals with the technical expertise and professional experience necessary to develop architectural and technical plans for building a warehouse.

Assumptions about the warehouse project

The warehouse:
- Has 2 stories and approximately 14,000 square feet (1,300.6 square meters). Each floor is 9 feet, 10 inches (3 meters) high.
- Is located in a periurban area of the country's most populous city.
- Is located on a land plot of 10,000 square feet (929 square meters), which is 100% owned by BuildCo and is accurately registered in the cadastre and land registry.

- Is a new construction (there was no previous construction on the land).
- Has complete architectural and technical plans.
- Will be connected to electricity, water, sewerage and one land phone line. The connection to each utility network will be 32 feet, 10 inches (10 meters) long.
- Will require a 10-ampere power connection and 140 kilowatts of electricity.
- Will be used for storing books.

Procedures

A procedure is any interaction of the company's employees or managers with external parties, including government agencies, public inspectors, notaries, the land registry and cadastre and technical experts apart from architects and engineers. Interactions between company employees, such as development of the warehouse plans and inspections conducted by employees, are not counted as procedures. Procedures that the company undergoes to connect to electricity, water, sewerage and phone services are included. All procedures that are legally or in practice required for building a warehouse are counted, even if they may be avoided in exceptional cases.

Time

Time is recorded in calendar days. The measure captures the median duration that local experts indicate is necessary to complete a procedure. It is assumed that the minimum time required for each procedure is 1 day. If a procedure can be accelerated legally for an additional cost, the fastest procedure is chosen. It is assumed that BuildCo does not waste time and commits to completing each remaining procedure without delay. The time that BuildCo spends on gathering information is ignored. It is assumed that BuildCo is aware of all building requirements and their sequence from the beginning.

Cost

Cost is recorded as a percentage of the country's income per capita. Only official costs are recorded. The building code, specific regulations and fee schedules and information from local experts are used as sources for costs. If several local partners provide different estimates, the median reported value is used. All the fees associated with completing the procedures to legally build a warehouse, including utility hook-up, are included.

Employing workers

Doing Business measures the regulation of employment, specifically as it affects the hiring and firing of workers and the rigidity of working hours. The data on employing workers are based on a detailed survey of employment regulations that is completed by local law firms. The employment laws of most countries are available online in the NATLEX database, published by the International Labour Organization. Laws and regulations as well as secondary sources are reviewed to ensure accuracy. Conflicting answers are further checked against 2 additional sources, including a local legal treatise on employment regulation.

To make the data comparable across countries, several assumptions about the worker and the business are used.

Assumptions about the worker

The worker:

- Is a nonexecutive, full-time male employee who has worked in the same company for 20 years.
- Earns a salary plus benefits equal to the country's average wage during the entire period of his employment.
- Is a lawful citizen with a wife and 2 children. The family resides in the country's most populous city.
- Is not a member of a labor union, unless membership is mandatory.

Assumptions about the business

The business:

- Is a limited liability company.
- Operates in the country's most populous city.
- Is 100% domestically owned.
- Operates in the manufacturing sector.
- Has 201 employees.
- Abides by every law and regulation but does not grant workers more benefits than what is legally mandated.
- Is subject to collective bargaining agreements in countries where such bargaining covers more than half the manufacturing sector.

Rigidity of employment index

The rigidity of employment index is the average of three subindices: a difficulty of hiring index, a rigidity of hours index and a difficulty of firing index. All the subindices have several components. And all take values between 0 and 100, with higher values indicating more rigid regulation.

The difficulty of hiring index measures (i) whether term contracts can be used only for temporary tasks; (ii) the maximum cumulative duration of term contracts; and (iii) the ratio of the minimum wage for a trainee or first-time employee to the average value added per worker. A country is assigned a score of 1 if term contracts can be used only for temporary tasks and a score of 0 if they can be used for any

task. A score of 1 is assigned if the maximum cumulative duration of term contracts is less than 3 years; 0.5 if it is between 3 and 5 years; and 0 if term contracts can last 5 years or more. Finally, a score of 1 is assigned if the ratio of the minimum wage to the average value added per worker is higher than 0.75; 0.67 for a ratio greater than 0.50 and less than or equal to 0.75; 0.33 for a ratio greater than 0.25 and less than or equal to 0.50; and 0 for a ratio less than or equal to 0.25. In the Central African Republic, for example, term contracts are allowed only for temporary tasks (a score of 1), and they can be used for a maximum of 2 years (a score of 1). The ratio of the mandated minimum wage to the value added per worker is 0.66 (a score of 0.67). Averaging the three subindices and scaling the index to 100 gives the Central African Republic a score of 89.

The rigidity of hours index has 5 components: (i) whether night work is unrestricted; (ii) whether weekend work is unrestricted; (iii) whether the workweek can consist of 5.5 days; (iv) whether the workweek can extend to 50 hours or more (including overtime) for 2 months a year; and (v) whether paid annual vacation is 21 working days or fewer. For each of these questions, if the answer is no, the country is assigned a score of 1; otherwise a score of 0 is assigned. For example, Montenegro imposes restrictions on night work (a score of 1) and weekend work (a score of 1), allows 5.5-day workweeks (a score of 0), permits 50-hour workweeks for 2 months (a score of 0) and requires paid vacation of 20 working days (a score of 0). Averaging the scores and scaling the result to 100 gives a final index of 40 for Montenegro.

The difficulty of firing index has 8 components: (i) whether redundancy is disallowed as a basis for terminating workers; (ii) whether the employer needs to notify a third party (such as a government agency) to terminate 1 redundant worker; (iii) whether the employer needs to notify a third party to terminate a group of more than 20 redundant workers; (iv) whether the employer needs approval from a third party to terminate 1 redundant worker; (v) whether the employer needs approval from a third party to terminate a group of more than 20 redundant workers; (vi) whether the law requires the employer to consider reassignment or retraining options before redundancy termination; (vii) whether priority rules apply for redundancies; and (viii) whether priority rules apply for reemployment. For the first question an answer of yes for workers of any income level gives a score of 10 and means that the rest of the questions do not apply. An answer of yes to question (iv) gives a score of 2. For every other question, if the answer is yes, a score of 1 is assigned; otherwise a score of 0 is given. Questions (i) and (iv), as the most restrictive regulations, have greater weight in the construction of the index.

In Tunisia, for example, redundancy is allowed as grounds for termination (a score of 0). An employer has to both notify a third party (a score of 1) and obtain its approval (a score of 2) to terminate a single redundant worker, and has to both notify a third party (a score of 1) and obtain its approval (a score of 1) to terminate a group of redundant workers. The law mandates consideration of retraining or alternative placement before termination (a score of 1). There are priority rules for termination (a score of 1) and reemployment (a score of 1). Adding up the scores and scaling to 100 gives a final index of 80 for Tunisia.

Nonwage labor cost

The nonwage labor cost indicator measures all social security payments (including retirement fund; sickness, maternity and health insurance; workplace injury; family allowance; and other obligatory contributions) and payroll taxes associated with hiring an employee in fiscal year 2005. The cost is expressed as a percentage of the worker's salary. In Bolivia, for example, the taxes paid by the employer amount to 13.7% of the worker's wages and include 10% for sickness, maternity

and temporary disability benefits; 1.7% for permanent disability and survivor benefits; and 2% for housing.

Firing cost

The firing cost indicator measures the cost of advance notice requirements, severance payments and penalties due when terminating a redundant worker, expressed in weekly wages. One month is recorded as 4 and 1/3 weeks. In Mozambique, for example, an employer is required to give 90 days' notice before a redundancy termination, and the severance pay for workers with 20 years of service equals 30 months of wages. No penalty is levied. Altogether, the employer pays the equivalent of 143 weeks of salary to dismiss the worker.

This methodology was developed in Botero and others (2004) and is adopted here with minor changes.

Registering property

Doing Business records the full sequence of procedures necessary when a business purchases land and a building to transfer the property title from the seller to the buyer so that the buyer can use the property for expanding its business, as collateral in taking new loans or, if necessary, to sell to another business. Every required procedure is included, whether it is the responsibility of the seller or the buyer or must be completed by a third party on their behalf. Local property lawyers and property registries provide information on required procedures as well as the time and cost to complete each of them.

To make the data comparable across countries, several assumptions about the business, the property and the procedures are used.

Assumptions about the business

The business:
- Is a limited liability company.
- Is located in a periurban area of the country's most populous city.
- Is 100% domestically and privately owned.
- Has 50 employees, all of whom are nationals.
- Performs general commercial activities.

Assumptions about the property

The property:
- Has a value of 50 times income per capita.
- Is fully owned by another domestic limited liability company.
- Has no mortgages attached and has been under the same ownership for the past 10 years.

- Is adequately measured and filed in the cadastre, registered in the land registry and free of title disputes.
- Is located in a periurban commercial zone, and no rezoning is required.
- Consists of land and a building. The land area is 6,000 square feet (557.4 square meters). A 2-story warehouse of 10,000 square feet (929 square meters) is located on the land. The warehouse is 10 years old, is in good condition and complies with all safety standards, building codes and other legal requirements. The property of land and building will be transferred in its entirety.
- Will not be subject to renovations or additional building following the purchase.
- Has no trees, natural water sources, natural reserves or historical monuments of any kind.
- Will not be used for special purposes, and no special permits, such as for residential use, industrial plants, waste storage or certain types of agricultural activities, are required.
- Has no occupants (legal or illegal), and no other party holds a legal interest in it.

Procedures

A procedure is defined as any interaction of the buyer or the seller, their agents (if an agent is legally or in practice required) or the property with external parties, including government agencies, inspectors, notaries and lawyers. Interactions between company officers and employees are not considered. All procedures that are legally or in practice required for registering property are recorded, even if they may be avoided in exceptional cases. It is assumed that the buyer follows the fastest legal option available and used by the general public. Although the business may use lawyers or other professionals where necessary in the registration process, it is assumed that it does not employ an outside facilitator in the registration process unless legally or in practice required to do so.

Time

Time is recorded in calendar days. The measure captures the median duration that property lawyers or registry officials indicate is necessary to complete a procedure. It is assumed that the minimum time required for each procedure is 1 day. Although procedures may take place simultaneously, they cannot start on the same day. It is assumed that the buyer does not waste time and commits to completing each remaining procedure without delay. If a procedure can be accelerated for an additional cost, the fastest legal procedure available and used by the general public is chosen. If procedures can be undertaken simultaneously, it is assumed that they are. It is assumed that the parties involved are aware of all regulations and their sequence from the beginning. Time spent on gathering information is not considered.

Cost

Cost is recorded as a percentage of the property value, assumed to be equivalent to 50 times income per capita. Only official costs required by law are recorded, including fees, transfer taxes, stamp duties and any other payment to the property registry, notaries, public agencies or lawyers. Other taxes, such as capital gains tax or value added tax, are excluded from the cost measure. If cost estimates differ among sources, the median reported value is used.

Getting credit

Doing Business constructs measures of the legal rights of borrowers and lenders and the sharing of credit information. The first set of indicators describes how well collateral and bankruptcy laws facilitate lending. The second set measures the coverage, scope, quality and accessibility of credit information available through public and private credit registries.

The data on the legal rights of borrowers and lenders are gathered through a survey of financial lawyers and verified through analysis of laws and regulations as well as public sources of information on collateral and bankruptcy laws. The data on credit information sharing are built in two stages. First, banking supervision authorities and public information sources are surveyed to confirm the presence of public credit registries and private credit information bureaus. Second, when applicable, a detailed survey on the public or private credit registry's structure, law and associated rules is administered to the credit registry. Survey responses are verified through several rounds of follow-up communication with respondents as well as by contacting third parties and consulting public sources. The survey data are confirmed through teleconference calls in most countries.

Strength of legal rights index

The strength of legal rights index measures the degree to which collateral and bankruptcy laws protect the rights of borrowers and lenders and thus facilitate lending. The index includes 7 aspects related to legal rights in collateral law and 3 aspects in bankruptcy law. A score of 1 is assigned for each of the following features of the laws:

- General rather than specific description of assets is permitted in collateral agreements.
- General rather than specific description of debt is permitted in collateral agreements.

- Any legal or natural person may grant or take security in the property.
- A unified registry operates that includes charges over movable property.
- Secured creditors have priority outside of bankruptcy.
- Secured creditors, rather than other parties such as government or workers, are paid first out of the proceeds from liquidating a bankrupt firm.
- Secured creditors are able to seize their collateral when a debtor enters reorganization; there is no "automatic stay" or "asset freeze" imposed by the court.
- Management does not stay during reorganization. An administrator is responsible for managing the business during reorganization.
- Parties may agree on enforcement procedures by contract.
- Creditors may both seize and sell collateral out of court without restriction.

The index ranges from 0 to 10, with higher scores indicating that collateral and bankruptcy laws are better designed to expand access to credit.

Depth of credit information index

The depth of credit information index measures rules affecting the scope, accessibility and quality of credit information available through either public or private credit registries. A score of 1 is assigned for each of the following 6 features of the credit information system:

- Both positive (for example, amount of loan and on-time repayment pattern) and negative (for instance, number and amount of defaults, late payments, bankruptcies) credit information is distributed.
- Data on both firms and individuals are distributed.
- Data from retailers, trade creditors or utilities as well as financial institutions are distributed.

- More than 2 years of historical data are distributed.
- Data on loans above 1% of income per capita are distributed.
- By law, borrowers have the right to access their data.

The index ranges from 0 to 6, with higher values indicating the availability of more credit information, from either a public registry or a private bureau, to facilitate lending decisions. In Turkey, for example, both a public and a private registry operate. Both distribute positive and negative information (a score of 1). The private bureau distributes data only on individuals, but the public registry covers firms as well as individuals (a score of 1). The public and private registries share data among financial institutions only; no data are collected from retailers or utilities (a score of 0). The private bureau distributes more than 2 years of historical data (a score of 1). The public registry collects data only on loans of $3,132 (66% of income per capita) or more, but the private bureau collects information on loans of any value (a score of 1). Borrowers have the right to access their data (a score of 1). Summing across the indicators gives Turkey a total score of 5.

Public credit registry coverage

The public credit registry coverage indicator reports the number of individuals and firms listed in a public credit registry with current information on repayment history, unpaid debts or credit outstanding. The number is expressed as a

percentage of the adult population. A public credit registry is defined as a database managed by the public sector, usually by the central bank or the superintendent of banks, that collects information on the creditworthiness of borrowers (persons or businesses) in the financial system and makes it available to financial institutions. If no public registry operates, the coverage value is 0.

Private credit bureau coverage

The private credit bureau coverage indicator reports the number of individuals or firms listed by a private credit bureau with current information on repayment history, unpaid debts or credit outstanding. The number is expressed as a percentage of the adult population. A private credit bureau is defined as a private firm or nonprofit organization that maintains a database on the creditworthiness of borrowers (persons or businesses) in the financial system and facilitates the exchange of credit information among banks and financial institutions. Credit investigative bureaus and credit reporting firms that do not directly facilitate information exchange between banks and other financial institutions are not considered. If no private bureau operates, the coverage value is 0.

This methodology was developed in Djankov, McLiesh and Shleifer (forthcoming) and is adopted here with minor changes.

Protecting investors

Doing Business measures the strength of minority shareholder protections against directors' misuse of corporate assets for personal gain. The indicators distinguish 3 dimensions of investor protection: transparency of transactions (extent of disclosure index), liability for self-dealing (extent of director liability index) and shareholders' ability to sue officers and directors for misconduct (ease of shareholder suits index). The data come from a survey of corporate lawyers and are based on company laws, court rules of evidence and securities regulations.

To make the data comparable across countries, several assumptions about the business and the transaction are used.

Assumptions about the business

The business (Buyer):

- Is a publicly traded corporation listed on the country's most important stock exchange. If the number of publicly traded companies listed on that exchange is less than 10, or if there is no stock exchange in the country, it is assumed that Buyer is a large private company with multiple shareholders.
- Has a board of directors and a chief executive officer (CEO) who may legally act on behalf of Buyer where permitted, even if this is not specifically required by law.

- Has only national shareholders.
- Has invested only in the country and has no subsidiaries or operations abroad.
- Is a food manufacturer.
- Has its own distribution network.

Assumptions about the transaction

- Mr. James is Buyer's controlling shareholder and a member of Buyer's board of directors. He owns 60% of Buyer and elected 2 directors to Buyer's 5-member board.
- Mr. James also owns 90% of Seller, a company that operates a chain of retail hardware stores. Seller recently closed a large number of its stores.
- Mr. James proposes to Buyer that it purchase Seller's unused fleet of trucks to expand Buyer's distribution of its food products. Buyer agrees. The price is equal to 10% of Buyer's assets and is higher than the market value.
- The proposed transaction is part of the company's ordinary course of business and is not outside the authority of the company.
- Buyer enters into the transaction. All required approvals are obtained, and all required disclosures made.
- The transaction is unfair to Buyer. Shareholders sue Mr. James and the other parties that approved the transaction.

Extent of disclosure index

The extent of disclosure index has 5 components: (i) what corporate body can provide legally sufficient approval for the transaction (a score of 0 is assigned if it is the CEO or the managing director alone; 1 if the board of directors or shareholders must vote and Mr. James is permitted to vote; 2 if the board of directors must vote and Mr. James is not permitted to vote; 3 if shareholders must vote and Mr. James is not permitted to vote); (ii) whether immediate disclosure of the transaction to the public, the shareholders or both is required (a score of 0 is assigned if no disclosure is required; 1 if disclosure on the terms of the transaction but not Mr. James's conflict of interest is required; 2 if disclosure on both the terms and Mr. James's conflict of interest is required); (iii) whether disclosure in the annual report is required (a score of 0 is assigned if no disclosure on the transaction is required; 1 if disclosure on the terms of the transaction but not Mr. James's conflict of interest is required; 2 if disclosure on both the terms and Mr. James's conflict of interest is required); (iv) whether disclosure by Mr. James to the board of directors is required (a score of 0 is assigned if no disclosure is required; 1 if a general disclosure of the existence of a conflict of interest is required without any specifics; 2 if full disclosure of all material facts relating to Mr. James's interest in the Buyer-Seller transaction is required); and (v) whether it is required that an external body, for example, an external auditor, review the transaction before it takes place (a score of 0 is assigned if no; 1 if yes).

The index ranges from 0 to 10, with higher values indicating greater disclosure. In Poland, for example, the board of directors must approve the transaction and Mr. James is not allowed to vote (a score of 2). Buyer is required to disclose immediately all information affecting the stock price, including the conflict of interest (a score of 2). In its annual report Buyer must also disclose the terms of the transaction and Mr. James's ownership in Buyer and Seller (a score of 2). Before the transaction Mr. James must disclose his conflict of interest to the other directors, but he is not required to provide specific information about it (a score of 1). Poland does not require an external body to review the transaction (a score of 0). Adding these numbers gives Poland a score of 7 on the extent of disclosure index.

Extent of director liability index

The extent of director liability index measures (i) a shareholder plaintiff's ability to hold Mr. James liable for damage the Buyer-Seller transaction causes to the company (a score of 0 is assigned if Mr. James cannot be held liable or can be held liable only for fraud or bad faith; 1 if Mr. James can be held liable only if he influenced the approval of the transaction or was negligent; 2 if Mr. James can be held liable when the transaction was unfair or prejudicial to the other shareholders); (ii) a shareholder plaintiff's ability to hold the approving body (the CEO or board of directors) liable for

damage the transaction causes to the company (a score of 0 is assigned if the approving body cannot be held liable or can be held liable only for fraud or bad faith; 1 if the approving body can be held liable for negligence; 2 if the approving body can be held liable when the transaction is unfair or prejudicial to the other shareholders); (iii) whether a court can void the transaction upon a successful claim by a shareholder plaintiff (a score of 0 is assigned if rescission is unavailable or is available only in case of fraud or bad faith; 1 if rescission is available when the transaction is oppressive or prejudicial to the other shareholders; 2 if rescission is available when the transaction is unfair or entails a conflict of interest); (iv) whether Mr. James pays damages for the harm caused to the company upon a successful claim by the shareholder plaintiff (a score of 0 is assigned if no; 1 if yes); (v) whether Mr. James repays profits made from the transaction upon a successful claim by the shareholder plaintiff (a score of 0 is assigned if no; 1 if yes); (vi) whether fines and imprisonment can be applied against Mr. James (a score of 0 is assigned if no; 1 if yes); and (vii) shareholder plaintiffs' ability to sue directly or derivatively for damage the transaction causes to the company (a score of 0 is assigned if suits are unavailable or are available only for shareholders holding more than 10% of the company's share capital; 1 if direct or derivative suits are available for shareholders holding 10% or less of share capital).

The index ranges from 0 to 10, with higher values indicating greater liability of directors. To hold Mr. James liable in Panama, for example, a plaintiff must prove that Mr. James influenced the approving body or acted negligently (a score of 1). To hold the other directors liable, a plaintiff must prove that they acted negligently (a score of 1). The unfair transaction cannot be voided (a score of 0). If Mr. James is found liable, he must pay damages (a score of 1) but he is not required to disgorge his profits (a score of 0). Mr. James cannot be fined or imprisoned (a score of 0). Direct suits are available for shareholders holding 10% or less of share capital (a score of 1). Adding these numbers gives Panama a score of 4 on the extent of director liability index.

Ease of shareholder suits index

The ease of shareholder suits index measures (i) the range of documents available to the shareholder plaintiff from the defendant and witnesses during trial (a score of 1 is assigned for each of the following types of documents available: information that the defendant has indicated he intends to rely on for his defense; information that directly proves specific facts in the plaintiff's claim; any information relevant to the subject matter of the claim; and any information that may lead to the discovery of relevant information); (ii) whether the plaintiff can directly examine the defendant and witnesses during trial (a score of 0 is assigned if no; 1 if yes, with prior approval of the questions by the judge; 2 if yes, without prior approval); (iii) whether the plaintiff can obtain any documents from the defendant without identifying them specifically (a score of 0 is assigned if no; 1 if yes); (iv) whether shareholders owning

10% or less of the company's share capital can request that a government inspector investigate the Buyer-Seller transaction (a score of 0 is assigned if no; 1 if yes); (v) whether shareholders owning 10% or less of the company's share capital have the right to inspect the transaction documents before filing suit (a score of 0 is assigned if no; 1 if yes); and (vi) whether the standard of proof for civil suits is lower than that for a criminal case (a score of 0 is assigned if no; 1 if yes).

The index ranges from 0 to 10, with higher values indicating greater powers of shareholders to challenge the transaction. In Greece, for example, the plaintiff can access documents that the defendant intends to rely on for his defense and that directly prove facts in the plaintiff's claim (a score of 2). The plaintiff can examine the defendant and witnesses during trial, though only with prior approval of the questions by the court (a score of 1). The plaintiff must specifically identify the documents being sought (for example, the Buyer-Seller purchase agreement of July 15, 2005) and cannot just request categories (for example, all documents related to the

transaction) (a score of 0). A shareholder holding 5% of Buyer's shares can request that a government inspector review suspected mismanagement by Mr. James and the CEO (a score of 1). And any shareholder can inspect the transaction documents before deciding whether to sue (a score of 1). The standard of proof for civil suits is the same as that for criminal suits (a score of 0). Adding these numbers gives Greece a score of 5 on the ease of shareholder suits index.

Strength of investor protection index

The strength of investor protection index is the average of the extent of disclosure index, the extent of director liability index and the ease of shareholder suits index. The index ranges from 0 to 10, with higher values indicating better investor protection.

This methodology was developed in Djankov, La Porta, Lopez-de-Silanes and Shleifer (2005) and is adopted here with minor changes.

Paying taxes

Doing Business records the tax that a medium-size company must pay or withhold in a given year, as well as measures of the administrative burden in paying taxes. Taxes are measured at all levels of government and include the profit or corporate income tax, social security contributions and labor taxes paid by the employer, property taxes, property transfer taxes, the dividend tax, the capital gains tax, the financial transactions tax, waste collection taxes and vehicle and road taxes.

To measure the tax paid by a standardized business and the complexity of a country's tax law, a case study is prepared with a set of financial statements and assumptions about transactions made over the year. Experts in each country compute the taxes owed in their jurisdiction based on the standardized case facts. Information on the frequency of filing, audits and other costs of compliance is also compiled. The project was developed and implemented in cooperation with PricewaterhouseCoopers.

To make the data comparable across countries, several assumptions about the business and the taxes are used.

Assumptions about the business

The business:
- Is a limited liability, taxable company. If there is more than one type of limited liability company in the country, the limited liability form most popular among domestic firms is chosen. Incorporation lawyers or the statistical office report the most popular form.
- Started operations on January 1, 2004. At that time the company purchased all the assets shown in its balance sheet and hired all its workers.
- Operates in the country's most populous city.

- Is 100% domestically owned and has 5 owners, all of whom are natural persons.
- Has a start-up capital of 102 times income per capita at the end of 2004.
- Performs general industrial or commercial activities. Specifically, it produces ceramic flowerpots and sells them at retail. It does not participate in foreign trade (no import or export) and does not handle products subject to a special tax regime, for example, liquor or tobacco.
- Owns 2 plots of land, 1 building, machinery, office equipment, computers and 1 truck and leases another truck.
- Does not qualify for investment incentives or any special benefits apart from those related to the age or size of the company.
- Has 60 employees—4 managers, 8 assistants and 48 workers. All are nationals, and 1 of the managers is also an owner.
- Has a turnover of 1,050 times income per capita.
- Makes a loss in the first year of operation.
- Has the same gross margin (pre-tax) across all economies.
- Distributes 50% of its profits as dividends to the owners at the end of the second year.
- Sells one of its plots of land at a profit during the second year.
- Is subject to a series of detailed assumptions on expenses and transactions to further standardize the case.

Assumptions about the taxes

- All the taxes paid or withheld in the second year of operation are recorded. A tax is considered distinct if it has a different name or is collected by a different agency. Taxes with the same name and agency, but charged at different rates depending on the business, are counted as the same tax.

- The number of times the company pays or withholds taxes in a year is the number of different taxes multiplied by the frequency of payment (or withholding) for each tax. The frequency of payment includes advance payments (or withholding) as well as regular payments (or withholding).

Tax payments

The tax payments indicator reflects the total number of taxes paid, the method of payment, the frequency of payment and the number of agencies involved for this standardized case during the second year of operation. It includes payments made by the company on consumption taxes, such as sales tax or value added tax. These taxes are traditionally withheld on behalf of the consumer. The number of payments takes into account electronic filing. Where full electronic filing is allowed, the tax is counted as paid once a year even if the payment is more frequent.

Time

Time is recorded in hours per year. The indicator measures the time to prepare, file and pay (or withhold) three major types of taxes: the corporate income tax, value added or sales tax and labor taxes, including payroll taxes and social security contributions. Preparation time includes the time to collect all information necessary to compute the tax payable. If separate accounting books must be kept for tax purposes—or separate calculations must be made for tax purposes—the time associated with these processes is included. Filing time includes the time to complete all necessary tax forms and make all necessary calculations. Payment time is the hours needed to make the payment online or at the tax office. When taxes are paid in person, the time includes delays while waiting.

Total tax rate

The total tax rate measures the amount of taxes payable by the business in the second year of operation, expressed as a share of commercial profits. *Doing Business 2007* reports tax rates for fiscal year 2005. The total amount of taxes is the sum of all the different taxes payable after accounting for deductions and exemptions. The taxes withheld (such as sales tax or value added tax) but not paid by the company are excluded. The taxes included can be divided into five categories: profit or corporate income tax, social security contributions and other labor taxes paid by the employer, property taxes, turnover taxes and other small taxes (such as municipal fees and vehicle and fuel taxes).

Commercial profits are defined as sales minus cost of goods sold, minus gross salaries, minus administrative expenses, minus other deductible expenses, minus deductible provisions, plus capital gains (from the property sale) minus interest expense, plus interest income and minus commercial depreciation. To compute the commercial depreciation, a straight-line depreciation method is applied with the following rates: 0% for the land, 5% for the building, 10% for the machinery, 33% for the computers, 20% for the office equipment, 20% for the truck and 10% for business development expenses.

The methodology is consistent with the total tax calculation applied by PricewaterhouseCoopers.

This methodology was developed in "Tax Burdens around the World," an ongoing research project by Simeon Djankov, Caralee McLiesh, Rita Ramalho and Andrei Shleifer.

Trading across borders

Doing Business compiles procedural requirements for exporting and importing a standardized cargo of goods. Every official procedure for exporting and importing the goods is recorded—from the contractual agreement between the two parties to the delivery of goods—along with the time and cost necessary for completion. All documents required for clearance of the goods across the border are also recorded. For exporting goods, procedures range from packing the goods at the factory to their departure from the port of exit. For importing goods, procedures range from the vessel's arrival at the port of entry to the cargo's delivery at the factory warehouse.

Local freight forwarders, shipping lines, customs brokers and port officials provide information on required documents and cost as well as the time to complete each procedure. To make the data comparable across countries, several assumptions about the business and the traded goods are used.

Assumptions about the business

The business:
- Has 200 or more employees.
- Is located in the country's most populous city.
- Is a private, limited liability company. It does not operate within an export processing zone or an industrial estate with special export or import privileges.
- Is domestically owned with no foreign ownership.
- Exports more than 10% of its sales.

Assumptions about the traded goods

The traded product travels in a dry-cargo, 20-foot, full container load. The product:
- Is not hazardous nor does it include military items.
- Does not require refrigeration or any other special environment.
- Does not require any special phytosanitary or environmental safety standards other than accepted international standards.

- Falls under one of the following Standard International Trade Classification (SITC) Revision categories:

    SITC 65: textile yarn, fabrics and made-up articles.

    SITC 84: articles of apparel and clothing accessories.

    SITC 07: coffee, tea, cocoa, spices and manufactures thereof.

Documents

All documents required to export and import the goods are recorded. It is assumed that the contract has already been agreed upon and signed by both parties. Documents include bank documents, customs declaration and clearance documents, port filing documents, import licenses and other official documents exchanged between the concerned parties. Documents filed simultaneously are considered different documents but with the same time frame for completion.

Time

Time is recorded in calendar days. The time calculation for a procedure starts from the moment it is initiated and runs until it is completed. If a procedure can be accelerated for an additional cost, the fastest legal procedure is chosen. It is assumed that neither the exporter nor the importer wastes time and that each commits to completing each remaining procedure without delay. Procedures that can be completed in parallel are measured as simultaneous for the purpose of measuring time. The waiting time between procedures (for example, during unloading of the cargo) is included in the measure.

Cost

Cost is recorded as the fees levied on a 20-foot container in United States dollars. All the fees associated with completing the procedures to export or import the goods are included. These include costs for documents, administrative fees for customs clearance and technical control, terminal handling charges and inland transport. The cost measure does not include tariffs or trade taxes. Only official costs are recorded.

Enforcing contracts

Indicators on enforcing contracts measure the efficiency of the judicial system in resolving a commercial dispute. The data are built by following the step-by-step evolution of a payment dispute before local courts. The data are collected through study of the codes of civil procedure and other court regulations as well as surveys completed by local litigation lawyers (and, in a quarter of the countries, by judges as well).

Assumptions about the case

- The value of the claim equals 200% of the country's income per capita.
- The plaintiff has fully complied with the contract (that is, the plaintiff is 100% right).
- The case represents a lawful transaction between businesses located in the country's most populous city.
- The plaintiff files a lawsuit to enforce the contract.
- A court in the most populous city decides the dispute.
- The defendant attempts to delay service of process but it is finally accomplished.
- The defendant opposes the complaint (default judgment is not an option) on the grounds that the delivered goods were not of adequate quality.
- The plaintiff introduces documentary evidence and calls one witness. The defendant calls one witness. Neither party presents objections.
- The judgment is in favor of the plaintiff and the defendant does not appeal the judgment.

- The plaintiff takes all required steps for prompt enforcement of the judgment. The debt is successfully collected through sale of the defendant's movable assets (such as a vehicle) at a public auction.

Procedures

A procedure is defined as any interaction mandated by law or court regulation between the parties, or between them and the judge (or administrator) or court officer. This includes steps to file the case, steps for trial and judgment and steps necessary to enforce the judgment.

Time

Time is recorded in calendar days, counted from the moment the plaintiff files the lawsuit in court until payment. This includes both the days when actions take place and the waiting periods between actions. The respondents make separate estimates of the average duration of different stages of dispute resolution: the completion of service of process (time to file the case), the issuance of judgment (time for the trial) and the moment of payment (time for enforcement).

Cost

Cost is recorded as a percentage of the claim, assumed to be equivalent to 200% of income per capita. Only official costs required by law are recorded, including court costs and average attorney fees where the use of attorneys is mandatory or common.

This methodology was developed in Djankov and others (2003) and is adopted here with minor changes.

Closing a business

Doing Business studies the time, cost and outcomes of bankruptcy proceedings involving domestic entities. The data are derived from survey responses by local insolvency lawyers and verified through a study of laws and regulations as well as public information on bankruptcy systems.

To make the data comparable across countries, several assumptions about the business and the case are used.

Assumptions about the business

The business:

- Is a limited liability company.
- Operates in the country's most populous city.
- Is 100% domestically owned, with the founder, who is also the chairman of the supervisory board, owning 51% (no other shareholder holds more than 5% of shares).
- Has downtown real estate, where it runs a hotel, as its major asset.
- Has a professional general manager.
- Has had average annual revenue of 1,000 times income per capita over the past 3 years.
- Has 201 employees and 50 suppliers, each of whom is owed money for the last delivery.
- Borrowed from a domestic bank 5 years ago (the loan has 10 years to full repayment) and bought real estate (the hotel building), using it as security for the bank loan.
- Has observed the payment schedule and all other conditions of the loan up to now.
- Has a mortgage, with the value of the mortgage principal being exactly equal to the market value of the hotel.

Assumptions about the case

- The business is experiencing liquidity problems. The company's loss in 2005 reduced its net worth to a negative figure. There is no cash to pay the bank interest or principal in full, due tomorrow. Therefore, the business defaults on its loan. Management believes that losses will be incurred in 2007 and 2008 as well.
- The bank holds a floating charge against the hotel in countries where floating charges are possible. If the law does not permit a floating charge but contracts commonly use some other provision to that effect, this provision is specified in the lending contract.
- The business has too many creditors to renegotiate out of court. It has the following options: a procedure aimed at rehabilitation or any procedure that will reorganize the business to permit further operation; a procedure aimed at liquidation; or a procedure aimed at selling the hotel, as a going concern or piecemeal, enforced either through court (or by a government authority like a debt collection agency) or out of court (receivership).

Time

Time is recorded in calendar years. It captures the estimated duration required to complete a bankruptcy. Information is collected on the sequence of the bankruptcy procedures and on whether any procedures can be carried out simultaneously. Delays due to legal derailment tactics that parties to the bankruptcy may use—in particular, the extension of response periods or appeals—are considered.

Cost

The cost of the bankruptcy proceedings is recorded as a percentage of the estate's value. The cost is calculated on the basis of survey responses by practicing insolvency lawyers. If several respondents report different estimates, the median reported value is used. Only official costs are recorded, including court costs as well as fees of insolvency practitioners, independent assessors, lawyers and accountants. The cost figures are averages of the estimates on a multiple-choice question, where the respondents choose among the following options: 0–2%, 3–5%, 6–8%, 9–10%, 11–18%, 19–25%, 26–33%, 34–50%, 51–75% and more than 75% of the estate value of the bankrupt business.

Recovery rate

The recovery rate is recorded as cents on the dollar recovered by claimants—creditors, tax authorities and employees—through the bankruptcy proceedings. The calculation takes into account whether the business is kept as a going concern during the proceedings, as well as bankruptcy costs and the loss in value due to the time spent closing down. If the business keeps operating, no value is lost on the initial claim, set at 100 cents on the dollar. If it does not, the initial 100 cents on the dollar are reduced to 70 cents on the dollar. Then the official costs of the insolvency procedure are deducted (1 cent for each percentage of the initial value). Finally, the value lost as a result of the time that the money remains tied up in insolvency procedures is taken into account, including the loss of value due to depreciation of the hotel furniture. Consistent with international accounting practice, the depreciation rate for furniture is taken to be 20%. The furniture is assumed to account for a quarter of the total value of assets. The recovery rate is the present value of the remaining proceeds, based on end-2005 lending rates from the International Monetary Fund's *International Financial Statistics*, supplemented with data from central banks.

This methodology was developed in "Efficiency in Bankruptcy," an ongoing research project by Simeon Djankov, Oliver Hart, Caralee McLiesh and Andrei Shleifer.

Ease of doing business

The ease of doing business index ranks economies from 1 to 175. The index is calculated as the ranking on the simple average of country percentile rankings on each of the 10 topics covered in *Doing Business 2007*. The ranking on each topic is the simple average of the percentile rankings on its component indicators (table 12.1).

One example: The ranking on starting a business is the average of the country percentile rankings on the procedures, time, cost and paid-in minimum capital requirement to register a business. In Iceland it takes 5 procedures, 5 days and 3% of annual income per capita in fees to open a business. The minimum capital required amounts to 16% of income per capita. On these 4 indicators Iceland ranks in the 7th, 1st, 8th and 48th percentiles. So on average, Iceland ranks in the 18th percentile on the ease of starting a business. It ranks in the 55th percentile on protecting investors, 18th percentile on trading across borders, 10th percentile on enforcing contracts, 7th percentile on closing a business and so on. Higher ranks indicate simpler regulation and stronger protections of property rights. The simple average of Iceland's percentile rankings on all topics is 20%. When all countries are ordered by their average percentile rank, Iceland is in 12th place.

Each indicator set studies a different aspect of the business environment. Country rankings vary, sometimes significantly, across indicator sets. For example, Iceland ranks in the 7th percentile on closing a business, its highest ranking, and in the 55th percentile on protecting investors, its lowest. This points to priorities for reform: Protecting investors is one place to start in further improving business conditions in Iceland. Across all 175 economies the average correlation coefficient between the 10 sets of indicators is 0.39, and the coefficients between any 2 sets of indicators range from 0.16 (between employing workers and trading across borders) to 0.66 (between closing a business and enforcing contracts). The low correlations suggest that countries rarely score universally well or universally badly on the indicators. In other words, there is much room for partial reform.

When an economy has no laws or regulations covering a specific area—for example bankruptcy—it receives a "no practice" mark. Similarly, if regulation exists but is never used in practice, or if a competing regulation prohibits such practice, the economy receives a "no practice" mark. This puts it at the bottom of the ranking.

The ease of doing business index is limited in scope. It does not account for a country's proximity to large markets, the quality of its infrastructure services (other than services related to trading across borders), the security of property from theft and looting, macroeconomic conditions or the strength of underlying institutions. There remains a large unfinished agenda for research into what regulation constitutes binding constraints, what package of reforms is most effective and how these issues are shaped by the country context. The *Doing Business* indicators provide a new empirical data set that may improve understanding of these issues.

Doing Business 2007 uses a simple method to calculate the top reformers (table 1.1). First, it selects the economies that reformed three or more of the ten *Doing Business* topics (table 12.2). This year, 23 economies met this criterion: Armenia, Australia, Bulgaria, China, Croatia, Czech Republic, El Salvador, France, Georgia, Ghana, Guatemala, India, Israel, Latvia, Lithuania, Mexico, Morocco, Nicaragua, Nigeria, Peru, Romania, Rwanda and Tanzania. Second, these selected economies are ranked on the percentage improvement in the ease of doing business from the previous year. For example, Mexico, Nicaragua, and Nigeria reformed in three aspects of business regulation each. But Mexico's rank improved from 75 to 44, Nicaragua's from 71 to 68 and Nigeria's from 102 to 90. These represent a 41%, 4%, and 12% improvement, respectively. Mexico therefore ranks ahead of Nigeria in the top ten reformers list; Nicaragua doesn't make it

This methodology was developed in Djankov, McLiesh and Ramalho (forthcoming) and adopted with minor changes here.

TABLE 12.1
Which indicators make up the ranking?

Starting a business Procedures, time, cost and paid-in minimum capital to open a new business	**Protecting investors** Indices of the extent of disclosure, extent of director liability and ease of shareholder suits
Dealing with licenses Procedures, time and cost of business inspections and licensing (construction industry)	**Paying taxes** Number of tax payments, time to prepare tax returns and total taxes as a share of commercial profits
Employing workers Difficulty of hiring index, rigidity of hours index, difficulty of firing index and firing cost	**Trading across borders** Documents, time and cost to export and import
Registering property Procedures, time and cost to register commercial real estate	**Enforcing contracts** Procedures, time and cost to resolve a commercial dispute
Getting credit Strength of legal rights index, depth of credit information index	**Closing a business** Recovery rate in bankruptcy

TABLE 12.2

■ Positive reform
● Negative reform

Economy	REFORMS IN 2005/06									
	Starting a business	Dealing with licenses	Employing workers	Registering property	Getting credit	Protecting investors	Paying taxes	Trading across borders	Enforcing contracts	Closing a business
Afghanistan										
Albania							■			
Algeria					■		■			
Angola										
Antigua and Barbuda	■						■			
Argentina			■							
Armenia	■	■		■	■					
Australia			■	■					■	
Austria										
Azerbaijan	■				■					
Bangladesh										
Belarus	■				●		■			
Belgium	■									
Belize										
Benin	■									
Bhutan										
Bolivia			●							
Bosnia and Herzegovina				■			■			
Botswana				■						
Brazil									■	
Bulgaria	■				■		■			
Burkina Faso	■									
Burundi									■	■
Cambodia		■						■		
Cameroon										
Canada		■								
Cape Verde										
Central African Republic				■			●			
Chad									■	
Chile										■
China	■				■	■		■		
Colombia						■		■		
Comoros										
Congo, Dem. Rep.										
Congo, Rep.										
Costa Rica										
Côte d'Ivoire				■						
Croatia	■			■					■	
Czech Republic	■				■		■			
Denmark					■				■	
Djibouti			●							
Dominica										
Dominican Republic					■		●		■	
Ecuador										
Egypt	■						■			
El Salvador	■			■	■					
Equatorial Guinea										
Eritrea		●								
Estonia							■		■	
Ethiopia	■									
Fiji										
Finland										
France		■			■			■	■	■
Gabon										
Gambia									■	
Georgia	■	■	■		■			■	■	
Germany		■				■				
Ghana				■			■	■		
Greece			■	■						

	REFORMS IN 2005/06									
Economy	Starting a business	Dealing with licenses	Employing workers	Registering property	Getting credit	Protecting investors	Paying taxes	Trading across borders	Enforcing contracts	Closing a business
Grenada										
Guatemala	■	■		■						
Guinea										
Guinea-Bissau							■			
Guyana									■	
Haiti										
Honduras	■				■					
Hong Kong, China						■		■		
Hungary					●		■			
Iceland										
India	■				■	■	■	■		
Indonesia	■									
Iran										
Iraq										
Ireland	■									
Israel					■	■	■			
Italy									■	■
Jamaica								■		
Japan	■				■					
Jordan								■		
Kazakhstan					■					
Kenya		■						■		
Kiribati										
Korea		■								■
Kuwait				■						
Kyrgyz Republic				■	■					
Lao PDR	■				■					
Latvia		■					■			■
Lebanon										
Lesotho	■						■			
Lithuania	■		■				■			
FYR Macedonia	■		■	●					■	
Madagascar	■									
Malawi										
Malaysia										
Maldives			●							
Mali		■		■						
Marshall Islands										
Mauritania				■						
Mauritius				■	■					
Mexico	■					■	■			
Micronesia	■									■
Moldova		■					■			
Mongolia										
Montenegro							■			
Morocco	■			■			■			
Mozambique	■									
Namibia										
Nepal										
Netherlands	■									
New Zealand		●				■				
Nicaragua				■	■			■		
Niger	■	■								
Nigeria				■				■	■	
Norway			●							
Oman										
Pakistan							■	■		
Palau	●									
Panama					■					

■ Positive reform
● Negative reform

Legend: ■ Positive reform ● Negative reform

Economy	Starting a business	Dealing with licenses	Employing workers	Registering property	Getting credit	Protecting investors	Paying taxes	Trading across borders	Enforcing contracts	Closing a business
Papua New Guinea										
Paraguay							■			
Peru	■				■	■			■	●
Philippines										
Poland						■				
Portugal	■									
Puerto Rico										■
Romania		■	■		■	■		■		■
Russia	■						■			
Rwanda	■						■		■	
Samoa										
São Tomé and Principe										
Saudi Arabia	■									
Senegal							■			
Serbia			●		■			■		■
Seychelles				■						
Sierra Leone							■			
Singapore										
Slovakia									■	■
Slovenia										
Solomon Islands										
South Africa				■						
Spain		■		■						
Sri Lanka							●			
St. Kitts and Nevis										
St. Lucia										
St. Vincent and the Grenadines										
Sudan							■			
Suriname										
Swaziland	●			■						
Sweden						■				
Switzerland	■						■			
Syria	■							■		
Taiwan, China										
Tajikistan										
Tanzania	■			■		■		■		
Thailand					■					
Timor-Leste		●								
Togo				●				■		
Tonga										
Trinidad and Tobago										
Tunisia						■				
Turkey							■			
Uganda	■			●						
Ukraine	■	■								
United Arab Emirates										
United Kingdom						■				
United States										■
Uruguay	■				■					
Uzbekistan							●			●
Vanuatu										
Venezuela				●	●			●		
Vietnam		■	■							
West Bank and Gaza										
Yemen							■			
Zambia										
Zimbabwe			●							

Indicator tables

Doing business indicators
Country tables

Economy	Starting a business				Dealing with licenses		
	Procedures (number)	Time (days)	Cost (% of income per capita)	Minimum capital (% of income per capita)	Procedures (number)	Time (days)	Cost (% of income per capita)
Afghanistan	3	8	67.4	0.0	..	..	..
Albania	11	39	22.4	36.7	22	344	286.8
Algeria	14	24	21.5	46.0	25	244	58.9
Angola	13	124	486.7	74.1	15	326	1239.2
Antigua and Barbuda	7	21	12.5	0.0	12	139	27.8
Argentina	15	32	12.1	5.6	23	288	46.3
Armenia	9	24	5.1	3.3	18	112	43.1
Australia	2	2	1.8	0.0	17	140	13.8
Austria	9	29	5.6	59.6	14	195	79.1
Azerbaijan	15	53	9.5	0.0	28	212	977.4
Bangladesh	8	37	87.6	0.0	13	185	272.3
Belarus	16	69	26.1	36.4	18	354	17.5
Belgium	4	27	5.8	21.8	15	184	61.8
Belize	9	45	57.5	0.0	12	66	30.9
Benin	7	31	173.3	379.1	16	333	338.9
Bhutan	10	62	16.6	0.0	26	204	263.5
Bolivia	15	50	140.6	3.8	14	183	196.0
Bosnia and Herzegovina	12	54	37.0	52.0	16	467	2423.4
Botswana	11	108	10.6	0.0	24	169	457.7
Brazil	17	152	9.9	0.0	19	460	179.9
Bulgaria	9	32	7.9	91.3	22	226	270.5
Burkina Faso	8	34	120.8	481.4	32	226	1247.5
Burundi	11	43	222.4	0.0	18	302	8808.2
Cambodia	10	86	236.4	66.2	28	181	1640.5
Cameroon	12	37	152.2	187.3	15	444	1165.6
Canada	2	3	0.9	0.0	15	77	117.9
Cape Verde	12	52	45.6	60.7	17	141	1526.0
Central African Republic	10	14	209.3	554.6	21	245	301.0
Chad	19	75	226.1	414.1	16	199	1139.1
Chile	9	27	9.8	0.0	12	171	114.2
China	13	35	9.3	213.1	29	367	84.0
Colombia	13	44	19.8	0.0	12	150	646.3
Comoros	11	23	192.3	291.7	17	196	80.9
Congo, Dem. Rep.	13	155	481.1	177.3	14	306	2281.9
Congo, Rep.	8	71	214.8	192.4	15	175	1243.0
Costa Rica	11	77	23.5	0.0	19	119	140.2
Côte d'Ivoire	11	45	134.1	226.7	22	569	196.3
Croatia	10	45	12.2	20.6	28	278	1164.1
Czech Republic	10	24	8.9	36.8	31	271	14.5
Denmark	3	5	0.0	44.6	7	70	67.8
Djibouti	11	37	222.0	571.4	15	203	1050.6
Dominica	5	19	30.0	0.0	11	195	82.1
Dominican Republic	10	73	30.2	1.1	17	165	240.1
Ecuador	14	65	31.8	7.7	19	149	83.7
Egypt	10	19	68.8	694.7	30	263	1002.0
El Salvador	10	26	75.6	119.7	22	144	201.0
Equatorial Guinea	20	136	100.7	13.1	19	156	364.9
Eritrea	13	76	115.9	449.8	NO PRACTICE	NO PRACTICE	NO PRACTICE
Estonia	6	35	5.1	34.3	13	117	34.3
Ethiopia	7	16	45.9	1083.8	12	133	1235.5
Fiji	8	46	25.8	0.0	16	114	41.7
Finland	3	14	1.1	27.1	17	56	108.0
France	7	8	1.1	0.0	10	155	75.0
Gabon	10	60	162.8	36.1	13	268	45.3
Gambia	8	27	292.1	119.7	17	145	276.8
Georgia	7	16	10.9	3.7	17	137	71.7
Germany	9	24	5.1	46.2	11	133	89.1
Ghana	12	81	49.6	23.2	16	127	1314.1
Greece	15	38	24.2	116.0	17	176	68.8

Economy	Starting a business				Dealing with licenses		
	Procedures (number)	Time (days)	Cost (% of income per capita)	Minimum capital (% of income per capita)	Procedures (number)	Time (days)	Cost (% of income per capita)
Grenada	4	52	37.2	0.0	8	142	36.4
Guatemala	13	30	52.1	26.4	23	390	496.5
Guinea	13	49	186.5	423.4	29	278	535.4
Guinea-Bissau	17	233	261.2	1028.9	11	161	2664.9
Guyana	8	46	100.2	0.0	17	202	94.7
Haiti	12	203	127.7	124.7	12	141	1003.0
Honduras	13	44	60.6	28.6	14	199	636.8
Hong Kong, China	5	11	3.3	0.0	22	160	23.3
Hungary	6	38	20.9	74.2	25	212	260.0
Iceland	5	5	3.1	15.9	19	111	15.7
India	11	35	73.7	0.0	20	270	606.0
Indonesia	12	97	86.7	83.4	19	224	311.0
Iran	8	47	5.4	1.3	21	668	684.5
Iraq	11	77	67.6	57.1	14	216	833.2
Ireland	4	19	0.3	0.0	10	181	22.2
Israel	5	34	5.1	0.0	21	215	91.1
Italy	9	13	15.2	10.4	17	284	142.3
Jamaica	6	8	9.4	0.0	14	242	417.5
Japan	8	23	7.5	0.0	11	96	19.8
Jordan	11	18	73.0	864.4	16	122	503.2
Kazakhstan	7	20	7.0	23.1	32	248	35.0
Kenya	13	54	46.3	0.0	11	170	37.6
Kiribati	6	21	50.0	27.0	14	174	545.2
Korea	12	22	15.2	299.7	14	52	175.9
Kuwait	13	35	1.6	100.8	26	149	210.1
Kyrgyz Republic	8	21	9.8	0.5	20	218	510.4
Lao PDR	8	163	17.3	0.0	24	192	204.1
Latvia	5	16	3.5	26.1	22	152	36.3
Lebanon	6	46	105.4	56.5	16	275	176.9
Lesotho	8	73	39.9	15.7	14	265	128.3
Lithuania	7	26	2.8	48.8	14	151	18.2
FYR Macedonia	10	18	7.4	112.0	18	222	89.8
Madagascar	10	21	35.0	373.1	19	297	387.1
Malawi	10	37	134.7	0.0	22	185	236.2
Malaysia	9	30	19.7	0.0	25	281	78.2
Maldives	5	13	18.1	6.6	10	118	40.2
Mali	13	42	201.9	519.8	15	209	1813.2
Marshall Islands	5	17	18.1	0.0	9	81	37.6
Mauritania	11	82	121.6	632.0	19	152	710.9
Mauritius	6	46	8.0	0.0	21	145	13.7
Mexico	8	27	14.2	12.5	12	142	104.5
Micronesia	7	16	135.9	0.0	15	73	21.3
Moldova	10	30	13.3	18.8	34	158	165.0
Mongolia	8	20	5.1	115.3	18	96	48.4
Montenegro	15	24	6.6	0.0	22	179	5869.2
Morocco	6	12	12.7	66.7	21	217	264.9
Mozambique	13	113	85.7	10.4	13	364	279.3
Namibia	10	95	18.0	0.0	11	105	134.9
Nepal	7	31	78.5	0.0	15	424	324.0
Netherlands	6	10	7.2	62.3	18	184	137.6
New Zealand	2	12	0.2	0.0	7	184	27.2
Nicaragua	6	39	131.6	0.0	12	192	1002.2
Niger	11	24	416.8	778.1	19	148	2986.7
Nigeria	9	43	54.4	29.0	16	465	238.2
Norway	4	13	2.5	25.1	13	104	50.4
Oman	9	34	4.5	84.7	16	242	883.1
Pakistan	11	24	21.3	0.0	12	218	972.9
Palau	8	28	4.9	13.1	23	114	6.8
Panama	7	19	23.9	0.0	22	121	114.7

Economy	Starting a business				Dealing with licenses		
	Procedures (number)	Time (days)	Cost (% of income per capita)	Minimum capital (% of income per capita)	Procedures (number)	Time (days)	Cost (% of income per capita)
Papua New Guinea	8	56	28.2	0.0	20	218	110.0
Paraguay	17	74	136.8	0.0	15	273	564.4
Peru	10	72	32.5	0.0	19	201	337.9
Philippines	11	48	18.7	1.8	23	197	113.4
Poland	10	31	21.4	204.4	25	322	85.6
Portugal	8	8	4.3	38.7	20	327	60.3
Puerto Rico	7	7	0.8	0.0	20	212	82.9
Romania	5	11	4.4	0.0	17	242	332.6
Russia	7	28	2.7	3.4	22	531	275.3
Rwanda	9	16	188.3	0.0	17	252	626.5
Samoa	9	35	45.5	0.0	19	88	105.1
São Tomé and Principe	10	144	147.2	0.0	16	259	1647.9
Saudi Arabia	13	39	58.6	1057.5	18	125	70.2
Senegal	10	58	112.6	269.6	15	185	151.6
Serbia	10	18	10.2	7.6	20	211	1946.7
Seychelles	9	38	9.1	0.0	22	147	51.3
Sierra Leone	9	26	1194.5	0.0	48	236	218.4
Singapore	6	6	0.8	0.0	11	129	22.0
Slovakia	9	25	4.8	39.1	13	272	17.1
Slovenia	9	60	9.4	16.1	14	207	122.2
Solomon Islands	7	57	68.9	0.0	13	74	501.1
South Africa	9	35	6.9	0.0	17	174	33.5
Spain	10	47	16.2	14.6	11	277	65.7
Sri Lanka	8	50	9.2	0.0	17	167	151.0
St. Kitts and Nevis	8	47	26.7	45.4	14	72	15.2
St. Lucia	6	40	25.9	0.0	9	139	34.9
St. Vincent and the Grenadines	8	12	33.8	0.0	11	74	10.6
Sudan	10	39	58.6	0.0	17	172	506.1
Suriname	13	694	153.8	1.4	14	431	196.3
Swaziland	13	61	41.1	0.0	11	114	97.1
Sweden	3	16	0.7	33.7	8	116	115.3
Switzerland	6	20	2.2	15.1	15	152	57.2
Syria	12	43	21.1	4233.5	20	134	298.0
Taiwan, China	8	48	4.6	200.0	32	206	231.9
Tajikistan	14	67	75.1	378.6	18	187	154.7
Tanzania	13	30	91.6	5.5	26	313	3796.6
Thailand	8	33	5.8	0.0	9	127	11.1
Timor-Leste	10	92	83.3	666.7	NO PRACTICE	NO PRACTICE	NO PRACTICE
Togo	13	53	252.7	539.7	14	273	1435.6
Tonga	4	32	10.3	0.0	15	81	174.6
Trinidad and Tobago	9	43	1.1	0.0	19	292	9.9
Tunisia	10	11	9.3	28.3	24	79	1031.9
Turkey	8	9	26.8	18.7	32	232	150.2
Uganda	17	30	114.0	0.0	19	156	832.8
Ukraine	10	33	9.2	198.8	18	242	186.5
United Arab Emirates	12	63	36.4	338.2	21	125	210.0
United Kingdom	6	18	0.7	0.0	19	115	68.9
United States	5	5	0.7	0.0	18	69	16.0
Uruguay	10	43	44.2	183.3	17	156	96.3
Uzbekistan	8	29	14.1	24.7	19	287	258.2
Vanuatu	8	39	61.3	0.0	7	82	398.9
Venezuela	16	141	25.4	0.0	13	276	388.4
Vietnam	11	50	44.5	0.0	14	133	56.4
West Bank and Gaza	12	93	324.7	1889.6	21	134	823.4
Yemen	12	63	228.0	2565.7	13	107	306.4
Zambia	6	35	29.9	1.9	16	196	1766.1
Zimbabwe	10	96	35.6	53.0	21	481	1509.6

Economy	Difficulty of hiring index (0–100)	Rigidity of hours index (0–100)	Difficulty of firing index (0–100)	Rigidity of employment index (0–100)	Nonwage labor cost (% of salary)	Firing cost (weeks of salary)	Procedures (number)	Time (days)	Cost (% of property value)
Afghanistan	67	40	30	46	0	4	11	252	9.5
Albania	44	40	30	38	31	64	7	47	3.6
Algeria	44	60	30	45	27	17	15	51	7.5
Angola	33	80	80	64	8	58	7	334	11.1
Antigua and Barbuda	11	0	20	10	9	52	5	26	13.0
Argentina	44	60	20	41	23	139	5	44	8.3
Armenia	33	40	20	31	18	13	3	4	0.4
Australia	0	0	10	3	21	4	5	5	4.8
Austria	11	60	40	37	31	56	3	32	4.5
Azerbaijan	33	40	40	38	22	22	7	61	0.3
Bangladesh	11	40	40	30	0	51	8	425	10.5
Belarus	0	40	40	27	39	22	7	231	0.1
Belgium	11	40	10	20	55	16	7	132	12.8
Belize	11	20	0	10	8	24	8	60	5.0
Benin	39	60	40	46	29	36	3	50	15.1
Bhutan	78	40	0	39	1	95	5	93	0.0
Bolivia	61	60	100	74	14	100	7	92	5.0
Bosnia and Herzegovina	56	40	30	42	15	33	7	331	5.0
Botswana	0	20	40	20	0	90	4	30	4.9
Brazil	67	60	0	42	37	37	14	47	4.0
Bulgaria	50	80	10	47	30	9	9	19	2.3
Burkina Faso	83	60	50	64	20	34	8	107	16.2
Burundi	78	60	40	59	7	26	5	94	17.9
Cambodia	56	60	30	49	0	39	7	56	4.6
Cameroon	28	60	80	56	16	33	5	93	18.7
Canada	11	0	0	4	14	28	6	10	1.7
Cape Verde	33	40	60	44	17	91	6	83	7.9
Central African Republic	89	80	50	73	18	22	3	69	11.7
Chad	39	60	80	60	21	36	6	44	21.2
Chile	33	20	20	24	3	52	6	31	1.3
China	11	20	40	24	44	91	3	32	3.1
Colombia	22	40	20	27	28	59	7	23	3.5
Comoros	39	60	40	46	0	100	5	24	20.8
Congo, Dem. Rep.	83	80	70	78	6	31	8	57	9.5
Congo, Rep.	78	60	70	69	29	41	7	137	27.2
Costa Rica	56	40	0	32	26	35	6	21	3.5
Côte d'Ivoire	44	80	10	45	18	49	6	32	14.3
Croatia	61	40	50	50	17	39	5	399	5.0
Czech Republic	33	20	30	28	35	22	4	123	3.0
Denmark	0	40	10	17	1	10	6	42	0.6
Djibouti	67	40	30	46	16	56	7	49	13.3
Dominica	11	20	20	17	7	58	4	40	13.0
Dominican Republic	56	40	30	42	14	88	7	107	5.1
Ecuador	44	60	50	51	12	135	10	20	3.9
Egypt	0	60	100	53	26	186	7	193	5.9
El Salvador	33	40	0	24	9	86	6	33	3.6
Equatorial Guinea	67	60	70	66	23	133	6	23	6.2
Eritrea	0	40	20	20	0	69	12	101	5.2
Estonia	33	80	60	58	34	35	3	51	0.7
Ethiopia	33	40	30	34	0	40	13	43	7.7
Fiji	22	40	0	21	9	28	3	48	12.0
Finland	44	60	40	48	25	26	3	14	4.0
France	67	60	40	56	47	32	9	183	6.8
Gabon	17	80	80	59	20	43	8	60	10.5
Gambia	0	40	40	27	11	9	5	371	7.6
Georgia	0	20	0	7	20	4	6	9	0.5
Germany	33	60	40	44	19	69	4	40	4.5
Ghana	11	40	50	34	13	178	7	382	1.9
Greece	44	80	50	58	31	69	12	23	3.8

Economy	Difficulty of hiring index (0–100)	Rigidity of hours index (0–100)	Difficulty of firing index (0–100)	Rigidity of employment index (0–100)	Nonwage labor cost (% of salary)	Firing cost (weeks of salary)	Procedures (number)	Time (days)	Cost (% of property value)
	Employing workers						Registering property		
Grenada	44	20	0	21	5	29	8	77	7.6
Guatemala	61	40	0	34	13	101	5	37	1.1
Guinea	33	60	30	41	27	26	6	104	15.6
Guinea-Bissau	100	60	70	77	22	87	9	211	13.2
Guyana	22	20	20	21	8	56	6	27	4.5
Haiti	11	40	20	24	11	26	5	683	8.7
Honduras	67	40	0	36	10	43	7	36	5.8
Hong Kong, China	0	0	0	0	5	62	5	54	5.0
Hungary	11	80	10	34	35	35	4	78	11.0
Iceland	33	60	0	31	12	13	3	4	2.4
India	33	20	70	41	17	56	6	62	7.8
Indonesia	61	20	50	44	10	108	7	42	10.5
Iran	78	60	10	49	23	91	9	36	10.5
Iraq	78	60	40	59	12	4	5	8	6.6
Ireland	28	40	30	33	11	49	5	38	10.3
Israel	0	60	20	27	6	91	7	144	7.5
Italy	61	60	40	54	42	2	8	27	0.9
Jamaica	11	0	0	4	12	61	5	54	13.5
Japan	28	60	0	29	13	9	6	14	4.1
Jordan	11	20	50	27	11	4	8	22	10.0
Kazakhstan	0	60	10	23	22	9	8	52	1.8
Kenya	33	20	30	28	4	47	8	73	4.1
Kiribati	0	0	50	17	8	4	5	513	0.1
Korea	11	60	30	34	18	91	7	11	6.3
Kuwait	0	40	0	13	11	43	8	55	0.5
Kyrgyz Republic	33	40	40	38	25	17	7	8	1.9
Lao PDR	11	40	60	37	5	19	9	135	4.2
Latvia	67	40	70	59	24	17	8	54	2.0
Lebanon	33	0	40	24	22	17	8	25	5.9
Lesotho	56	40	10	35	0	44	6	101	8.4
Lithuania	33	80	30	48	31	30	3	3	0.7
FYR Macedonia	61	60	40	54	33	22	6	98	3.5
Madagascar	72	60	40	57	18	30	8	134	11.6
Malawi	22	20	20	21	1	84	6	118	3.4
Malaysia	0	20	10	10	13	88	5	144	2.4
Maldives	0	0	0	0	0	9	NO PRACTICE	NO PRACTICE	NO PRACTICE
Mali	44	60	50	51	27	31	5	33	20.7
Marshall Islands	0	0	0	0	11	0	NO PRACTICE	NO PRACTICE	NO PRACTICE
Mauritania	67	60	50	59	16	31	4	49	5.2
Mauritius	0	40	50	30	6	35	6	210	15.8
Mexico	33	40	40	38	24	74	5	74	5.2
Micronesia	33	0	0	11	6	0	NO PRACTICE	NO PRACTICE	NO PRACTICE
Moldova	33	60	70	54	29	29	6	48	1.5
Mongolia	11	80	10	34	20	9	5	11	2.2
Montenegro	33	40	30	34	16	39	8	86	2.5
Morocco	100	40	50	63	18	85	4	46	4.4
Mozambique	83	60	20	54	4	143	8	42	5.4
Namibia	0	60	20	27	0	24	9	23	10.0
Nepal	67	20	70	52	10	90	3	5	6.4
Netherlands	17	40	70	42	18	17	2	5	6.2
New Zealand	11	0	10	7	1	0	2	2	0.1
Nicaragua	11	60	0	24	17	24	8	124	3.5
Niger	100	80	50	77	17	31	5	49	14.0
Nigeria	22	20	20	21	9	50	16	80	21.2
Norway	61	60	40	54	14	13	1	1	2.5
Oman	44	60	0	35	10	4	2	16	3.0
Pakistan	78	20	30	43	12	90	6	50	4.4
Palau	11	0	0	4	6	0	5	14	0.4
Panama	78	20	70	56	19	44	7	44	2.4

Economy	Employing workers						Registering property		
	Difficulty of hiring index (0–100)	Rigidity of hours index (0–100)	Difficulty of firing index (0–100)	Rigidity of employment index (0–100)	Nonwage labor cost (% of salary)	Firing cost (weeks of salary)	Procedures (number)	Time (days)	Cost (% of property value)
Papua New Guinea	11	20	0	10	10	39	4	72	5.1
Paraguay	56	60	60	59	17	113	6	46	2.0
Peru	44	60	80	61	10	52	5	33	3.3
Philippines	56	40	20	39	9	91	8	33	5.7
Poland	0	60	40	33	21	13	6	197	2.0
Portugal	33	60	60	51	24	99	5	81	7.4
Puerto Rico	56	20	20	32	8	0	8	15	1.4
Romania	33	80	40	51	33	3	8	150	1.9
Russia	33	60	40	44	31	17	6	52	0.3
Rwanda	56	60	30	49	5	26	5	371	9.6
Samoa	11	20	0	10	6	9	5	147	1.8
São Tomé and Principe	61	80	60	67	6	91	7	62	12.7
Saudi Arabia	0	20	0	7	11	80	4	4	0.0
Senegal	72	60	50	61	21	38	6	114	18.1
Serbia	33	40	40	38	18	27	6	111	5.4
Seychelles	33	20	50	34	25	39	4	33	7.0
Sierra Leone	78	60	50	63	10	329	8	235	15.6
Singapore	0	0	0	0	13	4	3	9	2.8
Slovakia	17	60	40	39	35	13	3	17	0.1
Slovenia	61	60	50	57	17	40	6	391	2.0
Solomon Islands	22	20	20	21	8	44	10	297	4.9
South Africa	44	40	40	41	2	24	6	23	8.9
Spain	78	60	50	63	30	56	3	17	7.2
Sri Lanka	0	20	60	27	15	178	8	63	5.1
St. Kitts and Nevis	0	20	20	13	10	60	6	81	13.3
St. Lucia	0	20	20	13	5	56	5	20	7.3
St. Vincent and the Grenadines	11	20	20	17	4	54	6	37	11.9
Sudan	56	60	50	55	25	118	6	9	3.3
Suriname	0	20	50	23	0	26	4	193	10.2
Swaziland	11	20	20	17	3	53	11	46	7.1
Sweden	28	60	40	43	33	26	1	2	3.0
Switzerland	0	60	10	23	14	13	4	16	0.4
Syria	0	40	50	30	17	80	4	34	27.9
Taiwan, China	78	60	30	56	11	91	3	5	6.2
Tajikistan	33	20	40	31	25	22	6	37	2.0
Tanzania	100	40	60	67	16	32	10	123	5.5
Thailand	33	20	0	18	5	54	2	2	6.3
Timor-Leste	67	20	50	46	0	34	NO PRACTICE	NO PRACTICE	NO PRACTICE
Togo	44	60	70	58	25	36	7	242	7.7
Tonga	0	20	0	7	0	0	4	108	10.2
Trinidad and Tobago	0	0	20	7	4	67	8	162	7.0
Tunisia	17	40	80	46	22	17	5	57	6.1
Turkey	56	60	30	49	22	95	8	9	3.2
Uganda	0	20	0	7	10	13	13	227	6.9
Ukraine	44	40	80	55	39	13	10	93	3.4
United Arab Emirates	0	60	0	20	13	84	3	6	2.0
United Kingdom	11	20	10	14	11	22	2	21	4.1
United States	0	0	0	0	8	0	4	12	0.5
Uruguay	33	60	0	31	6	31	8	66	7.1
Uzbekistan	33	40	30	34	31	30	12	97	10.5
Vanuatu	50	40	10	33	4	56	2	188	7.0
Venezuela	67	60	100	76	16	47	8	47	2.1
Vietnam	0	40	70	37	17	87	4	67	1.2
West Bank and Gaza	33	40	20	31	13	91	10	72	2.4
Yemen	0	60	40	33	9	17	6	21	3.9
Zambia	0	40	30	23	11	178	6	70	9.6
Zimbabwe	11	40	50	34	4	446	4	30	24.0

Economy	Getting credit				Protecting investors			
	Strength of legal rights index (0–10)	Depth of credit information index (0–6)	Public registry coverage (% of adults)	Private bureau coverage (% of adults)	Extent of disclosure index (0–10)	Extent of director liability index (0–10)	Ease of shareholder suits index (0–10)	Strength of investor protection index (0–10)
Afghanistan	0	0	0.0	0.0	0	0	2	0.7
Albania	9	0	0.0	0.0	0	5	3	2.7
Algeria	3	2	0.2	0.0	6	6	4	5.3
Angola	3	4	2.9	0.0	5	6	6	5.7
Antigua and Barbuda	6	0	0.0	0.0	4	8	7	6.3
Argentina	3	6	25.4	100.0	6	2	6	4.7
Armenia	5	3	1.5	0.0	5	2	8	5.0
Australia	9	5	0.0	100.0	8	2	7	5.7
Austria	5	6	1.2	39.9	2	5	4	3.7
Azerbaijan	7	4	1.1	0.0	4	1	8	4.3
Bangladesh	7	2	0.6	0.0	6	7	7	6.7
Belarus	2	3	0.0	0.0	1	3	7	3.7
Belgium	5	4	56.2	0.0	8	6	7	7.0
Belize	7	0	0.0	0.0	3	4	6	4.3
Benin	4	1	10.3	0.0	5	8	4	5.7
Bhutan	3	0	0.0	0.0	6	3	4	4.3
Bolivia	3	5	11.5	32.3	1	5	7	4.3
Bosnia and Herzegovina	8	5	0.0	22.9	3	6	6	5.0
Botswana	7	5	0.0	43.2	8	2	3	4.3
Brazil	2	5	9.2	43.0	5	7	4	5.3
Bulgaria	6	4	20.7	..	10	1	7	6.0
Burkina Faso	4	1	2.4	0.0	6	5	3	4.7
Burundi	2	1	0.1	0.0	..	..	..	..
Cambodia	0	0	0.0	0.0	5	9	2	5.3
Cameroon	3	2	3.4	0.0	8	2	6	5.3
Canada	7	6	0.0	100.0	8	9	8	8.3
Cape Verde	5	3	11.9	0.0	1	5	6	4.0
Central African Republic	3	2	1.1	0.0	4	6	7	5.7
Chad	4	1	0.2	0.0	3	4	7	4.7
Chile	4	6	31.3	19.3	8	6	5	6.3
China	2	4	10.2	0.0	10	1	4	5.0
Colombia	3	4	0.0	28.3	7	2	9	6.0
Comoros	3	0	0.0	0.0	6	4	5	5.0
Congo, Dem. Rep.	3	0	0.0	0.0	3	3	5	3.7
Congo, Rep.	3	2	1.4	0.0	4	5	6	5.0
Costa Rica	4	6	2.5	39.2	2	5	2	3.0
Côte d'Ivoire	3	1	3.1	0.0	6	5	3	4.7
Croatia	5	0	0.0	0.0	2	5	2	3.0
Czech Republic	6	5	3.5	51.0	2	5	8	5.0
Denmark	8	4	0.0	11.5	7	5	7	6.3
Djibouti	4	1	0.2	0.0	5	2	0	2.3
Dominica	6	0	0.0	0.0	4	8	7	6.3
Dominican Republic	4	6	11.9	57.1	5	0	7	4.0
Ecuador	3	5	15.2	43.7	1	5	6	4.0
Egypt	1	2	1.5	0.0	5	3	5	4.3
El Salvador	4	6	30.5	79.6	6	2	6	4.7
Equatorial Guinea	2	2	2.4	0.0	6	4	5	5.0
Eritrea	3	0	0.0	0.0	4	5	5	4.7
Estonia	4	5	0.0	18.2	8	4	6	6.0
Ethiopia	5	2	0.1	0.0	4	4	5	4.3
Fiji	7	4	0.0	33.4	3	8	8	6.3
Finland	6	5	0.0	14.9	6	4	7	5.7
France	5	4	12.3	0.0	10	1	5	5.3
Gabon	4	2	2.6	0.0	5	4	5	4.7
Gambia	4	0	0.0	0.0	2	1	5	2.7
Georgia	6	3	0.0	0.0	4	4	4	4.0
Germany	8	6	0.5	93.9	5	5	5	5.0
Ghana	5	0	0.0	0.0	7	5	6	6.0
Greece	3	4	0.0	37.5	1	3	5	3.0

Economy	Getting credit				Protecting investors			
	Strength of legal rights index (0–10)	Depth of credit information index (0–6)	Public registry coverage (% of adults)	Private bureau coverage (% of adults)	Extent of disclosure index (0–10)	Extent of director liability index (0–10)	Ease of shareholder suits index (0–10)	Strength of investor protection index (0–10)
Grenada	7	0	0.0	0.0	4	8	7	6.3
Guatemala	4	5	16.1	9.2	3	3	6	4.0
Guinea	4	1	0.0	0.0	5	7	2	4.7
Guinea-Bissau	3	1	1.0	0.0	0	5	6	3.7
Guyana	3	0	0.0	0.0	5	4	1	3.3
Haiti	3	2	0.7	0.0	4	3	4	3.7
Honduras	6	5	8.3	18.7	1	5	4	3.3
Hong Kong, China	10	5	0.0	64.5	10	8	9	9.0
Hungary	6	5	0.0	5.9	2	4	7	4.3
Iceland	7	5	0.0	100.0	4	5	6	5.0
India	5	3	0.0	6.1	7	4	7	6.0
Indonesia	5	2	8.4	0.2	8	5	3	5.3
Iran	5	3	13.7	0.0	5	4	0	3.0
Iraq	4	0	0.0	0.0	4	5	5	4.7
Ireland	8	5	0.0	100.0	10	6	9	8.3
Israel	8	5	0.0	100.0	7	9	9	8.3
Italy	3	5	7.0	67.8	7	2	6	5.0
Jamaica	6	0	0.0	0.0	4	8	4	5.3
Japan	6	6	0.0	..	7	6	8	7.0
Jordan	5	2	0.7	0.0	5	4	4	4.3
Kazakhstan	5	4	0.0	5.5	7	1	9	5.7
Kenya	8	2	0.0	0.1	4	2	10	5.3
Kiribati	6	0	0.0	0.0	6	5	7	6.0
Korea	6	5	0.0	76.6	7	2	7	5.3
Kuwait	4	3	0.0	16.1	7	7	5	6.3
Kyrgyz Republic	5	3	0.0	0.4	8	1	9	6.0
Lao PDR	2	0	0.0	0.0	0	3	3	2.0
Latvia	8	4	1.9	0.0	5	4	8	5.7
Lebanon	4	5	4.3	0.0	9	1	5	5.0
Lesotho	5	0	0.0	0.0	2	1	8	3.7
Lithuania	4	6	4.2	7.2	6	4	6	5.3
FYR Macedonia	6	3	2.1	0.0	5	6	4	5.0
Madagascar	2	1	0.3	0.0	5	6	6	5.7
Malawi	8	0	0.0	0.0	4	7	5	5.3
Malaysia	8	6	42.2	..	10	9	7	8.7
Maldives	4	0	0.0	0.0	0	8	8	5.3
Mali	3	1	2.9	0.0	6	5	3	4.7
Marshall Islands	5	0	0.0	0.0	2	0	8	3.3
Mauritania	5	1	0.2	0.0	..	..	..	..
Mauritius	6	1	10.2	0.0	6	8	9	7.7
Mexico	2	6	0.0	69.5	8	5	5	6.0
Micronesia	6	0	0.0	0.0	0	0	8	2.7
Moldova	6	0	0.0	0.0	7	1	6	4.7
Mongolia	5	3	10.2	0.0	5	8	6	6.3
Montenegro	7	0	0.0	0.0	5	8	6	6.3
Morocco	3	1	2.3	0.0	6	6	1	4.3
Mozambique	4	3	0.7	0.0	7	2	6	5.0
Namibia	5	5	0.0	35.2	5	5	6	5.3
Nepal	4	2	0.0	0.1	6	1	9	5.3
Netherlands	7	5	0.0	68.9	4	4	6	4.7
New Zealand	9	5	0.0	100.0	10	9	10	9.7
Nicaragua	4	5	12.5	3.4	4	5	6	5.0
Niger	3	1	1.2	0.0	4	5	5	4.7
Nigeria	7	0	0.0	0.0	6	7	4	5.7
Norway	6	4	0.0	100.0	7	6	7	6.7
Oman	3	1	17.5	0.0	8	5	3	5.3
Pakistan	4	4	0.3	1.1	6	6	7	6.3
Palau	5	0	0.0	0.0	0	0	8	2.7
Panama	6	6	0.0	59.8	3	4	7	4.7

Economy	Getting credit				Protecting investors			
	Strength of legal rights index (0–10)	Depth of credit information index (0–6)	Public registry coverage (% of adults)	Private bureau coverage (% of adults)	Extent of disclosure index (0–10)	Extent of director liability index (0–10)	Ease of shareholder suits index (0–10)	Strength of investor protection index (0–10)
Papua New Guinea	6	0	0.0	0.0	5	5	8	6.0
Paraguay	3	6	10.6	52.2	6	5	6	5.7
Peru	4	6	19.2	28.6	8	5	7	6.7
Philippines	3	3	0.0	4.8	1	2	7	3.3
Poland	4	4	0.0	38.1	7	2	9	6.0
Portugal	4	4	72.0	9.1	6	5	7	6.0
Puerto Rico	6	5	0.0	63.6	7	6	8	7.0
Romania	4	5	2.6	5.5	9	5	4	6.0
Russia	3	0	0.0	0.0	7	2	7	5.3
Rwanda	1	2	0.2	0.0	2	5	1	2.7
Samoa	7	0	0.0	0.0	5	6	8	6.3
São Tomé and Principe	5	0	0.0	0.0	6	1	6	4.3
Saudi Arabia	3	5	0.2	12.5	8	5	1	4.7
Senegal	3	1	4.7	0.0	4	4	4	4.0
Serbia	5	5	0.1	43.4	7	6	3	5.3
Seychelles	3	0	0.0	0.0	4	8	5	5.7
Sierra Leone	5	0	0.0	0.0	3	6	5	4.7
Singapore	9	4	0.0	38.6	10	9	9	9.3
Slovakia	9	3	1.0	45.3	2	4	7	4.3
Slovenia	6	3	2.9	0.0	3	8	6	5.7
Solomon Islands	4	0	0.0	0.0	3	7	7	5.7
South Africa	5	5	0.0	53.0	8	8	8	8.0
Spain	5	6	44.9	7.4	5	6	4	5.0
Sri Lanka	3	3	0.0	3.1	4	5	7	5.3
St. Kitts and Nevis	5	0	0.0	0.0	4	8	7	6.3
St. Lucia	6	0	0.0	0.0	4	8	7	6.3
St. Vincent and the Grenadines	7	0	0.0	0.0	4	8	7	6.3
Sudan	4	0	0.0	0.0	0	6	5	3.7
Suriname	5	0	0.0	0.0	2	2	5	3.0
Swaziland	6	5	0.0	39.0	1	1	5	2.3
Sweden	6	4	0.0	100.0	6	4	7	5.7
Switzerland	6	5	0.0	24.5	0	5	4	3.0
Syria	5	0	0.0	0.0	6	5	2	4.3
Taiwan, China	4	5	0.0	59.5	8	4	4	5.3
Tajikistan	4	0	0.0	0.0	0	0	5	1.7
Tanzania	5	0	0.0	0.0	3	4	7	4.7
Thailand	5	5	0.0	21.7	10	2	6	6.0
Timor-Leste	3	0	0.0	0.0	7	1	3	3.7
Togo	3	1	3.6	0.0	4	3	5	4.0
Tonga	5	0	0.0	0.0	3	3	8	4.7
Trinidad and Tobago	6	3	0.0	31.5	4	9	7	6.7
Tunisia	3	3	11.6	0.0	0	4	6	3.3
Turkey	3	5	6.7	..	8	4	4	5.3
Uganda	3	0	0.0	0.0	7	5	4	5.3
Ukraine	8	0	0.0	0.0	1	3	7	3.7
United Arab Emirates	3	2	1.7	0.0	4	7	2	4.3
United Kingdom	10	6	0.0	86.1	10	7	7	8.0
United States	7	6	0.0	100.0	7	9	9	8.3
Uruguay	4	6	13.2	85.3	3	4	8	5.0
Uzbekistan	3	0	0.0	0.0	4	6	3	4.3
Vanuatu	5	0	0.0	0.0	5	6	5	5.3
Venezuela	4	0	0.0	0.0	3	3	2	2.7
Vietnam	4	3	2.7	0.0	4	0	2	2.0
West Bank and Gaza	5	3	0.7	0.0	7	2	5	4.7
Yemen	3	2	0.1	0.0	6	4	3	4.3
Zambia	7	0	0.0	0.0	3	6	7	5.3
Zimbabwe	6	0	0.0	0.0	8	1	4	4.3

Economy	Paying taxes			Trading across borders					
	Payments (number per year)	Time (hours per year)	Total tax rate (% of profit)	Documents to export (number)	Time to export (days)	Cost to export (US$ per container)	Documents to import (number)	Time to import (days)	Cost to import (US$ per container)
Afghanistan	2	275	36.3	7	66	2,500	11	88	2,100
Albania	41	240	55.8	7	34	818	12	34	820
Algeria	61	504	76.4	9	15	1,606	9	22	1,886
Angola	42	272	64.4	6	74	1,800	10	85	2,225
Antigua and Barbuda	44	528	48.5	5	13	1,056	6	15	1,467
Argentina	34	615	116.8	6	16	1,470	7	21	1,750
Armenia	50	1120	42.5	7	34	1,600	6	37	1,750
Australia	11	107	52.2	6	9	795	5	12	945
Austria	20	272	56.1	4	8	803	5	9	843
Azerbaijan	36	1000	44.9	7	69	2,275	18	79	2,575
Bangladesh	17	400	40.3	7	35	902	16	57	1,287
Belarus	125	1188	186.1	7	33	1,472	7	36	1,472
Belgium	10	160	70.1	5	7	1,350	6	9	1,300
Belize	40	108	31.7	7	13	1,800	14	15	2,130
Benin	72	270	68.5	8	35	980	11	48	1,452
Bhutan	19	274	43.0	10	39	1,230	14	42	1,950
Bolivia	41	1080	80.3	12	26	1,110	12	36	1,230
Bosnia and Herzegovina	73	100	50.4	5	22	1,150	7	25	1,150
Botswana	24	140	53.3	6	37	524	9	42	1,159
Brazil	23	2600	71.7	7	18	895	6	24	1,145
Bulgaria	27	616	40.7	7	26	1,233	10	25	1,201
Burkina Faso	45	270	51.1	9	69	1,215	13	66	1,700
Burundi	40	140	286.7	12	80	3,625	14	124	3,705
Cambodia	27	121	22.3	8	36	736	12	45	816
Cameroon	39	1300	46.2	10	38	524	14	51	1,360
Canada	10	119	43.0	3	7	700	4	10	850
Cape Verde	49	100	54.4	4	18	533	9	16	533
Central African Republic	54	504	209.5	9	63	1,502	19	60	1,572
Chad	65	122	68.2	7	87	1,860	14	111	2,400
Chile	10	432	26.3	7	20	510	9	24	510
China	44	872	77.1	6	18	335	12	22	375
Colombia	68	456	82.8	6	34	1,745	11	35	1,773
Comoros	20	100	47.5	9	28	1,481	8	22	1,481
Congo, Dem. Rep.	34	312	235.4	8	64	3,120	12	92	3,308
Congo, Rep.	94	576	57.3	12	50	1,732	15	62	2,201
Costa Rica	41	402	83.0	7	36	660	13	42	660
Côte d'Ivoire	71	270	45.7	9	21	781	19	48	1,395
Croatia	39	196	37.1	7	26	1,250	9	18	1,250
Czech Republic	14	930	49.0	5	20	713	8	22	833
Denmark	18	135	31.5	3	5	540	3	5	540
Djibouti	36	114	41.7	15	25	2,035	14	26	2,035
Dominica	30	65	34.8	7	11	1,477	13	17	1,512
Dominican Republic	87	178	67.9	7	17	770	11	17	990
Ecuador	8	600	34.9	12	20	1,090	11	41	1,090
Egypt	41	536	50.4	8	20	1,014	8	25	1,049
El Salvador	66	224	27.4	7	22	515	12	30	515
Equatorial Guinea	48	212	62.4	6	26	1,203	6	50	1,203
Eritrea	18	216	86.3	11	69	935	18	69	1,185
Estonia	11	104	50.2	5	3	640	6	5	640
Ethiopia	20	212	32.8	8	46	1,700	11	52	2,455
Fiji	34	145	40.1	7	22	418	12	22	1,170
Finland	19	264	47.9	4	7	420	3	7	420
France	33	128	68.2	4	15	886	5	15	886
Gabon	27	272	48.3	4	19	4,000	10	26	4,031
Gambia	47	376	291.4	4	19	422	8	23	494
Georgia	35	423	37.8	8	13	1,370	11	15	1,370
Germany	32	105	57.1	4	6	731	4	6	750
Ghana	35	304	32.3	5	21	822	9	42	842
Greece	33	204	60.2	7	29	1,328	11	34	1,443

Economy	Paying taxes			Trading across borders					
	Payments (number per year)	Time (hours per year)	Total tax rate (% of profit)	Documents to export (number)	Time to export (days)	Cost to export (US$ per container)	Documents to import (number)	Time to import (days)	Cost to import (US$ per container)
Grenada	30	140	42.8	6	19	858	6	20	984
Guatemala	50	294	40.9	9	20	1,785	7	33	1,985
Guinea	55	416	49.4	7	43	510	12	56	2,785
Guinea-Bissau	47	208	47.5	8	27	1,656	9	26	1,749
Guyana	45	288	44.2	8	42	3,606	11	54	3,656
Haiti	53	160	40.5	8	58	1,298	9	60	1,304
Honduras	48	424	51.4	6	28	500	15	39	670
Hong Kong, China	4	80	28.8	2	6	425	2	5	425
Hungary	24	304	59.3	6	23	922	10	24	1,137
Iceland	18	140	27.9	7	15	469	6	15	443
India	59	264	81.1	10	27	864	15	41	1,244
Indonesia	52	576	37.2	7	25	546	10	30	675
Iran	28	292	46.4	5	26	700	11	38	1,220
Iraq	13	312	38.7	10	105	1,010	19	135	2,060
Ireland	8	76	25.8	5	7	1,146	4	14	1,139
Israel	33	225	39.1	5	15	340	5	16	700
Italy	15	360	76.0	8	15	1,253	16	21	1,291
Jamaica	72	414	52.3	6	19	1,750	7	20	1,350
Japan	15	350	52.8	5	11	789	7	11	847
Jordan	26	101	31.9	7	24	720	12	22	955
Kazakhstan	34	156	45.0	14	93	2,780	18	87	2,880
Kenya	17	432	74.2	11	25	1,980	9	45	2,325
Kiribati	16	120	34.4	3	11	1,300	2	8	1,300
Korea	27	290	30.9	5	12	780	8	12	1,040
Kuwait	14	118	55.7	5	18	675	11	27	1,170
Kyrgyz Republic	89	204	67.4	..	..	..	18	127	3,032
Lao PDR	31	180	32.5	12	66	1,420	16	78	1,690
Latvia	8	320	42.6	6	11	965	5	12	965
Lebanon	33	208	37.3	6	22	969	12	34	752
Lesotho	21	352	25.6	6	46	1,270	9	51	1,270
Lithuania	13	162	48.4	5	6	704	12	17	782
FYR Macedonia	54	96	43.5	10	32	1,070	10	35	1,070
Madagascar	25	304	43.2	8	48	982	11	48	1,282
Malawi	29	878	32.6	8	44	1,565	16	60	1,590
Malaysia	35	190	35.2	6	20	481	12	22	428
Maldives	1	0	9.3	8	15	1,000	9	21	1,784
Mali	60	270	50.0	10	66	1,752	16	61	2,680
Marshall Islands	20	128	66.6	..	..	..	9	15	2,115
Mauritania	61	696	104.3	9	25	3,733	7	40	3,733
Mauritius	7	158	24.8	5	16	683	7	16	683
Mexico	49	552	37.1	6	17	1,049	8	26	2,152
Micronesia	9	128	61.3	..	..	..	7	21	895
Moldova	44	250	48.8	7	33	1,185	7	35	1,285
Mongolia	42	204	32.2	11	66	3,007	10	74	3,030
Montenegro	75	208	33.9	6	19	1,515	8	17	1,715
Morocco	28	468	52.7	6	18	700	11	30	1,500
Mozambique	36	230	39.2	6	39	1,516	16	38	1,616
Namibia	34	..	25.6	9	32	1,672	14	25	1,549
Nepal	35	408	32.8	7	44	1,599	10	37	1,800
Netherlands	22	250	48.1	5	7	875	4	8	950
New Zealand	9	70	36.5	5	8	355	9	13	555
Nicaragua	64	240	66.4	5	36	1,020	5	38	1,020
Niger	44	270	46.0	..	..	..	19	89	3,266
Nigeria	35	1120	31.4	11	25	798	13	45	1,460
Norway	3	87	46.1	4	7	518	4	7	468
Oman	14	52	20.2	9	23	987	13	27	987
Pakistan	47	560	43.4	8	24	996	12	19	1,005
Palau	18	128	74.6	7	20	860	9	27	860
Panama	59	560	52.4	9	16	920	9	13	920

Economy	Paying taxes			Trading across borders					
	Payments (number per year)	Time (hours per year)	Total tax rate (% of profit)	Documents to export (number)	Time to export (days)	Cost to export (US$ per container)	Documents to import (number)	Time to import (days)	Cost to import (US$ per container)
Papua New Guinea	44	198	44.3	5	30	584	10	32	642
Paraguay	33	328	43.2	9	34	685	13	31	1,077
Peru	53	424	40.8	7	24	800	13	31	820
Philippines	59	94	53.0	6	18	1,336	7	20	1,336
Poland	43	175	38.4	6	19	2,260	7	26	2,260
Portugal	7	328	47.0	4	14	495	9	17	994
Puerto Rico	17	140	40.9	9	15	535	10	19	535
Romania	89	198	48.9	4	14	1,300	4	14	1,200
Russia	23	256	54.2	8	39	2,237	8	38	2,237
Rwanda	43	168	41.1	14	60	3,840	20	95	4,080
Samoa	36	224	22.1	7	15	1,120	8	19	1,265
São Tomé and Principe	42	424	55.2	8	27	490	10	29	577
Saudi Arabia	14	75	14.9	5	13	654	9	34	604
Senegal	59	696	47.7	6	22	978	10	26	1,674
Serbia	41	168	38.9	6	11	1,240	8	12	1,440
Seychelles	15	76	48.8	6	17	1,842	7	19	1,842
Sierra Leone	20	399	277.0	7	29	2,075	7	33	2,218
Singapore	16	30	28.8	5	6	382	6	3	333
Slovakia	30	344	48.9	9	20	1,015	8	21	1,050
Slovenia	34	272	39.4	9	20	1,070	11	24	1,107
Solomon Islands	33	80	33.6	8	15	805	5	12	788
South Africa	23	350	38.3	5	31	850	9	34	850
Spain	7	602	59.1	4	9	1,050	5	10	1,050
Sri Lanka	61	256	74.9	8	25	797	13	27	789
St. Kitts and Nevis	23	368	52.7	8	11	706	8	13	756
St. Lucia	16	41	31.5	5	9	1,053	8	19	1,163
St. Vincent and the Grenadines	21	208	33.6	7	15	756	6	13	1,354
Sudan	66	180	37.1	12	56	1,870	13	83	1,970
Suriname	17	199	27.8	7	16	905	7	15	815
Swaziland	34	104	39.5	9	9	1,857	14	35	1,950
Sweden	5	122	57.0	4	6	831	3	6	831
Switzerland	13	68	24.9	4	17	1,238	5	18	1,333
Syria	21	336	35.5	9	40	1,300	11	49	1,962
Taiwan, China	15	1104	35.8	8	14	747	8	14	747
Tajikistan	55	224	87.0	14	72	4,300	10	44	3,550
Tanzania	48	248	45.0	3	24	822	10	39	917
Thailand	46	104	40.2	9	24	848	12	22	1,042
Timor-Leste	15	640	59.2	6	32	700	11	37	700
Togo	51	270	48.3	7	32	463	9	41	695
Tonga	22	164	56.2	6	12	265	9	17	360
Trinidad and Tobago	28	114	37.2	5	9	693	7	13	1,093
Tunisia	45	268	58.8	5	18	770	8	29	600
Turkey	18	254	46.3	9	20	513	13	25	735
Uganda	31	237	32.2	12	42	1,050	19	67	2,945
Ukraine	98	2185	60.3	6	33	1,009	10	46	1,025
United Arab Emirates	15	12	15.0	4	18	392	6	16	398
United Kingdom	7	105	35.4	5	12	676	4	12	756
United States	10	325	46.0	6	9	625	5	9	625
Uruguay	41	300	27.6	9	22	552	9	25	666
Uzbekistan	130	152	122.3	10	44	2,550	18	139	3,970
Vanuatu	32	120	14.4	9	12	1,565	16	14	1,975
Venezuela	68	864	51.9	8	32	525	13	67	900
Vietnam	32	1050	41.6	6	35	701	9	36	887
West Bank and Gaza	50	154	31.5	7	27	705	7	41	755
Yemen	32	248	48.0	6	33	1,129	9	31	1,475
Zambia	36	131.5	22.2	16	60	2,500	19	62	2,640
Zimbabwe	59	216	37.0	9	52	3,175	15	66	4,565

Economy	Enforcing contracts			Closing a business		
	Procedures (number)	Time (days)	Cost (% of claim)	Time (years)	Cost (% of estate)	Recovery rate (cents on the dollar)
Afghanistan	..	1642	25.0	NO PRACTICE	NO PRACTICE	0.0
Albania	39	390	22.6	4.0	38	26.4
Algeria	49	397	10.3	2.5	7	41.7
Angola	47	1011	11.2	6.2	22	2.0
Antigua and Barbuda	48	297	10.7	3.0	1	37.3
Argentina	33	520	15.0	2.8	12	36.2
Armenia	24	185	14.0	1.9	4	42.0
Australia	19	181	12.8	1.0	8	79.7
Austria	23	342	9.0	1.1	18	73.7
Azerbaijan	27	267	19.8	2.7	8	32.5
Bangladesh	50	1442	45.7	4.0	8	24.9
Belarus	28	225	21.1	5.8	22	25.7
Belgium	27	328	9.5	0.9	4	86.4
Belize	51	892	18.0	1.0	23	63.6
Benin	49	720	29.7	4.0	15	23.7
Bhutan	34	275	20.2	NO PRACTICE	NO PRACTICE	0.0
Bolivia	47	591	10.5	1.8	15	37.6
Bosnia and Herzegovina	36	595	19.6	3.3	9	33.7
Botswana	26	501	24.8	1.3	15	64.7
Brazil	42	616	15.5	4.0	12	12.1
Bulgaria	34	440	14.0	3.3	9	34.4
Burkina Faso	41	446	95.4	4.0	9	26.4
Burundi	47	403	32.5	4.0	18	16.5
Cambodia	31	401	121.3	NO PRACTICE	NO PRACTICE	0.0
Cameroon	58	800	36.4	3.2	15	24.1
Canada	17	346	12.0	0.8	4	89.3
Cape Verde	40	465	15.0	NO PRACTICE	NO PRACTICE	0.0
Central African Republic	45	660	43.7	4.8	76	0.0
Chad	52	743	54.9	10.0	63	0.0
Chile	33	480	16.3	5.6	15	20.0
China	31	292	26.8	2.4	22	31.5
Colombia	37	1346	20.0	3.0	1	57.7
Comoros	60	721	29.4	NO PRACTICE	NO PRACTICE	0.0
Congo, Dem. Rep.	51	685	156.8	5.2	22	4.9
Congo, Rep.	47	560	45.6	3.0	24	19.4
Costa Rica	34	615	18.7	3.5	15	17.6
Côte d'Ivoire	25	525	29.5	2.2	18	33.8
Croatia	22	561	10.0	3.1	15	28.9
Czech Republic	21	820	14.1	9.2	15	18.5
Denmark	15	190	6.5	3.0	4	70.5
Djibouti	59	1225	27.0	5.0	18	15.9
Dominica	52	681	28.2	NO PRACTICE	NO PRACTICE	0.0
Dominican Republic	29	460	35.0	3.5	38	7.4
Ecuador	41	498	15.3	8.0	18	12.7
Egypt	55	1010	18.4	4.2	22	16.6
El Salvador	41	626	15.0	4.0	9	29.2
Equatorial Guinea	38	553	14.5	NO PRACTICE	NO PRACTICE	0.0
Eritrea	35	305	18.6	1.7	15	0.0
Estonia	25	275	11.5	3.0	9	39.9
Ethiopia	30	690	14.8	2.4	15	36.9
Fiji	26	397	62.1	1.8	38	20.8
Finland	27	228	5.9	0.9	4	89.1
France	21	331	11.8	1.9	9	48.0
Gabon	32	880	9.8	5.0	15	13.9
Gambia	26	247	35.9	3.0	15	31.4
Georgia	24	285	20.5	3.3	4	27.5
Germany	30	394	10.5	1.2	8	53.1
Ghana	29	552	13.0	1.9	22	24.7
Greece	22	730	12.7	2.0	9	46.3

Economy	Enforcing contracts			Closing a business		
	Procedures (number)	Time (days)	Cost (% of claim)	Time (years)	Cost (% of estate)	Recovery rate (cents on the dollar)
Grenada	50	583	22.1	NO PRACTICE	NO PRACTICE	0.0
Guatemala	36	1459	26.5	3.0	15	28.3
Guinea	44	276	43.8	3.8	8	17.5
Guinea-Bissau	40	1140	27.0	NO PRACTICE	NO PRACTICE	0.0
Guyana	30	661	24.2	2.0	42	13.7
Haiti	35	368	32.6	5.7	30	4.0
Honduras	36	480	30.4	3.8	8	23.0
Hong Kong, China	16	211	14.2	1.1	9	78.9
Hungary	21	335	9.6	2.0	15	39.7
Iceland	14	352	5.9	1.0	4	79.7
India	56	1420	35.7	10.0	9	13.0
Indonesia	34	570	126.5	5.5	18	11.8
Iran	23	520	12.0	4.5	9	19.7
Iraq	65	520	15.3	NO PRACTICE	NO PRACTICE	0.0
Ireland	18	217	21.1	0.4	9	87.9
Israel	31	585	22.1	4.0	23	43.9
Italy	40	1210	17.6	1.2	22	39.7
Jamaica	18	415	27.8	1.1	18	64.3
Japan	20	242	9.5	0.6	4	92.7
Jordan	43	342	16.2	4.3	9	28.2
Kazakhstan	37	183	11.5	3.3	18	23.6
Kenya	25	360	41.3	4.5	22	14.6
Kiribati	26	660	71.0	NO PRACTICE	NO PRACTICE	0.0
Korea	29	230	5.5	1.5	4	81.8
Kuwait	52	390	13.3	4.2	1	34.5
Kyrgyz Republic	44	140	12.0	4.0	15	14.9
Lao PDR	53	443	30.3	5.0	76	0.0
Latvia	21	240	11.8	3.0	13	34.8
Lebanon	39	721	27.8	4.0	22	19.0
Lesotho	58	695	10.6	2.6	8	36.6
Lithuania	24	166	8.6	1.7	7	50.5
FYR Macedonia	27	385	32.8	3.7	28	15.5
Madagascar	29	591	22.8	NO PRACTICE	NO PRACTICE	0.0
Malawi	40	337	136.5	2.6	30	13.2
Malaysia	31	450	21.3	2.3	15	38.7
Maldives	28	665	16.2	6.7	4	18.2
Mali	28	860	45.0	3.6	18	23.7
Marshall Islands	34	432	26.5	2.0	38	17.9
Mauritania	40	400	17.9	8.0	9	7.8
Mauritius	37	630	15.7	1.7	15	34.3
Mexico	37	415	20.0	1.8	18	63.2
Micronesia	25	775	77.0	5.3	38	3.1
Moldova	37	310	16.2	2.8	9	29.4
Mongolia	29	314	17.6	4.0	8	18.0
Montenegro	49	545	15.0	2.0	9	41.0
Morocco	42	615	16.5	1.8	18	35.1
Mozambique	38	1010	132.1	5.0	9	15.0
Namibia	31	270	28.3	1.5	15	41.3
Nepal	28	590	24.4	5.0	9	24.5
Netherlands	22	408	15.9	1.7	1	86.3
New Zealand	28	109	10.9	2.0	4	68.6
Nicaragua	20	486	21.8	2.2	15	34.3
Niger	33	360	42.0	5.0	18	14.2
Nigeria	23	457	27.0	1.5	22	32.1
Norway	14	277	9.0	0.9	1	91.1
Oman	41	598	12.9	4.0	4	35.4
Pakistan	55	880	22.6	2.8	4	39.9
Palau	43	622	33.2	1.0	23	38.2
Panama	45	686	50.0	2.5	18	32.3

	Enforcing contracts			Closing a business		
Economy	**Procedures** (number)	**Time** (days)	**Cost** (% of claim)	**Time** (years)	**Cost** (% of estate)	**Recovery rate** (cents on the dollar)
Papua New Guinea	22	440	110.3	3.0	23	24.1
Paraguay	46	478	39.8	3.9	9	15.4
Peru	35	300	34.7	3.1	7	31.8
Philippines	25	600	16.0	5.7	38	4.0
Poland	41	980	10.0	3.0	22	27.9
Portugal	24	495	14.5	2.0	9	75.0
Puerto Rico	43	620	16.1	3.8	8	56.0
Romania	43	335	10.7	4.6	9	19.9
Russia	31	178	13.5	3.8	9	28.7
Rwanda	27	310	43.2	NO PRACTICE	NO PRACTICE	0.0
Samoa	30	455	15.3	2.5	38	15.2
São Tomé and Principe	67	405	69.5	NO PRACTICE	NO PRACTICE	0.0
Saudi Arabia	44	360	20.0	2.8	22	27.3
Senegal	33	780	23.8	3.0	7	31.6
Serbia	33	635	12.7	2.7	23	22.6
Seychelles	29	720	13.0	NO PRACTICE	NO PRACTICE	0.0
Sierra Leone	58	515	227.3	2.6	42	8.7
Singapore	29	120	14.6	0.8	1	91.3
Slovakia	27	565	15.7	4.0	18	48.1
Slovenia	25	1350	15.2	2.0	8	44.9
Solomon Islands	25	455	69.8	1.0	38	23.3
South Africa	26	600	11.5	2.0	18	34.4
Spain	23	515	15.7	1.0	15	77.6
Sri Lanka	20	837	21.3	2.2	18	35.6
St. Kitts and Nevis	49	578	17.1	NO PRACTICE	NO PRACTICE	0.0
St. Lucia	51	635	31.2	2.0	9	42.2
St. Vincent and the Grenadines	52	394	22.2	NO PRACTICE	NO PRACTICE	0.0
Sudan	67	770	20.6	NO PRACTICE	NO PRACTICE	0.0
Suriname	29	1290	15.9	5.0	30	7.1
Swaziland	31	972	20.1	2.0	15	36.9
Sweden	19	208	5.9	2.0	9	75.7
Switzerland	22	215	11.0	3.0	4	47.1
Syria	47	872	21.9	4.1	9	29.6
Taiwan, China	28	510	16.6	0.8	4	89.5
Tajikistan	46	257	10.3	3.0	9	39.1
Tanzania	21	393	51.5	3.0	22	21.9
Thailand	26	425	17.5	2.7	36	42.6
Timor-Leste	69	1170	183.1	NO PRACTICE	NO PRACTICE	0.0
Togo	37	535	24.3	3.0	15	27.2
Tonga	30	510	47.0	2.7	22	25.6
Trinidad and Tobago	37	1340	30.5	NO PRACTICE	NO PRACTICE	0.0
Tunisia	21	481	17.3	1.3	7	51.2
Turkey	34	420	17.4	5.9	7	9.8
Uganda	19	484	35.2	2.2	30	40.4
Ukraine	28	183	16.0	2.9	42	8.7
United Arab Emirates	34	607	18.5	5.1	30	10.4
United Kingdom	19	229	16.8	1.0	6	85.2
United States	17	300	7.7	1.5	7	77.0
Uruguay	39	655	15.9	2.1	7	43.2
Uzbekistan	35	195	13.5	4.0	10	18.7
Vanuatu	24	430	64.0	2.6	38	40.0
Venezuela	41	435	28.7	4.0	38	6.7
Vietnam	37	295	31.0	5.0	15	18.0
West Bank and Gaza	26	700	20.2	NO PRACTICE	NO PRACTICE	0.0
Yemen	37	360	10.5	3.0	8	28.6
Zambia	21	404	28.7	3.1	9	22.0
Zimbabwe	33	410	26.9	3.3	22	0.1

AFGHANISTAN

Ease of doing business (rank)	162	South Asia Low income		GNI per capita (US$) Population (m)	270 24.8	

Starting a business (rank)	17	**Registering property** (rank)	169	**Trading across borders** (rank)	152
Procedures (number)	3	Procedures (number)	11	Documents to export (number)	7
Time (days)	8	Time (days)	252	Time to export (days)	66
Cost (% of income per capita)	67.4	Cost (% of property value)	9.5	Cost to export (US$ per container)	2,500
Minimum capital (% of income per capita)	0.0			Documents to import (number)	11
		Getting credit (rank)	174	Time to import (days)	88
Dealing with licenses (rank)	..	Strength of legal rights index (0–10)	0	Cost to import (US$ per container)	2,100
Procedures (number)	..	Depth of credit information index (0–6)	0		
Time (days)	..	Public registry coverage (% of adults)	0.0	**Enforcing contracts** (rank)	165
Cost (% of income per capita)	..	Private bureau coverage (% of adults)	0.0	Procedures (number)	..
				Time (days)	1642
Employing workers (rank)	74	**Protecting investors** (rank)	173	Cost (% of claim)	25.0
Difficulty of hiring index (0–100)	67	Extent of disclosure index (0–10)	0		
Rigidity of hours index (0–100)	40	Extent of director liability index (0–10)	0	**Closing a business** (rank)	151
Difficulty of firing index (0–100)	30	Ease of shareholder suits index (0–10)	2	Time (years)	NO PRACTICE
Rigidity of employment index (0–100)	46	Strength of investor protection index (0–10)	0.7	Cost (% of estate)	NO PRACTICE
Nonwage labor cost (% of salary)	0			Recovery rate (cents on the dollar)	0.0
Firing cost (weeks of salary)	4	**Paying taxes** (rank)	30		
		Payments (number per year)	2		
		Time (hours per year)	275		
		Total tax rate (% of profit)	36.3		

ALBANIA

Ease of doing business (rank)	120	Eastern Europe & Central Asia Lower middle income		GNI per capita (US$) Population (m)	2,580 3.1	

Starting a business (rank)	121	**Registering property** (rank)	76	**Trading across borders** (rank)	101
Procedures (number)	11	Procedures (number)	7	Documents to export (number)	7
Time (days)	39	Time (days)	47	Time to export (days)	34
Cost (% of income per capita)	22.4	Cost (% of property value)	3.6	Cost to export (US$ per container)	818
Minimum capital (% of income per capita)	36.7			Documents to import (number)	12
		Getting credit (rank)	48	Time to import (days)	34
Dealing with licenses (rank)	161	Strength of legal rights index (0–10)	9	Cost to import (US$ per container)	820
Procedures (number)	22	Depth of credit information index (0–6)	0		
Time (days)	344	Public registry coverage (% of adults)	0.0	**Enforcing contracts** (rank)	99
Cost (% of income per capita)	286.8	Private bureau coverage (% of adults)	0.0	Procedures (number)	39
				Time (days)	390
Employing workers (rank)	113	**Protecting investors** (rank)	162	Cost (% of claim)	22.6
Difficulty of hiring index (0–100)	44	Extent of disclosure index (0–10)	0		
Rigidity of hours index (0–100)	40	Extent of director liability index (0–10)	5	**Closing a business** (rank)	89
Difficulty of firing index (0–100)	30	Ease of shareholder suits index (0–10)	3	Time (years)	4.0
Rigidity of employment index (0–100)	38	Strength of investor protection index (0–10)	2.7	Cost (% of estate)	38
Nonwage labor cost (% of salary)	31			Recovery rate (cents on the dollar)	26.4
Firing cost (weeks of salary)	64	**Paying taxes** (rank)	125		
		Payments (number per year)	41		
		Time (hours per year)	240		
		Total tax rate (% of profit)	55.8		

ALGERIA

Ease of doing business (rank)	116	Middle East & North Africa Lower middle income		GNI per capita (US$) Population (m)	2,730 32.5	

Starting a business (rank)	120	**Registering property** (rank)	152	**Trading across borders** (rank)	109
Procedures (number)	14	Procedures (number)	15	Documents to export (number)	9
Time (days)	24	Time (days)	51	Time to export (days)	15
Cost (% of income per capita)	21.5	Cost (% of property value)	7.5	Cost to export (US$ per container)	1,606
Minimum capital (% of income per capita)	46.0			Documents to import (number)	9
		Getting credit (rank)	117	Time to import (days)	22
Dealing with licenses (rank)	117	Strength of legal rights index (0–10)	3	Cost to import (US$ per container)	1,886
Procedures (number)	25	Depth of credit information index (0–6)	2		
Time (days)	244	Public registry coverage (% of adults)	0.2	**Enforcing contracts** (rank)	61
Cost (% of income per capita)	58.9	Private bureau coverage (% of adults)	0.0	Procedures (number)	49
				Time (days)	397
Employing workers (rank)	93	**Protecting investors** (rank)	60	Cost (% of claim)	10.3
Difficulty of hiring index (0–100)	44	Extent of disclosure index (0–10)	6		
Rigidity of hours index (0–100)	60	Extent of director liability index (0–10)	6	**Closing a business** (rank)	41
Difficulty of firing index (0–100)	30	Ease of shareholder suits index (0–10)	4	Time (years)	2.5
Rigidity of employment index (0–100)	45	Strength of investor protection index (0–10)	5.3	Cost (% of estate)	7
Nonwage labor cost (% of salary)	27			Recovery rate (cents on the dollar)	41.7
Firing cost (weeks of salary)	17	**Paying taxes** (rank)	169		
		Payments (number per year)	61		
		Time (hours per year)	504		
		Total tax rate (% of profit)	76.4		

ANGOLA

		Sub-Saharan Africa			GNI per capita (US$)	1,350
Ease of doing business (rank)	156	Lower middle income			Population (m)	15.9

Starting a business (rank)	170	**Registering property** (rank)	161	**Trading across borders** (rank)	146
Procedures (number)	13	Procedures (number)	7	Documents to export (number)	6
Time (days)	124	Time (days)	334	Time to export (days)	74
Cost (% of income per capita)	486.7	Cost (% of property value)	11.1	Cost to export (US$ per container)	1,800
Minimum capital (% of income per capita)	74.1			Documents to import (number)	10
		Getting credit (rank)	83	Time to import (days)	85
Dealing with licenses (rank)	146	Strength of legal rights index (0–10)	3	Cost to import (US$ per container)	2,225
Procedures (number)	15	Depth of credit information index (0–6)	4		
Time (days)	326	Public registry coverage (% of adults)	2.9	**Enforcing contracts** (rank)	133
Cost (% of income per capita)	1239.2	Private bureau coverage (% of adults)	0.0	Procedures (number)	47
				Time (days)	1011
Employing workers (rank)	167	**Protecting investors** (rank)	46	Cost (% of claim)	11.2
Difficulty of hiring index (0–100)	33	Extent of disclosure index (0–10)	5		
Rigidity of hours index (0–100)	80	Extent of director liability index (0–10)	6	**Closing a business** (rank)	149
Difficulty of firing index (0–100)	80	Ease of shareholder suits index (0–10)	6	Time (years)	6.2
Rigidity of employment index (0–100)	64	Strength of investor protection index (0–10)	5.7	Cost (% of estate)	22
Nonwage labor cost (% of salary)	8			Recovery rate (cents on the dollar)	2.0
Firing cost (weeks of salary)	58	**Paying taxes** (rank)	142		
		Payments (number per year)	42		
		Time (hours per year)	272		
		Total tax rate (% of profit)	64.4		

ANTIGUA AND BARBUDA

		Latin America & Caribbean			GNI per capita (US$)	10,920
Ease of doing business (rank)	33	High income			Population (m)	0.1

Starting a business (rank)	22	**Registering property** (rank)	71	**Trading across borders** (rank)	47
Procedures (number)	7	Procedures (number)	5	Documents to export (number)	5
Time (days)	21	Time (days)	26	Time to export (days)	13
Cost (% of income per capita)	12.5	Cost (% of property value)	13.0	Cost to export (US$ per container)	1,056
Minimum capital (% of income per capita)	0.0			Documents to import (number)	6
		Getting credit (rank)	101	Time to import (days)	15
Dealing with licenses (rank)	15	Strength of legal rights index (0–10)	6	Cost to import (US$ per container)	1,467
Procedures (number)	12	Depth of credit information index (0–6)	0		
Time (days)	139	Public registry coverage (% of adults)	0.0	**Enforcing contracts** (rank)	47
Cost (% of income per capita)	27.8	Private bureau coverage (% of adults)	0.0	Procedures (number)	48
				Time (days)	297
Employing workers (rank)	40	**Protecting investors** (rank)	19	Cost (% of claim)	10.7
Difficulty of hiring index (0–100)	11	Extent of disclosure index (0–10)	4		
Rigidity of hours index (0–100)	0	Extent of director liability index (0–10)	8	**Closing a business** (rank)	54
Difficulty of firing index (0–100)	20	Ease of shareholder suits index (0–10)	7	Time (years)	3.0
Rigidity of employment index (0–100)	10	Strength of investor protection index (0–10)	6.3	Cost (% of estate)	1
Nonwage labor cost (% of salary)	9			Recovery rate (cents on the dollar)	37.3
Firing cost (weeks of salary)	52	**Paying taxes** (rank)	145		
		Payments (number per year)	44		
		Time (hours per year)	528		
		Total tax rate (% of profit)	48.5		

ARGENTINA

		Latin America & Caribbean			GNI per capita (US$)	4,470
Ease of doing business (rank)	101	Upper middle income			Population (m)	38.7

Starting a business (rank)	106	**Registering property** (rank)	74	**Trading across borders** (rank)	71
Procedures (number)	15	Procedures (number)	5	Documents to export (number)	6
Time (days)	32	Time (days)	44	Time to export (days)	16
Cost (% of income per capita)	12.1	Cost (% of property value)	8.3	Cost to export (US$ per container)	1,470
Minimum capital (% of income per capita)	5.6			Documents to import (number)	7
		Getting credit (rank)	48	Time to import (days)	21
Dealing with licenses (rank)	125	Strength of legal rights index (0–10)	3	Cost to import (US$ per container)	1,750
Procedures (number)	23	Depth of credit information index (0–6)	6		
Time (days)	288	Public registry coverage (% of adults)	25.4	**Enforcing contracts** (rank)	68
Cost (% of income per capita)	46.3	Private bureau coverage (% of adults)	100.0	Procedures (number)	33
				Time (days)	520
Employing workers (rank)	138	**Protecting investors** (rank)	99	Cost (% of claim)	15.0
Difficulty of hiring index (0–100)	44	Extent of disclosure index (0–10)	6		
Rigidity of hours index (0–100)	60	Extent of director liability index (0–10)	2	**Closing a business** (rank)	58
Difficulty of firing index (0–100)	20	Ease of shareholder suits index (0–10)	6	Time (years)	2.8
Rigidity of employment index (0–100)	41	Strength of investor protection index (0–10)	4.7	Cost (% of estate)	12
Nonwage labor cost (% of salary)	23			Recovery rate (cents on the dollar)	36.2
Firing cost (weeks of salary)	139	**Paying taxes** (rank)	161		
		Payments (number per year)	34		
		Time (hours per year)	615		
		Total tax rate (% of profit)	116.8		

ARMENIA

		Eastern Europe & Central Asia		GNI per capita (US$)	1,470
Ease of doing business (rank)	34	Lower middle income		Population (m)	3.0

Starting a business (rank)	46	**Registering property** (rank)	2	**Trading across borders** (rank)	119
Procedures (number)	9	Procedures (number)	3	Documents to export (number)	7
Time (days)	24	Time (days)	4	Time to export (days)	34
Cost (% of income per capita)	5.1	Cost (% of property value)	0.4	Cost to export (US$ per container)	1,600
Minimum capital (% of income per capita)	3.3			Documents to import (number)	6
		Getting credit (rank)	65	Time to import (days)	37
Dealing with licenses (rank)	36	Strength of legal rights index (0–10)	5	Cost to import (US$ per container)	1,750
Procedures (number)	18	Depth of credit information index (0–6)	3		
Time (days)	112	Public registry coverage (% of adults)	1.5		
Cost (% of income per capita)	43.1	Private bureau coverage (% of adults)	0.0	**Enforcing contracts** (rank)	18
				Procedures (number)	24
				Time (days)	185
Employing workers (rank)	41	**Protecting investors** (rank)	83	Cost (% of claim)	14.0
Difficulty of hiring index (0–100)	33	Extent of disclosure index (0–10)	5		
Rigidity of hours index (0–100)	40	Extent of director liability index (0–10)	2	**Closing a business** (rank)	40
Difficulty of firing index (0–100)	20	Ease of shareholder suits index (0–10)	8	Time (years)	1.9
Rigidity of employment index (0–100)	31	Strength of investor protection index (0–10)	5.0	Cost (% of estate)	4
Nonwage labor cost (% of salary)	18			Recovery rate (cents on the dollar)	42.0
Firing cost (weeks of salary)	13	**Paying taxes** (rank)	148		
		Payments (number per year)	50		
		Time (hours per year)	1120		
		Total tax rate (% of profit)	42.5		

AUSTRALIA

		OECD: High Income		GNI per capita (US$)	32,220
Ease of doing business (rank)	8	High income		Population (m)	20.3

Starting a business (rank)	2	**Registering property** (rank)	27	**Trading across borders** (rank)	23
Procedures (number)	2	Procedures (number)	5	Documents to export (number)	6
Time (days)	2	Time (days)	5	Time to export (days)	9
Cost (% of income per capita)	1.8	Cost (% of property value)	4.8	Cost to export (US$ per container)	795
Minimum capital (% of income per capita)	0.0			Documents to import (number)	5
		Getting credit (rank)	3	Time to import (days)	12
Dealing with licenses (rank)	29	Strength of legal rights index (0–10)	9	Cost to import (US$ per container)	945
Procedures (number)	17	Depth of credit information index (0–6)	5		
Time (days)	140	Public registry coverage (% of adults)	0.0		
Cost (% of income per capita)	13.8	Private bureau coverage (% of adults)	100.0	**Enforcing contracts** (rank)	7
				Procedures (number)	19
				Time (days)	181
Employing workers (rank)	9	**Protecting investors** (rank)	46	Cost (% of claim)	12.8
Difficulty of hiring index (0–100)	0	Extent of disclosure index (0–10)	8		
Rigidity of hours index (0–100)	0	Extent of director liability index (0–10)	2	**Closing a business** (rank)	12
Difficulty of firing index (0–100)	10	Ease of shareholder suits index (0–10)	7	Time (years)	1.0
Rigidity of employment index (0–100)	3	Strength of investor protection index (0–10)	5.7	Cost (% of estate)	8
Nonwage labor cost (% of salary)	21			Recovery rate (cents on the dollar)	79.7
Firing cost (weeks of salary)	4	**Paying taxes** (rank)	35		
		Payments (number per year)	11		
		Time (hours per year)	107		
		Total tax rate (% of profit)	52.2		

AUSTRIA

		OECD: High Income		GNI per capita (US$)	36,980
Ease of doing business (rank)	30	High income		Population (m)	8.2

Starting a business (rank)	74	**Registering property** (rank)	28	**Trading across borders** (rank)	15
Procedures (number)	9	Procedures (number)	3	Documents to export (number)	4
Time (days)	29	Time (days)	32	Time to export (days)	8
Cost (% of income per capita)	5.6	Cost (% of property value)	4.5	Cost to export (US$ per container)	803
Minimum capital (% of income per capita)	59.6			Documents to import (number)	5
		Getting credit (rank)	21	Time to import (days)	9
Dealing with licenses (rank)	50	Strength of legal rights index (0–10)	5	Cost to import (US$ per container)	843
Procedures (number)	14	Depth of credit information index (0–6)	6		
Time (days)	195	Public registry coverage (% of adults)	1.2		
Cost (% of income per capita)	79.1	Private bureau coverage (% of adults)	39.9	**Enforcing contracts** (rank)	14
				Procedures (number)	23
				Time (days)	342
Employing workers (rank)	103	**Protecting investors** (rank)	142	Cost (% of claim)	9.0
Difficulty of hiring index (0–100)	11	Extent of disclosure index (0–10)	2		
Rigidity of hours index (0–100)	60	Extent of director liability index (0–10)	5	**Closing a business** (rank)	19
Difficulty of firing index (0–100)	40	Ease of shareholder suits index (0–10)	4	Time (years)	1.1
Rigidity of employment index (0–100)	37	Strength of investor protection index (0–10)	3.7	Cost (% of estate)	18
Nonwage labor cost (% of salary)	31			Recovery rate (cents on the dollar)	73.7
Firing cost (weeks of salary)	56	**Paying taxes** (rank)	102		
		Payments (number per year)	20		
		Time (hours per year)	272		
		Total tax rate (% of profit)	56.1		

AZERBAIJAN

Ease of doing business (rank)	99	Eastern Europe & Central Asia		GNI per capita (US$)		1,240
		Lower middle income		Population (m)		8.4

Starting a business (rank)	96	**Registering property** (rank)	59	**Trading across borders** (rank)	158
Procedures (number)	15	Procedures (number)	7	Documents to export (number)	7
Time (days)	53	Time (days)	61	Time to export (days)	69
Cost (% of income per capita)	9.5	Cost (% of property value)	0.3	Cost to export (US$ per container)	2,275
Minimum capital (% of income per capita)	0.0			Documents to import (number)	18
		Getting credit (rank)	21	Time to import (days)	79
Dealing with licenses (rank)	162	Strength of legal rights index (0–10)	7	Cost to import (US$ per container)	2,575
Procedures (number)	28	Depth of credit information index (0–6)	4		
Time (days)	212	Public registry coverage (% of adults)	1.1	**Enforcing contracts** (rank)	34
Cost (% of income per capita)	977.4	Private bureau coverage (% of adults)	0.0	Procedures (number)	27
				Time (days)	267
Employing workers (rank)	66	**Protecting investors** (rank)	118	Cost (% of claim)	19.8
Difficulty of hiring index (0–100)	33	Extent of disclosure index (0–10)	4		
Rigidity of hours index (0–100)	40	Extent of director liability index (0–10)	1	**Closing a business** (rank)	70
Difficulty of firing index (0–100)	40	Ease of shareholder suits index (0–10)	8	Time (years)	2.7
Rigidity of employment index (0–100)	38	Strength of investor protection index (0–10)	4.3	Cost (% of estate)	8
Nonwage labor cost (% of salary)	22			Recovery rate (cents on the dollar)	32.5
Firing cost (weeks of salary)	22	**Paying taxes** (rank)	136		
		Payments (number per year)	36		
		Time (hours per year)	1000		
		Total tax rate (% of profit)	44.9		

BANGLADESH

Ease of doing business (rank)	88	South Asia		GNI per capita (US$)		470
		Low income		Population (m)		141.8

Starting a business (rank)	68	**Registering property** (rank)	167	**Trading across borders** (rank)	134
Procedures (number)	8	Procedures (number)	8	Documents to export (number)	7
Time (days)	37	Time (days)	425	Time to export (days)	35
Cost (% of income per capita)	87.6	Cost (% of property value)	10.5	Cost to export (US$ per container)	902
Minimum capital (% of income per capita)	0.0			Documents to import (number)	16
		Getting credit (rank)	48	Time to import (days)	57
Dealing with licenses (rank)	67	Strength of legal rights index (0–10)	7	Cost to import (US$ per container)	1,287
Procedures (number)	13	Depth of credit information index (0–6)	2		
Time (days)	185	Public registry coverage (% of adults)	0.6	**Enforcing contracts** (rank)	174
Cost (% of income per capita)	272.3	Private bureau coverage (% of adults)	0.0	Procedures (number)	50
				Time (days)	1442
Employing workers (rank)	75	**Protecting investors** (rank)	15	Cost (% of claim)	45.7
Difficulty of hiring index (0–100)	11	Extent of disclosure index (0–10)	6		
Rigidity of hours index (0–100)	40	Extent of director liability index (0–10)	7	**Closing a business** (rank)	93
Difficulty of firing index (0–100)	40	Ease of shareholder suits index (0–10)	7	Time (years)	4.0
Rigidity of employment index (0–100)	30	Strength of investor protection index (0–10)	6.7	Cost (% of estate)	8
Nonwage labor cost (% of salary)	0			Recovery rate (cents on the dollar)	24.9
Firing cost (weeks of salary)	51	**Paying taxes** (rank)	72		
		Payments (number per year)	17		
		Time (hours per year)	400		
		Total tax rate (% of profit)	40.3		

BELARUS

Ease of doing business (rank)	129	Eastern Europe & Central Asia		GNI per capita (US$)		2,760
		Lower middle income		Population (m)		9.8

Starting a business (rank)	148	**Registering property** (rank)	96	**Trading across borders** (rank)	113
Procedures (number)	16	Procedures (number)	7	Documents to export (number)	7
Time (days)	69	Time (days)	231	Time to export (days)	33
Cost (% of income per capita)	26.1	Cost (% of property value)	0.1	Cost to export (US$ per container)	1,472
Minimum capital (% of income per capita)	36.4			Documents to import (number)	7
		Getting credit (rank)	117	Time to import (days)	36
Dealing with licenses (rank)	84	Strength of legal rights index (0–10)	2	Cost to import (US$ per container)	1,472
Procedures (number)	18	Depth of credit information index (0–6)	3		
Time (days)	354	Public registry coverage (% of adults)	0.0	**Enforcing contracts** (rank)	36
Cost (% of income per capita)	17.5	Private bureau coverage (% of adults)	0.0	Procedures (number)	28
				Time (days)	225
Employing workers (rank)	31	**Protecting investors** (rank)	142	Cost (% of claim)	21.1
Difficulty of hiring index (0–100)	0	Extent of disclosure index (0–10)	1		
Rigidity of hours index (0–100)	40	Extent of director liability index (0–10)	3	**Closing a business** (rank)	91
Difficulty of firing index (0–100)	40	Ease of shareholder suits index (0–10)	7	Time (years)	5.8
Rigidity of employment index (0–100)	27	Strength of investor protection index (0–10)	3.7	Cost (% of estate)	22
Nonwage labor cost (% of salary)	39			Recovery rate (cents on the dollar)	25.7
Firing cost (weeks of salary)	22	**Paying taxes** (rank)	175		
		Payments (number per year)	125		
		Time (hours per year)	1188		
		Total tax rate (% of profit)	186.1		

BELGIUM

Ease of doing business (rank)	20

Starting a business (rank) — 37
Procedures (number) — 4
Time (days) — 27
Cost (% of income per capita) — 5.8
Minimum capital (% of income per capita) — 21.8

Dealing with licenses (rank) — 48
Procedures (number) — 15
Time (days) — 184
Cost (% of income per capita) — 61.8

Employing workers (rank) — 23
Difficulty of hiring index (0–100) — 11
Rigidity of hours index (0–100) — 40
Difficulty of firing index (0–100) — 10
Rigidity of employment index (0–100) — 20
Nonwage labor cost (% of salary) — 55
Firing cost (weeks of salary) — 16

OECD: High Income
High income

Registering property (rank) — 158
Procedures (number) — 7
Time (days) — 132
Cost (% of property value) — 12.8

Getting credit (rank) — 48
Strength of legal rights index (0–10) — 5
Depth of credit information index (0–6) — 4
Public registry coverage (% of adults) — 56.2
Private bureau coverage (% of adults) — 0.0

Protecting investors (rank) — 12
Extent of disclosure index (0–10) — 8
Extent of director liability index (0–10) — 6
Ease of shareholder suits index (0–10) — 7
Strength of investor protection index (0–10) — 7.0

Paying taxes (rank) — 60
Payments (number per year) — 10
Time (hours per year) — 160
Total tax rate (% of profit) — 70.1

GNI per capita (US$) — 35,700
Population (m) — 10.5

Trading across borders (rank) — 36
Documents to export (number) — 5
Time to export (days) — 7
Cost to export (US$ per container) — 1,350
Documents to import (number) — 6
Time to import (days) — 9
Cost to import (US$ per container) — 1,300

Enforcing contracts (rank) — 21
Procedures (number) — 27
Time (days) — 328
Cost (% of claim) — 9.5

Closing a business (rank) — 8
Time (years) — 0.9
Cost (% of estate) — 4
Recovery rate (cents on the dollar) — 86.4

BELIZE

Ease of doing business (rank)	56

Starting a business (rank) — 103
Procedures (number) — 9
Time (days) — 45
Cost (% of income per capita) — 57.5
Minimum capital (% of income per capita) — 0.0

Dealing with licenses (rank) — 4
Procedures (number) — 12
Time (days) — 66
Cost (% of income per capita) — 30.9

Employing workers (rank) — 14
Difficulty of hiring index (0–100) — 11
Rigidity of hours index (0–100) — 20
Difficulty of firing index (0–100) — 0
Rigidity of employment index (0–100) — 10
Nonwage labor cost (% of salary) — 8
Firing cost (weeks of salary) — 24

Latin America & Caribbean
Upper middle income

Registering property (rank) — 117
Procedures (number) — 8
Time (days) — 60
Cost (% of property value) — 5.0

Getting credit (rank) — 83
Strength of legal rights index (0–10) — 7
Depth of credit information index (0–6) — 0
Public registry coverage (% of adults) — 0.0
Private bureau coverage (% of adults) — 0.0

Protecting investors (rank) — 118
Extent of disclosure index (0–10) — 3
Extent of director liability index (0–10) — 4
Ease of shareholder suits index (0–10) — 6
Strength of investor protection index (0–10) — 4.3

Paying taxes (rank) — 33
Payments (number per year) — 40
Time (hours per year) — 108
Total tax rate (% of profit) — 31.7

GNI per capita (US$) — 3,500
Population (m) — 0.3

Trading across borders (rank) — 111
Documents to export (number) — 7
Time to export (days) — 13
Cost to export (US$ per container) — 1,800
Documents to import (number) — 14
Time to import (days) — 15
Cost to import (US$ per container) — 2,130

Enforcing contracts (rank) — 150
Procedures (number) — 51
Time (days) — 892
Cost (% of claim) — 18.0

Closing a business (rank) — 24
Time (years) — 1.0
Cost (% of estate) — 23
Recovery rate (cents on the dollar) — 63.6

BENIN

Ease of doing business (rank)	137

Starting a business (rank) — 126
Procedures (number) — 7
Time (days) — 31
Cost (% of income per capita) — 173.3
Minimum capital (% of income per capita) — 379.1

Dealing with licenses (rank) — 133
Procedures (number) — 16
Time (days) — 333
Cost (% of income per capita) — 338.9

Employing workers (rank) — 121
Difficulty of hiring index (0–100) — 39
Rigidity of hours index (0–100) — 60
Difficulty of firing index (0–100) — 40
Rigidity of employment index (0–100) — 46
Nonwage labor cost (% of salary) — 29
Firing cost (weeks of salary) — 36

Sub-Saharan Africa
Low income

Registering property (rank) — 85
Procedures (number) — 3
Time (days) — 50
Cost (% of property value) — 15.1

Getting credit (rank) — 117
Strength of legal rights index (0–10) — 4
Depth of credit information index (0–6) — 1
Public registry coverage (% of adults) — 10.3
Private bureau coverage (% of adults) — 0.0

Protecting investors (rank) — 46
Extent of disclosure index (0–10) — 5
Extent of director liability index (0–10) — 8
Ease of shareholder suits index (0–10) — 4
Strength of investor protection index (0–10) — 5.7

Paying taxes (rank) — 162
Payments (number per year) — 72
Time (hours per year) — 270
Total tax rate (% of profit) — 68.5

GNI per capita (US$) — 510
Population (m) — 8.4

Trading across borders (rank) — 130
Documents to export (number) — 8
Time to export (days) — 35
Cost to export (US$ per container) — 980
Documents to import (number) — 11
Time to import (days) — 48
Cost to import (US$ per container) — 1,452

Enforcing contracts (rank) — 162
Procedures (number) — 49
Time (days) — 720
Cost (% of claim) — 29.7

Closing a business (rank) — 98
Time (years) — 4.0
Cost (% of estate) — 15
Recovery rate (cents on the dollar) — 23.7

BHUTAN

		South Asia		GNI per capita (US$)	870
Ease of doing business (rank)	138	Low income		Population (m)	0.9

Starting a business (rank)	79	**Registering property** (rank)	41	**Trading across borders** (rank)	150
Procedures (number)	10	Procedures (number)	5	Documents to export (number)	10
Time (days)	62	Time (days)	93	Time to export (days)	39
Cost (% of income per capita)	16.6	Cost (% of property value)	0.0	Cost to export (US$ per container)	1,230
Minimum capital (% of income per capita)	0.0			Documents to import (number)	14
		Getting credit (rank)	159	Time to import (days)	42
Dealing with licenses (rank)	145	Strength of legal rights index (0–10)	3	Cost to import (US$ per container)	1,950
Procedures (number)	26	Depth of credit information index (0–6)	0		
Time (days)	204	Public registry coverage (% of adults)	0.0	**Enforcing contracts** (rank)	56
Cost (% of income per capita)	263.5	Private bureau coverage (% of adults)	0.0	Procedures (number)	34
				Time (days)	275
Employing workers (rank)	116	**Protecting investors** (rank)	118	Cost (% of claim)	20.2
Difficulty of hiring index (0–100)	78	Extent of disclosure index (0–10)	6		
Rigidity of hours index (0–100)	40	Extent of director liability index (0–10)	3	**Closing a business** (rank)	151
Difficulty of firing index (0–100)	0	Ease of shareholder suits index (0–10)	4	Time (years)	NO PRACTICE
Rigidity of employment index (0–100)	39	Strength of investor protection index (0–10)	4.3	Cost (% of estate)	NO PRACTICE
Nonwage labor cost (% of salary)	1			Recovery rate (cents on the dollar)	0.0
Firing cost (weeks of salary)	95	**Paying taxes** (rank)	68		
		Payments (number per year)	19		
		Time (hours per year)	274		
		Total tax rate (% of profit)	43.0		

BOLIVIA

		Latin America & Caribbean		GNI per capita (US$)	1,010
Ease of doing business (rank)	131	Lower middle income		Population (m)	9.2

Starting a business (rank)	149	**Registering property** (rank)	115	**Trading across borders** (rank)	135
Procedures (number)	15	Procedures (number)	7	Documents to export (number)	12
Time (days)	50	Time (days)	92	Time to export (days)	26
Cost (% of income per capita)	140.6	Cost (% of property value)	5.0	Cost to export (US$ per container)	1,110
Minimum capital (% of income per capita)	3.8			Documents to import (number)	12
		Getting credit (rank)	65	Time to import (days)	36
Dealing with licenses (rank)	57	Strength of legal rights index (0–10)	3	Cost to import (US$ per container)	1,230
Procedures (number)	14	Depth of credit information index (0–6)	5		
Time (days)	183	Public registry coverage (% of adults)	11.5	**Enforcing contracts** (rank)	98
Cost (% of income per capita)	196.0	Private bureau coverage (% of adults)	32.3	Procedures (number)	47
				Time (days)	591
Employing workers (rank)	174	**Protecting investors** (rank)	118	Cost (% of claim)	10.5
Difficulty of hiring index (0–100)	61	Extent of disclosure index (0–10)	1		
Rigidity of hours index (0–100)	60	Extent of director liability index (0–10)	5	**Closing a business** (rank)	53
Difficulty of firing index (0–100)	100	Ease of shareholder suits index (0–10)	7	Time (years)	1.8
Rigidity of employment index (0–100)	74	Strength of investor protection index (0–10)	4.3	Cost (% of estate)	15
Nonwage labor cost (% of salary)	14			Recovery rate (cents on the dollar)	37.6
Firing cost (weeks of salary)	100	**Paying taxes** (rank)	166		
		Payments (number per year)	41		
		Time (hours per year)	1080		
		Total tax rate (% of profit)	80.3		

BOSNIA AND HERZEGOVINA

		Eastern Europe & Central Asia		GNI per capita (US$)	2,440
Ease of doing business (rank)	95	Lower middle income		Population (m)	3.9

Starting a business (rank)	141	**Registering property** (rank)	139	**Trading across borders** (rank)	56
Procedures (number)	12	Procedures (number)	7	Documents to export (number)	5
Time (days)	54	Time (days)	331	Time to export (days)	22
Cost (% of income per capita)	37.0	Cost (% of property value)	5.0	Cost to export (US$ per container)	1,150
Minimum capital (% of income per capita)	52.0			Documents to import (number)	7
		Getting credit (rank)	7	Time to import (days)	25
Dealing with licenses (rank)	160	Strength of legal rights index (0–10)	8	Cost to import (US$ per container)	1,150
Procedures (number)	16	Depth of credit information index (0–6)	5		
Time (days)	467	Public registry coverage (% of adults)	0.0	**Enforcing contracts** (rank)	117
Cost (% of income per capita)	2423.4	Private bureau coverage (% of adults)	22.9	Procedures (number)	36
				Time (days)	595
Employing workers (rank)	95	**Protecting investors** (rank)	83	Cost (% of claim)	19.6
Difficulty of hiring index (0–100)	56	Extent of disclosure index (0–10)	3		
Rigidity of hours index (0–100)	40	Extent of director liability index (0–10)	6	**Closing a business** (rank)	69
Difficulty of firing index (0–100)	30	Ease of shareholder suits index (0–10)	6	Time (years)	3.3
Rigidity of employment index (0–100)	42	Strength of investor protection index (0–10)	5.0	Cost (% of estate)	9
Nonwage labor cost (% of salary)	15			Recovery rate (cents on the dollar)	33.7
Firing cost (weeks of salary)	33	**Paying taxes** (rank)	111		
		Payments (number per year)	73		
		Time (hours per year)	100		
		Total tax rate (% of profit)	50.4		

BOTSWANA

Ease of doing business (rank)	48

Sub-Saharan Africa	
Upper middle income	

GNI per capita (US$)	5,180
Population (m)	1.8

Starting a business (rank)	93
Procedures (number)	11
Time (days)	108
Cost (% of income per capita)	10.6
Minimum capital (% of income per capita)	0.0

Registering property (rank)	34
Procedures (number)	4
Time (days)	30
Cost (% of property value)	4.9

Trading across borders (rank)	89
Documents to export (number)	6
Time to export (days)	37
Cost to export (US$ per container)	524
Documents to import (number)	9
Time to import (days)	42
Cost to import (US$ per container)	1,159

Dealing with licenses (rank)	136
Procedures (number)	24
Time (days)	169
Cost (% of income per capita)	457.7

Getting credit (rank)	13
Strength of legal rights index (0–10)	7
Depth of credit information index (0–6)	5
Public registry coverage (% of adults)	0.0
Private bureau coverage (% of adults)	43.2

Enforcing contracts (rank)	77
Procedures (number)	26
Time (days)	501
Cost (% of claim)	24.8

Employing workers (rank)	62
Difficulty of hiring index (0–100)	0
Rigidity of hours index (0–100)	20
Difficulty of firing index (0–100)	40
Rigidity of employment index (0–100)	20
Nonwage labor cost (% of salary)	0
Firing cost (weeks of salary)	90

Protecting investors (rank)	118
Extent of disclosure index (0–10)	8
Extent of director liability index (0–10)	2
Ease of shareholder suits index (0–10)	3
Strength of investor protection index (0–10)	4.3

Closing a business (rank)	22
Time (years)	1.3
Cost (% of estate)	15
Recovery rate (cents on the dollar)	64.7

Paying taxes (rank)	67
Payments (number per year)	24
Time (hours per year)	140
Total tax rate (% of profit)	53.3

BRAZIL

Ease of doing business (rank)	121

Latin America & Caribbean	
Lower middle income	

GNI per capita (US$)	3,460
Population (m)	186.4

Starting a business (rank)	115
Procedures (number)	17
Time (days)	152
Cost (% of income per capita)	9.9
Minimum capital (% of income per capita)	0.0

Registering property (rank)	124
Procedures (number)	14
Time (days)	47
Cost (% of property value)	4.0

Trading across borders (rank)	53
Documents to export (number)	7
Time to export (days)	18
Cost to export (US$ per container)	895
Documents to import (number)	6
Time to import (days)	24
Cost to import (US$ per container)	1,145

Dealing with licenses (rank)	139
Procedures (number)	19
Time (days)	460
Cost (% of income per capita)	179.9

Getting credit (rank)	83
Strength of legal rights index (0–10)	2
Depth of credit information index (0–6)	5
Public registry coverage (% of adults)	9.2
Private bureau coverage (% of adults)	43.0

Enforcing contracts (rank)	120
Procedures (number)	42
Time (days)	616
Cost (% of claim)	15.5

Employing workers (rank)	99
Difficulty of hiring index (0–100)	67
Rigidity of hours index (0–100)	60
Difficulty of firing index (0–100)	0
Rigidity of employment index (0–100)	42
Nonwage labor cost (% of salary)	37
Firing cost (weeks of salary)	37

Protecting investors (rank)	60
Extent of disclosure index (0–10)	5
Extent of director liability index (0–10)	7
Ease of shareholder suits index (0–10)	4
Strength of investor protection index (0–10)	5.3

Closing a business (rank)	135
Time (years)	4.0
Cost (% of estate)	12
Recovery rate (cents on the dollar)	12.1

Paying taxes (rank)	151
Payments (number per year)	23
Time (hours per year)	2600
Total tax rate (% of profit)	71.7

BULGARIA

Ease of doing business (rank)	54

Eastern Europe & Central Asia	
Lower middle income	

GNI per capita (US$)	3,450
Population (m)	7.7

Starting a business (rank)	85
Procedures (number)	9
Time (days)	32
Cost (% of income per capita)	7.9
Minimum capital (% of income per capita)	91.3

Registering property (rank)	65
Procedures (number)	9
Time (days)	19
Cost (% of property value)	2.3

Trading across borders (rank)	104
Documents to export (number)	7
Time to export (days)	26
Cost to export (US$ per container)	1,233
Documents to import (number)	10
Time to import (days)	25
Cost to import (US$ per container)	1,201

Dealing with licenses (rank)	140
Procedures (number)	22
Time (days)	226
Cost (% of income per capita)	270.5

Getting credit (rank)	33
Strength of legal rights index (0–10)	6
Depth of credit information index (0–6)	4
Public registry coverage (% of adults)	20.7
Private bureau coverage (% of adults)	..

Enforcing contracts (rank)	52
Procedures (number)	34
Time (days)	440
Cost (% of claim)	14.0

Employing workers (rank)	100
Difficulty of hiring index (0–100)	50
Rigidity of hours index (0–100)	80
Difficulty of firing index (0–100)	10
Rigidity of employment index (0–100)	47
Nonwage labor cost (% of salary)	30
Firing cost (weeks of salary)	9

Protecting investors (rank)	33
Extent of disclosure index (0–10)	10
Extent of director liability index (0–10)	1
Ease of shareholder suits index (0–10)	7
Strength of investor protection index (0–10)	6.0

Closing a business (rank)	64
Time (years)	3.3
Cost (% of estate)	9
Recovery rate (cents on the dollar)	34.4

Paying taxes (rank)	107
Payments (number per year)	27
Time (hours per year)	616
Total tax rate (% of profit)	40.7

BURKINA FASO

Ease of doing business (rank)	163	Sub-Saharan Africa		GNI per capita (US$)	400
		Low income		Population (m)	13.2

Starting a business (rank)	131	**Registering property** (rank)	164	**Trading across borders** (rank)	154
Procedures (number)	8	Procedures (number)	8	Documents to export (number)	9
Time (days)	34	Time (days)	107	Time to export (days)	69
Cost (% of income per capita)	120.8	Cost (% of property value)	16.2	Cost to export (US$ per container)	1,215
Minimum capital (% of income per capita)	481.4			Documents to import (number)	13
		Getting credit (rank)	117	Time to import (days)	66
Dealing with licenses (rank)	168	Strength of legal rights index (0–10)	4	Cost to import (US$ per container)	1,700
Procedures (number)	32	Depth of credit information index (0–6)	1		
Time (days)	226	Public registry coverage (% of adults)	2.4	**Enforcing contracts** (rank)	143
Cost (% of income per capita)	1247.5	Private bureau coverage (% of adults)	0.0	Procedures (number)	41
				Time (days)	446
Employing workers (rank)	153	**Protecting investors** (rank)	99	Cost (% of claim)	95.4
Difficulty of hiring index (0–100)	83	Extent of disclosure index (0–10)	6		
Rigidity of hours index (0–100)	60	Extent of director liability index (0–10)	5	**Closing a business** (rank)	90
Difficulty of firing index (0–100)	50	Ease of shareholder suits index (0–10)	3	Time (years)	4.0
Rigidity of employment index (0–100)	64	Strength of investor protection index (0–10)	4.7	Cost (% of estate)	9
Nonwage labor cost (% of salary)	20			Recovery rate (cents on the dollar)	26.4
Firing cost (weeks of salary)	34	**Paying taxes** (rank)	129		
		Payments (number per year)	45		
		Time (hours per year)	270		
		Total tax rate (% of profit)	51.1		

BURUNDI

Ease of doing business (rank)	166	Sub-Saharan Africa		GNI per capita (US$)	100
		Low income		Population (m)	7.5

Starting a business (rank)	109	**Registering property** (rank)	132	**Trading across borders** (rank)	171
Procedures (number)	11	Procedures (number)	5	Documents to export (number)	12
Time (days)	43	Time (days)	94	Time to export (days)	80
Cost (% of income per capita)	222.4	Cost (% of property value)	17.9	Cost to export (US$ per container)	3,625
Minimum capital (% of income per capita)	0.0			Documents to import (number)	14
		Getting credit (rank)	159	Time to import (days)	124
Dealing with licenses (rank)	164	Strength of legal rights index (0–10)	2	Cost to import (US$ per container)	3,705
Procedures (number)	18	Depth of credit information index (0–6)	1		
Time (days)	302	Public registry coverage (% of adults)	0.1	**Enforcing contracts** (rank)	137
Cost (% of income per capita)	8808.2	Private bureau coverage (% of adults)	0.0	Procedures (number)	47
				Time (days)	403
Employing workers (rank)	132	**Protecting investors** (rank)	..	Cost (% of claim)	32.5
Difficulty of hiring index (0–100)	78	Extent of disclosure index (0–10)	..		
Rigidity of hours index (0–100)	60	Extent of director liability index (0–10)	..	**Closing a business** (rank)	121
Difficulty of firing index (0–100)	40	Ease of shareholder suits index (0–10)	..	Time (years)	4.0
Rigidity of employment index (0–100)	59	Strength of investor protection index (0–10)	..	Cost (% of estate)	18
Nonwage labor cost (% of salary)	7			Recovery rate (cents on the dollar)	16.5
Firing cost (weeks of salary)	26	**Paying taxes** (rank)	123		
		Payments (number per year)	40		
		Time (hours per year)	140		
		Total tax rate (% of profit)	286.7		

CAMBODIA

Ease of doing business (rank)	143	East Asia & Pacific		GNI per capita (US$)	380
		Low income		Population (m)	14.1

Starting a business (rank)	159	**Registering property** (rank)	100	**Trading across borders** (rank)	114
Procedures (number)	10	Procedures (number)	7	Documents to export (number)	8
Time (days)	86	Time (days)	56	Time to export (days)	36
Cost (% of income per capita)	236.4	Cost (% of property value)	4.6	Cost to export (US$ per container)	736
Minimum capital (% of income per capita)	66.2			Documents to import (number)	12
		Getting credit (rank)	174	Time to import (days)	45
Dealing with licenses (rank)	159	Strength of legal rights index (0–10)	0	Cost to import (US$ per container)	816
Procedures (number)	28	Depth of credit information index (0–6)	0		
Time (days)	181	Public registry coverage (% of adults)	0.0	**Enforcing contracts** (rank)	118
Cost (% of income per capita)	1640.5	Private bureau coverage (% of adults)	0.0	Procedures (number)	31
				Time (days)	401
Employing workers (rank)	124	**Protecting investors** (rank)	60	Cost (% of claim)	121.3
Difficulty of hiring index (0–100)	56	Extent of disclosure index (0–10)	5		
Rigidity of hours index (0–100)	60	Extent of director liability index (0–10)	9	**Closing a business** (rank)	151
Difficulty of firing index (0–100)	30	Ease of shareholder suits index (0–10)	2	Time (years)	NO PRACTICE
Rigidity of employment index (0–100)	49	Strength of investor protection index (0–10)	5.3	Cost (% of estate)	NO PRACTICE
Nonwage labor cost (% of salary)	0			Recovery rate (cents on the dollar)	0.0
Firing cost (weeks of salary)	39	**Paying taxes** (rank)	16		
		Payments (number per year)	27		
		Time (hours per year)	121		
		Total tax rate (% of profit)	22.3		

CAMEROON

Ease of doing business (rank)	152	Sub-Saharan Africa		GNI per capita (US$)	1,010		
		Lower middle income		Population (m)	16.3		

Starting a business (rank)	152	**Registering property** (rank)	131	**Trading across borders** (rank)	140
Procedures (number)	12	Procedures (number)	5	Documents to export (number)	10
Time (days)	37	Time (days)	93	Time to export (days)	38
Cost (% of income per capita)	152.2	Cost (% of property value)	18.7	Cost to export (US$ per container)	524
Minimum capital (% of income per capita)	187.3			Documents to import (number)	14
		Getting credit (rank)	117	Time to import (days)	51
Dealing with licenses (rank)	151	Strength of legal rights index (0–10)	3	Cost to import (US$ per container)	1,360
Procedures (number)	15	Depth of credit information index (0–6)	2		
Time (days)	444	Public registry coverage (% of adults)	3.4	**Enforcing contracts** (rank)	170
Cost (% of income per capita)	1165.6	Private bureau coverage (% of adults)	0.0	Procedures (number)	58
				Time (days)	800
Employing workers (rank)	135	**Protecting investors** (rank)	60	Cost (% of claim)	36.4
Difficulty of hiring index (0–100)	28	Extent of disclosure index (0–10)	8		
Rigidity of hours index (0–100)	60	Extent of director liability index (0–10)	2	**Closing a business** (rank)	96
Difficulty of firing index (0–100)	80	Ease of shareholder suits index (0–10)	6	Time (years)	3.2
Rigidity of employment index (0–100)	56	Strength of investor protection index (0–10)	5.3	Cost (% of estate)	15
Nonwage labor cost (% of salary)	16			Recovery rate (cents on the dollar)	24.1
Firing cost (weeks of salary)	33	**Paying taxes** (rank)	143		
		Payments (number per year)	39		
		Time (hours per year)	1300		
		Total tax rate (% of profit)	46.2		

CANADA

Ease of doing business (rank)	4	OECD: High Income		GNI per capita (US$)	32,600		
		High income		Population (m)	32.3		

Starting a business (rank)	1	**Registering property** (rank)	22	**Trading across borders** (rank)	8
Procedures (number)	2	Procedures (number)	6	Documents to export (number)	3
Time (days)	3	Time (days)	10	Time to export (days)	7
Cost (% of income per capita)	0.9	Cost (% of property value)	1.7	Cost to export (US$ per container)	700
Minimum capital (% of income per capita)	0.0			Documents to import (number)	4
		Getting credit (rank)	7	Time to import (days)	10
Dealing with licenses (rank)	32	Strength of legal rights index (0–10)	7	Cost to import (US$ per container)	850
Procedures (number)	15	Depth of credit information index (0–6)	6		
Time (days)	77	Public registry coverage (% of adults)	0.0	**Enforcing contracts** (rank)	16
Cost (% of income per capita)	117.9	Private bureau coverage (% of adults)	100.0	Procedures (number)	17
				Time (days)	346
Employing workers (rank)	13	**Protecting investors** (rank)	5	Cost (% of claim)	12.0
Difficulty of hiring index (0–100)	11	Extent of disclosure index (0–10)	8		
Rigidity of hours index (0–100)	0	Extent of director liability index (0–10)	9	**Closing a business** (rank)	5
Difficulty of firing index (0–100)	0	Ease of shareholder suits index (0–10)	8	Time (years)	0.8
Rigidity of employment index (0–100)	4	Strength of investor protection index (0–10)	8.3	Cost (% of estate)	4
Nonwage labor cost (% of salary)	14			Recovery rate (cents on the dollar)	89.3
Firing cost (weeks of salary)	28	**Paying taxes** (rank)	22		
		Payments (number per year)	10		
		Time (hours per year)	119		
		Total tax rate (% of profit)	43.0		

CAPE VERDE

Ease of doing business (rank)	125	Sub-Saharan Africa		GNI per capita (US$)	1,870		
		Lower middle income		Population (m)	0.5		

Starting a business (rank)	144	**Registering property** (rank)	122	**Trading across borders** (rank)	20
Procedures (number)	12	Procedures (number)	6	Documents to export (number)	4
Time (days)	52	Time (days)	83	Time to export (days)	18
Cost (% of income per capita)	45.6	Cost (% of property value)	7.9	Cost to export (US$ per container)	533
Minimum capital (% of income per capita)	60.7			Documents to import (number)	9
		Getting credit (rank)	65	Time to import (days)	16
Dealing with licenses (rank)	93	Strength of legal rights index (0–10)	5	Cost to import (US$ per container)	533
Procedures (number)	17	Depth of credit information index (0–6)	3		
Time (days)	141	Public registry coverage (% of adults)	11.9	**Enforcing contracts** (rank)	80
Cost (% of income per capita)	1526.0	Private bureau coverage (% of adults)	0.0	Procedures (number)	40
				Time (days)	465
Employing workers (rank)	137	**Protecting investors** (rank)	135	Cost (% of claim)	15.0
Difficulty of hiring index (0–100)	33	Extent of disclosure index (0–10)	1		
Rigidity of hours index (0–100)	40	Extent of director liability index (0–10)	5	**Closing a business** (rank)	151
Difficulty of firing index (0–100)	60	Ease of shareholder suits index (0–10)	6	Time (years)	NO PRACTICE
Rigidity of employment index (0–100)	44	Strength of investor protection index (0–10)	4.0	Cost (% of estate)	NO PRACTICE
Nonwage labor cost (% of salary)	17			Recovery rate (cents on the dollar)	0.0
Firing cost (weeks of salary)	91	**Paying taxes** (rank)	100		
		Payments (number per year)	49		
		Time (hours per year)	100		
		Total tax rate (% of profit)	54.4		

CENTRAL AFRICAN REPUBLIC

		Sub-Saharan Africa		GNI per capita (US$)	350
Ease of doing business (rank)	167	Low income		Population (m)	4.0

Starting a business (rank)	132	**Registering property** (rank)	92	**Trading across borders** (rank)	156
Procedures (number)	10	Procedures (number)	3	Documents to export (number)	9
Time (days)	14	Time (days)	69	Time to export (days)	63
Cost (% of income per capita)	209.3	Cost (% of property value)	11.7	Cost to export (US$ per container)	1,502
Minimum capital (% of income per capita)	554.6			Documents to import (number)	19
		Getting credit (rank)	117	Time to import (days)	60
Dealing with licenses (rank)	148	Strength of legal rights index (0–10)	3	Cost to import (US$ per container)	1,572
Procedures (number)	21	Depth of credit information index (0–6)	2		
Time (days)	245	Public registry coverage (% of adults)	1.1	**Enforcing contracts** (rank)	161
Cost (% of income per capita)	301.0	Private bureau coverage (% of adults)	0.0	Procedures (number)	45
				Time (days)	660
Employing workers (rank)	160	**Protecting investors** (rank)	46	Cost (% of claim)	43.7
Difficulty of hiring index (0–100)	89	Extent of disclosure index (0–10)	4		
Rigidity of hours index (0–100)	80	Extent of director liability index (0–10)	6	**Closing a business** (rank)	151
Difficulty of firing index (0–100)	50	Ease of shareholder suits index (0–10)	7	Time (years)	4.8
Rigidity of employment index (0–100)	73	Strength of investor protection index (0–10)	5.7	Cost (% of estate)	76
Nonwage labor cost (% of salary)	18			Recovery rate (cents on the dollar)	0.0
Firing cost (weeks of salary)	22	**Paying taxes** (rank)	171		
		Payments (number per year)	54		
		Time (hours per year)	504		
		Total tax rate (% of profit)	209.5		

CHAD

		Sub-Saharan Africa		GNI per capita (US$)	400
Ease of doing business (rank)	172	Low income		Population (m)	9.7

Starting a business (rank)	174	**Registering property** (rank)	122	**Trading across borders** (rank)	157
Procedures (number)	19	Procedures (number)	6	Documents to export (number)	7
Time (days)	75	Time (days)	44	Time to export (days)	87
Cost (% of income per capita)	226.1	Cost (% of property value)	21.2	Cost to export (US$ per container)	1,860
Minimum capital (% of income per capita)	414.1			Documents to import (number)	14
		Getting credit (rank)	117	Time to import (days)	111
Dealing with licenses (rank)	114	Strength of legal rights index (0–10)	4	Cost to import (US$ per container)	2,400
Procedures (number)	16	Depth of credit information index (0–6)	1		
Time (days)	199	Public registry coverage (% of adults)	0.2	**Enforcing contracts** (rank)	171
Cost (% of income per capita)	1139.1	Private bureau coverage (% of adults)	0.0	Procedures (number)	52
				Time (days)	743
Employing workers (rank)	148	**Protecting investors** (rank)	99	Cost (% of claim)	54.9
Difficulty of hiring index (0–100)	39	Extent of disclosure index (0–10)	3		
Rigidity of hours index (0–100)	60	Extent of director liability index (0–10)	4	**Closing a business** (rank)	151
Difficulty of firing index (0–100)	80	Ease of shareholder suits index (0–10)	7	Time (years)	10.0
Rigidity of employment index (0–100)	60	Strength of investor protection index (0–10)	4.7	Cost (% of estate)	63
Nonwage labor cost (% of salary)	21			Recovery rate (cents on the dollar)	0.0
Firing cost (weeks of salary)	36	**Paying taxes** (rank)	132		
		Payments (number per year)	65		
		Time (hours per year)	122		
		Total tax rate (% of profit)	68.2		

CHILE

		Latin America & Caribbean		GNI per capita (US$)	5,870
Ease of doing business (rank)	28	Upper middle income		Population (m)	16.3

Starting a business (rank)	32	**Registering property** (rank)	30	**Trading across borders** (rank)	44
Procedures (number)	9	Procedures (number)	6	Documents to export (number)	7
Time (days)	27	Time (days)	31	Time to export (days)	20
Cost (% of income per capita)	9.8	Cost (% of property value)	1.3	Cost to export (US$ per container)	510
Minimum capital (% of income per capita)	0.0			Documents to import (number)	9
		Getting credit (rank)	33	Time to import (days)	24
Dealing with licenses (rank)	40	Strength of legal rights index (0–10)	4	Cost to import (US$ per container)	510
Procedures (number)	12	Depth of credit information index (0–6)	6		
Time (days)	171	Public registry coverage (% of adults)	31.3	**Enforcing contracts** (rank)	73
Cost (% of income per capita)	114.2	Private bureau coverage (% of adults)	19.3	Procedures (number)	33
				Time (days)	480
Employing workers (rank)	58	**Protecting investors** (rank)	19	Cost (% of claim)	16.3
Difficulty of hiring index (0–100)	33	Extent of disclosure index (0–10)	8		
Rigidity of hours index (0–100)	20	Extent of director liability index (0–10)	6	**Closing a business** (rank)	107
Difficulty of firing index (0–100)	20	Ease of shareholder suits index (0–10)	5	Time (years)	5.6
Rigidity of employment index (0–100)	24	Strength of investor protection index (0–10)	6.3	Cost (% of estate)	15
Nonwage labor cost (% of salary)	3			Recovery rate (cents on the dollar)	20.0
Firing cost (weeks of salary)	52	**Paying taxes** (rank)	37		
		Payments (number per year)	10		
		Time (hours per year)	432		
		Total tax rate (% of profit)	26.3		

CHINA

		East Asia & Pacific		GNI per capita (US$)	1,740
Ease of doing business (rank)	93	Lower middle income		Population (m)	1304.5

Starting a business (rank)	128	**Registering property** (rank)	21	**Trading across borders** (rank)	38
Procedures (number)	13	Procedures (number)	3	Documents to export (number)	6
Time (days)	35	Time (days)	32	Time to export (days)	18
Cost (% of income per capita)	9.3	Cost (% of property value)	3.1	Cost to export (US$ per container)	335
Minimum capital (% of income per capita)	213.1			Documents to import (number)	12
		Getting credit (rank)	101	Time to import (days)	22
Dealing with licenses (rank)	153	Strength of legal rights index (0–10)	2	Cost to import (US$ per container)	375
Procedures (number)	29	Depth of credit information index (0–6)	4		
Time (days)	367	Public registry coverage (% of adults)	10.2	**Enforcing contracts** (rank)	63
Cost (% of income per capita)	84.0	Private bureau coverage (% of adults)	0.0	Procedures (number)	31
				Time (days)	292
Employing workers (rank)	78	**Protecting investors** (rank)	83	Cost (% of claim)	26.8
Difficulty of hiring index (0–100)	11	Extent of disclosure index (0–10)	10		
Rigidity of hours index (0–100)	20	Extent of director liability index (0–10)	1	**Closing a business** (rank)	75
Difficulty of firing index (0–100)	40	Ease of shareholder suits index (0–10)	4	Time (years)	2.4
Rigidity of employment index (0–100)	24	Strength of investor protection index (0–10)	5.0	Cost (% of estate)	22
Nonwage labor cost (% of salary)	44			Recovery rate (cents on the dollar)	31.5
Firing cost (weeks of salary)	91	**Paying taxes** (rank)	168		
		Payments (number per year)	44		
		Time (hours per year)	872		
		Total tax rate (% of profit)	77.1		

COLOMBIA

		Latin America & Caribbean		GNI per capita (US$)	2,290
Ease of doing business (rank)	79	Lower middle income		Population (m)	45.6

Starting a business (rank)	90	**Registering property** (rank)	56	**Trading across borders** (rank)	128
Procedures (number)	13	Procedures (number)	7	Documents to export (number)	6
Time (days)	44	Time (days)	23	Time to export (days)	34
Cost (% of income per capita)	19.8	Cost (% of property value)	3.5	Cost to export (US$ per container)	1,745
Minimum capital (% of income per capita)	0.0			Documents to import (number)	11
		Getting credit (rank)	83	Time to import (days)	35
Dealing with licenses (rank)	60	Strength of legal rights index (0–10)	3	Cost to import (US$ per container)	1,773
Procedures (number)	12	Depth of credit information index (0–6)	4		
Time (days)	150	Public registry coverage (% of adults)	0.0	**Enforcing contracts** (rank)	141
Cost (% of income per capita)	646.3	Private bureau coverage (% of adults)	28.3	Procedures (number)	37
				Time (days)	1346
Employing workers (rank)	77	**Protecting investors** (rank)	33	Cost (% of claim)	20.0
Difficulty of hiring index (0–100)	22	Extent of disclosure index (0–10)	7		
Rigidity of hours index (0–100)	40	Extent of director liability index (0–10)	2	**Closing a business** (rank)	26
Difficulty of firing index (0–100)	20	Ease of shareholder suits index (0–10)	9	Time (years)	3.0
Rigidity of employment index (0–100)	27	Strength of investor protection index (0–10)	6.0	Cost (% of estate)	1
Nonwage labor cost (% of salary)	28			Recovery rate (cents on the dollar)	57.7
Firing cost (weeks of salary)	59	**Paying taxes** (rank)	172		
		Payments (number per year)	68		
		Time (hours per year)	456		
		Total tax rate (% of profit)	82.8		

COMOROS

		Sub-Saharan Africa		GNI per capita (US$)	640
Ease of doing business (rank)	144	Low income		Population (m)	0.6

Starting a business (rank)	136	**Registering property** (rank)	83	**Trading across borders** (rank)	118
Procedures (number)	11	Procedures (number)	5	Documents to export (number)	9
Time (days)	23	Time (days)	24	Time to export (days)	28
Cost (% of income per capita)	192.3	Cost (% of property value)	20.8	Cost to export (US$ per container)	1,481
Minimum capital (% of income per capita)	291.7			Documents to import (number)	8
		Getting credit (rank)	159	Time to import (days)	22
Dealing with licenses (rank)	68	Strength of legal rights index (0–10)	3	Cost to import (US$ per container)	1,481
Procedures (number)	17	Depth of credit information index (0–6)	0		
Time (days)	196	Public registry coverage (% of adults)	0.0	**Enforcing contracts** (rank)	167
Cost (% of income per capita)	80.9	Private bureau coverage (% of adults)	0.0	Procedures (number)	60
				Time (days)	721
Employing workers (rank)	149	**Protecting investors** (rank)	83	Cost (% of claim)	29.4
Difficulty of hiring index (0–100)	39	Extent of disclosure index (0–10)	6		
Rigidity of hours index (0–100)	60	Extent of director liability index (0–10)	4	**Closing a business** (rank)	151
Difficulty of firing index (0–100)	40	Ease of shareholder suits index (0–10)	5	Time (years)	NO PRACTICE
Rigidity of employment index (0–100)	46	Strength of investor protection index (0–10)	5.0	Cost (% of estate)	NO PRACTICE
Nonwage labor cost (% of salary)	0			Recovery rate (cents on the dollar)	0.0
Firing cost (weeks of salary)	100	**Paying taxes** (rank)	34		
		Payments (number per year)	20		
		Time (hours per year)	100		
		Total tax rate (% of profit)	47.5		

CONGO, DEM. REP.

		Sub-Saharan Africa		GNI per capita (US$)	120
Ease of doing business (rank)	175	Low income		Population (m)	57.5

Starting a business (rank)	172	**Registering property** (rank)	141	**Trading across borders** (rank)	159
Procedures (number)	13	Procedures (number)	8	Documents to export (number)	8
Time (days)	155	Time (days)	57	Time to export (days)	64
Cost (% of income per capita)	481.1	Cost (% of property value)	9.5	Cost to export (US$ per container)	3,120
Minimum capital (% of income per capita)	177.3			Documents to import (number)	12
		Getting credit (rank)	159	Time to import (days)	92
Dealing with licenses (rank)	140	Strength of legal rights index (0–10)	3	Cost to import (US$ per container)	3,308
Procedures (number)	14	Depth of credit information index (0–6)	0		
Time (days)	306	Public registry coverage (% of adults)	0.0	**Enforcing contracts** (rank)	171
Cost (% of income per capita)	2281.9	Private bureau coverage (% of adults)	0.0	Procedures (number)	51
				Time (days)	685
Employing workers (rank)	170	**Protecting investors** (rank)	142	Cost (% of claim)	156.8
Difficulty of hiring index (0–100)	83	Extent of disclosure index (0–10)	3		
Rigidity of hours index (0–100)	80	Extent of director liability index (0–10)	3	**Closing a business** (rank)	145
Difficulty of firing index (0–100)	70	Ease of shareholder suits index (0–10)	5	Time (years)	5.2
Rigidity of employment index (0–100)	78	Strength of investor protection index (0–10)	3.7	Cost (% of estate)	22
Nonwage labor cost (% of salary)	6			Recovery rate (cents on the dollar)	4.9
Firing cost (weeks of salary)	31	**Paying taxes** (rank)	147		
		Payments (number per year)	34		
		Time (hours per year)	312		
		Total tax rate (% of profit)	235.4		

CONGO, REP.

		Sub-Saharan Africa		GNI per capita (US$)	950
Ease of doing business (rank)	171	Lower middle income		Population (m)	4.0

Starting a business (rank)	146	**Registering property** (rank)	163	**Trading across borders** (rank)	166
Procedures (number)	8	Procedures (number)	7	Documents to export (number)	12
Time (days)	71	Time (days)	137	Time to export (days)	50
Cost (% of income per capita)	214.8	Cost (% of property value)	27.2	Cost to export (US$ per container)	1,732
Minimum capital (% of income per capita)	192.4			Documents to import (number)	15
		Getting credit (rank)	117	Time to import (days)	62
Dealing with licenses (rank)	95	Strength of legal rights index (0–10)	3	Cost to import (US$ per container)	2,201
Procedures (number)	15	Depth of credit information index (0–6)	2		
Time (days)	175	Public registry coverage (% of adults)	1.4	**Enforcing contracts** (rank)	155
Cost (% of income per capita)	1243.0	Private bureau coverage (% of adults)	0.0	Procedures (number)	47
				Time (days)	560
Employing workers (rank)	163	**Protecting investors** (rank)	83	Cost (% of claim)	45.6
Difficulty of hiring index (0–100)	78	Extent of disclosure index (0–10)	4		
Rigidity of hours index (0–100)	60	Extent of director liability index (0–10)	5	**Closing a business** (rank)	110
Difficulty of firing index (0–100)	70	Ease of shareholder suits index (0–10)	6	Time (years)	3.0
Rigidity of employment index (0–100)	69	Strength of investor protection index (0–10)	5.0	Cost (% of estate)	24
Nonwage labor cost (% of salary)	29			Recovery rate (cents on the dollar)	19.4
Firing cost (weeks of salary)	41	**Paying taxes** (rank)	170		
		Payments (number per year)	94		
		Time (hours per year)	576		
		Total tax rate (% of profit)	57.3		

COSTA RICA

		Latin America & Caribbean		GNI per capita (US$)	4,590
Ease of doing business (rank)	105	Upper middle income		Population (m)	4.3

Starting a business (rank)	99	**Registering property** (rank)	37	**Trading across borders** (rank)	100
Procedures (number)	11	Procedures (number)	6	Documents to export (number)	7
Time (days)	77	Time (days)	21	Time to export (days)	36
Cost (% of income per capita)	23.5	Cost (% of property value)	3.5	Cost to export (US$ per container)	660
Minimum capital (% of income per capita)	0.0			Documents to import (number)	13
		Getting credit (rank)	33	Time to import (days)	42
Dealing with licenses (rank)	57	Strength of legal rights index (0–10)	4	Cost to import (US$ per container)	660
Procedures (number)	19	Depth of credit information index (0–6)	6		
Time (days)	119	Public registry coverage (% of adults)	2.5	**Enforcing contracts** (rank)	114
Cost (% of income per capita)	140.2	Private bureau coverage (% of adults)	39.2	Procedures (number)	34
				Time (days)	615
Employing workers (rank)	65	**Protecting investors** (rank)	156	Cost (% of claim)	18.7
Difficulty of hiring index (0–100)	56	Extent of disclosure index (0–10)	2		
Rigidity of hours index (0–100)	40	Extent of director liability index (0–10)	5	**Closing a business** (rank)	118
Difficulty of firing index (0–100)	0	Ease of shareholder suits index (0–10)	2	Time (years)	3.5
Rigidity of employment index (0–100)	32	Strength of investor protection index (0–10)	3.0	Cost (% of estate)	15
Nonwage labor cost (% of salary)	26			Recovery rate (cents on the dollar)	17.6
Firing cost (weeks of salary)	35	**Paying taxes** (rank)	160		
		Payments (number per year)	41		
		Time (hours per year)	402		
		Total tax rate (% of profit)	83.0		

CÔTE D'IVOIRE

		Sub-Saharan Africa		GNI per capita (US$)	840
Ease of doing business (rank)	141	Low income		Population (m)	18.2

Starting a business (rank)	154	**Registering property** (rank)	101	**Trading across borders** (rank)	132
Procedures (number)	11	Procedures (number)	6	Documents to export (number)	9
Time (days)	45	Time (days)	32	Time to export (days)	21
Cost (% of income per capita)	134.1	Cost (% of property value)	14.3	Cost to export (US$ per container)	781
Minimum capital (% of income per capita)	226.7			Documents to import (number)	19
		Getting credit (rank)	143	Time to import (days)	48
Dealing with licenses (rank)	158	Strength of legal rights index (0–10)	3	Cost to import (US$ per container)	1,395
Procedures (number)	22	Depth of credit information index (0–6)	1		
Time (days)	569	Public registry coverage (% of adults)	3.1	**Enforcing contracts** (rank)	92
Cost (% of income per capita)	196.3	Private bureau coverage (% of adults)	0.0	Procedures (number)	25
				Time (days)	525
Employing workers (rank)	133	**Protecting investors** (rank)	99	Cost (% of claim)	29.5
Difficulty of hiring index (0–100)	44	Extent of disclosure index (0–10)	6		
Rigidity of hours index (0–100)	80	Extent of director liability index (0–10)	5	**Closing a business** (rank)	68
Difficulty of firing index (0–100)	10	Ease of shareholder suits index (0–10)	3	Time (years)	2.2
Rigidity of employment index (0–100)	45	Strength of investor protection index (0–10)	4.7	Cost (% of estate)	18
Nonwage labor cost (% of salary)	18			Recovery rate (cents on the dollar)	33.8
Firing cost (weeks of salary)	49	**Paying taxes** (rank)	134		
		Payments (number per year)	71		
		Time (hours per year)	270		
		Total tax rate (% of profit)	45.7		

CROATIA

		Eastern Europe & Central Asia		GNI per capita (US$)	8,060
Ease of doing business (rank)	124	Upper middle income		Population (m)	4.4

Starting a business (rank)	100	**Registering property** (rank)	109	**Trading across borders** (rank)	92
Procedures (number)	10	Procedures (number)	5	Documents to export (number)	7
Time (days)	45	Time (days)	399	Time to export (days)	26
Cost (% of income per capita)	12.2	Cost (% of property value)	5.0	Cost to export (US$ per container)	1,250
Minimum capital (% of income per capita)	20.6			Documents to import (number)	9
		Getting credit (rank)	117	Time to import (days)	18
Dealing with licenses (rank)	170	Strength of legal rights index (0–10)	5	Cost to import (US$ per container)	1,250
Procedures (number)	28	Depth of credit information index (0–6)	0		
Time (days)	278	Public registry coverage (% of adults)	0.0	**Enforcing contracts** (rank)	28
Cost (% of income per capita)	1164.1	Private bureau coverage (% of adults)	0.0	Procedures (number)	22
				Time (days)	561
Employing workers (rank)	130	**Protecting investors** (rank)	156	Cost (% of claim)	10.0
Difficulty of hiring index (0–100)	61	Extent of disclosure index (0–10)	2		
Rigidity of hours index (0–100)	40	Extent of director liability index (0–10)	5	**Closing a business** (rank)	80
Difficulty of firing index (0–100)	50	Ease of shareholder suits index (0–10)	2	Time (years)	3.1
Rigidity of employment index (0–100)	50	Strength of investor protection index (0–10)	3.0	Cost (% of estate)	15
Nonwage labor cost (% of salary)	17			Recovery rate (cents on the dollar)	28.9
Firing cost (weeks of salary)	39	**Paying taxes** (rank)	58		
		Payments (number per year)	39		
		Time (hours per year)	196		
		Total tax rate (% of profit)	37.1		

CZECH REPUBLIC

		Eastern Europe & Central Asia		GNI per capita (US$)	10,710
Ease of doing business (rank)	52	Upper middle income		Population (m)	10.2

Starting a business (rank)	74	**Registering property** (rank)	58	**Trading across borders** (rank)	41
Procedures (number)	10	Procedures (number)	4	Documents to export (number)	5
Time (days)	24	Time (days)	123	Time to export (days)	20
Cost (% of income per capita)	8.9	Cost (% of property value)	3.0	Cost to export (US$ per container)	713
Minimum capital (% of income per capita)	36.8			Documents to import (number)	8
		Getting credit (rank)	21	Time to import (days)	22
Dealing with licenses (rank)	110	Strength of legal rights index (0–10)	6	Cost to import (US$ per container)	833
Procedures (number)	31	Depth of credit information index (0–6)	5		
Time (days)	271	Public registry coverage (% of adults)	3.5	**Enforcing contracts** (rank)	57
Cost (% of income per capita)	14.5	Private bureau coverage (% of adults)	51.0	Procedures (number)	21
				Time (days)	820
Employing workers (rank)	45	**Protecting investors** (rank)	83	Cost (% of claim)	14.1
Difficulty of hiring index (0–100)	33	Extent of disclosure index (0–10)	2		
Rigidity of hours index (0–100)	20	Extent of director liability index (0–10)	5	**Closing a business** (rank)	113
Difficulty of firing index (0–100)	30	Ease of shareholder suits index (0–10)	8	Time (years)	9.2
Rigidity of employment index (0–100)	28	Strength of investor protection index (0–10)	5.0	Cost (% of estate)	15
Nonwage labor cost (% of salary)	35			Recovery rate (cents on the dollar)	18.5
Firing cost (weeks of salary)	22	**Paying taxes** (rank)	110		
		Payments (number per year)	14		
		Time (hours per year)	930		
		Total tax rate (% of profit)	49.0		

DENMARK

		OECD: High Income		GNI per capita (US$)	47,390
Ease of doing business (rank)	7	High income		Population (m)	5.4

Starting a business (rank)	14	**Registering property** (rank)	36	**Trading across borders** (rank)	3
Procedures (number)	3	Procedures (number)	6	Documents to export (number)	3
Time (days)	5	Time (days)	42	Time to export (days)	5
Cost (% of income per capita)	0.0	Cost (% of property value)	0.6	Cost to export (US$ per container)	540
Minimum capital (% of income per capita)	44.6			Documents to import (number)	3
		Getting credit (rank)	13	Time to import (days)	5
		Strength of legal rights index (0–10)	8	Cost to import (US$ per container)	540
Dealing with licenses (rank)	6	Depth of credit information index (0–6)	4		
Procedures (number)	7	Public registry coverage (% of adults)	0.0	**Enforcing contracts** (rank)	1
Time (days)	70	Private bureau coverage (% of adults)	11.5	Procedures (number)	15
Cost (% of income per capita)	67.8			Time (days)	190
		Protecting investors (rank)	19	Cost (% of claim)	6.5
Employing workers (rank)	15	Extent of disclosure index (0–10)	7		
Difficulty of hiring index (0–100)	0	Extent of director liability index (0–10)	5	**Closing a business** (rank)	20
Rigidity of hours index (0–100)	40	Ease of shareholder suits index (0–10)	7	Time (years)	3.0
Difficulty of firing index (0–100)	10	Strength of investor protection index (0–10)	6.3	Cost (% of estate)	4
Rigidity of employment index (0–100)	17			Recovery rate (cents on the dollar)	70.5
Nonwage labor cost (% of salary)	1				
Firing cost (weeks of salary)	10	**Paying taxes** (rank)	15		
		Payments (number per year)	18		
		Time (hours per year)	135		
		Total tax rate (% of profit)	31.5		

DJIBOUTI

		Middle East & North Africa		GNI per capita (US$)	1,020
Ease of doing business (rank)	161	Lower middle income		Population (m)	0.8

Starting a business (rank)	157	**Registering property** (rank)	137	**Trading across borders** (rank)	148
Procedures (number)	11	Procedures (number)	7	Documents to export (number)	15
Time (days)	37	Time (days)	49	Time to export (days)	25
Cost (% of income per capita)	222.0	Cost (% of property value)	13.3	Cost to export (US$ per container)	2,035
Minimum capital (% of income per capita)	571.4			Documents to import (number)	14
		Getting credit (rank)	117	Time to import (days)	26
		Strength of legal rights index (0–10)	4	Cost to import (US$ per container)	2,035
Dealing with licenses (rank)	106	Depth of credit information index (0–6)	1		
Procedures (number)	15	Public registry coverage (% of adults)	0.2	**Enforcing contracts** (rank)	169
Time (days)	203	Private bureau coverage (% of adults)	0.0	Procedures (number)	59
Cost (% of income per capita)	1050.6			Time (days)	1225
		Protecting investors (rank)	168	Cost (% of claim)	27.0
Employing workers (rank)	125	Extent of disclosure index (0–10)	5		
Difficulty of hiring index (0–100)	67	Extent of director liability index (0–10)	2	**Closing a business** (rank)	122
Rigidity of hours index (0–100)	40	Ease of shareholder suits index (0–10)	0	Time (years)	5.0
Difficulty of firing index (0–100)	30	Strength of investor protection index (0–10)	2.3	Cost (% of estate)	18
Rigidity of employment index (0–100)	46			Recovery rate (cents on the dollar)	15.9
Nonwage labor cost (% of salary)	16				
Firing cost (weeks of salary)	56	**Paying taxes** (rank)	51		
		Payments (number per year)	36		
		Time (hours per year)	114		
		Total tax rate (% of profit)	41.7		

DOMINICA

		Latin America & Caribbean		GNI per capita (US$)	3,790
Ease of doing business (rank)	72	Upper middle income		Population (m)	0.1

Starting a business (rank)	24	**Registering property** (rank)	78	**Trading across borders** (rank)	97
Procedures (number)	5	Procedures (number)	4	Documents to export (number)	7
Time (days)	19	Time (days)	40	Time to export (days)	11
Cost (% of income per capita)	30.0	Cost (% of property value)	13.0	Cost to export (US$ per container)	1,477
Minimum capital (% of income per capita)	0.0			Documents to import (number)	13
		Getting credit (rank)	101	Time to import (days)	17
		Strength of legal rights index (0–10)	6	Cost to import (US$ per container)	1,512
Dealing with licenses (rank)	51	Depth of credit information index (0–6)	0		
Procedures (number)	11	Public registry coverage (% of adults)	0.0	**Enforcing contracts** (rank)	159
Time (days)	195	Private bureau coverage (% of adults)	0.0	Procedures (number)	52
Cost (% of income per capita)	82.1			Time (days)	681
		Protecting investors (rank)	19	Cost (% of claim)	28.2
Employing workers (rank)	50	Extent of disclosure index (0–10)	4		
Difficulty of hiring index (0–100)	11	Extent of director liability index (0–10)	8	**Closing a business** (rank)	151
Rigidity of hours index (0–100)	20	Ease of shareholder suits index (0–10)	7	Time (years)	NO PRACTICE
Difficulty of firing index (0–100)	20	Strength of investor protection index (0–10)	6.3	Cost (% of estate)	NO PRACTICE
Rigidity of employment index (0–100)	17			Recovery rate (cents on the dollar)	0.0
Nonwage labor cost (% of salary)	7				
Firing cost (weeks of salary)	58	**Paying taxes** (rank)	20		
		Payments (number per year)	30		
		Time (hours per year)	65		
		Total tax rate (% of profit)	34.8		

DOMINICAN REPUBLIC

		Latin America & Caribbean		GNI per capita (US$)	2,370
Ease of doing business (rank)	117	Lower middle income		Population (m)	8.9

Starting a business (rank)	119	**Registering property** (rank)	126	**Trading across borders** (rank)	55
Procedures (number)	10	Procedures (number)	7	Documents to export (number)	7
Time (days)	73	Time (days)	107	Time to export (days)	17
Cost (% of income per capita)	30.2	Cost (% of property value)	5.1	Cost to export (US$ per container)	770
Minimum capital (% of income per capita)	1.1			Documents to import (number)	11
		Getting credit (rank)	33	Time to import (days)	17
Dealing with licenses (rank)	77	Strength of legal rights index (0–10)	4	Cost to import (US$ per container)	990
Procedures (number)	17	Depth of credit information index (0–6)	6		
Time (days)	165	Public registry coverage (% of adults)	11.9	**Enforcing contracts** (rank)	108
Cost (% of income per capita)	240.1	Private bureau coverage (% of adults)	57.1	Procedures (number)	29
				Time (days)	460
Employing workers (rank)	127	**Protecting investors** (rank)	135	Cost (% of claim)	35.0
Difficulty of hiring index (0–100)	56	Extent of disclosure index (0–10)	5		
Rigidity of hours index (0–100)	40	Extent of director liability index (0–10)	0	**Closing a business** (rank)	142
Difficulty of firing index (0–100)	30	Ease of shareholder suits index (0–10)	7	Time (years)	3.5
Rigidity of employment index (0–100)	42	Strength of investor protection index (0–10)	4.0	Cost (% of estate)	38
Nonwage labor cost (% of salary)	14			Recovery rate (cents on the dollar)	7.4
Firing cost (weeks of salary)	88	**Paying taxes** (rank)	146		
		Payments (number per year)	87		
		Time (hours per year)	178		
		Total tax rate (% of profit)	67.9		

ECUADOR

		Latin America & Caribbean		GNI per capita (US$)	2,630
Ease of doing business (rank)	123	Lower middle income		Population (m)	13.2

Starting a business (rank)	139	**Registering property** (rank)	84	**Trading across borders** (rank)	126
Procedures (number)	14	Procedures (number)	10	Documents to export (number)	12
Time (days)	65	Time (days)	20	Time to export (days)	20
Cost (% of income per capita)	31.8	Cost (% of property value)	3.9	Cost to export (US$ per container)	1,090
Minimum capital (% of income per capita)	7.7			Documents to import (number)	11
		Getting credit (rank)	65	Time to import (days)	41
Dealing with licenses (rank)	60	Strength of legal rights index (0–10)	3	Cost to import (US$ per container)	1,090
Procedures (number)	19	Depth of credit information index (0–6)	5		
Time (days)	149	Public registry coverage (% of adults)	15.2	**Enforcing contracts** (rank)	96
Cost (% of income per capita)	83.7	Private bureau coverage (% of adults)	43.7	Procedures (number)	41
				Time (days)	498
Employing workers (rank)	161	**Protecting investors** (rank)	135	Cost (% of claim)	15.3
Difficulty of hiring index (0–100)	44	Extent of disclosure index (0–10)	1		
Rigidity of hours index (0–100)	60	Extent of director liability index (0–10)	5	**Closing a business** (rank)	134
Difficulty of firing index (0–100)	50	Ease of shareholder suits index (0–10)	6	Time (years)	8.0
Rigidity of employment index (0–100)	51	Strength of investor protection index (0–10)	4.0	Cost (% of estate)	18
Nonwage labor cost (% of salary)	12			Recovery rate (cents on the dollar)	12.7
Firing cost (weeks of salary)	135	**Paying taxes** (rank)	53		
		Payments (number per year)	8		
		Time (hours per year)	600		
		Total tax rate (% of profit)	34.9		

EGYPT

		Middle East & North Africa		GNI per capita (US$)	1,250
Ease of doing business (rank)	165	Lower middle income		Population (m)	74.0

Starting a business (rank)	125	**Registering property** (rank)	141	**Trading across borders** (rank)	83
Procedures (number)	10	Procedures (number)	7	Documents to export (number)	8
Time (days)	19	Time (days)	193	Time to export (days)	20
Cost (% of income per capita)	68.8	Cost (% of property value)	5.9	Cost to export (US$ per container)	1,014
Minimum capital (% of income per capita)	694.7			Documents to import (number)	8
		Getting credit (rank)	159	Time to import (days)	25
Dealing with licenses (rank)	169	Strength of legal rights index (0–10)	1	Cost to import (US$ per container)	1,049
Procedures (number)	30	Depth of credit information index (0–6)	2		
Time (days)	263	Public registry coverage (% of adults)	1.5	**Enforcing contracts** (rank)	157
Cost (% of income per capita)	1002.0	Private bureau coverage (% of adults)	0.0	Procedures (number)	55
				Time (days)	1010
Employing workers (rank)	144	**Protecting investors** (rank)	118	Cost (% of claim)	18.4
Difficulty of hiring index (0–100)	0	Extent of disclosure index (0–10)	5		
Rigidity of hours index (0–100)	60	Extent of director liability index (0–10)	3	**Closing a business** (rank)	120
Difficulty of firing index (0–100)	100	Ease of shareholder suits index (0–10)	5	Time (years)	4.2
Rigidity of employment index (0–100)	53	Strength of investor protection index (0–10)	4.3	Cost (% of estate)	22
Nonwage labor cost (% of salary)	26			Recovery rate (cents on the dollar)	16.6
Firing cost (weeks of salary)	186	**Paying taxes** (rank)	144		
		Payments (number per year)	41		
		Time (hours per year)	536		
		Total tax rate (% of profit)	50.4		

EL SALVADOR

		Latin America & Caribbean		GNI per capita (US$)	2,450
Ease of doing business (rank)	71	Lower middle income		Population (m)	6.9

Starting a business (rank)	123	**Registering property** (rank)	49	**Trading across borders** (rank)	58
Procedures (number)	10	Procedures (number)	6	Documents to export (number)	7
Time (days)	26	Time (days)	33	Time to export (days)	22
Cost (% of income per capita)	75.6	Cost (% of property value)	3.6	Cost to export (US$ per container)	515
Minimum capital (% of income per capita)	119.7			Documents to import (number)	12
		Getting credit (rank)	33	Time to import (days)	30
Dealing with licenses (rank)	90	Strength of legal rights index (0–10)	4	Cost to import (US$ per container)	515
Procedures (number)	22	Depth of credit information index (0–6)	6		
Time (days)	144	Public registry coverage (% of adults)	30.5	**Enforcing contracts** (rank)	116
Cost (% of income per capita)	201.0	Private bureau coverage (% of adults)	79.6	Procedures (number)	41
				Time (days)	626
Employing workers (rank)	70	**Protecting investors** (rank)	99	Cost (% of claim)	15.0
Difficulty of hiring index (0–100)	33	Extent of disclosure index (0–10)	6		
Rigidity of hours index (0–100)	40	Extent of director liability index (0–10)	2	**Closing a business** (rank)	79
Difficulty of firing index (0–100)	0	Ease of shareholder suits index (0–10)	6	Time (years)	4.0
Rigidity of employment index (0–100)	24	Strength of investor protection index (0–10)	4.7	Cost (% of estate)	9
Nonwage labor cost (% of salary)	9			Recovery rate (cents on the dollar)	29.2
Firing cost (weeks of salary)	86	**Paying taxes** (rank)	85		
		Payments (number per year)	66		
		Time (hours per year)	224		
		Total tax rate (% of profit)	27.4		

EQUATORIAL GUINEA

		Sub-Saharan Africa		GNI per capita (US$)	14,497
Ease of doing business (rank)	150	Upper middle income		Population (m)	0.5

Starting a business (rank)	162	**Registering property** (rank)	57	**Trading across borders** (rank)	96
Procedures (number)	20	Procedures (number)	6	Documents to export (number)	6
Time (days)	136	Time (days)	23	Time to export (days)	26
Cost (% of income per capita)	100.7	Cost (% of property value)	6.2	Cost to export (US$ per container)	1,203
Minimum capital (% of income per capita)	13.1			Documents to import (number)	6
		Getting credit (rank)	143	Time to import (days)	50
Dealing with licenses (rank)	96	Strength of legal rights index (0–10)	2	Cost to import (US$ per container)	1,203
Procedures (number)	19	Depth of credit information index (0–6)	2		
Time (days)	156	Public registry coverage (% of adults)	2.4	**Enforcing contracts** (rank)	91
Cost (% of income per capita)	364.9	Private bureau coverage (% of adults)	0.0	Procedures (number)	38
				Time (days)	553
Employing workers (rank)	172	**Protecting investors** (rank)	83	Cost (% of claim)	14.5
Difficulty of hiring index (0–100)	67	Extent of disclosure index (0–10)	6		
Rigidity of hours index (0–100)	60	Extent of director liability index (0–10)	4	**Closing a business** (rank)	151
Difficulty of firing index (0–100)	70	Ease of shareholder suits index (0–10)	5	Time (years)	NO PRACTICE
Rigidity of employment index (0–100)	66	Strength of investor protection index (0–10)	5.0	Cost (% of estate)	NO PRACTICE
Nonwage labor cost (% of salary)	23			Recovery rate (cents on the dollar)	0.0
Firing cost (weeks of salary)	133	**Paying taxes** (rank)	137		
		Payments (number per year)	48		
		Time (hours per year)	212		
		Total tax rate (% of profit)	62.4		

ERITREA

		Sub-Saharan Africa		GNI per capita (US$)	220
Ease of doing business (rank)	170	Low income		Population (m)	4.4

Starting a business (rank)	168	**Registering property** (rank)	153	**Trading across borders** (rank)	151
Procedures (number)	13	Procedures (number)	12	Documents to export (number)	11
Time (days)	76	Time (days)	101	Time to export (days)	69
Cost (% of income per capita)	115.9	Cost (% of property value)	5.2	Cost to export (US$ per container)	935
Minimum capital (% of income per capita)	449.8			Documents to import (number)	18
		Getting credit (rank)	159	Time to import (days)	69
Dealing with licenses (rank)	173	Strength of legal rights index (0–10)	3	Cost to import (US$ per container)	1,185
Procedures (number)	NO PRACTICE	Depth of credit information index (0–6)	0		
Time (days)	NO PRACTICE	Public registry coverage (% of adults)	0.0	**Enforcing contracts** (rank)	58
Cost (% of income per capita)	NO PRACTICE	Private bureau coverage (% of adults)	0.0	Procedures (number)	35
				Time (days)	305
Employing workers (rank)	55	**Protecting investors** (rank)	99	Cost (% of claim)	18.6
Difficulty of hiring index (0–100)	0	Extent of disclosure index (0–10)	4		
Rigidity of hours index (0–100)	40	Extent of director liability index (0–10)	5	**Closing a business** (rank)	151
Difficulty of firing index (0–100)	20	Ease of shareholder suits index (0–10)	5	Time (years)	1.7
Rigidity of employment index (0–100)	20	Strength of investor protection index (0–10)	4.7	Cost (% of estate)	15
Nonwage labor cost (% of salary)	0			Recovery rate (cents on the dollar)	0.0
Firing cost (weeks of salary)	69	**Paying taxes** (rank)	101		
		Payments (number per year)	18		
		Time (hours per year)	216		
		Total tax rate (% of profit)	86.3		

ESTONIA

		Eastern Europe & Central Asia		GNI per capita (US$)	9,100
Ease of doing business (rank)	17	Upper middle income		Population (m)	1.3

Starting a business (rank)	51
Procedures (number)	6
Time (days)	35
Cost (% of income per capita)	5.1
Minimum capital (% of income per capita)	34.3

Dealing with licenses (rank)	13
Procedures (number)	13
Time (days)	117
Cost (% of income per capita)	34.3

Employing workers (rank)	151
Difficulty of hiring index (0–100)	33
Rigidity of hours index (0–100)	80
Difficulty of firing index (0–100)	60
Rigidity of employment index (0–100)	58
Nonwage labor cost (% of salary)	34
Firing cost (weeks of salary)	35

Registering property (rank)	23
Procedures (number)	3
Time (days)	51
Cost (% of property value)	0.7

Getting credit (rank)	48
Strength of legal rights index (0–10)	4
Depth of credit information index (0–6)	5
Public registry coverage (% of adults)	0.0
Private bureau coverage (% of adults)	18.2

Protecting investors (rank)	33
Extent of disclosure index (0–10)	8
Extent of director liability index (0–10)	4
Ease of shareholder suits index (0–10)	6
Strength of investor protection index (0–10)	6.0

Paying taxes (rank)	29
Payments (number per year)	11
Time (hours per year)	104
Total tax rate (% of profit)	50.2

Trading across borders (rank)	6
Documents to export (number)	5
Time to export (days)	3
Cost to export (US$ per container)	640
Documents to import (number)	6
Time to import (days)	5
Cost to import (US$ per container)	640

Enforcing contracts (rank)	20
Procedures (number)	25
Time (days)	275
Cost (% of claim)	11.5

Closing a business (rank)	47
Time (years)	3.0
Cost (% of estate)	9
Recovery rate (cents on the dollar)	39.9

ETHIOPIA

		Sub-Saharan Africa		GNI per capita (US$)	160
Ease of doing business (rank)	97	Low income		Population (m)	71.3

Starting a business (rank)	95
Procedures (number)	7
Time (days)	16
Cost (% of income per capita)	45.9
Minimum capital (% of income per capita)	1083.8

Dealing with licenses (rank)	59
Procedures (number)	12
Time (days)	133
Cost (% of income per capita)	1235.5

Employing workers (rank)	79
Difficulty of hiring index (0–100)	33
Rigidity of hours index (0–100)	40
Difficulty of firing index (0–100)	30
Rigidity of employment index (0–100)	34
Nonwage labor cost (% of salary)	0
Firing cost (weeks of salary)	40

Registering property (rank)	146
Procedures (number)	13
Time (days)	43
Cost (% of property value)	7.7

Getting credit (rank)	83
Strength of legal rights index (0–10)	5
Depth of credit information index (0–6)	2
Public registry coverage (% of adults)	0.1
Private bureau coverage (% of adults)	0.0

Protecting investors (rank)	118
Extent of disclosure index (0–10)	4
Extent of director liability index (0–10)	4
Ease of shareholder suits index (0–10)	5
Strength of investor protection index (0–10)	4.3

Paying taxes (rank)	31
Payments (number per year)	20
Time (hours per year)	212
Total tax rate (% of profit)	32.8

Trading across borders (rank)	149
Documents to export (number)	8
Time to export (days)	46
Cost to export (US$ per container)	1,700
Documents to import (number)	11
Time to import (days)	52
Cost to import (US$ per container)	2,455

Enforcing contracts (rank)	82
Procedures (number)	30
Time (days)	690
Cost (% of claim)	14.8

Closing a business (rank)	55
Time (years)	2.4
Cost (% of estate)	15
Recovery rate (cents on the dollar)	36.9

FIJI

		East Asia & Pacific		GNI per capita (US$)	3,280
Ease of doing business (rank)	31	Lower middle income		Population (m)	0.8

Starting a business (rank)	55
Procedures (number)	8
Time (days)	46
Cost (% of income per capita)	25.8
Minimum capital (% of income per capita)	0.0

Dealing with licenses (rank)	27
Procedures (number)	16
Time (days)	114
Cost (% of income per capita)	41.7

Employing workers (rank)	28
Difficulty of hiring index (0–100)	22
Rigidity of hours index (0–100)	40
Difficulty of firing index (0–100)	0
Rigidity of employment index (0–100)	21
Nonwage labor cost (% of salary)	9
Firing cost (weeks of salary)	28

Registering property (rank)	71
Procedures (number)	3
Time (days)	48
Cost (% of property value)	12.0

Getting credit (rank)	21
Strength of legal rights index (0–10)	7
Depth of credit information index (0–6)	4
Public registry coverage (% of adults)	0.0
Private bureau coverage (% of adults)	33.4

Protecting investors (rank)	19
Extent of disclosure index (0–10)	3
Extent of director liability index (0–10)	8
Ease of shareholder suits index (0–10)	8
Strength of investor protection index (0–10)	6.3

Paying taxes (rank)	49
Payments (number per year)	34
Time (hours per year)	145
Total tax rate (% of profit)	40.1

Trading across borders (rank)	70
Documents to export (number)	7
Time to export (days)	22
Cost to export (US$ per container)	418
Documents to import (number)	12
Time to import (days)	22
Cost to import (US$ per container)	1,170

Enforcing contracts (rank)	86
Procedures (number)	26
Time (days)	397
Cost (% of claim)	62.1

Closing a business (rank)	106
Time (years)	1.8
Cost (% of estate)	38
Recovery rate (cents on the dollar)	20.8

FINLAND

		OECD: High Income		GNI per capita (US$)	37,460
Ease of doing business (rank)	14	High income		Population (m)	5.2

Starting a business (rank)	18	**Registering property** (rank)	15	**Trading across borders** (rank)	2
Procedures (number)	3	Procedures (number)	3	Documents to export (number)	4
Time (days)	14	Time (days)	14	Time to export (days)	7
Cost (% of income per capita)	1.1	Cost (% of property value)	4.0	Cost to export (US$ per container)	420
Minimum capital (% of income per capita)	27.1			Documents to import (number)	3
		Getting credit (rank)	21	Time to import (days)	7
Dealing with licenses (rank)	35	Strength of legal rights index (0–10)	6	Cost to import (US$ per container)	420
Procedures (number)	17	Depth of credit information index (0–6)	5		
Time (days)	56	Public registry coverage (% of adults)	0.0	**Enforcing contracts** (rank)	13
Cost (% of income per capita)	108.0	Private bureau coverage (% of adults)	14.9	Procedures (number)	27
				Time (days)	228
Employing workers (rank)	111	**Protecting investors** (rank)	46	Cost (% of claim)	5.9
Difficulty of hiring index (0–100)	44	Extent of disclosure index (0–10)	6		
Rigidity of hours index (0–100)	60	Extent of director liability index (0–10)	4	**Closing a business** (rank)	6
Difficulty of firing index (0–100)	40	Ease of shareholder suits index (0–10)	7	Time (years)	0.9
Rigidity of employment index (0–100)	48	Strength of investor protection index (0–10)	5.7	Cost (% of estate)	4
Nonwage labor cost (% of salary)	25			Recovery rate (cents on the dollar)	89.1
Firing cost (weeks of salary)	26	**Paying taxes** (rank)	75		
		Payments (number per year)	19		
		Time (hours per year)	264		
		Total tax rate (% of profit)	47.9		

FRANCE

		OECD: High Income		GNI per capita (US$)	34,810
Ease of doing business (rank)	35	High income		Population (m)	60.7

Starting a business (rank)	12	**Registering property** (rank)	160	**Trading across borders** (rank)	26
Procedures (number)	7	Procedures (number)	9	Documents to export (number)	4
Time (days)	8	Time (days)	183	Time to export (days)	15
Cost (% of income per capita)	1.1	Cost (% of property value)	6.8	Cost to export (US$ per container)	886
Minimum capital (% of income per capita)	0.0			Documents to import (number)	5
		Getting credit (rank)	48	Time to import (days)	15
Dealing with licenses (rank)	26	Strength of legal rights index (0–10)	5	Cost to import (US$ per container)	886
Procedures (number)	10	Depth of credit information index (0–6)	4		
Time (days)	155	Public registry coverage (% of adults)	12.3	**Enforcing contracts** (rank)	19
Cost (% of income per capita)	75.0	Private bureau coverage (% of adults)	0.0	Procedures (number)	21
				Time (days)	331
Employing workers (rank)	134	**Protecting investors** (rank)	60	Cost (% of claim)	11.8
Difficulty of hiring index (0–100)	67	Extent of disclosure index (0–10)	10		
Rigidity of hours index (0–100)	60	Extent of director liability index (0–10)	1	**Closing a business** (rank)	32
Difficulty of firing index (0–100)	40	Ease of shareholder suits index (0–10)	5	Time (years)	1.9
Rigidity of employment index (0–100)	56	Strength of investor protection index (0–10)	5.3	Cost (% of estate)	9
Nonwage labor cost (% of salary)	47			Recovery rate (cents on the dollar)	48.0
Firing cost (weeks of salary)	32	**Paying taxes** (rank)	92		
		Payments (number per year)	33		
		Time (hours per year)	128		
		Total tax rate (% of profit)	68.2		

GABON

		Sub-Saharan Africa		GNI per capita (US$)	5,010
Ease of doing business (rank)	132	Upper middle income		Population (m)	1.4

Starting a business (rank)	142	**Registering property** (rank)	149	**Trading across borders** (rank)	112
Procedures (number)	10	Procedures (number)	8	Documents to export (number)	4
Time (days)	60	Time (days)	60	Time to export (days)	19
Cost (% of income per capita)	162.8	Cost (% of property value)	10.5	Cost to export (US$ per container)	4,000
Minimum capital (% of income per capita)	36.1			Documents to import (number)	10
		Getting credit (rank)	101	Time to import (days)	26
Dealing with licenses (rank)	54	Strength of legal rights index (0–10)	4	Cost to import (US$ per container)	4,031
Procedures (number)	13	Depth of credit information index (0–6)	2		
Time (days)	268	Public registry coverage (% of adults)	2.6	**Enforcing contracts** (rank)	77
Cost (% of income per capita)	45.3	Private bureau coverage (% of adults)	0.0	Procedures (number)	32
				Time (days)	880
Employing workers (rank)	159	**Protecting investors** (rank)	99	Cost (% of claim)	9.8
Difficulty of hiring index (0–100)	17	Extent of disclosure index (0–10)	5		
Rigidity of hours index (0–100)	80	Extent of director liability index (0–10)	4	**Closing a business** (rank)	130
Difficulty of firing index (0–100)	80	Ease of shareholder suits index (0–10)	5	Time (years)	5.0
Rigidity of employment index (0–100)	59	Strength of investor protection index (0–10)	4.7	Cost (% of estate)	15
Nonwage labor cost (% of salary)	20			Recovery rate (cents on the dollar)	13.9
Firing cost (weeks of salary)	43	**Paying taxes** (rank)	94		
		Payments (number per year)	27		
		Time (hours per year)	272		
		Total tax rate (% of profit)	48.3		

GAMBIA

		Sub-Saharan Africa		GNI per capita (US$)	290
Ease of doing business (rank)	113	Low income		Population (m)	1.5

Starting a business (rank)	124
Procedures (number)	8
Time (days)	27
Cost (% of income per capita)	292.1
Minimum capital (% of income per capita)	119.7

Registering property (rank)	130
Procedures (number)	5
Time (days)	371
Cost (% of property value)	7.6

Trading across borders (rank)	24
Documents to export (number)	4
Time to export (days)	19
Cost to export (US$ per container)	422
Documents to import (number)	8
Time to import (days)	23
Cost to import (US$ per container)	494

Dealing with licenses (rank)	73
Procedures (number)	17
Time (days)	145
Cost (% of income per capita)	276.8

Getting credit (rank)	143
Strength of legal rights index (0–10)	4
Depth of credit information index (0–6)	0
Public registry coverage (% of adults)	0.0
Private bureau coverage (% of adults)	0.0

Enforcing contracts (rank)	53
Procedures (number)	26
Time (days)	247
Cost (% of claim)	35.9

Employing workers (rank)	25
Difficulty of hiring index (0–100)	0
Rigidity of hours index (0–100)	40
Difficulty of firing index (0–100)	40
Rigidity of employment index (0–100)	27
Nonwage labor cost (% of salary)	11
Firing cost (weeks of salary)	9

Protecting investors (rank)	162
Extent of disclosure index (0–10)	2
Extent of director liability index (0–10)	1
Ease of shareholder suits index (0–10)	5
Strength of investor protection index (0–10)	2.7

Closing a business (rank)	76
Time (years)	3.0
Cost (% of estate)	15
Recovery rate (cents on the dollar)	31.4

Paying taxes (rank)	165
Payments (number per year)	47
Time (hours per year)	376
Total tax rate (% of profit)	291.4

GEORGIA

		Eastern Europe & Central Asia		GNI per capita (US$)	1,350
Ease of doing business (rank)	37	Lower middle income		Population (m)	4.5

Starting a business (rank)	36
Procedures (number)	7
Time (days)	16
Cost (% of income per capita)	10.9
Minimum capital (% of income per capita)	3.7

Registering property (rank)	16
Procedures (number)	6
Time (days)	9
Cost (% of property value)	0.5

Trading across borders (rank)	95
Documents to export (number)	8
Time to export (days)	13
Cost to export (US$ per container)	1,370
Documents to import (number)	11
Time to import (days)	15
Cost to import (US$ per container)	1,370

Dealing with licenses (rank)	42
Procedures (number)	17
Time (days)	137
Cost (% of income per capita)	71.7

Getting credit (rank)	48
Strength of legal rights index (0–10)	6
Depth of credit information index (0–6)	3
Public registry coverage (% of adults)	0.0
Private bureau coverage (% of adults)	0.0

Enforcing contracts (rank)	32
Procedures (number)	24
Time (days)	285
Cost (% of claim)	20.5

Employing workers (rank)	6
Difficulty of hiring index (0–100)	0
Rigidity of hours index (0–100)	20
Difficulty of firing index (0–100)	0
Rigidity of employment index (0–100)	7
Nonwage labor cost (% of salary)	20
Firing cost (weeks of salary)	4

Protecting investors (rank)	135
Extent of disclosure index (0–10)	4
Extent of director liability index (0–10)	4
Ease of shareholder suits index (0–10)	4
Strength of investor protection index (0–10)	4.0

Closing a business (rank)	86
Time (years)	3.3
Cost (% of estate)	4
Recovery rate (cents on the dollar)	27.5

Paying taxes (rank)	104
Payments (number per year)	35
Time (hours per year)	423
Total tax rate (% of profit)	37.8

GERMANY

		OECD: High Income		GNI per capita (US$)	34,580
Ease of doing business (rank)	21	High income		Population (m)	82.5

Starting a business (rank)	66
Procedures (number)	9
Time (days)	24
Cost (% of income per capita)	5.1
Minimum capital (% of income per capita)	46.2

Registering property (rank)	42
Procedures (number)	4
Time (days)	40
Cost (% of property value)	4.5

Trading across borders (rank)	7
Documents to export (number)	4
Time to export (days)	6
Cost to export (US$ per container)	731
Documents to import (number)	4
Time to import (days)	6
Cost to import (US$ per container)	750

Dealing with licenses (rank)	21
Procedures (number)	11
Time (days)	133
Cost (% of income per capita)	89.1

Getting credit (rank)	3
Strength of legal rights index (0–10)	8
Depth of credit information index (0–6)	6
Public registry coverage (% of adults)	0.5
Private bureau coverage (% of adults)	93.9

Enforcing contracts (rank)	29
Procedures (number)	30
Time (days)	394
Cost (% of claim)	10.5

Employing workers (rank)	129
Difficulty of hiring index (0–100)	33
Rigidity of hours index (0–100)	60
Difficulty of firing index (0–100)	40
Rigidity of employment index (0–100)	44
Nonwage labor cost (% of salary)	19
Firing cost (weeks of salary)	69

Protecting investors (rank)	83
Extent of disclosure index (0–10)	5
Extent of director liability index (0–10)	5
Ease of shareholder suits index (0–10)	5
Strength of investor protection index (0–10)	5.0

Closing a business (rank)	28
Time (years)	1.2
Cost (% of estate)	8
Recovery rate (cents on the dollar)	53.1

Paying taxes (rank)	73
Payments (number per year)	32
Time (hours per year)	105
Total tax rate (% of profit)	57.1

GHANA

		Sub-Saharan Africa		GNI per capita (US$)	450
Ease of doing business (rank)	94	Low income		Population (m)	22.1

Starting a business (rank)	145	**Registering property** (rank)	113	**Trading across borders** (rank)	61
Procedures (number)	12	Procedures (number)	7	Documents to export (number)	5
Time (days)	81	Time (days)	382	Time to export (days)	21
Cost (% of income per capita)	49.6	Cost (% of property value)	1.9	Cost to export (US$ per container)	822
Minimum capital (% of income per capita)	23.2			Documents to import (number)	9
		Getting credit (rank)	117	Time to import (days)	42
Dealing with licenses (rank)	83	Strength of legal rights index (0–10)	5	Cost to import (US$ per container)	842
Procedures (number)	16	Depth of credit information index (0–6)	0		
Time (days)	127	Public registry coverage (% of adults)	0.0	**Enforcing contracts** (rank)	50
Cost (% of income per capita)	1314.1	Private bureau coverage (% of adults)	0.0	Procedures (number)	29
				Time (days)	552
Employing workers (rank)	120	**Protecting investors** (rank)	33	Cost (% of claim)	13.0
Difficulty of hiring index (0–100)	11	Extent of disclosure index (0–10)	7		
Rigidity of hours index (0–100)	40	Extent of director liability index (0–10)	5	**Closing a business** (rank)	94
Difficulty of firing index (0–100)	50	Ease of shareholder suits index (0–10)	6	Time (years)	1.9
Rigidity of employment index (0–100)	34	Strength of investor protection index (0–10)	6.0	Cost (% of estate)	22
Nonwage labor cost (% of salary)	13			Recovery rate (cents on the dollar)	24.7
Firing cost (weeks of salary)	178	**Paying taxes** (rank)	77		
		Payments (number per year)	35		
		Time (hours per year)	304		
		Total tax rate (% of profit)	32.3		

GREECE

		OECD: High Income		GNI per capita (US$)	19,670
Ease of doing business (rank)	109	High income		Population (m)	11.1

Starting a business (rank)	140	**Registering property** (rank)	94	**Trading across borders** (rank)	123
Procedures (number)	15	Procedures (number)	12	Documents to export (number)	7
Time (days)	38	Time (days)	23	Time to export (days)	29
Cost (% of income per capita)	24.2	Cost (% of property value)	3.8	Cost to export (US$ per container)	1,328
Minimum capital (% of income per capita)	116.0			Documents to import (number)	11
		Getting credit (rank)	83	Time to import (days)	34
Dealing with licenses (rank)	55	Strength of legal rights index (0–10)	3	Cost to import (US$ per container)	1,443
Procedures (number)	17	Depth of credit information index (0–6)	4		
Time (days)	176	Public registry coverage (% of adults)	0.0	**Enforcing contracts** (rank)	48
Cost (% of income per capita)	68.8	Private bureau coverage (% of adults)	37.5	Procedures (number)	22
				Time (days)	730
Employing workers (rank)	166	**Protecting investors** (rank)	156	Cost (% of claim)	12.7
Difficulty of hiring index (0–100)	44	Extent of disclosure index (0–10)	1		
Rigidity of hours index (0–100)	80	Extent of director liability index (0–10)	3	**Closing a business** (rank)	34
Difficulty of firing index (0–100)	50	Ease of shareholder suits index (0–10)	5	Time (years)	2.0
Rigidity of employment index (0–100)	58	Strength of investor protection index (0–10)	3.0	Cost (% of estate)	9
Nonwage labor cost (% of salary)	31			Recovery rate (cents on the dollar)	46.3
Firing cost (weeks of salary)	69	**Paying taxes** (rank)	108		
		Payments (number per year)	33		
		Time (hours per year)	204		
		Total tax rate (% of profit)	60.2		

GRENADA

		Latin America & Caribbean		GNI per capita (US$)	3,920
Ease of doing business (rank)	73	Upper middle income		Population (m)	0.1

Starting a business (rank)	50	**Registering property** (rank)	145	**Trading across borders** (rank)	84
Procedures (number)	4	Procedures (number)	8	Documents to export (number)	6
Time (days)	52	Time (days)	77	Time to export (days)	19
Cost (% of income per capita)	37.2	Cost (% of property value)	7.6	Cost to export (US$ per container)	858
Minimum capital (% of income per capita)	0.0			Documents to import (number)	6
		Getting credit (rank)	83	Time to import (days)	20
Dealing with licenses (rank)	12	Strength of legal rights index (0–10)	7	Cost to import (US$ per container)	984
Procedures (number)	8	Depth of credit information index (0–6)	0		
Time (days)	142	Public registry coverage (% of adults)	0.0	**Enforcing contracts** (rank)	143
Cost (% of income per capita)	36.4	Private bureau coverage (% of adults)	0.0	Procedures (number)	50
				Time (days)	583
Employing workers (rank)	34	**Protecting investors** (rank)	19	Cost (% of claim)	22.1
Difficulty of hiring index (0–100)	44	Extent of disclosure index (0–10)	4		
Rigidity of hours index (0–100)	20	Extent of director liability index (0–10)	8	**Closing a business** (rank)	151
Difficulty of firing index (0–100)	0	Ease of shareholder suits index (0–10)	7	Time (years)	NO PRACTICE
Rigidity of employment index (0–100)	21	Strength of investor protection index (0–10)	6.3	Cost (% of estate)	NO PRACTICE
Nonwage labor cost (% of salary)	5			Recovery rate (cents on the dollar)	0.0
Firing cost (weeks of salary)	29	**Paying taxes** (rank)	45		
		Payments (number per year)	30		
		Time (hours per year)	140		
		Total tax rate (% of profit)	42.8		

GUATEMALA

		Latin America & Caribbean		GNI per capita (US$)	2,400
Ease of doing business (rank)	118	Lower middle income		Population (m)	12.6

Starting a business (rank)	130	**Registering property** (rank)	26	**Trading across borders** (rank)	122
Procedures (number)	13	Procedures (number)	5	Documents to export (number)	9
Time (days)	30	Time (days)	37	Time to export (days)	20
Cost (% of income per capita)	52.1	Cost (% of property value)	1.1	Cost to export (US$ per container)	1,785
Minimum capital (% of income per capita)	26.4			Documents to import (number)	7
		Getting credit (rank)	48	Time to import (days)	33
Dealing with licenses (rank)	165	Strength of legal rights index (0–10)	4	Cost to import (US$ per container)	1,985
Procedures (number)	23	Depth of credit information index (0–6)	5		
Time (days)	390	Public registry coverage (% of adults)	16.1	**Enforcing contracts** (rank)	149
Cost (% of income per capita)	496.5	Private bureau coverage (% of adults)	9.2	Procedures (number)	36
				Time (days)	1459
Employing workers (rank)	105	**Protecting investors** (rank)	135	Cost (% of claim)	26.5
Difficulty of hiring index (0–100)	61	Extent of disclosure index (0–10)	3		
Rigidity of hours index (0–100)	40	Extent of director liability index (0–10)	3	**Closing a business** (rank)	83
Difficulty of firing index (0–100)	0	Ease of shareholder suits index (0–10)	6	Time (years)	3.0
Rigidity of employment index (0–100)	34	Strength of investor protection index (0–10)	4.0	Cost (% of estate)	15
Nonwage labor cost (% of salary)	13			Recovery rate (cents on the dollar)	28.3
Firing cost (weeks of salary)	101	**Paying taxes** (rank)	122		
		Payments (number per year)	50		
		Time (hours per year)	294		
		Total tax rate (% of profit)	40.9		

GUINEA

		Sub-Saharan Africa		GNI per capita (US$)	370
Ease of doing business (rank)	157	Low income		Population (m)	9.4

Starting a business (rank)	165	**Registering property** (rank)	147	**Trading across borders** (rank)	129
Procedures (number)	13	Procedures (number)	6	Documents to export (number)	7
Time (days)	49	Time (days)	104	Time to export (days)	43
Cost (% of income per capita)	186.5	Cost (% of property value)	15.6	Cost to export (US$ per container)	510
Minimum capital (% of income per capita)	423.4			Documents to import (number)	12
		Getting credit (rank)	117	Time to import (days)	56
Dealing with licenses (rank)	166	Strength of legal rights index (0–10)	4	Cost to import (US$ per container)	2,785
Procedures (number)	29	Depth of credit information index (0–6)	1		
Time (days)	278	Public registry coverage (% of adults)	0.0	**Enforcing contracts** (rank)	121
Cost (% of income per capita)	535.4	Private bureau coverage (% of adults)	0.0	Procedures (number)	44
				Time (days)	276
Employing workers (rank)	85	**Protecting investors** (rank)	99	Cost (% of claim)	43.8
Difficulty of hiring index (0–100)	33	Extent of disclosure index (0–10)	5		
Rigidity of hours index (0–100)	60	Extent of director liability index (0–10)	7	**Closing a business** (rank)	119
Difficulty of firing index (0–100)	30	Ease of shareholder suits index (0–10)	2	Time (years)	3.8
Rigidity of employment index (0–100)	41	Strength of investor protection index (0–10)	4.7	Cost (% of estate)	8
Nonwage labor cost (% of salary)	27			Recovery rate (cents on the dollar)	17.5
Firing cost (weeks of salary)	26	**Paying taxes** (rank)	156		
		Payments (number per year)	55		
		Time (hours per year)	416		
		Total tax rate (% of profit)	49.4		

GUINEA-BISSAU

		Sub-Saharan Africa		GNI per capita (US$)	180
Ease of doing business (rank)	173	Low income		Population (m)	1.6

Starting a business (rank)	175	**Registering property** (rank)	171	**Trading across borders** (rank)	125
Procedures (number)	17	Procedures (number)	9	Documents to export (number)	8
Time (days)	233	Time (days)	211	Time to export (days)	27
Cost (% of income per capita)	261.2	Cost (% of property value)	13.2	Cost to export (US$ per container)	1,656
Minimum capital (% of income per capita)	1028.9			Documents to import (number)	9
		Getting credit (rank)	143	Time to import (days)	26
Dealing with licenses (rank)	78	Strength of legal rights index (0–10)	3	Cost to import (US$ per container)	1,749
Procedures (number)	11	Depth of credit information index (0–6)	1		
Time (days)	161	Public registry coverage (% of adults)	1.0	**Enforcing contracts** (rank)	154
Cost (% of income per capita)	2664.9	Private bureau coverage (% of adults)	0.0	Procedures (number)	40
				Time (days)	1140
Employing workers (rank)	173	**Protecting investors** (rank)	142	Cost (% of claim)	27.0
Difficulty of hiring index (0–100)	100	Extent of disclosure index (0–10)	0		
Rigidity of hours index (0–100)	60	Extent of director liability index (0–10)	5	**Closing a business** (rank)	151
Difficulty of firing index (0–100)	70	Ease of shareholder suits index (0–10)	6	Time (years)	NO PRACTICE
Rigidity of employment index (0–100)	77	Strength of investor protection index (0–10)	3.7	Cost (% of estate)	NO PRACTICE
Nonwage labor cost (% of salary)	22			Recovery rate (cents on the dollar)	0.0
Firing cost (weeks of salary)	87	**Paying taxes** (rank)	109		
		Payments (number per year)	47		
		Time (hours per year)	208		
		Total tax rate (% of profit)	47.5		

GUYANA

		Latin America & Caribbean		GNI per capita (US$)	1,010
Ease of doing business (rank)	136	Lower middle income		Population (m)	0.8

Starting a business (rank)	78	**Registering property** (rank)	52	**Trading across borders** (rank)	155
Procedures (number)	8	Procedures (number)	6	Documents to export (number)	8
Time (days)	46	Time (days)	27	Time to export (days)	42
Cost (% of income per capita)	100.2	Cost (% of property value)	4.5	Cost to export (US$ per container)	3,606
Minimum capital (% of income per capita)	0.0			Documents to import (number)	11
		Getting credit (rank)	159	Time to import (days)	54
Dealing with licenses (rank)	74	Strength of legal rights index (0–10)	3	Cost to import (US$ per container)	3,656
Procedures (number)	17	Depth of credit information index (0–6)	0		
Time (days)	202	Public registry coverage (% of adults)	0.0	**Enforcing contracts** (rank)	122
Cost (% of income per capita)	94.7	Private bureau coverage (% of adults)	0.0	Procedures (number)	30
				Time (days)	661
Employing workers (rank)	60	**Protecting investors** (rank)	151	Cost (% of claim)	24.2
Difficulty of hiring index (0–100)	22	Extent of disclosure index (0–10)	5		
Rigidity of hours index (0–100)	20	Extent of director liability index (0–10)	4	**Closing a business** (rank)	131
Difficulty of firing index (0–100)	20	Ease of shareholder suits index (0–10)	1	Time (years)	2.0
Rigidity of employment index (0–100)	21	Strength of investor protection index (0–10)	3.3	Cost (% of estate)	42
Nonwage labor cost (% of salary)	8			Recovery rate (cents on the dollar)	13.7
Firing cost (weeks of salary)	56	**Paying taxes** (rank)	121		
		Payments (number per year)	45		
		Time (hours per year)	288		
		Total tax rate (% of profit)	44.2		

HAITI

		Latin America & Caribbean		GNI per capita (US$)	450
Ease of doing business (rank)	139	Low income		Population (m)	8.5

Starting a business (rank)	167	**Registering property** (rank)	135	**Trading across borders** (rank)	138
Procedures (number)	12	Procedures (number)	5	Documents to export (number)	8
Time (days)	203	Time (days)	683	Time to export (days)	58
Cost (% of income per capita)	127.7	Cost (% of property value)	8.7	Cost to export (US$ per container)	1,298
Minimum capital (% of income per capita)	124.7			Documents to import (number)	9
		Getting credit (rank)	117	Time to import (days)	60
Dealing with licenses (rank)	60	Strength of legal rights index (0–10)	3	Cost to import (US$ per container)	1,304
Procedures (number)	12	Depth of credit information index (0–6)	2		
Time (days)	141	Public registry coverage (% of adults)	0.7	**Enforcing contracts** (rank)	107
Cost (% of income per capita)	1003.0	Private bureau coverage (% of adults)	0.0	Procedures (number)	35
				Time (days)	368
Employing workers (rank)	37	**Protecting investors** (rank)	142	Cost (% of claim)	32.6
Difficulty of hiring index (0–100)	11	Extent of disclosure index (0–10)	4		
Rigidity of hours index (0–100)	40	Extent of director liability index (0–10)	3	**Closing a business** (rank)	146
Difficulty of firing index (0–100)	20	Ease of shareholder suits index (0–10)	4	Time (years)	5.7
Rigidity of employment index (0–100)	24	Strength of investor protection index (0–10)	3.7	Cost (% of estate)	30
Nonwage labor cost (% of salary)	11			Recovery rate (cents on the dollar)	4.1
Firing cost (weeks of salary)	26	**Paying taxes** (rank)	87		
		Payments (number per year)	53		
		Time (hours per year)	160		
		Total tax rate (% of profit)	40.5		

HONDURAS

		Latin America & Caribbean		GNI per capita (US$)	1,190
Ease of doing business (rank)	111	Lower middle income		Population (m)	7.2

Starting a business (rank)	138	**Registering property** (rank)	89	**Trading across borders** (rank)	85
Procedures (number)	13	Procedures (number)	7	Documents to export (number)	6
Time (days)	44	Time (days)	36	Time to export (days)	28
Cost (% of income per capita)	60.6	Cost (% of property value)	5.8	Cost to export (US$ per container)	500
Minimum capital (% of income per capita)	28.6			Documents to import (number)	15
		Getting credit (rank)	21	Time to import (days)	39
Dealing with licenses (rank)	88	Strength of legal rights index (0–10)	6	Cost to import (US$ per container)	670
Procedures (number)	14	Depth of credit information index (0–6)	5		
Time (days)	199	Public registry coverage (% of adults)	8.3	**Enforcing contracts** (rank)	124
Cost (% of income per capita)	636.8	Private bureau coverage (% of adults)	18.7	Procedures (number)	36
				Time (days)	480
Employing workers (rank)	81	**Protecting investors** (rank)	151	Cost (% of claim)	30.4
Difficulty of hiring index (0–100)	67	Extent of disclosure index (0–10)	1		
Rigidity of hours index (0–100)	40	Extent of director liability index (0–10)	5	**Closing a business** (rank)	102
Difficulty of firing index (0–100)	0	Ease of shareholder suits index (0–10)	4	Time (years)	3.8
Rigidity of employment index (0–100)	36	Strength of investor protection index (0–10)	3.3	Cost (% of estate)	8
Nonwage labor cost (% of salary)	10			Recovery rate (cents on the dollar)	23.0
Firing cost (weeks of salary)	43	**Paying taxes** (rank)	152		
		Payments (number per year)	48		
		Time (hours per year)	424		
		Total tax rate (% of profit)	51.4		

HONG KONG, CHINA

		East Asia & Pacific		GNI per capita (US$)	27,670
Ease of doing business (rank)	5	High income		Population (m)	6.9

Starting a business (rank)	5
Procedures (number)	5
Time (days)	11
Cost (% of income per capita)	3.3
Minimum capital (% of income per capita)	0.0

Dealing with licenses (rank)	64
Procedures (number)	22
Time (days)	160
Cost (% of income per capita)	23.3

Employing workers (rank)	16
Difficulty of hiring index (0–100)	0
Rigidity of hours index (0–100)	0
Difficulty of firing index (0–100)	0
Rigidity of employment index (0–100)	0
Nonwage labor cost (% of salary)	5
Firing cost (weeks of salary)	62

Registering property (rank)	60
Procedures (number)	5
Time (days)	54
Cost (% of property value)	5.0

Getting credit (rank)	2
Strength of legal rights index (0–10)	10
Depth of credit information index (0–6)	5
Public registry coverage (% of adults)	0.0
Private bureau coverage (% of adults)	64.5

Protecting investors (rank)	3
Extent of disclosure index (0–10)	10
Extent of director liability index (0–10)	8
Ease of shareholder suits index (0–10)	9
Strength of investor protection index (0–10)	9.0

Paying taxes (rank)	5
Payments (number per year)	4
Time (hours per year)	80
Total tax rate (% of profit)	28.8

Trading across borders (rank)	1
Documents to export (number)	2
Time to export (days)	6
Cost to export (US$ per container)	425
Documents to import (number)	2
Time to import (days)	5
Cost to import (US$ per container)	425

Enforcing contracts (rank)	10
Procedures (number)	16
Time (days)	211
Cost (% of claim)	14.2

Closing a business (rank)	14
Time (years)	1.1
Cost (% of estate)	9
Recovery rate (cents on the dollar)	78.9

HUNGARY

		Eastern Europe & Central Asia		GNI per capita (US$)	10,030
Ease of doing business (rank)	66	Upper middle income		Population (m)	10.1

Starting a business (rank)	87
Procedures (number)	6
Time (days)	38
Cost (% of income per capita)	20.9
Minimum capital (% of income per capita)	74.2

Dealing with licenses (rank)	143
Procedures (number)	25
Time (days)	212
Cost (% of income per capita)	260.0

Employing workers (rank)	90
Difficulty of hiring index (0–100)	11
Rigidity of hours index (0–100)	80
Difficulty of firing index (0–100)	10
Rigidity of employment index (0–100)	34
Nonwage labor cost (% of salary)	35
Firing cost (weeks of salary)	35

Registering property (rank)	103
Procedures (number)	4
Time (days)	78
Cost (% of property value)	11.0

Getting credit (rank)	21
Strength of legal rights index (0–10)	6
Depth of credit information index (0–6)	5
Public registry coverage (% of adults)	0.0
Private bureau coverage (% of adults)	5.9

Protecting investors (rank)	118
Extent of disclosure index (0–10)	2
Extent of director liability index (0–10)	4
Ease of shareholder suits index (0–10)	7
Strength of investor protection index (0–10)	4.3

Paying taxes (rank)	118
Payments (number per year)	24
Time (hours per year)	304
Total tax rate (% of profit)	59.3

Trading across borders (rank)	76
Documents to export (number)	6
Time to export (days)	23
Cost to export (US$ per container)	922
Documents to import (number)	10
Time to import (days)	24
Cost to import (US$ per container)	1,137

Enforcing contracts (rank)	12
Procedures (number)	21
Time (days)	335
Cost (% of claim)	9.6

Closing a business (rank)	48
Time (years)	2.0
Cost (% of estate)	15
Recovery rate (cents on the dollar)	39.7

ICELAND

		OECD: High Income		GNI per capita (US$)	46,320
Ease of doing business (rank)	12	High income		Population (m)	0.3

Starting a business (rank)	16
Procedures (number)	5
Time (days)	5
Cost (% of income per capita)	3.1
Minimum capital (% of income per capita)	15.9

Dealing with licenses (rank)	30
Procedures (number)	19
Time (days)	111
Cost (% of income per capita)	15.7

Employing workers (rank)	42
Difficulty of hiring index (0–100)	33
Rigidity of hours index (0–100)	60
Difficulty of firing index (0–100)	0
Rigidity of employment index (0–100)	31
Nonwage labor cost (% of salary)	12
Firing cost (weeks of salary)	13

Registering property (rank)	8
Procedures (number)	3
Time (days)	4
Cost (% of property value)	2.4

Getting credit (rank)	13
Strength of legal rights index (0–10)	7
Depth of credit information index (0–6)	5
Public registry coverage (% of adults)	0.0
Private bureau coverage (% of adults)	100.0

Protecting investors (rank)	83
Extent of disclosure index (0–10)	4
Extent of director liability index (0–10)	5
Ease of shareholder suits index (0–10)	6
Strength of investor protection index (0–10)	5.0

Paying taxes (rank)	13
Payments (number per year)	18
Time (hours per year)	140
Total tax rate (% of profit)	27.9

Trading across borders (rank)	18
Documents to export (number)	7
Time to export (days)	15
Cost to export (US$ per container)	469
Documents to import (number)	6
Time to import (days)	15
Cost to import (US$ per container)	443

Enforcing contracts (rank)	8
Procedures (number)	14
Time (days)	352
Cost (% of claim)	5.9

Closing a business (rank)	13
Time (years)	1.0
Cost (% of estate)	4
Recovery rate (cents on the dollar)	79.7

INDIA

		South Asia		GNI per capita (US$)	720
Ease of doing business (rank)	134	Low income		Population (m)	1094.6

Starting a business (rank)	88	**Registering property** (rank)	110	**Trading across borders** (rank)	139
Procedures (number)	11	Procedures (number)	6	Documents to export (number)	10
Time (days)	35	Time (days)	62	Time to export (days)	27
Cost (% of income per capita)	73.7	Cost (% of property value)	7.8	Cost to export (US$ per container)	864
Minimum capital (% of income per capita)	0.0			Documents to import (number)	15
		Getting credit (rank)	65	Time to import (days)	41
Dealing with licenses (rank)	155	Strength of legal rights index (0–10)	5	Cost to import (US$ per container)	1,244
Procedures (number)	20	Depth of credit information index (0–6)	3		
Time (days)	270	Public registry coverage (% of adults)	0.0	**Enforcing contracts** (rank)	173
Cost (% of income per capita)	606.0	Private bureau coverage (% of adults)	6.1	Procedures (number)	56
				Time (days)	1420
Employing workers (rank)	112	**Protecting investors** (rank)	33	Cost (% of claim)	35.7
Difficulty of hiring index (0–100)	33	Extent of disclosure index (0–10)	7		
Rigidity of hours index (0–100)	20	Extent of director liability index (0–10)	4	**Closing a business** (rank)	133
Difficulty of firing index (0–100)	70	Ease of shareholder suits index (0–10)	7	Time (years)	10.0
Rigidity of employment index (0–100)	41	Strength of investor protection index (0–10)	6.0	Cost (% of estate)	9
Nonwage labor cost (% of salary)	17			Recovery rate (cents on the dollar)	13.0
Firing cost (weeks of salary)	56	**Paying taxes** (rank)	158		
		Payments (number per year)	59		
		Time (hours per year)	264		
		Total tax rate (% of profit)	81.1		

INDONESIA

		East Asia & Pacific		GNI per capita (US$)	1,280
Ease of doing business (rank)	135	Lower middle income		Population (m)	220.6

Starting a business (rank)	161	**Registering property** (rank)	120	**Trading across borders** (rank)	60
Procedures (number)	12	Procedures (number)	7	Documents to export (number)	7
Time (days)	97	Time (days)	42	Time to export (days)	25
Cost (% of income per capita)	86.7	Cost (% of property value)	10.5	Cost to export (US$ per container)	546
Minimum capital (% of income per capita)	83.4			Documents to import (number)	10
		Getting credit (rank)	83	Time to import (days)	30
Dealing with licenses (rank)	131	Strength of legal rights index (0–10)	5	Cost to import (US$ per container)	675
Procedures (number)	19	Depth of credit information index (0–6)	2		
Time (days)	224	Public registry coverage (% of adults)	8.4	**Enforcing contracts** (rank)	145
Cost (% of income per capita)	311.0	Private bureau coverage (% of adults)	0.2	Procedures (number)	34
				Time (days)	570
Employing workers (rank)	140	**Protecting investors** (rank)	60	Cost (% of claim)	126.5
Difficulty of hiring index (0–100)	61	Extent of disclosure index (0–10)	8		
Rigidity of hours index (0–100)	20	Extent of director liability index (0–10)	5	**Closing a business** (rank)	136
Difficulty of firing index (0–100)	50	Ease of shareholder suits index (0–10)	3	Time (years)	5.5
Rigidity of employment index (0–100)	44	Strength of investor protection index (0–10)	5.3	Cost (% of estate)	18
Nonwage labor cost (% of salary)	10			Recovery rate (cents on the dollar)	11.8
Firing cost (weeks of salary)	108	**Paying taxes** (rank)	133		
		Payments (number per year)	52		
		Time (hours per year)	576		
		Total tax rate (% of profit)	37.2		

IRAN

		Middle East & North Africa		GNI per capita (US$)	2,770
Ease of doing business (rank)	119	Lower middle income		Population (m)	67.7

Starting a business (rank)	64	**Registering property** (rank)	143	**Trading across borders** (rank)	87
Procedures (number)	8	Procedures (number)	9	Documents to export (number)	5
Time (days)	47	Time (days)	36	Time to export (days)	26
Cost (% of income per capita)	5.4	Cost (% of property value)	10.5	Cost to export (US$ per container)	700
Minimum capital (% of income per capita)	1.3			Documents to import (number)	11
		Getting credit (rank)	65	Time to import (days)	38
Dealing with licenses (rank)	167	Strength of legal rights index (0–10)	5	Cost to import (US$ per container)	1,220
Procedures (number)	21	Depth of credit information index (0–6)	3		
Time (days)	668	Public registry coverage (% of adults)	13.7	**Enforcing contracts** (rank)	33
Cost (% of income per capita)	684.5	Private bureau coverage (% of adults)	0.0	Procedures (number)	23
				Time (days)	520
Employing workers (rank)	141	**Protecting investors** (rank)	156	Cost (% of claim)	12.0
Difficulty of hiring index (0–100)	78	Extent of disclosure index (0–10)	5		
Rigidity of hours index (0–100)	60	Extent of director liability index (0–10)	4	**Closing a business** (rank)	109
Difficulty of firing index (0–100)	10	Ease of shareholder suits index (0–10)	0	Time (years)	4.5
Rigidity of employment index (0–100)	49	Strength of investor protection index (0–10)	3.0	Cost (% of estate)	9
Nonwage labor cost (% of salary)	23			Recovery rate (cents on the dollar)	19.7
Firing cost (weeks of salary)	91	**Paying taxes** (rank)	96		
		Payments (number per year)	28		
		Time (hours per year)	292		
		Total tax rate (% of profit)	46.4		

IRAQ

Ease of doing business (rank)	145	Middle East & North Africa Lower middle income		GNI per capita (US$)	1,188
				Population (m)	28.8

Starting a business (rank)	150	**Registering property** (rank)	37	**Trading across borders** (rank)	164
Procedures (number)	11	Procedures (number)	5	Documents to export (number)	10
Time (days)	77	Time (days)	8	Time to export (days)	105
Cost (% of income per capita)	67.6	Cost (% of property value)	6.6	Cost to export (US$ per container)	1,010
Minimum capital (% of income per capita)	57.1			Documents to import (number)	19
				Time to import (days)	135
Dealing with licenses (rank)	97	**Getting credit** (rank)	143	Cost to import (US$ per container)	2,060
Procedures (number)	14	Strength of legal rights index (0–10)	4		
Time (days)	216	Depth of credit information index (0–6)	0	**Enforcing contracts** (rank)	131
Cost (% of income per capita)	833.2	Public registry coverage (% of adults)	0.0	Procedures (number)	65
		Private bureau coverage (% of adults)	0.0	Time (days)	520
Employing workers (rank)	114			Cost (% of claim)	15.3
Difficulty of hiring index (0–100)	78	**Protecting investors** (rank)	99		
Rigidity of hours index (0–100)	60	Extent of disclosure index (0–10)	4	**Closing a business** (rank)	151
Difficulty of firing index (0–100)	40	Extent of director liability index (0–10)	5	Time (years)	NO PRACTICE
Rigidity of employment index (0–100)	59	Ease of shareholder suits index (0–10)	5	Cost (% of estate)	NO PRACTICE
Nonwage labor cost (% of salary)	12	Strength of investor protection index (0–10)	4.7	Recovery rate (cents on the dollar)	0.0
Firing cost (weeks of salary)	4				
		Paying taxes (rank)	47		
		Payments (number per year)	13		
		Time (hours per year)	312		
		Total tax rate (% of profit)	38.7		

IRELAND

Ease of doing business (rank)	10	OECD: High Income High income		GNI per capita (US$)	40,150
				Population (m)	4.2

Starting a business (rank)	6	**Registering property** (rank)	80	**Trading across borders** (rank)	30
Procedures (number)	4	Procedures (number)	5	Documents to export (number)	5
Time (days)	19	Time (days)	38	Time to export (days)	7
Cost (% of income per capita)	0.3	Cost (% of property value)	10.3	Cost to export (US$ per container)	1,146
Minimum capital (% of income per capita)	0.0			Documents to import (number)	4
				Time to import (days)	14
Dealing with licenses (rank)	20	**Getting credit** (rank)	7	Cost to import (US$ per container)	1,139
Procedures (number)	10	Strength of legal rights index (0–10)	8		
Time (days)	181	Depth of credit information index (0–6)	5	**Enforcing contracts** (rank)	24
Cost (% of income per capita)	22.2	Public registry coverage (% of adults)	0.0	Procedures (number)	18
		Private bureau coverage (% of adults)	100.0	Time (days)	217
Employing workers (rank)	83			Cost (% of claim)	21.1
Difficulty of hiring index (0–100)	28	**Protecting investors** (rank)	5		
Rigidity of hours index (0–100)	40	Extent of disclosure index (0–10)	10	**Closing a business** (rank)	7
Difficulty of firing index (0–100)	30	Extent of director liability index (0–10)	6	Time (years)	0.4
Rigidity of employment index (0–100)	33	Ease of shareholder suits index (0–10)	9	Cost (% of estate)	9
Nonwage labor cost (% of salary)	11	Strength of investor protection index (0–10)	8.3	Recovery rate (cents on the dollar)	87.9
Firing cost (weeks of salary)	49				
		Paying taxes (rank)	2		
		Payments (number per year)	8		
		Time (hours per year)	76		
		Total tax rate (% of profit)	25.8		

ISRAEL

Ease of doing business (rank)	26	Middle East & North Africa High income		GNI per capita (US$)	18,620
				Population (m)	6.9

Starting a business (rank)	15	**Registering property** (rank)	150	**Trading across borders** (rank)	13
Procedures (number)	5	Procedures (number)	7	Documents to export (number)	5
Time (days)	34	Time (days)	144	Time to export (days)	15
Cost (% of income per capita)	5.1	Cost (% of property value)	7.5	Cost to export (US$ per container)	340
Minimum capital (% of income per capita)	0.0			Documents to import (number)	5
				Time to import (days)	16
Dealing with licenses (rank)	101	**Getting credit** (rank)	7	Cost to import (US$ per container)	700
Procedures (number)	21	Strength of legal rights index (0–10)	8		
Time (days)	215	Depth of credit information index (0–6)	5	**Enforcing contracts** (rank)	110
Cost (% of income per capita)	91.1	Public registry coverage (% of adults)	0.0	Procedures (number)	31
		Private bureau coverage (% of adults)	100.0	Time (days)	585
Employing workers (rank)	82			Cost (% of claim)	22.1
Difficulty of hiring index (0–100)	0	**Protecting investors** (rank)	5		
Rigidity of hours index (0–100)	60	Extent of disclosure index (0–10)	7	**Closing a business** (rank)	36
Difficulty of firing index (0–100)	20	Extent of director liability index (0–10)	9	Time (years)	4.0
Rigidity of employment index (0–100)	27	Ease of shareholder suits index (0–10)	9	Cost (% of estate)	23
Nonwage labor cost (% of salary)	6	Strength of investor protection index (0–10)	8.3	Recovery rate (cents on the dollar)	43.9
Firing cost (weeks of salary)	91				
		Paying taxes (rank)	62		
		Payments (number per year)	33		
		Time (hours per year)	225		
		Total tax rate (% of profit)	39.1		

ITALY

		OECD: High Income		GNI per capita (US$)	30,010
Ease of doing business (rank)	82	High income		Population (m)	57.5

Starting a business (rank)	52	**Registering property** (rank)	53	**Trading across borders** (rank)	110
Procedures (number)	9	Procedures (number)	8	Documents to export (number)	8
Time (days)	13	Time (days)	27	Time to export (days)	15
Cost (% of income per capita)	15.2	Cost (% of property value)	0.9	Cost to export (US$ per container)	1,253
Minimum capital (% of income per capita)	10.4			Documents to import (number)	16
		Getting credit (rank)	65	Time to import (days)	21
Dealing with licenses (rank)	104	Strength of legal rights index (0–10)	3	Cost to import (US$ per container)	1,291
Procedures (number)	17	Depth of credit information index (0–6)	5		
Time (days)	284	Public registry coverage (% of adults)	7.0	**Enforcing contracts** (rank)	141
Cost (% of income per capita)	142.3	Private bureau coverage (% of adults)	67.8	Procedures (number)	40
				Time (days)	1210
Employing workers (rank)	101	**Protecting investors** (rank)	83	Cost (% of claim)	17.6
Difficulty of hiring index (0–100)	61	Extent of disclosure index (0–10)	7		
Rigidity of hours index (0–100)	60	Extent of director liability index (0–10)	2	**Closing a business** (rank)	49
Difficulty of firing index (0–100)	40	Ease of shareholder suits index (0–10)	6	Time (years)	1.2
Rigidity of employment index (0–100)	54	Strength of investor protection index (0–10)	5.0	Cost (% of estate)	22
Nonwage labor cost (% of salary)	42			Recovery rate (cents on the dollar)	39.7
Firing cost (weeks of salary)	2	**Paying taxes** (rank)	117		
		Payments (number per year)	15		
		Time (hours per year)	360		
		Total tax rate (% of profit)	76.0		

JAMAICA

		Latin America & Caribbean		GNI per capita (US$)	3,400
Ease of doing business (rank)	50	Lower middle income		Population (m)	2.7

Starting a business (rank)	10	**Registering property** (rank)	107	**Trading across borders** (rank)	74
Procedures (number)	6	Procedures (number)	5	Documents to export (number)	6
Time (days)	8	Time (days)	54	Time to export (days)	19
Cost (% of income per capita)	9.4	Cost (% of property value)	13.5	Cost to export (US$ per container)	1,750
Minimum capital (% of income per capita)	0.0			Documents to import (number)	7
		Getting credit (rank)	101	Time to import (days)	20
Dealing with licenses (rank)	93	Strength of legal rights index (0–10)	6	Cost to import (US$ per container)	1,350
Procedures (number)	14	Depth of credit information index (0–6)	0		
Time (days)	242	Public registry coverage (% of adults)	0.0	**Enforcing contracts** (rank)	46
Cost (% of income per capita)	417.5	Private bureau coverage (% of adults)	0.0	Procedures (number)	18
				Time (days)	415
Employing workers (rank)	26	**Protecting investors** (rank)	60	Cost (% of claim)	27.8
Difficulty of hiring index (0–100)	11	Extent of disclosure index (0–10)	4		
Rigidity of hours index (0–100)	0	Extent of director liability index (0–10)	8	**Closing a business** (rank)	23
Difficulty of firing index (0–100)	0	Ease of shareholder suits index (0–10)	4	Time (years)	1.1
Rigidity of employment index (0–100)	4	Strength of investor protection index (0–10)	5.3	Cost (% of estate)	18
Nonwage labor cost (% of salary)	12			Recovery rate (cents on the dollar)	64.3
Firing cost (weeks of salary)	61	**Paying taxes** (rank)	163		
		Payments (number per year)	72		
		Time (hours per year)	414		
		Total tax rate (% of profit)	52.3		

JAPAN

		OECD: High Income		GNI per capita (US$)	38,980
Ease of doing business (rank)	11	High income		Population (m)	128.0

Starting a business (rank)	18	**Registering property** (rank)	39	**Trading across borders** (rank)	19
Procedures (number)	8	Procedures (number)	6	Documents to export (number)	5
Time (days)	23	Time (days)	14	Time to export (days)	11
Cost (% of income per capita)	7.5	Cost (% of property value)	4.1	Cost to export (US$ per container)	789
Minimum capital (% of income per capita)	0.0			Documents to import (number)	7
		Getting credit (rank)	13	Time to import (days)	11
Dealing with licenses (rank)	2	Strength of legal rights index (0–10)	6	Cost to import (US$ per container)	847
Procedures (number)	11	Depth of credit information index (0–6)	6		
Time (days)	96	Public registry coverage (% of adults)	0.0	**Enforcing contracts** (rank)	5
Cost (% of income per capita)	19.8	Private bureau coverage (% of adults)	..	Procedures (number)	20
				Time (days)	242
Employing workers (rank)	36	**Protecting investors** (rank)	12	Cost (% of claim)	9.5
Difficulty of hiring index (0–100)	28	Extent of disclosure index (0–10)	7		
Rigidity of hours index (0–100)	60	Extent of director liability index (0–10)	6	**Closing a business** (rank)	1
Difficulty of firing index (0–100)	0	Ease of shareholder suits index (0–10)	8	Time (years)	0.6
Rigidity of employment index (0–100)	29	Strength of investor protection index (0–10)	7.0	Cost (% of estate)	4
Nonwage labor cost (% of salary)	13			Recovery rate (cents on the dollar)	92.7
Firing cost (weeks of salary)	9	**Paying taxes** (rank)	98		
		Payments (number per year)	15		
		Time (hours per year)	350		
		Total tax rate (% of profit)	52.8		

JORDAN

		Middle East & North Africa		GNI per capita (US$)	2,500
Ease of doing business (rank)	78	Lower middle income		Population (m)	5.4

Starting a business (rank)	133	**Registering property** (rank)	110	**Trading across borders** (rank)	78
Procedures (number)	11	Procedures (number)	8	Documents to export (number)	7
Time (days)	18	Time (days)	22	Time to export (days)	24
Cost (% of income per capita)	73.0	Cost (% of property value)	10.0	Cost to export (US$ per container)	720
Minimum capital (% of income per capita)	864.4			Documents to import (number)	12
		Getting credit (rank)	83	Time to import (days)	22
		Strength of legal rights index (0–10)	5	Cost to import (US$ per container)	955
Dealing with licenses (rank)	70	Depth of credit information index (0–6)	2		
Procedures (number)	16	Public registry coverage (% of adults)	0.7	**Enforcing contracts** (rank)	75
Time (days)	122	Private bureau coverage (% of adults)	0.0	Procedures (number)	43
Cost (% of income per capita)	503.2			Time (days)	342
		Protecting investors (rank)	118	Cost (% of claim)	16.2
Employing workers (rank)	30	Extent of disclosure index (0–10)	5		
Difficulty of hiring index (0–100)	11	Extent of director liability index (0–10)	4	**Closing a business** (rank)	84
Rigidity of hours index (0–100)	20	Ease of shareholder suits index (0–10)	4	Time (years)	4.3
Difficulty of firing index (0–100)	50	Strength of investor protection index (0–10)	4.3	Cost (% of estate)	9
Rigidity of employment index (0–100)	27			Recovery rate (cents on the dollar)	28.2
Nonwage labor cost (% of salary)	11	**Paying taxes** (rank)	18		
Firing cost (weeks of salary)	4	Payments (number per year)	26		
		Time (hours per year)	101		
		Total tax rate (% of profit)	31.9		

KAZAKHSTAN

		Eastern Europe & Central Asia		GNI per capita (US$)	2,930
Ease of doing business (rank)	63	Lower middle income		Population (m)	15.1

Starting a business (rank)	40	**Registering property** (rank)	76	**Trading across borders** (rank)	172
Procedures (number)	7	Procedures (number)	8	Documents to export (number)	14
Time (days)	20	Time (days)	52	Time to export (days)	93
Cost (% of income per capita)	7.0	Cost (% of property value)	1.8	Cost to export (US$ per container)	2,780
Minimum capital (% of income per capita)	23.1			Documents to import (number)	18
		Getting credit (rank)	48	Time to import (days)	87
		Strength of legal rights index (0–10)	5	Cost to import (US$ per container)	2,880
Dealing with licenses (rank)	119	Depth of credit information index (0–6)	4		
Procedures (number)	32	Public registry coverage (% of adults)	0.0	**Enforcing contracts** (rank)	27
Time (days)	248	Private bureau coverage (% of adults)	5.5	Procedures (number)	37
Cost (% of income per capita)	35.0			Time (days)	183
		Protecting investors (rank)	46	Cost (% of claim)	11.5
Employing workers (rank)	22	Extent of disclosure index (0–10)	7		
Difficulty of hiring index (0–100)	0	Extent of director liability index (0–10)	1	**Closing a business** (rank)	100
Rigidity of hours index (0–100)	60	Ease of shareholder suits index (0–10)	9	Time (years)	3.3
Difficulty of firing index (0–100)	10	Strength of investor protection index (0–10)	5.7	Cost (% of estate)	18
Rigidity of employment index (0–100)	23			Recovery rate (cents on the dollar)	23.6
Nonwage labor cost (% of salary)	22	**Paying taxes** (rank)	66		
Firing cost (weeks of salary)	9	Payments (number per year)	34		
		Time (hours per year)	156		
		Total tax rate (% of profit)	45.0		

KENYA

		Sub-Saharan Africa		GNI per capita (US$)	530
Ease of doing business (rank)	83	Low income		Population (m)	34.3

Starting a business (rank)	111	**Registering property** (rank)	115	**Trading across borders** (rank)	145
Procedures (number)	13	Procedures (number)	8	Documents to export (number)	11
Time (days)	54	Time (days)	73	Time to export (days)	25
Cost (% of income per capita)	46.3	Cost (% of property value)	4.1	Cost to export (US$ per container)	1,980
Minimum capital (% of income per capita)	0.0			Documents to import (number)	9
		Getting credit (rank)	33	Time to import (days)	45
		Strength of legal rights index (0–10)	8	Cost to import (US$ per container)	2,325
Dealing with licenses (rank)	24	Depth of credit information index (0–6)	2		
Procedures (number)	11	Public registry coverage (% of adults)	0.0	**Enforcing contracts** (rank)	67
Time (days)	170	Private bureau coverage (% of adults)	0.1	Procedures (number)	25
Cost (% of income per capita)	37.6			Time (days)	360
		Protecting investors (rank)	60	Cost (% of claim)	41.3
Employing workers (rank)	68	Extent of disclosure index (0–10)	4		
Difficulty of hiring index (0–100)	33	Extent of director liability index (0–10)	2	**Closing a business** (rank)	128
Rigidity of hours index (0–100)	20	Ease of shareholder suits index (0–10)	10	Time (years)	4.5
Difficulty of firing index (0–100)	30	Strength of investor protection index (0–10)	5.3	Cost (% of estate)	22
Rigidity of employment index (0–100)	28			Recovery rate (cents on the dollar)	14.6
Nonwage labor cost (% of salary)	4	**Paying taxes** (rank)	126		
Firing cost (weeks of salary)	47	Payments (number per year)	17		
		Time (hours per year)	432		
		Total tax rate (% of profit)	74.2		

KIRIBATI

		East Asia & Pacific		GNI per capita (US$)	1,390
Ease of doing business (rank)	60	Lower middle income		Population (m)	0.1

Starting a business (rank)	72	**Registering property** (rank)	62	**Trading across borders** (rank)	31
Procedures (number)	6	Procedures (number)	5	Documents to export (number)	3
Time (days)	21	Time (days)	513	Time to export (days)	11
Cost (% of income per capita)	50.0	Cost (% of property value)	0.1	Cost to export (US$ per container)	1,300
Minimum capital (% of income per capita)	27.1			Documents to import (number)	2
		Getting credit (rank)	101	Time to import (days)	8
Dealing with licenses (rank)	76	Strength of legal rights index (0–10)	6	Cost to import (US$ per container)	1,300
Procedures (number)	14	Depth of credit information index (0–6)	0		
Time (days)	174	Public registry coverage (% of adults)	0.0	**Enforcing contracts** (rank)	136
Cost (% of income per capita)	545.2	Private bureau coverage (% of adults)	0.0	Procedures (number)	26
				Time (days)	660
Employing workers (rank)	18	**Protecting investors** (rank)	33	Cost (% of claim)	71.0
Difficulty of hiring index (0–100)	0	Extent of disclosure index (0–10)	6		
Rigidity of hours index (0–100)	0	Extent of director liability index (0–10)	5	**Closing a business** (rank)	151
Difficulty of firing index (0–100)	50	Ease of shareholder suits index (0–10)	7	Time (years)	NO PRACTICE
Rigidity of employment index (0–100)	17	Strength of investor protection index (0–10)	6.0	Cost (% of estate)	NO PRACTICE
Nonwage labor cost (% of salary)	8			Recovery rate (cents on the dollar)	0.0
Firing cost (weeks of salary)	4	**Paying taxes** (rank)	14		
		Payments (number per year)	16		
		Time (hours per year)	120		
		Total tax rate (% of profit)	34.4		

KOREA

		OECD: High Income		GNI per capita (US$)	15,830
Ease of doing business (rank)	23	High income		Population (m)	48.3

Starting a business (rank)	116	**Registering property** (rank)	67	**Trading across borders** (rank)	28
Procedures (number)	12	Procedures (number)	7	Documents to export (number)	5
Time (days)	22	Time (days)	11	Time to export (days)	12
Cost (% of income per capita)	15.2	Cost (% of property value)	6.3	Cost to export (US$ per container)	780
Minimum capital (% of income per capita)	299.7			Documents to import (number)	8
		Getting credit (rank)	21	Time to import (days)	12
Dealing with licenses (rank)	28	Strength of legal rights index (0–10)	6	Cost to import (US$ per container)	1,040
Procedures (number)	14	Depth of credit information index (0–6)	5		
Time (days)	52	Public registry coverage (% of adults)	0.0	**Enforcing contracts** (rank)	17
Cost (% of income per capita)	175.9	Private bureau coverage (% of adults)	76.6	Procedures (number)	29
				Time (days)	230
Employing workers (rank)	110	**Protecting investors** (rank)	60	Cost (% of claim)	5.5
Difficulty of hiring index (0–100)	11	Extent of disclosure index (0–10)	7		
Rigidity of hours index (0–100)	60	Extent of director liability index (0–10)	2	**Closing a business** (rank)	11
Difficulty of firing index (0–100)	30	Ease of shareholder suits index (0–10)	7	Time (years)	1.5
Rigidity of employment index (0–100)	34	Strength of investor protection index (0–10)	5.3	Cost (% of estate)	4
Nonwage labor cost (% of salary)	18			Recovery rate (cents on the dollar)	81.8
Firing cost (weeks of salary)	91	**Paying taxes** (rank)	48		
		Payments (number per year)	27		
		Time (hours per year)	290		
		Total tax rate (% of profit)	30.9		

KUWAIT

		Middle East & North Africa		GNI per capita (US$)	24,040
Ease of doing business (rank)	46	High income		Population (m)	2.5

Starting a business (rank)	104	**Registering property** (rank)	69	**Trading across borders** (rank)	54
Procedures (number)	13	Procedures (number)	8	Documents to export (number)	5
Time (days)	35	Time (days)	55	Time to export (days)	18
Cost (% of income per capita)	1.6	Cost (% of property value)	0.5	Cost to export (US$ per container)	675
Minimum capital (% of income per capita)	100.8			Documents to import (number)	11
		Getting credit (rank)	83	Time to import (days)	27
Dealing with licenses (rank)	109	Strength of legal rights index (0–10)	4	Cost to import (US$ per container)	1,170
Procedures (number)	26	Depth of credit information index (0–6)	3		
Time (days)	149	Public registry coverage (% of adults)	0.0	**Enforcing contracts** (rank)	79
Cost (% of income per capita)	210.1	Private bureau coverage (% of adults)	16.1	Procedures (number)	52
				Time (days)	390
Employing workers (rank)	20	**Protecting investors** (rank)	19	Cost (% of claim)	13.3
Difficulty of hiring index (0–100)	0	Extent of disclosure index (0–10)	7		
Rigidity of hours index (0–100)	40	Extent of director liability index (0–10)	7	**Closing a business** (rank)	63
Difficulty of firing index (0–100)	0	Ease of shareholder suits index (0–10)	5	Time (years)	4.2
Rigidity of employment index (0–100)	13	Strength of investor protection index (0–10)	6.3	Cost (% of estate)	1
Nonwage labor cost (% of salary)	11			Recovery rate (cents on the dollar)	34.5
Firing cost (weeks of salary)	43	**Paying taxes** (rank)	41		
		Payments (number per year)	14		
		Time (hours per year)	118		
		Total tax rate (% of profit)	55.7		

KYRGYZ REPUBLIC

Ease of doing business (rank)	90

Starting a business (rank)	41
Procedures (number)	8
Time (days)	21
Cost (% of income per capita)	9.8
Minimum capital (% of income per capita)	0.5

Dealing with licenses (rank)	143
Procedures (number)	20
Time (days)	218
Cost (% of income per capita)	510.4

Employing workers (rank)	63
Difficulty of hiring index (0–100)	33
Rigidity of hours index (0–100)	40
Difficulty of firing index (0–100)	40
Rigidity of employment index (0–100)	38
Nonwage labor cost (% of salary)	25
Firing cost (weeks of salary)	17

Eastern Europe & Central Asia
Low income

Registering property (rank)	31
Procedures (number)	7
Time (days)	8
Cost (% of property value)	1.9

Getting credit (rank)	65
Strength of legal rights index (0–10)	5
Depth of credit information index (0–6)	3
Public registry coverage (% of adults)	0.0
Private bureau coverage (% of adults)	0.4

Protecting investors (rank)	33
Extent of disclosure index (0–10)	8
Extent of director liability index (0–10)	1
Ease of shareholder suits index (0–10)	9
Strength of investor protection index (0–10)	6.0

Paying taxes (rank)	150
Payments (number per year)	89
Time (hours per year)	204
Total tax rate (% of profit)	67.4

GNI per capita (US$)	440
Population (m)	5.2

Trading across borders (rank)	173
Documents to export (number)	..
Time to export (days)	..
Cost to export (US$ per container)	..
Documents to import (number)	18
Time to import (days)	127
Cost to import (US$ per container)	3,032

Enforcing contracts (rank)	38
Procedures (number)	44
Time (days)	140
Cost (% of claim)	12.0

Closing a business (rank)	127
Time (years)	4.0
Cost (% of estate)	15
Recovery rate (cents on the dollar)	14.9

LAO PDR

Ease of doing business (rank)	159

Starting a business (rank)	73
Procedures (number)	8
Time (days)	163
Cost (% of income per capita)	17.3
Minimum capital (% of income per capita)	0.0

Dealing with licenses (rank)	130
Procedures (number)	24
Time (days)	192
Cost (% of income per capita)	204.1

Employing workers (rank)	71
Difficulty of hiring index (0–100)	11
Rigidity of hours index (0–100)	40
Difficulty of firing index (0–100)	60
Rigidity of employment index (0–100)	37
Nonwage labor cost (% of salary)	5
Firing cost (weeks of salary)	19

East Asia & Pacific
Low income

Registering property (rank)	148
Procedures (number)	9
Time (days)	135
Cost (% of property value)	4.2

Getting credit (rank)	173
Strength of legal rights index (0–10)	2
Depth of credit information index (0–6)	0
Public registry coverage (% of adults)	0.0
Private bureau coverage (% of adults)	0.0

Protecting investors (rank)	170
Extent of disclosure index (0–10)	0
Extent of director liability index (0–10)	3
Ease of shareholder suits index (0–10)	3
Strength of investor protection index (0–10)	2.0

Paying taxes (rank)	36
Payments (number per year)	31
Time (hours per year)	180
Total tax rate (% of profit)	32.5

GNI per capita (US$)	440
Population (m)	5.9

Trading across borders (rank)	161
Documents to export (number)	12
Time to export (days)	66
Cost to export (US$ per container)	1,420
Documents to import (number)	16
Time to import (days)	78
Cost to import (US$ per container)	1,690

Enforcing contracts (rank)	146
Procedures (number)	53
Time (days)	443
Cost (% of claim)	30.3

Closing a business (rank)	151
Time (years)	5.0
Cost (% of estate)	76
Recovery rate (cents on the dollar)	0.0

LATVIA

Ease of doing business (rank)	24

Starting a business (rank)	25
Procedures (number)	5
Time (days)	16
Cost (% of income per capita)	3.5
Minimum capital (% of income per capita)	26.1

Dealing with licenses (rank)	65
Procedures (number)	22
Time (days)	152
Cost (% of income per capita)	36.3

Employing workers (rank)	123
Difficulty of hiring index (0–100)	67
Rigidity of hours index (0–100)	40
Difficulty of firing index (0–100)	70
Rigidity of employment index (0–100)	59
Nonwage labor cost (% of salary)	24
Firing cost (weeks of salary)	17

Eastern Europe & Central Asia
Upper middle income

Registering property (rank)	82
Procedures (number)	8
Time (days)	54
Cost (% of property value)	2.0

Getting credit (rank)	13
Strength of legal rights index (0–10)	8
Depth of credit information index (0–6)	4
Public registry coverage (% of adults)	1.9
Private bureau coverage (% of adults)	0.0

Protecting investors (rank)	46
Extent of disclosure index (0–10)	5
Extent of director liability index (0–10)	4
Ease of shareholder suits index (0–10)	8
Strength of investor protection index (0–10)	5.7

Paying taxes (rank)	52
Payments (number per year)	8
Time (hours per year)	320
Total tax rate (% of profit)	42.6

GNI per capita (US$)	6,760
Population (m)	2.3

Trading across borders (rank)	28
Documents to export (number)	6
Time to export (days)	11
Cost to export (US$ per container)	965
Documents to import (number)	5
Time to import (days)	12
Cost to import (US$ per container)	965

Enforcing contracts (rank)	11
Procedures (number)	21
Time (days)	240
Cost (% of claim)	11.8

Closing a business (rank)	62
Time (years)	3.0
Cost (% of estate)	13
Recovery rate (cents on the dollar)	34.8

LEBANON

		Middle East & North Africa		GNI per capita (US$)	6,180
Ease of doing business (rank)	86	Upper middle income		Population (m)	3.6
Starting a business (rank)	116	**Registering property** (rank)	95	**Trading across borders** (rank)	82
Procedures (number)	6	Procedures (number)	8	Documents to export (number)	6
Time (days)	46	Time (days)	25	Time to export (days)	22
Cost (% of income per capita)	105.4	Cost (% of property value)	5.9	Cost to export (US$ per container)	969
Minimum capital (% of income per capita)	56.5			Documents to import (number)	12
		Getting credit (rank)	48	Time to import (days)	34
Dealing with licenses (rank)	99	Strength of legal rights index (0–10)	4	Cost to import (US$ per container)	752
Procedures (number)	16	Depth of credit information index (0–6)	5		
Time (days)	275	Public registry coverage (% of adults)	4.3	**Enforcing contracts** (rank)	148
Cost (% of income per capita)	176.9	Private bureau coverage (% of adults)	0.0	Procedures (number)	39
				Time (days)	721
Employing workers (rank)	43	**Protecting investors** (rank)	83	Cost (% of claim)	27.8
Difficulty of hiring index (0–100)	33	Extent of disclosure index (0–10)	9		
Rigidity of hours index (0–100)	0	Extent of director liability index (0–10)	1	**Closing a business** (rank)	111
Difficulty of firing index (0–100)	40	Ease of shareholder suits index (0–10)	5	Time (years)	4.0
Rigidity of employment index (0–100)	24	Strength of investor protection index (0–10)	5.0	Cost (% of estate)	22
Nonwage labor cost (% of salary)	22			Recovery rate (cents on the dollar)	19.0
Firing cost (weeks of salary)	17	**Paying taxes** (rank)	54		
		Payments (number per year)	33		
		Time (hours per year)	208		
		Total tax rate (% of profit)	37.3		

LESOTHO

		Sub-Saharan Africa		GNI per capita (US$)	960
Ease of doing business (rank)	114	Lower middle income		Population (m)	1.8
Starting a business (rank)	113	**Registering property** (rank)	129	**Trading across borders** (rank)	121
Procedures (number)	8	Procedures (number)	6	Documents to export (number)	6
Time (days)	73	Time (days)	101	Time to export (days)	46
Cost (% of income per capita)	39.9	Cost (% of property value)	8.4	Cost to export (US$ per container)	1,270
Minimum capital (% of income per capita)	15.7			Documents to import (number)	9
		Getting credit (rank)	117	Time to import (days)	51
Dealing with licenses (rank)	75	Strength of legal rights index (0–10)	5	Cost to import (US$ per container)	1,270
Procedures (number)	14	Depth of credit information index (0–6)	0		
Time (days)	265	Public registry coverage (% of adults)	0.0	**Enforcing contracts** (rank)	130
Cost (% of income per capita)	128.3	Private bureau coverage (% of adults)	0.0	Procedures (number)	58
				Time (days)	695
Employing workers (rank)	91	**Protecting investors** (rank)	142	Cost (% of claim)	10.6
Difficulty of hiring index (0–100)	56	Extent of disclosure index (0–10)	2		
Rigidity of hours index (0–100)	40	Extent of director liability index (0–10)	1	**Closing a business** (rank)	57
Difficulty of firing index (0–100)	10	Ease of shareholder suits index (0–10)	8	Time (years)	2.6
Rigidity of employment index (0–100)	35	Strength of investor protection index (0–10)	3.7	Cost (% of estate)	8
Nonwage labor cost (% of salary)	0			Recovery rate (cents on the dollar)	36.6
Firing cost (weeks of salary)	44	**Paying taxes** (rank)	44		
		Payments (number per year)	21		
		Time (hours per year)	352		
		Total tax rate (% of profit)	25.6		

LITHUANIA

		Eastern Europe & Central Asia		GNI per capita (US$)	7,050
Ease of doing business (rank)	16	Upper middle income		Population (m)	3.4
Starting a business (rank)	48	**Registering property** (rank)	3	**Trading across borders** (rank)	32
Procedures (number)	7	Procedures (number)	3	Documents to export (number)	5
Time (days)	26	Time (days)	3	Time to export (days)	6
Cost (% of income per capita)	2.8	Cost (% of property value)	0.7	Cost to export (US$ per container)	704
Minimum capital (% of income per capita)	48.8			Documents to import (number)	12
		Getting credit (rank)	33	Time to import (days)	17
Dealing with licenses (rank)	23	Strength of legal rights index (0–10)	4	Cost to import (US$ per container)	782
Procedures (number)	14	Depth of credit information index (0–6)	6		
Time (days)	151	Public registry coverage (% of adults)	4.2	**Enforcing contracts** (rank)	4
Cost (% of income per capita)	18.2	Private bureau coverage (% of adults)	7.2	Procedures (number)	24
				Time (days)	166
Employing workers (rank)	119	**Protecting investors** (rank)	60	Cost (% of claim)	8.6
Difficulty of hiring index (0–100)	33	Extent of disclosure index (0–10)	6		
Rigidity of hours index (0–100)	80	Extent of director liability index (0–10)	4	**Closing a business** (rank)	30
Difficulty of firing index (0–100)	30	Ease of shareholder suits index (0–10)	6	Time (years)	1.7
Rigidity of employment index (0–100)	48	Strength of investor protection index (0–10)	5.3	Cost (% of estate)	7
Nonwage labor cost (% of salary)	31			Recovery rate (cents on the dollar)	50.5
Firing cost (weeks of salary)	30	**Paying taxes** (rank)	40		
		Payments (number per year)	13		
		Time (hours per year)	162		
		Total tax rate (% of profit)	48.4		

FYR MACEDONIA

		Eastern Europe & Central Asia		GNI per capita (US$)	2,830
Ease of doing business (rank)	92	Lower middle income		Population (m)	2.0

Starting a business (rank)	76	**Registering property** (rank)	87	**Trading across borders** (rank)	127
Procedures (number)	10	Procedures (number)	6	Documents to export (number)	10
Time (days)	18	Time (days)	98	Time to export (days)	32
Cost (% of income per capita)	7.4	Cost (% of property value)	3.5	Cost to export (US$ per container)	1,070
Minimum capital (% of income per capita)	112.0			Documents to import (number)	10
		Getting credit (rank)	48	Time to import (days)	35
Dealing with licenses (rank)	86	Strength of legal rights index (0–10)	6	Cost to import (US$ per container)	1,070
Procedures (number)	18	Depth of credit information index (0–6)	3		
Time (days)	222	Public registry coverage (% of adults)	2.1	**Enforcing contracts** (rank)	72
Cost (% of income per capita)	89.8	Private bureau coverage (% of adults)	0.0	Procedures (number)	27
				Time (days)	385
Employing workers (rank)	117	**Protecting investors** (rank)	83	Cost (% of claim)	32.8
Difficulty of hiring index (0–100)	61	Extent of disclosure index (0–10)	5		
Rigidity of hours index (0–100)	60	Extent of director liability index (0–10)	6	**Closing a business** (rank)	123
Difficulty of firing index (0–100)	40	Ease of shareholder suits index (0–10)	4	Time (years)	3.7
Rigidity of employment index (0–100)	54	Strength of investor protection index (0–10)	5.0	Cost (% of estate)	28
Nonwage labor cost (% of salary)	33			Recovery rate (cents on the dollar)	15.5
Firing cost (weeks of salary)	22	**Paying taxes** (rank)	79		
		Payments (number per year)	54		
		Time (hours per year)	96		
		Total tax rate (% of profit)	43.5		

MADAGASCAR

		Sub-Saharan Africa		GNI per capita (US$)	290
Ease of doing business (rank)	149	Low income		Population (m)	18.6

Starting a business (rank)	110	**Registering property** (rank)	162	**Trading across borders** (rank)	131
Procedures (number)	10	Procedures (number)	8	Documents to export (number)	8
Time (days)	21	Time (days)	134	Time to export (days)	48
Cost (% of income per capita)	35.0	Cost (% of property value)	11.6	Cost to export (US$ per container)	982
Minimum capital (% of income per capita)	373.1			Documents to import (number)	11
		Getting credit (rank)	159	Time to import (days)	48
Dealing with licenses (rank)	152	Strength of legal rights index (0–10)	2	Cost to import (US$ per container)	1,282
Procedures (number)	19	Depth of credit information index (0–6)	1		
Time (days)	297	Public registry coverage (% of adults)	0.3	**Enforcing contracts** (rank)	106
Cost (% of income per capita)	387.1	Private bureau coverage (% of adults)	0.0	Procedures (number)	29
				Time (days)	591
Employing workers (rank)	136	**Protecting investors** (rank)	46	Cost (% of claim)	22.8
Difficulty of hiring index (0–100)	72	Extent of disclosure index (0–10)	5		
Rigidity of hours index (0–100)	60	Extent of director liability index (0–10)	6	**Closing a business** (rank)	151
Difficulty of firing index (0–100)	40	Ease of shareholder suits index (0–10)	6	Time (years)	NO PRACTICE
Rigidity of employment index (0–100)	57	Strength of investor protection index (0–10)	5.7	Cost (% of estate)	NO PRACTICE
Nonwage labor cost (% of salary)	18			Recovery rate (cents on the dollar)	0.0
Firing cost (weeks of salary)	30	**Paying taxes** (rank)	86		
		Payments (number per year)	25		
		Time (hours per year)	304		
		Total tax rate (% of profit)	43.2		

MALAWI

		Sub-Saharan Africa		GNI per capita (US$)	160
Ease of doing business (rank)	110	Low income		Population (m)	12.9

Starting a business (rank)	89	**Registering property** (rank)	90	**Trading across borders** (rank)	153
Procedures (number)	10	Procedures (number)	6	Documents to export (number)	8
Time (days)	37	Time (days)	118	Time to export (days)	44
Cost (% of income per capita)	134.7	Cost (% of property value)	3.4	Cost to export (US$ per container)	1,565
Minimum capital (% of income per capita)	0.0			Documents to import (number)	16
		Getting credit (rank)	65	Time to import (days)	60
Dealing with licenses (rank)	117	Strength of legal rights index (0–10)	8	Cost to import (US$ per container)	1,590
Procedures (number)	22	Depth of credit information index (0–6)	0		
Time (days)	185	Public registry coverage (% of adults)	0.0	**Enforcing contracts** (rank)	134
Cost (% of income per capita)	236.2	Private bureau coverage (% of adults)	0.0	Procedures (number)	40
				Time (days)	337
Employing workers (rank)	68	**Protecting investors** (rank)	60	Cost (% of claim)	136.5
Difficulty of hiring index (0–100)	22	Extent of disclosure index (0–10)	4		
Rigidity of hours index (0–100)	20	Extent of director liability index (0–10)	7	**Closing a business** (rank)	132
Difficulty of firing index (0–100)	20	Ease of shareholder suits index (0–10)	5	Time (years)	2.6
Rigidity of employment index (0–100)	21	Strength of investor protection index (0–10)	5.3	Cost (% of estate)	30
Nonwage labor cost (% of salary)	1			Recovery rate (cents on the dollar)	13.2
Firing cost (weeks of salary)	84	**Paying taxes** (rank)	90		
		Payments (number per year)	29		
		Time (hours per year)	878		
		Total tax rate (% of profit)	32.6		

MALAYSIA

		East Asia & Pacific		GNI per capita (US$)	4,960
Ease of doing business (rank)	25	Upper middle income		Population (m)	25.3

Starting a business (rank)	71	**Registering property** (rank)	66	**Trading across borders** (rank)	46
Procedures (number)	9	Procedures (number)	5	Documents to export (number)	6
Time (days)	30	Time (days)	144	Time to export (days)	20
Cost (% of income per capita)	19.7	Cost (% of property value)	2.4	Cost to export (US$ per container)	481
Minimum capital (% of income per capita)	0.0			Documents to import (number)	12
		Getting credit (rank)	3	Time to import (days)	22
Dealing with licenses (rank)	137	Strength of legal rights index (0–10)	8	Cost to import (US$ per container)	428
Procedures (number)	25	Depth of credit information index (0–6)	6		
Time (days)	281	Public registry coverage (% of adults)	42.2	**Enforcing contracts** (rank)	81
Cost (% of income per capita)	78.2	Private bureau coverage (% of adults)	..	Procedures (number)	31
				Time (days)	450
Employing workers (rank)	38	**Protecting investors** (rank)	4	Cost (% of claim)	21.3
Difficulty of hiring index (0–100)	0	Extent of disclosure index (0–10)	10		
Rigidity of hours index (0–100)	20	Extent of director liability index (0–10)	9	**Closing a business** (rank)	51
Difficulty of firing index (0–100)	10	Ease of shareholder suits index (0–10)	7	Time (years)	2.3
Rigidity of employment index (0–100)	10	Strength of investor protection index (0–10)	8.7	Cost (% of estate)	15
Nonwage labor cost (% of salary)	13			Recovery rate (cents on the dollar)	38.7
Firing cost (weeks of salary)	88	**Paying taxes** (rank)	49		
		Payments (number per year)	35		
		Time (hours per year)	190		
		Total tax rate (% of profit)	35.2		

MALDIVES

		South Asia		GNI per capita (US$)	2,390
Ease of doing business (rank)	53	Lower middle income		Population (m)	0.3

Starting a business (rank)	31	**Registering property** (rank)	172	**Trading across borders** (rank)	91
Procedures (number)	5	Procedures (number)	NO PRACTICE	Documents to export (number)	8
Time (days)	13	Time (days)	NO PRACTICE	Time to export (days)	15
Cost (% of income per capita)	18.1	Cost (% of property value)	NO PRACTICE	Cost to export (US$ per container)	1,000
Minimum capital (% of income per capita)	6.6			Documents to import (number)	9
		Getting credit (rank)	143	Time to import (days)	21
Dealing with licenses (rank)	9	Strength of legal rights index (0–10)	4	Cost to import (US$ per container)	1,784
Procedures (number)	10	Depth of credit information index (0–6)	0		
Time (days)	118	Public registry coverage (% of adults)	0.0	**Enforcing contracts** (rank)	83
Cost (% of income per capita)	40.2	Private bureau coverage (% of adults)	0.0	Procedures (number)	28
				Time (days)	665
Employing workers (rank)	5	**Protecting investors** (rank)	60	Cost (% of claim)	16.2
Difficulty of hiring index (0–100)	0	Extent of disclosure index (0–10)	0		
Rigidity of hours index (0–100)	0	Extent of director liability index (0–10)	8	**Closing a business** (rank)	114
Difficulty of firing index (0–100)	0	Ease of shareholder suits index (0–10)	8	Time (years)	6.7
Rigidity of employment index (0–100)	0	Strength of investor protection index (0–10)	5.3	Cost (% of estate)	4
Nonwage labor cost (% of salary)	0			Recovery rate (cents on the dollar)	18.2
Firing cost (weeks of salary)	9	**Paying taxes** (rank)	1		
		Payments (number per year)	1		
		Time (hours per year)	0		
		Total tax rate (% of profit)	9.3		

MALI

		Sub-Saharan Africa		GNI per capita (US$)	380
Ease of doing business (rank)	155	Low income		Population (m)	13.5

Starting a business (rank)	163	**Registering property** (rank)	93	**Trading across borders** (rank)	167
Procedures (number)	13	Procedures (number)	5	Documents to export (number)	10
Time (days)	42	Time (days)	33	Time to export (days)	66
Cost (% of income per capita)	201.9	Cost (% of property value)	20.7	Cost to export (US$ per container)	1,752
Minimum capital (% of income per capita)	519.8			Documents to import (number)	16
		Getting credit (rank)	143	Time to import (days)	61
Dealing with licenses (rank)	122	Strength of legal rights index (0–10)	3	Cost to import (US$ per container)	2,680
Procedures (number)	15	Depth of credit information index (0–6)	1		
Time (days)	209	Public registry coverage (% of adults)	2.9	**Enforcing contracts** (rank)	140
Cost (% of income per capita)	1813.2	Private bureau coverage (% of adults)	0.0	Procedures (number)	28
				Time (days)	860
Employing workers (rank)	131	**Protecting investors** (rank)	99	Cost (% of claim)	45.0
Difficulty of hiring index (0–100)	44	Extent of disclosure index (0–10)	6		
Rigidity of hours index (0–100)	60	Extent of director liability index (0–10)	5	**Closing a business** (rank)	99
Difficulty of firing index (0–100)	50	Ease of shareholder suits index (0–10)	3	Time (years)	3.6
Rigidity of employment index (0–100)	51	Strength of investor protection index (0–10)	4.7	Cost (% of estate)	18
Nonwage labor cost (% of salary)	27			Recovery rate (cents on the dollar)	23.7
Firing cost (weeks of salary)	31	**Paying taxes** (rank)	141		
		Payments (number per year)	60		
		Time (hours per year)	270		
		Total tax rate (% of profit)	50.0		

MARSHALL ISLANDS

		East Asia & Pacific		GNI per capita (US$)	2,930
Ease of doing business (rank)	87	Lower middle income		Population (m)	0.1

Starting a business (rank)	13	**Registering property** (rank)	172	**Trading across borders** (rank)	90
Procedures (number)	5	Procedures (number)	NO PRACTICE	Documents to export (number)	..
Time (days)	17	Time (days)	NO PRACTICE	Time to export (days)	..
Cost (% of income per capita)	18.1	Cost (% of property value)	NO PRACTICE	Cost to export (US$ per container)	..
Minimum capital (% of income per capita)	0.0			Documents to import (number)	9
		Getting credit (rank)	117	Time to import (days)	15
Dealing with licenses (rank)	5	Strength of legal rights index (0–10)	5	Cost to import (US$ per container)	2,115
Procedures (number)	9	Depth of credit information index (0–6)	0		
Time (days)	81	Public registry coverage (% of adults)	0.0	**Enforcing contracts** (rank)	103
Cost (% of income per capita)	37.6	Private bureau coverage (% of adults)	0.0	Procedures (number)	34
				Time (days)	432
Employing workers (rank)	1	**Protecting investors** (rank)	151	Cost (% of claim)	26.5
Difficulty of hiring index (0–100)	0	Extent of disclosure index (0–10)	2		
Rigidity of hours index (0–100)	0	Extent of director liability index (0–10)	0	**Closing a business** (rank)	117
Difficulty of firing index (0–100)	0	Ease of shareholder suits index (0–10)	8	Time (years)	2.0
Rigidity of employment index (0–100)	0	Strength of investor protection index (0–10)	3.3	Cost (% of estate)	38
Nonwage labor cost (% of salary)	11			Recovery rate (cents on the dollar)	17.9
Firing cost (weeks of salary)	0	**Paying taxes** (rank)	69		
		Payments (number per year)	20		
		Time (hours per year)	128		
		Total tax rate (% of profit)	66.6		

MAURITANIA

		Sub-Saharan Africa		GNI per capita (US$)	560
Ease of doing business (rank)	148	Low income		Population (m)	3.1

Starting a business (rank)	164	**Registering property** (rank)	55	**Trading across borders** (rank)	142
Procedures (number)	11	Procedures (number)	4	Documents to export (number)	9
Time (days)	82	Time (days)	49	Time to export (days)	25
Cost (% of income per capita)	121.6	Cost (% of property value)	5.2	Cost to export (US$ per container)	3,733
Minimum capital (% of income per capita)	632.0			Documents to import (number)	7
		Getting credit (rank)	101	Time to import (days)	40
Dealing with licenses (rank)	105	Strength of legal rights index (0–10)	5	Cost to import (US$ per container)	3,733
Procedures (number)	19	Depth of credit information index (0–6)	1		
Time (days)	152	Public registry coverage (% of adults)	0.2	**Enforcing contracts** (rank)	85
Cost (% of income per capita)	710.9	Private bureau coverage (% of adults)	0.0	Procedures (number)	40
				Time (days)	400
Employing workers (rank)	142	**Protecting investors** (rank)	..	Cost (% of claim)	17.9
Difficulty of hiring index (0–100)	67	Extent of disclosure index (0–10)	..		
Rigidity of hours index (0–100)	60	Extent of director liability index (0–10)	..	**Closing a business** (rank)	141
Difficulty of firing index (0–100)	50	Ease of shareholder suits index (0–10)	..	Time (years)	8.0
Rigidity of employment index (0–100)	59	Strength of investor protection index (0–10)	..	Cost (% of estate)	9
Nonwage labor cost (% of salary)	16			Recovery rate (cents on the dollar)	7.8
Firing cost (weeks of salary)	31	**Paying taxes** (rank)	173		
		Payments (number per year)	61		
		Time (hours per year)	696		
		Total tax rate (% of profit)	104.3		

MAURITIUS

		Sub-Saharan Africa		GNI per capita (US$)	5,260
Ease of doing business (rank)	32	Upper middle income		Population (m)	1.2

Starting a business (rank)	30	**Registering property** (rank)	156	**Trading across borders** (rank)	21
Procedures (number)	6	Procedures (number)	6	Documents to export (number)	5
Time (days)	46	Time (days)	210	Time to export (days)	16
Cost (% of income per capita)	8.0	Cost (% of property value)	15.8	Cost to export (US$ per container)	683
Minimum capital (% of income per capita)	0.0			Documents to import (number)	7
		Getting credit (rank)	83	Time to import (days)	16
Dealing with licenses (rank)	49	Strength of legal rights index (0–10)	6	Cost to import (US$ per container)	683
Procedures (number)	21	Depth of credit information index (0–6)	1		
Time (days)	145	Public registry coverage (% of adults)	10.2	**Enforcing contracts** (rank)	109
Cost (% of income per capita)	13.7	Private bureau coverage (% of adults)	0.0	Procedures (number)	37
				Time (days)	630
Employing workers (rank)	64	**Protecting investors** (rank)	11	Cost (% of claim)	15.7
Difficulty of hiring index (0–100)	0	Extent of disclosure index (0–10)	6		
Rigidity of hours index (0–100)	40	Extent of director liability index (0–10)	8	**Closing a business** (rank)	67
Difficulty of firing index (0–100)	50	Ease of shareholder suits index (0–10)	9	Time (years)	1.7
Rigidity of employment index (0–100)	30	Strength of investor protection index (0–10)	7.7	Cost (% of estate)	15
Nonwage labor cost (% of salary)	6			Recovery rate (cents on the dollar)	34.3
Firing cost (weeks of salary)	35	**Paying taxes** (rank)	11		
		Payments (number per year)	7		
		Time (hours per year)	158		
		Total tax rate (% of profit)	24.8		

MEXICO

		Latin America & Caribbean		GNI per capita (US$)		7,310
Ease of doing business (rank)	43	Upper middle income		Population (m)		103.1

Starting a business (rank)	61	**Registering property** (rank)	79	**Trading across borders** (rank)	86
Procedures (number)	8	Procedures (number)	5	Documents to export (number)	6
Time (days)	27	Time (days)	74	Time to export (days)	17
Cost (% of income per capita)	14.2	Cost (% of property value)	5.2	Cost to export (US$ per container)	1,049
Minimum capital (% of income per capita)	12.5			Documents to import (number)	8
		Getting credit (rank)	65	Time to import (days)	26
Dealing with licenses (rank)	30	Strength of legal rights index (0–10)	2	Cost to import (US$ per container)	2,152
Procedures (number)	12	Depth of credit information index (0–6)	6		
Time (days)	142	Public registry coverage (% of adults)	0.0	**Enforcing contracts** (rank)	87
Cost (% of income per capita)	104.5	Private bureau coverage (% of adults)	69.5	Procedures (number)	37
				Time (days)	415
Employing workers (rank)	108	**Protecting investors** (rank)	33	Cost (% of claim)	20.0
Difficulty of hiring index (0–100)	33	Extent of disclosure index (0–10)	8		
Rigidity of hours index (0–100)	40	Extent of director liability index (0–10)	5	**Closing a business** (rank)	25
Difficulty of firing index (0–100)	40	Ease of shareholder suits index (0–10)	5	Time (years)	1.8
Rigidity of employment index (0–100)	38	Strength of investor protection index (0–10)	6.0	Cost (% of estate)	18
Nonwage labor cost (% of salary)	24			Recovery rate (cents on the dollar)	63.2
Firing cost (weeks of salary)	74	**Paying taxes** (rank)	126		
		Payments (number per year)	49		
		Time (hours per year)	552		
		Total tax rate (% of profit)	37.1		

MICRONESIA

		East Asia & Pacific		GNI per capita (US$)		2,300
Ease of doing business (rank)	106	Lower middle income		Population (m)		0.1

Starting a business (rank)	39	**Registering property** (rank)	172	**Trading across borders** (rank)	40
Procedures (number)	7	Procedures (number)	NO PRACTICE	Documents to export (number)	..
Time (days)	16	Time (days)	NO PRACTICE	Time to export (days)	..
Cost (% of income per capita)	135.9	Cost (% of property value)	NO PRACTICE	Cost to export (US$ per container)	..
Minimum capital (% of income per capita)	0.0			Documents to import (number)	7
		Getting credit (rank)	101	Time to import (days)	21
Dealing with licenses (rank)	11	Strength of legal rights index (0–10)	6	Cost to import (US$ per container)	895
Procedures (number)	15	Depth of credit information index (0–6)	0		
Time (days)	73	Public registry coverage (% of adults)	0.0	**Enforcing contracts** (rank)	139
Cost (% of income per capita)	21.3	Private bureau coverage (% of adults)	0.0	Procedures (number)	25
				Time (days)	775
Employing workers (rank)	12	**Protecting investors** (rank)	162	Cost (% of claim)	77.0
Difficulty of hiring index (0–100)	33	Extent of disclosure index (0–10)	0		
Rigidity of hours index (0–100)	0	Extent of director liability index (0–10)	0	**Closing a business** (rank)	148
Difficulty of firing index (0–100)	0	Ease of shareholder suits index (0–10)	8	Time (years)	5.3
Rigidity of employment index (0–100)	11	Strength of investor protection index (0–10)	2.7	Cost (% of estate)	38
Nonwage labor cost (% of salary)	6			Recovery rate (cents on the dollar)	3.1
Firing cost (weeks of salary)	0	**Paying taxes** (rank)	45		
		Payments (number per year)	9		
		Time (hours per year)	128		
		Total tax rate (% of profit)	61.3		

MOLDOVA

		Eastern Europe & Central Asia		GNI per capita (US$)		880
Ease of doing business (rank)	103	Lower middle income		Population (m)		4.2

Starting a business (rank)	84	**Registering property** (rank)	47	**Trading across borders** (rank)	105
Procedures (number)	10	Procedures (number)	6	Documents to export (number)	7
Time (days)	30	Time (days)	48	Time to export (days)	33
Cost (% of income per capita)	13.3	Cost (% of property value)	1.5	Cost to export (US$ per container)	1,185
Minimum capital (% of income per capita)	18.8			Documents to import (number)	7
		Getting credit (rank)	101	Time to import (days)	35
Dealing with licenses (rank)	119	Strength of legal rights index (0–10)	6	Cost to import (US$ per container)	1,285
Procedures (number)	34	Depth of credit information index (0–6)	0		
Time (days)	158	Public registry coverage (% of adults)	0.0	**Enforcing contracts** (rank)	55
Cost (% of income per capita)	165.0	Private bureau coverage (% of adults)	0.0	Procedures (number)	37
				Time (days)	310
Employing workers (rank)	128	**Protecting investors** (rank)	99	Cost (% of claim)	16.2
Difficulty of hiring index (0–100)	33	Extent of disclosure index (0–10)	7		
Rigidity of hours index (0–100)	60	Extent of director liability index (0–10)	1	**Closing a business** (rank)	78
Difficulty of firing index (0–100)	70	Ease of shareholder suits index (0–10)	6	Time (years)	2.8
Rigidity of employment index (0–100)	54	Strength of investor protection index (0–10)	4.7	Cost (% of estate)	9
Nonwage labor cost (% of salary)	29			Recovery rate (cents on the dollar)	29.4
Firing cost (weeks of salary)	29	**Paying taxes** (rank)	119		
		Payments (number per year)	44		
		Time (hours per year)	250		
		Total tax rate (% of profit)	48.8		

MONGOLIA

		East Asia & Pacific		GNI per capita (US$)	690
Ease of doing business (rank)	45	Low income		Population (m)	2.6

Starting a business (rank)	55	**Registering property** (rank)	17	**Trading across borders** (rank)	162
Procedures (number)	8	Procedures (number)	5	Documents to export (number)	11
Time (days)	20	Time (days)	11	Time to export (days)	66
Cost (% of income per capita)	5.1	Cost (% of property value)	2.2	Cost to export (US$ per container)	3,007
Minimum capital (% of income per capita)	115.3			Documents to import (number)	10
		Getting credit (rank)	65	Time to import (days)	74
Dealing with licenses (rank)	34	Strength of legal rights index (0–10)	5	Cost to import (US$ per container)	3,030
Procedures (number)	18	Depth of credit information index (0–6)	3		
Time (days)	96	Public registry coverage (% of adults)	10.2	**Enforcing contracts** (rank)	41
Cost (% of income per capita)	48.4	Private bureau coverage (% of adults)	0.0	Procedures (number)	29
				Time (days)	314
Employing workers (rank)	61	**Protecting investors** (rank)	19	Cost (% of claim)	17.6
Difficulty of hiring index (0–100)	11	Extent of disclosure index (0–10)	5		
Rigidity of hours index (0–100)	80	Extent of director liability index (0–10)	8	**Closing a business** (rank)	115
Difficulty of firing index (0–100)	10	Ease of shareholder suits index (0–10)	6	Time (years)	4.0
Rigidity of employment index (0–100)	34	Strength of investor protection index (0–10)	6.3	Cost (% of estate)	8
Nonwage labor cost (% of salary)	20			Recovery rate (cents on the dollar)	18.0
Firing cost (weeks of salary)	9	**Paying taxes** (rank)	56		
		Payments (number per year)	42		
		Time (hours per year)	204		
		Total tax rate (% of profit)	32.2		

MONTENEGRO

		Eastern Europe & Central Asia		GNI per capita (US$)	3,600
Ease of doing business (rank)	70	Lower middle income		Population (m)	0.6

Starting a business (rank)	83	**Registering property** (rank)	106	**Trading across borders** (rank)	80
Procedures (number)	15	Procedures (number)	8	Documents to export (number)	6
Time (days)	24	Time (days)	86	Time to export (days)	19
Cost (% of income per capita)	6.6	Cost (% of property value)	2.5	Cost to export (US$ per container)	1,515
Minimum capital (% of income per capita)	0.0			Documents to import (number)	8
		Getting credit (rank)	83	Time to import (days)	17
Dealing with licenses (rank)	154	Strength of legal rights index (0–10)	7	Cost to import (US$ per container)	1,715
Procedures (number)	22	Depth of credit information index (0–6)	0		
Time (days)	179	Public registry coverage (% of adults)	0.0	**Enforcing contracts** (rank)	115
Cost (% of income per capita)	5869.2	Private bureau coverage (% of adults)	0.0	Procedures (number)	49
				Time (days)	545
Employing workers (rank)	76	**Protecting investors** (rank)	19	Cost (% of claim)	15.0
Difficulty of hiring index (0–100)	33	Extent of disclosure index (0–10)	5		
Rigidity of hours index (0–100)	40	Extent of director liability index (0–10)	8	**Closing a business** (rank)	43
Difficulty of firing index (0–100)	30	Ease of shareholder suits index (0–10)	6	Time (years)	2.0
Rigidity of employment index (0–100)	34	Strength of investor protection index (0–10)	6.3	Cost (% of estate)	9
Nonwage labor cost (% of salary)	16			Recovery rate (cents on the dollar)	41.0
Firing cost (weeks of salary)	39	**Paying taxes** (rank)	97		
		Payments (number per year)	75		
		Time (hours per year)	208		
		Total tax rate (% of profit)	33.9		

MOROCCO

		Middle East & North Africa		GNI per capita (US$)	1,730
Ease of doing business (rank)	115	Lower middle income		Population (m)	30.2

Starting a business (rank)	47	**Registering property** (rank)	45	**Trading across borders** (rank)	77
Procedures (number)	6	Procedures (number)	4	Documents to export (number)	6
Time (days)	12	Time (days)	46	Time to export (days)	18
Cost (% of income per capita)	12.7	Cost (% of property value)	4.4	Cost to export (US$ per container)	700
Minimum capital (% of income per capita)	66.7			Documents to import (number)	11
		Getting credit (rank)	143	Time to import (days)	30
Dealing with licenses (rank)	133	Strength of legal rights index (0–10)	3	Cost to import (US$ per container)	1,500
Procedures (number)	21	Depth of credit information index (0–6)	1		
Time (days)	217	Public registry coverage (% of adults)	2.3	**Enforcing contracts** (rank)	127
Cost (% of income per capita)	264.9	Private bureau coverage (% of adults)	0.0	Procedures (number)	42
				Time (days)	615
Employing workers (rank)	156	**Protecting investors** (rank)	118	Cost (% of claim)	16.5
Difficulty of hiring index (0–100)	100	Extent of disclosure index (0–10)	6		
Rigidity of hours index (0–100)	40	Extent of director liability index (0–10)	6	**Closing a business** (rank)	61
Difficulty of firing index (0–100)	50	Ease of shareholder suits index (0–10)	1	Time (years)	1.8
Rigidity of employment index (0–100)	63	Strength of investor protection index (0–10)	4.3	Cost (% of estate)	18
Nonwage labor cost (% of salary)	18			Recovery rate (cents on the dollar)	35.1
Firing cost (weeks of salary)	85	**Paying taxes** (rank)	128		
		Payments (number per year)	28		
		Time (hours per year)	468		
		Total tax rate (% of profit)	52.7		

MOZAMBIQUE

Ease of doing business (rank)	140	Sub-Saharan Africa			GNI per capita (US$)	310
		Low income			Population (m)	19.8

Starting a business (rank)	153	**Registering property** (rank)	105	**Trading across borders** (rank)	141
Procedures (number)	13	Procedures (number)	8	Documents to export (number)	6
Time (days)	113	Time (days)	42	Time to export (days)	39
Cost (% of income per capita)	85.7	Cost (% of property value)	5.4	Cost to export (US$ per container)	1,516
Minimum capital (% of income per capita)	10.4			Documents to import (number)	16
		Getting credit (rank)	83	Time to import (days)	38
Dealing with licenses (rank)	103	Strength of legal rights index (0–10)	4	Cost to import (US$ per container)	1,616
Procedures (number)	13	Depth of credit information index (0–6)	3		
Time (days)	364	Public registry coverage (% of adults)	0.7	**Enforcing contracts** (rank)	168
Cost (% of income per capita)	279.3	Private bureau coverage (% of adults)	0.0	Procedures (number)	38
				Time (days)	1010
Employing workers (rank)	157	**Protecting investors** (rank)	83	Cost (% of claim)	132.1
Difficulty of hiring index (0–100)	83	Extent of disclosure index (0–10)	7		
Rigidity of hours index (0–100)	60	Extent of director liability index (0–10)	2	**Closing a business** (rank)	126
Difficulty of firing index (0–100)	20	Ease of shareholder suits index (0–10)	6	Time (years)	5.0
Rigidity of employment index (0–100)	54	Strength of investor protection index (0–10)	5.0	Cost (% of estate)	9
Nonwage labor cost (% of salary)	4			Recovery rate (cents on the dollar)	15.0
Firing cost (weeks of salary)	143	**Paying taxes** (rank)	80		
		Payments (number per year)	36		
		Time (hours per year)	230		
		Total tax rate (% of profit)	39.2		

NAMIBIA

Ease of doing business (rank)	42	Sub-Saharan Africa			GNI per capita (US$)	2,990
		Lower middle income			Population (m)	2.0

Starting a business (rank)	86	**Registering property** (rank)	127	**Trading across borders** (rank)	144
Procedures (number)	10	Procedures (number)	9	Documents to export (number)	9
Time (days)	95	Time (days)	23	Time to export (days)	32
Cost (% of income per capita)	18.0	Cost (% of property value)	10.0	Cost to export (US$ per container)	1,672
Minimum capital (% of income per capita)	0.0			Documents to import (number)	14
		Getting credit (rank)	33	Time to import (days)	25
Dealing with licenses (rank)	19	Strength of legal rights index (0–10)	5	Cost to import (US$ per container)	1,549
Procedures (number)	11	Depth of credit information index (0–6)	5		
Time (days)	105	Public registry coverage (% of adults)	0.0	**Enforcing contracts** (rank)	64
Cost (% of income per capita)	134.9	Private bureau coverage (% of adults)	35.2	Procedures (number)	31
				Time (days)	270
Employing workers (rank)	44	**Protecting investors** (rank)	60	Cost (% of claim)	28.3
Difficulty of hiring index (0–100)	0	Extent of disclosure index (0–10)	5		
Rigidity of hours index (0–100)	60	Extent of director liability index (0–10)	5	**Closing a business** (rank)	42
Difficulty of firing index (0–100)	20	Ease of shareholder suits index (0–10)	6	Time (years)	1.5
Rigidity of employment index (0–100)	27	Strength of investor protection index (0–10)	5.3	Cost (% of estate)	15
Nonwage labor cost (% of salary)	0			Recovery rate (cents on the dollar)	41.3
Firing cost (weeks of salary)	24	**Paying taxes** (rank)	28		
		Payments (number per year)	34		
		Time (hours per year)	..		
		Total tax rate (% of profit)	25.6		

NEPAL

Ease of doing business (rank)	100	South Asia			GNI per capita (US$)	270
		Low income			Population (m)	27.1

Starting a business (rank)	49	**Registering property** (rank)	25	**Trading across borders** (rank)	136
Procedures (number)	7	Procedures (number)	3	Documents to export (number)	7
Time (days)	31	Time (days)	5	Time to export (days)	44
Cost (% of income per capita)	78.5	Cost (% of property value)	6.4	Cost to export (US$ per container)	1,599
Minimum capital (% of income per capita)	0.0			Documents to import (number)	10
		Getting credit (rank)	101	Time to import (days)	37
Dealing with licenses (rank)	127	Strength of legal rights index (0–10)	4	Cost to import (US$ per container)	1,800
Procedures (number)	15	Depth of credit information index (0–6)	2		
Time (days)	424	Public registry coverage (% of adults)	0.0	**Enforcing contracts** (rank)	105
Cost (% of income per capita)	324.0	Private bureau coverage (% of adults)	0.1	Procedures (number)	28
				Time (days)	590
Employing workers (rank)	150	**Protecting investors** (rank)	60	Cost (% of claim)	24.4
Difficulty of hiring index (0–100)	67	Extent of disclosure index (0–10)	6		
Rigidity of hours index (0–100)	20	Extent of director liability index (0–10)	1	**Closing a business** (rank)	95
Difficulty of firing index (0–100)	70	Ease of shareholder suits index (0–10)	9	Time (years)	5.0
Rigidity of employment index (0–100)	52	Strength of investor protection index (0–10)	5.3	Cost (% of estate)	9
Nonwage labor cost (% of salary)	10			Recovery rate (cents on the dollar)	24.5
Firing cost (weeks of salary)	90	**Paying taxes** (rank)	88		
		Payments (number per year)	35		
		Time (hours per year)	408		
		Total tax rate (% of profit)	32.8		

NETHERLANDS

		OECD: High Income		GNI per capita (US$)	36,620
Ease of doing business (rank)	22	High income		Population (m)	16.3

Starting a business (rank)	38
Procedures (number)	6
Time (days)	10
Cost (% of income per capita)	7.2
Minimum capital (% of income per capita)	62.3

Dealing with licenses (rank)	80
Procedures (number)	18
Time (days)	184
Cost (% of income per capita)	137.6

Employing workers (rank)	86
Difficulty of hiring index (0–100)	17
Rigidity of hours index (0–100)	40
Difficulty of firing index (0–100)	70
Rigidity of employment index (0–100)	42
Nonwage labor cost (% of salary)	18
Firing cost (weeks of salary)	17

Registering property (rank)	20
Procedures (number)	2
Time (days)	5
Cost (% of property value)	6.2

Getting credit (rank)	13
Strength of legal rights index (0–10)	7
Depth of credit information index (0–6)	5
Public registry coverage (% of adults)	0.0
Private bureau coverage (% of adults)	68.9

Protecting investors (rank)	99
Extent of disclosure index (0–10)	4
Extent of director liability index (0–10)	4
Ease of shareholder suits index (0–10)	6
Strength of investor protection index (0–10)	4.7

Paying taxes (rank)	82
Payments (number per year)	22
Time (hours per year)	250
Total tax rate (% of profit)	48.1

Trading across borders (rank)	16
Documents to export (number)	5
Time to export (days)	7
Cost to export (US$ per container)	875
Documents to import (number)	4
Time to import (days)	8
Cost to import (US$ per container)	950

Enforcing contracts (rank)	31
Procedures (number)	22
Time (days)	408
Cost (% of claim)	15.9

Closing a business (rank)	9
Time (years)	1.7
Cost (% of estate)	1
Recovery rate (cents on the dollar)	86.3

NEW ZEALAND

		OECD: High Income		GNI per capita (US$)	25,960
Ease of doing business (rank)	2	High income		Population (m)	4.1

Starting a business (rank)	3
Procedures (number)	2
Time (days)	12
Cost (% of income per capita)	0.2
Minimum capital (% of income per capita)	0.0

Dealing with licenses (rank)	18
Procedures (number)	7
Time (days)	184
Cost (% of income per capita)	27.2

Employing workers (rank)	10
Difficulty of hiring index (0–100)	11
Rigidity of hours index (0–100)	0
Difficulty of firing index (0–100)	10
Rigidity of employment index (0–100)	7
Nonwage labor cost (% of salary)	1
Firing cost (weeks of salary)	0

Registering property (rank)	1
Procedures (number)	2
Time (days)	2
Cost (% of property value)	0.1

Getting credit (rank)	3
Strength of legal rights index (0–10)	9
Depth of credit information index (0–6)	5
Public registry coverage (% of adults)	0.0
Private bureau coverage (% of adults)	100.0

Protecting investors (rank)	1
Extent of disclosure index (0–10)	10
Extent of director liability index (0–10)	9
Ease of shareholder suits index (0–10)	10
Strength of investor protection index (0–10)	9.7

Paying taxes (rank)	10
Payments (number per year)	9
Time (hours per year)	70
Total tax rate (% of profit)	36.5

Trading across borders (rank)	12
Documents to export (number)	5
Time to export (days)	8
Cost to export (US$ per container)	355
Documents to import (number)	9
Time to import (days)	13
Cost to import (US$ per container)	555

Enforcing contracts (rank)	15
Procedures (number)	28
Time (days)	109
Cost (% of claim)	10.9

Closing a business (rank)	21
Time (years)	2.0
Cost (% of estate)	4
Recovery rate (cents on the dollar)	68.6

NICARAGUA

		Latin America & Caribbean		GNI per capita (US$)	910
Ease of doing business (rank)	67	Lower middle income		Population (m)	5.5

Starting a business (rank)	62
Procedures (number)	6
Time (days)	39
Cost (% of income per capita)	131.6
Minimum capital (% of income per capita)	0.0

Dealing with licenses (rank)	82
Procedures (number)	12
Time (days)	192
Cost (% of income per capita)	1002.2

Employing workers (rank)	32
Difficulty of hiring index (0–100)	11
Rigidity of hours index (0–100)	60
Difficulty of firing index (0–100)	0
Rigidity of employment index (0–100)	24
Nonwage labor cost (% of salary)	17
Firing cost (weeks of salary)	24

Registering property (rank)	127
Procedures (number)	8
Time (days)	124
Cost (% of property value)	3.5

Getting credit (rank)	48
Strength of legal rights index (0–10)	4
Depth of credit information index (0–6)	5
Public registry coverage (% of adults)	12.5
Private bureau coverage (% of adults)	3.4

Protecting investors (rank)	83
Extent of disclosure index (0–10)	4
Extent of director liability index (0–10)	5
Ease of shareholder suits index (0–10)	6
Strength of investor protection index (0–10)	5.0

Paying taxes (rank)	153
Payments (number per year)	64
Time (hours per year)	240
Total tax rate (% of profit)	66.4

Trading across borders (rank)	72
Documents to export (number)	5
Time to export (days)	36
Cost to export (US$ per container)	1,020
Documents to import (number)	5
Time to import (days)	38
Cost to import (US$ per container)	1,020

Enforcing contracts (rank)	49
Procedures (number)	20
Time (days)	486
Cost (% of claim)	21.8

Closing a business (rank)	66
Time (years)	2.2
Cost (% of estate)	15
Recovery rate (cents on the dollar)	34.3

NIGER

Ease of doing business (rank)	160	Sub-Saharan Africa		GNI per capita (US$)		240
		Low income		Population (m)		14.0

Starting a business (rank)	147	**Registering property** (rank)	103	**Trading across borders** (rank)	174
Procedures (number)	11	Procedures (number)	5	Documents to export (number)	..
Time (days)	24	Time (days)	49	Time to export (days)	..
Cost (% of income per capita)	416.8	Cost (% of property value)	14.0	Cost to export (US$ per container)	..
Minimum capital (% of income per capita)	778.1			Documents to import (number)	19
		Getting credit (rank)	143	Time to import (days)	89
Dealing with licenses (rank)	126	Strength of legal rights index (0–10)	3	Cost to import (US$ per container)	3,266
Procedures (number)	19	Depth of credit information index (0–6)	1		
Time (days)	148	Public registry coverage (% of adults)	1.2	**Enforcing contracts** (rank)	104
Cost (% of income per capita)	2986.7	Private bureau coverage (% of adults)	0.0	Procedures (number)	33
				Time (days)	360
Employing workers (rank)	168	**Protecting investors** (rank)	99	Cost (% of claim)	42.0
Difficulty of hiring index (0–100)	100	Extent of disclosure index (0–10)	4		
Rigidity of hours index (0–100)	80	Extent of director liability index (0–10)	5	**Closing a business** (rank)	129
Difficulty of firing index (0–100)	50	Ease of shareholder suits index (0–10)	5	Time (years)	5.0
Rigidity of employment index (0–100)	77	Strength of investor protection index (0–10)	4.7	Cost (% of estate)	18
Nonwage labor cost (% of salary)	17			Recovery rate (cents on the dollar)	14.2
Firing cost (weeks of salary)	31	**Paying taxes** (rank)	115		
		Payments (number per year)	44		
		Time (hours per year)	270		
		Total tax rate (% of profit)	46.0		

NIGERIA

Ease of doing business (rank)	108	Sub-Saharan Africa		GNI per capita (US$)		560
		Low income		Population (m)		131.5

Starting a business (rank)	118	**Registering property** (rank)	170	**Trading across borders** (rank)	137
Procedures (number)	9	Procedures (number)	16	Documents to export (number)	11
Time (days)	43	Time (days)	80	Time to export (days)	25
Cost (% of income per capita)	54.4	Cost (% of property value)	21.2	Cost to export (US$ per container)	798
Minimum capital (% of income per capita)	29.0			Documents to import (number)	13
		Getting credit (rank)	83	Time to import (days)	45
Dealing with licenses (rank)	129	Strength of legal rights index (0–10)	7	Cost to import (US$ per container)	1,460
Procedures (number)	16	Depth of credit information index (0–6)	0		
Time (days)	465	Public registry coverage (% of adults)	0.0	**Enforcing contracts** (rank)	66
Cost (% of income per capita)	238.2	Private bureau coverage (% of adults)	0.0	Procedures (number)	23
				Time (days)	457
Employing workers (rank)	56	**Protecting investors** (rank)	46	Cost (% of claim)	27.0
Difficulty of hiring index (0–100)	22	Extent of disclosure index (0–10)	6		
Rigidity of hours index (0–100)	20	Extent of director liability index (0–10)	7	**Closing a business** (rank)	72
Difficulty of firing index (0–100)	20	Ease of shareholder suits index (0–10)	4	Time (years)	1.5
Rigidity of employment index (0–100)	21	Strength of investor protection index (0–10)	5.7	Cost (% of estate)	22
Nonwage labor cost (% of salary)	9			Recovery rate (cents on the dollar)	32.1
Firing cost (weeks of salary)	50	**Paying taxes** (rank)	105		
		Payments (number per year)	35		
		Time (hours per year)	1120		
		Total tax rate (% of profit)	31.4		

NORWAY

Ease of doing business (rank)	9	OECD: High Income		GNI per capita (US$)		59,590
		High income		Population (m)		4.6

Starting a business (rank)	21	**Registering property** (rank)	6	**Trading across borders** (rank)	5
Procedures (number)	4	Procedures (number)	1	Documents to export (number)	4
Time (days)	13	Time (days)	1	Time to export (days)	7
Cost (% of income per capita)	2.5	Cost (% of property value)	2.5	Cost to export (US$ per container)	518
Minimum capital (% of income per capita)	25.1			Documents to import (number)	4
		Getting credit (rank)	33	Time to import (days)	7
Dealing with licenses (rank)	14	Strength of legal rights index (0–10)	6	Cost to import (US$ per container)	468
Procedures (number)	13	Depth of credit information index (0–6)	4		
Time (days)	104	Public registry coverage (% of adults)	0.0	**Enforcing contracts** (rank)	3
Cost (% of income per capita)	50.4	Private bureau coverage (% of adults)	100.0	Procedures (number)	14
				Time (days)	277
Employing workers (rank)	109	**Protecting investors** (rank)	15	Cost (% of claim)	9.0
Difficulty of hiring index (0–100)	61	Extent of disclosure index (0–10)	7		
Rigidity of hours index (0–100)	60	Extent of director liability index (0–10)	6	**Closing a business** (rank)	3
Difficulty of firing index (0–100)	40	Ease of shareholder suits index (0–10)	7	Time (years)	0.9
Rigidity of employment index (0–100)	54	Strength of investor protection index (0–10)	6.7	Cost (% of estate)	1
Nonwage labor cost (% of salary)	14			Recovery rate (cents on the dollar)	91.1
Firing cost (weeks of salary)	13	**Paying taxes** (rank)	16		
		Payments (number per year)	3		
		Time (hours per year)	87		
		Total tax rate (% of profit)	46.1		

OMAN

Ease of doing business (rank)	55	Middle East & North Africa		GNI per capita (US$)	9,070
		Upper middle income		Population (m)	2.6

Starting a business (rank)	81
Procedures (number)	9
Time (days)	34
Cost (% of income per capita)	4.5
Minimum capital (% of income per capita)	84.7

Dealing with licenses (rank)	127
Procedures (number)	16
Time (days)	242
Cost (% of income per capita)	883.1

Employing workers (rank)	51
Difficulty of hiring index (0–100)	44
Rigidity of hours index (0–100)	60
Difficulty of firing index (0–100)	0
Rigidity of employment index (0–100)	35
Nonwage labor cost (% of salary)	10
Firing cost (weeks of salary)	4

Registering property (rank)	14
Procedures (number)	2
Time (days)	16
Cost (% of property value)	3.0

Getting credit (rank)	143
Strength of legal rights index (0–10)	3
Depth of credit information index (0–6)	1
Public registry coverage (% of adults)	17.5
Private bureau coverage (% of adults)	0.0

Protecting investors (rank)	60
Extent of disclosure index (0–10)	8
Extent of director liability index (0–10)	5
Ease of shareholder suits index (0–10)	3
Strength of investor protection index (0–10)	5.3

Paying taxes (rank)	3
Payments (number per year)	14
Time (hours per year)	52
Total tax rate (% of profit)	20.2

Trading across borders (rank)	115
Documents to export (number)	9
Time to export (days)	23
Cost to export (US$ per container)	987
Documents to import (number)	13
Time to import (days)	27
Cost to import (US$ per container)	987

Enforcing contracts (rank)	101
Procedures (number)	41
Time (days)	598
Cost (% of claim)	12.9

Closing a business (rank)	60
Time (years)	4.0
Cost (% of estate)	4
Recovery rate (cents on the dollar)	35.4

PAKISTAN

Ease of doing business (rank)	74	South Asia		GNI per capita (US$)	690
		Low income		Population (m)	155.8

Starting a business (rank)	54
Procedures (number)	11
Time (days)	24
Cost (% of income per capita)	21.3
Minimum capital (% of income per capita)	0.0

Dealing with licenses (rank)	89
Procedures (number)	12
Time (days)	218
Cost (% of income per capita)	972.9

Employing workers (rank)	126
Difficulty of hiring index (0–100)	78
Rigidity of hours index (0–100)	20
Difficulty of firing index (0–100)	30
Rigidity of employment index (0–100)	43
Nonwage labor cost (% of salary)	12
Firing cost (weeks of salary)	90

Registering property (rank)	68
Procedures (number)	6
Time (days)	50
Cost (% of property value)	4.4

Getting credit (rank)	65
Strength of legal rights index (0–10)	4
Depth of credit information index (0–6)	4
Public registry coverage (% of adults)	0.3
Private bureau coverage (% of adults)	1.1

Protecting investors (rank)	19
Extent of disclosure index (0–10)	6
Extent of director liability index (0–10)	6
Ease of shareholder suits index (0–10)	7
Strength of investor protection index (0–10)	6.3

Paying taxes (rank)	140
Payments (number per year)	47
Time (hours per year)	560
Total tax rate (% of profit)	43.4

Trading across borders (rank)	98
Documents to export (number)	8
Time to export (days)	24
Cost to export (US$ per container)	997
Documents to import (number)	12
Time to import (days)	19
Cost to import (US$ per container)	1,005

Enforcing contracts (rank)	163
Procedures (number)	55
Time (days)	880
Cost (% of claim)	22.6

Closing a business (rank)	46
Time (years)	2.8
Cost (% of estate)	4
Recovery rate (cents on the dollar)	39.9

PALAU

Ease of doing business (rank)	62	East Asia & Pacific		GNI per capita (US$)	7,630
		Upper middle income		Population (m)	0.1

Starting a business (rank)	45
Procedures (number)	8
Time (days)	28
Cost (% of income per capita)	4.9
Minimum capital (% of income per capita)	13.1

Dealing with licenses (rank)	42
Procedures (number)	23
Time (days)	114
Cost (% of income per capita)	6.8

Employing workers (rank)	7
Difficulty of hiring index (0–100)	11
Rigidity of hours index (0–100)	0
Difficulty of firing index (0–100)	0
Rigidity of employment index (0–100)	4
Nonwage labor cost (% of salary)	6
Firing cost (weeks of salary)	0

Registering property (rank)	13
Procedures (number)	5
Time (days)	14
Cost (% of property value)	0.4

Getting credit (rank)	117
Strength of legal rights index (0–10)	5
Depth of credit information index (0–6)	0
Public registry coverage (% of adults)	0.0
Private bureau coverage (% of adults)	0.0

Protecting investors (rank)	162
Extent of disclosure index (0–10)	0
Extent of director liability index (0–10)	0
Ease of shareholder suits index (0–10)	8
Strength of investor protection index (0–10)	2.7

Paying taxes (rank)	70
Payments (number per year)	18
Time (hours per year)	128
Total tax rate (% of profit)	74.6

Trading across borders (rank)	66
Documents to export (number)	7
Time to export (days)	20
Cost to export (US$ per container)	860
Documents to import (number)	9
Time to import (days)	27
Cost to import (US$ per container)	860

Enforcing contracts (rank)	151
Procedures (number)	43
Time (days)	622
Cost (% of claim)	33.2

Closing a business (rank)	52
Time (years)	1.0
Cost (% of estate)	23
Recovery rate (cents on the dollar)	38.2

PANAMA

		Latin America & Caribbean		GNI per capita (US$)	4,630
Ease of doing business (rank)	81	Upper middle income		Population (m)	3.2

Starting a business (rank)	26	**Registering property** (rank)	63	**Trading across borders** (rank)	57
Procedures (number)	7	Procedures (number)	7	Documents to export (number)	9
Time (days)	19	Time (days)	44	Time to export (days)	16
Cost (% of income per capita)	23.9	Cost (% of property value)	2.4	Cost to export (US$ per container)	920
Minimum capital (% of income per capita)	0.0			Documents to import (number)	9
		Getting credit (rank)	13	Time to import (days)	13
Dealing with licenses (rank)	72	Strength of legal rights index (0–10)	6	Cost to import (US$ per container)	920
Procedures (number)	22	Depth of credit information index (0–6)	6		
Time (days)	121	Public registry coverage (% of adults)	0.0	**Enforcing contracts** (rank)	164
Cost (% of income per capita)	114.7	Private bureau coverage (% of adults)	59.8	Procedures (number)	45
				Time (days)	686
Employing workers (rank)	139	**Protecting investors** (rank)	99	Cost (% of claim)	50.0
Difficulty of hiring index (0–100)	78	Extent of disclosure index (0–10)	3		
Rigidity of hours index (0–100)	20	Extent of director liability index (0–10)	4	**Closing a business** (rank)	71
Difficulty of firing index (0–100)	70	Ease of shareholder suits index (0–10)	7	Time (years)	2.5
Rigidity of employment index (0–100)	56	Strength of investor protection index (0–10)	4.7	Cost (% of estate)	18
Nonwage labor cost (% of salary)	19			Recovery rate (cents on the dollar)	32.3
Firing cost (weeks of salary)	44	**Paying taxes** (rank)	164		
		Payments (number per year)	59		
		Time (hours per year)	560		
		Total tax rate (% of profit)	52.4		

PAPUA NEW GUINEA

		East Asia & Pacific		GNI per capita (US$)	660
Ease of doing business (rank)	57	Low income		Population (m)	5.9

Starting a business (rank)	69	**Registering property** (rank)	64	**Trading across borders** (rank)	52
Procedures (number)	8	Procedures (number)	4	Documents to export (number)	5
Time (days)	56	Time (days)	72	Time to export (days)	30
Cost (% of income per capita)	28.2	Cost (% of property value)	5.1	Cost to export (US$ per container)	584
Minimum capital (% of income per capita)	0.0			Documents to import (number)	10
		Getting credit (rank)	101	Time to import (days)	32
Dealing with licenses (rank)	102	Strength of legal rights index (0–10)	6	Cost to import (US$ per container)	642
Procedures (number)	20	Depth of credit information index (0–6)	0		
Time (days)	218	Public registry coverage (% of adults)	0.0	**Enforcing contracts** (rank)	88
Cost (% of income per capita)	110.0	Private bureau coverage (% of adults)	0.0	Procedures (number)	22
				Time (days)	440
Employing workers (rank)	19	**Protecting investors** (rank)	33	Cost (% of claim)	110.3
Difficulty of hiring index (0–100)	11	Extent of disclosure index (0–10)	5		
Rigidity of hours index (0–100)	20	Extent of director liability index (0–10)	5	**Closing a business** (rank)	97
Difficulty of firing index (0–100)	0	Ease of shareholder suits index (0–10)	8	Time (years)	3.0
Rigidity of employment index (0–100)	10	Strength of investor protection index (0–10)	6.0	Cost (% of estate)	23
Nonwage labor cost (% of salary)	10			Recovery rate (cents on the dollar)	24.1
Firing cost (weeks of salary)	39	**Paying taxes** (rank)	91		
		Payments (number per year)	44		
		Time (hours per year)	198		
		Total tax rate (% of profit)	44.3		

PARAGUAY

		Latin America & Caribbean		GNI per capita (US$)	1,280
Ease of doing business (rank)	112	Lower middle income		Population (m)	6.2

Starting a business (rank)	135	**Registering property** (rank)	48	**Trading across borders** (rank)	117
Procedures (number)	17	Procedures (number)	6	Documents to export (number)	9
Time (days)	74	Time (days)	46	Time to export (days)	34
Cost (% of income per capita)	136.8	Cost (% of property value)	2.0	Cost to export (US$ per container)	685
Minimum capital (% of income per capita)	0.0			Documents to import (number)	13
		Getting credit (rank)	48	Time to import (days)	31
Dealing with licenses (rank)	124	Strength of legal rights index (0–10)	3	Cost to import (US$ per container)	1,077
Procedures (number)	15	Depth of credit information index (0–6)	6		
Time (days)	273	Public registry coverage (% of adults)	10.6	**Enforcing contracts** (rank)	147
Cost (% of income per capita)	564.4	Private bureau coverage (% of adults)	52.2	Procedures (number)	46
				Time (days)	478
Employing workers (rank)	169	**Protecting investors** (rank)	46	Cost (% of claim)	39.8
Difficulty of hiring index (0–100)	56	Extent of disclosure index (0–10)	6		
Rigidity of hours index (0–100)	60	Extent of director liability index (0–10)	5	**Closing a business** (rank)	124
Difficulty of firing index (0–100)	60	Ease of shareholder suits index (0–10)	6	Time (years)	3.9
Rigidity of employment index (0–100)	59	Strength of investor protection index (0–10)	5.7	Cost (% of estate)	9
Nonwage labor cost (% of salary)	17			Recovery rate (cents on the dollar)	15.4
Firing cost (weeks of salary)	113	**Paying taxes** (rank)	103		
		Payments (number per year)	33		
		Time (hours per year)	328		
		Total tax rate (% of profit)	43.2		

COUNTRY TABLES 135

PERU

Ease of doing business (rank)	65

Latin America & Caribbean
Lower middle income

GNI per capita (US$)	2,610
Population (m)	28.0

Starting a business (rank)	92
Procedures (number)	10
Time (days)	72
Cost (% of income per capita)	32.5
Minimum capital (% of income per capita)	0.0

Registering property (rank)	32
Procedures (number)	5
Time (days)	33
Cost (% of property value)	3.3

Trading across borders (rank)	93
Documents to export (number)	7
Time to export (days)	24
Cost to export (US$ per container)	800
Documents to import (number)	13
Time to import (days)	31
Cost to import (US$ per container)	820

Dealing with licenses (rank)	121
Procedures (number)	19
Time (days)	201
Cost (% of income per capita)	337.9

Getting credit (rank)	33
Strength of legal rights index (0–10)	4
Depth of credit information index (0–6)	6
Public registry coverage (% of adults)	19.2
Private bureau coverage (% of adults)	28.6

Enforcing contracts (rank)	95
Procedures (number)	35
Time (days)	300
Cost (% of claim)	34.7

Employing workers (rank)	158
Difficulty of hiring index (0–100)	44
Rigidity of hours index (0–100)	60
Difficulty of firing index (0–100)	80
Rigidity of employment index (0–100)	61
Nonwage labor cost (% of salary)	10
Firing cost (weeks of salary)	52

Protecting investors (rank)	15
Extent of disclosure index (0–10)	8
Extent of director liability index (0–10)	5
Ease of shareholder suits index (0–10)	7
Strength of investor protection index (0–10)	6.7

Closing a business (rank)	73
Time (years)	3.1
Cost (% of estate)	7
Recovery rate (cents on the dollar)	31.8

Paying taxes (rank)	135
Payments (number per year)	53
Time (hours per year)	424
Total tax rate (% of profit)	40.8

PHILIPPINES

Ease of doing business (rank)	126

East Asia & Pacific
Lower middle income

GNI per capita (US$)	1,300
Population (m)	83.1

Starting a business (rank)	108
Procedures (number)	11
Time (days)	48
Cost (% of income per capita)	18.7
Minimum capital (% of income per capita)	1.8

Registering property (rank)	98
Procedures (number)	8
Time (days)	33
Cost (% of property value)	5.7

Trading across borders (rank)	63
Documents to export (number)	6
Time to export (days)	18
Cost to export (US$ per container)	1,336
Documents to import (number)	7
Time to import (days)	20
Cost to import (US$ per container)	1,336

Dealing with licenses (rank)	113
Procedures (number)	23
Time (days)	197
Cost (% of income per capita)	113.4

Getting credit (rank)	101
Strength of legal rights index (0–10)	3
Depth of credit information index (0–6)	3
Public registry coverage (% of adults)	0.0
Private bureau coverage (% of adults)	4.8

Enforcing contracts (rank)	59
Procedures (number)	25
Time (days)	600
Cost (% of claim)	16.0

Employing workers (rank)	118
Difficulty of hiring index (0–100)	56
Rigidity of hours index (0–100)	40
Difficulty of firing index (0–100)	20
Rigidity of employment index (0–100)	39
Nonwage labor cost (% of salary)	9
Firing cost (weeks of salary)	91

Protecting investors (rank)	151
Extent of disclosure index (0–10)	1
Extent of director liability index (0–10)	2
Ease of shareholder suits index (0–10)	7
Strength of investor protection index (0–10)	3.3

Closing a business (rank)	147
Time (years)	5.7
Cost (% of estate)	38
Recovery rate (cents on the dollar)	4.0

Paying taxes (rank)	106
Payments (number per year)	59
Time (hours per year)	94
Total tax rate (% of profit)	53.0

POLAND

Ease of doing business (rank)	75

Eastern Europe & Central Asia
Upper middle income

GNI per capita (US$)	7,110
Population (m)	38.2

Starting a business (rank)	114
Procedures (number)	10
Time (days)	31
Cost (% of income per capita)	21.4
Minimum capital (% of income per capita)	204.4

Registering property (rank)	86
Procedures (number)	6
Time (days)	197
Cost (% of property value)	2.0

Trading across borders (rank)	102
Documents to export (number)	6
Time to export (days)	19
Cost to export (US$ per container)	2,260
Documents to import (number)	7
Time to import (days)	26
Cost to import (US$ per container)	2,260

Dealing with licenses (rank)	146
Procedures (number)	25
Time (days)	322
Cost (% of income per capita)	85.6

Getting credit (rank)	65
Strength of legal rights index (0–10)	4
Depth of credit information index (0–6)	4
Public registry coverage (% of adults)	0.0
Private bureau coverage (% of adults)	38.1

Enforcing contracts (rank)	112
Procedures (number)	41
Time (days)	980
Cost (% of claim)	10.0

Employing workers (rank)	49
Difficulty of hiring index (0–100)	0
Rigidity of hours index (0–100)	60
Difficulty of firing index (0–100)	40
Rigidity of employment index (0–100)	33
Nonwage labor cost (% of salary)	21
Firing cost (weeks of salary)	13

Protecting investors (rank)	33
Extent of disclosure index (0–10)	7
Extent of director liability index (0–10)	2
Ease of shareholder suits index (0–10)	9
Strength of investor protection index (0–10)	6.0

Closing a business (rank)	85
Time (years)	3.0
Cost (% of estate)	22
Recovery rate (cents on the dollar)	27.9

Paying taxes (rank)	71
Payments (number per year)	43
Time (hours per year)	175
Total tax rate (% of profit)	38.4

PORTUGAL

Ease of doing business (rank)	40	OECD: High Income		GNI per capita (US$)	16,170
		High income		Population (m)	10.6

Starting a business (rank)	33	**Registering property** (rank)	98	**Trading across borders** (rank)	27
Procedures (number)	8	Procedures (number)	5	Documents to export (number)	4
Time (days)	8	Time (days)	81	Time to export (days)	14
Cost (% of income per capita)	4.3	Cost (% of property value)	7.4	Cost to export (US$ per container)	495
Minimum capital (% of income per capita)	38.7			Documents to import (number)	9
		Getting credit (rank)	65	Time to import (days)	17
Dealing with licenses (rank)	115	Strength of legal rights index (0–10)	4	Cost to import (US$ per container)	994
Procedures (number)	20	Depth of credit information index (0–6)	4		
Time (days)	327	Public registry coverage (% of adults)	72.0	**Enforcing contracts** (rank)	35
Cost (% of income per capita)	60.3	Private bureau coverage (% of adults)	9.1	Procedures (number)	24
				Time (days)	495
Employing workers (rank)	155	**Protecting investors** (rank)	33	Cost (% of claim)	14.5
Difficulty of hiring index (0–100)	33	Extent of disclosure index (0–10)	6		
Rigidity of hours index (0–100)	60	Extent of director liability index (0–10)	5	**Closing a business** (rank)	18
Difficulty of firing index (0–100)	60	Ease of shareholder suits index (0–10)	7	Time (years)	2.0
Rigidity of employment index (0–100)	51	Strength of investor protection index (0–10)	6.0	Cost (% of estate)	9
Nonwage labor cost (% of salary)	24			Recovery rate (cents on the dollar)	75.0
Firing cost (weeks of salary)	99	**Paying taxes** (rank)	61		
		Payments (number per year)	7		
		Time (hours per year)	328		
		Total tax rate (% of profit)	47.0		

PUERTO RICO

Ease of doing business (rank)	19	Latin America & Caribbean		GNI per capita (US$)	13,648
		High income		Population (m)	3.9

Starting a business (rank)	8	**Registering property** (rank)	46	**Trading across borders** (rank)	50
Procedures (number)	7	Procedures (number)	8	Documents to export (number)	9
Time (days)	7	Time (days)	15	Time to export (days)	15
Cost (% of income per capita)	0.8	Cost (% of property value)	1.4	Cost to export (US$ per container)	535
Minimum capital (% of income per capita)	0.0			Documents to import (number)	10
		Getting credit (rank)	21	Time to import (days)	19
Dealing with licenses (rank)	91	Strength of legal rights index (0–10)	6	Cost to import (US$ per container)	535
Procedures (number)	20	Depth of credit information index (0–6)	5		
Time (days)	212	Public registry coverage (% of adults)	0.0	**Enforcing contracts** (rank)	127
Cost (% of income per capita)	82.9	Private bureau coverage (% of adults)	63.6	Procedures (number)	43
				Time (days)	620
Employing workers (rank)	33	**Protecting investors** (rank)	12	Cost (% of claim)	16.1
Difficulty of hiring index (0–100)	56	Extent of disclosure index (0–10)	7		
Rigidity of hours index (0–100)	20	Extent of director liability index (0–10)	6	**Closing a business** (rank)	27
Difficulty of firing index (0–100)	20	Ease of shareholder suits index (0–10)	8	Time (years)	3.8
Rigidity of employment index (0–100)	32	Strength of investor protection index (0–10)	7.0	Cost (% of estate)	8
Nonwage labor cost (% of salary)	8			Recovery rate (cents on the dollar)	56.0
Firing cost (weeks of salary)	0	**Paying taxes** (rank)	26		
		Payments (number per year)	17		
		Time (hours per year)	140		
		Total tax rate (% of profit)	40.9		

ROMANIA

Ease of doing business (rank)	49	Eastern Europe & Central Asia		GNI per capita (US$)	3,830
		Upper middle income		Population (m)	21.6

Starting a business (rank)	7	**Registering property** (rank)	114	**Trading across borders** (rank)	35
Procedures (number)	5	Procedures (number)	8	Documents to export (number)	4
Time (days)	11	Time (days)	150	Time to export (days)	14
Cost (% of income per capita)	4.4	Cost (% of property value)	1.9	Cost to export (US$ per container)	1,300
Minimum capital (% of income per capita)	0.0			Documents to import (number)	4
		Getting credit (rank)	48	Time to import (days)	14
Dealing with licenses (rank)	116	Strength of legal rights index (0–10)	4	Cost to import (US$ per container)	1,200
Procedures (number)	17	Depth of credit information index (0–6)	5		
Time (days)	242	Public registry coverage (% of adults)	2.6	**Enforcing contracts** (rank)	45
Cost (% of income per capita)	332.6	Private bureau coverage (% of adults)	5.5	Procedures (number)	43
				Time (days)	335
Employing workers (rank)	101	**Protecting investors** (rank)	33	Cost (% of claim)	10.7
Difficulty of hiring index (0–100)	33	Extent of disclosure index (0–10)	9		
Rigidity of hours index (0–100)	80	Extent of director liability index (0–10)	5	**Closing a business** (rank)	108
Difficulty of firing index (0–100)	40	Ease of shareholder suits index (0–10)	4	Time (years)	4.6
Rigidity of employment index (0–100)	51	Strength of investor protection index (0–10)	6.0	Cost (% of estate)	9
Nonwage labor cost (% of salary)	33			Recovery rate (cents on the dollar)	19.9
Firing cost (weeks of salary)	3	**Paying taxes** (rank)	131		
		Payments (number per year)	89		
		Time (hours per year)	198		
		Total tax rate (% of profit)	48.9		

RUSSIA

		Eastern Europe & Central Asia		GNI per capita (US$)	4,460
Ease of doing business (rank)	96	Upper middle income		Population (m)	143.2

Starting a business (rank)	33
Procedures (number)	7
Time (days)	28
Cost (% of income per capita)	2.7
Minimum capital (% of income per capita)	3.4

Dealing with licenses (rank)	163
Procedures (number)	22
Time (days)	531
Cost (% of income per capita)	275.3

Employing workers (rank)	87
Difficulty of hiring index (0–100)	33
Rigidity of hours index (0–100)	60
Difficulty of firing index (0–100)	40
Rigidity of employment index (0–100)	44
Nonwage labor cost (% of salary)	31
Firing cost (weeks of salary)	17

Registering property (rank)	44
Procedures (number)	6
Time (days)	52
Cost (% of property value)	0.3

Getting credit (rank)	159
Strength of legal rights index (0–10)	3
Depth of credit information index (0–6)	0
Public registry coverage (% of adults)	0.0
Private bureau coverage (% of adults)	0.0

Protecting investors (rank)	60
Extent of disclosure index (0–10)	7
Extent of director liability index (0–10)	2
Ease of shareholder suits index (0–10)	7
Strength of investor protection index (0–10)	5.3

Paying taxes (rank)	98
Payments (number per year)	23
Time (hours per year)	256
Total tax rate (% of profit)	54.2

Trading across borders (rank)	143
Documents to export (number)	8
Time to export (days)	39
Cost to export (US$ per container)	2,237
Documents to import (number)	8
Time to import (days)	38
Cost to import (US$ per container)	2,237

Enforcing contracts (rank)	25
Procedures (number)	31
Time (days)	178
Cost (% of claim)	13.5

Closing a business (rank)	81
Time (years)	3.8
Cost (% of estate)	9
Recovery rate (cents on the dollar)	28.7

RWANDA

		Sub-Saharan Africa		GNI per capita (US$)	230
Ease of doing business (rank)	158	Low income		Population (m)	9.0

Starting a business (rank)	58
Procedures (number)	9
Time (days)	16
Cost (% of income per capita)	188.3
Minimum capital (% of income per capita)	0.0

Dealing with licenses (rank)	133
Procedures (number)	17
Time (days)	252
Cost (% of income per capita)	626.5

Employing workers (rank)	106
Difficulty of hiring index (0–100)	56
Rigidity of hours index (0–100)	60
Difficulty of firing index (0–100)	30
Rigidity of employment index (0–100)	49
Nonwage labor cost (% of salary)	5
Firing cost (weeks of salary)	26

Registering property (rank)	134
Procedures (number)	5
Time (days)	371
Cost (% of property value)	9.6

Getting credit (rank)	159
Strength of legal rights index (0–10)	1
Depth of credit information index (0–6)	2
Public registry coverage (% of adults)	0.2
Private bureau coverage (% of adults)	0.0

Protecting investors (rank)	162
Extent of disclosure index (0–10)	2
Extent of director liability index (0–10)	5
Ease of shareholder suits index (0–10)	1
Strength of investor protection index (0–10)	2.7

Paying taxes (rank)	83
Payments (number per year)	43
Time (hours per year)	168
Total tax rate (% of profit)	41.1

Trading across borders (rank)	175
Documents to export (number)	14
Time to export (days)	60
Cost to export (US$ per container)	3,840
Documents to import (number)	20
Time to import (days)	95
Cost to import (US$ per container)	4,080

Enforcing contracts (rank)	69
Procedures (number)	27
Time (days)	310
Cost (% of claim)	43.2

Closing a business (rank)	151
Time (years)	NO PRACTICE
Cost (% of estate)	NO PRACTICE
Recovery rate (cents on the dollar)	0.0

SAMOA

		East Asia & Pacific		GNI per capita (US$)	2,090
Ease of doing business (rank)	41	Lower middle income		Population (m)	0.2

Starting a business (rank)	91
Procedures (number)	9
Time (days)	35
Cost (% of income per capita)	45.5
Minimum capital (% of income per capita)	0.0

Dealing with licenses (rank)	51
Procedures (number)	19
Time (days)	88
Cost (% of income per capita)	105.1

Employing workers (rank)	11
Difficulty of hiring index (0–100)	11
Rigidity of hours index (0–100)	20
Difficulty of firing index (0–100)	0
Rigidity of employment index (0–100)	10
Nonwage labor cost (% of salary)	6
Firing cost (weeks of salary)	9

Registering property (rank)	60
Procedures (number)	5
Time (days)	147
Cost (% of property value)	1.8

Getting credit (rank)	83
Strength of legal rights index (0–10)	7
Depth of credit information index (0–6)	0
Public registry coverage (% of adults)	0.0
Private bureau coverage (% of adults)	0.0

Protecting investors (rank)	19
Extent of disclosure index (0–10)	5
Extent of director liability index (0–10)	6
Ease of shareholder suits index (0–10)	8
Strength of investor protection index (0–10)	6.3

Paying taxes (rank)	42
Payments (number per year)	36
Time (hours per year)	224
Total tax rate (% of profit)	22.1

Trading across borders (rank)	62
Documents to export (number)	7
Time to export (days)	15
Cost to export (US$ per container)	1,120
Documents to import (number)	8
Time to import (days)	19
Cost to import (US$ per container)	1,265

Enforcing contracts (rank)	54
Procedures (number)	30
Time (days)	455
Cost (% of claim)	15.3

Closing a business (rank)	125
Time (years)	2.5
Cost (% of estate)	38
Recovery rate (cents on the dollar)	15.2

SAO TOME AND PRINCIPE

Ease of doing business (rank)	169	Sub-Saharan Africa		GNI per capita (US$)	390
		Low income		Population (m)	0.2

Starting a business (rank)	122	**Registering property** (rank)	144	**Trading across borders** (rank)	69
Procedures (number)	10	Procedures (number)	7	Documents to export (number)	8
Time (days)	144	Time (days)	62	Time to export (days)	27
Cost (% of income per capita)	147.2	Cost (% of property value)	12.7	Cost to export (US$ per container)	490
Minimum capital (% of income per capita)	0.0			Documents to import (number)	10
		Getting credit (rank)	117	Time to import (days)	29
Dealing with licenses (rank)	142	Strength of legal rights index (0–10)	5	Cost to import (US$ per container)	577
Procedures (number)	16	Depth of credit information index (0–6)	0		
Time (days)	259	Public registry coverage (% of adults)	0.0	**Enforcing contracts** (rank)	152
Cost (% of income per capita)	1647.9	Private bureau coverage (% of adults)	0.0	Procedures (number)	67
				Time (days)	405
Employing workers (rank)	175	**Protecting investors** (rank)	118	Cost (% of claim)	69.5
Difficulty of hiring index (0–100)	61	Extent of disclosure index (0–10)	6		
Rigidity of hours index (0–100)	80	Extent of director liability index (0–10)	1	**Closing a business** (rank)	151
Difficulty of firing index (0–100)	60	Ease of shareholder suits index (0–10)	6	Time (years)	NO PRACTICE
Rigidity of employment index (0–100)	67	Strength of investor protection index (0–10)	4.3	Cost (% of estate)	NO PRACTICE
Nonwage labor cost (% of salary)	6			Recovery rate (cents on the dollar)	0.0
Firing cost (weeks of salary)	91	**Paying taxes** (rank)	149		
		Payments (number per year)	42		
		Time (hours per year)	424		
		Total tax rate (% of profit)	55.2		

SAUDI ARABIA

Ease of doing business (rank)	38	Middle East & North Africa		GNI per capita (US$)	11,770
		High income		Population (m)	24.6

Starting a business (rank)	156	**Registering property** (rank)	4	**Trading across borders** (rank)	33
Procedures (number)	13	Procedures (number)	4	Documents to export (number)	5
Time (days)	39	Time (days)	4	Time to export (days)	13
Cost (% of income per capita)	58.6	Cost (% of property value)	0.0	Cost to export (US$ per container)	654
Minimum capital (% of income per capita)	1057.5			Documents to import (number)	9
		Getting credit (rank)	65	Time to import (days)	34
Dealing with licenses (rank)	44	Strength of legal rights index (0–10)	3	Cost to import (US$ per container)	605
Procedures (number)	18	Depth of credit information index (0–6)	5		
Time (days)	125	Public registry coverage (% of adults)	0.2	**Enforcing contracts** (rank)	97
Cost (% of income per capita)	70.2	Private bureau coverage (% of adults)	12.5	Procedures (number)	44
				Time (days)	360
Employing workers (rank)	21	**Protecting investors** (rank)	99	Cost (% of claim)	20.0
Difficulty of hiring index (0–100)	0	Extent of disclosure index (0–10)	8		
Rigidity of hours index (0–100)	20	Extent of director liability index (0–10)	5	**Closing a business** (rank)	87
Difficulty of firing index (0–100)	0	Ease of shareholder suits index (0–10)	1	Time (years)	2.8
Rigidity of employment index (0–100)	7	Strength of investor protection index (0–10)	4.7	Cost (% of estate)	22
Nonwage labor cost (% of salary)	11			Recovery rate (cents on the dollar)	27.3
Firing cost (weeks of salary)	80	**Paying taxes** (rank)	6		
		Payments (number per year)	14		
		Time (hours per year)	75		
		Total tax rate (% of profit)	14.9		

SENEGAL

Ease of doing business (rank)	146	Sub-Saharan Africa		GNI per capita (US$)	710
		Low income		Population (m)	11.7

Starting a business (rank)	150	**Registering property** (rank)	151	**Trading across borders** (rank)	94
Procedures (number)	10	Procedures (number)	6	Documents to export (number)	6
Time (days)	58	Time (days)	114	Time to export (days)	22
Cost (% of income per capita)	112.6	Cost (% of property value)	18.1	Cost to export (US$ per container)	978
Minimum capital (% of income per capita)	269.6			Documents to import (number)	10
		Getting credit (rank)	143	Time to import (days)	26
Dealing with licenses (rank)	66	Strength of legal rights index (0–10)	3	Cost to import (US$ per container)	1,674
Procedures (number)	15	Depth of credit information index (0–6)	1		
Time (days)	185	Public registry coverage (% of adults)	4.7	**Enforcing contracts** (rank)	138
Cost (% of income per capita)	151.6	Private bureau coverage (% of adults)	0.0	Procedures (number)	33
				Time (days)	780
Employing workers (rank)	152	**Protecting investors** (rank)	135	Cost (% of claim)	23.8
Difficulty of hiring index (0–100)	72	Extent of disclosure index (0–10)	4		
Rigidity of hours index (0–100)	60	Extent of director liability index (0–10)	4	**Closing a business** (rank)	74
Difficulty of firing index (0–100)	50	Ease of shareholder suits index (0–10)	4	Time (years)	3.0
Rigidity of employment index (0–100)	61	Strength of investor protection index (0–10)	4.0	Cost (% of estate)	7
Nonwage labor cost (% of salary)	21			Recovery rate (cents on the dollar)	31.6
Firing cost (weeks of salary)	38	**Paying taxes** (rank)	159		
		Payments (number per year)	59		
		Time (hours per year)	696		
		Total tax rate (% of profit)	47.7		

SERBIA

| Ease of doing business (rank) | 68 | Eastern Europe & Central Asia
Lower middle income | | GNI per capita (US$) | 3,280 |
| | | | | Population (m) | 10.0 |

Starting a business (rank)	60
Procedures (number)	10
Time (days)	18
Cost (% of income per capita)	10.2
Minimum capital (% of income per capita)	7.6

Registering property (rank)	110
Procedures (number)	6
Time (days)	111
Cost (% of property value)	5.4

Trading across borders (rank)	51
Documents to export (number)	6
Time to export (days)	11
Cost to export (US$ per container)	1,240
Documents to import (number)	8
Time to import (days)	12
Cost to import (US$ per container)	1,440

Dealing with licenses (rank)	157
Procedures (number)	20
Time (days)	211
Cost (% of income per capita)	1946.7

Getting credit (rank)	33
Strength of legal rights index (0–10)	5
Depth of credit information index (0–6)	5
Public registry coverage (% of adults)	0.1
Private bureau coverage (% of adults)	43.4

Enforcing contracts (rank)	76
Procedures (number)	33
Time (days)	635
Cost (% of claim)	12.7

Employing workers (rank)	73
Difficulty of hiring index (0–100)	33
Rigidity of hours index (0–100)	40
Difficulty of firing index (0–100)	40
Rigidity of employment index (0–100)	38
Nonwage labor cost (% of salary)	18
Firing cost (weeks of salary)	27

Protecting investors (rank)	60
Extent of disclosure index (0–10)	7
Extent of director liability index (0–10)	6
Ease of shareholder suits index (0–10)	3
Strength of investor protection index (0–10)	5.3

Closing a business (rank)	103
Time (years)	2.7
Cost (% of estate)	23
Recovery rate (cents on the dollar)	22.6

Paying taxes (rank)	64
Payments (number per year)	41
Time (hours per year)	168
Total tax rate (% of profit)	38.9

SEYCHELLES

| Ease of doing business (rank) | 84 | Sub-Saharan Africa
Upper middle income | | GNI per capita (US$) | 8,290 |
| | | | | Population (m) | 0.1 |

Starting a business (rank)	42
Procedures (number)	9
Time (days)	38
Cost (% of income per capita)	9.1
Minimum capital (% of income per capita)	0.0

Registering property (rank)	50
Procedures (number)	4
Time (days)	33
Cost (% of property value)	7.0

Trading across borders (rank)	81
Documents to export (number)	6
Time to export (days)	17
Cost to export (US$ per container)	1,842
Documents to import (number)	7
Time to import (days)	19
Cost to import (US$ per container)	1,842

Dealing with licenses (rank)	69
Procedures (number)	22
Time (days)	147
Cost (% of income per capita)	51.3

Getting credit (rank)	159
Strength of legal rights index (0–10)	3
Depth of credit information index (0–6)	0
Public registry coverage (% of adults)	0.0
Private bureau coverage (% of adults)	0.0

Enforcing contracts (rank)	73
Procedures (number)	29
Time (days)	720
Cost (% of claim)	13.0

Employing workers (rank)	84
Difficulty of hiring index (0–100)	33
Rigidity of hours index (0–100)	20
Difficulty of firing index (0–100)	50
Rigidity of employment index (0–100)	34
Nonwage labor cost (% of salary)	25
Firing cost (weeks of salary)	39

Protecting investors (rank)	46
Extent of disclosure index (0–10)	4
Extent of director liability index (0–10)	8
Ease of shareholder suits index (0–10)	5
Strength of investor protection index (0–10)	5.7

Closing a business (rank)	151
Time (years)	NO PRACTICE
Cost (% of estate)	NO PRACTICE
Recovery rate (cents on the dollar)	0.0

Paying taxes (rank)	24
Payments (number per year)	15
Time (hours per year)	76
Total tax rate (% of profit)	48.8

SIERRA LEONE

| Ease of doing business (rank) | 168 | Sub-Saharan Africa
Low income | | GNI per capita (US$) | 220 |
| | | | | Population (m) | 5.5 |

Starting a business (rank)	80
Procedures (number)	9
Time (days)	26
Cost (% of income per capita)	1194.5
Minimum capital (% of income per capita)	0.0

Registering property (rank)	168
Procedures (number)	8
Time (days)	235
Cost (% of property value)	15.6

Trading across borders (rank)	124
Documents to export (number)	7
Time to export (days)	29
Cost to export (US$ per container)	2,075
Documents to import (number)	7
Time to import (days)	33
Cost to import (US$ per container)	2,218

Dealing with licenses (rank)	156
Procedures (number)	48
Time (days)	236
Cost (% of income per capita)	218.4

Getting credit (rank)	117
Strength of legal rights index (0–10)	5
Depth of credit information index (0–6)	0
Public registry coverage (% of adults)	0.0
Private bureau coverage (% of adults)	0.0

Enforcing contracts (rank)	166
Procedures (number)	58
Time (days)	515
Cost (% of claim)	227.3

Employing workers (rank)	171
Difficulty of hiring index (0–100)	78
Rigidity of hours index (0–100)	60
Difficulty of firing index (0–100)	50
Rigidity of employment index (0–100)	63
Nonwage labor cost (% of salary)	10
Firing cost (weeks of salary)	329

Protecting investors (rank)	99
Extent of disclosure index (0–10)	3
Extent of director liability index (0–10)	6
Ease of shareholder suits index (0–10)	5
Strength of investor protection index (0–10)	4.7

Closing a business (rank)	140
Time (years)	2.6
Cost (% of estate)	42
Recovery rate (cents on the dollar)	8.7

Paying taxes (rank)	138
Payments (number per year)	20
Time (hours per year)	399
Total tax rate (% of profit)	277.0

SINGAPORE

		East Asia & Pacific		GNI per capita (US$)	27,490
Ease of doing business (rank)	1	High income		Population (m)	4.4

Starting a business (rank)	11	**Registering property** (rank)	12	**Trading across borders** (rank)	4
Procedures (number)	6	Procedures (number)	3	Documents to export (number)	5
Time (days)	6	Time (days)	9	Time to export (days)	6
Cost (% of income per capita)	0.8	Cost (% of property value)	2.8	Cost to export (US$ per container)	382
Minimum capital (% of income per capita)	0.0			Documents to import (number)	6
		Getting credit (rank)	7	Time to import (days)	3
Dealing with licenses (rank)	8	Strength of legal rights index (0–10)	9	Cost to import (US$ per container)	333
Procedures (number)	11	Depth of credit information index (0–6)	4		
Time (days)	129	Public registry coverage (% of adults)	0.0	**Enforcing contracts** (rank)	23
Cost (% of income per capita)	22.0	Private bureau coverage (% of adults)	38.6	Procedures (number)	29
				Time (days)	120
Employing workers (rank)	3	**Protecting investors** (rank)	2	Cost (% of claim)	14.6
Difficulty of hiring index (0–100)	0	Extent of disclosure index (0–10)	10		
Rigidity of hours index (0–100)	0	Extent of director liability index (0–10)	9	**Closing a business** (rank)	2
Difficulty of firing index (0–100)	0	Ease of shareholder suits index (0–10)	9	Time (years)	0.8
Rigidity of employment index (0–100)	0	Strength of investor protection index (0–10)	9.3	Cost (% of estate)	1
Nonwage labor cost (% of salary)	13			Recovery rate (cents on the dollar)	91.3
Firing cost (weeks of salary)	4	**Paying taxes** (rank)	8		
		Payments (number per year)	16		
		Time (hours per year)	30		
		Total tax rate (% of profit)	28.8		

SLOVAKIA

		Eastern Europe & Central Asia		GNI per capita (US$)	7,950
Ease of doing business (rank)	36	Upper middle income		Population (m)	5.4

Starting a business (rank)	63	**Registering property** (rank)	5	**Trading across borders** (rank)	88
Procedures (number)	9	Procedures (number)	3	Documents to export (number)	9
Time (days)	25	Time (days)	17	Time to export (days)	20
Cost (% of income per capita)	4.8	Cost (% of property value)	0.1	Cost to export (US$ per container)	1,015
Minimum capital (% of income per capita)	39.1			Documents to import (number)	8
		Getting credit (rank)	13	Time to import (days)	21
Dealing with licenses (rank)	47	Strength of legal rights index (0–10)	9	Cost to import (US$ per container)	1,050
Procedures (number)	13	Depth of credit information index (0–6)	3		
Time (days)	272	Public registry coverage (% of adults)	1.0	**Enforcing contracts** (rank)	59
Cost (% of income per capita)	17.1	Private bureau coverage (% of adults)	45.3	Procedures (number)	27
				Time (days)	565
Employing workers (rank)	72	**Protecting investors** (rank)	118	Cost (% of claim)	15.7
Difficulty of hiring index (0–100)	17	Extent of disclosure index (0–10)	2		
Rigidity of hours index (0–100)	60	Extent of director liability index (0–10)	4	**Closing a business** (rank)	31
Difficulty of firing index (0–100)	40	Ease of shareholder suits index (0–10)	7	Time (years)	4.0
Rigidity of employment index (0–100)	39	Strength of investor protection index (0–10)	4.3	Cost (% of estate)	18
Nonwage labor cost (% of salary)	35			Recovery rate (cents on the dollar)	48.1
Firing cost (weeks of salary)	13	**Paying taxes** (rank)	113		
		Payments (number per year)	30		
		Time (hours per year)	344		
		Total tax rate (% of profit)	48.9		

SLOVENIA

		Eastern Europe & Central Asia		GNI per capita (US$)	17,350
Ease of doing business (rank)	61	High income		Population (m)	2.0

Starting a business (rank)	98	**Registering property** (rank)	97	**Trading across borders** (rank)	108
Procedures (number)	9	Procedures (number)	6	Documents to export (number)	9
Time (days)	60	Time (days)	391	Time to export (days)	20
Cost (% of income per capita)	9.4	Cost (% of property value)	2.0	Cost to export (US$ per container)	1,070
Minimum capital (% of income per capita)	16.1			Documents to import (number)	11
		Getting credit (rank)	48	Time to import (days)	24
Dealing with licenses (rank)	63	Strength of legal rights index (0–10)	6	Cost to import (US$ per container)	1,107
Procedures (number)	14	Depth of credit information index (0–6)	3		
Time (days)	207	Public registry coverage (% of adults)	2.9	**Enforcing contracts** (rank)	84
Cost (% of income per capita)	122.2	Private bureau coverage (% of adults)	0.0	Procedures (number)	25
				Time (days)	1350
Employing workers (rank)	146	**Protecting investors** (rank)	46	Cost (% of claim)	15.2
Difficulty of hiring index (0–100)	61	Extent of disclosure index (0–10)	3		
Rigidity of hours index (0–100)	60	Extent of director liability index (0–10)	8	**Closing a business** (rank)	35
Difficulty of firing index (0–100)	50	Ease of shareholder suits index (0–10)	6	Time (years)	2.0
Rigidity of employment index (0–100)	57	Strength of investor protection index (0–10)	5.7	Cost (% of estate)	8
Nonwage labor cost (% of salary)	17			Recovery rate (cents on the dollar)	44.9
Firing cost (weeks of salary)	40	**Paying taxes** (rank)	84		
		Payments (number per year)	34		
		Time (hours per year)	272		
		Total tax rate (% of profit)	39.4		

SOLOMON ISLANDS

		East Asia & Pacific		GNI per capita (US$)	590
Ease of doing business (rank)	69	Low income		Population (m)	0.5

Starting a business (rank)	76	Registering property (rank)	159	Trading across borders (rank)	34
Procedures (number)	7	Procedures (number)	10	Documents to export (number)	8
Time (days)	57	Time (days)	297	Time to export (days)	15
Cost (% of income per capita)	68.9	Cost (% of property value)	4.9	Cost to export (US$ per container)	805
Minimum capital (% of income per capita)	0.0			Documents to import (number)	5
		Getting credit (rank)	143	Time to import (days)	12
		Strength of legal rights index (0–10)	4	Cost to import (US$ per container)	788
Dealing with licenses (rank)	40	Depth of credit information index (0–6)	0		
Procedures (number)	13	Public registry coverage (% of adults)	0.0		
Time (days)	74	Private bureau coverage (% of adults)	0.0	Enforcing contracts (rank)	102
Cost (% of income per capita)	501.1			Procedures (number)	25
				Time (days)	455
Employing workers (rank)	53	Protecting investors (rank)	46	Cost (% of claim)	69.8
Difficulty of hiring index (0–100)	22	Extent of disclosure index (0–10)	3		
Rigidity of hours index (0–100)	20	Extent of director liability index (0–10)	7	Closing a business (rank)	101
Difficulty of firing index (0–100)	20	Ease of shareholder suits index (0–10)	7	Time (years)	1.0
Rigidity of employment index (0–100)	21	Strength of investor protection index (0–10)	5.7	Cost (% of estate)	38
Nonwage labor cost (% of salary)	8			Recovery rate (cents on the dollar)	23.3
Firing cost (weeks of salary)	44	Paying taxes (rank)	23		
		Payments (number per year)	33		
		Time (hours per year)	80		
		Total tax rate (% of profit)	33.6		

SOUTH AFRICA

		Sub-Saharan Africa		GNI per capita (US$)	4,960
Ease of doing business (rank)	29	Upper middle income		Population (m)	45.2

Starting a business (rank)	57	Registering property (rank)	69	Trading across borders (rank)	67
Procedures (number)	9	Procedures (number)	6	Documents to export (number)	5
Time (days)	35	Time (days)	23	Time to export (days)	31
Cost (% of income per capita)	6.9	Cost (% of property value)	8.9	Cost to export (US$ per container)	850
Minimum capital (% of income per capita)	0.0			Documents to import (number)	9
		Getting credit (rank)	33	Time to import (days)	34
		Strength of legal rights index (0–10)	5	Cost to import (US$ per container)	850
Dealing with licenses (rank)	45	Depth of credit information index (0–6)	5		
Procedures (number)	17	Public registry coverage (% of adults)	0.0		
Time (days)	174	Private bureau coverage (% of adults)	53.0	Enforcing contracts (rank)	43
Cost (% of income per capita)	33.5			Procedures (number)	26
				Time (days)	600
Employing workers (rank)	87	Protecting investors (rank)	9	Cost (% of claim)	11.5
Difficulty of hiring index (0–100)	44	Extent of disclosure index (0–10)	8		
Rigidity of hours index (0–100)	40	Extent of director liability index (0–10)	8	Closing a business (rank)	65
Difficulty of firing index (0–100)	40	Ease of shareholder suits index (0–10)	8	Time (years)	2.0
Rigidity of employment index (0–100)	41	Strength of investor protection index (0–10)	8.0	Cost (% of estate)	18
Nonwage labor cost (% of salary)	2			Recovery rate (cents on the dollar)	34.4
Firing cost (weeks of salary)	24	Paying taxes (rank)	74		
		Payments (number per year)	23		
		Time (hours per year)	350		
		Total tax rate (% of profit)	38.3		

SPAIN

		OECD: High Income		GNI per capita (US$)	25,360
Ease of doing business (rank)	39	High income		Population (m)	43.4

Starting a business (rank)	102	Registering property (rank)	33	Trading across borders (rank)	25
Procedures (number)	10	Procedures (number)	3	Documents to export (number)	4
Time (days)	47	Time (days)	17	Time to export (days)	9
Cost (% of income per capita)	16.2	Cost (% of property value)	7.2	Cost to export (US$ per container)	1,050
Minimum capital (% of income per capita)	14.6			Documents to import (number)	5
		Getting credit (rank)	21	Time to import (days)	10
		Strength of legal rights index (0–10)	5	Cost to import (US$ per container)	1,050
Dealing with licenses (rank)	53	Depth of credit information index (0–6)	6		
Procedures (number)	11	Public registry coverage (% of adults)	44.9		
Time (days)	277	Private bureau coverage (% of adults)	7.4	Enforcing contracts (rank)	42
Cost (% of income per capita)	65.7			Procedures (number)	23
				Time (days)	515
Employing workers (rank)	161	Protecting investors (rank)	83	Cost (% of claim)	15.7
Difficulty of hiring index (0–100)	78	Extent of disclosure index (0–10)	5		
Rigidity of hours index (0–100)	60	Extent of director liability index (0–10)	6	Closing a business (rank)	15
Difficulty of firing index (0–100)	50	Ease of shareholder suits index (0–10)	4	Time (years)	1.0
Rigidity of employment index (0–100)	63	Strength of investor protection index (0–10)	5.0	Cost (% of estate)	15
Nonwage labor cost (% of salary)	30			Recovery rate (cents on the dollar)	77.6
Firing cost (weeks of salary)	56	Paying taxes (rank)	112		
		Payments (number per year)	7		
		Time (hours per year)	602		
		Total tax rate (% of profit)	59.1		

SRI LANKA

		South Asia		GNI per capita (US$)	1,160
Ease of doing business (rank)	89	Lower middle income		Population (m)	19.6

Starting a business (rank)	44	**Registering property** (rank)	125	**Trading across borders** (rank)	99
Procedures (number)	8	Procedures (number)	8	Documents to export (number)	8
Time (days)	50	Time (days)	63	Time to export (days)	25
Cost (% of income per capita)	9.2	Cost (% of property value)	5.1	Cost to export (US$ per container)	797
Minimum capital (% of income per capita)	0.0			Documents to import (number)	13
		Getting credit (rank)	101	Time to import (days)	27
Dealing with licenses (rank)	71	Strength of legal rights index (0–10)	3	Cost to import (US$ per container)	789
Procedures (number)	17	Depth of credit information index (0–6)	3		
Time (days)	167	Public registry coverage (% of adults)	0.0	**Enforcing contracts** (rank)	90
Cost (% of income per capita)	151.0	Private bureau coverage (% of adults)	3.1	Procedures (number)	20
				Time (days)	837
Employing workers (rank)	98	**Protecting investors** (rank)	60	Cost (% of claim)	21.3
Difficulty of hiring index (0–100)	0	Extent of disclosure index (0–10)	4		
Rigidity of hours index (0–100)	20	Extent of director liability index (0–10)	5	**Closing a business** (rank)	59
Difficulty of firing index (0–100)	60	Ease of shareholder suits index (0–10)	7	Time (years)	2.2
Rigidity of employment index (0–100)	27	Strength of investor protection index (0–10)	5.3	Cost (% of estate)	18
Nonwage labor cost (% of salary)	15			Recovery rate (cents on the dollar)	35.6
Firing cost (weeks of salary)	178	**Paying taxes** (rank)	157		
		Payments (number per year)	61		
		Time (hours per year)	256		
		Total tax rate (% of profit)	74.9		

ST. KITTS AND NEVIS

		Latin America & Caribbean		GNI per capita (US$)	8,210
Ease of doing business (rank)	85	Upper middle income		Population (m)	0.1

Starting a business (rank)	105	**Registering property** (rank)	136	**Trading across borders** (rank)	37
Procedures (number)	8	Procedures (number)	6	Documents to export (number)	8
Time (days)	47	Time (days)	81	Time to export (days)	11
Cost (% of income per capita)	26.7	Cost (% of property value)	13.3	Cost to export (US$ per container)	706
Minimum capital (% of income per capita)	45.4			Documents to import (number)	8
		Getting credit (rank)	117	Time to import (days)	13
Dealing with licenses (rank)	7	Strength of legal rights index (0–10)	5	Cost to import (US$ per container)	756
Procedures (number)	14	Depth of credit information index (0–6)	0		
Time (days)	72	Public registry coverage (% of adults)	0.0	**Enforcing contracts** (rank)	135
Cost (% of income per capita)	15.2	Private bureau coverage (% of adults)	0.0	Procedures (number)	49
				Time (days)	578
Employing workers (rank)	35	**Protecting investors** (rank)	19	Cost (% of claim)	17.1
Difficulty of hiring index (0–100)	0	Extent of disclosure index (0–10)	4		
Rigidity of hours index (0–100)	20	Extent of director liability index (0–10)	8	**Closing a business** (rank)	151
Difficulty of firing index (0–100)	20	Ease of shareholder suits index (0–10)	7	Time (years)	NO PRACTICE
Rigidity of employment index (0–100)	13	Strength of investor protection index (0–10)	6.3	Cost (% of estate)	NO PRACTICE
Nonwage labor cost (% of salary)	10			Recovery rate (cents on the dollar)	0.0
Firing cost (weeks of salary)	60	**Paying taxes** (rank)	116		
		Payments (number per year)	23		
		Time (hours per year)	368		
		Total tax rate (% of profit)	52.7		

ST. LUCIA

		Latin America & Caribbean		GNI per capita (US$)	4,800
Ease of doing business (rank)	27	Upper middle income		Population (m)	0.2

Starting a business (rank)	43	**Registering property** (rank)	51	**Trading across borders** (rank)	45
Procedures (number)	6	Procedures (number)	5	Documents to export (number)	5
Time (days)	40	Time (days)	20	Time to export (days)	9
Cost (% of income per capita)	25.9	Cost (% of property value)	7.3	Cost to export (US$ per container)	1,053
Minimum capital (% of income per capita)	0.0			Documents to import (number)	8
		Getting credit (rank)	101	Time to import (days)	19
Dealing with licenses (rank)	10	Strength of legal rights index (0–10)	6	Cost to import (US$ per container)	1,163
Procedures (number)	9	Depth of credit information index (0–6)	0		
Time (days)	139	Public registry coverage (% of adults)	0.0	**Enforcing contracts** (rank)	160
Cost (% of income per capita)	34.9	Private bureau coverage (% of adults)	0.0	Procedures (number)	51
				Time (days)	635
Employing workers (rank)	29	**Protecting investors** (rank)	19	Cost (% of claim)	31.2
Difficulty of hiring index (0–100)	0	Extent of disclosure index (0–10)	4		
Rigidity of hours index (0–100)	20	Extent of director liability index (0–10)	8	**Closing a business** (rank)	39
Difficulty of firing index (0–100)	20	Ease of shareholder suits index (0–10)	7	Time (years)	2.0
Rigidity of employment index (0–100)	13	Strength of investor protection index (0–10)	6.3	Cost (% of estate)	9
Nonwage labor cost (% of salary)	5			Recovery rate (cents on the dollar)	42.2
Firing cost (weeks of salary)	56	**Paying taxes** (rank)	9		
		Payments (number per year)	16		
		Time (hours per year)	41		
		Total tax rate (% of profit)	31.5		

ST. VINCENT AND THE GRENADINES

		Latin America & Caribbean			GNI per capita (US$)	3,590
Ease of doing business (rank)	44	Upper middle income			Population (m)	0.1

Starting a business (rank)	29	**Registering property** (rank)	101	**Trading across borders** (rank)	48
Procedures (number)	8	Procedures (number)	6	Documents to export (number)	7
Time (days)	12	Time (days)	37	Time to export (days)	15
Cost (% of income per capita)	33.8	Cost (% of property value)	11.9	Cost to export (US$ per container)	756
Minimum capital (% of income per capita)	0.0			Documents to import (number)	6
				Time to import (days)	13
Dealing with licenses (rank)	1	**Getting credit** (rank)	83	Cost to import (US$ per container)	1,354
Procedures (number)	11	Strength of legal rights index (0–10)	7		
Time (days)	74	Depth of credit information index (0–6)	0		
Cost (% of income per capita)	10.6	Public registry coverage (% of adults)	0.0	**Enforcing contracts** (rank)	125
		Private bureau coverage (% of adults)	0.0	Procedures (number)	52
				Time (days)	394
Employing workers (rank)	48	**Protecting investors** (rank)	19	Cost (% of claim)	22.2
Difficulty of hiring index (0–100)	11	Extent of disclosure index (0–10)	4		
Rigidity of hours index (0–100)	20	Extent of director liability index (0–10)	8	**Closing a business** (rank)	151
Difficulty of firing index (0–100)	20	Ease of shareholder suits index (0–10)	7	Time (years)	NO PRACTICE
Rigidity of employment index (0–100)	17	Strength of investor protection index (0–10)	6.3	Cost (% of estate)	NO PRACTICE
Nonwage labor cost (% of salary)	4			Recovery rate (cents on the dollar)	0.0
Firing cost (weeks of salary)	54	**Paying taxes** (rank)	32		
		Payments (number per year)	21		
		Time (hours per year)	208		
		Total tax rate (% of profit)	33.6		

SUDAN

		Sub-Saharan Africa			GNI per capita (US$)	640
Ease of doing business (rank)	154	Low income			Population (m)	36.2

Starting a business (rank)	82	**Registering property** (rank)	29	**Trading across borders** (rank)	165
Procedures (number)	10	Procedures (number)	6	Documents to export (number)	12
Time (days)	39	Time (days)	9	Time to export (days)	56
Cost (% of income per capita)	58.6	Cost (% of property value)	3.3	Cost to export (US$ per container)	1,870
Minimum capital (% of income per capita)	0.0			Documents to import (number)	13
				Time to import (days)	83
Dealing with licenses (rank)	92	**Getting credit** (rank)	143	Cost to import (US$ per container)	1,970
Procedures (number)	17	Strength of legal rights index (0–10)	4		
Time (days)	172	Depth of credit information index (0–6)	0		
Cost (% of income per capita)	506.1	Public registry coverage (% of adults)	0.0	**Enforcing contracts** (rank)	158
		Private bureau coverage (% of adults)	0.0	Procedures (number)	67
				Time (days)	770
Employing workers (rank)	164	**Protecting investors** (rank)	142	Cost (% of claim)	20.6
Difficulty of hiring index (0–100)	56	Extent of disclosure index (0–10)	0		
Rigidity of hours index (0–100)	60	Extent of director liability index (0–10)	6	**Closing a business** (rank)	151
Difficulty of firing index (0–100)	50	Ease of shareholder suits index (0–10)	5	Time (years)	NO PRACTICE
Rigidity of employment index (0–100)	55	Strength of investor protection index (0–10)	3.7	Cost (% of estate)	NO PRACTICE
Nonwage labor cost (% of salary)	25			Recovery rate (cents on the dollar)	0.0
Firing cost (weeks of salary)	118	**Paying taxes** (rank)	93		
		Payments (number per year)	66		
		Time (hours per year)	180		
		Total tax rate (% of profit)	37.1		

SURINAME

		Latin America & Caribbean			GNI per capita (US$)	2,540
Ease of doing business (rank)	122	Lower middle income			Population (m)	0.4

Starting a business (rank)	158	**Registering property** (rank)	120	**Trading across borders** (rank)	43
Procedures (number)	13	Procedures (number)	4	Documents to export (number)	7
Time (days)	694	Time (days)	193	Time to export (days)	16
Cost (% of income per capita)	153.8	Cost (% of property value)	10.2	Cost to export (US$ per container)	905
Minimum capital (% of income per capita)	1.4			Documents to import (number)	7
				Time to import (days)	15
Dealing with licenses (rank)	100	**Getting credit** (rank)	117	Cost to import (US$ per container)	815
Procedures (number)	14	Strength of legal rights index (0–10)	5		
Time (days)	431	Depth of credit information index (0–6)	0		
Cost (% of income per capita)	196.3	Public registry coverage (% of adults)	0.0	**Enforcing contracts** (rank)	111
		Private bureau coverage (% of adults)	0.0	Procedures (number)	29
				Time (days)	1290
Employing workers (rank)	39	**Protecting investors** (rank)	156	Cost (% of claim)	15.9
Difficulty of hiring index (0–100)	0	Extent of disclosure index (0–10)	2		
Rigidity of hours index (0–100)	20	Extent of director liability index (0–10)	2	**Closing a business** (rank)	143
Difficulty of firing index (0–100)	50	Ease of shareholder suits index (0–10)	5	Time (years)	5.0
Rigidity of employment index (0–100)	23	Strength of investor protection index (0–10)	3.0	Cost (% of estate)	30
Nonwage labor cost (% of salary)	0			Recovery rate (cents on the dollar)	7.1
Firing cost (weeks of salary)	26	**Paying taxes** (rank)	21		
		Payments (number per year)	17		
		Time (hours per year)	199		
		Total tax rate (% of profit)	27.8		

SWAZILAND

		Sub-Saharan Africa		GNI per capita (US$)	2,280
Ease of doing business (rank)	76	Lower middle income		Population (m)	1.1

Starting a business (rank)	112	**Registering property** (rank)	140	**Trading across borders** (rank)	133
Procedures (number)	13	Procedures (number)	11	Documents to export (number)	9
Time (days)	61	Time (days)	46	Time to export (days)	9
Cost (% of income per capita)	41.1	Cost (% of property value)	7.1	Cost to export (US$ per container)	1,857
Minimum capital (% of income per capita)	0.0			Documents to import (number)	14
		Getting credit (rank)	21	Time to import (days)	35
Dealing with licenses (rank)	16	Strength of legal rights index (0–10)	6	Cost to import (US$ per container)	1,950
Procedures (number)	11	Depth of credit information index (0–6)	5		
Time (days)	114	Public registry coverage (% of adults)	0.0	**Enforcing contracts** (rank)	132
Cost (% of income per capita)	97.1	Private bureau coverage (% of adults)	39.0	Procedures (number)	31
				Time (days)	972
Employing workers (rank)	47	**Protecting investors** (rank)	168	Cost (% of claim)	20.1
Difficulty of hiring index (0–100)	11	Extent of disclosure index (0–10)	1		
Rigidity of hours index (0–100)	20	Extent of director liability index (0–10)	1	**Closing a business** (rank)	56
Difficulty of firing index (0–100)	20	Ease of shareholder suits index (0–10)	5	Time (years)	2.0
Rigidity of employment index (0–100)	17	Strength of investor protection index (0–10)	2.3	Cost (% of estate)	15
Nonwage labor cost (% of salary)	3			Recovery rate (cents on the dollar)	36.9
Firing cost (weeks of salary)	53	**Paying taxes** (rank)	38		
		Payments (number per year)	34		
		Time (hours per year)	104		
		Total tax rate (% of profit)	39.5		

SWEDEN

		OECD: High Income		GNI per capita (US$)	41,060
Ease of doing business (rank)	13	High income		Population (m)	9.0

Starting a business (rank)	20	**Registering property** (rank)	7	**Trading across borders** (rank)	9
Procedures (number)	3	Procedures (number)	1	Documents to export (number)	4
Time (days)	16	Time (days)	2	Time to export (days)	6
Cost (% of income per capita)	0.7	Cost (% of property value)	3.0	Cost to export (US$ per container)	831
Minimum capital (% of income per capita)	33.7			Documents to import (number)	3
		Getting credit (rank)	33	Time to import (days)	6
Dealing with licenses (rank)	17	Strength of legal rights index (0–10)	6	Cost to import (US$ per container)	831
Procedures (number)	8	Depth of credit information index (0–6)	4		
Time (days)	116	Public registry coverage (% of adults)	0.0	**Enforcing contracts** (rank)	2
Cost (% of income per capita)	115.3	Private bureau coverage (% of adults)	100.0	Procedures (number)	19
				Time (days)	208
Employing workers (rank)	94	**Protecting investors** (rank)	46	Cost (% of claim)	5.9
Difficulty of hiring index (0–100)	28	Extent of disclosure index (0–10)	6		
Rigidity of hours index (0–100)	60	Extent of director liability index (0–10)	4	**Closing a business** (rank)	17
Difficulty of firing index (0–100)	40	Ease of shareholder suits index (0–10)	7	Time (years)	2.0
Rigidity of employment index (0–100)	43	Strength of investor protection index (0–10)	5.7	Cost (% of estate)	9
Nonwage labor cost (% of salary)	33			Recovery rate (cents on the dollar)	75.7
Firing cost (weeks of salary)	26	**Paying taxes** (rank)	39		
		Payments (number per year)	5		
		Time (hours per year)	122		
		Total tax rate (% of profit)	57.0		

SWITZERLAND

		OECD: High Income		GNI per capita (US$)	54,930
Ease of doing business (rank)	15	High income		Population (m)	7.4

Starting a business (rank)	27	**Registering property** (rank)	11	**Trading across borders** (rank)	49
Procedures (number)	6	Procedures (number)	4	Documents to export (number)	4
Time (days)	20	Time (days)	16	Time to export (days)	17
Cost (% of income per capita)	2.2	Cost (% of property value)	0.4	Cost to export (US$ per container)	1,238
Minimum capital (% of income per capita)	15.1			Documents to import (number)	5
		Getting credit (rank)	21	Time to import (days)	18
Dealing with licenses (rank)	38	Strength of legal rights index (0–10)	6	Cost to import (US$ per container)	1,333
Procedures (number)	15	Depth of credit information index (0–6)	5		
Time (days)	152	Public registry coverage (% of adults)	0.0	**Enforcing contracts** (rank)	9
Cost (% of income per capita)	57.2	Private bureau coverage (% of adults)	24.5	Procedures (number)	22
				Time (days)	215
Employing workers (rank)	24	**Protecting investors** (rank)	156	Cost (% of claim)	11.0
Difficulty of hiring index (0–100)	0	Extent of disclosure index (0–10)	0		
Rigidity of hours index (0–100)	60	Extent of director liability index (0–10)	5	**Closing a business** (rank)	33
Difficulty of firing index (0–100)	10	Ease of shareholder suits index (0–10)	4	Time (years)	3.0
Rigidity of employment index (0–100)	23	Strength of investor protection index (0–10)	3.0	Cost (% of estate)	4
Nonwage labor cost (% of salary)	14			Recovery rate (cents on the dollar)	47.1
Firing cost (weeks of salary)	13	**Paying taxes** (rank)	7		
		Payments (number per year)	13		
		Time (hours per year)	68		
		Total tax rate (% of profit)	24.9		

SYRIA

		Middle East & North Africa		GNI per capita (US$)	1,380
Ease of doing business (rank)	130	Lower middle income		Population (m)	19.0

Starting a business (rank)	142
Procedures (number)	12
Time (days)	43
Cost (% of income per capita)	21.1
Minimum capital (% of income per capita)	4233.5

Dealing with licenses (rank)	87
Procedures (number)	20
Time (days)	134
Cost (% of income per capita)	298.0

Employing workers (rank)	89
Difficulty of hiring index (0–100)	0
Rigidity of hours index (0–100)	40
Difficulty of firing index (0–100)	50
Rigidity of employment index (0–100)	30
Nonwage labor cost (% of salary)	17
Firing cost (weeks of salary)	80

Registering property (rank)	88
Procedures (number)	4
Time (days)	34
Cost (% of property value)	27.9

Getting credit (rank)	117
Strength of legal rights index (0–10)	5
Depth of credit information index (0–6)	0
Public registry coverage (% of adults)	0.0
Private bureau coverage (% of adults)	0.0

Protecting investors (rank)	118
Extent of disclosure index (0–10)	6
Extent of director liability index (0–10)	5
Ease of shareholder suits index (0–10)	2
Strength of investor protection index (0–10)	4.3

Paying taxes (rank)	59
Payments (number per year)	21
Time (hours per year)	336
Total tax rate (% of profit)	35.5

Trading across borders (rank)	147
Documents to export (number)	9
Time to export (days)	40
Cost to export (US$ per container)	1,300
Documents to import (number)	11
Time to import (days)	49
Cost to import (US$ per container)	1,962

Enforcing contracts (rank)	153
Procedures (number)	47
Time (days)	872
Cost (% of claim)	21.9

Closing a business (rank)	77
Time (years)	4.1
Cost (% of estate)	9
Recovery rate (cents on the dollar)	29.6

TAIWAN, CHINA

		East Asia & Pacific		GNI per capita (US$)	16,170
Ease of doing business (rank)	47	High income		Population (m)	22.9

Starting a business (rank)	94
Procedures (number)	8
Time (days)	48
Cost (% of income per capita)	4.6
Minimum capital (% of income per capita)	200.0

Dealing with licenses (rank)	148
Procedures (number)	32
Time (days)	206
Cost (% of income per capita)	231.9

Employing workers (rank)	154
Difficulty of hiring index (0–100)	78
Rigidity of hours index (0–100)	60
Difficulty of firing index (0–100)	30
Rigidity of employment index (0–100)	56
Nonwage labor cost (% of salary)	11
Firing cost (weeks of salary)	91

Registering property (rank)	24
Procedures (number)	3
Time (days)	5
Cost (% of property value)	6.2

Getting credit (rank)	48
Strength of legal rights index (0–10)	4
Depth of credit information index (0–6)	5
Public registry coverage (% of adults)	0.0
Private bureau coverage (% of adults)	59.5

Protecting investors (rank)	60
Extent of disclosure index (0–10)	8
Extent of director liability index (0–10)	4
Ease of shareholder suits index (0–10)	4
Strength of investor protection index (0–10)	5.3

Paying taxes (rank)	78
Payments (number per year)	15
Time (hours per year)	1104
Total tax rate (% of profit)	35.8

Trading across borders (rank)	42
Documents to export (number)	8
Time to export (days)	14
Cost to export (US$ per container)	747
Documents to import (number)	8
Time to import (days)	14
Cost to import (US$ per container)	747

Enforcing contracts (rank)	62
Procedures (number)	28
Time (days)	510
Cost (% of claim)	16.6

Closing a business (rank)	4
Time (years)	0.8
Cost (% of estate)	4
Recovery rate (cents on the dollar)	89.5

TAJIKISTAN

		Eastern Europe & Central Asia		GNI per capita (US$)	330
Ease of doing business (rank)	133	Low income		Population (m)	6.5

Starting a business (rank)	166
Procedures (number)	14
Time (days)	67
Cost (% of income per capita)	75.1
Minimum capital (% of income per capita)	378.6

Dealing with licenses (rank)	85
Procedures (number)	18
Time (days)	187
Cost (% of income per capita)	154.7

Employing workers (rank)	52
Difficulty of hiring index (0–100)	33
Rigidity of hours index (0–100)	20
Difficulty of firing index (0–100)	40
Rigidity of employment index (0–100)	31
Nonwage labor cost (% of salary)	25
Firing cost (weeks of salary)	22

Registering property (rank)	40
Procedures (number)	6
Time (days)	37
Cost (% of property value)	2.0

Getting credit (rank)	143
Strength of legal rights index (0–10)	4
Depth of credit information index (0–6)	0
Public registry coverage (% of adults)	0.0
Private bureau coverage (% of adults)	0.0

Protecting investors (rank)	172
Extent of disclosure index (0–10)	0
Extent of director liability index (0–10)	0
Ease of shareholder suits index (0–10)	5
Strength of investor protection index (0–10)	1.7

Paying taxes (rank)	154
Payments (number per year)	55
Time (hours per year)	224
Total tax rate (% of profit)	87.0

Trading across borders (rank)	163
Documents to export (number)	14
Time to export (days)	72
Cost to export (US$ per container)	4,300
Documents to import (number)	10
Time to import (days)	44
Cost to import (US$ per container)	3,550

Enforcing contracts (rank)	39
Procedures (number)	46
Time (days)	257
Cost (% of claim)	10.3

Closing a business (rank)	50
Time (years)	3.0
Cost (% of estate)	9
Recovery rate (cents on the dollar)	39.1

TANZANIA

| | | Sub-Saharan Africa | | GNI per capita (US$) | 340 |
| Ease of doing business (rank) | 142 | Low income | | Population (m) | 38.3 |

Starting a business (rank)	127	Registering property (rank)	157	Trading across borders (rank)	67
Procedures (number)	13	Procedures (number)	10	Documents to export (number)	3
Time (days)	30	Time (days)	123	Time to export (days)	24
Cost (% of income per capita)	91.6	Cost (% of property value)	5.5	Cost to export (US$ per container)	822
Minimum capital (% of income per capita)	5.5			Documents to import (number)	10
		Getting credit (rank)	117	Time to import (days)	39
Dealing with licenses (rank)	172	Strength of legal rights index (0–10)	5	Cost to import (US$ per container)	917
Procedures (number)	26	Depth of credit information index (0–6)	0		
Time (days)	313	Public registry coverage (% of adults)	0.0	Enforcing contracts (rank)	65
Cost (% of income per capita)	3796.6	Private bureau coverage (% of adults)	0.0	Procedures (number)	21
				Time (days)	393
Employing workers (rank)	143	Protecting investors (rank)	99	Cost (% of claim)	51.5
Difficulty of hiring index (0–100)	100	Extent of disclosure index (0–10)	3		
Rigidity of hours index (0–100)	40	Extent of director liability index (0–10)	4	Closing a business (rank)	105
Difficulty of firing index (0–100)	60	Ease of shareholder suits index (0–10)	7	Time (years)	3.0
Rigidity of employment index (0–100)	67	Strength of investor protection index (0–10)	4.7	Cost (% of estate)	22
Nonwage labor cost (% of salary)	16			Recovery rate (cents on the dollar)	21.9
Firing cost (weeks of salary)	32	Paying taxes (rank)	113		
		Payments (number per year)	48		
		Time (hours per year)	248		
		Total tax rate (% of profit)	45.0		

THAILAND

| | | East Asia & Pacific | | GNI per capita (US$) | 2,750 |
| Ease of doing business (rank) | 18 | Lower middle income | | Population (m) | 64.2 |

Starting a business (rank)	28	Registering property (rank)	18	Trading across borders (rank)	103
Procedures (number)	8	Procedures (number)	2	Documents to export (number)	9
Time (days)	33	Time (days)	2	Time to export (days)	24
Cost (% of income per capita)	5.8	Cost (% of property value)	6.3	Cost to export (US$ per container)	848
Minimum capital (% of income per capita)	0.0			Documents to import (number)	12
		Getting credit (rank)	33	Time to import (days)	22
Dealing with licenses (rank)	3	Strength of legal rights index (0–10)	5	Cost to import (US$ per container)	1,042
Procedures (number)	9	Depth of credit information index (0–6)	5		
Time (days)	127	Public registry coverage (% of adults)	0.0	Enforcing contracts (rank)	44
Cost (% of income per capita)	11.1	Private bureau coverage (% of adults)	21.7	Procedures (number)	26
				Time (days)	425
Employing workers (rank)	46	Protecting investors (rank)	33	Cost (% of claim)	17.5
Difficulty of hiring index (0–100)	33	Extent of disclosure index (0–10)	10		
Rigidity of hours index (0–100)	20	Extent of director liability index (0–10)	2	Closing a business (rank)	38
Difficulty of firing index (0–100)	0	Ease of shareholder suits index (0–10)	6	Time (years)	2.7
Rigidity of employment index (0–100)	18	Strength of investor protection index (0–10)	6.0	Cost (% of estate)	36
Nonwage labor cost (% of salary)	5			Recovery rate (cents on the dollar)	42.6
Firing cost (weeks of salary)	54	Paying taxes (rank)	57		
		Payments (number per year)	46		
		Time (hours per year)	104		
		Total tax rate (% of profit)	40.2		

TIMOR-LESTE

| | | East Asia & Pacific | | GNI per capita (US$) | 750 |
| Ease of doing business (rank) | 174 | Low income | | Population (m) | 1.0 |

Starting a business (rank)	160	Registering property (rank)	172	Trading across borders (rank)	73
Procedures (number)	10	Procedures (number)	NO PRACTICE	Documents to export (number)	6
Time (days)	92	Time (days)	NO PRACTICE	Time to export (days)	32
Cost (% of income per capita)	83.3	Cost (% of property value)	NO PRACTICE	Cost to export (US$ per container)	700
Minimum capital (% of income per capita)	666.7			Documents to import (number)	11
		Getting credit (rank)	159	Time to import (days)	37
Dealing with licenses (rank)	173	Strength of legal rights index (0–10)	3	Cost to import (US$ per container)	700
Procedures (number)	NO PRACTICE	Depth of credit information index (0–6)	0		
Time (days)	NO PRACTICE	Public registry coverage (% of adults)	0.0	Enforcing contracts (rank)	175
Cost (% of income per capita)	NO PRACTICE	Private bureau coverage (% of adults)	0.0	Procedures (number)	69
				Time (days)	1170
Employing workers (rank)	115	Protecting investors (rank)	142	Cost (% of claim)	183.1
Difficulty of hiring index (0–100)	67	Extent of disclosure index (0–10)	7		
Rigidity of hours index (0–100)	20	Extent of director liability index (0–10)	1	Closing a business (rank)	151
Difficulty of firing index (0–100)	50	Ease of shareholder suits index (0–10)	3	Time (years)	NO PRACTICE
Rigidity of employment index (0–100)	46	Strength of investor protection index (0–10)	3.7	Cost (% of estate)	NO PRACTICE
Nonwage labor cost (% of salary)	0			Recovery rate (cents on the dollar)	0.0
Firing cost (weeks of salary)	35	Paying taxes (rank)	124		
		Payments (number per year)	15		
		Time (hours per year)	640		
		Total tax rate (% of profit)	59.2		

TOGO

		Sub-Saharan Africa		GNI per capita (US$)	350
Ease of doing business (rank)	151	Low income		Population (m)	6.1

Starting a business (rank)	169	**Registering property** (rank)	155	**Trading across borders** (rank)	64
Procedures (number)	13	Procedures (number)	7	Documents to export (number)	7
Time (days)	53	Time (days)	242	Time to export (days)	32
Cost (% of income per capita)	252.7	Cost (% of property value)	7.7	Cost to export (US$ per container)	463
Minimum capital (% of income per capita)	539.7			Documents to import (number)	9
		Getting credit (rank)	143	Time to import (days)	41
Dealing with licenses (rank)	132	Strength of legal rights index (0–10)	3	Cost to import (US$ per container)	695
Procedures (number)	14	Depth of credit information index (0–6)	1		
Time (days)	273	Public registry coverage (% of adults)	3.6	**Enforcing contracts** (rank)	123
Cost (% of income per capita)	1435.6	Private bureau coverage (% of adults)	0.0	Procedures (number)	37
				Time (days)	535
Employing workers (rank)	145	**Protecting investors** (rank)	135	Cost (% of claim)	24.3
Difficulty of hiring index (0–100)	44	Extent of disclosure index (0–10)	4		
Rigidity of hours index (0–100)	60	Extent of director liability index (0–10)	3	**Closing a business** (rank)	88
Difficulty of firing index (0–100)	70	Ease of shareholder suits index (0–10)	5	Time (years)	3.0
Rigidity of employment index (0–100)	58	Strength of investor protection index (0–10)	4.0	Cost (% of estate)	15
Nonwage labor cost (% of salary)	25			Recovery rate (cents on the dollar)	27.2
Firing cost (weeks of salary)	36	**Paying taxes** (rank)	130		
		Payments (number per year)	51		
		Time (hours per year)	270		
		Total tax rate (% of profit)	48.3		

TONGA

		East Asia & Pacific		GNI per capita (US$)	2,190
Ease of doing business (rank)	51	Lower middle income		Population (m)	0.1

Starting a business (rank)	23	**Registering property** (rank)	108	**Trading across borders** (rank)	17
Procedures (number)	4	Procedures (number)	4	Documents to export (number)	6
Time (days)	32	Time (days)	108	Time to export (days)	12
Cost (% of income per capita)	10.3	Cost (% of property value)	10.2	Cost to export (US$ per container)	265
Minimum capital (% of income per capita)	0.0			Documents to import (number)	9
		Getting credit (rank)	117	Time to import (days)	17
Dealing with licenses (rank)	37	Strength of legal rights index (0–10)	5	Cost to import (US$ per container)	360
Procedures (number)	15	Depth of credit information index (0–6)	0		
Time (days)	81	Public registry coverage (% of adults)	0.0	**Enforcing contracts** (rank)	126
Cost (% of income per capita)	174.6	Private bureau coverage (% of adults)	0.0	Procedures (number)	30
				Time (days)	510
Employing workers (rank)	4	**Protecting investors** (rank)	99	Cost (% of claim)	47.0
Difficulty of hiring index (0–100)	0	Extent of disclosure index (0–10)	3		
Rigidity of hours index (0–100)	20	Extent of director liability index (0–10)	3	**Closing a business** (rank)	92
Difficulty of firing index (0–100)	0	Ease of shareholder suits index (0–10)	8	Time (years)	2.7
Rigidity of employment index (0–100)	7	Strength of investor protection index (0–10)	4.7	Cost (% of estate)	22
Nonwage labor cost (% of salary)	0			Recovery rate (cents on the dollar)	25.6
Firing cost (weeks of salary)	0	**Paying taxes** (rank)	81		
		Payments (number per year)	22		
		Time (hours per year)	164		
		Total tax rate (% of profit)	56.2		

TRINIDAD AND TOBAGO

		Latin America & Caribbean		GNI per capita (US$)	10,440
Ease of doing business (rank)	59	Upper middle income		Population (m)	1.3

Starting a business (rank)	35	**Registering property** (rank)	154	**Trading across borders** (rank)	22
Procedures (number)	9	Procedures (number)	8	Documents to export (number)	5
Time (days)	43	Time (days)	162	Time to export (days)	9
Cost (% of income per capita)	1.1	Cost (% of property value)	7.0	Cost to export (US$ per container)	693
Minimum capital (% of income per capita)	0.0			Documents to import (number)	7
		Getting credit (rank)	48	Time to import (days)	13
Dealing with licenses (rank)	81	Strength of legal rights index (0–10)	6	Cost to import (US$ per container)	1,093
Procedures (number)	19	Depth of credit information index (0–6)	3		
Time (days)	292	Public registry coverage (% of adults)	0.0	**Enforcing contracts** (rank)	156
Cost (% of income per capita)	9.9	Private bureau coverage (% of adults)	31.5	Procedures (number)	37
				Time (days)	1340
Employing workers (rank)	27	**Protecting investors** (rank)	15	Cost (% of claim)	30.5
Difficulty of hiring index (0–100)	0	Extent of disclosure index (0–10)	4		
Rigidity of hours index (0–100)	0	Extent of director liability index (0–10)	9	**Closing a business** (rank)	151
Difficulty of firing index (0–100)	20	Ease of shareholder suits index (0–10)	7	Time (years)	NO PRACTICE
Rigidity of employment index (0–100)	7	Strength of investor protection index (0–10)	6.7	Cost (% of estate)	NO PRACTICE
Nonwage labor cost (% of salary)	5			Recovery rate (cents on the dollar)	0.0
Firing cost (weeks of salary)	67	**Paying taxes** (rank)	27		
		Payments (number per year)	28		
		Time (hours per year)	114		
		Total tax rate (% of profit)	37.2		

TUNISIA

		Middle East & North Africa		GNI per capita (US$)	2,890
Ease of doing business (rank)	80	Lower middle income		Population (m)	10.0

Starting a business (rank)	59	**Registering property** (rank)	71	**Trading across borders** (rank)	39
Procedures (number)	10	Procedures (number)	5	Documents to export (number)	5
Time (days)	11	Time (days)	57	Time to export (days)	18
Cost (% of income per capita)	9.3	Cost (% of property value)	6.1	Cost to export (US$ per container)	770
Minimum capital (% of income per capita)	28.3			Documents to import (number)	8
		Getting credit (rank)	101	Time to import (days)	29
Dealing with licenses (rank)	110	Strength of legal rights index (0–10)	3	Cost to import (US$ per container)	600
Procedures (number)	24	Depth of credit information index (0–6)	3		
Time (days)	79	Public registry coverage (% of adults)	11.6	**Enforcing contracts** (rank)	40
Cost (% of income per capita)	1031.9	Private bureau coverage (% of adults)	0.0	Procedures (number)	21
				Time (days)	481
Employing workers (rank)	92	**Protecting investors** (rank)	151	Cost (% of claim)	17.3
Difficulty of hiring index (0–100)	17	Extent of disclosure index (0–10)	0		
Rigidity of hours index (0–100)	40	Extent of director liability index (0–10)	4	**Closing a business** (rank)	29
Difficulty of firing index (0–100)	80	Ease of shareholder suits index (0–10)	6	Time (years)	1.3
Rigidity of employment index (0–100)	46	Strength of investor protection index (0–10)	3.3	Cost (% of estate)	7
Nonwage labor cost (% of salary)	22			Recovery rate (cents on the dollar)	51.2
Firing cost (weeks of salary)	17	**Paying taxes** (rank)	139		
		Payments (number per year)	45		
		Time (hours per year)	268		
		Total tax rate (% of profit)	58.8		

TURKEY

		Eastern Europe & Central Asia		GNI per capita (US$)	4,710
Ease of doing business (rank)	91	Upper middle income		Population (m)	72.6

Starting a business (rank)	53	**Registering property** (rank)	54	**Trading across borders** (rank)	79
Procedures (number)	8	Procedures (number)	8	Documents to export (number)	9
Time (days)	9	Time (days)	9	Time to export (days)	20
Cost (% of income per capita)	26.8	Cost (% of property value)	3.2	Cost to export (US$ per container)	513
Minimum capital (% of income per capita)	18.7			Documents to import (number)	13
		Getting credit (rank)	65	Time to import (days)	25
Dealing with licenses (rank)	148	Strength of legal rights index (0–10)	3	Cost to import (US$ per container)	735
Procedures (number)	32	Depth of credit information index (0–6)	5		
Time (days)	232	Public registry coverage (% of adults)	6.7	**Enforcing contracts** (rank)	70
Cost (% of income per capita)	150.2	Private bureau coverage (% of adults)	..	Procedures (number)	34
				Time (days)	420
Employing workers (rank)	146	**Protecting investors** (rank)	60	Cost (% of claim)	17.4
Difficulty of hiring index (0–100)	56	Extent of disclosure index (0–10)	8		
Rigidity of hours index (0–100)	60	Extent of director liability index (0–10)	4	**Closing a business** (rank)	138
Difficulty of firing index (0–100)	30	Ease of shareholder suits index (0–10)	4	Time (years)	5.9
Rigidity of employment index (0–100)	49	Strength of investor protection index (0–10)	5.3	Cost (% of estate)	7
Nonwage labor cost (% of salary)	22			Recovery rate (cents on the dollar)	9.8
Firing cost (weeks of salary)	95	**Paying taxes** (rank)	65		
		Payments (number per year)	18		
		Time (hours per year)	254		
		Total tax rate (% of profit)	46.3		

UGANDA

		Sub-Saharan Africa		GNI per capita (US$)	280
Ease of doing business (rank)	107	Low income		Population (m)	28.8

Starting a business (rank)	107	**Registering property** (rank)	166	**Trading across borders** (rank)	160
Procedures (number)	17	Procedures (number)	13	Documents to export (number)	12
Time (days)	30	Time (days)	227	Time to export (days)	42
Cost (% of income per capita)	114.0	Cost (% of property value)	6.9	Cost to export (US$ per container)	1,050
Minimum capital (% of income per capita)	0.0			Documents to import (number)	19
		Getting credit (rank)	159	Time to import (days)	67
Dealing with licenses (rank)	110	Strength of legal rights index (0–10)	3	Cost to import (US$ per container)	2,945
Procedures (number)	19	Depth of credit information index (0–6)	0		
Time (days)	156	Public registry coverage (% of adults)	0.0	**Enforcing contracts** (rank)	71
Cost (% of income per capita)	832.8	Private bureau coverage (% of adults)	0.0	Procedures (number)	19
				Time (days)	484
Employing workers (rank)	8	**Protecting investors** (rank)	60	Cost (% of claim)	35.2
Difficulty of hiring index (0–100)	0	Extent of disclosure index (0–10)	7		
Rigidity of hours index (0–100)	20	Extent of director liability index (0–10)	5	**Closing a business** (rank)	44
Difficulty of firing index (0–100)	0	Ease of shareholder suits index (0–10)	4	Time (years)	2.2
Rigidity of employment index (0–100)	7	Strength of investor protection index (0–10)	5.3	Cost (% of estate)	30
Nonwage labor cost (% of salary)	10			Recovery rate (cents on the dollar)	40.4
Firing cost (weeks of salary)	13	**Paying taxes** (rank)	43		
		Payments (number per year)	31		
		Time (hours per year)	237		
		Total tax rate (% of profit)	32.2		

UKRAINE

		Eastern Europe & Central Asia		GNI per capita (US$)	1,520
Ease of doing business (rank)	128	Lower middle income		Population (m)	47.1

Starting a business (rank)	101	**Registering property** (rank)	133	**Trading across borders** (rank)	106
Procedures (number)	10	Procedures (number)	10	Documents to export (number)	6
Time (days)	33	Time (days)	93	Time to export (days)	33
Cost (% of income per capita)	9.2	Cost (% of property value)	3.4	Cost to export (US$ per container)	1,009
Minimum capital (% of income per capita)	198.8			Documents to import (number)	10
		Getting credit (rank)	65	Time to import (days)	46
Dealing with licenses (rank)	107	Strength of legal rights index (0–10)	8	Cost to import (US$ per container)	1,025
Procedures (number)	18	Depth of credit information index (0–6)	0		
Time (days)	242	Public registry coverage (% of adults)	0.0	**Enforcing contracts** (rank)	26
Cost (% of income per capita)	186.5	Private bureau coverage (% of adults)	0.0	Procedures (number)	28
				Time (days)	183
Employing workers (rank)	107	**Protecting investors** (rank)	142	Cost (% of claim)	16.0
Difficulty of hiring index (0–100)	44	Extent of disclosure index (0–10)	1		
Rigidity of hours index (0–100)	40	Extent of director liability index (0–10)	3	**Closing a business** (rank)	139
Difficulty of firing index (0–100)	80	Ease of shareholder suits index (0–10)	7	Time (years)	2.9
Rigidity of employment index (0–100)	55	Strength of investor protection index (0–10)	3.7	Cost (% of estate)	42
Nonwage labor cost (% of salary)	39			Recovery rate (cents on the dollar)	8.7
Firing cost (weeks of salary)	13	**Paying taxes** (rank)	174		
		Payments (number per year)	98		
		Time (hours per year)	2185		
		Total tax rate (% of profit)	60.3		

UNITED ARAB EMIRATES

		Middle East & North Africa		GNI per capita (US$)	23,770
Ease of doing business (rank)	77	High income		Population (m)	4.5

Starting a business (rank)	155	**Registering property** (rank)	8	**Trading across borders** (rank)	10
Procedures (number)	12	Procedures (number)	3	Documents to export (number)	4
Time (days)	63	Time (days)	6	Time to export (days)	18
Cost (% of income per capita)	36.4	Cost (% of property value)	2.0	Cost to export (US$ per container)	392
Minimum capital (% of income per capita)	338.2			Documents to import (number)	6
		Getting credit (rank)	117	Time to import (days)	16
Dealing with licenses (rank)	79	Strength of legal rights index (0–10)	3	Cost to import (US$ per container)	398
Procedures (number)	21	Depth of credit information index (0–6)	2		
Time (days)	125	Public registry coverage (% of adults)	1.7	**Enforcing contracts** (rank)	112
Cost (% of income per capita)	210.0	Private bureau coverage (% of adults)	0.0	Procedures (number)	34
				Time (days)	607
Employing workers (rank)	57	**Protecting investors** (rank)	118	Cost (% of claim)	18.5
Difficulty of hiring index (0–100)	0	Extent of disclosure index (0–10)	4		
Rigidity of hours index (0–100)	60	Extent of director liability index (0–10)	7	**Closing a business** (rank)	137
Difficulty of firing index (0–100)	0	Ease of shareholder suits index (0–10)	2	Time (years)	5.1
Rigidity of employment index (0–100)	20	Strength of investor protection index (0–10)	4.3	Cost (% of estate)	30
Nonwage labor cost (% of salary)	13			Recovery rate (cents on the dollar)	10.4
Firing cost (weeks of salary)	84	**Paying taxes** (rank)	3		
		Payments (number per year)	15		
		Time (hours per year)	12		
		Total tax rate (% of profit)	15.0		

UNITED KINGDOM

		OECD: High Income		GNI per capita (US$)	37,600
Ease of doing business (rank)	6	High income		Population (m)	60.2

Starting a business (rank)	9	**Registering property** (rank)	19	**Trading across borders** (rank)	14
Procedures (number)	6	Procedures (number)	2	Documents to export (number)	5
Time (days)	18	Time (days)	21	Time to export (days)	12
Cost (% of income per capita)	0.7	Cost (% of property value)	4.1	Cost to export (US$ per container)	676
Minimum capital (% of income per capita)	0.0			Documents to import (number)	4
		Getting credit (rank)	1	Time to import (days)	12
Dealing with licenses (rank)	46	Strength of legal rights index (0–10)	10	Cost to import (US$ per container)	756
Procedures (number)	19	Depth of credit information index (0–6)	6		
Time (days)	115	Public registry coverage (% of adults)	0.0	**Enforcing contracts** (rank)	22
Cost (% of income per capita)	68.9	Private bureau coverage (% of adults)	86.1	Procedures (number)	19
				Time (days)	229
Employing workers (rank)	17	**Protecting investors** (rank)	9	Cost (% of claim)	16.8
Difficulty of hiring index (0–100)	11	Extent of disclosure index (0–10)	10		
Rigidity of hours index (0–100)	20	Extent of director liability index (0–10)	7	**Closing a business** (rank)	10
Difficulty of firing index (0–100)	10	Ease of shareholder suits index (0–10)	7	Time (years)	1.0
Rigidity of employment index (0–100)	14	Strength of investor protection index (0–10)	8.0	Cost (% of estate)	6
Nonwage labor cost (% of salary)	11			Recovery rate (cents on the dollar)	85.2
Firing cost (weeks of salary)	22	**Paying taxes** (rank)	12		
		Payments (number per year)	7		
		Time (hours per year)	105		
		Total tax rate (% of profit)	35.4		

UNITED STATES

		OECD: High Income		GNI per capita (US$)	43,740
Ease of doing business (rank)	3	High income		Population (m)	296.5

Starting a business (rank)	3	**Registering property** (rank)	10	**Trading across borders** (rank)	11
Procedures (number)	5	Procedures (number)	4	Documents to export (number)	6
Time (days)	5	Time (days)	12	Time to export (days)	9
Cost (% of income per capita)	0.7	Cost (% of property value)	0.5	Cost to export (US$ per container)	625
Minimum capital (% of income per capita)	0.0			Documents to import (number)	5
		Getting credit (rank)	7	Time to import (days)	9
Dealing with licenses (rank)	22	Strength of legal rights index (0–10)	7	Cost to import (US$ per container)	625
Procedures (number)	18	Depth of credit information index (0–6)	6		
Time (days)	69	Public registry coverage (% of adults)	0.0	**Enforcing contracts** (rank)	6
Cost (% of income per capita)	16.0	Private bureau coverage (% of adults)	100.0	Procedures (number)	17
				Time (days)	300
Employing workers (rank)	1	**Protecting investors** (rank)	5	Cost (% of claim)	7.7
Difficulty of hiring index (0–100)	0	Extent of disclosure index (0–10)	7		
Rigidity of hours index (0–100)	0	Extent of director liability index (0–10)	9	**Closing a business** (rank)	16
Difficulty of firing index (0–100)	0	Ease of shareholder suits index (0–10)	9	Time (years)	1.5
Rigidity of employment index (0–100)	0	Strength of investor protection index (0–10)	8.3	Cost (% of estate)	7
Nonwage labor cost (% of salary)	8			Recovery rate (cents on the dollar)	77.0
Firing cost (weeks of salary)	0	**Paying taxes** (rank)	63		
		Payments (number per year)	10		
		Time (hours per year)	325		
		Total tax rate (% of profit)	46.0		

URUGUAY

		Latin America & Caribbean		GNI per capita (US$)	4,360
Ease of doing business (rank)	64	Upper middle income		Population (m)	3.5

Starting a business (rank)	134	**Registering property** (rank)	138	**Trading across borders** (rank)	59
Procedures (number)	10	Procedures (number)	8	Documents to export (number)	9
Time (days)	43	Time (days)	66	Time to export (days)	22
Cost (% of income per capita)	44.2	Cost (% of property value)	7.1	Cost to export (US$ per container)	552
Minimum capital (% of income per capita)	183.3			Documents to import (number)	9
		Getting credit (rank)	33	Time to import (days)	25
Dealing with licenses (rank)	56	Strength of legal rights index (0–10)	4	Cost to import (US$ per container)	666
Procedures (number)	17	Depth of credit information index (0–6)	6		
Time (days)	156	Public registry coverage (% of adults)	13.2	**Enforcing contracts** (rank)	119
Cost (% of income per capita)	96.3	Private bureau coverage (% of adults)	85.3	Procedures (number)	39
				Time (days)	655
Employing workers (rank)	58	**Protecting investors** (rank)	83	Cost (% of claim)	15.9
Difficulty of hiring index (0–100)	33	Extent of disclosure index (0–10)	3		
Rigidity of hours index (0–100)	60	Extent of director liability index (0–10)	4	**Closing a business** (rank)	37
Difficulty of firing index (0–100)	0	Ease of shareholder suits index (0–10)	8	Time (years)	2.1
Rigidity of employment index (0–100)	31	Strength of investor protection index (0–10)	5.0	Cost (% of estate)	7
Nonwage labor cost (% of salary)	6			Recovery rate (cents on the dollar)	43.2
Firing cost (weeks of salary)	31	**Paying taxes** (rank)	76		
		Payments (number per year)	41		
		Time (hours per year)	300		
		Total tax rate (% of profit)	27.6		

UZBEKISTAN

		Eastern Europe & Central Asia		GNI per capita (US$)	510
Ease of doing business (rank)	147	Low income		Population (m)	26.6

Starting a business (rank)	70	**Registering property** (rank)	165	**Trading across borders** (rank)	169
Procedures (number)	8	Procedures (number)	12	Documents to export (number)	10
Time (days)	29	Time (days)	97	Time to export (days)	44
Cost (% of income per capita)	14.1	Cost (% of property value)	10.5	Cost to export (US$ per container)	2,550
Minimum capital (% of income per capita)	24.7			Documents to import (number)	18
		Getting credit (rank)	159	Time to import (days)	139
Dealing with licenses (rank)	138	Strength of legal rights index (0–10)	3	Cost to import (US$ per container)	3,970
Procedures (number)	19	Depth of credit information index (0–6)	0		
Time (days)	287	Public registry coverage (% of adults)	0.0	**Enforcing contracts** (rank)	30
Cost (% of income per capita)	258.2	Private bureau coverage (% of adults)	0.0	Procedures (number)	35
				Time (days)	195
Employing workers (rank)	67	**Protecting investors** (rank)	118	Cost (% of claim)	13.5
Difficulty of hiring index (0–100)	33	Extent of disclosure index (0–10)	4		
Rigidity of hours index (0–100)	40	Extent of director liability index (0–10)	6	**Closing a business** (rank)	112
Difficulty of firing index (0–100)	30	Ease of shareholder suits index (0–10)	3	Time (years)	4.0
Rigidity of employment index (0–100)	34	Strength of investor protection index (0–10)	4.3	Cost (% of estate)	10
Nonwage labor cost (% of salary)	31			Recovery rate (cents on the dollar)	18.7
Firing cost (weeks of salary)	30	**Paying taxes** (rank)	155		
		Payments (number per year)	130		
		Time (hours per year)	152		
		Total tax rate (% of profit)	122.3		

VANUATU

		East Asia & Pacific		GNI per capita (US$)	1,600
Ease of doing business (rank)	58	Lower middle income		Population (m)	0.2

Starting a business (rank)	65	**Registering property** (rank)	91	**Trading across borders** (rank)	120
Procedures (number)	8	Procedures (number)	2	Documents to export (number)	9
Time (days)	39	Time (days)	188	Time to export (days)	12
Cost (% of income per capita)	61.3	Cost (% of property value)	7.0	Cost to export (US$ per container)	1,565
Minimum capital (% of income per capita)	0.0			Documents to import (number)	16
		Getting credit (rank)	117	Time to import (days)	14
Dealing with licenses (rank)	33	Strength of legal rights index (0–10)	5	Cost to import (US$ per container)	1,975
Procedures (number)	7	Depth of credit information index (0–6)	0		
Time (days)	82	Public registry coverage (% of adults)	0.0	**Enforcing contracts** (rank)	88
Cost (% of income per capita)	398.9	Private bureau coverage (% of adults)	0.0	Procedures (number)	24
				Time (days)	430
Employing workers (rank)	96	**Protecting investors** (rank)	60	Cost (% of claim)	64.0
Difficulty of hiring index (0–100)	50	Extent of disclosure index (0–10)	5		
Rigidity of hours index (0–100)	40	Extent of director liability index (0–10)	6	**Closing a business** (rank)	45
Difficulty of firing index (0–100)	10	Ease of shareholder suits index (0–10)	5	Time (years)	2.6
Rigidity of employment index (0–100)	33	Strength of investor protection index (0–10)	5.3	Cost (% of estate)	38
Nonwage labor cost (% of salary)	4			Recovery rate (cents on the dollar)	40.0
Firing cost (weeks of salary)	56	**Paying taxes** (rank)	19		
		Payments (number per year)	32		
		Time (hours per year)	120		
		Total tax rate (% of profit)	14.4		

VENEZUELA

		Latin America & Caribbean		GNI per capita (US$)	4,810
Ease of doing business (rank)	164	Upper middle income		Population (m)	26.6

Starting a business (rank)	129	**Registering property** (rank)	75	**Trading across borders** (rank)	116
Procedures (number)	16	Procedures (number)	8	Documents to export (number)	8
Time (days)	141	Time (days)	47	Time to export (days)	32
Cost (% of income per capita)	25.4	Cost (% of property value)	2.1	Cost to export (US$ per container)	525
Minimum capital (% of income per capita)	0.0			Documents to import (number)	13
		Getting credit (rank)	143	Time to import (days)	67
Dealing with licenses (rank)	98	Strength of legal rights index (0–10)	4	Cost to import (US$ per container)	900
Procedures (number)	13	Depth of credit information index (0–6)	0		
Time (days)	276	Public registry coverage (% of adults)	0.0	**Enforcing contracts** (rank)	129
Cost (% of income per capita)	388.4	Private bureau coverage (% of adults)	0.0	Procedures (number)	41
				Time (days)	435
Employing workers (rank)	165	**Protecting investors** (rank)	162	Cost (% of claim)	28.7
Difficulty of hiring index (0–100)	67	Extent of disclosure index (0–10)	3		
Rigidity of hours index (0–100)	60	Extent of director liability index (0–10)	3	**Closing a business** (rank)	144
Difficulty of firing index (0–100)	100	Ease of shareholder suits index (0–10)	2	Time (years)	4.0
Rigidity of employment index (0–100)	76	Strength of investor protection index (0–10)	2.7	Cost (% of estate)	38
Nonwage labor cost (% of salary)	16			Recovery rate (cents on the dollar)	6.7
Firing cost (weeks of salary)	47	**Paying taxes** (rank)	167		
		Payments (number per year)	68		
		Time (hours per year)	864		
		Total tax rate (% of profit)	51.9		

VIETNAM

		East Asia & Pacific		GNI per capita (US$)	620
Ease of doing business (rank)	104	Low income		Population (m)	83.0

Starting a business (rank)	97	**Registering property** (rank)	34	**Trading across borders** (rank)	75
Procedures (number)	11	Procedures (number)	4	Documents to export (number)	6
Time (days)	50	Time (days)	67	Time to export (days)	35
Cost (% of income per capita)	44.5	Cost (% of property value)	1.2	Cost to export (US$ per container)	701
Minimum capital (% of income per capita)	0.0			Documents to import (number)	9
		Getting credit (rank)	83	Time to import (days)	36
Dealing with licenses (rank)	25	Strength of legal rights index (0–10)	4	Cost to import (US$ per container)	887
Procedures (number)	14	Depth of credit information index (0–6)	3		
Time (days)	133	Public registry coverage (% of adults)	2.7	**Enforcing contracts** (rank)	94
Cost (% of income per capita)	56.4	Private bureau coverage (% of adults)	0.0	Procedures (number)	37
				Time (days)	295
Employing workers (rank)	104	**Protecting investors** (rank)	170	Cost (% of claim)	31.0
Difficulty of hiring index (0–100)	0	Extent of disclosure index (0–10)	4		
Rigidity of hours index (0–100)	40	Extent of director liability index (0–10)	0	**Closing a business** (rank)	116
Difficulty of firing index (0–100)	70	Ease of shareholder suits index (0–10)	2	Time (years)	5.0
Rigidity of employment index (0–100)	37	Strength of investor protection index (0–10)	2.0	Cost (% of estate)	15
Nonwage labor cost (% of salary)	17			Recovery rate (cents on the dollar)	18.0
Firing cost (weeks of salary)	87	**Paying taxes** (rank)	120		
		Payments (number per year)	32		
		Time (hours per year)	1050		
		Total tax rate (% of profit)	41.6		

WEST BANK AND GAZA

Ease of doing business (rank)	127	Middle East & North Africa		
		Lower middle income		

Starting a business (rank)	173	**Registering property** (rank)	118
Procedures (number)	12	Procedures (number)	10
Time (days)	93	Time (days)	72
Cost (% of income per capita)	324.7	Cost (% of property value)	2.4
Minimum capital (% of income per capita)	1889.6		

GNI per capita (US$) 953
Population (m) 3.6

Trading across borders (rank)	65
Documents to export (number)	7
Time to export (days)	27
Cost to export (US$ per container)	705
Documents to import (number)	7
Time to import (days)	41
Cost to import (US$ per container)	755

Dealing with licenses (rank)	108
Procedures (number)	21
Time (days)	134
Cost (% of income per capita)	823.4

Getting credit (rank)	65
Strength of legal rights index (0–10)	5
Depth of credit information index (0–6)	3
Public registry coverage (% of adults)	0.7
Private bureau coverage (% of adults)	0.0

Enforcing contracts (rank)	100
Procedures (number)	26
Time (days)	700
Cost (% of claim)	20.2

Employing workers (rank)	97
Difficulty of hiring index (0–100)	33
Rigidity of hours index (0–100)	40
Difficulty of firing index (0–100)	20
Rigidity of employment index (0–100)	31
Nonwage labor cost (% of salary)	13
Firing cost (weeks of salary)	91

Protecting investors (rank)	99
Extent of disclosure index (0–10)	7
Extent of director liability index (0–10)	2
Ease of shareholder suits index (0–10)	5
Strength of investor protection index (0–10)	4.7

Closing a business (rank)	151
Time (years)	NO PRACTICE
Cost (% of estate)	NO PRACTICE
Recovery rate (cents on the dollar)	0.0

Paying taxes (rank)	55
Payments (number per year)	50
Time (hours per year)	154
Total tax rate (% of profit)	31.5

YEMEN

Ease of doing business (rank)	98	Middle East & North Africa		
		Low income		

Starting a business (rank)	171	**Registering property** (rank)	43
Procedures (number)	12	Procedures (number)	6
Time (days)	63	Time (days)	21
Cost (% of income per capita)	228.0	Cost (% of property value)	3.9
Minimum capital (% of income per capita)	2565.7		

GNI per capita (US$) 600
Population (m) 21.0

Trading across borders (rank)	107
Documents to export (number)	6
Time to export (days)	33
Cost to export (US$ per container)	1,129
Documents to import (number)	9
Time to import (days)	31
Cost to import (US$ per container)	1,475

Dealing with licenses (rank)	39
Procedures (number)	13
Time (days)	107
Cost (% of income per capita)	306.4

Getting credit (rank)	117
Strength of legal rights index (0–10)	3
Depth of credit information index (0–6)	2
Public registry coverage (% of adults)	0.1
Private bureau coverage (% of adults)	0.0

Enforcing contracts (rank)	37
Procedures (number)	37
Time (days)	360
Cost (% of claim)	10.5

Employing workers (rank)	53
Difficulty of hiring index (0–100)	0
Rigidity of hours index (0–100)	60
Difficulty of firing index (0–100)	40
Rigidity of employment index (0–100)	33
Nonwage labor cost (% of salary)	9
Firing cost (weeks of salary)	17

Protecting investors (rank)	118
Extent of disclosure index (0–10)	6
Extent of director liability index (0–10)	4
Ease of shareholder suits index (0–10)	3
Strength of investor protection index (0–10)	4.3

Closing a business (rank)	82
Time (years)	3.0
Cost (% of estate)	8
Recovery rate (cents on the dollar)	28.6

Paying taxes (rank)	89
Payments (number per year)	32
Time (hours per year)	248
Total tax rate (% of profit)	48.0

ZAMBIA

Ease of doing business (rank)	102	Sub-Saharan Africa		
		Low income		

Starting a business (rank)	67	**Registering property** (rank)	119
Procedures (number)	6	Procedures (number)	6
Time (days)	35	Time (days)	70
Cost (% of income per capita)	29.9	Cost (% of property value)	9.6
Minimum capital (% of income per capita)	1.9		

GNI per capita (US$) 490
Population (m) 11.7

Trading across borders (rank)	170
Documents to export (number)	16
Time to export (days)	60
Cost to export (US$ per container)	2,500
Documents to import (number)	19
Time to import (days)	62
Cost to import (US$ per container)	2,640

Dealing with licenses (rank)	123
Procedures (number)	16
Time (days)	196
Cost (% of income per capita)	1766.1

Getting credit (rank)	83
Strength of legal rights index (0–10)	7
Depth of credit information index (0–6)	0
Public registry coverage (% of adults)	0.0
Private bureau coverage (% of adults)	0.0

Enforcing contracts (rank)	51
Procedures (number)	21
Time (days)	404
Cost (% of claim)	28.7

Employing workers (rank)	80
Difficulty of hiring index (0–100)	0
Rigidity of hours index (0–100)	40
Difficulty of firing index (0–100)	30
Rigidity of employment index (0–100)	23
Nonwage labor cost (% of salary)	11
Firing cost (weeks of salary)	178

Protecting investors (rank)	60
Extent of disclosure index (0–10)	3
Extent of director liability index (0–10)	6
Ease of shareholder suits index (0–10)	7
Strength of investor protection index (0–10)	5.3

Closing a business (rank)	104
Time (years)	3.1
Cost (% of estate)	9
Recovery rate (cents on the dollar)	22.0

Paying taxes (rank)	25
Payments (number per year)	36
Time (hours per year)	132
Total tax rate (% of profit)	22.2

ZIMBABWE

Ease of doing business (rank)	153

Starting a business (rank) 137
Procedures (number) 10
Time (days) 96
Cost (% of income per capita) 35.6
Minimum capital (% of income per capita) 53.0

Dealing with licenses (rank) 171
Procedures (number) 21
Time (days) 481
Cost (% of income per capita) 1509.6

Employing workers (rank) 122
Difficulty of hiring index (0–100) 11
Rigidity of hours index (0–100) 40
Difficulty of firing index (0–100) 50
Rigidity of employment index (0–100) 34
Nonwage labor cost (% of salary) 4
Firing cost (weeks of salary) 446

Sub-Saharan Africa
Low income

Registering property (rank) 80
Procedures (number) 4
Time (days) 30
Cost (% of property value) 24.0

Getting credit (rank) 101
Strength of legal rights index (0–10) 6
Depth of credit information index (0–6) 0
Public registry coverage (% of adults) 0.0
Private bureau coverage (% of adults) 0.0

Protecting investors (rank) 118
Extent of disclosure index (0–10) 8
Extent of director liability index (0–10) 1
Ease of shareholder suits index (0–10) 4
Strength of investor protection index (0–10) 4.3

Paying taxes (rank) 95
Payments (number per year) 59
Time (hours per year) 216
Total tax rate (% of profit) 37.0

GNI per capita (US$)	340
Population (m)	13.0

Trading across borders (rank) 168
Documents to export (number) 9
Time to export (days) 52
Cost to export (US$ per container) 3,175
Documents to import (number) 15
Time to import (days) 66
Cost to import (US$ per container) 4,565

Enforcing contracts (rank) 93
Procedures (number) 33
Time (days) 410
Cost (% of claim) 26.9

Closing a business (rank) 150
Time (years) 3.3
Cost (% of estate) 22
Recovery rate (cents on the dollar) 0.1

Acknowledgments

Contact details for local partners are available
on the *Doing Business* website at
http://www.doingbusiness.org

Doing Business 2007 was prepared by a team led by Simeon Djankov and Caralee McLiesh under the general direction of Michael Klein. The team comprised Svetlana Bagaudinova, Marie-Lily Delion, Jacqueline den Otter, Allen Dennis, Penelope Fidas, Monica Hanssen, Sabine Hertveldt, Benjamin Horne, Melissa Johns, Joanna Kata-Blackman, Adam Larson, Julien Levis, Darshini Manraj, Dana Omran, Rita Ramalho, Sylvia Solf, Caroline van Coppenolle, Adriana Vicentini, Lihong Wang, Jelani Wilkins and Justin Yap. Mema Beye, Hania Dawood and Francoise-Helene Schorosch assisted in the months prior to publication.

Oliver Hart, Rafael La Porta and Andrei Shleifer provided academic advice on the project. The paying taxes project was conducted in partnership with PricewaterhouseCoopers, led by Robert Morris with Kelly Murray and Penny Vaughn. The protecting investors and enforcing contracts projects were conducted in partnership with the Lex Mundi association, led by Carl Anduri and Sam Nolen. The Ministry for Foreign Affairs of Iceland funded the expansion of the sample to 20 small economies. Paul Holtz and Alison Strong edited the manuscript. Nadine Shamounki Ghannam and Suzanne Smith provided editorial and marketing advice. Gerry Quinn designed the report and the graphs.

Individual chapters were refereed by a panel of experts comprising Irina Astrakhan, Teresa Barger, Alexander Berg, David Bernstein, Penelope Brook, Tony Burns, Mierta Capaul, Stijn Claessens, Jacqueline Coolidge, Michael Engelschalk, Mario Gamboa-Cavazos, Luke Haggarty, Linn Hammergren, Catherine Anne Hickey, Leora Klapper, Arvo Kuddo, Peter Ladegaard, Richard Messick, Andrei Mikhnev, Claudio Montenegro, Tatiana Nenova, Sanda Putnina, Dory Reiling, Adolfo Rouillon, Jorge Saba Arbache, Jolyne Sanjak, Sevi Simavi, Inderbir Singh Dhingra, Kalanidhi Subbarao, Richard Symonds, Vijay Tata and Mahesh Uttamchandani.

The full draft report was reviewed by Demba Ba, Francois Bourguignon, Susan Goldmark, Arvind Gupta, Ernesto May, Fernando Montes-Negret, Vikram Nehru, Michele de Nevers, Guillermo Perry, Mohammad Zia Qureshi and Tevfik Mehmet Yaprak. We are grateful for comments and review provided by the World Bank Group's country and private sector teams.

The online service of the *Doing Business* database is managed by the Private Sector Development Knowledge Management Unit of the World Bank Group.

The report was made possible by the generous contribution of more than 5,000 lawyers, accountants, judges, business people and public officials in 175 economies. Quotations in this report are from local partners unless otherwise indicated. The names of those wishing to be acknowledged individually are listed below. Contact details are posted on the *Doing Business* website at http://www.doingbusiness.org.

GLOBAL CONTRIBUTORS

ALLEN & OVERY LLP

BAKER & McKENZIE

BOOZ ALLEN HAMILTON INC.

CLEARY, GOTTLIEB, STEEN & HAMILTON LLP

LEX MUNDI, ASSOCIATION OF INDEPENDENT LAW FIRMS

PRICEWATERHOUSECOOPERS

SDV INTERNATIONAL LOGISTICS

REGIONAL CONTRIBUTORS

ACZALAW

Robert Hughes
IKRP ROKAS & PARTNERS

AFGHANISTAN

Taqi-ud-din Ahmad
A.F. FERGUSON & CO.

Shafic Gawhari
MINISTRY OF COMMERCE

Parwana Hasan
AWLPA

Rashid Ibrahim
A.F. FERGUSON & CO.

Visal Khan
MANDVIWALLA & ZAFAR

Yasin Khosti
SOCIETY OF AFGHAN ARCHITECTS AND ENGINEERS

Gaurav Kukreja
AFGHAN CONTAINER TRANSPORT CO.

Khalid Mahmood
A.F. FERGUSON & CO.

Zahoor Malla
GLOBALINK LOGISTICS GROUP

Mehmood Y. Mandviwalla
MANDVIWALLA & ZAFAR

John D. McDonald
BAKER & McKENZIE, LLP

Salman Nasim
A.F. FERGUSON & CO.

Soli Parakh
A.F. FERGUSON & CO.

Abdul Rahman Watanwal
MBC CONSTRUCTION

Charles Clinton
ALTAI CONSULTING

Zaid Mohseni
ZAMOH

Omar Zakhilwal
AFGHANISTAN INVESTMENT SUPPORT AGENCY

ALBANIA

Artur Asllani
STUDIO LEGALE TONUCCI

Alban Caushi
KALO & ASSOCIATES

Sokol Elmazi
BOGA & ASSOCIATES

Jola Gjuzi
KALO & ASSOCIATES

Vilma Gjyshi
KALO & ASSOCIATES

Shkelqim Kerluku
IKRP ROKAS & PARTNERS

Kledi Kodra
PRICEWATERHOUSECOOPERS

Genci Krasniqi
KALO & ASSOCIATES

Georgios K. Lemonis
IKRP ROKAS & PARTNERS

Vojo Malo
BOGA & ASSOCIATES

Andi Memi
HOXHA, MEMI & HOXHA

Albert Muratti
SHEGA GROUP

Loreta Peci
PRICEWATERHOUSECOOPERS

Laura Qorlaze
PRICEWATERHOUSECOOPERS

Oltiana Rexhepai
IKRP ROKAS & PARTNERS

Spyridon Tsallas
IKRP ROKAS & PARTNERS

Zamira Xhaferri
IKRP ROKAS & PARTNERS

ALGERIA

Branka Achari-Djokic
BANK OF ALGERIA

Adnane Bouchaib
BOUCHAIB LAW FIRM

Samir Boukider
GHELLAL & MEKERBA

Samir Djelliout
CABINET SATOR

Mourad Dubert
ARCHITECTE

Malik Elkettas
ELKETTAS INTERNATIONAL

Mohamed El Amine Haddad
GHELLAL & MEKERBA

Samir Hamouda
CABINET SAMIR HAMOUDA

Mustapha Hamza
HAMZALAW OFFICE

Jérôme Le Hec
LANDWELL & ASSOCIÉS - PRICEWATERHOUSECOOPERS

Michel Lecerf
LANDWELL & ASSOCIÉS - PRICEWATERHOUSECOOPERS

Adnane Merad
ETUDE DE ME KADDOUR MERAD

Gerard Morin
LANDWELL & ASSOCIÉS - PRICEWATERHOUSECOOPERS

Feriel Oulounis
CABINET SAMIR HAMOUDA

Fares Ouzegdouh
MAERSK LOGISTICS

Dominique Rolland
LANDWELL & ASSOCIÉS - PRICEWATERHOUSECOOPERS

Badredine Saadi
AX-CONSULT, AGENCE D'ARCHITECTURE ET D'URBANISME

Mohamed Sator
CABINET SATOR

Mohamed Smati
AVOCAT

Marc Veuillot
LANDWELL & ASSOCIÉS - PRICEWATERHOUSECOOPERS

Tarik Zahzah
GHELLAL & MEKERBA

Nabiha Zerigui
CABINET SAMIR HAMOUDA

ANGOLA

Fernando Barros
PRICEWATERHOUSECOOPERS

Alain Brachet
SDV AMI INTERNATIONAL LOGISTICS

Paulo Caldeira

Pedro Calixto
PRICEWATERHOUSECOOPERS

José Alberto Cardoso
CÂMARA DE COMÉRCIO E INDÚSTRIA DE ANGOLA

Nahary Cardoso
FÁTIMA FREITAS ADVOGADOS

Ruth Chitas

Esperança Costa
ALEXANDRE PEGADO - ESCRITÓRIO DE ADVOGADOS

Benard de Buor
SDV AMI INTERNATIONAL LOGISTICS

Judith De Fatima Dos Santos Lima
NATIONAL BANK OF ANGOLA

Yves Flodrops
SDV AMI INTERNATIONAL LOGISTICS

Fernando Fortes
GUICHÉ ÚNICO DE EMPRESA

Fátima Freitas
FÁTIMA FREITAS ADVOGADOS

Aymeric Frisch
SDV AMI INTERNATIONAL LOGISTICS

Julian Ince
PRICEWATERHOUSECOOPERS

Teresinha Lopes
FARIA DE BASTOS, SEBASTIÃO E LOPES ADVOGADOS

Nita Palhota
ATS LOGISTICS CO.

Elisa Rangel Nunes
RANGEL, NUNES & TERESA

Arsénio Silva
GUICHÉ ÚNICO DE EMPRESA

ANTIGUA AND BARBUDA

Eleanor R. Clark
CLARKE & CLARKE

Carden Conliffe Clarke
COMMODORE & ASSOCIATES

Neil Coates
PRICEWATERHOUSECOOPERS

Vernon Edwards
FREIGHT FORWARDING AND DECONSOLIDATING

Ann Henry
HENRY & BURNETTE

Philip Isaacs
OBM LTD.

Hugh C. Marshall
MARSHALL & CO.

Brian O'Dornellas
OBM LTD.

Laurie Roberts
REGISTRY

Patricia Simon-Forde
CHAMBERS PATRICIA SIMON-FORDE

Denzil Solomon
DEVELOPMENT CONTROL AUTHORITY

Christian Sydney
CHRISTIAN, WALWYN & ASSOCIATES

Charles Walwyn
PRICEWATERHOUSECOOPERS

Marietta Warren
INTERFREIGHT LTD.

Hesketh A. Williams
LABOUR DEPARTMENT

ARGENTINA

Lisandro A. Allende
BRONS & SALAS ABOGADOS

Vanesa Balda
VITALE, MANOFF & FEILBOGEN

Mariano Carricart
FORNIELES ABOGADOS

Pablo Cavallaro
ESTUDIO CAVALLARO ABOGADOS

Carlos Marcelo D'Alessio
UNION INTERNACIONAL DEL NOTARIADO

Oscar Alberto del Rio
CENTRAL BANK OF ARGENTINA

Andres M. Edelstein
PRICEWATERHOUSECOOPERS

Lilian Falcon
PRICEWATERHOUSECOOPERS

María Fraguas
NICHOLSON Y CANO

Ignacio Funes de Rioja
FUNES DE RIOJA & ASOCIADOS, MEMBER OF IUS LABORIS

Santiago Laclau
MARVAL, O'FARRELL & MAIRAL, MEMBER OF LEX MUNDI

Agustina Larriera
ALFARO ABOGADOS

María del Rosario Martínez
ALFARO ABOGADOS

Miguel P. Murray
MURRAY, d'ANDRÉ, ISASMENDI & SIRITO DE ZAVALÍA

Alfredo Miguel O'Farrell
MARVAL, O'FARRELL & MAIRAL, MEMBER OF LEX MUNDI

Enrique Pugliano
ORGANIZACIÓN VERAZ S.A., IN AFFILIATION WITH EQUIFAX INC.

Ignacio Rodriguez
PRICEWATERHOUSECOOPERS

Adolfo Rouillon
WORLD BANK GROUP

Patricia Ruhman Seggiaro
MARVAL, O'FARRELL & MAIRAL, MEMBER OF LEX MUNDI

Jorge San Martin
PRICEWATERHOUSECOOPERS

Liliana Segade
QUATTRINI, LAPRIDA & ASOCIADOS

Angelica Sola
MARVAL, O'FARRELL & MAIRAL, MEMBER OF LEX MUNDI

Alfredo Suarez
ASOCIACION ARGENTINA DE AGENTES DE CARGA INTERNACIONAL

Eduardo J. Viñales
FUNES DE RIOJA & ASOCIADOS, MEMBER OF IUS LABORIS

Carlos Zima
PRICEWATERHOUSECOOPERS

ARMENIA

Karen Andreasyan
DEFENSE LTD.

Artak Arzoyan
CENTRAL BANK OF ARMENIA

Ron J. Barden
PRICEWATERHOUSECOOPERS

Svetlana Bilyk
PRICEWATERHOUSECOOPERS

Mher Grigoryan
LEGAL ADVISOR

Bela Gutidze
PRICEWATERHOUSECOOPERS

Sargis H. Martirosyan
TRANS-ALLIANCE

Jorge Intriago
PRICEWATERHOUSECOOPERS

Artashes F. Kakoyan
INVESTMENT LAW GROUP LLC

Vahe Kakoyan
INVESTMENT LAW GROUP LLC

Ludmila Kosarenko
PRICEWATERHOUSECOOPERS

Maria Livinska
PRICEWATERHOUSECOOPERS

Arsen Matikyan
ALFATRANS LTD.

Suren Melikyan
KPMG

Eduard Mesropyan
JINJ LTD.

Aram Poghosyan
Grant Thornton Amyot

Hayk Sahakyan
State Committee of the Real Property Cadastre

David Sargsyan
Ameria CJSC

Tigran Serobyan
KPMG

Rusa Sreseli
PricewaterhouseCoopers

Hakob Tadevosyan
Grant Thornton Amyot

Matthew Tallarovic
PricewaterhouseCoopers

Liana Yordanyan
Ter-Tachatyan Legal and Business Consulting

AUSTRALIA

Matthew Allison
Baycorp Advantage

Sarah Bergin
Allens Arthur Robinson

Alexis Biancardi
PricewaterhouseCoopers

Lynda Brumm
PricewaterhouseCoopers

David Buda
Cowley Hearne Lawyers

Greg Channell
Department of Lands

Nyssa Cherry
Atanaskovic Hartnell

Daniel Clough
Victorian Bar

Michael Croker
PricewaterhouseCoopers

David Cross
Deacons

Steven Fleming
Allens Arthur Robinson

Mark Geniale
Office of State Revenue, NSW Treasury

Penny Grau
Clayton Utz, member of Lex Mundi

Jacqueline Hassarati
PricewaterhouseCoopers

Eric Herding
Panalpina World Transport

Paul James
Clayton Utz, member of Lex Mundi

Doug Jones AM
Clayton Utz, member of Lex Mundi

Khal Katrib
Office of State Revenue, NSW Treasury

Edward Nicholas
Clayton Utz, member of Lex Mundi

Ann Previtera
PricewaterhouseCoopers

Michael Quinlan
Allens Arthur Robinson

Robert Riddell
Gadens Lawyers

Phil Rosser
Sydney Ports Corporation

Luke Sayers
PricewaterhouseCoopers

Ron Schaffer
Clayton Utz, member of Lex Mundi

Dean Schiller

Neil Wilson
PricewaterhouseCoopers

Irene Yeung
PricewaterhouseCoopers

David Zwi
Cowley Hearne Lawyers

AUSTRIA

Gerhard Antenreiter
Dr. Gerhard Antenreiter, Civil Law Notary

Austrian Customs - Ministry of Finance

Georg Bahn
Freshfields Bruckhaus Deringer

Brandstetter Pritz & Partner

Ernst Biebl
PricewaterhouseCoopers

Doris Buxbaum
Binder Grösswang Rechtsanwälte

Martin Eckel
Eiselsberg Natlacen Walderdorff Cancola

Jana Eichmeyer
Kunz Schima Wallentin Rechtsanwälte KEG, member of Ius Laboris

Julian Feichtinger
Cerha Hempel & Spiegelfeld Hlawati, member of Lex Mundi

Ferdinand Graf
Graf, Maxl & Pitkowitz

Andreas Hable
Binder Grösswang Rechtsanwälte

Harald Heschl
Consumer Credit Information

Rudolf Kaindl
Koehler, Kaindl, Duerr & Partner, Civil Law Notaries

Alexander Klauser
Brauneis, Klauser & Prandl

Rudolf Krickl
PricewaterhouseCoopers

Ulrike Langwallner
Schoenherr Rechtsanwaelte

Gregor Maderbacher
Brauneis, Klauser & Prandl

Peter Madl
Schoenherr Rechtsanwaelte

Irene Mandl
Austrian Institute for SME Research

Wolfgang Messeritsch
National Bank of Austria

Michael Podesser
PricewaterhouseCoopers

Friedrich Roedler
PricewaterhouseCoopers

Georg Schima
Kunz Schima Wallentin Rechtsanwälte KEG, member of Ius Laboris

Andrea Schwartz
Kunz Schima Wallentin Rechtsanwälte KEG, member of Ius Laboris

Benedikt Spiegelfeld
Cerha Hempel & Spiegelfeld Hlawati, member of Lex Mundi

Michael Stelzer
Graf, Maxl & Pitkowitz

Birgit Vogt-Majarek
Kunz Schima Wallentin Rechtsanwälte KEG, member of Ius Laboris

Lothar Wachter
Wolf Theiss

Klaus Woschnak
Notar Dr. Klaus Woschnak

Angela Zaffalon
Cerha Hempel & Spiegelfeld Hlawati, member of Lex Mundi

AZERBAIJAN

Eldar Adilzade
IFC Corporate Governance Project

Anar Aliyev
IFC Corporate Governance Project

Mushfig Aliyev
PricewaterhouseCoopers

Roman Alloyarov
OMNI Consultants

Ismayil Askerov
Ledingham Chalmers

Rufat Aslanli
National Bank of Azerbaijan

Alum Bati
Salans Hertzfeld & Heilbronn Law Firm

Rizvan Gubiyev
PricewaterhouseCoopers

Arif Guliyev
PricewaterhouseCoopers

Emin Huseynov
National Bank of Azerbaijan

Gunduz Karimov
Baker & McKenzie

Vugar Mammadov
PricewaterhouseCoopers

Kamal Mammadzade
Salans

Efendiyeva Mehriban
Michael Wilson & Partners Ltd.

Namik Novruzov
BM International LLC

Movlan Pashayev
PricewaterhouseCoopers

John Quinn
ACE Forwarding Ltd.

Kanan Safarov
Attorney-at-Law

Emma Silyayeva
Salans Hertzfeld & Heilbronn Law Firm

Ismail Zargarli
OMNI Consultants

BANGLADESH

Nahid Afreen
The Law Associates, member of Lex Mundi

Jasim Ahmed
Bangladesh Container Lines Ltd.

Sahahuddin Ahmed
Dr. Kamal Hossain & Associates

Sahabuddin Ahmed
Dutch-Bangla Bank Foundation

Badrul Ahsan
A. Qasem & Co. / PricewaterhouseCoopers

Tanjib-ul Alam
Dr. Kamal Hossain & Associates

Abdullah Al-Masud
Prime Bank Ltd.

Nurul Amin

Ashfaq Amin
Integrated Transportation Services Ltd., Agent of Panalpina

Ad. Asaduzzaman
Syed Ashtiaq Ahmed & Associates

Isbahul Bar Chowdhury
Prime Bank Ltd.

Md. Halim Bepari
Halim Law Associate

Gouranga Chakraborty
Bank of Bangladesh

Shirin Chaudhury

Jamilur Reza Choudhury

A.B.M. Nasirud Doulah
Doulah & Doulah Advocates

A.B.M. Shamsud Doulah
Doulah & Doulah Advocates

A.B.M. Badrud Doulah
Doulah & Doulah Advocates

Moin Ghani
Dr. Kamal Hossain & Associates

Mainul Haque
Bank of Bangladesh

Aneek Haque
Haque and Associates

Raquibul Haque Miah

Shamsul Hasan

Syed Afzal Hasan Uddin
Syed Ashtiaq Ahmed & Associates

Azmal Hossain

Kamal Hossain

Rafiqul Islam
Judicial Service Association

M. Moksadul Islam
Legal Steps

Amir-Ul Islam
The Law Associates, member of Lex Mundi

Karishma Jahan

Ahsanul Kabir

Sohel Kasem
A. Qasem & Co. / PricewaterhouseCoopers

Khurram Khan
Standard Chartered Bank

Khondker Shamsuddin Mahmood
Advisers' Legal Alliance

Q.M. Mahtab-Uz-Zaman
BRAC University

Kazi Abdul Mannan

Abdul Qayyum
Ministry of Commerce

Mirza Quamrul Hasan

Golam Rabbani
Prime Bank Ltd.

Mizanur Rahaman
Ministry of Law, Justice and Parliamentary Affairs

Habibur Rahman
The Law Counsel

Mohammed Razack

Abdur Razzaq
The Law Counsel

Quazi Reza-Ul Hoque
ERGO Legal Counsels

Omar Sadat

Imran Siddiq
The Law Counsel

Munir Uddin Ahamed

Rafique Ul-Huq
Huq & Co.

BELARUS

Ivan Alievich
Mikhel and Partners

Kiryl Apanasevich
Vlasova and Partners

Ron J. Barden
PricewaterhouseCoopers

Svetlana Bilyk
PricewaterhouseCoopers

Vladimir G. Biruk
Capital Group

Anastasia Bondar
INSTAR Logistics

Alexander Botian
Borovtsov & Salei

Igor Dankov
PricewaterhouseCoopers

Gennadiy Glinskiy
DICSA International Group of Lawyers

Alexandr Ignatov
National Bank of the Republic of Belarus

Jorge Intriago
PricewaterhouseCoopers

Igor Ishchenko
PricewaterhouseCoopers

Alena Ivanova
ABA CEELI

Alexander Khrapoutsky
LAW FIRM JUREXPERT GROUP

Alexander Korneiko
AHLERS

Olga Sergeevna Kuryleva
BELARUS STATE UNIVERSITY

Maria Livinska
PRICEWATERHOUSECOOPERS

Konstantin Mikhel
MIKHEL AND PARTNERS

Evgeniya Motina
INSTITUTE OF STATE AND LAW, NATIONAL ACADEMY OF SCIENCE

Maksim Salahub
VLASOVA AND PARTNERS

Anton Vashkevich
BOROVTSOV & SALEI

Alexander Vasilevsky
VALEX CONSULT

Ekaterina Zabello
VLASOVA AND PARTNERS

BELGIUM

ALLEN & OVERY LLP

Hubert Andre-Dumont
McGUIREWOODS LLP

Hugo Callens
ELEGIS

Koen Cooreman
PRICEWATERHOUSECOOPERS

COUR DE CASSATION

Steven de Schrijver
VAN BAEL & BELLIS

Olivier Debray
CLAEYS & ENGELS, MEMBER OF IUS LABORIS

Frank Dierckx
PRICEWATERHOUSECOOPERS

Edmond Dierinck
ECT LOGISTICS

David Du Pont
ASHURST

EUBELIUS ATTORNEYS

Pierrette Fraisse
SERVICE PUBLIC FEDERAL FINANCES

Pamela R. Gonzales de Cordova
LOYENS

Sandrine Hirsch
SIMONT BRAUN

Grégory Jurion
PRICEWATERHOUSECOOPERS

Jean Philippe Lebeau
PALAIS DE JUSTICE

Stephan Legein
CUSTOMS ADMINISTRATION

Luc Legon
PRICEWATERHOUSECOOPERS

Axel Maeterlinck
SIMONT BRAUN

Robert Meunier
NOTARY

Carl Meyntjens
ASHURST

Aurore Mons delle Roche
PRICEWATERHOUSECOOPERS

Didier Muraille
NATIONAL BANK OF BELGIUM

Fannia Polet
ALTIUS

Tim Roelans
ELEGIS

Frédéric Souchon
PRICEWATERHOUSECOOPERS

Peter Van Melkebeke
NOTAIRES BERQUIN

Suzy Vande Wiele
LOYENS

Bart Vanham
PRICEWATERHOUSECOOPERS

Tom Vantroyen
ALTIUS

Gregory Verpoorten
PRICEWATERHOUSECOOPERS

Yves Voeten
PRICEWATERHOUSECOOPERS

BELIZE

Emil Arguelles
ARGUELLES & COMPANY

Liesje Barrow Chung
BARROW & CO.

Emory K. Bennett
YOUNG'S ENGINEERING CONSULTANCY LTD.

Rudy Castillo
BELIZE BANK LIMITED

Julian Castillo FCCA
CASTILLO SANCHEZ & BURRELL, LLP

Julius Espat
STRUKTURE ARCHITECTS

Gian C. Gandhi
INTERNATIONAL FINANCIAL SERVICES COMMISSION

Mirna Lara
EUROCARIBE BELIZE SHIPPING SERVICES

Fred Lumor
FRED LUMOR & CO.

Andrew Marshalleck
BARROW & CO.

Tania Moody
BARROW & WILLIAMS

Kareem D. Musa
MUSA & BALDERAMOS

Sharon JJA Pitts-Robateau
PITTS & ELRINGTON

Patricia Rodriguez
BELIZE COMPANIES REGISTRY LTD.

Catherine Smith
BELIZE COMPANIES REGISTRY LTD.

Troy Smith
BELIZE CITY COUNCIL

Dale L. Trujeque
BELIZE CITY COUNCIL

Saidi M. Vaccaro
ORION CORPORATE SERVICES LTD.

Lionel L. R. Welch
SUPREME COURT OF BELIZE

Ivan Williams
MINISTRY OF EDUCATION AND LABOUR

Carlton N. Young
YOUNG'S ENGINEERING CONSULTANCY LTD.

Michael C.E. Young S.C.
YOUNGS LAW FIRM

Philip Zuniga
ATTORNEY-AT-LAW

BENIN

Victoire Agbanrin-Elisha
AVOCAT À LA COUR

Saïdou Agbantou
CABINET AGBANTOU SAIDOU

Cosme Ahouansou
SA-APB

Rafikou Alabi
CABINET ME ALABI

Mochtar Alidou
BANQUE RÉGIONALE DE SOLIDARITÉ

Innocent Sourou Avognon
MINISTÈRE DE LA JUSTICE ET DE LA LEGISLATION

Constantin Azon
BSIC

Charles Badou
CABINET EDGAR-YVES MONNOU

Clifton Best
DIAMOND BANK

Agnes A. Campbell
CABINET D'AVOCATS CAMPBELL & ASSOCIES

Michèle A.O. Carrena
TRIBUNAL DE PREMIÈRE INSTANCE DE COTONOU

Jacques Chareyre
FIDAFRICA / PRICEWATERHOUSECOOPERS

Alice Codjia-Sohouenou
CABINET AGBANTOU SAIDOU

Veronique Akankoussi Deguenon
ETUDE ME VERONIQUE AKANKOUSSI DEGUENON

Placide T. Ganmavo
TRIBUNAL DE PREMIÈRE INSTANCE DE COTONOU

Luc-M. C. Gnacadja
IMOTEPH

Bernard Gourlaouen
SOCIÉTÉ GÉNÉRALE DE BANQUES AU BÉNIN

Denis Hazoume
CONTINENTAL BANK

Jean-Luc Labonte
FINANCIAL BANK

Dominique Lales
ORYX S.A.

Edouard Messou
FIDAFRICA / PRICEWATERHOUSECOOPERS

Edgar-Yves Mpoy
CABINET EDGAR-YVES MONNOU

Philippe Nadaud
BANQUE DE L'HABITAT DU BÉNIN

Severin-Maxime Quenum
SPA BABA BODY & QUENUM

Patrick Saizonou
EQUIPBAIL

Zakari Djibril Sambaou
ATTORNEY-AT-LAW

Jean Pierre Sancerne
SDV SAGA - GROUPE BOLLORE

Dominique Taty
FIDAFRICA / PRICEWATERHOUSECOOPERS

Jean Bosco Todjinou
ORDRE DES ARCHITECTES

Fousseni Traore
FIDAFRICA / PRICEWATERHOUSECOOPERS

Dieudonne Vignon
CREDIT AFRICAIN

Jean Claude Wognin
FIDAFRICA / PRICEWATERHOUSECOOPERS

Gilles Guerard
ECOBANK

Cyrille Laleye
ECOBANK

BHUTAN

Loknath Chapagai
MINISTRY OF TRADE & INDUSTRY

Tashi Delek
OFFICE OF LEGAL AFFAIRS

Eden Dema
ROYAL MONETARY AUTHORITY

Kincho Dorjee
CARGO & COURIER CO.

Rinzin Dorji
MINISTRY OF TRADE & INDUSTRY

Dophu Dorji
ROYAL SECURITIES EXCHANGE

T.C. Ghimirey

N.B. Gurung
DHL

Kenzang Gyeltshen
DHL

B.B. Kalden
DZONGKHAG THRIMKIDUENSA

Bap Kinga
CHAMBER OF COMMERCE & INDUSTRY

Kunzang
MINISTRY OF FINANCE

Subarna Lama
MINISTRY OF TRADE & INDUSTRY

Sonam Lhendup
MINISTRY OF TRADE & INDUSTRY

Karma Lotey
YANGPHEL ADVENTURE TRAVEL

Mon Bahadur Monger
MANAGING PROPRIETOR

Mr. Naichu
CHAMBER OF COMMERCE & INDUSTRY

Sangay Penjore
THIMPU MUNICIPAL CORPORATION

Prakash Rasaily
CITY LEGAL UNIT

Dasho Shera Lhendup
WANGDUE DISTRICT COURT

Dawa Sherpa
SHERPA CONSULTANCY

SUPERINTENDENCY OF BANKS AND FINANCIAL ENTITIES

Ugen Takchhu
SURVEY AND LAND RECORDS OFFICE, MINISTRY OF AGRICULTURE

Norbu Tsering
ROYAL COURT OF JUSTICE

Kipchu Tshering

Karma Tshering

Game Tshering
CONSTRUCTION ASSOCIATION OF BHUTAN

Tandin Tshering
MINISTRY OF TRADE & INDUSTRY

Tsering Wangchuck
ROYAL COURT OF JUSTICE

Sonam P. Wangdi

Nima Wangdi

Deki Wangmo
BHUTAN NATIONAL BANK

Tashi Wangmo
MINISTRY OF LABOUR AND HUMAN RESOURCES

Tshering Yangchen
ROYAL MONETARY AUTHORITY

Tashi Yezer
ROYAL SECURITIES EXCHANGE

BOLIVIA

Carolina Aguiree Urioste
BUFETE AGUIRRE

Fernando Aguirre
BUFETE AGUIRRE

Adrián Barrenechea Bazoberry
CRIALES, URCULLO & ANTEZANA

Francisco Bollini Roca
GUEVARA & GUTIÉRREZ S.C. SERVICIOS LEGALES

Cintya Burgoa
PRICEWATERHOUSECOOPERS

Liliana Ching
PRICEWATERHOUSECOOPERS

Jose A. Criales
CRIALES, URCULLO & ANTEZANA

Primitivo Gutiérrez
GUEVARA & GUTIÉRREZ S.C. SERVICIOS LEGALES

Ana Carola Guzman Gonzales
SALAZAR, SALAZAR & ASOCIADOS

Gonzalo Mendieta Romero
MENDIETA ROMERO & ASOCIADOS

Oscar Antonio Plaza Ponte
ENTIDAD DE SERVICIOS DE INFORMACIÓN ENSERBIC S.A.

Julio Quintanilla Quiroga
QUINTANILLA & SORIA

Fabian Rabinovich
PRICEWATERHOUSECOOPERS

Fernando Rojas
C.R. & F. ROJAS, MEMBER OF LEX MUNDI

Sergio Salazar-Machicado
SALAZAR, SALAZAR & ASOCIADOS

Sandra Salinas
C.R. & F. Rojas, member of Lex Mundi

Edmond Tondu
Bolivian Intermodal Container

A. Mauricio Torrico Galindo
Quintanilla & Soria

Miguel Vertiz
PricewaterhouseCoopers

BOSNIA AND HERZEGOVINA

Edisa Bakovic
DLA Weiss - Tessbach

Mark Davidson
PricewaterhouseCoopers

Petros Doukas
IKRP Rokas & Partners

Senada Havic
LRC Credit Bureau

Nikola M. Jankovi
Lansky, Ganzger & Partner d.o.o.

Muhidin Kari
Law Office of Emir Kovaevi

Emmanuel Koenig
PricewaterhouseCoopers

Emir Kovaevi
Law Office of Emir Kovaevi

Branko Mari
Branko & Vladimir Mari

Nedzida Salihovic-Whalen
DLA Weiss - Tessbach

Hasib Salkic
Intersped dd Sarajevo

Adin Serdarevic
PricewaterhouseCoopers

Daniela Terzic
DLA Weiss - Tessbach

Bojana Tkalcic-Djulic
Lawyers' Office Bojana Tkalcic-Djulic & Olodar Prebanic

Ruzica Topic
Ruzika Topic Law Firm

Spyridon Tsallas
IKRP Rokas & Partners

BOTSWANA

Susan Anne Aird
Minchin & Kelly

Jinabhai Akheel
Magang & Co.

Neill Armstrong
Armstrongs Attorneys, member of Lex Mundi

Mark Badenhorst
PricewaterhouseCoopers

John Carr-Hartley
Armstrongs Attorneys, member of Lex Mundi

Uttum Corea
PricewaterhouseCoopers

Paul De Chalain
PricewaterhouseCoopers

Elias M. Dewah

Diba M. Diba
Minchin & Kelly

Edward W. Fashole-Luke II
Luke & Associates

J. M. Griffiths
Minchin & Kelly

Max Gunasekera
PricewaterhouseCoopers

Nigel Haynes
Manica Botswana Pty. Ltd.

L. Jayawickrama
PricewaterhouseCoopers

Akheel Jinabhai
Magang & Co.

Tiro Kayawe
Citizen Entrepreneurial Development Agency

Tsholofelo Kokorwe

Godwin Kunda

Ezekiel Lungu
Lands Department

Elizabeth Macharia
Chibanda, Makgaleme & Co.

Mr. Magang
Magang & Co.

Mercia Makgaleme
Chibanda, Makgaleme & Co.

Wayne Mambwe
Roscoe Bonna Valuers

Mmasekgoa Masire-Mwamba

Patience Matengu
Citizen Entrepreneurial Development Agency

T.T.K. Matome

Kgaotsang Matthews

Colin McVey
Landflow Solutions Pty. Ltd.

Claude Mojafi

Ontiretse Monagen

Viola Morgan

Jack Allan Mutua
Tectura International, Botswana

Alfred Ngowi
University of Botswana

Kwadwo Osei-Ofei
Hazel Todd Attorneys

Suren Perera
PricewaterhouseCoopers

Joao Salbany
Minchin & Kelly

Morag Swift
Minchin & Kelly

Ludo Tema

Tally Tshekiso
Caratex Botswana

Thata Tshukudu
Roscoe Bonna Valuers

Angelica Waibale-Muganga
Armstrongs Attorneys, member of Lex Mundi

Dave Williams
Minchin & Kelly

Richard Wright

Sipho Ziga
Armstrongs Attorneys, member of Lex Mundi

BRAZIL

Andrea Acerbi
Felsberg e Associados

Tania Mara Coelho de Almeida Costa
Secretaria de Inspecao do Trabalho

Gilberto Deon Corrêa Junior
Veirano Advogados

Sidinei Corrêa Marques
Banco Central do Brasil

José Ricardo dos Santos Luz Júnior
Duarte Garcia, Caselli Guimarães e Terra Advogados

Thomas Benes Felsberg
Felsberg e Associados

Susan Christina Forster
Fischer & Forster Advogados

Michelle Giraldi
PricewaterhouseCoopers

Karina Goldberg Britto
Lefosse Advogados, in cooperation with Linklaters

Adriana Grizante
PricewaterhouseCoopers

Luiz Felipe Guimarães Santoro
Demarest e Almeida, member of Lex Mundi

Esther Jerussalmy
Araújo e Policastro Advogados

Carlos Lacia
PricewaterhouseCoopers

Ricardo Loureiro
SERASA S.A.

Verônica Madureira Pereira
Viseu, Castro, Cunha e Oricchio Advogados

Rodrigo Matos
Cargo Logistics do Brasil

Eduardo Augusto Mattar
Pinheiro Guimarães, Advogados

Cássio Mesquita Barros
Mesquita Barros Advogados, member of Ius Laboris

Laercio Nascimento
Nascimento Imoveis

Andrea Oricchio Kirsh
Viseu, Castro, Cunha e Oricchio Advogados

Maria Fernanda Pecora
Veirano Advogados

Cacilda Pedrosa Vieira
Nascimento Imoveis

Fabio Luis Pereira Barboza
Viseu, Castro, Cunha e Oricchio Advogados

Andréa Pitthan Françolin
De Vivo, Whitaker e Castro Advogados

Eliane Ribeiro Gago
Duarte Garcia, Caselli Guimarães e Terra Advogados

Karina Romano
Demarest e Almeida, member of Lex Mundi

Elaine Shimoda
SERASA S.A.

Leonardo Soares de Oliveira
Secretaria de Inspecao do Trabalho

Marcos Tiraboschi
Veirano Advogados

Pedro Vitor Araujo da Costa
Escritorio de Advocacia Gouvêa Vieira

Flavia Warde
Demarest e Almeida, member of Lex Mundi

Beatriz Ryoko Yamashita
Fischer & Forster Advogados

BULGARIA

Svetlin Adrianov
Lega InterConsult - Penkov, Markov and Partners, member of Lex Mundi

Nikolai Bozhilov
Unimasters Logistics Group

Dimitar Danailov
Georgiev, Todorov & Co.

Bogdan Drenski
Georgiev, Todorov & Co.

Daniela Dzabarova
IKRP Rokas & Partners

Polina Ganeva
Landwell Bulgaria

Alexander Georgiev
Dobrev, Kinkin, Lyutskanov & Partners

Ralitsa Gougleva
Djingov, Gouginski, Kyutchukov & Velichkov

Orlin Hadjiiski
PricewaterhouseCoopers

Monika Hristova
IKRP Rokas & Partners

Ginka Iskrova
PricewaterhouseCoopers

Nedyalko Mitev Ivanov
IKRP Rokas & Partners

Mina Kapsazova
PricewaterhouseCoopers

Nickolay Kiskinov
Lega InterConsult - Penkov, Markov and Partners, member of Lex Mundi

Radostina Krasteva
PricewaterhouseCoopers

Dessislava Loukarova
Arsiv, Natchev, Ganeva

Totyu Maldenov
Ministry of Labour and Social Policy

Jordan Manahilov
Bulgarian National Bank

Marina Marinova
Georgiev, Todorov & Co.

Ivan Markov
Lega InterConsult - Penkov, Markov and Partners, member of Lex Mundi

Krasimir Merdzhov
PricewaterhouseCoopers

Vladimir Natchev
Arsiv, Natchev, Ganeva

Yordan Naydenov
Borislav Boyanov & Co.

Darina Oresharova
Experian-Scorex Bulgaria

Vladimir Penkov
Lega InterConsult - Penkov, Markov and Partners, member of Lex Mundi

Kalina Tchakarova
Djingov, Gouginski, Kyutchukov & Velichkov

Svilen Todorov
Legacom Antov & Partners

Irina Tsvetkova
PricewaterhouseCoopers

Stefan Tzakov
Kambourov & Partners

Angel Kalaidjiev
Dimitrov, Petrov & Co.

BURKINA FASO

Dieudonne Bonkoungou
Cabinet Ouedraogo & Bonkoungou

Jacques Chareyre
FIDAFRICA / PricewaterhouseCoopers

Jean Claude Gnamien
FIDAFRICA / PricewaterhouseCoopers

Charles Ki-Zerbo
BCEAO

Evelyne Mandessi Bell
Cabinet Ouedraogo & Bonkoungou

Edouard Messou
PricewaterhouseCoopers

Serge Messou
FIDAFRICA / PricewaterhouseCoopers

Anna T. Ouattara-Sory
Cabinet MePaulin Salambéré

Marie Ouedraogo
Barreau du Burkina Faso

Oumarou Ouedraogo
Cabinet Ouedraogo & Bonkoungou

Hamidou Savadogo
Avocat

Barterlé Mathieu Some
Attorney-at-Law

Dominique Taty
FIDAFRICA / PricewaterhouseCoopers

Fousseni Traore
FIDAFRICA / PricewaterhouseCoopers

Jean Claude Wognin
FIDAFRICA / PricewaterhouseCoopers

Bouba Yaguibou
Yaguibou & Yanogo

Gilles Yameogo
Barreau du Burkina Faso

Ousmane Prosper Zoungrana
Chevalier de l'Orde National

Birika Jean Claude Bonzi

Amélie Nebie-Bayala
eDONEC, EDUCATOR ONE CONSULTING

BURUNDI

BANQUE DE LA RÉPUBLIQUE DU BURUNDI

Anatole Miburo
CABINET ANATOLE MIBURO

MINISTÈRE DE LA JUSTICE

Tharcisse Ntakiyica
BARREAU DU BURUNDI

Denis Ntibandetse
ATTORNEY-AT-LAW

François Nyamoya
AVOCAT

Fabien Segatwa
ETUDE ME SEGATWA

Gabriel Sinarinzi
CABINET MEGABRIEL SINARINZI

Rubeya Willy
BARREAU DU BURUNDI

CAMBODIA

Ngov Chong
PRICEWATERHOUSECOOPERS

Martin Desautels
DFDL MEKONG LAW GROUP

David Fitzgerald
PRICEWATERHOUSECOOPERS

Naryth H. Hem
B.N.G., ADVOCATES & SOLICITORS

Richard Irwin
PRICEWATERHOUSECOOPERS

Song Khun
RAF INT'L FORWARDING INC.

David King
KPMG

Avy Kong Putheavy
DIRKSEN FLIPSE DORAN & LE

Jean Loi
PRICEWATERHOUSECOOPERS

Tayseng Ly
DFDL MEKONG LAW GROUP

Nimmith Men
ARBITRATION COUNCIL FOUNDATION

Seakirin Neak
B.N.G. - ADVOCATES & SOLICITORS

Roger Ouk
PRICEWATERHOUSECOOPERS

Ham Phea
MINISTRY OF LABOR AND VOCATIONAL TRAINING

Matt Rendall
SCIARONI & ASSOCIATES

Sovan Sa
ATTORNEY-AT-LAW

Denora Sarin
SARIN & ASSOCIATES

Socheata Seng
B.N.G., ADVOCATES & SOLICITORS

Sorya Sin
SHA TRANSPORT EXPRESS CO. LTD.

Christine Soutif
SDV CAMBODGE LTD.

Ly Tayseng
DFDL MEKONG LAW GROUP

CAMEROON

Lucy Asuagbor
COURT OF APPEALS OF BUEA

Feh H. Baaboh
HENRY SAMUELSON & CO.

David Boyo
JING & PARTNERS

Jacques Chareyre
FIDAFRICA / PRICEWATERHOUSECOOPERS

Emmanuel Ekobo
CABINET EKOBO

Isabelle Fomukong
CABINET FOMUKONG

Caroline Idrissou-Belingar
BEAC

Paul Jing
JING & PARTNERS

Jean Aimet Kounga
ABENG LAW FIRM

Kumfa Jude Kwenyui
JURIS CONSUL LAW FIRM

Buergi Marcel
PANALPINA WORLD TRANSPORT LTD.

CANADA

David Bish
GOODMANS LLP

Michael S. Bondy
PRICEWATERHOUSECOOPERS

Jay A. Carfagnini
GOODMANS LLP

Larry Chapman
PRICEWATERHOUSECOOPERS

Susan Clifford
OSLER, HOSKIN & HARCOURT LLP

John Craig
HEENAN BLAIKIE LLP, MEMBER OF IUS LABORIS

Michael Davies
OSLER, HOSKIN & HARCOURT LLP

Gian Fortuna
KENAIDAN CONTRACTING LTD.

Karen Grant
TRANSUNION

Pamela S. Hughes
BLAKE, CASSELS & GRAYDON, MEMBER OF LEX MUNDI

Joshua Kochath
COMAGE CONTAINER LINES

Melanie N. Laskey
PRICEWATERHOUSECOOPERS

Grace Lee
PRICEWATERHOUSECOOPERS

Richard Marcovitz
PRICEWATERHOUSECOOPERS

Shelley Munro
OSLER, HOSKIN & HARCOURT LLP

Dera Nevin
BLAKE, CASSELS & GRAYDON, MEMBER OF LEX MUNDI

Paula Rochwerger
HEENAN BLAIKIE LLP, MEMBER OF IUS LABORIS

Harris M. Rosen
SHIBLEY RIGHTON LLP

Paul Schabas
BLAKE, CASSELS & GRAYDON, MEMBER OF LEX MUNDI

Cynthia Seifried
BLAKE, CASSELS & GRAYDON, MEMBER OF LEX MUNDI

CAPE VERDE

Hermínio Afonso
PRICEWATERHOUSECOOPERS

Vasco Carvalho Oliveira Ramos
ENGIC

Ilíldio Cruz
GABINETE DE ADVOCACIA CONSULTORIA E PROCURADORIA JURIDICA

Victor Adolfo de Pinto Osório
ATTORNEY-AT-LAW

João Dono
MARIA JOÃO DE NOVAIS ADVOGADOS - MIRANDA ALLIANCE

Joana Gomes Rosa
ATTORNEY-AT-LAW

Ana Denise Lima Barber
WV CONSULTORES

Joao M. A. Mendes
AUDITEC

Eldetrudes Neves
ARAUJO, NEVES & SANTOS

Ricardo G. Pereira
BDO CAPEAUDIT

José Manuel Pinto Monteiro
ADVOGADOS E JURISCONSULTORES - JC FONSECA, JM PINTO MONTEIRO, LIGIA FONSECA

Armando J.F. Rodrigues
PRICEWATERHOUSECOOPERS

Tito Lívio Santos Oliveira Ramos

Henrique Semedo Borges
HENRIQUE SEMEDO BORGES ADVOGADO

João Carlos Tavares Fidalgo
BANQUE CENTRALE

Mr. Teixeira

Tereza Teixeira B. Amado
AMADO & MEDINA ADVOGADAS

Fatima Varela
BANQUE CENTRALE

Henrique Veiga
HENRIQUE VEIGA ADVOGADO

CENTRAL AFRICAN REPUBLIC

Mackfoy Amiect
CBCA - COMMERCIAL BANK

Jean Noel Bangue
COUR D'APPEL DE BANGUI

Emile Bizon
CABINET TIANGAYE - UNIVERSITÉ DE BANGUI

Jacques Boti
MINISTÈRE DE LA FONCTION PUBLIQUE, DU TRAVAIL, DE LA SÉCURITÉ SOCIALE ET DE L'INSERTION PROFESSIONELLE DES JEUNES

Maurice Dibert-Dollet
MINISTÈRE DE LA JUSTICE

Marie-Edith Douzima-Lawson
CABINET DOUZIMA

Sylvestre Gouendji
INSPECTEUR DU TRAVAIL ET DES LOIS SOCIALES

Caroline Idrissou-Belingar
BEAC

Francois Kayema
GREFFIER EN CHEF, COMMISSAIRE PRISEUR

Noel Kelembho
SDV CENTRAFRIQUE - GROUPE BOLLORE

Christian Lindo - Yando
BEAC

Timothee M'beto
SDV CENTRAFRIQUE - GROUPE BOLLORE

Yves Namkomkoina
TRIBUNAL DE COMMERCE DE BANGUI

Jean Baptiste Nouganga
BUREAU COMPTABLE FISCAL - CABINET NOUGANGA

CHAD

Nathé Amady
AVOCAT

Jacques Chareyre
FIDAFRICA / PRICEWATERHOUSECOOPERS

Thomas Dingamgoto
CABINET THOMAS DINGAMGOTO

Nadjita Francis Ngarhodjim

Mr. Froud
FGP

Johann Hopf
STAT CTBL AGENT

Matthias Hubert
FIDAFRICA / PRICEWATERHOUSECOOPERS

Caroline Idrissou-Belingar
BEAC

Gerard Leclaire
INGÉNIERIE & ARCHITECTURE

Bechir Madet
OFFICE NOTARIAL

Naramadji Mekonné
CLERC D'HUISSIER DE JUSTICE

Nadjita Francis Ngarhodjim
ATTORNEY-AT-LAW

Nicolas Ronzié
FIDAFRICA / PRICEWATERHOUSECOOPERS

Sobdibé Zoua
LAW FIRM SCPP

CHILE

CAREY Y CIA LAW FIRM

Leticia Acosta Aguirre
REDLINES FORWARDING

Jorge Benitez Urrutia
URRUTIA & CIA

Enrique Benitez Urrutia
URRUTIA & CIA

Jimena Bronfman
GUERRERO, OLIVOS NOVOA Y ERRAZURIZ

Miguel Capo Valdez
BESALCO S.A.

Mariana Castro
CAREY Y CIA LAW FIRM

Camilo Cortés
ALESSANDRI & COMPAÑÍA

Sebastian Diaz
PRICEWATERHOUSECOOPERS

Cristian Eyzaguirre
CLARO & CÍA., ABOGADOS, MEMBER OF LEX MUNDI

Silvio Figari Napoli
DATABUSINESS

Juan Pablo Gonzalez M.
GUERRERO, OLIVOS, NOVOA Y ERRÁZURIZ

Pedro Pablo Gutierrez
CAREY Y CIA LAW FIRM

Fernando Jamarne
ALESSANDRI & COMPAÑÍA

Nicolas Luco
CLARO & CÍA., ABOGADOS, MEMBER OF LEX MUNDI

Miguel Massone
PRICEWATERHOUSECOOPERS

Carmen Paz Cruz Lozano
CAMARA CHILENA DE LA CONSTRUCCION

Daniela Peña Fergadiott
BARROS & ERRÁZURIZ

Alfonso Reymond Larrain
CHADWICK & ALDUNATE ABOGADOS

Roberto Carlos Rivas
PRICEWATERHOUSECOOPERS

Edmundo Rojas García
CONSERVADOR DE BIENES RAICES DE SANTIAGO

María Agnes Salah
CAREY Y CIA LAW FIRM

María Eugenia Sandoval Gouet
PRICEWATERHOUSECOOPERS

Eduardo Torreti
BARROS LETELIER & CÍA.

Sebastián Yunge
GUERRERO, OLIVOS NOVOA Y ERRAZURIZ

CHINA

Rico Chan
BAKER & MCKENZIE

Rex Chan
PRICEWATERHOUSECOOPERS

Yan-Hua Chau
JUN HE LAW OFFICE, MEMBER OF LEX MUNDI

Jie Chen
JUN HE LAW OFFICES, MEMBER OF LEX MUNDI

Eu Jin Chua
CLIFFORD CHANCE

Leo Ge
GLOBAL STAR LOGISTICS CO. LTD.

Alexander Gong
BAKER & MCKENZIE

Kejun Guo
DEHENG LAW OFFICE

Hew Kian Heong
PINSENT MASONS

Maggie Jiang
PRICEWATERHOUSECOOPERS

He Jun
DEHENG LAW OFFICE

Guo Kejun
DEHENG LAW OFFICE

Edward E. Lehman
LEHMAN, LEE & XU

Linfei Liu
JUN HE LAW OFFICE, MEMBER OF LEX MUNDI

George Luo
PINSENT MASONS

Han Shen
DAVIS POLK & WARDWELL

Xuehua Wang
BEIJING HUANZHONG & PARTNERS

Li Wang
DEHENG LAW OFFICE

Celia Wang
PRICEWATERHOUSECOOPERS

Cassie Wong
PRICEWATERHOUSECOOPERS

Wang Xuehua
BEIJING HUANZHONG & PARTNERS

Xiaochuan Yang
PRICEWATERHOUSECOOPERS

Emma Zhang
DEHENG LAW OFFICE

Fengli Zhang
BEIJING HUANZHONG & PARTNERS

COLOMBIA

Felipe Arbouin
PINILLA, GONZÁLEZ & PRIETO

Jose Arias
GÓMEZ-PINZÓN ABOGADOS

Patricia Arrázola Bustillo
GÓMEZ-PINZÓN ABOGADOS

Jaime Alberto Arrubla Paucar
CORTE SUPREMA DE JUSTICIA

Pablo Barraquer-Uprimny
BRIGARD & URRUTIA, MEMBER OF LEX MUNDI

Juliana Bazzani Botero
JOSÉ LLOREDA CAMACHO & Co.

Leonardo Calderón
COLEGIO DE REGISTRADORES DE INSTRUMENTOS PÚBLICOS DE COLOMBIA

Dario Cardenas Navas
CARDENAS & CARDENAS

Mauricio Carvajal Cordoba
MINISTRY OF FINANCE

Felipe Cuberos
PRIETO & CARRIZOSA S.A.

Ignacio Durán
COMPUTEC - DATACRÉDITO

Gustavo Flores
SOCIEDAD PORTUARIA REGIONAL DE CARTAGENA

Carlos Fradique-Méndez
BRIGARD & URRUTIA, MEMBER OF LEX MUNDI

Santiago Gutiérrez
JOSÉ LLOREDA CAMACHO & Co.

Gabriela Mancero
CAVELIER ABOGADOS

Margarita María Núñez
Andrés Millán Pineda
GÓMEZ-PINZÓN ABOGADOS

Jinni Pastrana
JOSÉ LLOREDA CAMACHO & Co.

Carlos Felipe Pinilla Acevedo
PINILLA, GONZÁLEZ & PRIETO

Rodrigo Prieto Martinez
PINILLA, GONZÁLEZ & PRIETO

Juan Carlos Ruiz
JOSÉ LLOREDA CAMACHO & Co.

Paula Samper Salazar
GÓMEZ-PINZÓN ABOGADOS

Felipe Sandoval Villamil
GÓMEZ-PINZÓN ABOGADOS

Gustavo Tamayo
JOSÉ LLOREDA CAMACHO & Co.

Julia Uribe
CAVELIER ABOGADOS

Carlos Urrutia Jr.
BRIGARD & URRUTIA, MEMBER OF LEX MUNDI

COMOROS

Ahmed Abdallah
3A COMORES

Kamal Abdallah
3A COMORES

Mohamed Abdallah Halifa
GROUPE HASSANATI SOILIHI - GROUPE HASOIL

Chabani Abdallah Halifa
GROUPE HASSANATI SOILIHI - GROUPE HASOIL

Aboubakar Abdou
PRESIDENT DE L'ILE AUTONOME DE LA GRANDE COMORE

Djoussouf Abi
DIRECTION RÉGIONALE DES AFFAIRES FONCIÈRES ET DOMANIALES

Hassani Adili
ELECTRICITÉ ET EAU DES COMORES

Harimia Ahmed Ali
MINISTÈRE DE LA JUSTICE

Hassani Assoumani
CVP BIOCOM

Ali Mohamed Choybou
PALAIS DE LA JUSTICE

Francisco Edgar
COTECNA INSPECTION S.A.

Remy Grondin
VITOGAZ COMORES

Halima Houhadji
BANQUE DE DEVELOPPEMENT DE COMORES

Haroussi Idrissa
TRIBUNAL DE PREMIERE INSTANCE DE MORONI

Ahamada Mahamoudou
AVOCAT À LA COUR

Zainaba Mohamed
FONDS D'APPUI AU DÉVELOPPEMENT COMMUNAUTAIRE

Said Ibrahim Mourad
ANCIEN MAGISTRAT

Ibrahim A. Mzimba
CABINET MZIMBA AVOCATS

Said Ali Natukouddine
BANQUE DE DEVELOPPEMENT DE COMORES

Eric Pierard

Mihidhoir Sagaf

Tourqui Said Abdallah
BANQUE DE DEVELOPPEMENT DE COMORES

Mohamed Salipi
TRIBUNAL DE PREMIERE INSTANCE DE MORONI

Houdhoir Soilihi

Youssouf Yahaya
IMPOTS DE LA GRANDE COMORE

CONGO, DEM. REP.

Anthony Nkinzo
FIDAFRICA / PRICEWATERHOUSECOOPERS

R. Rigo

Louis-Odilon Alaguillaume
PROCREDIT BANK

Siku Beya
CABINET LUGUNDA LUMBAMBA

Jean Adolphe Bitenu
ANAPI

Jacques Chareyre
FIDAFRICA / PRICEWATERHOUSECOOPERS

Victor Crespel Musafiri
FEDERATION DES ENTREPRISES

Fabienne De Greef
CABINET G.B. MOKA NGOLO & ASSOCIES

Yves Debiesme
SDV AGETRAF

Lambert S. Djunga
CABINET DJUNGA & RISASI

David Guarnieri
FIDAFRICA / PRICEWATERHOUSECOOPERS

Paul Kabongo Tshibangu
CABINET PAUL KABONGO

Emery Kalamba
KALAMBA & ASSOCIES

Ambroise Kamukuny
CABINET TSHIBANGU ET ASSOCIES

G. Le Dourain

Francis Lugunda Lumbamba
CABINET LUGUNDA LUMBAMBA

Andre Malangu Muabila
CABINET FAMILLE

Babala Mangala
GTS EXPRESS

Roger Masamba Makela
AVOCAT, DOYEN DE FACULTÉ

Jean Claude Mbaki Siluzaku
CABINET MBAKI ET ASSOCIÉS

Bernard Claude Mbu Ne Letang
CABINET DE MEMBU NE LETANG

Tanayi Mbuy-Mbiye
CABINET MBUY-MBIYE & ASSOCIÉS

Oliver Meisenberg
PROCREDIT BANK

Polycarpe Kabasele Mfumu Tshishimbi
CABINET KABASELE - MFUMU & ASSOCIES

Louman Mpoy
CABINET MPOY-LOUMAN & ASSOCIÉS

Mwema Mulungi Mbuyu
ANAPI

Jacques Munday
CABINET NTOTO

Thierry Mutombo Kalonji
ANAPI

Marius Muzembe Mpungu
CABINET KABASELE - MFUMU & ASSOCIES

Honore Njibikila Nkonka
FEDERATION DES ENTREPRISES

Leon Nzimbi
PRICEWATERHOUSECOOPERS

Albert Okitosomba
RAWBANK

Otton Oligo Mbelia Kanalia
ANAPI

Pierre Risasi
CABINET DJUNGA & RISASI

Christie Madudu Sulubika
CABINET G.B. MOKA NGOLO & ASSOCIÉS

Toto Wa Kinkela Leon
CABINET TOTO

CONGO, REP.

Prosper Bianga
CONSEIL DU BARREAU DE BRAZZAVILLE

Prosper Bizitou
PRICEWATERHOUSECOOPERS

André Blaise Bolle
BANQUE COFIPA

Daniel Bolletot
BUREAU VERITAS

David Bourion
PRICEWATERHOUSECOOPERS

Jacques Chareyre
FIDAFRICA / PRICEWATERHOUSECOOPERS

Claude Coelho
CABINET D'AVOCAT CLAUDE COELHO

Johan Coetzer
PANALPINA

Gerard Devillers
CABINET GERARD DEVILLERS

Thomas Djolani
CONSEIL DE L'ORDRE NATIONAL

Jean-Philippe Esseau
CABINET ESSEAU

Mathias Essereke
CABINET D'AVOCAT CLAUDE COELHO

Ludovic Désiré Essou
CABINET ESSOU

Caroline Idrissou-Belingar
BEAC

Gaston Ifoko
TRIBUNAL DE COMMERCE DE BRAZZAVILLE

Bruno Jacquet
CABINET ESSOU

Philippe Jarry
SAGA CONGO - BOLLORE GROUP

Eric Jpouele
TRIBUNAL DE COMMERCE DE BRAZZAVILLE

Mr. Lendongo
TRIBUNAL DE COMMERCE DE BRAZZAVILLE

Salomon Louboula
NOTAIRE

Jerome Loutete
TRIBUNAL D'INSTANCE DE MAKELEKELE ET DE BACONGO

Thierry Mamimoue
CABINET D'AVOCATS JEAN PETRO

Jean-Claude Marc
BUREAU VERITAS

Françoise Mbongo
CABINET MBONGO

Jean Petro
CABINET D'AVOCATS JEAN PETRO

Francis Sassa
CABINET D'AVOCATS JEAN PETRO

COSTA RICA

Alejandro Antillon
PACHECO COTO

Carlos Barrantes
PRICEWATERHOUSECOOPERS

Eduardo Calderón
BUFETE FACIO & CAÑAS, MEMBER OF LEX MUNDI

Luis Manuel Castro
BLP ABOGADOS

Silvia Chacon Bolaños
ALFREDO FOURNIER & ASOCIADOS

Ludovino Colón Sánchez
PRICEWATERHOUSECOOPERS

Daniel de LaGarza
J. DE CANO ESTUDIO LEGAL

Freddy Fachler
PACHECO COTO

Alejandro Fernandez
PRICEWATERHOUSECOOPERS

Luis E. Fernandez
TRANSUNION

Octavio Fournier
ALFREDO FOURNIER & ASOCIADOS

Alfredo Fournier-Beeche
ALFREDO FOURNIER & ASOCIADOS

Victor Andrés Gómez
PRICEWATERHOUSECOOPERS

Tomás F. Guardia
BUFETE FACIO & CAÑAS, MEMBER OF LEX MUNDI

Mariano Jimenez
BLP ABOGADOS

Eduardo Lopez
PRICEWATERHOUSECOOPERS

Ivannia Méndez Rodríguez
OLLER ABOGADOS

Eduardo Montoya Solano
SUPERINTENDENCIA GENERAL DE ENTIDADES FINANCIERAS

Ramon Ortega
PRICEWATERHOUSECOOPERS

Roger Petersen
ALLIANCE LAW GROUP, SRL

Walter Anderson Salomons
JAPDEVA - PORT LIMON

Dagoberto Sibaja Morales
REGISTRO NACIONAL DE COSTA RICA

Jose Antonio Sueiras
INTER-MOVES SG GLOBAL S.A.

CÔTE D'IVOIRE

Marie Pascale Aphing Kouassi
CABINET JEAN-FRANÇOIS CHAUVEAU

César Asman
CABINET N'GOAN, ASMAN & ASSOCIÉS

Jacques Chareyre
FIDAFRICA / PRICEWATERHOUSECOOPERS

Jean-François Chauveau
CABINET JEAN-FRANÇOIS CHAUVEAU

Guillaume Dufeaux
SDV CÔTE D'IVOIRE

Jean Claude Gnamien
FIDAFRICA / PRICEWATERHOUSECOOPERS

Charles Ki-Zerbo
BCEAO

Kouame Klemet
CABINET JEAN-FRANÇOIS CHAUVEAU

Gerard Kone Dogbemin
SCPA NAMBEYA-DOGBEMIN ET ASSOCIÉS

Serge Messou
FIDAFRICA / PRICEWATERHOUSECOOPERS

Edouard Messou
PRICEWATERHOUSECOOPERS

Georges N'Goan
CABINET N'GOAN, ASMAN & ASSOCIÉS

Patricia Nguessan
CABINET JEAN-FRANÇOIS CHAUVEAU

Zinda Sawadogo
CABINET JEAN-FRANÇOIS CHAUVEAU

Dominique Taty
FIDAFRICA / PRICEWATERHOUSECOOPERS

Fousseni Traore
FIDAFRICA / PRICEWATERHOUSECOOPERS

Nadia Vanie
CABINET N'GOAN, ASMAN & ASSOCIÉS

Abbé Yao
SCPA DOGUÉ-ABBÉ YAO & ASSOCIÉS

Léon Désiré Zalo
MINISTÈRE D'ETAT, MINISTÈRE DE L'AGRICULTURE

CROATIA

Andrea August
HITRO.HR

Ivo Bijeli
PRICEWATERHOUSECOOPERS

Zoran Bohacek
CROATIAN BANKING ASSOCIATION

Esther Bronic
PRICEWATERHOUSECOOPERS

Stefanija Cukman
JURIC LAW OFFICES

Sasa Divjak
DIVJAK, TOPI & BAHTIJAREVI

Ivan Duic
VUKMIR LAW OFFICE

Lidija Hanzek
HROK

Marija Haramija
KORPER & HARAMIJA

Irina Jelcic
HANZEKOVIC, RADAKOVIC & PARTNERS, MEMBER OF LEX MUNDI

Sanja Juric
JURIC LAW OFFICES

Mirna Kette
PRICEWATERHOUSECOOPERS

Helena Konjevod
KOEL PROMET D.O.O.

Tarja Krehic-Djuranovic
LAW OFFICE LACMANOVIC

Don Markusic
PRICEWATERHOUSECOOPERS

Iain McGuire
PRICEWATERHOUSECOOPERS

Sanja Porobija
POROBIJA & POROBIJA LAW FIRM

Tatjana Radmilovic
PRICEWATERHOUSECOOPERS

Gordan Rotkvi
PRICEWATERHOUSECOOPERS

Ana Sihtar
SIHTAR ATTORNEYS-AT-LAW

Ivan Simac
ATTORNEY-AT-LAW

Lidija Stopfer
VUKMIR LAW OFFICE

Iva Tokic
POROBIJA & POROBIJA LAW FIRM

Hrvoje Vidan
LAW FIRM IVEKOVIC & VIDAN

Eugen Zadravec
EUGEN ZADRAVEC LAW FIRM

Ivana Zovko
DIVJAK, TOPI & BAHTIJAREVI

CZECH REPUBLIC

Elsebeth Aaes-Jørgensen
ALLEN & OVERY, PRAHA ADVOKÁTNÍ KANCELÁ

Stephen B. Booth
PRICEWATERHOUSECOOPERS

Jiri Cerny
PETERKA & PARTNERS V.O.S.

Roman Grones
GLEISS LUTZ ADVOKATI

Gabriela Hájková
PETERKA & PARTNERS V.O.S.

Jarmila Hanzalova
PROCHÁZKA RANDL KUBR, MEMBER OF IUS LABORIS & LEX MUNDI

David Hora
PRICEWATERHOUSECOOPERS

Vít Horáek
GLATZOVÁ & CO. LAW OFFICES PRAGUE

Sarka Jandova
PROCHÁZKA RANDL KUBR, MEMBER OF IUS LABORIS & LEX MUNDI

Petr Kucera
CCB - CZECH BANKING CREDIT BUREAU

Tomas Liptak
PRICEWATERHOUSECOOPERS

Jiri Markvart
AMBRUZ & DARK ADVOKÁTI, V.O.S.

Karol Marsovszky
WOLF THEISS

Lenka Mrazova
PRICEWATERHOUSECOOPERS

David Musil
PRICEWATERHOUSECOOPERS

Jarmila Musilova

Jörg Nürnberger
DLA WEISS - TESSBACH

Athanassios Pantazopoulos
IKRP ROKAS & PARTNERS

Martina Pavelkova
PANALPINA CZECH S.R.O.

Jana Pavlasova
SQUIRE, SANDERS & DEMPSEY

Pavla Prikrylova
PETERKA & PARTNERS V.O.S.

Natasa Randlová
PROCHÁZKA RANDL KUBR, MEMBER OF IUS LABORIS & LEX MUNDI

Tomas Richter
CLIFFORD CHANCE

Tereza Ihoková
PROCHÁZKA RANDL KUBR, MEMBER OF IUS LABORIS & LEX MUNDI

Zdenek Rosicky
SQUIRE, SANDERS & DEMPSEY

Rena Trojánková
LINKLATERS & ALLIANCE

Ludík Vrána
LINKLATERS & ALLIANCE

Katerina Vyslouzilova
AMBRUZ & DARK ADVOKÁTI, V.O.S.

Marketa Zachova
VEJMELKA & WÜNSCH

DENMARK

Elsebeth Aaes-Jørgensen
NORBOM & VINDING, MEMBER OF IUS LABORIS

Jonas Bøgelund
GORRISSEN FEDERSPIEL KIERKEGAARD

Ole Borch
BECH-BRUUN LAW FIRM

CITY COURT OF COPENHAGEN

Mogens Ebeling
JONAS BRUUN

Eivind Einersen
PHILIP & PARTNERE

Arne J. Gehring
PRICEWATERHOUSECOOPERS

Joern S. Hansen
RKI KREDIT INFORMATION A.S.

Anette Henriksen
PRICEWATERHOUSECOOPERS

Jens Hjortskov
PHILIP & PARTNERE

Jørgen B. Jepsen
KROMANN REUMERT, MEMBER OF LEX MUNDI

Susanne Madsen
KROMANN REUMERT, MEMBER OF LEX MUNDI

Carsten Melgaard
PRICEWATERHOUSECOOPERS

Karin L. Nielsen
PRICEWATERHOUSECOOPERS

Thomas Olsen
PANALPINA DENMARK

Claus Kaare Pedersen
PHILIP & PARTNERE

Bente Skovgaard Risvig
RKI KREDIT INFORMATION A.S.

Jan Hoej Soerensen
RKI KREDIT INFORMATION A.S.

Jens Steen Jensen
KROMANN REUMERT, MEMBER OF LEX MUNDI

Henrik Stenbjerre
KROMANN REUMERT, MEMBER OF LEX MUNDI

Mikael Stenstrup
PRICEWATERHOUSECOOPERS

Kim Trenskow
KROMANN REUMERT, MEMBER OF LEX MUNDI

Knud Villemoes Hansen
NATIONAL SURVEY AND CADASTRE - DENMARK/KORT- OG MATRIKELSTYRELSEN

Benedicte Wiberg
PRICEWATERHOUSECOOPERS

Torben Wolsted
PRICEWATERHOUSECOOPERS

DJIBOUTI

Rahma Abdi Adbillahi
BANQUE CENTRALE

Koran Ahmed Aouled
ETUDE NOTARIALE

Luigi Bahari Bahari
GROUPEMENT COSMEZZ DJIBOUTI S.A.

Hasna Barakat Daoud
CABINET D'AVOCAT

Wabat Daoud
AVOCAT

Jean Phillipe Delarue
SOCIETE MARITIME L. SAVON ET RIES

Luc Deruyer
SOCIETE MARITIME L. SAVON ET RIES

Félix Emok N'Dolo
CHD GROUP

Cosimo Federici
GROUPEMENT COSMEZZ DJIBOUTI S.A.

Djama M. Haid
BANQUE CENTRALE DE DJIBOUTI

Mariam Hamadou Ali
MINISTRY OF FINANCE

Ibrahim Hamadou Hassan
BANQUE POUR LE COMMERCE ET L'INDUSTRIE

Mr. Lanto
GROUPEMENT COSMEZZ DJIBOUTI S.A.

Fatouma Mahamoud Hassan

Alain Martinet

Mayank Metha
MAERSK SEALAND LINE MANAGER

Simon Mibrathu
MINISTRY OF FINANCE

Abdallah Mohammed Kamil
ETUDE NOTARIALE

Ali Moussa

Mohamed Omar Ibrahim
CABINET D'EXPERTISE COMPTABLE ET D'AUDIT

Mohamed Omar Mohamed
AVOCAT A LA COUR

Ahmed Osman
BANQUE CENTRALE DE DJIBOUTI

Mohamed Oubah
SOCIETE MARITIME L. SAVON ET RIES

Jerome Passicos
SOCIETE MARITIME L. SAVON ET RIES

Aicha Youssouf
CABINET D'EXPERTISE COMPTABLE ET D'AUDIT

Abdillahi Aidid Farah
AVOCAT À LA COUR

Ali Dini
AVOCAT À LA COUR

DOMINICA

Anthony Atkinson
PRICEWATERHOUSECOOPERS

Joelle AV Harris
HARRIS & HARRIS

Eddie Beaupierre
ELEMENT AGENCIES

Gerald D. Burton
GERALD D. BURTON'S CHAMBERS

Jofrrey C.G. Harris
HARRIS & HARRIS

Marvlyn Estrado
KPB CHARTERED ACCOUNTANTS

Noelize N. Knight
GERALD D. BURTON'S CHAMBERS

Alick C. Lawrence
ATTORNEY-AT-LAW

Severin McKenzie
MCKENZIE ARCHITECTURAL & CONSTRUCTION SERVICES INC.

Richard Peterkin
PRICEWATERHOUSECOOPERS

Joan K.R. Prevost
PREVOST & ROBERTS

Mark Riddle
DOMINICA ELECTRICITY SERVICE LTD.

Arthur R. Smith
LABOUR DEPARTMENT

Eddison St. Jean
DOMINICA ELECTRICITY SERVICE LTD.

Duncan G. Stowe
DUNCAN G. STOWE CHAMBERS

Charles Tibbits
PRICEWATERHOUSECOOPERS

Laurina A. Vidal
ATTORNEY-AT-LAW

Dawn Yearwood
ATTORNEY-AT-LAW

Stephen Isodore
ATTORNEY-AT-LAW

DOMINICAN REPUBLIC

Rhadys Abre de Polanco
UNION INTERNACIONAL DEL NOTARIADO LATINO

Joanna M. Bonnelly Ginebra
SQUIRE SANDERS & DEMPSEY PENA PRIETO GAMUNDI

Caroline Bono
PRICEWATERHOUSECOOPERS

Ludovino Colón Sánchez
PRICEWATERHOUSECOOPERS

Robinson Cuello Shanlate
PROGRAMA DE MODERNIZACIÓN DE LA JURISDICCIÓN DE TIERRAS

Sarah de León
HEADRICK RIZIK ALVAREZ & FERNANDEZ

Alejandro Fernandez
PRICEWATERHOUSECOOPERS

Mary Fernández Rodríguez
HEADRICK RIZIK ALVAREZ & FERNANDEZ

Wilson Gomez Ramirez
SUPREMA CORTE DE JUSTICIA

Pablo Gonzalez Tapia
BIAGGI & MESSINA

Fabio Guzman
GUZMÁN ARIZA & ASOCIADOS

Philippe Lescuras
PANALPINA

José Antonio Logroño Morales
ADAMS GUZMAN & ASOCIADOS

José Ramón Logroño Morales
ADAMS GUZMAN & ASOCIADOS

Ramon Ortega
PRICEWATERHOUSECOOPERS

Andrea Paniagua
PRICEWATERHOUSECOOPERS

Maria Portes
CASTILLO Y CASTILLO

Claudia Roca
HEADRICK RIZIK ALVAREZ & FERNANDEZ

Wendy Sanchez
TransUNION

Wilfredo Senior
HEADRICK RIZIK ALVAREZ & FERNANDEZ

Claudia Taveras
HEADRICK RIZIK ALVAREZ & FERNANDEZ

Mariana Vargas Gaurilova
PELLERANO & HERRERA, MEMBER OF LEX MUNDI

ECUADOR

Pablo Aguirre
PRICEWATERHOUSECOOPERS

Luciano Almeida
PRICEWATERHOUSECOOPERS

Diego Cabezas-Klaere
CABEZAS & CABEZAS-KLAERE

Luis Cascante
MOELLER, GÓMEZ-LINCE & CÍA

Fernando Coral
PANALPINA

Jose Durán
MOELLER, GÓMEZ-LINCE & CÍA

Rodrigo Espinosa
SUPERINTENDENCIA DE BANCOS E SEGUROS

Jorge Eduardo Fernandez Perdomo
DATACREDITO

Juan Carlos Gallegos
GALLEGOS, VALAREZO & NEIRA

Myriam Rosales Garces
SUPERINTENDENCIA DE BANCOS E SEGUROS

Juan Manuel Marchán
PÉREZ, BUSTAMANTE Y PONCE, MEMBER OF LEX MUNDI

Heinz Moeller Freile
MOELLER, GÓMEZ-LINCE & CÍA

Paulina Montesdeoca De Bustamante
MACIAS HURTADO & MACIAS

Jorge Paz Durini
PAZ & HOROWITZ

Xavier Amador Pino
ESTUDIO JURIDICO AMADOR

Sandra Reed
PÉREZ, BUSTAMANTE Y PONCE, MEMBER OF LEX MUNDI

Maria de los Angeles Roman
FABARA & COMPAÑIA ABOGADOS

Jose Rumazo-Arcos
PÉREZ, BUSTAMANTE Y PONCE, MEMBER OF LEX MUNDI

EGYPT

Abdel Aal Aly
AFIFI WORLD TRANSPORT

Eman Abdelbakey
PRICEWATERHOUSECOOPERS / MANSOUR & CO.

Rasha Abdel-Hakim

Amal Afifi
EL OTEIFI LAW OFFICE

Arig Ali
TROWERS & HAMLINS

Alaa Amer
MINISTRY OF MANPOWER AND MIGRATION

Tim Armsby
TROWERS & HAMLINS

George Atalla

Ingy Badawy
SHALAKANY LAW OFFICE, MEMBER OF LEX MUNDI

Alah Bassyouni

Rania Bata
SARWAT A. SHAHID LAW FIRM

Tim Bueher

Heather Carpenter
PRICEWATERHOUSECOOPERS / MANSOUR & CO.

E. Yehia H. El Bably
EL BABLY LAW FIRM

Samir El Tagy
MINISTRY OF MANPOWER AND MIGRATION

Yasmine Elabassy
PRICEWATERHOUSECOOPERS / MANSOUR & CO.

Ashraf Elibrachy
IBRACHY LAW FIRM

Tarek El-Marsafawy
ADEL KAMEL & ASSOCIATES

Amr ElMonayer
PRICEWATERHOUSECOOPERS / MANSOUR & CO.

Mohamed Fahim
PRICEWATERHOUSECOOPERS / MANSOUR & CO.

Zeinab Saieed Gohar
CENTRAL BANK OF EGYPT

A.G. Hassan

Manuel Henriques

Sarah Hinton
TROWERS & HAMLINS

Sadeyaa Ibrahim
MINISTRY OF MANPOWER AND MIGRATION

Ashraf Ihab
SHALAKANY LAW OFFICE, MEMBER OF LEX MUNDI

Stephan Jäger
KRAUSS AMERELLER HENKENBORG

Karim Adel Kamel
ADEL KAMEL & ASSOCIATES

Mohamed Kamel
AL KAMEL LAW

Ghada Kaptan
SHALAKANY LAW OFFICE, MEMBER OF LEX MUNDI

Adel Kheir
ADEL KHEIR LAW OFFICE

Kamel M.

Dr. Magadi
EGYPTIAN CENTER FOR ECONOMIC STUDIES

Sherif Mansour
PRICEWATERHOUSECOOPERS / MANSOUR & CO.

Hoda Mohamed Etman

Alan Morley

Ashraf Nadhoury
ATTORNEY-AT-LAW

Ragia Omran
SHALAKANY LAW OFFICE, MEMBER OF LEX MUNDI

Ingy Rasekh
MENA ASSOCIATES

Tarek F. Riad
KOSHERI, RASHED & RIAD INTERNATIONAL LAW FIRM

Maria Rodriguez

Khaled Sewelam

Safwat Sobhy
PRICEWATERHOUSECOOPERS / MANSOUR & CO.

Ahmed Weshahi
SHALAKANY LAW OFFICE, MEMBER OF LEX MUNDI

Louise Williams
INDEPENDENT CONSULTANT

Tamima Yehia
SHALAKANY LAW OFFICE, MEMBER OF LEX MUNDI

Mona Zulficar
SHALAKANY LAW OFFICE, MEMBER OF LEX MUNDI

EL SALVADOR

Francisco Armando Arias Rivera
F.A. ARIAS & MUÑOZ

Lilliam Arrieta Carsana
ARRIETA BUSTAMANTE

Irene Arrieta de Díaz Nuila
ARRIETA BUSTAMANTE

Ricardo A. Cevallos
CONSORTIUM - DELGADO & CEVALLOS

Walter A. Chavez
GOLD SERVICE / MSI

Ludovino Colón Sánchez
PRICEWATERHOUSECOOPERS

María Eugenia de Castenada
ACZALAW

Mayra de Morán
PRESIDENTIAL PROGRAM "EL SALVADOR EFICIENTE"

Manuel del Valle Menendez
REGISTRY

Maria Martha Delgado Molina
ESPINO, NIETO, UMAÑA & ASOCIADOS

Alejandro Fernandez
PRICEWATERHOUSECOOPERS

Otto Guzman
PRICEWATERHOUSECOOPERS, S.A. DE C.V.

Ernesto Hempe
PRICEWATERHOUSECOOPERS, S.A. DE C.V.

Juan Carlos Herrera
F.A. ARIAS & MUÑOZ

Thelma Dinora Lizama de Osorio
SUPERINTENDENCIA DEL SISTEMA FINANCIERO

Karla Maley Guzman
ARRIETA BUSTAMANTE

Astrud Maria Melendez
PROCREDITO - TRANSUNION CENTRAL AMERICA

Mauricio Melhado
GOLD SERVICE S.A. DE C.V.

Antonio R. Mendez Llort
ROMERO PINEDA & ASOCIADOS, MEMBER OF LEX MUNDI

Jose Navas
ALL WORLD CARGO, SA DE CV

James W. Newton
BOOZ ALLEN HAMILTON

Maria Eugenia Olmedo de Castaneda
ACZALAW

Ramon Ortega
PRICEWATERHOUSECOOPERS

Carlos Oviedo
CONSORTIUM - DELGADO & CEVALLOS

Monica Guadalupe Pineda Machuca
ACZALAW

Ana Patricia Portillo Reyes
GUANDIQUE SEGOVIA QUINTANILLA

Carlos Roberto Alfaro
PRICEWATERHOUSECOOPERS, S.A. DE C.V.

Manuel Francisco Telles Suvillaga
LEXINCORP

Mauricio Antonio Urrutia Urrutia
SUPERINTENDENCIA DEL SISTEMA FINANCIERO

EQUATORIAL GUINEA

Jose Angel Borrico Moises
FISCAL LAWYER

Jacques Chareyre
FIDAFRICA / PRICEWATERHOUSECOOPERS

Augustin Chicampo Barila
DISTRICT COURT

Leoncio-Mitogo Edjang Avoro
ATTORNEY-AT-LAW

Pedro Nsue Ela Eyang
NOTARY

Caroline Idrissou-Belingar
BEAC

Heidi Johansen
GLOBALTRANS

Benoit Kanyandekme
BK ARCHITECTS SL

Mariam Laine
AIR FREIGHT

Sébastien Lechêne
FIDAFRICA / PRICEWATERHOUSECOOPERS

Franck Mamelin
PANALPINA TRANSPORTES - MUNDIALES GUINEA ECUATORIAL S.A.R.L.

Francisco Javier Mbe Ngomo
ATTORNEY-AT-LAW

Paulino Mbo Obama
OFICINA DE ESTUDIEOS - ATEG

Ponciano Mbomio Nvo

Diosdado Nchama
MINISTRY OF MINING

Solvador-Ondo Ncume Oye
ATTORNEY-AT-LAW

Honorio Ndong Obama
ATTORNEY-AT-LAW

Jenaro Obuno Ela
ATTORNEY-AT-LAW

Antonio-Pascual Oko Ebobo
ATTORNEY-AT-LAW

Jose-Antonio Lluch Ondo
Matojo
ATTORNEY-AT-LAW

Vicente-Nse Ondo-Mitogo
CORTE SUPREMA DE JUSTICIA

Reginaldo Egido Panades
ATTORNEY-AT-LAW

Caroline Traverse
FIDAFRICA /
PRICEWATERHOUSECOOPERS

ERITREA

Ali Reza Abdolhussein
ELMI OLINDO & CO.

Rahel Abera
BERHANE GILA-MICHAEL LAW
FIRM

Tadesse Beraki
TRADE PROMOTION AGENCY

Leghese Ghebremedhin
Seyoum
ADVOCATE & COUNSELOR
AT LAW

Berhane Gila-Michael
BERHANE GILA-MICHAEL LAW
FIRM

Fessahaie Habte
ATTORNEY-AT-LAW AND
LEGAL CONSULTANT

Kebreab Habte Michael
LEGAL COUNSELING

Mebrahtom Habtemariam
PUBLIC FACILITATION OFFICE

Mulgheta Hailu
TEFERI BERHANE &
MULGHETA HAILU LAW FIRM

Michael Joseph
ERNST & YOUNG EAST AFRICA

Mesfin Makonnen Mebrahtu
ADVOCATE & COUNSELOR
AT LAW

Ataklti H. Mariam
COMMERCIAL COURT

Chief Justice Mercurius
MINISTRY OF JUSTICE

Tekeste Mesghenna
MTD ENTERPRISES PLC

Akberom Tedla
ERITREAN NATIONAL
CHAMBER OF COMMERCE

Alem Tesfai
BUSINESS LICENSE OFFICE

Belay Tewelde
REMATCO

ESTONIA

Aet Bergmann
LAW OFFICE TARK & CO.

Cameron Greaves
PRICEWATERHOUSECOOPERS

Heili Haabu
LAW OFFICE RAIDLA &
PARTNERS

Andres Juss
ESTONIAN LAND BOARD

Peep Kalamae
PRICEWATERHOUSECOOPERS

Iren Koplimets
PRICEWATERHOUSECOOPERS

Ermo Kosk
LEPIK & LUHAÄÄR LAWIN,
MEMBER OF LEX MUNDI

Igor Kostjuk
HOUGH, HÜBNER, HÜTT &
PARTNERS

Konstantin Kotivnenko

Villu Kõve
ESTONIAN SUPREME COURT

Kristi Kullerkup
LAW OFFICE TARK & CO.

Aare Kurist
PRICEWATERHOUSECOOPERS

LEXTAL LAW OFFICE

Lea Liigus
SORAINEN LAW OFFICES

Jaan Lindmäe
LAW OFFICE TARK & CO.

Indrek Link
HOUGH, HÜBNER, HÜTT &
PARTNERS

Karin Madisson
SORAINEN LAW OFFICES

Marko Mehilane
LEPIK & LUHAÄÄR LAWIN,
MEMBER OF LEX MUNDI

Veiko Meos
KREDIIDIINFO A.S.

Margus Mugu
LUIGA MODY HÄÄL BORENIUS

Toomas Prangli
ADVOKAADIBÜROO SORAINEN
LAW OFFICES

Ants Ratas
ECF&S AGNETS LTD.

Merle Saaliste
ADVOKAADIBÜROO SORAINEN
LAW OFFICES

Katrin Sarap
ADVOKAADIBÜROO SORAINEN
LAW OFFICES

Villi Töntson
PRICEWATERHOUSECOOPERS

Triin Toomemets
ADVOKAADIBÜROO SORAINEN
LAW OFFICES

Maarja Torga
LEPIK & LUHAÄÄR LAWIN,
MEMBER OF LEX MUNDI

Karolina Ullmann
MAQS LAW FIRM
ADVOKAADIBÜROO

Toomas Vaher
RAIDLA & PARTNERS

Vesse Võhma

ETHIOPIA

Getachew Afrasa
TADESSE, GETACHEW & ABATE
LAW OFFICE

Bekure Assefa
BEKURE ASSEFA LAW OFFICE

Befekadu Assefa Gonefa
LEWA PLC

Teshome Gabre-Mariam
Bokan
TESHOME GABRE-MARIAM
LAW FIRM

Teferra Demiss
LEGAL AND INSURANCE
CONSULTANT AND ATTORNEY

Giancarlo Elmi
ELMI OLINDO & CO. PLC -
GENERAL CONTRACTOR

Shimelise Eshete
MIDROC CONSTRUCTION
PLC

Nega Getahun
CITY ADMINISTRATION OF
ADDIS ABABA

Berhane Ghebray
BERHANE GHEBRAY &
ASSOCIATES

Solomon Gizaw
HST & CO.

Abebe T. Kasay
ATTORNEY-AT-LAW

Getachew Kebede
PACKFORD INTERNATIONAL,
ETHIOPIA

Belay Kebede Alemu
ATTORNEY AND CONSULTANT
AT LAW

Aberra Ketsela

Habtu Wolde Kiros
HABTU AND ASSOCIATES

Tadesse Kiros
TADESSE, GETACHEW & ABATE
LAW OFFICE

Getachew Kitaw Yitateku
ETHIOPIAN BAR ASSOCIATION

Debebe Legesse

Lakew Lemma

Mebratu Misghina
LEGAL ADVISER

Woldegabriel Naizghi
HST & CO.

Getahun Nana
NATIONAL BANK OF ETHIOPIA

Hailye Sahle Seifu
ATTORNEY-AT-LAW

Mekuria Tafassa
FIRAWRARI TAFESSA LEGAL
FIRM

Wolde Tsadik Someno
MINISTRY OF TRADE &
INDUSTRY

Amsale Tsehaye
AMSALE TSEHAYE &
ASSOCIATES LAW OFFICE

Marcos Weldesenbet
LAW FIRM MARCOS
WELDESENBET

Abate Yimer
TADESSE, GETACHEW & ABATE
LAW OFFICE

Tesfaye Zemedkun
CITY ADMINISTRATION OF
ADDIS ABABA

FIJI

John Apted
MUNRO LEYS NOTARIES
PUBLIC

Nehla Basawaiya
MUNRO LEYES NOTARIES
PUBLIC

Williams Wylie Clarke
HOWARDS LAWYERS

Delores Elliott
DATABUREAU, BAYCORP
ADVANTAGE

Dominique Fischer
UNIVERSITY OF THE SOUTH
PACIFIC

Anthea S. Fong
CROMPTONS

Richard Krishnan Naidu
MUNRO LEYS NOTARIES
PUBLIC

Haroon Latif
LATEEF & LATEEF

Richard Krishnan Naidu
MUNRO LEYES NOTARIES
PUBLIC

Ramesh Prakash
MISHRA PRAKASH &
ASSOCIATES

Jenny Seeto
PRICEWATERHOUSECOOPERS

Suruj Sharma
PATEL SHARMA & ASSOCIATES,
NOTARY PUBLIC

Shayne Sorby
HOWARDS LAWYERS

Chirk Yam
PRICEWATERHOUSECOOPERS

FINLAND

Markku Aaltonen
CONFEDERATION OF FINNISH
CONSTRUCTION INDUSTRIES

Claudio Busi
CASTREN & SNELLMAN

Mikko Eerola
WASELIUS & WIST

Johannes Frände
ROSCHIER HOLMBERG
ATTORNEYS LTD., MEMBER OF
IUS LABORIS & LEX MUNDI

Tuula Gottleben
HEDMAN OSBORNE CLARKE

Markku Hakkarainen
PRICEWATERHOUSECOOPERS
OY - SVH

Johanna Haltia-Tapio
HANNES SNELLMAN

Harry Hedman
HEDMAN OSBORNE CLARKE

Berndt Heikel
HANNES SNELLMAN

Jenni Hupli
CASTREN & SNELLMAN

Pekka Jaatinen
CASTREN & SNELLMAN

Juuso Jokela
SUOMEN ASIAKASTIETO OY
- FINSKA

Bernt Juthstrom
ROSCHIER HOLMBERG
ATTORNEYS LTD., MEMBER OF
IUS LABORIS & LEX MUNDI

Ilkka Kajas
PRICEWATERHOUSECOOPERS
OY - SVH

Risto Löf
PRICEWATERHOUSECOOPERS
OY - SVH

Tuomas Lukkarinen
NATIONAL LAND SURVEY OF
FINLAND

Natalia Malgina
HEDMAN OSBORNE CLARKE

Mikko Mali
KROGERUS & CO.

Eva Nordman
ROSCHIER HOLMBERG
ATTORNEYS LTD., MEMBER OF
IUS LABORIS & LEX MUNDI

Vesa-Pekka Nuotio
PRICEWATERHOUSECOOPERS
OY - SVH

Johan Nybergh
HANNES SNELLMAN

Maarit Pokkinen
PRICEWATERHOUSECOOPERS
OY - SVH

Sami Rautiainen
CASTREN & SNELLMAN

Mikko Reinikainen
PRICEWATERHOUSECOOPERS
OY - SVH

Kai Soini
PRICEWATERHOUSECOOPERS
OY - SVH

Ville Sulonen
PANALPINA FINLAND

Sarah Tahkala
HANNES SNELLMAN

Susanna Tiihonen
ROSCHIER HOLMBERG
ATTORNEYS LTD., MEMBER OF
IUS LABORIS & LEX MUNDI

Irmeli Timonen
HANNES SNELLMAN

Carita Wallgren
ROSCHIER HOLMBERG
ATTORNEYS LTD., MEMBER OF
IUS LABORIS & LEX MUNDI

FRANCE

Antoine Azam-Darley
AZAM-DARLEY & ASSOCIÉS

Christopher Baker
SKADDEN, ARPS, SLATE,
MEAGHER & FLOM LLP

Guillaume Barbier
LANDWELL & ASSOCIÉS -
PRICEWATERHOUSECOOPERS

Aurélie Besloin
LANDWELL & ASSOCIÉS -
PRICEWATERHOUSECOOPERS

Arnaud Chastel
LANDWELL & ASSOCIÉS -
PRICEWATERHOUSECOOPERS

Frédérique Chifflot Bourgeois
AVOCAT AU BARREAU DE
PARIS

Christian Courivaud
SCP COURIVAUD - MORANGE
- VOLNIAC

Anne Creelman
VATIER & ASSOCIÉS

Bernard de Rasque de Laval
CONSEIL SUPÉRIEUR DU
NOTARIAT

François de Verdière
CLEARY, GOTTLIEB, STEEN &
HAMILTON LLP

Albane Henry de Villeneuve
LANDWELL & ASSOCIÉS -
PRICEWATERHOUSECOOPERS

Jean-Paul Decorps
NOTARY

Aurèle Delors
CLEARY, GOTTLIEB, STEEN &
HAMILTON LLP

François Fauvet
FAUVET, LA GIRAUDIÈRE &
ASSOCIÉS

Jean-Pierre Fiquet
Landwell & Associés - PricewaterhouseCoopers

Sylvie Ghesquiere
Banque de France

Xavier-Philippe Gruwez
Saint Georges Conseil Avocats

Marc Jobert
Jobert & Associés

Renaud Jouffroy
Landwell & Associés - PricewaterhouseCoopers

Jennifer Juvenal
Landwell & Associés - PricewaterhouseCoopers

Gerard Kaeufling
Notary

Carol Khoury
Jones Day

Daniel Arthur Laprès
Cabinet d'Avocats

Christophe Leclere
Landwell & Associés - PricewaterhouseCoopers

Sébastien Lecoeur
Cleary, Gottlieb, Steen & Hamilton LLP

David Malamed
Gide Loyrette Nouel, member of Lex Mundi

Elise Mannent
Cleary, Gottlieb, Steen & Hamilton LLP

Jean-Louis Martin
Jones Day

Michel Ledoeuff
SDV Logistique Internationale

Alain Moreau
UINL/Conrseil Superieur du Notariat

Catherine Peulvé
Cleary, Gottlieb, Steen & Hamilton LLP

Etienne Pichat
Allez & Associés

Jacques Pourciel
Notary

Bernard Reynis
SCP Reynis & Associés

Jacques Röder
Skadden, Arps, Slate, Meagher & Flom LLP

Notaire Roussel
Conseil Supérieur du Notariat

Annie Sauve
Banque de France

Alexia Simon
Azam-Darley & Associés

Virginie Vinas
CGI

Philippe Xavier-Bender
Gide Loyrette Nouel, member of Lex Mundi

GABON

Y.A. Adetona
Cabinet Fidexce S.A.R.L.

Justine Agondjo-Reteno
Avocate

Itchola Mano Alade
Avocate

Philippe Alexandre
Attorney-at-Law

Gianni Ardizzone
Attorney-at-Law

Jacques Chareyre
FIDAFRICA / PricewaterhouseCoopers

Francois Coron
Panalpina

Leopold Effah
Avocat à la Cour

Augustin Fang
Cabinet Oyane-Ondo

Laurent Guiral
FIDAFRICA / PricewaterhouseCoopers

Caroline Idrissou-Belingar
BEAC

Samuel Josso
FIDAFRICA / PricewaterhouseCoopers

Ntoutoume Lubin
Avocate

Orphée Yvan Mandji
Agence de Promotions des Investissements Privés

Pelagie Massamba
FIDAFRICA / PricewaterhouseCoopers

Bongho Mavoungou
Attorney-at-Law

J. Zassi Mikala
Avocat à la Cour

Ruben Mindonga
Cabinet Me Anguiler

Mba Ndong
Attorney-at-Law

Thierry Ngomo
ArchiPro International

Francois Nguema Ebane
Cabinet Atelier 5A

Josette Olendo
Cabinet Olendo

C. Apollinaire Ondo Mve
Cour d'Appel Judiciaire de Libreville

Christophe Relongoue
FIDAFRICA / PricewaterhouseCoopers

Laurent Boris Skitt
Agence de Promotions des Investissements Privés

GAMBIA

Rodolphe K. Akoto
Maersk Gambia Ltd.

Cherno Alieu Jallow
Deloitte & Touche, member of Deloitte Touche Tohmatsu

Awa Bah
Department of State for Justice

Alpha Amadou Barry
Deloitte & Touche, member of Deloitte Touche Tohmatsu

Amie N. Bensouda
Amie Bensouda & Co.

Amie Joof Conteh
Kunni Boy Chambers

Ida Denise Drameh
Ida D. Drameh & Associates

Kumba Jameh
Attorney-at-Law

M.K. Krubally
All As One, Inc.

Tijan Mbye
Maj Consult Ltd.

Thomas Nielsen
Gambia Shipping Agencies

Augustus J. Prom
Augustus Prom Chartered Certified Accountants

Mary Abdoulie Samba Christensen
Legal Practitioner

Joseph Sarre
Gambia Architectural and Planning Consultants

Howsoon B. Semega-Janneh
Attorney-at-Law

Hawa Sisay-Sabally
Supreme Court

Mabel Yamoa
High Court

GEORGIA

Eka Abashidze
Association for the Protection of Landowners' Rights

Mushfig Aliyev
PricewaterhouseCoopers

Zurab Antelidze
Ministry of Finance

Ekaterine Avaliani
Ministry of Economic Development

Natalia Babakishvili
Mgaloblishvili, Kipiani, Dzidziguri Law Firm

Nino Bakhtadze
National Agency of Public Registry

Merab Barbakadze

Sopo Begiashvili
Millennium Challenge Georgia Fund

Sandro Bibilashvili
BGI Advisory Services Georgia

Zaza Bibilashvili
BGI Legal

Jen Braswell
Booz Allen Hamilton

Vazha Chopikashvili
National Agency of Public Registry

Tea Dabrundasvili
National Agency of Public Registry

Amy Denman
American Chamber of Commerce in Georgia

Stuart Duncan
Land and Permitting Manager

Jaba Ebanoidze
Association for the Protection of Landowners' Rights

David Egiashvili
National Agency of Public Registry

Revaz Enukidze
Ministry of Environment

Irine Gabriadze
USAID

Irina Gordeladze
USAID

David Gosney
USAID

Rizvan Gubiyev
PricewaterhouseCoopers

Arif Guliyev
PricewaterhouseCoopers

Bela Gutidze
PricewaterhouseCoopers

David Kakabadze
Georgian Legal Partnership

Nugzar Kavtaradze
Federation of Georgian Businessmen

Marina Khatiashvili
Georgian Real Estate Association

Victor Kipiani
Mgaloblishvili, Kipiani, Dzidziguri Law Firm

Konstantin Kublashvili
Supreme Court

Kakha Kuchava
USAID

Aieti Kukava
Alliance Group Holding

Jim McNicholas
Booz Allen Hamilton

Avto Namicheishvili
Begiashvili & Co.

Stephanos Orestis
USAID

Sopho Roinishvili
PricewaterhouseCoopers

Soso Salukvadz
KfW

Joseph Salukvadze
Cadastre and Land Register Project

Sandro Shakhov
GTZ

Lela Shatirishvili
Tbilisi Title Company

Nick Skhirtladze
Federation of Georgian Businessmen

Irakli Songulia
Association for the Protection of Landowners' Rights

Rusa Sreseli
PricewaterhouseCoopers

Matthew Tallarovic
PricewaterhouseCoopers

Tamara Tevdoradze
BGI Advisory Services Georgia

GERMANY

Allen & Overy LLP

Gabriele Apfelbacher
Cleary, Gottlieb, Steen & Hamilton LLP

Wulf Bach
Schufa

Dirk Baumgardt
PricewaterhouseCoopers AG

Henning Berger
White & Case

Klaus Berner
Nörr Stiefenhofer Lutz, member of Lex Mundi

Jennifer Bierly-Seipp
Gassner Stockmann & Kollegen

Pia Dorfmueller
PricewaterhouseCoopers AG

Dieter Endres
PricewaterhouseCoopers AG

Sigrun Erber-Faller
Notare Erber-Faller und Voran

Klaus Günther
Linklaters Oppenhoff & Rädler

Robert Gutte
Cleary, Gottlieb, Steen & Hamilton LLP

Malte Hansen
Cleary, Gottlieb, Steen & Hamilton LLP

Manfred Heinrich
Deutsche Bundesbank

Silvanne Helle
Linklaters Oppenhoff & Rädler

Götz-Sebastian Hök
Law Firm Dr. Hök, Stieglmeier & Kollegen

Andre Jahn
Law Firm Dr. Hök, Stieglmeier & Kollegen

Bernard Khun
Lovells

Thomas Kopp
Cleary, Gottlieb, Steen & Hamilton LLP

Peter Limmer
Notare Dr. Limmer & Dr. Friederich

Frank Lohrmann
Cleary, Gottlieb, Steen & Hamilton LLP

Werner Meier
Cleary, Gottlieb, Steen & Hamilton LLP

Werner M. Mues
C·B·H Rechtsanwälte, member of Ius Laboris

Daniel Panajotow
Cleary, Gottlieb, Steen & Hamilton LLP

Jan Christoph Pfeffer
Cleary, Gottlieb, Steen & Hamilton LLP

Peter Polke
Cleary, Gottlieb, Steen & Hamilton LLP

Klaus Riehmer
Cleary, Gottlieb, Steen & Hamilton LLP

Christoph Schauenburg
*CLEARY, GOTTLIEB, STEEN &
HAMILTON LLP*

Hanno Sperlich
*CLEARY, GOTTLIEB, STEEN &
HAMILTON LLP*

Holger Thomas
SJ BERWIN LLP

Tobias Tillmann
*CLEARY, GOTTLIEB, STEEN &
HAMILTON LLP*

Heiko Vogt
*PANALPINA WELTTRANSPORT
GMBH*

Wilhelm Zeddies
*SURVEYING AUTHORITIES -
ADV c/o LGN*

GHANA

Stella Ackwerh
LAND TITLE REGISTRY

Shaira Adamali
PRICEWATERHOUSECOOPERS

Larry Adjetey
LAW TRUST COMPANY

Nene Amegatcher
*SAM OKUDZETO &
ASSOCIATES*

Wilfred Anim-Odame
LAND VALUATION BOARD

Reginald Bannerman
*BRUCE-LYLE BANNERMAN &
THOMPSON*

Kojo Bentsi-Enchill
*BENTSI-ENCHILL & LETSA,
MEMBER OF LEX MUNDI*

Charles Egan
PRICEWATERHOUSECOOPERS

Willie Fugar
FUGAR & COMPANY

David A. Hesse
HESSE & HESSE

Rosa Kudoadzi
*BENTSI-ENCHILL & LETSA,
MEMBER OF LEX MUNDI*

George Kwatia
PRICEWATERHOUSECOOPERS

Kenneth D. Laryea
LARYEA, LARYEA & CO. P.C.

David Nukator
*DOCK TO DOOR SHIPPING
LTD.*

Darcy White
PRICEWATERHOUSECOOPERS

GREECE

Georgios B. Bazinas
*ANAGNOSTOPOULOS BAZINAS
FIFIS*

Panayotis Bernitsas
*M & P BERNITSAS LAW
OFFICES*

Alkistis Christofilou
IKRP ROKAS & PARTNERS

Helen Dikonimaki
*TEIRESIAS S.A. INTERBANKING
INFORMATION SYSTEMS*

Maira Galani
IKRP ROKAS & PARTNERS

Eirini Eleftheria Galinou
*PROFESSOR K. KREMALIS &
PARTNERS, MEMBER OF IUS
LABORIS*

Yanos Gramatidis
*BAHAS, GRAMATIDIS &
PARTNERS*

Peter Kapasouris
*TEIRESIAS S.A. INTERBANKING
INFORMATION SYSTEMS*

Catherine M. Karatzas
KARATZAS & PARTNERS

Konstantinos Karlis
*BUSINESS SOLUTIONS S.A. /
PRICEWATERHOUSECOOPERS*

Fotini D. Katrakaza
LAW OFFICE T. J. KOUTALIDIS

Dimitris Katsadakis
*ORPHEE BEINOGLOU INTL.
FORWARDERS*

Constantinos Klissouras
*ANAGNOSTOPOULOS BAZINAS
FIFIS*

Alexandra Kondyli
KARATZAS & PARTNERS

Nicholas Kontizas
*ZEPOS & YANNOPOULOS,
MEMBER OF LEX MUNDI*

Panos Koromantzos
*BAHAS, GRAMATIDIS &
PARTNERS*

Ioanna Koulouri
*PROFESSOR K. KREMALIS &
PARTNERS, MEMBER OF IUS
LABORIS*

Yannis Kourniotis
*M & P BERNITSAS LAW
OFFICES*

Vassiliki G. Lazarakou
*ZEPOS & YANNOPOULOS,
MEMBER OF LEX MUNDI*

Evi Martinovits
IKRP ROKAS & PARTNERS

Effie G. Mitsopoulou
*KYRIAKIDES - GEOGROPOULOS
LAW FIRM*

Vassiliki Ntziora
*PROFESSOR K. KREMALIS &
PARTNERS, MEMBER OF IUS
LABORIS*

Stefanos Petropoulakos
*PROFESSOR K. KREMALIS &
PARTNERS, MEMBER OF IUS
LABORIS*

Chryssiis Poulakou
*KYRIAKIDES - GEOGROPOULOS
LAW FIRM*

Vasiliki Salaka
KARATZAS & PARTNERS

George Samothrakis
PRICEWATERHOUSECOOPERS

SARANTITIS LAW FIRM

Vassiliki Strantzia
*BUSINESS SOLUTIONS S.A. /
PRICEWATERHOUSECOOPERS*

Charles Tibbits
PRICEWATERHOUSECOOPERS

Spyridon Tsallas
IKRP ROKAS & PARTNERS

Antonios Tsavdaridis
IKRP ROKAS & PARTNERS

Vicky Xourafa
*KYRIAKIDES - GEOGROPOULOS
LAW FIRM*

Freddy Yatracou
PRICEWATERHOUSECOOPERS

GRENADA

Anthony Atkinson
PRICEWATERHOUSECOOPERS

Alain Bain
*MINISTRY OF FOREIGN
AFFAIRS AND INTERNATIONAL
TRADE*

Robert Branch
SUPREME COURT

Andrew DeBourg
MINISTRY OF LABOR

Ruggles Ferguson
GRANADA BAR ASSOCIATION

Claudia Francis
PRICEWATERHOUSECOOPERS

Cosmas George
FREIGHT FORWARDER

Cyrius Griffith
MINISTRY OF LABOR

Kelvin Jacobs
CREATIVE DESIGN

Nigel John
*JOSEPH JOHN & ASSOCIATES
LTD.*

Claudette Joseph
AMICUS ATTORNEYS

Kurt LaBarrie
CREATIVE DESIGN

Dickon Mitchell
*GRANT JOSEPH & CO.,
MEMBER OF LEX MUNDI*

Niel Noel
*HENRY HUDSON - PHILLIPS
& CO.*

Richard Peterkin
PRICEWATERHOUSECOOPERS

Raymond Anthony
RAYMOND ANTHONY & CO.

Ian H. Sandy
AMICUS ATTORNEYS

David Sinclair
*GRENADA CONTRACTORS
ASSOCIATION / SINCLAIR
ENTERPRISES LTD.*

Trevor St. Bernard
LEWIS & RENWICK

Phinsley St. Louis
ST. LOUIS SERVICE

Avril Trotman
MINISTRY OF LEGAL AFFAIRS

Roselyn Wilkinson
*WILKINSON, WILKINSON &
WILKINSON*

GUATEMALA

Ruby Asturias
ACZALAW

Nico Asturias
ATTORNEY-AT-LAW

Maria de los Angeles Barillas
Buchhalter
SARAVIA & MUÑOZ

Julio Roberto Berduo
PALACIOS & ASOCIADOS

Mario Adolfo Búcaro Flores
DÍAZ-DURAN & ASOCIADOS

Sergio Raúl Calderón
Mancilla

Rodrigo Callejas Aquino
CARRILLO & ASOCIADOS

Juan Pablo Carrasco de
Groote
DÍAZ-DURÁN & ASOCIADOS

Alfonso Carrillo
CARRILLO & ASOCIADOS

Arabella Castro Quiñones
ATTORNEY-AT-LAW

Luis Pedro Cazali Leal
PALACIOS & ASOCIADOS

Leonel E. Chinchilla Recinos
REGISTRO MERCANTIL

Ludovino Colón Sánchez
PRICEWATERHOUSECOOPERS

Isabel Coma de Samayoa
CARRILLO & ASOCIADOS

Guillermo Lopez Cordero
BUFETE LOPEZ CORDERO

Michael Daniels Toriello

Rolando Díaz
PRICEWATERHOUSECOOPERS

Estuardo Enrique Echeverria
Nova
*UNIDAD DE CDR Y
CONTROL DE LA CALIDAD,
SUPERINTENDENCIA DE
BANCOS*

Juan Pedro Falla
RUIZ SKINNER-KLEE & RUIZ

Alejandro Fernandez
PRICEWATERHOUSECOOPERS

Rudolfo Fuentes
BAC / CREDOMATIC

Jorge Gálvez
BAC / CREDOMATIC

Carolina Gándara
ACZALAW

Rafael Garavito
GARAVITO, MUADI & MURGA

Claudia Maria Gordinez Soto
LEXINCORP

Maria Isabel Luján
Zilbermann
*QUIÑONES, IBARGÜEN &
LUJÁN*

Estuardo Mata Palmieri
*QUIÑONES, IBARGUEN &
LUJAN, S.C.*

Eduardo Mayora Alvarado
*MAYORA & MAYORA, MEMBER
OF LEX MUNDI*

Eduardo Mayora Dawe
*MAYORA & MAYORA, MEMBER
OF LEX MUNDI*

Edgar Mendoza
PRICEWATERHOUSECOOPERS

Amarilis Ondina Navas
Portillo
*BELTRANENA, DE LA CERDA Y
CHAVEZ*

Jose Orive
F.A. ARIAS & MUÑOZ

Ramon Ortega
PRICEWATERHOUSECOOPERS

Marco Antonio Palacios
PALACIOS & ASOCIADOS

Edgardo Pérez
BANCO UNO

Fernando Quezado Toruño

Arabella Castro Quiñones
*REGISTRADORA GENERAL DE
LA PROPIEDAD*

Evelyn Rebuli
*QUIÑONES, IBARGUEN &
LUJAN*

Jose A. Rodríguez
REGISTRO MERCANTIL

Alfredo Rodriguez-Mahuad
*CONSORTIUM - RODRIGUEZ,
ARCHILA, CASTELLANOS,
SOLARES & AGUILAR, S.C.*

Jorge Rolando Barrios

Edgar Ruiz
LEXINCORP

Sylvia Ruiz Hochstetter
RUIZ SKINNER-KLEE & RUIZ

Isabel Samayoa
CARRILLO Y ASOCIADOS

Jorge Martínez Sanche
*RODRIGUEZ-MAHUAD Y
CASTELLANOS*

Salvador A. Saravia Castillo
SARAVIA & MUÑOZ

Arelis Torres de Alfaro
*UNIDAD DE CDR Y
CONTROL DE LA CALIDAD,
SUPERINTENDENCIA DE
BANCOS*

Estuardo Toruño
DIRECTOR CORPORATIVO

Fernando Quezado Toruño
*QUEZADA TORUÑO &
ASOCIADOS*

Elmer Vargas
ACZALAW

Ernesto Viteri Arriola
VITERI & VITERI

GUINEA

Alpha Bakar Barry
*CABINET ME ALPHA BAKAR
BARRY*

Barry Boubacar
JURIFIS CONSULT GUINEE

Jacques Chareyre
*FIDAFRICA /
PRICEWATERHOUSECOOPERS*

Ibrahima Diakite
LANDNET

Ibrahima Sory Sow
BANQUE CENTRALE - B.C.R.G.

Dominique Taty
*FIDAFRICA /
PRICEWATERHOUSECOOPERS*

Cheick Mohamed Tidjane
Sylla
BANQUE CENTRALE - B.C.R.G.

GUINEA-BISSAU

José Alves Té
*DIRECÇÃO - GERAL DE
IDENTIFICAÇÃO CIVIL, DOS
REGISTOS E DO NOTARIADO*

Mr. Ribeiro

Felicidade Brito Abelha
BCEAO

Jaimantino Co
*DIRECÇÃO - GERAL DO
COMERCIO, MINISTERIO DO
COMERCIO, INDUSTRIA E
ARTESANATO*

Francisco Correia
*PROJECTO DE REABILITACAO
E DESENVOLVIMENTO DO
SECTOR PRIVADO*

Rui Paulo Coutinho de
Mascarenhas Ataíde
Law School in Bissau

Daniel dos Santos Nunes
Agribissau

Josue Gomes de Almeida

Munira Jauad Ribeiro
Attorney-at-Law

Charles Ki-Zerbo
BCEAO

Octávio Lopes
*Octávio Lopes Advogados
- Miranda Alliance*

Miguel Mango
Audi-Conta Lda

Armando Mango
*Ordem dos Advogados da
Guiné-Bissau*

V. Marcelino
BCEAO

Adelaida Mesa D'Almeida
Attorney-at-Law

Jaló Pires
*Comissao Nacional da
Ohada*

Rogério Reis
Rogério Reis Despachante

Armando J.F. Rodrigues
PricewaterhouseCoopers

A.Ussumane So
Losser Lda

Carlos Vamain
*Projecto de Reabilitacao
e Desenvolvimento do
Sector Privado*

Jan Van Maanen

João (Daniel) Vaz Jr.
TransVaz, Lda

GUYANA

Chapman & Trotman

Ashton Chase
Attorney-at-Law

Desmond Correia
Correia & Correia Ltd.

Rexford Jackson
*Singh, Doodnauth Law
Firm*

Hughes, Fields & Stoby

Godwin F. McPherson
*Critchlow Labour
College*

Christopher Ram
Ram & McRae

William H. Sampson
*Lincoln Chambers &
Associates*

Josephine Whitehead

Troy Williams
Ram & McRae

Roger Yearwood
*Britton, Hamilton &
Adams*

HAITI

Jean Baptiste Brown
Brown Law Firm

Steve Christian Brown
Brown Law Firm

*Cabinet Hudicourt-
Woolley*

Raoul Celestin
*Les Entreprises
Commerciales J. Nadal S.A.*

Jocelyne Désinor

Alexandre Joseph Dieunor
*Cabinet Alexandre-
Donatien*

Enerlio Gassant
Cabinet Gassant

Marc Hebert Ignace
*Banque de la République
d'Haiti*

Enedland Jabouin
*Cabinet Jabouin Regis
Descardes*

Robert LaForest
Cabinet LaForest

Kareen T. Laplanche
UN Habitat

Garry Lhérisson

Louis Gary Lissade
Cabinet Lissade

Mr. Palliant
*Ordre des Comptables
Professionels Agrees
d'Haiti*

Jean Frederic Sales
Cabinet Sales

Salim Succar
Cabinet Lissade

HONDURAS

Fernando Aguilera
*Committee for the
Simplification of
Administration for
Companies, National
Competitiveness Program*

Dario Antunez
Instituto de la Propiedad

Gustavo Martin Arguello
ACZALAW

Ricardo Arias
Office of the President

Isaías Barahona
Instituto de la Propiedad

Yolanda Betancourt
*Cámara de Comercio e
Industrias de Tegucigalpa*

Jonathan Brooks
*Millennium Challenge
Corporation*

Amilcar Bulnes
*Cámara de Comercio e
Industrias de Tegucigalpa*

Tatiana Zelaya Bustamante
TransUnion

Daniel Bustillo
*Confederation of National
Federaciones y Patronotes*

Mario Bustillos
*Cámara de Comercio e
Industrias de Tegucigalpa*

Maria del Carmen Jovel
PricewaterhouseCoopers

Jorge Omar Casco
Bufete Casco & Asociados

Janeth Castañeda
*Cropa Panalpina
Tegucigalpa Honduras*

Maria del Carmen Chevez
Sosa
*Comision Nacional de
Bancos y Seguros*

Ludovino Colón Sánchez
PricewaterhouseCoopers

Francisco Guillermo Durón
Lopez
Bufete Durón

Allan Elvir
Lexincorp

Alejandro Fernandez
PricewaterhouseCoopers

Jorge Fu
PricewaterhouseCoopers

Porfirio Fuentes
*Office of the Environment,
Agriculture and
Commerce, USAID*

Lawrence Groo
Booz Allen Hamilton

Santiago Herrera
*Foundation for Investment
and Export Development*

German E. Leitzelar H.
*Despacho Legal Leitzelar
y Asociados*

Rene Lopez Rodezno
*Lopez Rodezno &
Asociados*

Armida Maria Lopez Villela
de Arguello
ACZALAW

Mario Maldonado
Instituto de la Propiedad

Dennis Matamoros Batson
Arias & Muñoz

Maria Elena Matute Cruz
Palacio de Justicia

Juan Carlos Mejia Cotto
Instituto de la Propiedad

Henry Merriam
*Fundación para El
Desarrollo Municipal*

Ramon E. Morales
PricewaterhouseCoopers

Roger Marin
*Asociación de Ahorro
y Prestamao para la
Micro, Pequeña y Mediana
Empresa S.A.*

Ramon Ortega
PricewaterhouseCoopers

Jose Ramon Paz
J.R. Paz & Asociados

Susan Perdomo
ACZALAW

Mauricio Quinonez
PricewaterhouseCoopers

Dino Rietti
ARQUITECNIC

José Rafael Rivera Ferrari
J.R. Paz & Asociados

Enrique Rodriguez Burchard
Abogados y Asesores SRL

Octavio Sanchez
Instituto de la Propiedad

Maria Lidia Solano
Banking Association

HONG KONG,
CHINA

Allen & Overy

Charles D. Booth
University of Hawaii

Agatha Chan
PricewaterhouseCoopers

Nicholas Chan
Squire, Sanders & Dempsey

Albert P.C. Chan
*Hong Kong Polytechnic
University*

Gaven Cheong
Clifford Chance

Winnie Cheung
Land Registry

Glenda Fung
*Johnson Stokes & Master,
member of Lex Mundi*

Tammy Goh
*Johnson Stokes & Master,
member of Lex Mundi*

Rod Houng-Lee
PricewaterhouseCoopers

Magdalena Kwan
Transunion Ltd.

David Lawrence
Deacons

Candas Lee
*Burke, Fung & Li
Solicitors*

Tommy Li
*Burke, Fung & Li
Solicitors*

Angie Lim
*Hong Kong Association
of Freight Forwarding &
Logistics*

Dickson Lo
Maunsell AECOM Group

Nina Sze
*Johnson Stokes & Master,
member of Lex Mundi*

Yi Ting Tam
Ching Mason & Associates

Sara Tong
Temple Chambers

Stephen Vine
Angela Wang & Co.

Susanne Wong
*Hong Kong Economic &
Trade Office, Washington,
D.C.*

Raymond Wong
*Johnson Stokes & Master,
member of Lex Mundi*

Raymond Wong
PricewaterhouseCoopers

Alexander Yuen
Transunion Ltd.

HUNGARY

Allen & Overy LLP

Krisztián Bácsi
*Hungarian Customs and
Finance Guard*

Barbara Barcsik
PricewaterhouseCoopers

Péter Berethalmi
*Nagy és Trócsányi Law
Office, member of Lex
Mundi*

Judit Bókai

Hedi Bozsonyik
*Szecskay Attorneys-at-
Law*

*BISZ Central Credit
Information Ltd.*

Zsuzsanna Cseri
*Bárd, Cseri & Partners Law
Firm*

Zsofia Domotor
PricewaterhouseCoopers

Gabriella Erdos
PricewaterhouseCoopers

Gábor Fejes
*Oppenheim ès Tàrsai,
Freshfields Bruckhaus
Dering*

Anna Gaspar
Build & Econ Hungary

Peter Gerendasi
PricewaterhouseCoopers

Andrea Jádi Németh
*Haarmann Hemmelrath &
Partner*

Zoltan Krausz
Build & Econ Hungary

Petra Lencs
*Bárd, Cseri & Partners Law
Firm*

Dora Mathe
PricewaterhouseCoopers

Peter Mihaly
PricewaterhouseCoopers

Sandor Nemeth
*Szecskay Ügyvédi Iroda,
Attorneys-at-Law*

Csaba Pigler
*Nagy és Trócsányi Law
Office, member of Lex
Mundi*

Tamás Saád
Build & Econ Hungary

*Sándor Szegedi Szent-Ivány
& Komáromi*

Csaba Szabó
*Dessewffy, Dávid és Társai
Ügyvédi Iroda*

András Szecskay
*Szecskay Attorneys-at-
Law*

Tibor Torok
PricewaterhouseCoopers

Ádám Tóth
Civil Law Notary

Vera Várkonyi
Civil Law Notary

ICELAND

Heiar Asberg Atlason
*LOGOS, member of Lex
Mundi*

Skuli Th. Fjeldsted
*Fjeldsted, Blöndal &
Fjeldsted*

Erlendur Gíslason
*LOGOS, member of Lex
Mundi*

Reynir Grétarsson
Lánstraust Ltd.

Ingibjörg Gubjartsdóttir

Margrét Hauksdóttir
Fasteignamat rikisins

Jóhannes R. Jóhannsson
JURIS LAW OFFICE

Erlingur E. Jónasson
ISTAK

Hrobjartur Jonatansson
AM PRAXIS LAW OFFICES

Tómas J. Jónsson
LÖGFRÆISTOFU REYKJAVÍKUR

LEX LAW OFFICES

Kari Hrafn Kjartansson
LANDWELL

Ragna Matthíasdóttir
ISTAK

Bragi Ragnarsson
EIMSKIPAFÉLAG ÍSLANDS EHF

Eyvindur Sólnes

Gunnar Sturluson
LOGOS, MEMBER OF LEX MUNDI

Stefán A. Svensson
JURIS LAW OFFICE

Tómas Orvaldsson

INDIA

Richa Agarwal
PRICEWATERHOUSECOOPERS

Amit Bahl
PRICEWATERHOUSECOOPERS

Harshala Chandorkar
CREDIT INFORMATION BUREAU LTD.

Ashutosh Chaturvedi
PRICEWATERHOUSECOOPERS

Harminder Chawla
CHAWLA & CO.

Rahul Garg
PRICEWATERHOUSECOOPERS

Nirmala Gill
LITTLE & CO.

Nityanand Gupta
PRICEWATERHOUSECOOPERS

Akil Hirani
MAJMUDAR & CO.

Toral Jhaveri
FOX MANDAL

KACHWAHA & PARTNERS

Himesh Kampani
PRICEWATERHOUSECOOPERS

Mukesh Kumar
CHAWLA & CO.

Parveen Kumar
PARNAMI OVERSEAS LOGISTICS PVT. LTD.

Manish Madhukar
INFINI JURIDIQUE

Som Mandal
FOX MANDAL

Vipender Mann
CHAWLA & CO.

Satish Mehta
DUN & BRADSTREET SAME LTD.

Dara Mehta
LITTLE & CO.

Saurabh Misra
FOX MANDAL

Satish Murthi
MURTI AND MURTI INTERNATIONAL LAW PRACTICE

Anshoo Nayar
FOX MANDAL

Janak Pandya
NISHITH DESAI ASSOCIATES

Shreyas Patel
FOX MANDAL

K.V. Ramesh
KOCHHAR & CO.

Dipak Rao
SINGHANIA & PARTNERS

Abhishek Saket
INFINI JURIDIQUE

Radhika Sankaran
FOX MANDAL

Tapas Sen
NATIONAL INSTITUTE OF PUBLIC FINANCE AND POLICY

Vikram Shroff
NISHITH DESAI ASSOCIATES

Ravinder Singhania
SINGHANIA & PARTNERS

INDONESIA

Benjamin Abrams
JAKARTA ADVISORY SERVICES

Almer Apon
PT BUANA MAS CITRA LESTARI

Firdaus Asikin
PT PRIMA WAHANA CARAKA / PRICEWATERHOUSECOOPERS

Hamud M. Balfas
ALI BUDIARDJO, NUGROHO, REKSODIPUTRO, MEMBER OF LEX MUNDI

BANK INDONESIA

Fabian Buddy Pascoal
HANAFIAH PONGGAWA BANGUN

Jenny Budiman
MAKARIM & TAIRA S.

Ayik Candrawulan Gunadi
ALI BUDIARDJO, NUGROHO, REKSODIPUTRO, MEMBER OF LEX MUNDI

Ira A. Eddymurthy
SSEK INDONESIAN LEGAL CONSULTANTS

Iqbal Hadromi
HADROMI & PARTNERS LAW FIRM

Rika Hardaini
MAKARIM & TAIRA S.

Ray Headifen
PRICEWATERHOUSECOOPERS

Darrell R. Johnson
SSEK INDONESIAN LEGAL CONSULTANTS

Galinar Kartakusuma
MAKARIM & TAIRA S.

Winita E. Kusnandar
KUSNANDAR & CO.

Bill MacDonald
PRICEWATERHOUSECOOPERS

Paul O'Brien
PRICEWATERHOUSECOOPERS

Hartono Parbudi
BIRO KREDIT

Brigitta I. Rahayoe
BRIGITTA I. RAHAYOE & SYAMSUDDIN

Haryanto Sahari
PRICEWATERHOUSECOOPERS

Arfidea Dwi Saraswati
SSEK INDONESIAN LEGAL CONSULTANTS

Indra Setiawan Jamin
ALI BUDIARDJO, NUGROHO, REKSODIPUTRO, MEMBER OF LEX MUNDI

Bambang Soelaksono
SMERU RESEARCH INSTITUTE

Ernst G. Tehuteru
ALI BUDIARDJO, NUGROHO, REKSODIPUTRO, MEMBER OF LEX MUNDI

Christian Teo
CHRISTIAN TEO & ASSOCIATES

Gatot Triprasetio
WIDYAWAN & PARTNERS

Pudji Wahjuni Purbo
MAKARIM & TAIRA S.

Robertus Winarto
PT PRIMA WAHANA CARAKA / PRICEWATERHOUSECOOPERS

Ferry Zulkarnaen
WIDYAWAN & PARTNERS

IRAN

Mohammad Adib
ADIB LAW FIRM

Behrooz Akhlaghi
INTERNATIONAL LAW OFFICE DR. BEHROOZ AKHLAGHI & ASSOCIATES

Reza Askari
FOREIGN LEGAL AFFAIRS GROUP

Mohammad Badamchi
HAMI LEGAL SERVICES

Shirin Ozra Entezari
DR. SHIRIN O. ENTEZARI & ASSOCIATES

Behzad Feizi
AGAHAN & CO.

Saeed Hashemian
ADIB LAW FIRM

Mozaffar Mohammadian
TEEMA BAR INTERNATIONAL TRANSPORT CO.

Shahla Pournazeri
LAW OFFICES OF SHAHLA POURNAZERI & ASSOCIATES

Yahya Rayegani
RAYEGANI LAW OFFICE

DR. JAMAL SEIFI & ASSOCIATES

Mostafa Shahabi
TAVAKOLI & SHAHABI

Shahb Shahabi
DR. SHIRIN O. ENTEZARI & ASSOCIATES

Mohammad Reza Shojaedinni
CENTRAL BANK OF IRAN

Michael Stevenson
PRICEWATERHOUSECOOPERS

IRAQ

Hadeel Salih Abboud Al-Janabi
MENA ASSOCIATES

Salim Ahad
DANA FREIGHT SERVICE

Farquad Al-Salman
F.H. AL-SALMAN & CO.

Florian Amereller
AMERELLER RECHTSANWÄLTE

Blund Faridoon Arif Najeb
PRIVATE LAWYER

Munaf Hammed Muhammed
PRIVATE LAWYER

Husam A. Hatim
AL FADHAA CO. LTD.

Munthir Hasan Mahmoud
AL FADHAA CO. LTD.

Imad Makki
AL QARYA GROUP CO.

Adil Sinjakli
AL SUWAIDI & CO.

IRELAND

Andrew Bates
DILLON EUSTACE

Alan Browning
LK SHIELDS SOLICITORS, MEMBER OF IUS LABORIS

Jonathan Cullen
LK SHIELDS SOLICITORS, MEMBER OF IUS LABORIS

Eoin Cunneen
LK SHIELDS SOLICITORS, MEMBER OF IUS LABORIS

Richard Curran
LK SHIELDS SOLICITORS, MEMBER OF IUS LABORIS

Gavin Doherty
EUGENE F. COLLINS SOLICITORS

John Doyle
DILLON EUSTACE

Gillian Dully
LK SHIELDS SOLICITORS, MEMBER OF IUS LABORIS

Melissa Jennings
ARTHUR COX, MEMBER OF LEX MUNDI

Colm Kelly
PRICEWATERHOUSECOOPERS

Niamh Loughran
DILLON EUSTACE

Damien Mannion
LK SHIELDS SOLICITORS, MEMBER OF IUS LABORIS

Niav Ohiggins
ARTHUR COX, MEMBER OF LEX MUNDI

Matt O'Keeffe
PRICEWATERHOUSECOOPERS

Barry O'Neill
EUGENE F. COLLINS SOLICITORS

Sinead Power
IRISH CREDIT BUREAU

Lynne Rae
PRICEWATERHOUSECOOPERS

Gavin Simons
EUGENE F. COLLINS SOLICITORS

Fiona Thornton
LK SHIELDS SOLICITORS, MEMBER OF IUS LABORIS

Colm Walsh
IRISH INTERNATIONAL FREIGHT ASSOCIATION

Ted Williams
ARTHUR COX, MEMBER OF LEX MUNDI

ISRAEL

Ronen Bar-Even
WEISS, PORAT & CO.

Paul Baris
YIGAL ARNON & CO.

Ofer Bar-On
SHAVIT BAR-ON GAL-ON TZIN NOV YAGUR, LAW OFFICES

Ron Ben-Menachem
WEIL, GOTSHAL & MANGES, LLP

Dina Brown
ELCHANAN LANDAU LAW OFFICES

Koby Cohen
KESSELMAN & KESSELMAN

Clifford Davis
S. HOROWITZ & CO., MEMBER OF LEX MUNDI

Roee Hecht
SHAVIT BAR-ON GAL-ON TZIN NOV YAGUR, LAW OFFICES

Aaron Jaffe
YIGAL ARNON & CO.

Izeev Katz
KESSELMAN & KESSELMAN

Vered Kirshner
KESSELMAN & KESSELMAN

Gideon Koren
BEN ZVI KOREN & CO. LAW OFFICES

Orna Kornreich-Cohen
SHAVIT BAR-ON GAL-ON TZIN NOV YAGUR, LAW OFFICES

Michelle Liberman
S. HOROWITZ & CO., MEMBER OF LEX MUNDI

Aryeh Rachelin
BEN ZVI KOREN & CO. LAW OFFICES

Gerry Seligman
KESSELMAN & KESSELMAN

Daniel Singerman
BUSINESS DATA ISRAEL PERSONAL CHECK

Zeev Weiss
WEISS, PORAT & CO.

Shlomi Zehavi
KESSELMAN & KESSELMAN

ITALY

ALLEN & OVERY

Roberto Argeri
CLEARY, GOTTLIEB, STEEN & HAMILTON LLP

Tommaso Ariani
CLEARY, GOTTLIEB, STEEN & HAMILTON LLP

Maria Pia Ascenzo
BANK OF ITALY

Francesco Attaguile
NOTARY

Roberto Bonsignore
Cleary, Gottlieb, Steen & Hamilton LLP

Simon Botto
Cleary, Gottlieb, Steen & Hamilton LLP

Carlo Bruno
Ashurst

Sergio Calderara
Nunziante Magrone

Domenico Colella
Portolano Colella Cavallo Prosperetti Studio Legale

Mattia Colonnelli de Gasperis
Freshfields Bruckhaus Deringer

Massimo Cremona
Studio Pirola

CRIF S.P.A.

Antonio de Martinis
Spasaro De Martinis Law Firm

Claudio Di Falco
Cleary, Gottlieb, Steen & Hamilton LLP

Emanuele Ferrari
Studio Notarile Ferrari

Pier Andrea Fré Torelli Massini
Carabba & Partners

Linda Frigo
Studio Legale Macchi di Cellere e Gangemi

Vincenzo Giannantonio
Ashurst

Federico Guasti
Notary

Giovanni Izzo
Abbatescianni Studio Legale e Tributario

Ignazio la Candia
Studio Pirola

Giancarlo Laurini
Notary

Stefano Macchi di Cellere
Jones Day

Maria Georgia Magno
Cleary, Gottlieb, Steen & Hamilton LLP

Fabrizio Mariotti
Studio Legale Beltramo

Maria Grazia Medici
Verusio e Cosmelli Studio Legale

Mario Miccoli
Notary

Valeria Morossini
Toffoletto e Soci Law Firm, member of Ius Laboris

Alessandra Palladini
Cleary, Gottlieb, Steen & Hamilton LLP

Paolo Pasqualis
Notary

Paolo Pedrazzoli
Notary

Alessandro Pellegrini
Cleary, Gottlieb, Steen & Hamilton LLP

Giuseppe Ramondelli
Studio Legale Notarile Di Fabio Ramondelli Cantamagli

Giovanni Sandicchi
Cleary, Gottlieb, Steen & Hamilton LLP

Lamberto Schiona
Studio legale Gambino

Piervincenzo Spasaro
Spasaro De Martinis Law Firm

Vittorio Tadei
Chiomenti Studio Legale, member of Lex Mundi

Silvio Tersilla
Studio Legale Lovells

Franco Toffoletto
Toffoletto e Soci Law Firm, member of Ius Laboris

Daniele Tombesi
Panalpina Trasporti Mondiali S.p.A.

Luca Tufarelli
Ristuccia & Tufarelli

Benedetta Vannini
Cleary, Gottlieb, Steen & Hamilton LLP

Giovanni Verusio
Verusio e Cosmelli Studio Legale

JAMAICA

Neville Boxe
Incorporated Masterbuilders Association of Jamaica

Eric Crawford
PricewaterhouseCoopers

Nicole Foga
Foga Daley & Co.

Dave García
Myers, Fletcher & Gordon, member of Lex Mundi

Tamara Green
Myers, Fletcher & Gordon, member of Lex Mundi

Michael Hall
PricewaterhouseCoopers

Corrine N. Henry
Myers, Fletcher & Gordon, member of Lex Mundi

Alicia Hussey
Myers, Fletcher & Gordon, member of Lex Mundi

Christofer Kennedy
Eagle and Whale Ltd.

Noel Mcken
Kier Construction - Kier Group PLC

Viveen Morrison
PricewaterhouseCoopers

Jerome Spencer
Myers, Fletcher & Gordon, member of Lex Mundi

Humprey Taylor
Taylor Construction Ltd.

Karen Wilson
Rattray, Patterson, Rattray

JAPAN

Shinichiro Abe
Bingham McCutchen

Adachi, Henderson, Miyatake & Fujita

Miho Arimura
Hatasawa & Wakai Law Firm

Credit Information Center Corp.

Shigeru Hasegawa
PricewaterhouseCoopers / Zeirishi-Hojin ChuoAoyama

Tamotsu Hatasawa
Hatasawa & Wakai Law Firm

Kaoru Hattori
Asahi Koma Law Offices, member of Lex Mundi

Wakako Isaka
Asahi Koma Law Offices, member of Lex Mundi

Kotaku Kimu
PricewaterhouseCoopers / Zeirishi-Hojin ChuoAoyama

Nobuaki Matsuoka
Yamaguchi International

Yoko Oshima
Cleary, Gottlieb, Steen & Hamilton LLP

Tetsuro Sato
Asahi Koma Law Offices, member of Lex Mundi

Alvin Hiromasa Shiozaki
Asahi Koma Law Offices, member of Lex Mundi

Hiroyuki Suzuki
PricewaterhouseCoopers / Zeirishi-Hojin ChuoAoyama

Tsunemasa Terai
Cleary, Gottlieb, Steen & Hamilton LLP

Kenji Utsumi
Nagashima Ohno & Tsunematsu

Akio Yamamoto
Kajima Corporation

Setsuko Yufu
Atsumi & Partners

JORDAN

Iyad Abdin
Elite Manufacturing

Ibrahim Abunameh
Law & Arbitration Centre

Oubay Al-Baghdadi

Eman M. Al-Dabbas
International Business Legal Associates

Arafat Alfayoumi
Central Bank of Jordan

Sharif Ali Zu'bi
Ministry of Industry and Trade

Jamal Al-Jabiri
USAID

Ghaith Bakri
Jordan Enterprise Development Corporation

Alaa Batayneh
Jordan Customs

Francis J. Bawab
PricewaterhouseCoopers

Lori Brock
Booz Allen Hamilton

Khalil Burgan
Al Burgan Handicrafts

Saleh Abd El-Ati
Ali Sharif Zu'bi & Sharif Ali Zu'bi, member of Lex Mundi

Maurice Girigs
Nathan Associates

Tariq Hammouri
Hammouri & Partners

Mohammed Harthy
Harthy Textile Industrial Est.

George Hazboun
University of Jordan

Walter Hekala
Chemonics International Inc.

Ruba Jaradat
USAID

Sa'ed Karajah

Basel Kawar
Amin Kawar & Sons

Youssef S. Khalilieh
Rajai Dajani & Associates Law Office

Khaled Khateeb
I.C.A. Group

Rasha Laswi
Zalloum & Laswi Law Firm

Dureid Mahasneh
T. Gargour and Fils Shipping

Firas Malhas
International Business Legal Associates

Khaldoun Nazer
Khalifeh & Partners

Mohammed Obeidat
Jordan Customs

Diana Putman
USAID

Majdi Qubti
Bawabet Al-Sharq Handicrafts

Stephan Stephan
Bawab & Co. / PricewaterhouseCoopers

Anna Maria Toth Salameh
American Chamber of Commerce in Jordan

Rose Wazani
American Chamber of Commerce in Jordan

Tayseer Younis
Jordan Customs

Azzam Zalloum
Zalloum & Laswi Law Firm

Iyad Zawaideh
Ali Sharif Zu'bi & Sharif Ali Zu'bi, member of Lex Mundi

KAZAKHSTAN

Anvar Akhmedov
First Credit Bureau

Yermek Aubakirov
Michael Wilson & Partners Ltd.

Sabina Barayeva
JSC Kazkommerts Bank

Sanzhan N. Burambayev
Aequitas Law Firm

Yulia Chumachenko
Aequitas Law Firm

Almaz Dosserbekov
Denton Wilde Sapte

Courtney Fowler
PricewaterhouseCoopers

Katherine Garkavets
PricewaterhouseCoopers

Semion Issyk
Aequitas Law Firm

Aliya K. Iztleuova
McGuireWoods LLP

Dinara M. Jarmukhanova
McGuireWoods LLP

Thomas Johnson
Denton Wilde Sapte

Elena Kaeva
PricewaterhouseCoopers

Yekaterina Kim
Michael Wilson & Partners Ltd.

Abdulkhamid Muminov
PricewaterhouseCoopers

Ruslan Murzashev
McGuireWoods LLP

Marat Kh. Muzdubaev
LeBoeuf, Lamb, Greene & MacRae

Kamilya T. Nurpeissova
LeBoeuf, Lamb, Greene & MacRae

Yulia Penzova
Aequitas Law Firm

Natalya Revenko
PricewaterhouseCoopers

Elvis Roberts
M & M Logistics

Tatyana Suleyeva
Aequitas Law Firm

Matthew Tallarovic
PricewaterhouseCoopers

Aliya Utegaliyeva
PricewaterhouseCoopers

Natalya A. Yelizarova
Zhakenov & Partners, in partnership with White & Jones LLP

Valerie A. Zhakenov
Zhakenov & Partners, in partnership with White & Jones LLP

Yeranbek Zhussupov
Zanger Law Firm

KENYA

Shaira Adamali
PricewaterhouseCoopers

George Akoto
Akoto & Co.

Amoyo Andibo
Metropol East Africa Ltd.

Peter Chekwony
OCEAN ALLIANCE LOGISTICS

Philip Coulson
KAPLAN & STRATTON

Oliver Fowler
KAPLAN & STRATTON

Fiona Fox
CHUNGA ASSOCIATES

Peter Gachuhi
KAPLAN & STRATTON

Sheetal Kapila
ANJARWALLA & KHANNA ADVOCATES

Kamau Karori
ISEME, KAMAU & MAEMA ADVOCATES

Hamish Keith
DALY & FIGGIS ADVOCATES

Jinaro Kibet
OCHIENG, ONYANGO, KIBET & OHAGA

Anne Kimotho
PRICEWATERHOUSECOOPERS

Morris Kimuli
B. M. MUSAU & CO. ADVOCATES

Anthony Kiruma
MUTHOGA, GATURU & COMPANY ADVOCATES

Alexandra Kontos
WALKER KONTOS ADVOCATES

William Maema
ISEME, KAMAU & MAEMA ADVOCATES

Georges Maina
AMERITRANS FREIGHT INTERNATIONAL

Gavin McEwen
PRICEWATERHOUSECOOPERS

Amyn Musa
ANJARWALLA & KHANNA ADVOCATES

Benjamin Musau
B. M. MUSAU & CO. ADVOCATES

Washington Muthamiah
ALEXANDRIA FREIGHT FORWARDERS LTD.

Janet Mutua
B. M. MUSAU & CO. ADVOCATES

Lee Muthoga
MUTHOGA, GATURU & COMPANY ADVOCATES

Sam Mwara
KENYA PRIVATE SECTOR ALLIANCE

Gladys Mwariri
B. M. MUSAU & CO. ADVOCATES

Wachira Ndege
CREDIT REFERENCE BUREAU AFRICA LTD.

Benson Njiru
B. M. MUSAU & CO. ADVOCATES

Virginia Nzioka
B. M. MUSAU & CO. ADVOCATES

Richard Omwela
HAMILTON HARRISON & MATHEWS LAW FIRM

Tom Onyango
OCHIENG, ONYANGO, KIBET & OHAGA

Jack Ranguma
KENYA REVENUE AUTHORITY

Sonal Sejpal
ANJARWALLA & KHANNA ADVOCATES

Meenal Shah
PRICEWATERHOUSECOOPERS

Dipak Shah
PRICEWATERHOUSECOOPERS

Rina Thakar
WALKER KONTOS ADVOCATES

Francisca Tibo
PRICEWATERHOUSECOOPERS

Julius Wako
DALY & FIGGIS ADVOCATES

KIRIBATI

Aomoro Amten
OFFICE OF THE PEOPLE'S LAWYER

Banuera Berina
MP

Kautuna Kaitara
KIRIBATI CUSTOMS SERVICE

Greg MacPherson
AUSTRALIAN HIGH COMMISSION

Paul McLaughlin
CA'BELLA BETIO CONSTRUCTION

Tekaai Mikaere
SHIPPING AGENCY OF KIRIBATI

Lawrence Muller
BETIO CITY COUNCIL

Matereta Raiman
MINISTRY OF FINANCE AND ECONOMIC DEVELOPMENT

Romano Reo
LAND MANAGEMENT DIVISION

Tonganibea Tamoa
KIRIBATI CUSTOMS SERVICE

Karotu Tiba
OFFICE OF THE PEOPLE'S LAWYER

Arawaia Tiira
MINISTRY OF LABOUR AND HUMAN RESOURCES DEVELOPMENT

KOREA

C.W. Hyun
KIM & CHANG

Young-Cheol Jeong
WOO YUN KANG JEONG & HAN

Mia Kim
KIM & CHANG

Keunyeop Kim
PANALPINA IAF LTD.

Dae-Geun Kim
PRICEWATERHOUSECOOPERS

Dong-Bum Kim
PRICEWATERHOUSECOOPERS

Sung Jin Kim
WOO YUN KANG JEONG & HAN

Wonhyung Kim
YOON YANG KIM SHIN & YU

KOREA INFORMATION SERVICE

Sung Whan Lee
AHNSE LAW OFFICES

Hongnam Lim
PRICEWATERHOUSECOOPERS

Sung-Ho Moon
HORIZON (JIPYUNG) LAW GROUP

Sang Il Park
HWANG MOK PARK P.C., MEMBER OF LEX MUNDI

J. T. Park
KIM & CHANG

Ae-Ryun Rho
KIM & CHANG

Jeong Seo
DAEJEON DISTRICT COURT

Hi-Taek Shin
KIM & CHANG

Mina Yoo
PRICEWATERHOUSECOOPERS

Mi-Sook Yoon
PRICEWATERHOUSECOOPERS

Ando Yun
PRICEWATERHOUSECOOPERS

KUWAIT

Ihab Abbas
AL-FAHAD & CO., DELOITTE & TOUCHE

Labeed Abdal
LAW FIRM OF LABEED ABDAL

Hossam Abdullah
AL SARRAF & AL RUWAYEH, IN ASSOCIATION WITH STEPHENSON HARWOOD

Abdullah Al-Ayoub
ABDULLAH KH. AL-AYOUB & ASSOCIATES, MEMBER OF LEX MUNDI

Mishari M. Al-Ghazali
LAW OFFICES OF MISHARI AL-GHAZALI

Reema Ali
ALI & PARTNERS

Tim Bullock
AL-FAHAD & CO., DELOITTE & TOUCHE

Answer Ben Essa
CREDIT INFORMATION NETWORK

Sam Habbas
AL SARRAF & AL RUWAYEH, IN ASSOCIATION WITH STEPHENSON HARWOOD

Mazen A. Khoursheed
PPIC

KYRGYZ REPUBLIC

Omurbek Abdyrakhmanov
ENTREPRENEURS' UNION

Ilshat Ahmetov
ATTORNEY-AT-LAW

Jannat Aidazalieva
GLOBALLINK

Anarkan Akerova
IFC

Bekbolot Bekiev
MINISTRY OF JUSTICE

Baktiyar Djusuev
ARD / CHECCHI COMMERCIAL LAW PROJECT

Akjoltoi Elebesova
CREDIT INFORMATION BUREAU ISHENIM

Courtney Fowler
PRICEWATERHOUSECOOPERS

Kucheryavaya Galina
ATTORNEY-AT-LAW

Katherine Garkavets
PRICEWATERHOUSECOOPERS

Aibek Ismailov
ATTORNEY-AT-LAW

Mirulan Jamshitov

Bob Jurik
PRICEWATERHOUSECOOPERS

Elena Kaeva
PRICEWATERHOUSECOOPERS

Gulnara Kalikova
KALIKOVA & ASSOCIATES, LAW FIRM

Asel Kenenbaeva
LAW FIRM "PARTNER"

Tatiana Kim
INTERNATIONAL ENTREPRENEURSHIP FUND

Galina Kucherayvaya
USAID

Aida Mamarazieva
KENTOR CJSC

Kamila Mateeva
AMERICAN UNIVERSITY - CENTRAL ASIA

Gulmira McHale
IFC

Abdulkhamid Muminov
PRICEWATERHOUSECOOPERS

Meerim Nurkamilova
LAW FIRM "PARTNER"

Karlygash Ospankulova
KALIKOVA & ASSOCIATES, LAW FIRM

Natalya Revenko
PRICEWATERHOUSECOOPERS

Nikolai Soubbotin
IFC

Venera Sydykova
ARD / CHECCHI COMMERCIAL LAW PROJECT

Matthew Tallarovic
PRICEWATERHOUSECOOPERS

Aziz Usupov
KALIKOVA & ASSOCIATES, LAW FIRM

Aliya Utegaliyeva
PRICEWATERHOUSECOOPERS

Umar Shavurov
ATTORNEY-AT-LAW

Natalia Shirshova

LAO PDR

Xaynari Chanthala
PRICEWATERHOUSECOOPERS

Martin Desautels
DFDL MEKONG LAW GROUP

David Fitzgerald
PRICEWATERHOUSECOOPERS

Grant Follet
DFDL MEKONG LAW GROUP

Intong Oudom
SENEOUDOM TRADING CO. LTD.

Isabelle Robineau
DFDL MEKONG LAW GROUP

Maligna Saignavongs
LAO BAR ASSOCIATION

Simmaly Vongsack
BANK OF LAO PDR

LATVIA

Laura Ausekle
LATVIJAS BANKA

Ilze Baltmane
BALTMANE & BITANS LAW OFFICE

Elina Bedanova
LEJINS, TORGANS & PARTNERS

Mikus Buls
KLAVINS & SLAIDINS, MEMBER OF LEX MUNDI

Andis Burkevics
SORAINEN LAW OFFICES

Andis Conka
LATVIJAS BANKA

Zlata Elksnina-Zascirinska
PRICEWATERHOUSECOOPERS

Aldis Gobzems
LEJINS, TORGANS & PARTNERS

Cameron Greaves
PRICEWATERHOUSECOOPERS

Edvins Kapostins
STATE LAND SERVICE OF THE REPUBLIC OF LATVIA

Filip Klavins
KLAVINS & SLAIDINS, MEMBER OF LEX MUNDI

Aija Klavinska
PRICEWATERHOUSECOOPERS

Ludmila Kornijenko
BLUEGER & PLAUDE

Indrikis Liepa
LIEPA, SKOPINA, BORENIUS

Janis Loze

Lidija Plica
RIGA REGIONAL COURT

Inese Rendeniece

Dace Silava-Tomsone
LEJINS, TORGANS & PARTNERS

Sarmis Spilbergs
KLAVINS & SLAIDINS, MEMBER OF LEX MUNDI

Zane Stalberga-Markvarte
LAW OFFICE MARKVARTE & PARTNERS

Kristine Stege
BALTMANE & BITANS LAW OFFICE

Brigita Terauda
SORAINEN LAW OFFICES

Baiba Vevere
LATVIJAS BANKA

Daiga Zivtia
KLAVINS & SLAIDINS, MEMBER OF LEX MUNDI

LEBANON

Nadim Abboud
LAW OFFICE OF A. ABBOUD & ASSOCIATES

Zeina Abi Chahine
NABIL ABDEL-MALE

Jean Baroudi
BAROUDI & ASSOCIATES

Theodore De Mar Youssef
*Badri & Salim El Meouchi
Law Firm*

Chadia El Meouchi
*Badri & Salim El Meouchi
Law Firm*

Ramzi George
PricewaterhouseCoopers

Dania George
PricewaterhouseCoopers

Bassel Habiby
PricewaterhouseCoopers

George Jabre
George Jabre & Associates

Fady Jamaleddine
Jamaleddine Law Firm

Georges Kadige
Kadige & Kadige Law Firm

Albert Laham
*Law Office of Albert
Laham*

Nabil Mallat
Hyam Mallat Law Offices

Georges Mallat
Hyam Mallat Law Offices

Rachad Medawar
El Khoury Law Firm

Fadi Moghaizel
*Moghaizel Law Offices,
member of Lex Mundi*

Mario Mohanna
George Jabre & Associates

Choucair Najib
Banque du Liban

Toufic Nehme
*Law Office of Albert
Laham*

Mazen Rasamny
*Badri & Salim El Meouchi
Law Firm*

Mireille Richa
*Badri & Salim El Meouchi
Law Firm*

Elias A. Saadé
*Moghaizel Law Offices,
member of Lex Mundi*

Camille C. Sifri
PricewaterhouseCoopers

Nady Tyan
*Law Offices of Tyan &
Zgheib*

LESOTHO

Mark Badenhorst
PricewaterhouseCoopers

Paul De Chalain
PricewaterhouseCoopers

Thuso Green
Sechaba Consultants

Palesa Khabele
*Law Faculty of the
National University*

Erle Koomets
PricewaterhouseCoopers

Vuelva Kotelo

Qhalehang Letsika
Mei & Mei Attorneys Inc.

Tseliso Daniel Makhaphela
*Ministry of Local
Government*

Keketso (John) Maleka

Mathias H. Matshe
Sheeran & Associates

Zwelakhe Mda

Thabo Moetsane
Thetsane Wholesalers

Deborah Mofolo
*Mofolo, Tau-Thabane and
Company*

Popsiso Molapo

Tseliso Monapathi
High Court

Thabo Mpaka
Mpaka Chambers

T. Ntaoane
NedBank Lesotho Ltd.

Relebohile Ntene

Theodore Ntlatlapa
DNT Architects

S.K. Phafane

Eprahim Potsane

Peter Sands
SDV Transami Pty. Ltd.

Borenahabokhethe Sekoneyla

Lindiwe Sephomolo
*Association of Lesotho
Employers and Business*

Mathias Sheeran
Sheeran & Associates

Mark Webber
Harley & Morris

LITHUANIA

Kristina Bartuseviciene
PricewaterhouseCoopers

Andrius Bogdanovicius
Infobankas UAB

Dovil Burgien
*Law Firm Lideika,
Petrauskas, Valinas ir
partneriai LAWIN, member
of Lex Mundi*

Tomas Davidonis
Sorainen Law Offices

Giedre Domkute-
Lukauskiene
*Law Firm AAA Baltic
Service Company*

Dalia Foigt
*D. Foigt and Partners/
Regija*

Rolandas Galvenas
*Law Firm Lideika,
Petrauskas, Valinas ir
partneriai LAWIN, member
of Lex Mundi*

Cameron Greaves
PricewaterhouseCoopers

Indr Jonaityt
*Law Firm Lideika,
Petrauskas, Valinas ir
partneriai LAWIN, member
of Lex Mundi*

Mindaugas Kikis
*Law Firm Lideika,
Petrauskas, Valinas ir
partneriai LAWIN, member
of Lex Mundi*

Egidijus Kundelis
PricewaterhouseCoopers

Mindaugas Lescius
Sorainen Law Offices

Rasa Lubauskait
Ministry of Finance

Linas Paulius Margevicius

Bronislovas Mikuta
*State Enterprise Centre of
Registers*

Lina Mockeliunaite
PricewaterhouseCoopers

Nerijus Nedzinskas
PricewaterhouseCoopers

Ramnas Petraviius
*Law Firm Lideika,
Petrauskas, Valinas ir
partneriai LAWIN, member
of Lex Mundi*

Aidas Petrosius
SE Centre of Registers

Kazimieras Ramonas
Bank of Lithuania

Rimantas Simaitis
*Court of Appeal of
Lithuania*

Laimonas Skibarka
*Law Firm Lideika,
Petrauskas, Valinas ir
partneriai LAWIN, member
of Lex Mundi*

Sarune Smeleviciute
PricewaterhouseCoopers

Jurate Stulgyte
PricewaterhouseCoopers

Mindaugas Vaiciunas
*D. Foigt and Partners/
Regija*

Rolandas Valiunas
*Law Firm Lideika,
Petrauskas, Valinas ir
partneriai LAWIN, member
of Lex Mundi*

Darius Zabiela
*Law Firm Zabiela,
Zabielaite & Partners*

Audrius vybas
*Bernotas & Dominas
Glimstedt*

MACEDONIA, FYR

Zoran Andonovski
Law Office Polenak

Zlatko Antevski
Lawyers Antevski

Benita Beleskova
IKRP Rokas & Partners

Biljana Cakmakova
*Mens Legis Cakmakova
Advocates*

Frosina Celeska
*National Bank of the
Republic of Macedonia*

Zoran Cvetanoski
*State Authority for
Geodetic Works*

Nikola Dinevski
Central Register

Aleksandra Donevska
Lawyers Antevski

Theodoros Giannitsakis
IKRP Rokas & Partners

Kosta Gligorievski
Central Register

Biljana Joanidis
*Law & Patent Office
Joanidis*

Dejan Knezovic
*Law Office Knezovic &
Associates*

Rudi Lazarevski
PricewaterhouseCoopers

Nikola Lazarov
*Macedonia Court
Modernization Project*

Sanja Iliovska Madzovska
*National Bank of the
Republic of Macedonia*

Valerjan Monevski
Monevski Law Firm

Irena Petkovska
Lawyers Antevski

Tatjana Popovski Buloski
Law Office Polenak

Ljubica Ruben
Mens Legis

Charapich Sinisha
*TIR - International
Freight Forwarders*

Atanas Stojanoski
IKRP Rokas & Partners

Nake Stojanovski
Central Register

Joseph J. Traficanti Jr.
*Macedonia Court
Modernization Project*

Vladimir Vasilevski
Betasped

Zlatko Nobuski
Notary Chamber

MADAGASCAR

Lalao Andriamanga
Guide

Harimahefa Andriamitantsoa
*Tribunal de Première
Instance*

Josoa Lucien Andrianelinjaka
Banque Centrale

Philippe Buffier
Espace Ingénierie

Jacques Chareyre
*FIDAFRICA /
PricewaterhouseCoopers*

Guy Escarfail
Bureau de Liaison SGS

Isabelle Gachie
*Centre d'Information
Technique et Economique*

Raphaël Jakoba
*Madagascar Conseil
International*

Rakoto Manantsoa
*Madagascar Conseil
International*

Pascaline R. Rasamoeliarisoa
*Deloitte, member
of Deloitte Touche
Tohmatsu*

Sahondra Rabenarivo
*Keyserlingk - Rabenarivo
Associés*

Anthony Rabibisoa
Maersk Logistics S.A.

Allain Hubert Rajoelina
*MeAllain Hubert
Rajoelina*

Joachin Rakotonoelina
CMA CGM

Laingoniaina
Ramarimbahoaka
*Madagascar Conseil
International*

Zakazo Ranaivoson
*Cabinet de Conseils
d'Entreprises*

André Randranto
Ancien Bâtonnier

William Randrianarivelo
*FIDAFRICA /
PricewaterhouseCoopers*

Sahondra Rasoarisoa
*Deloitte, member
of Deloitte Touche
Tohmatsu*

Théodore Raveloarison
*JARY - Bureau d'Etudes
Architecture Ingenierie*

Andriamisa Ravelomanana
*FIDAFRICA /
PricewaterhouseCoopers*

Jean Marcel Razafimahenina
*Deloitte, member
of Deloitte Touche
Tohmatsu*

Njiva Razanatsoa
Banque Centrale

Olivier Ribot
*FIDAFRICA /
PricewaterhouseCoopers*

Lala Zoelison
*Centre d'Information
Technique et Economique*

MALAWI

Sylvia Ali

Mark Badenhorst
PricewaterhouseCoopers

Jai Banda
Sacranie, Gow & Co.

Kevin M. Carpenter
PricewaterhouseCoopers

Kashinath Chaturvedi

Alan Chinula

Paul De Chalain
PricewaterhouseCoopers

William Finseth

Stuart Forster
*U.K. Department
for International
Development*

Jim Ghobede
PricewaterhouseCoopers

Roseline Gramani

Silvester Kalembera

Anthony Kamanga SC
Ministry of Justice

Justice Kapanda

J.R. Kaphweleza Banda

Andrews Katuya
Savjani & Co.

Bansri Lakhani
Scranie, Gow & Co.

Shabir Latif
Scranie, Gow & Co.

P.D. Mlauzi
Attorney-at-Law

Chikosa Mozesi Silungwe
Malawi Law Commission

Eggrey Mpango
STUTTSFORDS INTERNATIONAL REMOVALS

Davis Mthakati Njobnu

Shepher Mumba
SAVJANI & CO.

Vincent J. Mzumara
MINISTRY OF JUSTICE

Benard Ndau

Isaac Nsamala

D.A. Ravel
WILSON & MORGAN

Richard Record

David Russell

Krishna Savjani
SAVJANI & ASSOCIATES LAW FIRM

Duncan Singano
SAVJANI & ASSOCIATES LAW FIRM

Alick C.E. Sukasuka

Samuel Tembenu

Macleod J. Tsilizani

Don Whayo
KNIGHT FRANK

MALAYSIA

Wilfred Abraham
ZUL RAFIQUE & PARTNERS, ADVOCATES & SOLICITORS

Zain Azlan
ZAIN & CO.

BANK NEGARA

Jennifer Chang
PRICEWATERHOUSECOOPERS

Huey Yueh Chang
PRICEWATERHOUSECOOPERS

Hong Yun Chang
TAY & PARTNERS

See Guat Har
SHEARN DELAMORE & CO.

Chuan Keat Khoo
PRICEWATERHOUSECOOPERS

Wee Leng Lee
PRICEWATERHOUSECOOPERS

Theresa Lim
PRICEWATERHOUSECOOPERS

Koon Huan Lim
SKRINE & CO., MEMBER OF LEX MUNDI

Caesar Loong
RASLAN - LOONG

Rajendra Navaratnam
AZMAN, DAVIDSON & CO.

Dinesh Ratnarajah
AZMAN, DAVIDSON & CO.

Loganath Sabapathy
LOGAN SABAPATHY & CO.

Tharminder Singh
LOGAN SABAPATHY & CO.

Francis Tan
AZMAN, DAVIDSON & CO.

Wynnee Tan
PRICEWATERHOUSECOOPERS

Chung Tze Keong
CTOS SDN BHD

Heng Choon Wan
PRICEWATERHOUSECOOPERS

Peter Wee
PRICEWATERHOUSECOOPERS

Chong Wah Wong
SKRINE & CO., MEMBER OF LEX MUNDI

Melina Yong
RASLAN - LOONG

Datuk Zainun Ali
HIGH COURT OF MALAYSIA

MALDIVES

Mohamed Abdulazeez
AIMA CONSTRUCTION CO.

Jatindra Bhattray
PRICEWATERHOUSECOOPERS

Ali Hussain Didi
MINISTRY OF HOME AFFAIRS

Mohamed Fizan
SHAH, HUSSAIN & CO., BARRISTERS & ATTORNEYS

S. Gayen

Mohamed Hameed
ANTRAC MALDIVES PVT. LTD.

Shaaheen Hameed
PREMIER CHAMBERS

Nadiya Hassan

Serene Ho Oi Khuen

Abdul Rasheed Ibrahim
CUSTOMS SERVICE

Ahmed Ifthikhar
MINISTRY OF ECONOMIC DEVELOPMENT AND TRADE

Hon Jameel
MINISTRY OF JUSTICE

Hassan Latheef
MUNAVVAR & ASSOCIATES LAW FIRM

Idham Muizz Adnan
MINISTRY OF ECONOMIC DEVELOPMENT AND TRADE

Ahmed Muizzu
MUIZZU, SUOOD & CO.

Mohamed Munavvar
MUNAVVAR & ASSOCIATES LAW FIRM

Ibrahim Muththalib
ASSOCIATION OF CONSTRUCTION INDUSTRY

Ibrahim Naeem
MONETARY AUTHORITY

Jack Niedenthal

Sriyani Perera
PRICEWATERHOUSECOOPERS

Shabab Rasheed
CIVIL COURT

Mazlan Rasheed
SHAH, HUSSAIN & CO., BARRISTERS & ATTORNEYS

Mohamed Saeed
FIHALHOHI

Fathimath Shafeegah

Shuaib M. Shah
SHAH, HUSSAIN & CO., BARRISTERS & ATTORNEYS

Aisha Shujune Muhammad
MINISTRY OF JUSTICE

Hussain Siraj
MINISTRY OF HIGHER EDUCATION, EMPLOYMENT AND SOCIAL SECURITY

Abdullah Waheed

Sarath Weerakoon
HSBC

Lubna Zahir Hussain
LAW COMMISSION OF THE MALDIVES

MALI

Diop Mohamed Abdoulaye
SDV MALI

Koffi Alinon
UNIVERSITY MANDE BUKARI

Baya Berthe

Amadou Camara
ETUDE DE MEAMADOU CAMARA

Jacques Chareyre
FIDAFRICA / PRICEWATERHOUSECOOPERS

Alassne Diallo
ETUDE ME DIALLO ALASSANE

Djeneba Diop
SCP D'AVOCAT DIOP-DIALLO

M. Domptail
SDV MALI

Seydou Ibrahim Maiga
CABINET D'AVOCATS SEYDOU IBRAHIM MAIGA

Mamadou Keita-Kanda
CHAMBER OF NOTARIES

Charles Ki-Zerbo
BCEAO

Dembele Fatoumata Kone
ASSOCIATION DES ANCIENS PARTICIPANTS DE L'IDLO

Edouard Messou
PRICEWATERHOUSECOOPERS

Aida Niare-Toure
JURIFIS CONSULT SCPA

Touré Sekou
ASSEMBLE NATIONALE

Malick Badara Sow
ATELIER D'ARCHITECTURE ET D'URBANISME

Dominique Taty
FIDAFRICA / PRICEWATERHOUSECOOPERS

Ahmadou Toure
ETUDE DE NOTAIRE

Fousseni Traore
FIDAFRICA / PRICEWATERHOUSECOOPERS

Jean Claude Wognin
FIDAFRICA / PRICEWATERHOUSECOOPERS

MARSHALL ISLANDS

Kenneth Barden
MINISTRY OF FINANCE

S. Posesi Fanua Bloomfield
OFFICE OF THE ATTORNEY GENERAL

Ave R. Gimao Jr.
MARSHALL ISLANDS SOCIAL SECURITY ADMINISTRATION

Ben Graham
CONSULTANT

Jerry Kramer
PACIFIC INTERNATIONAL, INC.

Amentha Matthew
LAND REGISTRATION ADMINISTRATION AUTHORITY

James M. Myazoe
TRUST COMPANY OF THE MARSHALL ISLANDS, INC.

Philip A. Okney
LAND REGISTRATION ADMINISTRATION AUTHORITY

Liz Rodick
EZ PRICE MART

Samuel L. Smith
SMITH BROTHERS BUSINESS SOLUTIONS

David M. Strauss
ATTORNEY-AT-LAW

Tony Tomlinson
BECA INTERNATIONAL CONSULTANTS LTD.

Philip Welch
MICRONESIAN SHIPPING AGENCIES

Bori Ysawa
ROBERT REIMERS ENTERPRISES, INC.

MAURITANIA

Jacques Chareyre
FIDAFRICA / PRICEWATERHOUSECOOPERS

Adama Demba Diop
ATTORNEY-AT-LAW

Cheikhani Jules
CABINET ME JULES

Saliou Niang
FIDAFRICA / PRICEWATERHOUSECOOPERS

Moulaye El Ghali Ould
AVOCAT

Yarba Ould Ahmed Saleh
CABINET ME SIDIYA

Ahmed Salem Ould Bouhoubeyni
CABINET BOUHOUBEYNI

Maouloud Vall Ould Hady Seyid
ETUDE HADY

Sidi Mohamed Ould Mohamed Lemine
CHAMBRE COMMERCIALE AUPRÈS DE LA COUR D'APPEL DE NOUAKCHOTT

Ahmed Ould Radhi
BANQUE CENTRALE

Aliou Sall
ASSURIM

MAURITIUS

Robert Bigaignon
PRICEWATERHOUSECOOPERS

Urmila Boolell
BANYMANDHUB BOOLELL CHAMBERS

Thierry Chellen
BENOIT CHAMBERS

D. Chinien
COMPANIES DIVISION

Bert C. Cunningham
CUSTOMS AND EXCISE DEPARTMENT

Zulfi J. Currimjee
ZAC ASSOCIATES LTD.

Marc Daruty de Granpre
DARUTY DE GRANDPRE ARCHITECTS ASSOCIATES LTD.

Martine de Fleuriot de la Colinière
DE COMARMOND & KOENIG, MEMBER OF LEX MUNDI

Catherine de Rosnay
LEGIS & PARTNERS

Bernard d'Hotman de Villiers
NOTAIRE

Ramesh Doma
PRICEWATERHOUSECOOPERS

Robert Ferrat
LEGIS & PARTNERS

B.R. Gujadhur
BANK OF MAURITIUS

Thierry Koenig
DE COMARMOND & KOENIG, MEMBER OF LEX MUNDI

Subhash Lallah
LALLAH CHAMBERS

Didier Lenette
PRICEWATERHOUSECOOPERS

Shakeel Mohamed
MOHAMED CHAMBERS LAW OFFICES

Jean-Pierre Montocchio

Shaukat Oozeer

Camille Poulettey
DE COMARMOND & KOENIG, MEMBER OF LEX MUNDI

Rishi Pursem

Ram L. Roy
PRICEWATERHOUSECOOPERS

Yeung Sik Yuen
ATTORNEY-AT-LAW

Deviantee Sobarun

Pascal Sullivan
PRICEWATERHOUSECOOPERS

Pritish Teeluck
DSL STAR EXPRESS

Muhammad R.C. Uteem
JERRIAH & UTEEM CHAMBERS

Yeung Yin In David
DSL STAR EXPRESS

MEXICO

Carlos Angulo
BAKER & MCKENZIE

Francisco Samuel Arias González
UINL

Oscar O. Cano
ADEATH LOGISTICS S.A. DE C.V.

María Casas Lopez
BAKER & MCKENZIE

Oscar de la Vega
BASHAM, RINGE Y CORREA, MEMBER OF IUS LABORIS & LEX MUNDI

Ignacio Diaque
BAKER & MCKENZIE

Mariano Enriquez-Mejia
BAKER & MCKENZIE

Salvador Esquivel Bernal
PRICEWATERHOUSECOOPERS

Carlos Frias
PRICEWATERHOUSECOOPERS

Gerardo Garreto-Chavez
Barrera, Siqueiros y Torres Landa

Teresa Gómez Neri
Goodrich, Riquelme y Asociados, member of Lex Mundi

Eugenia Gonzalez
Goodrich, Riquelme y Asociados, member of Lex Mundi

Jose Antonio Gonzalez Anaya
Ministry of Finance

Carlos Grimm
Baker & McKenzie

Mario A. Gutiérrez
PricewaterhouseCoopers

Luz Helena Lopez
PricewaterhouseCoopers

Gerardo Lozano Alarcon
Holland & Knight - Gallástegui y Lozano, S.C.

Carlos Montemayor
PricewaterhouseCoopers

Hector Munez

Enrique Nort
Comision Nacional Bancaria y de Valores

Jorge León Orantes Vallejo
Goodrich, Riquelme y Asociados, member of Lex Mundi

Bernardo Perez Fernandez Del Castillo
Notario 23 del DF

Pablo Perezalonso Eguía
Ritch Mueller, S.C.

Irela Robles Victory
Secretaria de Desarrollo Economico

Adrián Salgado Morante
COMAD, S.C.

Jorge Sanchez
Goodrich, Riquelme y Asociados, member of Lex Mundi

Cristina Sanchez-Urtiz
Miranda, Estavillo, Staines y Pizarro-Suarez

Monica Schiaffino Pérez
Basham, Ringe y Correa, member of Ius Laboris & Lex Mundi

Patricia Schroeder
PricewaterhouseCoopers

Juan Francisco Torres-Landa
Barrera, Siqueiros y Torres Landa

MICRONESIA

Eric Akamigbo

Kenneth Barden
Ministry of Finance

Wayne Bricknell

Lam Dang
Congress of the FSM

Stephen V. Finnen
Stephen Finnen's Law Corporation

FSM Supreme Court

Doug Hastings

Andrea S. Hillyer
Attorney-at-Law

Salvadore Jacob

Stevenson A. Joseph
FSM Development Bank

Patrick Mackenzie
Bank of FSM

Silberio S. Mathias
FSM Social Security Administration

Wendolin I. Mendiola
Court of Land Tenure, Judiciary Branch

Kevin Pelep
Office of the Registrar of Corporations

Marcelo Peterson
Foreign Investment Board, Pohnpei State Government

Craig D. Reffner
Law Office of Fredrick L. Ramp

Salomon Saimon
Pohnpei State Government

Joe Vitt
Pohnpei Transfer & Storage, Inc.

MOLDOVA

Rene Bijvoet
PricewaterhouseCoopers

David A. Brodsky
Brodsky Uskov Looper Reed & Partners

Victor Burunsus
World Bank Group

Andrian Candu
PricewaterhouseCoopers

Octavian Cazac
Turcan & Turcan

Svetlana Ceban
PricewaterhouseCoopers

Gabriela Cunev
PricewaterhouseCoopers

Inga Grecu-Stavila
First Cadastre Project Implementation Office

Boyan Kolev
SRL Constructproject

Mihaela Mitroi
PricewaterhouseCoopers

Irina Moghiliova
Brodsky Uskov Looper Reed & Partners

Nelea Moraru
PricewaterhouseCoopers

Carolina Muravetchi
Turcan & Turcan

Alexandra Placinta
PricewaterhouseCoopers

Natalia Ples
PricewaterhouseCoopers

Pirnevu Ruslan
Quehenberger-Hellmann Moldova SRL

Maximenco Serghei
BSMB Legal Counsellors

Oleg Surduleac
Brodsky Uskov Looper Reed & Partners

Alexander Turcan
Turcan & Turcan

Irina Verhovetchi
BSMB Legal Counsellors

MONGOLIA

Telenged Baast
MTT Mongolian Transport Team LLC

Bayarmaa Badarch
Lynch & Mahoney

Javzan Battogtokh
Credit Information Bureau

Batzaya Bodikhuu
Anand & Anand Advocates

Bayar Budragchaa
Lehman, Lee & Xu

Courtney Fowler
PricewaterhouseCoopers

Battsetseg Ganbold
Anderson & Anderson

Katherine Garkavets
PricewaterhouseCoopers

Batmunkh Javkhlant
Anderson & Anderson

Bob Jurik
PricewaterhouseCoopers

Elena Kaeva
PricewaterhouseCoopers

Daniel Mahoney
Lynch & Mahoney

Abdulkhamid Muminov
PricewaterhouseCoopers

Natalya Revenko
PricewaterhouseCoopers

Matthew Tallarovic
PricewaterhouseCoopers

Tsogt Tsend
Administrative Court of Capital City

Tsets Law Firm

Aliya Utegaliyeva
PricewaterhouseCoopers

N. Zorigt
Tuushin Company Limited

Solongo Zulbaatar
Anderson & Anderson

MONTENEGRO

Mike Ahern

Mladen Bojani
New Securities Exchange Montenegro

Vasilije Boskovi
Law Firm Boskovi

Stela Boskovi
Central Bank of Montenegro

Mirjana Izmovi
Central Bank of Montenegro

Goran Darmanovi
CMC Construction

Vladimir Dasi
Bojovi & Dasi

Igor Djurikovi
Crnogorska Komercijalna Banka AD Podgorica

Tamara Durutovi
Law Office Vukoti - Durutovi

Boidar Gogi
Montecco INC

Jelena Ilinci
Prelevi Law Firm

Rina Ivanevi
Secretariat for Urban Planning and Construction

Petar Ivanovi
Montenegrin Investment Promotion Agency

Rado Kastratovi
Kastratovi Law Office

Darko Konjevi
Montenegro Business Alliance

Maja Krsti
PricewaterhouseCoopers

Nikola Martinovi
Martinovi Law Office

Budimka Mikovi
Center for Entrepreneurship and Economic Development

Borislav Mijovi
Mercedes-Benz - Ljetopis Automotive d.o.o.

Sneana Mili
Central Bank of Montenegro

Nenad M. Novakovi
Law Office Novakovi

Predrag Pavlii
Montecco INC

Zorica Peshi
Law Office Vujaci

Dragana Radevi
Center for Entrepreneurship and Economic Development

Budimir Raikovi
Montenegrin Union of Employers

Milena Roncevi
Prelevi Law Firm

Igor V. Stijovi
Igor Stijovi Law Office

Marko Tintor
Central Bank of Montenegro

Sasha Vujaci
Law Office Vujaci

Judge Vujoevi
Commercial Court of Montenegro

MOROCCO

Younes Anibar
Cabinet Younes Anibar

Mr. Aziz
Globex Maritime Co.

Maria Belafia
Cabinet MeBelafia

Myriam Emmanuelle Bennani
Amin Hajji & Associés Association d'Avocats

Richard Cantin
Naciri & Associés / Gide Loyrette Nouel, member of Lex Mundi

Maha Dassouli
Bank Al-Maghrib

Fatima Erradi
PricewaterhouseCoopers

Amin Hajji

Mohamed Ibn Abdeljalil
Cabinet Me Mohamed Ibn Abdeljalil

Azeddine Kabbaj
Barreau de Casablanca

Abdelwaret Kabbaj
PricewaterhouseCoopers

Nadia Kettani
Kettani Law Firm

Ali Kettani Law Office

Abdelmajid Khachai
Baker & McKenzie, Wong & Leow

Haddaoui Khalil
Bank Al-Maghrib

Ahmed Lahrache
Bank Al-Maghrib

Anis Mahfoud
CMS Bureau Francis Lefebvre

Hicham Naciri
Naciri & Associes / Gide Loyrette Nouel, member of Lex Mundi

Morgane Saint-Jalmes
Kettani Law Firm

Houcine Sefrioui
Conseiller Executif Union Internationale du Notariat

MOZAMBIQUE

Ibrahim Agigi
Sal & Caldeira, Advogados e Consultores, Lda

Louise Alston

Mark Badenhorst
PricewaterhouseCoopers

Banco de Moçambique

José Manuel Caldeira
Sal & Caldeira, Advogados e Consultores, Lda

Padro E. Chambe
Mo Cargo SARL

Joao Chiboleca

Pedro Couto
H. Gamito, Couto, Gonçalves Pereira e Castelo Branco & Associados

Paul De Chalain
PricewaterhouseCoopers

Maria João Dionísio
Pimenta, Dionísio e Associados

Maria Isabel Fernandes
PricewaterhouseCoopers

Telmo Ferreira
H. Gamito, Couto, Gonçalves Pereira e Castelo Branco & Associados

Adrian Frey
Mozlegal Lda

Isabel Garcia
Silvia Garcia Advogados & Consultores

Jennifer Garvey
KPMG Auditoria e Consultoria

Rufino Lucas

Manuel Didier Malunga
NATIONAL DIRECTORATE OF REGISTRY AND NOTARIES

Xiluva Matavele
SAL & CALDEIRA, ADVOGADOS E CONSULTORES, LDA

José Mucavele

Lara Narcy
H. GAMITO, COUTO, GONÇALVES PEREIRA E CASTELO BRANCO & ASSOCIADOS

Auxílio Eugénio Nhabanga
FERNANDA LOPES & ASSOCIADOS, ADVOGADOS

Emilio R. Nhamissitane
ADVOGADO

Paulo Pimenta
PIMENTA, DIONÍSIO E ASSOCIADOS

António de Vasconcelos Porto
VASCONCELOS PORTO & ASSOCIADOS

Malaika Ribeiro
PRICEWATERHOUSECOOPERS

Luís Filipe Rodrigues
SAL & CALDEIRA, ADVOGADOS E CONSULTORES, LDA

Carlos Sousa Brito
CARLOS DE SOUSA E BRITO & ASSOCIADOS

Christopher Tanner
FAO REPRESENTATION

Mariam Bibi Umarji
SAL & CALDEIRA, ADVOGADOS E CONSULTORES, LDA

Mario Ussene
CACM

Robert Walker
PRICEWATERHOUSECOOPERS

NAMIBIA

John Ali Ipinge
FIRST NATIONAL BANK

Mark Badenhorst
PRICEWATERHOUSECOOPERS

Douglas Ball
USAID

Hanno D. Bossau
H.D. BOSSAU & CO.

Chris Brandt
CHRIS BRANDT & ASSOCIATES

Natasha Cochrane
P.F. KOEP & CO.

Tina Dooley-Jones
USAID

Jurie Engelbrecht
FIRST NATIONAL BANK

Hans-Bruno Gerdes
ENGLING, STRITTER & PARTNERS

Hennie Gous
PRICEWATERHOUSECOOPERS

Chris Gouws
PRICEWATERHOUSECOOPERS

Andreas Hans Gerdes
ENGLING, STRITTER & PARTNERS

Michael Hill
PUPKEWITZ HOLDINGS

Jorrie Jordaan
FIRST NATIONAL BANK

Tjakarenga Kamuhanga Hoveka

Peter Koep
P.F. KOEP & CO.

Erle Koomets
PRICEWATERHOUSECOOPERS

Lorinda Koorts
P.F. KOEP & CO.

G.F. Köpplinger
G.F. KÖPPLINGER LEGAL PRACTITIONERS

Willem Carel Kotze
P.F. KOEP & CO.

John Mandy
NAMIBIAN STOCK EXCHANGE

Kerry McNamara
MCNAMARA & ASSOCIATES

Charlotte Morland
FIRST NATIONAL BANK

Richard Mueller
P.F. KOEP & CO.

Charity Mwiya
NAMIBIA CHAMBER OF COMMERCE AND INDUSTRY

Browny Nceba Mutrifa

Kauna Ndilula
BANK WINDHOEK

Carina Oberholzer
PRICEWATERHOUSECOOPERS

Eckart Pfeifer
FISHER, QUARMBY & PFEIFER

Harold Pupkewitz
PUPKEWITZ HOLDINGS

Sanath Reddy
USAID

Gerald Riedel
PRICEWATERHOUSECOOPERS

Renate Rossler
P.F. KOEP & CO.

Marin Scholling
NEDBANK

Retha Steinmann
LAW SOCIETY OF NAMIBIA

Nangula Uaandja
PRICEWATERHOUSECOOPERS

Patrick Uaurikirua
KAUTA, BASSON & KAMUHANGA INC.

Marius van Breda
TRANSUNION ITC

Paul A. E. Wolff
MANICA GROUP NAMIBIA PTY. LTD.

NEPAL

Madhu Sudan Agrawal
STANDARD CHARTERED BANK NEPAL LTD.

Janak Bhandari
GLOBAL LAW ASSOCIATES

Parshuram Chetri
NEPAL BANK LTD.

Purna Chitra

Basu Dahal
HIMALAYAN BANK

Komal Prakash Ghimire

Tika Ram Ghimire
DEPARTMENT OF LAND REVENUE AND REFORM

Ashok Man Kapali
SHANGRI-LA FREIGHT PVT. LTD.

Shrawan Khanal

Satish Krishna Kharel
ADVOCATE

Parshuram Koirala
ADVOCATE

Namgyal Lama
NEPAL FREIGHT FORWARDERS ASSOCIATION

Indra Lohani

Surendra Man Pradhan

Bijaya Mishra
PRADHAN & ASSOCIATES

Kailash Prasad Neupane
NEPAL TELECOMMUNICATIONS AUTHORITY

Matrika Niraula
NIRAULA LAW CHAMBER

Bodhraj Niroula

Megh Raj Pokhrel

Devendra Pradhan
PRADHAN & ASSOCIATES

Bharat Raj Upreti
PIONEER LAW ASSOCIATES

Gorakh Rana

Kumar Regmi
REGMI LAW ASSOCIATES

Yubaraj Sangroula

Purna Man Shakya
RELIANCE LAW FIRM

Madan Krishna Sharma
CSC & CO. / PRICEWATERHOUSECOOPERS

Kusum Shrestha

Ramji Shrestha

Saroj Shrestha

Sudheer Shrestha

Prem Shanker Shrestha
CREDIT INFORMATION BUREAU LTD.

Anil Kumar Sinha
SINHA-VERMA LAW CONCERN

Sajjan Thapa
DHRUBA BAR SINGH THAPA & ASSOCIATES

G.D. Udas
REGISTRAR OF COMPANIES

Peter Ward
NEPAL BANK LTD.

NETHERLANDS

Bas Aalbers
PRICEWATERHOUSECOOPERS BELASTINGADVISEURS NV

ALLEN & OVERY LLP

Jurgen Baas
PRICEWATERHOUSECOOPERS BELASTINGADVISEURS NV

Henri Bentfort van Valkenburg
HOUTHOFF BURUMA, MEMBER OF LEX MUNDI

Barteline A. Cnossen
DE BRAUW BLACKSTONE WESTBROEK

Margriet H. de Boer
DE BRAUW BLACKSTONE WESTBROEK

Rolef de Weijs
HOUTHOFF BURUMA, MEMBER OF LEX MUNDI

Michel Gadron
MAERSK BENELUX B.V.

Jeroen Holland
NAUTA DUTILH ATTORNEYS

Steef Janssen
PRICEWATERHOUSECOOPERS BELASTINGADVISEURS NV

Jaap Koster
HOUTHOFF BURUMA, MEMBER OF LEX MUNDI

Joop Lobstein
STICHTING BUREAU KREDIET REGISTRATIE

Christianne Noordermeer Van Loo
PRICEWATERHOUSECOOPERS BELASTINGADVISEURS NV

Frans Oomen
PRICEWATERHOUSECOOPERS BELASTINGADVISEURS NV

Mark G. Rebergen
DE BRAUW BLACKSTONE WESTBROEK

Hugo Reumkens
VAN DOORNE

Stefan Sagel
DE BRAUW BLACKSTONE WESTBROEK

Rutger Schimmelpenninck
HOUTHOFF BURUMA, MEMBER OF LEX MUNDI

Robert Schrage
ROYAL NETHERLANDS NOTARIAL ORGANIZATION

Remco van der Linden
PRICEWATERHOUSECOOPERS BELASTINGADVISEURS NV

Paul van der Molen
CADASTRE, LAND REGISTRY AND MAPPING AGENCY

Els van der Riet
HOUTHOFF BURUMA, MEMBER OF LEX MUNDI

A. van der Zwaan
MAERSK BENELUX B.V.

Jan Carel van Dorp
PRICEWATERHOUSECOOPERS BELASTINGADVISEURS NV

Jasper Van Schijndel
PRICEWATERHOUSECOOPERS BELASTINGADVISEURS NV

Michiel Wesseling
HOUTHOFF BURUMA, MEMBER OF LEX MUNDI

NEW ZEALAND

Douglas Seymour Alderslade
CHAPMAN TRIPP

Matthew Allison
BAYCORP ADVANTAGE

Kevin Best
PRICEWATERHOUSECOOPERS

Geoff Bevan
CHAPMAN TRIPP

Peter Boyce
PRICEWATERHOUSECOOPERS

Niels Campbell
BELL GULLY

Shelley Cave
SIMPSON GRIERSON, MEMBER OF LEX MUNDI

John Cuthbertson
PRICEWATERHOUSECOOPERS

Chris Gordon
BELL GULLY

Hershla Ifwersen
SIMPSON GRIERSON, MEMBER OF LEX MUNDI

Jeffrey Lai
MINTER ELLISON RUDD WATTS

Wanita Lala
PRICEWATERHOUSECOOPERS

Russell Lawn
BUILDLAW - KUMEU-HUAPAI LAW CENTRE

Aaron Lloyd
MINTER ELLISON RUDD WATTS

Robbie Muir
LAND INFORMATION NEW ZEALAND

Emily Neale
BAYCORP ADVANTAGE

Lester Roy Dempster
CONVEYANCERS NZ LTD.

Murray Tingey
BELL GULLY

Michael McLean Toepfer
HESKETH HENRY

Louise Treacy
SIMPSON GRIERSON, MEMBER OF LEX MUNDI

Ben Upton
SIMPSON GRIERSON, MEMBER OF LEX MUNDI

Richard Wilson
JACKSON RUSSELL

NICARAGUA

Jasmina Almanza Diaz
NICARAGUAN CUSTOMS SERVICE

Bertha Argüello de Rizo
F.A. ARIAS & MUÑOZ

Roberto Argüello Villavicencio
F.A. ARIAS & MUÑOZ

David Urcuyo Báez
PRICEWATERHOUSECOOPERS

Minerva Bellorin
ACZALAW

Silvio Bendana
PRICEWATERHOUSECOOPERS

María José Bendaña Guerrero
BENDAÑA & BENDAÑA

Ricardo Bendaña Guerrero
BENDAÑA & BENDAÑA

Rodrigo Caldera

Thelma Carrion

Humberto Carrión
CARRIÓN, SOMARRIBA & ASOCIADOS

Ludovino Colón Sánchez
PRICEWATERHOUSECOOPERS

Sergio David Corrales Montenegro

Fanny Cuadra López

Gloria Maria de Alvarado
ALVARADO Y ASOCIADOS, MEMBER OF LEX MUNDI

Mercedes Deshon Mantica

Luis Chávez Escoto
MUNGUÍA, VIDAURRE, CHÁVEZ

Maricarmen Espinosa

Hernán Estrada
LEXINCORP

Alejandro Fernandez
PRICEWATERHOUSECOOPERS

Eduardo Garcia Herdocia

Martin Garcia Raudez
ACZALAW

Maria Jose Guerrero
F.A. ARIAS & MUÑOZ

Mario Adolfo Gutierrez Avendano
ACZALAW

Aida Maria Herdocia

Socorro Herrera

Mauricio Horvilleur

Ernesto Huezo Castillo

Eduardo Martínez

Byron Mejia
ATTORNEY-AT-LAW

Jorge Molina
CETREX

Yali Molina Palacios
PALACIOS, MOLINA, Y ASOCIADOS

Oscar Montes

Jacinto Obregon Sanchez
BUFETE JURIDICO OBREGON Y ASOCIADOS

José Aníbal Olivas Cajinas
ALVARADO Y ASOCIADOS, MEMBER OF LEX MUNDI

Ramon Ortega
PRICEWATERHOUSECOOPERS

Francisco Ortega Gonzalez
HUECK, MANZANARES & ORTEGA

Carlos Reynaldo Lacayo

Ana Rizo
F.A. ARIAS & MUÑOZ

César Carlos Porras Rosses
ALVARADO Y ASOCIADOS, MEMBER OF LEX MUNDI

Julio E. Sequeira
ATTORNEY-AT-LAW

Arnulfo Somarriba
TRANSUNION

Rodrigo Taboada
TABOADA Y ASOCIADOS

Evenor Valdivia

Gustavo Adolfo Vargas
F.A. ARIAS & MUÑOZ

Santiago Vega

Rolando Zambrana Arias

Soledad Zeledon O.
ATTORNEY-AT-LAW

NIGER

Alidou Adam
CABINET ALIDOU ADAM

Djibo Aïssatou
ETUDE DE MEDJIBO AÏSSATOU

Aliou Amadou
SCPA MANDELA

Issiaka Boukari
CENTRE DE FORMALITES DES ENTREPRISES

Jacques Chareyre
FIDAFRICA / PRICEWATERHOUSECOOPERS

Moussa Coulibaly
CABINET D'AVOCATS SOUNA-COULIBALY

Hassane Djibo
TRIBUNAL DE GRANDE INSTANCE HORS CLASSE DE NIAMEY

Sani Halilou
MAERSK S.A.

Charles Ki-Zerbo
BCEAO

Bernar-Oliver Kouaovi
CABINET KOUAOVI

Fati Kountche-Adji
CABINET FATI KOUNTCHE

Marc Lebihan
CABINET MARC LEBIHAN & COLLABORATEURS

Diallo Rayanatou Loutou
CABINET LOUTOU, ARCHITECTES

Saadou Maiguizo
BUREAU D'ETUDES TECHNIQUES D'ASSISTANCE ET DE SURVEILLANCE EN CONSTRUCTION CIVILE

Marie-Virginie Mamoudou
CHAMBRE NATIONALE DES NOTAIRES DU NIGER

Edouard Messou
PRICEWATERHOUSECOOPERS

Yayé Mounkaïla
AVOCAT À LA COUR

Moukaïla Nouhou Hamani
COUR SUPREME

Laurent Puerta
SDV - NIGER

Abdou Yacouba Saïdou
CABINET ASPAU

Daouda Samna
SCPA MANDELA

Dominique Taty
FIDAFRICA / PRICEWATERHOUSECOOPERS

Fousseni Traore
FIDAFRICA / PRICEWATERHOUSECOOPERS

Jean Claude Wognin
FIDAFRICA / PRICEWATERHOUSECOOPERS

Souleymane Yankori
SOCIETE CIVILE PROFESSIONNELLE D'AVOCATS YANKORI ET ASSOCIÉS

Hadizatou Zaroumey Gambo
BCEAO

NIGERIA

Oluseyi Abiodun Akinwunmi
AKINWUNMI & BUSARI

Olaleye Adebiyi
ALUKO & OYEBODE

Olu Funke Adekoya
AELEX PARTNERS

Bukkie Adewuyi
PRICEWATERHOUSECOOPERS

Daniel Agbor
UDO UDOMA & BELO-OSAGIE

Ken Aitken
PRICEWATERHOUSECOOPERS

Adolphous Akwumakwuhie

Henrotte Alexandre
SDV NIGERIA - LAGOS

Onikepo Animashaun
LAGOS STATE GOVERNMENT

Taiwo Ayedun
CREDIT REGISTRY SERVICES LTD.

Ndubisi Chuks Nwasike
FIRSTCOUNSEL FIRM

Kofo Dosekun
ALUKO & OYEBODE

Oyinda Ehiwere
UDO UDOMA & BELO-OSAGIE

Anse Agu Ezetah
CHIEF LAW AGU EZETAH & CO.

Babatunde Fagbohunlu
ALUKO & OYEBODE

Kevin Gager
U.K. DEPARTMENT FOR INTERNATIONAL DEVELOPMENT

Atinuke Ipaye
JUDGE

Ade Ipaye
SPECIAL ADVISOR TO THE GOVERNOR ON LAGOS STATE

Steve Kanyatte
PRICEWATERHOUSECOOPERS

Alayo Ogunbiyi
ABDULAI, TAIWO & CO.

Steve Okello
PRICEWATERHOUSECOOPERS

Patrick Okonjo
OKONJO, ODIAWA & EBIE

Dozie Okwuosah
CENTRAL BANK OF NIGERIA

Tolulope Olanrewaju
PRICEWATERHOUSECOOPERS

Henrietta Onaga
PRICEWATERHOUSECOOPERS

Gbenga Oyebode
ALUKO & OYEBODE

Oludare Senbore
ALUKO & OYEBODE

Olufemi Sunmonu
FEMI SUNMONU & ASSOCIATES

Ladi Taiwo
ABDULAI, TAIWO & CO.

Tunji Tiamiyu
MULTIFREIGHTLOGISTICS NIG LTD.

Aniekan Ukpanah
UDO UDOMA & BELO-OSAGIE

Adamu M. Usman
F.O. AKINRELE & CO.

NORWAY

Jan L. Backer
WIKBORG, REIN & CO.

Morten Beck
PRICEWATERHOUSECOOPERS

Stig Berge
THOMMESSEN KREFTING GREVE LUND AS, MEMBER OF LEX MUNDI

Petter Bjerke
THOMMESSEN KREFTING GREVE LUND AS, MEMBER OF LEX MUNDI

Elena Busch
NORWEGIAN MAPPING AUTHORITY, CADASTRE AND LAND REGISTRY, CENTRE FOR PROPERTY RIGHTS AND DEVELOPMENT

Lars Carlsson
CREDITINFORM A.S.

Carl Christiansen
RAEDER ADVOKATFIRMA

Knut Ekern
PRICEWATERHOUSECOOPERS

Jorunn Eriksson
CREDITINFORM A.S.

Stein Fagerhaug
THOMMESSEN KREFTING GREVE LUND AS, MEMBER OF LEX MUNDI

Amund Fougner
HJORT, MEMBER OF IUS LABORIS

Odd Hylland
PRICEWATERHOUSECOOPERS

Tove Ihle-Hansen
PRICEWATERHOUSECOOPERS

Niels Kiaer
RIME & CO. ADVOKATFIRMA DA

Bjørn H. Kise
ADVOKATFIRMA VOGT & WIIG A.S.

Jorgen Lund
THOMMESSEN KREFTING GREVE LUND AS, MEMBER OF LEX MUNDI

Thomas Nordgård
ADVOKATFIRMA VOGT & WIIG A.S.

Ole Kristian Olsby
WIKBORG, REIN & CO.

Helge Onsrud
NORWEGIAN MAPPING AUTHORITY, CADASTRE AND LAND REGISTRY, CENTRE FOR PROPERTY RIGHTS AND DEVELOPMENT

Johan Ratvik
ADVOKATFIRMA DLA NORDIC DA

Finn Rime
RIME & CO. ADVOKATFIRMA DA

Tore Ruud
OVERSEAS SHIPPING AS

Dag Halfdan Sem
PORT OF OSLO

Vegard Sivertsen
DELOITTE & TOUCHE TOHMATSU

Bernt Olav Steinland
ADVOKATFIRMAET SELMER D.A.

Svein Sulland
ADVOKATFIRMAET SELMER D.A.

Anne Ulset Sande
KVALE & CO. ANS

Eirik Vikanes
THOMMESSEN KREFTING GREVE LUND AS, MEMBER OF LEX MUNDI

OMAN

Zubaida Fakir Mohamed Al Balushi
BANKING SURVEILLANCE DEPARTMENT

Mohsin Al Haddad
MOHSIN AL-HADAD & AMUR AL-KIYUMI & PARTNERS

Mohammed Al Shahri
JANASHAL & SHAHRI

Said Al Shahry
SAID AL SHAHRY LAW OFFICE

Hamad bin Rashid Al-Alawi

Hassan Al-Ansari

Mohsin Ahmed Alawi Al-Hadad
MOHSIN AL-HADAD & AMUR AL-KIYUMI & PARTNERS

Saif Al-Saidi
DR. SAIF AL-SAIDI ADVOCATES & LEGAL CONSULTANTS

Hamad M. Al-Sharji

Mona Taha Amer
SALAM AL-NA'BI AND MONA AMER LAWYERS & LEGAL CONSULTANCY

Naveen K. Amin

Sean Angle
TROWERS & HAMLINS

M.O. Baidab
ATTORNEY-AT-LAW

Samer Dahdal

Mehreen B. Elahi
AL ALAWI, MANSOOR JAMAL & CO.

Abshaer M. Elgalal
DR. SAIF AL-SAIDI ADVOCATES & LEGAL CONSULTANTS

Nasser Jaber Abdul Hamid Al-Tabib
DR. SAIF AL-SAIDI ADVOCATES & LEGAL CONSULTANTS

Sohaib Ishaque
AL ALAWI, MANSOOR JAMAL & CO.

Abraham Jacob
MOHSIN AL-HADAD & AMUR AL-KIYUMI & PARTNERS

Maqbool Khabori
AL KHABORI LEGAL CONSULTANTS

Abdullah Salem Khamis Al-Etim

Christopher Knight
TROWERS & HAMLINS

S.M. Kulkarni

P.E. Lalachen MJ, LLB
HASSAN AL ANSARI LEGAL CONSULTANCY

S. Madhu

Pushpa Malani
PRICEWATERHOUSECOOPERS

Mansoor Jamal Malik
AL ALAWI, MANSOOR JAMAL & CO.

Ali Adam Mohamed
RAJAB AL KATHIRI & ASSOCIATES, LEGAL CONSULTANTS

Ala'a Eldin Mohammed
ABU-GHAZALEH INTELLECTUAL PROPERTY

Subha Mohan
SAID AL SHAHRY LAW OFFICE

Mr. Muntasir

Khalid Rhamtalah Al-Badwi

Charles Schofield

Paul Suddaby
PRICEWATERHOUSECOOPERS

Joseph Sunil
AGE MAERSK

Jeff Todd
PRICEWATERHOUSECOOPERS

PAKISTAN

Ali Jafar Abidi
STATE BANK OF PAKISTAN

Taqi-ud-din Ahmad
A.F. FERGUSON & CO.

Waheed Ahmad
AKHTAR SHABIR LAW ASSOCIATES

Masood Ahmed
ABRAHAM & SARWANA

Farooq Akhtar
AZAM CHAUDHRY LAW ASSOCIATES

Ahmad Syed Akhter
GROUP 'O' PYRAMID LOGISTICS GROUP

Mohammad Azam Chaudhry
AZAM CHAUDHRY LAW ASSOCIATES

Nadia Chaudhry
AZAM CHAUDHRY LAW ASSOCIATES

Fouad Rashid Dar
TARGET LOGISTICS INTL. PRIVATE LIMITED

Faisal Daudpota
KHALID DAUDPOTA & CO.

Ikram Fayaz
QAMAR ABBAS & CO.

Maria Ghaznavi
RIZVI, ISA, AFRIDI & ANGELL, MEMBER OF LEX MUNDI

Irfan Mir Halepota
LAW FIRM IRFAN M. HALEPOTA

Rashid Ibrahim
A.F. FERGUSON & CO.

Tariq Nasim Jan
DATACHECK PVT. LTD.

Mansoor Khan

Shadana Khan
AZAM CHAUDHRY LAW ASSOCIATES

Arif Khan
QAMAR ABBAS & CO.

Suleman Khan
RIZVI, ISA, AFRIDI & ANGELL, MEMBER OF LEX MUNDI

Khalid Mahmood
A.F. FERGUSON & CO.

Mahvash Malik
RIZVI, ISA, AFRIDI & ANGELL, MEMBER OF LEX MUNDI

Hasnain Naqvee
RIZVI, ISA, AFRIDI & ANGELL, MEMBER OF LEX MUNDI

Salman Nasim
A.F. FERGUSON & CO.

Neelofar Nawab
RIZVI, ISA, AFRIDI & ANGELL, MEMBER OF LEX MUNDI

Soli Parakh
A.F. FERGUSON & CO.

Abdul Rahman
QAMAR ABBAS & CO.

Jawad A. Sarwana
ABRAHAM & SARWANA

Huma Shah
SHEIKH SHAH RANA & IJAZ

Haider Shamsi
HAIDER SHAMSI AND CO.

Salman Talibuddin
KABRAJI & TALIBUDDIN

Saleem uz Zaman
KABRAJI & TALIBUDDIN

PALAU

Kenneth Barden
MINISTRY OF FINANCE

Ricardo R. Bausoch
MINISTRY OF FINANCE

Jeffrey L. Beattie
OFFICE OF THE ATTORNEY GENERAL

Cristina C. Castro
WESTERN CAROLINE TRADING CO.

Yukiwo P. Dengokl

Lolita Gibbons-Decheny
KOROR PLANNING AND ZONING OFFICE

Rebechong Bill Iskawa
MINISTRY OF FINANCE

Erin E. Johnson
OFFICE OF THE ATTORNEY GENERAL

Wilbert Kamerang

William Keldermans
PALAU SHIPPING COMPANY, INC.

Kevin N. Kirk
LAW OFFICE OF KIRK AND SHADEL

Lourdes F. Materne
SUPREME COURT

Kuniwo Nakamura
BELAU TRANSFER & TERMINAL CO. GROUP

Rose Ongalibang
SUPREME COURT

Frederick W. Reynolds
OFFICE OF THE ATTORNEY GENERAL

William L. Ridpath
RIDPATH & RAGLE

David Shadel
LAW OFFICE OF KIRK AND SHADEL

Peter C. Tsao
WESTERN CAROLINE TRADING CO.

PANAMA

Ludovino Colón Sánchez
PRICEWATERHOUSECOOPERS

Julio Cesar Contreras III
AROSEMENA, NORIEGA & CONTRERAS, MEMBER OF LEX MUNDI

Ricardo Eskildsen Morales
ESKILDSEN & ESKILDSEN

Alejandro Fernandez
PRICEWATERHOUSECOOPERS

Jorge Garrido
GARRIDO & GARRIDO

Jorge R. González
ARIAS, ALEMAN & MORA

Khiet Le Trinh
SUCRE, ARIAS & REYES

Eduardo Lee
PRICEWATERHOUSECOOPERS

Michelle Martinelli
PRICEWATERHOUSECOOPERS

Veronica Nativi
SUCRE, ARIAS & REYES

José Miguel Navarrete
AROSEMENA, NORIEGA & CONTRERAS, MEMBER OF LEX MUNDI

Ramon Ortega
PRICEWATERHOUSECOOPERS

Alfredo Ramírez Jr.
ALFARO, FERRER AND RAMÍREZ

Luz María Salamina
ASOCIACIÓN PANAMEÑA DE CRÉDITO

Ramon Varela
MORGAN & MORGAN

Francisco Vega
PRICEWATERHOUSECOOPERS

PAPUA NEW GUINEA

Rob Aarvold
STEAMSHIPS SHIPPING & TRANSPORT

Christine Bai
GADENS LAWYERS

Lynette Baratai-Pokas
CELCOR INC.

Tyson Boboro
ALLENS ARTHUR ROBINSON

Vincent Bull
ALLENS ARTHUR ROBINSON

David Caradus
PRICEWATERHOUSECOOPERS

Rio Fiocco
POSMAN KUA AISI LAWYERS, in association with MALLESON STEPHEN JAQUES

Richard Flynn
BLAKE DAWSON WALDRON

Winifred T. Kamit
GADENS LAWYERS

Gaudi Kidu
STRUCTON ARCHITECTS, LTD.

John Leahy
PRICEWATERHOUSECOOPERS

Linda Levett
PRICEWATERHOUSECOOPERS

Anthony Smare
ALLENS ARTHUR ROBINSON

Thomas Taberia
PRICEWATERHOUSECOOPERS

PARAGUAY

Perla Alderete
VOUGA & OLMEDO

Betharram Ardissone
FIORIO, CARDOZO & ALVARADO

Hugo Berkemeyer
BERKEMEYER ATTORNEYS & COUNSELORS

Luis A. Breuer
BERKEMEYER ATTORNEYS & COUNSELORS

Esteban Burt
PERONI, SOSA, TELLECHEA, BURT & NARVAJA, MEMBER OF LEX MUNDI

Julio Gonzalez Caballero
BANCO CENTRAL DEL PARAGUAY

Adriana Casati
VOUGA & OLMEDO

Ramón Antonio Castillo Saenz
INFORMCONF S.A.

Maria Debattisti
SERVIMEX SACI

Lorena Dolsa
BERKEMEYER ATTORNEYS & COUNSELORS

Daniel Elicetche
PRICEWATERHOUSECOOPERS

Ana Laura Godin
PRICEWATERHOUSECOOPERS

Nadia Gorostiaga
PRICEWATERHOUSECOOPERS

Larisa Guillen
PRICEWATERHOUSECOOPERS

María Antonia Gwynn
BERKEMEYER ATTORNEYS & COUNSELORS

Karina Lozano
PRICEWATERHOUSECOOPERS

Adriana M. Casati Allegretti
VOUGA & OLMEDO

Carmela Martinez
PRICEWATERHOUSECOOPERS

Roberto Moreno Rodriguez Alcala
MORENO RUFFINELLI & ASOCIADOS

Armindo Riquelme
FIORIO, CARDOZO & ALVARADO

Maria Gloria Trigüis
BERKEMEYER ATTORNEYS & COUNSELORS

Rodolfo Vouga Muller
VOUGA & OLMEDO

PERU

Humberto Allemant
PRICEWATERHOUSECOOPERS / DONGO-SORIA, GAVEGLIO Y ASOCIADOS SOCIEDAD CIVIL

Jimy Francisco Atunga Rios
MAV LOGISTICA Y TRANSPORTE S.A.

Guilhermo Alceu Auler Soto
FORSYTH & ARBE ABOGADOS

Juan Luis Avendaño Cisneros
MIRANDA & AMADO ABOGADOS

Luís Fuentes Villarán
BARRIOS FUENTES URQUIAGA

Anabelí González
ESTUDIO FERRERO ABOGADOS

Pedro Grados Smith
SUPERINTENDENCY OF BANKING, INSURANCE AND PRIVATE PENSION FUND ADMINISTRATORS

Rafael Lengua
BENITES, DE LAS CASAS, FORNO & UGAZ ABOGADOS

Herles Loayza Casimiro
CAMARA PERUANA DE LA CONSTRUCCION

Raul Lozano-Merino
PEÑA, LOZANO, FAURA & ASOCIADOS

Jesús Matos
ESTUDIO OLAECHEA, MEMBER OF LEX MUNDI

José Antonio Olaechea
ESTUDIO OLAECHEA, MEMBER OF LEX MUNDI

Willy Pedreski
BENITES, DE LAS CASAS, FORNO & UGAZ ABOGADOS

Diego Sanchez
PRICEWATERHOUSECOOPERS

Sergio Valencoso
CERTICOM

Walter Vasquez Vejarano
CORTE SUPREMA DE JUSTICIA

Javier De La Vega
PRICEWATERHOUSECOOPERS

Carlos Vegas Quintana
CAMARA PERUANA DE LA CONSTRUCCION

Manuel Villa-García
ESTUDIO OLAECHEA, MEMBER OF LEX MUNDI

Julio Wong Abad
CORTE SUPREMA DE JUSTICIA

Maria Zavala Valladares
CORTE SUPERIOR DE LIMA

PHILIPPINES

Ofelia Abueg-Sta. Maria
LAND REGISTRATION ADMINISTRATION AUTHORITY

Manuel Batallones
BAP CREDIT BUREAU

Rusvie Cadiz
ACF LOGISTICS WORLDWIDE

Cecile M.E. Caro
SYCIP SALAZAR HERNANDEZ & GATMAITAN

Connie G. Chu
ROMULO, MABANTA, BUENAVENTURA, SAYOC & DE LOS ANGELES, MEMBER OF LEX MUNDI

Emerico de Guzman
ANGARA ABELLO CONCEPCION REGALA & CRUZ

Melva M. Evangelista-Valdez
JIMENEZ GONZALES LIWANAG BELLO VALDEZ CALUYA & FERNANDEZ

Tadeo F. Hilado
ANGARA ABELLO CONCEPCION REGALA & CRUZ

Rafael H.E. Khan
Siguion Reyna Montecillo & Ongsiako

Genevieve Limbo
PricewaterhouseCoopers / Isla Lipana & Co.

Tammy Lipana
PricewaterhouseCoopers / Isla Lipana & Co.

Jesuito Morallos
Follosco Morallos & Herce

Nicanor N. Padilla
Siguion Reyna Montecillo & Ongsiako

Emmanuel C. Paras
SyCip Salazar Hernandez & Gatmaitan

Zaber Protacio
PricewaterhouseCoopers / Isla Lipana & Co.

Teodore Regala
Angara Abello Concepcion Regala & Cruz

Ricardo J. Romulo
Romulo, Mabanta, Buenaventura, Sayoc & de los Angeles, member of Lex Mundi

Riza Faith Ybanez
SyCip Salazar Hernandez & Gatmaitan

Jazmin Banal
Romulo, Mabanta, Buenaventura, Sayoc & de los Angeles, member of Lex Mundi

POLAND

Allen & Overy A. Pdzich Sp.k.

Ewa Auleytner
Gide Loyrette Nouel Polska

Jozef Banach
PricewaterhouseCoopers

Grzegorz Banasiuk
Gide Loyrette Nouel Polska

Aleksander Borowicz
Biuro Informacji Kredytowej

Bozena Ciosek
Wierzbowski i Wspólnicy

Rafal Dziedzic
Gide Loyrette Nouel Polska

Michal Górski
Bumar Ltd.

Michaela Guevska
PricewaterhouseCoopers

Piotr Kaim
PricewaterhouseCoopers

Tamasz Kanski
Soltysinski Kawecki & Szlezak, member of Ius Laboris

Marta Karmiska
Gide Loyrette Nouel Polska

Micha Kocur
Gide Loyrette Nouel

Piotr Kowalski
PricewaterhouseCoopers

Joanna Luzak
Soltysinski Kawecki & Szlezak, member of Ius Laboris

Lukasz Mróz
Kancelaria Adwokacka Nikiel i Zacharzewski

Dariusz Okolski
Okolski Law Office

Weronica Pelc
Wardyski i Wspólnicy

Sylvia Petrovskaya
Gide Loyrette Nouel Polska

Bartomiej Raczkowski
Soltysinski Kawecki & Szlezak, member of Ius Laboris

Anna Ratajczyk
Gide Loyrette Nouel Polska

Dariusz Wojciech Rzadkowski
Kancelaria Notarialna S.C.

Piotr Sadownik
Gide Loyrette Nouel Polska

Magdalena Smigrocka
PricewaterhouseCoopers

Anna Sowinskaya
Gide Loyrette Nouel Polska

Ewelina Stobiecka
Haarmann Hemmelrath & Partner

Dariusz Tokarczuk
Gide Loyrette Nouel Polska

Dariusz Wasylkowski
Wardyski i Wspólnicy

Krzysztof Wierzbowski
Wierzbowski i Wspólnicy

Ewa Winiewska

Jaroslaw Wysocki
Head Office of Geodesy and Cartography

PORTUGAL

Paula Alcântara Feliciano
Barros, Sobral, G. Gomes & Associados

Rui Amendoeira
Miranda Correia Amendoeira & Associados

Filipa Arantes Pedroso

Manuel P. Barrocas
Barrocas & Alves Pereira

Carlos Bernardes
PricewaterhouseCoopers

Pedro de Almeida Cabral
Macedo Vitorino e Associados

Miguel de Avillez Pereira
Abreu, Cardigos & Associados

João Cadete de Matos
Banco de Portugal

Carlos de Sousa e Brito
Carlos de Sousa e Brito & Associados

John Duggan
PricewaterhouseCoopers

António Luís Figueiredo
Directorate General of Registry & Notary Civil Service

Jorge Figueiredo
PricewaterhouseCoopers

Sónia Gonçalves Anjo
Barros, Sobral, G. Gomes & Associados

Frederico Gonçalves Pereira
Vieira de Almeida & Associados

Maria Manuel Leitão Marques
UCMA

Jorge Pedro Lopes
Polytechnic Institute of Bragança

Marta Elisa Machado
PricewaterhouseCoopers

Ana Margarida Maia
Miranda Correia Amendoeira & Associados

Paulo Lowndes Marques
Abreu & Marques, Vinhas e Associados

Rita Marques
PricewaterhouseCoopers

Fernando Marta
Credinformacoes

Joao Moucheira
Directorate General of Registry & Notary Civil Service

Vitorino Oliveira
Directorate General of Registry & Notary Civil Service

Acácio Pita Negrão
Abreu & Marques, Vinhas e Associados

Pedro Porto Dordio
António Frutuoso de Melo e Associados

Inês Reis
Carlos Aguiar, P. Pinto & Associados, member of Ius Laboris

Cristina Cabral Ribeiro
Barrocas & Alves Pereira

PUERTO RICO

Tomás Acevedo
McConnell Valdés

Antonio A. Arias Larcada
McConnell Valdés

James A. Arroyo
TransUnion De Puerto Rico

Fernando J. Bonilla
Puerto Rico Ports Authority

Samuel Céspedes Jr.
McConnell Valdés

Harry Cook
McConnell Valdés

Antonio Escudero-Viera
McConnell Valdés

Juan Carlos Fortuno Fas
Fortuno & Fortuno Fas, C.S.P.

Sary Iglesias
PricewaterhouseCoopers

Myriam E. Matos-Bermudez
Sosa Llorens, Cruz Neris & Associates

Rubén M. Medina-Lugo
Cancio, Nadal, Rivera & Díaz

Keila Ortega
Ralph Vallone Jr., Law Offices

Francis Pagan
Ralph Vallone Jr., Law Offices

Victor Rodriguez
Multitransport & Marine Co.

Victor Rodriguez
PricewaterhouseCoopers

Jorge Ruiz Montilla
McConnell Valdes

Roberto Santa Maria
PricewaterhouseCoopers

ROMANIA

Romulus Badea
PricewaterhouseCoopers

Dan Badin
PricewaterhouseCoopers

Constantin Barbu

Rene Bijvoet
PricewaterhouseCoopers

Ligia Buzsor
PricewaterhouseCoopers

Cristina Clujescu
PricewaterhouseCoopers

Anamaria Corbescu
Salans

Diana Coroaba
PricewaterhouseCoopers

Florin Covaciu

Dorin Coza
Babiuc Sulica Protopopescu Vonica

Anca Danilescu
Zamfirescu Racoi Predoiu Law Partnership

Razvan Dinca
Stoica & Asociatii, Attorneys-at-Law

Arina Dobrescu
McGregor & Partners S.C.A.

Ion Dragulin
National Bank of Romania

Laura Duca
Nestor Nestor Diculescu Kingston Petersen, member of Lex Mundi

Serban Epure

Razvan Filcescu

Gina Gheorghe
Tanasescu, Leaua, Cadar & Asociatii

Veronica Grunzsnicki
Babiuc Sulica Protopopescu Vonica

Barry Kolodkin
Independent consultant

Michael Kowalski

Florian Kubinschi

Crenguta Leaua
Tanasescu, Leaua, Cadar & Asociatii

Alina Manescu
PricewaterhouseCoopers

Oana Manuceanu
PricewaterhouseCoopers

Corina Mararu

Neil McGregor
McGregor & Partners S.C.A.

Obie L. Moore
Salans

Simona Nanescu

Manuela M. Nestor
Nestor Nestor Diculescu Kingston Petersen, member of Lex Mundi

Theodor Catalin Nicolescu
Theodor Nicolescu Law Office

Mihaela Popescu

Andrei Savescu
Savescu & Associates

Christina Spyridon
IKRP Rokas & Partners

Theodor Stanescu

Martin Stobbs

Dan Stoica
ROMPAK

Cristiana Stoica
Stoica & Asociatii Attorneys-at-Law

Stefano Stoppani

Sorin Corneliu Stratula
Nestor Nestor Diculescu Kingston Petersen, member of Lex Mundi

Simona Tartacuta

Roxana Teodorovici
PricewaterhouseCoopers

Potyesz Tiberu
Bitrans Ltd., member of World Mediatrans Group

Criton Tornaritis

Catalin Tripon
Attorney-at-Law

Tatiana Urimescu
National Union of Romanian Notaries

Andreea Vatui
PricewaterhouseCoopers

Dumitru Viorel Manescu
National Union of Romanian Notaries

Cristina Virtopeanu
Nestor Nestor Diculescu Kingston Petersen, member of Lex Mundi

Gabriel Voinescu
Zamfirescu Racoi Predoiu Law Partnership

Perry V. Zizzi
Salans

RUSSIA

Allen & Overy Legal Services

Darya Angelo
Law Firm ALRUD

Olga Anisimova
Orrick, Herrington & Sutcliffe LLP

Arsen Ayupov
Law Firm ALRUD

Pavel Bakoulev
DLA Piper Rudnick Gray Cary

Denis A. Bazlov
Cleary, Gottlieb, Steen & Hamilton LLP

Besedin Avakov Tarasov & Partners

Julia Borozdna
Baker & McKenzie

Mikhail Buzyuk
Trans-Business Group

Ilya Fedyaev
Orrick, Herrington & Sutcliffe LLP

Tatyana Fokina
Herbert Smith CIS LLP

Olga Fonotova
Macleod Dixon

Zulma George
PricewaterhouseCoopers

Marlena Hurley
TransUnion CRIF Decision Solution

Irina Im
PricewaterhouseCoopers

Denis Ivanov
Cleary, Gottlieb, Steen & Hamilton LLP

Konstantin Karpushin
PricewaterhouseCoopers

Loulia Koroleva
Gide Loyrette Nouel Vostok

David Lasfargue

Stepan Lubavsky
Baker & McKenzie

Sergey Lubimov
DLA Piper Rudnick Gray Cary

Anton Malkov
Cleary, Gottlieb, Steen & Hamilton LLP

Dmitry I. Melnikov
Cleary, Gottlieb, Steen & Hamilton LLP

Victoria Mischenko
Orrick, Herrington & Sutcliffe LLP

Reena Ohri
Gide Loyrette Nouel Vostok

Lev Orkin
APL Company

Evgeny Reyzman
Baker & McKenzie

Jason Sande
Macleod Dixon

Scott Senecal
Cleary, Gottlieb, Steen & Hamilton LLP

Evgeny Sheenko
PricewaterhouseCoopers

Andrey Shpak
PricewaterhouseCoopers

Steven Snaith
PricewaterhouseCoopers

Yulia Solomakhina
Cleary, Gottlieb, Steen & Hamilton LLP

Irina Strizhakova
Andreas Neocleous & Co., Legal Consultants

Diliara Taktashova
Cleary, Gottlieb, Steen & Hamilton LLP

Victor Topadze
Gide Loyrette Nouel Vostok

Elena Trubitsina
CMS Cameron McKenna

Andrey Zhdanov
Baker & McKenzie

RWANDA

François Bikolimana
Cabinet Augeco Sarl

Patricia Hajabakiga
Ministère des Terres, Environnement, Forêts, Eau et Ressources Naturelles

Busingye Johnston
Ministry of Justice

Annie Kairaba-Kyambadde
Rwanda Initiative for Sustainable Development / LandNet

Désiré Kamanzi
Kamanzi, Ntaganira & Associates

Angelique Kantengwa
National Bank of Rwanda

Tharcisse Karugarama
Rwandan High Court

Isaïe Mhayimana
Cabinet d'Avocats Mhayimana

Jean Marie Vianney Mugemana
Barreau de Kigali

Richard Mugisha
Trust Law Chambers

Eric Nsengimana
World Freight SARL

Benjamin Ntaganira
Kamanzi, Ntaganira & Associates, Corporate Lawyers

André Verbruggen
Cabinet d'Architecture AVA

SAMOA

Robert Barlow
Krase, Enari & Barlow

Denis Bracy
Land Registration Adviser

Jerry Brunt
Brunt & Keli

Lawrie Burich
L. Burich, Building Contractors

Murray Drake
Drake & Co.

Ruby Drake
Drake & Co.

Chris Grant
Land Equity International

George Latu
Latu Ey Lawyers

Ming C. Leung Wai
Leung Wai Law Firm

Leulua'iali'i Tasi Malifa
Sogilaw

Kevin Nettle
Land Equity International

Arthur R. Penn
Lesa ma Penn

Maiava Peteru
Attorney-at-Law

Kim Ralston
Latu Ey Lawyers

Sala Theodore S. Toalepai
Samoa Shippigng Service Limited

Raymond Schuster
Office of the Attorney General

Keilani Soloi
Soloi Survey Services

Grace Stowers
Stevensons Lawyers

Toleafoa Toailoa
Toailoa R.S.

Semi Leung Wai
Semi Leung Wai Law Firm

SÃO TOMÉ AND PRINCIPE

André Aureliano Aragão
Advogado

Fernando Barros
PricewaterhouseCoopers

Pedro Calixto
PricewaterhouseCoopers

Edmar Carvalho
Miranda, Correia, Amendoeira & Associados

Mr. Cavaco
Irmãos Cavaco Construcções Santomenses S.A.

Mr. Ceciliano
Direcção de Registros e Notariados

Frederico da Glória

Pascoal Daio
Advogado & Consultor

Celicia de Deus Lima
J. Palms Advogados

Acácio Elba Bonfim

Ms. Elisangela
Direcção de Comércio

Agostinho Q.S.A. Fernandes
Directorate of Taxes

Julian Ince
PricewaterhouseCoopers

Maria do Céu Silveira
Direcção dos Serviços Geográficos e Cadastrais

Carlos Stock
Direcção de Registros e Notariados

Kiluange Tiny
JuriSTEP

Mr. Valeriano
Direcção de Registros e Notariados

SAUDI ARABIA

Ali Abedi
The Alliance of Abbas F. Ghazzawi & Co. and Hammad & Al-Mehdar

Belal Talal Al Ghazzawi
Al-Ghazzawi Professional Association

Talal Amin Al Ghazzawi
Al-Ghazzawi Professional Association

Abdullah Al-Hashim
The Law Firm of Yousef and Mohammed Al-Jaddan

Mohammed Al-Jaddan
The Law Firm of Yousef and Mohammed Al-Jaddan

Mohammad S. Aba Al-Khail
Saudi Arabian Monetary Agency

Nabil Abdullah Al-Mubarak
Saudi Credit Bureau - SIMAH

Sami Al-Sarraj
Al Juraid & Company / PricewaterhouseCoopers

John Beaumont
The Law Firm of Yousef and Mohammed Al-Jaddan

Adel Elsaid
Panalpina / Ghassan

Abou Bakr Gadour
Toban Law Firm

Majed Mohammed Garoub
Law Firm of Majed M. Garoub

Taj Eldin M. Hassan
Al-Ghazzawi Professional Association

David K. Johnson
Al Juraid & Company / PricewaterhouseCoopers

Hassan Mahassni
Law Offices of Hassan Mahassni

Ceyda Okur
The Alliance of Abbas F. Ghazzawi & Co. and Hammad & Al-Mehdar

Samer Pharaon
Abu-Ghazaleh Legal

George Sayen
Legal Advisors in association with Baker & McKenzie Ltd.

Sameh M. Toban
Toban Law Firm

Abdul Aziz Zaibag
Alzaibag Consultants

Soudki Zawaydeh
Al Juraid & Company / PricewaterhouseCoopers

Ebaish Zebar
The Law Firm of Salah Al-Hejailany

SENEGAL

Cyrille Adandedjan
A.G.T. Agrotechnic

Cosme Ahouansou

Mochtar Alidou

Constantin Azon

Ameth Ba
Cabinet Ba & Tandian

Clifton Best

Jacques Chareyre
FIDAFRICA / PricewaterhouseCoopers

Magatte Dabo
Transfret Dakar

Gnagna Dienna

Vignon Dieudonne

Rita Fall
Agence chargée de la Promotion de l'Investissement et des Grands Travaux

Oumy Gaye
Centre de Formalites des Entreprises

Sandy Gillio

Hycinthe César Gomis
Tribunal Regional de Dakar

Bernard Gourlaouen

Mame Adama Gueye
SCP Mame Adama Gueye & Associes

Denis Hazoume

Khaled Houda
Cabinet Kanjo Koita

Oumy Kalsoum Gaye

Sidy Abdallah Kanouté
Etude Me Idy Kanouté

Charles Ki-Zerbo
BCEAO

Jean-Luc Labonte

Mamadou Mbaye
SCP Mame Adama Gueye & Associes

Ibrahima Mbodj
Etude MeIbrahima Mbodj

Ndjaye Mbodj
Etude MeIbrahima Mbodj

Moustapha N'Doye
Attorney-at-Law

Papa Ndiaye
Cour d'Appel de Dakar

Ndéné Ndiaye
Guedel Ndiaye & Associes

Birane Niang

Saliou Niang
FIDAFRICA / PricewaterhouseCoopers

Nadaud Philippe

Michelle Renous
Société Générale de Banque au Senegal

Patrick Saizonou

Pap Oumar Sakho
Attorney-at-Law

Amadou C. Sall
Agence Chargée de la Promotion de l'Investissement et des Grands Travaux

Daniel Sedar Senghor
ETUDE DE ME SEDAR SENGHOR

Mor Talla Tandian
ETUDE BA & TANDIAN

Jean Paul Thibault
TRIBUNAL RÉGIONAL HORS CLASSE DE DAKAR

Olivier Wybo
FIDAFRICA / PRICEWATERHOUSECOOPERS

SERBIA

Mike Ahern
PRICEWATERHOUSECOOPERS

Irina Astrakhan
WORLD BANK

Rade Backovic
ASSOCIATION OF SERBIAN BANKS

Bojana Bregovic
WOLF THEISS

Nataa V. Cvetianin
LAW OFFICES JANKOVI, POPOVI & MITI

Jelena Djokic
PRICEWATERHOUSECOOPERS

Horst Ebhardt
WOLF THEISS

Jelena S. Gazidova
LAW OFFICES JANKOVI, POPOVI & MITI

Oliver Haussmann
MORAVCEVIC, VOJNOVIC & ZDRAVKOVIC O.A.D. U SARADNJI SA SCHOENHER

Jovana Ilic
PRICEWATERHOUSECOOPERS

Scott Jacobs

Nikola M. Jankovi
LAW OFFICES JANKOVI, POPOVI & MITI

Nikola Jekic
HAYHURST ROBINSON LAW OFFICES

Tom Jersild
INDEPENDENT CONSULTANT

Dubravka Kosic
STUDIO LEGALE SUTTI

Vidak Kovacevic
WOLF THEISS

Miladin Maglov

Andreja Marusic
NATIONAL BANK OF SERBIA AND MONTENEGRO

Katarina Nedeljkovic
KATARINA NEDELJKOVIC LAW OFFICE

Dimitrij Nikolic
CARGO TEAM

Milan Parivodic

Maja Piscevic

Srdja M. Popovic
LAW OFFICES POPOVIC, POPOVIC, SAMARDZIJA & POPOVIC

Oliver Radosavljevic

Milan Samarzdic
ATTORNEY-AT-LAW

Petar Stojanovic
JOKSOVIC, STOJANOVIC & PARTNERS

Lidija Tomasovic
LAW OFFICES POPOVIC, POPOVIC, SAMARDZIJA & POPOVIC

Snezana Tosic

Mirko Vasiljevic

Nikoleta Vucenovic

Relja Zdravkovic
MORAVCEVIC, VOJNOVIC & ZDRAVKOVIC O.A.D. U SARADNJI SA SCHOENHER

Milos Zivkovic
ZIVKOVIC & SAMARDZIC LAW OFFICE

SEYCHELLES

Gerry Adam
MAHE SHIPPING

Hughes N. Adam
LAND MARINE LTD.

Benneth Alphonse
EMPLOYMENT DEPARTMENT

Jules G. Baker
SEYCHELLES PORTS AUTHORITY

France Gonzalves Bonte
BARRISTER & ATTORNEY-AT-LAW, NOTARY PUBLIC

Philippe Boulle
INTERSHORE CONSULT PTY. LTD.

Francis Chang-Sam
LAW CHAMBERS OF FRANCIS CHANG-SAM

Andre D. Ciseau
SEYCHELLES PORTS AUTHORITY

Alex Ellenberger
LOCUS ARCHITECTURE PTY. LTD.

Samia Govinden
REGISTRATION DIVISION

Daniel Houareau
SEYCHELLES PORTS AUTHORITY

Shelton M. Jolicoeur
INTERNATIONAL LAW & CORPORATE SERVICES PTY. LTD.

Pesi Pardiwalla
TWOMEY LABLACHE PARDIWALLA

Bernard L. Pool
POOL & PATEL

Serge Rouillon
AARTI CHAMBERS

Kieran B. Shah
BARRISTER-AT-LAW AND ATTORNEY-AT-LAW

Nicole Tirant-Gherardi
SEYCHELLES CHAMBER OF COMMERCE & INDUSTRY

Robert Victor
MINISTRY OF LAND USE AND HABITAT

SIERRA LEONE

Shaira Adamali
PRICEWATERHOUSECOOPERS

Henry Akin Macauley

Mohamed Bangura
ROBERTS AND PARTNERS

Denis Cordel
BOLLORÉ DTI - SDV

Mariama Dumbuya
RENNER THOMAS & CO.

Charles Egan
PRICEWATERHOUSECOOPERS

Jean Marcel Gariador
BOLLORÉ DTI - SDV

Jamesina King
BASMA & MACAULAY

George Kwatia
PRICEWATERHOUSECOOPERS

Centus Macauley
ROBERTS AND PARTNERS

Emmanuel Roberts
ROBERTS AND PARTNERS

Susan Sisty
BASMA & MACAULAY

SIERRA LEONE COMMERCIAL BANK

Darcy White
PRICEWATERHOUSECOOPERS

Amy Wright
WRIGHT & CO., BARRISTERS & SOLICITORS

Rowland S.V. Wright
WRIGHT & CO., BARRISTERS & SOLICITORS

SINGAPORE

Kala Anandarajah
RAJAH & TANN

Sam Bonifant
CLIFFORD CHANCE WONG PTE. LTD.

Jennifer Chia
TSMP LAW CORPORATION

Paula Eastwood
PRICEWATERHOUSECOOPERS

Chi Duan Gooi
DONALDSON & BURKINSHAW, MEMBER OF LEX MUNDI

Deepak Kaul
PRICEWATERHOUSECOOPERS

Nanda Kumar
CLIFFORD CHANCE WONG PTE. LTD.

Joseph Lai
JTC CORPORATION

Aloysius Leng
ABRAHAMLOW

Audrey Su Yin Ng
KELVIN CHIA PARTNERSHIP

Beng Hong Ong
WONG TAN & MOLLY LIM LLC

See Tiat Quek
PRICEWATERHOUSECOOPERS

Mark Rowley
CREDIT BUREAU SINGAPORE

Cynthia Tan
WONG TAN & MOLLY LIM LLC

Siu Ing Teng
SINGAPORE LAND AUTHORITY

David Shih Yee Teo
DONALDSON & BURKINSHAW, MEMBER OF LEX MUNDI

Shen Yi Thio
TSMP LAW CORPORATION

Han Li Toh
THE SUBORDINATE COURTS OF SINGAPORE

SLOVAKIA

ALLEN & OVERY BRATISLAVA S.R.O.

Radmila Benkova
PRICEWATERHOUSECOOPERS

Margareta Boskova
PRICEWATERHOUSECOOPERS

Todd Bradshaw
PRICEWATERHOUSECOOPERS

Jana Brezinova
DEDÁK & PARTNERS, S.R.O.

Katarina echová
ECHOVÁ RAKOVSK, MEMBER OF LEX MUNDI

Ondej Duek
PETERKA & PARTNERS

Dana Ferencikova
PRICEWATERHOUSECOOPERS

Zuzana Gaalova
ECHOVÁ RAKOVSK, MEMBER OF LEX MUNDI

Georgina Galova
PRICEWATERHOUSECOOPERS

Viera Gregorova
PETERKA & PARTNERS

Martin Javorcek
CMS CARNOGURSK

Tomá Kamenec
DEDÁK & PARTNERS, S.R.O.

Jan Korecky
CMS CARNOGURSK

Michal Luknar
SQUIRE, SANDERS & DEMPSEY

Tomá Maretta
ECHOVÁ RAKOVSK, MEMBER OF LEX MUNDI

Jana Moravcikova
ECHOVÁ RAKOVSK, MEMBER OF LEX MUNDI

Lenka Okaiková
PETERKA & PARTNERS

PANALPINA WELTTRANSPORT GMBH

Kristína Rúsková
PETERKA & PARTNERS

Michaela petková
GEODESY, CARTOGRAPHY AND CADASTRE AUTHORITY

Roman Turok-Hetes
NATIONAL BANK OF SLOVAKIA

Zuzana Valerova
PRICEWATERHOUSECOOPERS

Clare Vernon
PRICEWATERHOUSECOOPERS

Zuzana Wallova
NATIONAL BANK OF SLOVAKIA

WOLF THEISS

Dagmar Zukalova
LINKLATERS S.R.O.

SLOVENIA

Crtomir Borec
PRICEWATERHOUSECOOPERS

Natasa Bozovic
BANK OF SLOVENIA

Erika Braniselj
NOTARKA

Zarja Cibej
SCHOENHERR CONSULTING D.O.O.

Nada Drobnic
DELOITTE & TOUCHE TOHMATSU

Mrs. Fajdiga

Sreo Jadek
LAW OFFICE JADEK & PENSA

Aleksandra Jemc
LAW OFFICE JADEK & PENSA

Janos Kelemen
PRICEWATERHOUSECOOPERS

Lucijan Klemencic
PRICEWATERHOUSECOOPERS

Barbara Kozaric
DELOITTE & TOUCHE TOHMATSU

Bozena Lipej

Danilo Marinovic
PRICEWATERHOUSECOOPERS

Iain McGuire
PRICEWATERHOUSECOOPERS

Mitja Novak
MITJA JELENIC NOVAK

Janja Ovsenik
PRICEWATERHOUSECOOPERS

Ura Penca
LAW OFFICE JADEK & PENSA

Pavle Pensa
LAW OFFICE JADEK & PENSA

Natasa Pipan Nahtigal
ELIH, ELIH, JANEZIC & JARKOVIC

Mr. Ravnihar

Simon Seibert
PRICEWATERHOUSECOOPERS

Renata Terbenc
LAW OFFICE JADEK & PENSA

Renata Terbenc Trus
LAW OFFICE JADEK & PENSA

Saa Strahini
COLJA, ROJS & PARTNERJI LAW FIRM

Matthias Wahl
SCHOENHERR RECHTSANWAELTE

Ms. Zibrik

Mateja Zorko

SOLOMON ISLANDS

James Apaniai
JAMES APANIAI LAWYERS

Don Boykin
PACIFIC ARCHITECTS

Atkin Fakaia
MINISTRY OF COMMERCE INDUSTRIES AND EMPLOYMENT

Paul Griffiths
RAMSI LAW & JUSTICE PROGRAM

Clay Kerswell
CUSTOMS MODERNIZATION PROJECT

James McGovern
RAMSI LAW & JUSTICE PROGRAM

Wayne Morris
PRICEWATERHOUSECOOPERS

Haelo Pelu
DEPUTY REGISTRAR GENERAL

Andrew Radclyff
BARRISTER & SOLICITOR

Peter Rapasia
SOLOMON ISLANDS CUSTOMS

Roselle R. Rosales
PACIFIC ARCHITECTS

Gregory Joseph Sojnocki
PRICEWATERHOUSECOOPERS

Gerald Stenzil
TRADCO SHIPPING

John Sullivan
SOL - LAW

Gabriel Suri
SURI'S LEGAL PRACTICE

Phillip Tagini
MONASH UNIVERSITY

Julia Tijaja
*MINISTRY OF COMMERCE
INDUSTRIES AND
EMPLOYMENT*

Billy Titiulu
PACIFIC LAWYERS

SOUTH AFRICA

Mark Badenhorst
PRICEWATERHOUSECOOPERS

Heidi Bell
*BOWMAN GILFILLAN, MEMBER
OF LEX MUNDI*

Paul Coetser
BRINK COHEN LE ROUX

Paul De Chalain
PRICEWATERHOUSECOOPERS

Gretchen De Smit
EDWARD NATHAN

Miranda Feinstein
EDWARD NATHAN

Tim Gordon-Grant
*BOWMAN GILFILLAN, MEMBER
OF LEX MUNDI*

Roelof Grové
ADAMS & ADAMS

Erle Koomets
PRICEWATERHOUSECOOPERS

Victor Mesquita
MANICA AFRICA

Jenny Murphy
SAFCOR PANALPINA

Eamonn Quinn
*EAMONN DAVID QUINN
ATTORNEY*

Peter Sands
SDV TRANSAMI PTY. LTD

Ivan Tshinangwe
VAN HULSTEYNS ATTORNEYS

Claire Tucker
*BOWMAN GILFILLAN, MEMBER
OF LEX MUNDI*

Jacques van Wyk
CLIFFE DEKKER

Llevellyn Van Wyk
CSIR

Ralph Zulman
*SUPREME COURT OF APPEAL
OF SOUTH AFRICA*

SPAIN

Basilio Aguirre
*REGISTRO DE LA PROPIEDAD
DE ESPAÑA*

ALLEN & OVERY

Siro Arias
*LANDWELL, ABOGADOS Y
ASESORES FISCALES*

Juan Bolás Alfonso
NOTARIADO

Cristina Calvo
ASHURST

Jaume Cornudella
*LANDWELL, ABOGADOS Y
ASESORES FISCALES*

Fernando de la Puente Alfaro
*COLEGIO DE REGISTRADORES
DE LA PROPIEDAD Y
MERCANTILES DE ESPAÑA*

Iván Delgado
PÉREZ-LLORCA

Juan Francisco Delgado de
Miguel

Rossanna D'Onza
BAKER & MCKENZIE MADRID

*EXPERIAN BUREAU DE
CREDITO*

Alejandro Ferreres Comella
*URÍA & MENÉNDEZ, MEMBER
OF LEX MUNDI*

Guillermo Frühbeck
*DR. FRÜHBECK ABOGADOS Y
ECONOMISTAS*

José Manuel García Collantes
NOTARIADO

Juan Ignacio Gomeza Villa
NOTARIO DE BILBAO

Ana Just
IURIS VALLS ABOGADOS

Daniel Marin
GÓMEZ-ACEBO & POMBO

Andres Monereo Velasco
*MONEREO, MEYER &
MARINEL-LO ABOGADOS*

Juan Manuel Pardiñas Aranda
EQUIFAX IBERICA

Jose Luis Perales Sanz
NOTARIADO

Pedro Pérez-Llorca Zamora
PÉREZ-LLORCA

Roser Ràfols
ROCA JUNYENT ADVOCATS

Ricardo Rebate Labrandero
*SÁNCHEZ PINTADO, NÚÑEZ &
ASOCIADOS*

Carlos Rivadulla Oliva
CLIFFORD CHANCE

Enrique Rodriguez
ALTIUS S.A.

Eduardo Rodríguez-Rovira
*URÍA & MENÉNDEZ, MEMBER
OF LEX MUNDI*

María Gracia Rubio
BAKER & MCKENZIE MADRID

Iñigo Sagardoy de Simón
*SAGARDOY & ABOGADOS,
MEMBER OF IUS LABORIS*

Pilar Salinas
*SÁNCHEZ PINTADO, NÚÑEZ &
ASOCIADOS*

Sönke Schlaich
*MONEREO, MEYER &
MARINEL-LO ABOGADOS*

Julia Testigen
*DR. FRÜHBECK ABOGADOS Y
ECONOMISTAS*

Carlos Valls
IURIS VALLS ABOGADOS

SRI LANKA

Ayomi Aluwihare-
Gunawardene
*F.J. & G. DE SARAM, MEMBER
OF LEX MUNDI*

N.P.H. Amarasena
*CREDIT INFORMATION
BUREAU*

Sharmela de Silva
TIRUCHELVAM ASSOCIATES

Savantha De Saram
D.L. & F. DE SARAM

Amila Fernando
JULIUS & CREASY

Chandrahani Gamage
SUDATH PERERA ASSOCIATES

Anandhiy Gunawardhana
JULIUS & CREASY

Mahes Jeyadevan
PRICEWATERHOUSECOOPERS

Ramani Muttettuwegama
TICHURELVAM ASSOCIATES

Asiri Perera
MIT CARGO LTD.

Rujaratnam Senathi Rajah
JULIUS & CREASY

J.H.P. Ratnayeke
PAUL RATNAYEKE ASSOCIATES

Diluka Rodrigo

Daya Weeraratne
PRICEWATERHOUSECOOPERS

John Wilson Jr.
JOHN WILSON PARTNERS

ST. KITTS AND
NEVIS

Nicholas Brisbane
N. BRISBANE & ASSOCIATES

Jamaine Buchanan
*MINISTRY OF SUSTAINABLE
DEVELOPMENT*

Camilla Cato
WEBSTER DYRUD MITCHELL

Idris Fidela Clarke
*FINANCIAL SERVICES
DEPARTMENT*

Neil Coates
PRICEWATERHOUSECOOPERS

Patricia Dublin
DUBLIN AND JOHNSON

Kamsha Graham
*WALWYNLAW BARRISTERS &
SOLICITORS*

Dahlia Joseph
*DANIEL BRANTLEY &
ASSOCIATES*

Pearletta Lanns
HIGH COURT OF JUSTICE

Marcella Liburd
BRYANT & LIBURD

L. Everette Martin
*EASTERN CARIBBEAN CENTRAL
BANK, SECURITIES EXCHANGE*

Jeoffrey Nisbett
JEFFREY & NISBETTS

Miselle O'Brian
DUBLIN AND JOHNSON

R & T DESIGN-BUILD
CONSULTANTS

Clifford Thomas
DEPARTMENT OF LABOUR

Vernon S. Veira
VEIRA, GRANT & ASSOCIATES

Charles Walwyn
PRICEWATERHOUSECOOPERS

Leonora Walwynlaw
*WALWYNLAW BARRISTERS &
SOLICITORS*

ST. LUCIA

Thaddeus M. Antoine
FRANCIS & ANTOINE

Anthony Atkinson
PRICEWATERHOUSECOOPERS

Mac Stephen Aubertin
*DEPARTMENT OF LABOUR
RELATIONS*

Candace Cadasse
NICHOLAS JOHN & CO.

Mary Juliana Charles
GORDON, GORDON & CO.

Willibald Charles
KAPARRAN SHIPPING

Carol J. Gedeon
CHANCERY CHAMBERS

Bradley Paul
BRADLEY PAUL ASSOCIATES

Richard Peterkin
PRICEWATERHOUSECOOPERS

Trevor Philipe
*TREVOR PHILIPE AGENCIES
LTD.*

Kim Camille St. Rose
GORDON, GORDON & CO.

Charles Tibbits
PRICEWATERHOUSECOOPERS

Leandra Gabrielle Verneuil
GORDON, GORDON & CO.

Andie A. Wilkie
GORDON, GORDON & CO.

ST. VINCENT AND
THE GRENADINES

Anthony Atkinson
PRICEWATERHOUSECOOPERS

Kay Bacchus-Browne
*KAY BACCHUS-BROWNE
CHAMBERS*

Theodore Browne
ATTORNEY-AT-LAW

Ms. Campbell

Agnes E. Cato
CATO & CATO

Mira E. Commissiong
EQUITY CHAMBERS

Rosann N.D. Cummings
*HUGHES & CUMMINGS,
MEMBER OF LEX MUNDI*

Paula E. David
*SAUNDERS & HUGGINS,
BARRISTERS AND SOLICITORS*

DEPARTMENT OF LABOUR

Layne Errol
ATTORNEY-AT-LAW

Sean Joachim
CARIBTRANS

Ada Johnson
ATTORNEY-AT-LAW

Moulton Mayers
*MOULTON MAYERS
ARCHITECTS*

Floyd A. Patterson
PANNELL KERR FORSTER

Richard Peterkin
PRICEWATERHOUSECOOPERS

Charles Tibbits
PRICEWATERHOUSECOOPERS

Arthur Williams

Douglas L.A. Williams
*LAW FIRM OF PHILLIPS &
WILLIAMS*

Andrea Young-Lewis
*COMMERCE AND
INTELLECTUAL PROPERTY
OFFICE*

SUDAN

Khalid Mohamed Abdalla
*HIGH COURT, AND MEMBER
OF SPLM*

Abdullah Abozaid
*LAW OFFICE OF ABDULLAH A.
ABOZAID*

Malik Aggar Ayar

Al Fadel Ahmed Al Mahdi
AL MAHDI LAW OFFICE

Khalda Ali
ATTORNEY-AT-LAW

Hyder Altom
ATTORNEY-AT-LAW

Omer Abdel Ati
OMER ABDEL ATI LAW FIRM

Nahed Atif Ismail
COMMERCIAL COURT

Saite M. El Hag

El Tagini O. El Karib
ATTORNEY-AT-LAW

Ashraf A.H. El Neil
*MAHMOUD ELSHEIKH OMER &
ASSOCIATES*

Tariq Mahmoud Elsheikh
Omer
*MAHMOUD ELSHEIKH OMER &
ASSOCIATES*

Osman Yousif Ibrahim
*RASHMIEL FOR DEVELOPMENT
& CONSTRUCTION LTD.*

Samia Karamalla

Tariq Kisha
MAHIDUN CONTRACTING CO.

Emad Hassan Musnad
LEGAL CONSULTANT

Mohamed Osman

Osman Mekki Osman
*HOUSE OF LEGAL
CONSULTANCIES & SERVICES
LTD.*

Manal Osman Ali
ATTORNEY-AT-LAW

Murtada Shawki
ATTORNEY-AT-LAW

Abdel Gadir Warsama Ghalib
*DR. ABDEL GADIR WARSAMA
GHALIB & ASSOCIATES LEGAL
FIRM*

Tag Eldin Yamani Sadig
Montag Trading & Engineering Co. Ltd.

SURINAME

Jim D. Bousaid
Hakrinbank NV

Anoeschka Debipersad
A.E. Debipersad & Associates

Consuelo-Andrea Denz
Tjong A. Hung Belastingadviseurs

Angèle J. Karg
BDO AbrahamsRaijmann & Partners

Johan Kastelein
KDV Architects

R.J.S. Kensenhuis
NBM Groep

Femke Loning
Jos Steeman Shipping nv

Stanley Marica
LawFirm Marica

Anouschka Nabibaks
BDO AbrahamsRaijmann & Partners

R.M.F. Oemar
AdvocatenKantoor Oemar

Nannan Panday
Nannan Panday Lawyers

Rita Ramdat
Chamber of Commerce & Industry

E.M. Ranchor
High Court of Justice of Suriname

Roy Shyamnarain
Tjong A Hung Belastingadviseurs

R.A. Soerdjbalie
Notaris

M.M. Tjon a Ten
Hakrinbank NV

John van Alen
Vabi N.V.

P. Wolfran
Brokad

SWAZILAND

Rosslyn Carrington
Ernst & Young

Judith Marie Currie
Currie & Sibandze

Veli Dlamini

Vincent Galeromeloe

E.J. Henwood
Cloete Corporate

Phumlile Tina Khoza
Robinson Bertram

Paul Lewis
PricewaterhouseCoopers

Andrew Linsey
PricewaterhouseCoopers

C.J. Littler
C.J. Littler & Co.

Phiwa Mabuza
Mendip Investments

Service Magagula

Mangaliso Magagula
Magagula & Hlophe

Nledi Makhubu
TransUnion ITC

Theo Mason
PricewaterhouseCoopers

Mandisa Matsebula
Kemp Thomson Inc.

Mr. Mnisi
Sharp Freight SWD Pty. Ltd.

Jerome Ndzimandze
Speed Limit Construction

Knox Nxumalo
Robinson Bertram

José Rodrigues
Rodrigues & Associates

P.M. Shilubane
P.M. Shilubane & Associates

Pieter Smoor
Building Design Group

Caroline Sullivan
KPMG

Thomo Themba
Asymptotes Architects

UC AB

Magreit van der Walt
Attorney-at-Law

Bradford Mark Walker
BradWalker Architects

SWEDEN

Mats Berter
Magnusson Wahlin Qvist Stanbrook Advokat

Pernilla Carring
Advokatfirman Lindahl

Henric Diefke

Roger Gavelin
PricewaterhouseCoopers

Magnus Graner
Advokatfirman Lindahl

Olof Hallberg
Advokatfirman Lindahl

Lars Hartzell
Elmzell Advokatbyrå HB, member of Ius Laboris

Bengt Kjellson
Lantmäteriet

Jesper Kuschel

Susanne Öhbom
Hökerberg & Söderqvist Advokatbyrå KB

Karl-Arne Olsson
Gärde Wesslau

Mattias Örnulf
Hökerberg & Söderqvist Advokatbyrå KB

Martin Pagrotsky
Vinge KB Advokatfirman, member of Lex Mundi

Christa Persson
Panalpina Sweden AB

Jesper Schönbeck
Vinge KB Advokatfirman, member of Lex Mundi

Stefan Sjöblom
Panalpina Sweden AB

Hedda Stiernstedt
PricewaterhouseCoopers

Robert Wikholm
Vinge KB Advokatfirman, member of Lex Mundi

Camilla Wikland
Magnusson Wahlin Qvist Stanbrook Advokat

SWITZERLAND

Peter R. Altenburger
Altenburger & Partners

Beat M. Barthold
Froriep Renggli

Beat Büchler
SBI Gruppe der Schweizerischen Bauindustrie

Bernhard G. Burkard
Notariat Bernhard Burkard

Philippe de Salis
Borel & Barbey

Fiona Deucher
Altenburger & Partners

Suzanne Eckert
Wenger Plattner

Erwin Griesshammer
Vischer Attorneys-at-Law

Rainer Hepberger
PricewaterhouseCoopers

Hans R. Hintermeister
ZEK Switzerland

Urs Klöti
Pestalozzi Lachenal Patry, member of Lex Mundi

Michael Kramer
Pestalozzi Lachenal Patry, member of Lex Mundi

Thomas Leppert
PricewaterhouseCoopers

Wassilos Lytras
Maersk Logistics Ltd.

Michel Merlotti
Conseiller Permanent de l'UINL

Pierre Natural
Notaire

Martin Oesch
Pestalozzi Lachenal Patry, member of Lex Mundi

Christoph Rechsteiner
PricewaterhouseCoopers

Katja Roppelt
PricewaterhouseCoopers

Guy-Philippe Rubeli
Pestalozzi Lachenal Patry, member of Lex Mundi

Christian Schilly
Pestalozzi Lachenal Patry, member of Lex Mundi

Martina Schmid
PricewaterhouseCoopers

Daniel Schmitz
PricewaterhouseCoopers

Daniel Steudler
Swiss Federal Directorate of Cadastral Surveying

Barbara Stöckli-Klaus
Froriep Renggli

Jacques Tissot
Registre Foncier

Andrin Waldburger
PricewaterhouseCoopers

Marcel Zehnder
PricewaterhouseCoopers

Urs Zenger
Handelsregisteramt Kanton Zürich

SYRIA

Mouazza Al Ashhab
Auditing Consulting Accounting Center

Kanaan Al-Ahmar
Al-Ahmar & Partners, Attorneys and Legal Advisors

Bisher Al-Houssami
Al-Israa Int'l Freight Forwarder

Hani Bitar
Syrian Arab Consultants Law Office

Riad Daoudi
Syrian Arab Consultants Law Office

Antoun Joubran
Syrian Arab Consultants Law Office

Fady Kardous
Kardous Law Office

Mazen Khaddour
Law Office of M. Khaddour

Moussa Mitry
Damascus University / Louka & Mitry Law Office

Gabriel Oussi
Syrian Arab Consultants Law Office

Housam Safadi
Safadi Bureau

TAIWAN, CHINA

Don Bennett
Yangming Partners

Victor Chang
LCS & Partners

John Chen
Formosa Transnational, Attorneys-at-Law

Edgar Y. Chen
Tsar & Tsai Law Firm, member of Lex Mundi

Hui-ling Chen
Winkler Partners

Jenny Chen
Winkler Partners

Chun-Yih Cheng
Formosa Transnational, Attorneys-at-Law

Julie Chu
Jones Day

Serina Chung
Jones Day

Yuling Hsu
Formosa Transnational, Attorneys-at-Law

Margaret Huang
LCS & Partners

Zue Min Hwang
Asia World Engineering & Construction Co.

James J.M. Hwang
Tsar & Tsai Law Firm, member of Lex Mundi

Charles Hwang
Yangming Partners

Wen-Horng Kao
PricewaterhouseCoopers

Wayne Lee
Yangming Partners

Jeffrey Lin
Joint Credit Information Center

Rich Lin
LCS & Partners

Shing-Ping Liu
PricewaterhouseCoopers

J.F. Pun
Chen, Shyuu & Pun

Megan Shao
Winkler Partners

C.F. Tsai
Deep & Far, Attorneys-at-Law

Andrew Yeh
Panalpina Taipei

TAJIKISTAN

Bakhtiyor Abdulhamidov
Akhmedov, Azizov & Abdulhamidov, Attorneys

Shavkat Akhmedov
Akhmedov, Azizov & Abdulhamidov, Attorneys

Hassan Aliev
IFC / MIGA Project

Hassan Aliev
IFC / MIGA Project

Courtney Fowler
PricewaterhouseCoopers

Katherine Garkavets
PricewaterhouseCoopers

Bob Jurik
PricewaterhouseCoopers

Elena Kaeva
PricewaterhouseCoopers

Abdulkhamid Muminov
PricewaterhouseCoopers

Natalya Revenko
PricewaterhouseCoopers

Manizha Sharifova
Attorney-at-Law

Matthew Tallarovic
PricewaterhouseCoopers

Aliya Utegaliyeva
PricewaterhouseCoopers

TANZANIA

Johnson Jasson
Johnson Jasson & Associates, Advocates

Leopold Thomas Kalunga
Kalunga & Co. Advocates

Wilbert Kapinga
Mkono & Co. Law Firm

Nimrod Mkono
Mkono & Co. Law Firm

Albert Msangi
Commissioner of Lands

Alex Nguluma
Rex Attorneys

Conrad Nyukuri
PRICEWATERHOUSECOOPERS

Charles R.B. Rwechungura
MAAJAR, RWECHUNGURA,
NGULUMA & MAKANI

Rishit Shah
PRICEWATERHOUSECOOPERS

Mohamed H. Sumar
SUMAR VARMA ASSOCIATES

David Tarimo
PRICEWATERHOUSECOOPERS

Krista van Winkelhof
FK LAW CHAMBERS

THAILAND

ALLEN & OVERY CO., LTD.

Chalee Chantanayingyong
SECURITIES AND EXCHANGE
COMMISSION

Chinnavat Chinsangaram
WHITE & CASE

John Fotiadis
TILLEKE & GIBBINS
INTERNATIONAL LTD., MEMBER
OF LEX MUNDI

Niwat Kanjanapumin
NATIONAL CREDIT BUREAU
CO. LTD.

Suwat Kerdphon
BANGKOK METROPOLITAN
LAND OFFICE

Samma Kitsin
NATIONAL CREDIT BUREAU
CO. LTD.

William Lehane
SIAM PREMIER INTERNATIONAL
LAW OFFICE LTD.

Narong Leungbootnak
KHON KAEN UNIVERSITY

Sakchai Limsiripothong
WHITE & CASE

Nipa Pakdeechanuan
DEJ-UDOM & ASSOCIATES

PANALPINA WORLD
TRANSPORT LTD.

Jane Puranananda
DEJ-UDOM & ASSOCIATES

Wanna Rakyao
THAILAND LAND TITLING
PROJECT OFFICE

Michael Ramirez
TILLEKE & GIBBINS
INTERNATIONAL LTD., MEMBER
OF LEX MUNDI

Piyanuj Ratprasatporn
TILLEKE & GIBBINS
INTERNATIONAL LTD., MEMBER
OF LEX MUNDI

Dussadee Rattanopas
TILLEKE & GIBBINS
INTERNATIONAL LTD., MEMBER
OF LEX MUNDI

Thavorn Rujivanarom
PRICEWATERHOUSECOOPERS

Sawat Sangkavisit
SIAM PREMIER INTERNATIONAL
LAW OFFICE LTD.

Suttipong Srisaard
PRICEWATERHOUSECOOPERS

Harold K. Vickery Jr.
VICKERY & WORACHAI LTD.

Pimvimol Vipamaneerut
TILLEKE & GIBBINS
INTERNATIONAL LTD., MEMBER
OF LEX MUNDI

TIMOR-LESTE

Zacarias Albano da Costa
USAID / DAI

Jose Pedro Camoes
TIMOR-LESTE LEGAL AID
LBH-TL

Rui Castro
PRIVATE INVESTOR

Candido da Conceição
ECONOMIC GROWTH
PROGRAM

CONSULTORIA DE LEI

Georgina de Mello
PIU - SEP

Vital dos Santos
VSP - VITAL DOS SANTOS &
PARTNERS

Hau Kium Foo
CHINESE BUSINESS
ASSOCIATION

Rui Gomes
UNDP

Eusebio Guterres
LAIFET CONSULTANT AND
ADVOCACY

Americo Laia
TIMOR TELECOM, SA

Eric Mancini
SDV LOGISTICS

Francisco Soares
SERVICO DO IMPOSTO DE
TIMOR-LESTE

Pedro Sousa
MINISTRY OF JUSTICE

Stephen Vance
USAID

TOGO

Jean-Marie Adenka
CABINET ADENKA

Martial Akakpo
SCP MARTIAL AKAKPO,
SOCIÉTÉ D'AVOCATS

Adzewoda Ametsiagbe
DIRECTION GÉNÉRALE
DE L'URBANISME ET DE
L'HABITAT

Coffi Alexis Aquereburu
CABINET ME A.C.
AQUEREBURU

Jacques Chareyre
FIDAFRICA /
PRICEWATERHOUSECOOPERS

Denis Cordel
BOLLORÉ DTI - SDV

Charles Ki-Zerbo
BCEAO

John Kokou
CABINET D'AVOCATS KOKOU

Edouard Messou
PRICEWATERHOUSECOOPERS

Adjémida Douato Soededjede
SAFECO

Dominique Taty
FIDAFRICA /
PRICEWATERHOUSECOOPERS

Fousseni Traore
FIDAFRICA /
PRICEWATERHOUSECOOPERS

Jean Claude Wognin
FIDAFRICA /
PRICEWATERHOUSECOOPERS

TONGA

Inoke Afu
DATELINE SHIPPING & TRAVEL
LTD.

William Edwards
TONGASAT

Tomasi Fakahua
SIONE TOMASI NAITE
FAKAHUA LAW OFFICE

David Garrett
GARRETT & ASSOCIATES

Penisimani L. Latu
INTELLECTUAL PROPERTY AND
COMPANY REGISTRAR

Lee Miller
WASTE MANAGEMENT LTD.

Laki M. Niu
LAKI NIU OFFICES

Teimumu Tapueluelu-Schock
WESTPAC BANK OF TONGA

Lesina Tonga
LESINA TONGA LAW FIRM

Petunia Tupou
FUNGATEIKI LAW OFFICE

Mele Tupou
ATTORNEY-AT-LAW

Diana Warner
SKIP'S CUSTOM JOINERY LTD.

TRINIDAD AND TOBAGO

Rehana Ali
EMPLOYERS' CONSULTATIVE
ASSOCIATION

Tara Mary Allum
FITZWILLIAM STONE FURNESS-
SMITH & MORGAN

Rolph Balgobin
THE UNIVERSITY OF WEST
INDIES

Angelique Bart
PRICEWATERHOUSECOOPERS

Steve Beckles
R.D. RAMPERSAD & CO.

Linda M. Besson
EMPLOYERS' CONSULTATIVE
ASSOCIATION

Cecil Camacho
LEX CARIBBEAN

Lisa Chamely-Aqui
AMERICAN CHAMBER OF
COMMERCE OF TRINIDAD &
TOBAGO

Colvin Chen
GILLESPIIE & STEEL LTD.

Stephanie Daly

Luis Dini
HSMDT LTD.

Nicole Ferreira-Aaron
M. HAMEL-SMITH & CO.,
MEMBER OF LEX MUNDI

Philip Hamel-Smith
M. HAMEL-SMITH & CO.,
MEMBER OF LEX MUNDI

Marlon Holder
FIRST CITIZENS BANK

Peter Inglefield
PRICEWATERHOUSECOOPERS

Vishma Jaisingh
FITZWILLIAM STONE FURNESS-
SMITH & MORGAN

Nadia Sharon Kangaloo
FITZWILLIAM STONE FURNESS-
SMITH & MORGAN

Helen Llanos
INFOLINK SERVICES LTD.

Ramesh Lutchman
TRANSUNION

Resha Mahabir
MINISTRY OF TRADE &
INDUSTRY

Kurt Andrew Anthony Miller
FITZWILLIAM STONE FURNESS-
SMITH & MORGAN

Celeste Mohammed
M. HAMEL-SMITH & CO.,
MEMBER OF LEX MUNDI

Alvaro Montenegro
HSMDT LTD.

Yolanda Morales
HSMDT LTD.

Jon Paul Mouttet
FITZWILLIAM STONE FURNESS-
SMITH & MORGAN

Grégory Pantin
M. HAMEL-SMITH & CO.,
MEMBER OF LEX MUNDI

Ronald Patience
CARGO CONSOLIDATORS
AGENCY LTD.

Natalie Paul-Harry
MINISTRY OF TRADE &
INDUSTRY

Jacqueline Quamina
REPUBLIC BANK LTD.

Hollick Rajkumar

Mark Ramkerrysingh
FITZWILLIAM STONE FURNESS-
SMITH & MORGAN

Ronald Ramkissoon
REPUBLIC BANK LTD.

Ramdath Dave Rampersad
R.D. RAMPERSAD & CO.

RBTT BANK LTD.

Myrna Robinson-Walters
M. HAMEL-SMITH & CO.,
MEMBER OF LEX MUNDI

Bryan Rooplal
EMPLOYERS' CONSULTATIVE
ASSOCIATION

Helen Ross
M. HAMEL-SMITH & CO.,
MEMBER OF LEX MUNDI

Stephen A. Singh
LEX CARRIBBEAN

Jonathan Walker
M. HAMEL-SMITH & CO.,
MEMBER OF LEX MUNDI

Allyson West
PRICEWATERHOUSECOOPERS

Phillip Xavier
CARGO CONSOLIDATORS
AGENCY LTD.

TUNISIA

Mohamed Moncef Barouni
AVOCATS CONSEILS REUNIS

Elyès Ben Mansour
GAIJI AND BEN MANSOUR

Kamel Ben Salah
GIDE LOYRETTE NOUEL

Abdelfatah Benahji
FERCHIOU & ASSOCIATES
MEZIOU KNANI

Faiza Feki
CENTRAL BANK OF TUNISIA

Abderrahmen Fendri
CONSEIL AUDIT FORMATION
CAF SARL

Amel Ferchichi
GIDE LOYRETTE NOUEL

Noureddine Ferchiou
FERCHIOU & ASSOCIATES
MEZIOU KNANI

Marie Louise Gam
CONSEIL AUDIT FORMATION
CAF SARL

Olfa Jaziri
CONSEIL AUDIT FORMATION
CAF SARL

Sami Kallel
KALLEL & ASSOCIATES

Amina Larbi
GIDE LOYRETTE NOUEL

Mabrouk Maalaoui
CONSEIL AUDIT FORMATION
CAF SARL

Radhi Meddeb
COMETE ENGINEERING

Faouzi Mili
MILI AND ASSOCIATES

Sakoudi Ridha
A.T.I.S.

Imed Tanazefti
GIDE LOYRETTE NOUEL

TURKEY

Inanc Akalin
PAKSOY & CO.

Müjdem Aksoy
LAW OFFICES OF M.
FADLULLAH CERRAHOGLU

Ekin Altintas
PRICEWATERHOUSECOOPERS

Koray Altunordu
PEKIN & PEKIN, MEMBER OF
LEX MUNDI

Elvan Aziz
PAKSOY & CO.

M. Fadlullah Cerrahoglu

Devrim Çukur
ÇUKUR & YILMAZ

Rüçhan Derici
3E DANŽMANLŽK LTD. TI.

Kazim Derman
KREDI KAYIT BUREAU

Dilara Duman
SARIIBRAHIMOGLU LAW
OFFICE

Sezin Gruner
PEKIN & PEKIN, MEMBER OF
LEX MUNDI

Onur Gülsaran
LAW OFFICES OF M.
FADLULLAH CERRAHOGLU

Rufat Gunay
CENTRAL BANK OF THE
REPUBLIC OF TURKEY

Hande Hamevi
PEKIN & PEKIN, MEMBER OF
LEX MUNDI

Ceren Kartari
Cakmak Ortak Avukat Burosu

Sukran Kizilot
Pekin & Pekin, member of Lex Mundi

Sezin Okkan
Pekin & Pekin, member of Lex Mundi

Sebnem Onder
Cakmak Ortak Avukat Burosu

Fethi Pekin
Pekin & Pekin, member of Lex Mundi

Umut Postlu
Pekin & Pekin, member of Lex Mundi

Faruk Sabuncu
PricewaterhouseCoopers

Bilge Saltan
Mehmet Gün & Co.

Y. Selim Sariibrahimoglu
Sariibrahimoglu Law Office

Elif Tezcan
Pekin & Bayar Law Firm

H. Barž Yalçžn
PricewaterhouseCoopers

Aysegül Yalçinmani
Law Offices of M. Fadlullah Cerrahoglu

Orhan Yavuz Maviolu
Alkan Deniz Maviolu Dilmen Law Office

Serap Zuvin
Serap Zuvin Law Offices

UGANDA

Russell Eastaugh
PricewaterhouseCoopers

Charles Kalu Kalumiya
Kampala Associated Advocates

Jalia Kangave
PricewaterhouseCoopers

Assumpta Kemigisha
Nangwala, Rezida & Co., Advocates

Robert Kiggundu
Arch Forum Ltd.

David F.K. Mpanga
A.F. Mpanga, Advocates

Paul Frobisher Mugambwa
PricewaterhouseCoopers

Jimmy M Muyanja
Muyanja & Associates

Rachel Mwanje Musoke
Mugerwa & Masembe, Advocates

Alex Rezida
Nangwala, Rezida & Co., Advocates

Wycliffe Sebulime
PricewaterhouseCoopers

Ezekiel Tuma
Registry

Ben Turyasingura
Registry

Ronald Tusingwire
Kampala Associated Advocates

Osborne Wanyoike
PricewaterhouseCoopers

UKRAINE

Andrey Astopov
Astapov Lawyers International Law Group

Ron J. Barden
PricewaterhouseCoopers

Svetlana Bilyk
PricewaterhouseCoopers

Natalia Dotsenko-Belous
Konnov & Sozanovsky

Jorge Intriago
PricewaterhouseCoopers

Igor Ishchenko
PricewaterhouseCoopers

Yevgeniy Karpov
Astapov Lawyers International Law Group

Sergei Konnov
Konnov & Sozanovsky

Tatyana Kuzmenko
Astapov Lawyers International Law Group

Maria Livinska
PricewaterhouseCoopers

Ilona Melnichuk
Konnov & Sozanovsky

Victor Nevmerzhitsky
PricewaterhouseCoopers

Sergiy Onishchenko
Chadbourne and Parke

Oleksandr Padalka
Shevchenko Didkovskiy & Partners

Alexey Pokotylo
Konnov & Sozanovsky

Savva P. Poliakov
Grischenko & Partners

Anna Putintseva
Chadbourne and Parke

Oleg Shevchuk
Proxen & Partners

Markian Silecky
The Silecky Firm

Igor Svetchkar
Shevchenko Didkovskiy & Partners

Alexey Yanov
Law Firm IP & C. Consult

UNITED ARAB EMIRATES

Abdul Wahid Abdul Rahim Sultan Al Ulama

Saeed Abdulla Al Hamiz
Central Bank of the UAE

Theresa Abrefa
Berrymans Lace Mawer

Ishraga Abutaha
Al Suwaidi & Co.

Naveed Ahmed
Trowers & Hamlins

Khaled Amin
Shalakany Law Office, member of Lex Mundi

Desmond Balendra
Panalpina Gulf LLC

Jennifer Bibbings
Trowers & Hamlins

Samer Hamzeh

Sydene Helwick
Al Suwaidi & Co.

Walid Karam
Habib Al Mulla & Co.

Shahid M. Khan
Al Roken & Associates

Suneer Kumar
Al Suwaidi & Co.

Charles S. Laubach
Afridi & Angell, member of Lex Mundi

Valeria Lysenko

Sanjay Manchanda
PricewaterhouseCoopers

Khulood Obaid

Henrik Petersen

Ahmed Abdul Raheem Mahmoud
Emirates Advocates

Dean Rolfe
PricewaterhouseCoopers

Mohamed Rouchdi
Attorney-at-Law

Natalie Seeff
Trowers & Hamlins

Razan Shuqair
Al Suwaidi & Co.

Michael Stevenson
PricewaterhouseCoopers

Neil Taylor

Sham Yaghi
Dubai Municipality

UNITED KINGDOM

Allen & Overy

Gregory Campbell
Cleary, Gottlieb, Steen & Hamilton LLP

Richard Collier-Keywood
PricewaterhouseCoopers

Simon Cookson
Ashurst

Kerry Coston
PricewaterhouseCoopers

Laura Cram
Ashurst

David Crosthwaite
Davis Langdon

T.A.R. Curran
Cleary, Gottlieb, Steen & Hamilton LLP

Rupert Elderkin
Cleary, Gottlieb, Steen & Hamilton LLP

Experian Ltd.

Nick Francis
PricewaterhouseCoopers

Paul Samuel Gilbert
Finers Stephens Innocent

Helen Gorty
Simmons and Simmons

Neville Howlett
PricewaterhouseCoopers

Sandro Knecht
Panalpina

Sarah Lawson
Denton Wilde Sapte

Richard Lister
Lewis Silkin Solicitors, member of Ius Laboris

Charles Mayo
Simmons and Simmons

John Meadows
HM Land Registry, England and Wales

Jeremy Ray
PricewaterhouseCoopers

Paul Sillis
Collyer-Bristow

Michael Steiner
Denton Wilde Sapte

John Whiting
PricewaterhouseCoopers

Amy Allen
Booz Allen Hamilton

UNITED STATES

Luke A. Barefoot
Cleary, Gottlieb, Steen & Hamilton LLP

David Barksdale
Cleary, Gottlieb, Steen & Hamilton LLP

Victor Chiu
Cleary, Gottlieb, Steen & Hamilton LLP

Brian E. Clark
APM Terminals N.A.

Richard Conza
Cleary, Gottlieb, Steen & Hamilton LLP

Joshua L. Ditelberg
Seyfarth Shaw LLP, member of Ius Laboris

Desmond Eppel
Cleary, Gottlieb, Steen & Hamilton LLP

John Fedun
Thelen Reid & Priest LLP

Craig Foil
APM Terminals N.A.

Janet Ford
Cleary, Gottlieb, Steen & Hamilton LLP

Lindsee P. Granfield
Cleary, Gottlieb, Steen & Hamilton LLP

Christopher D. Hale
Cleary, Gottlieb, Steen & Hamilton LLP

Jonel Jordan
TransUnion

Arthur Kohn
Cleary, Gottlieb, Steen & Hamilton LLP

Fiana Kwasnik
Cleary, Gottlieb, Steen & Hamilton LLP

Michael Lazerwitz
Cleary, Gottlieb, Steen & Hamilton LLP

Gregory A. Lee
PricewaterhouseCoopers

Bradford L. Livingston
Seyfarth Shaw LLP, member of Ius Laboris

Paul Marquardt
Cleary, Gottlieb, Steen & Hamilton LLP

Janet Morris
Cleary, Gottlieb, Steen & Hamilton LLP

Robert Morris
PricewaterhouseCoopers

Kelly J. Murray
PricewaterhouseCoopers

David Nelson
Panalpina Inc.

David Newberg
Collier, Halpern, Newberg, Nolletti, & Bock

Samuel Nolen
Richards, Layton & Finger, P.A., member of Lex Mundi

Sean O'Neal
Cleary, Gottlieb, Steen & Hamilton LLP

Stephen Raslavich
United States Bankruptcy Court

Lillian E. Rice
Cleary, Gottlieb, Steen & Hamilton LLP

Sandra Rocks
Cleary, Gottlieb, Steen & Hamilton LLP

David Snyder
Snyder & Snyder, LLP

Sarah Ten Siethoff
Cleary, Gottlieb, Steen & Hamilton LLP

Frederick Turner
Snyder & Snyder, LLP

Penny Vaughn
PricewaterhouseCoopers

URUGUAY

César I. Aroztegui
Aroztegui & Asociados / Brons & Salas

Luis Baccino
Aroztegui & Asociados / Brons & Salas

Ady Beitler
Estudio Bergstein

Jonás Bergstein
Estudio Bergstein

Corina Bove
Guyer & Regules, member of Lex Mundi

Carlos Brandes
Guyer & Regules, member of Lex Mundi

Juan Pablo Croce Urbina
Union Internacional del Notariado

María Durán
Hughes & Hughes

Noelia Eiras
Hughes & Hughes

Gabriel Ejgenberg
Estudio Bergstein

Fabrizio Fava
Panalpina

Marcelo Femenías
Bado, Kuster, Zerbino & Rachetti

Juan Federico Fischer
LVM Attorneys-at-Law

Federico Formen
LVM Attorneys-at-Law

Sergio Franco
PRICEWATERHOUSECOOPERS

Daniel Garcia
PRICEWATERHOUSECOOPERS

Ariel Imken
BANCO CENTRAL DEL URUGUAY

Alfredo Inciarte Blanco
PEREZ DEL CASTILLO, NAVARRO, INCIARTE, GARI

Nelly Kleckin
ESTUDIO BERGSTEIN

Ricardo Mezzera
ESTUDIO DR. MEZZERA

Matilde Milicevic Santana
CLEARING DE INFORMES

Felipe Muxi
LVM ATTORNEYS-AT-LAW

Ricardo Olivera-García
OLIVERA & DELPIAZZO

Bruno Santin
ESTUDIO JURÍDICO MUXÍ & ASOCIADOS

Maria Jose Santos
PRICEWATERHOUSECOOPERS

Eliana Sartori
PRICEWATERHOUSECOOPERS

Fiorella Taborelli
PRICEWATERHOUSECOOPERS

Alvaro Tarabal
GUYER & REGULES, MEMBER OF LEX MUNDI

UZBEKISTAN

Bekhzod Abdurazzakov
DENTON WILDE SAPTE

Hairullah Akramhodjaev
PRICEWATERHOUSECOOPERS

Umid A. Aripdjanov
GRATA LAW FIRM

Jamol Askarov
CHADBOURNE AND PARKE

Abduaziz Azizov
BOOZ ALLEN HAMILTON

Sitora Babajanova
GLOBALINK CASPIAN

Irina Gosteva
DENTON WILDE SAPTE

Elena Kaeva
PRICEWATERHOUSECOOPERS

Mouborak Kambarova
DENTON WILDE SAPTE

Abdulkhamid Muminov
PRICEWATERHOUSECOOPERS

Sergio Purin
AHLERS

Akmal Rustamov
PRICEWATERHOUSECOOPERS

Alishar Sagatov

Alexander Samborsky
NATIONAL CENTRE OF GEODESY AND CARTOGRAPHY

Laziza Walter
GRATA LAW FIRM

VANUATU

George Boar
PACIFIC LAWYERS

Christopher Dawson
DAWSON BUILDERS

Geoffrey Gee
GEOFFREY GEE & PARTNERS

Silas Charles Hakwa
SILAS CHARLES HAKWA & ASSOCIATES

Anita Jowitt
UNIVERSITY OF THE SOUTH PACIFIC

Chris Kernot
FAMOUS PACIFIC SHIPPING

Jonathan Law
HAWKES LAW, CHARTERED ACCOUNTANTS

Joe W. Ligo
VANUATU INVESTMENT PROMOTION AUTHORITY

John Malcolm
GEOFFREY GEE & PARTNERS

John Malcolm

Juris Ozols

Mark Stafford
BDO BARRETT AND PARTNERS

VENEZUELA

Jorge Acedo-Prato
HOET PELAEZ CASTILLO & DUQUE, MEMBER OF LEX MUNDI

Rinaldo Mauricio Alcalá
PANALPINA C.A.

Francisco Aleman Planchart
TINOCO, TRAVIESO, PLANCHART & NUÑEZ

Servio T. Altuve Jr.
SERVIO T. ALTUVE R. & ASOCIADOS

María Corina Arocha
ESPIÑEIRA, SHELDON Y ASOCIADOS / PRICEWATERHOUSECOOPERS

Mercedes Briceño
CONAPRI

Alvaro Briceño
ITP CONSULTORES

Henrique Castillo G.
TRAVIESO EVANS ARRIA RENGEL & PAZ

Arturo de Sola Lander
DE SOLA PATE & BROWN

Carlos G. Dominguez
HOET PELAEZ CASTILLO & DUQUE, MEMBER OF LEX MUNDI

María Paola D'Onghia Inciarte
HOET PELAEZ CASTILLO & DUQUE, MEMBER OF LEX MUNDI

María Inés Fernández
BANCO VENEZOLANO DE CREDITO

Germán A. García-Velutini
VENCRED

Alejandro Giolito
ESPIÑEIRA, SHELDON Y ASOCIADOS / PRICEWATERHOUSECOOPERS

Diego Gonzalez Crespo
CASAS RINCON GONZALEZ RUBIO & ASOCIADOS

Alvaro Gonzalez-Ravelo
ESCRITORIO CALCANO-VETANCOURT

Ruben Gotberg
ESPIÑEIRA, SHELDON Y ASOCIADOS / PRICEWATERHOUSECOOPERS

Lorenzo E. Marturet D.
TRAVIESO EVANS ARRIA RENGEL & PAZ

Luiz Ignacio Mendoza
RODRIGUEZ & MENDOZA

Patricia Milano Hernández
DE SOLA PATE & BROWN

Luis Fernando Miranda E.
ESPIÑEIRA, SHELDON Y ASOCIADOS / PRICEWATERHOUSECOOPERS

Bruno Parales
LOGISTICA TSM, C.A.

Fernando Pelaez-Pier
HOET PELAEZ CASTILLO & DUQUE, MEMBER OF LEX MUNDI

Gustavo Enrique Planchart Pocaterra
TINOCO, TRAVIESO, PLANCHART & NUÑEZ

Carlos Plaza
BAKER & MCKENZIE

Eduardo Porcarelli
CONAPRI

Alfonso Porras
BAKER & MCKENZIE

Oscar Ignacio Torres
TRAVIESO EVANS ARRIA RENGEL & PAZ

Carlos Velandia Sanchez
ASOCIACIÓN VENEZOLANA DE DERECHO REGISTRAL

VIETNAM

Nicholas Audier
GIDE LOYRETTE NOUEL

John Bentley
STAR

David Brunell
USAID

Frederick Burke
BAKER & MCKENZIE

Doan Chiên
GIDE LOYRETTE NOUEL

Uan Pham Cong
STATE BANK OF VIETNAM

Giles Thomas Cooper
BAKER & MCKENZIE

Nguyen Dinh Cung
MINISTRY OF PLANNING AND INVESTMENT

John Davis
STAR

Tran Anh Duc
VILAF - HONG DUC LAW FIRM

Bernadette Fahy
GIDE LOYRETTE NOUEL

David Fitzgerald
PRICEWATERHOUSECOOPERS

Do Hong Hanh
USAID

Richard Irwin
PRICEWATERHOUSECOOPERS

Alice Krauss Stokke
UNIVERSITY OF WASHINGTON SCHOOL OF LAW

Le Thi Loc
YKVN

Bill Magennis
PHILLIPS FOX

Nguyen Tuan Minh
TILLEKE & GIBBINS INTERNATIONAL LTD., MEMBER OF LEX MUNDI

Suong Dao Nguyen
JOHNSON STOKES & MASTER, MEMBER OF LEX MUNDI

Mai Nguyen
JOHNSON STOKES & MASTER, MEMBER OF LEX MUNDI

Linh D. Nguyen
VILAF - HONG DUC LAW FIRM

Hong Ha Nguyen
JOHNSON STOKES & MASTER, MEMBER OF LEX MUNDI

Anne-Laure Nguyen Trung Hoang
BAKER & MCKENZIE LLP

Viet D. Phan
TRAN H. N. & ASSOCIATES

Le Quang Phong
INTECO LTD. INTERNATIONAL FREIGHT FORWARDER

Tran Tuan Phong
VILAF - HONG DUC LAW FIRM

Hoang Phong-Anh
GIDE LOYRETTE NOUEL

Nasir PKM Abdul
FLÉCHEUX, NGO & ASSOCIÉS

Truong Nhat Quang
YKVN

Van Thi Quynh Dinh
PRICEWATERHOUSECOOPERS

Dinh Quynh Van
PRICEWATERHOUSECOOPERS

Martin Rama
WORLD BANK

David Ray
VIETNAM COMPETITIVENESS INITIATIVE, USAID

Yee Chung Seck
BAKER & MCKENZIE

Robert Strahota
U.S. SECURITIES AND EXCHANGE COMMISSION

Sri Swaminathan
VILAF - HONG DUC LAW FIRM

Ho Dang Thanh Huyen
PRICEWATERHOUSECOOPERS

Le Thi Thanh Loan
USAID

Do Thi Thu Ha
PRICEWATERHOUSECOOPERS

Dao Thi Thu Hien
FLÉCHEUX, NGO & ASSOCIÉS

Phan Nguyen Toan
LEADCO

Thanh Ha Tran
BAKER & MCKENZIE

V.N. Trinh
PANALPINA WORLD TRANSPORT

Nguyen Anh Tuan
YKVN

Pham Nghiem Xuan Bac
VISION & ASSOCIATES

WEST BANK AND GAZA

Ashraf R. Al-Far
HOUSE OF LAW & ADVOCACY

Omar Al-Huroub
COMPANIES REGISTRY, MINISTRY OF ECONOMY AND TRADE-INDUSTRY

Safwan Al-Nather
MINISTRY OF NATIONAL ECONOMY

Hassan Al-Qudsi
PALESTINE REAL ESTATE INVESTMENT CO.

Sharhabeel Al-Zaeem
SHARHABEEL AL-ZAEEM AND ASSOCIATES

Haytham L. Al-Zu'bi
AL-ZU'BI LAW OFFICE, ADVOCATES AND LEGAL CONSULTANTS

Ameed Z. Anani
HOUSE OF LAW & ADVOCACY

Khalil Ansara
ARKAN

Nada Atrash
ARCHITECT, ARCHITECTURE & DESIGN

Charlie Deeb
BDO NATIONAL BROTHERS

Ali Faroun
PALESTINIAN MONETARY AUTHORITY

Philip Farrage
BDO NATIONAL BROTHERS

Suheil K. Gedeon
COMMERCIAL BANK OF PALESTINE

Riyad Halki

Hiba Husseini
HUSSEINI AND HUSSEINI

Rami Husseini
HUSSEINI AND HUSSEINI

Marwan W. Jadon
LAW OFFICE OF MARWAN JADON

Fadi Kattan

Mohamed Khader
LAUSANNE TRADING CONSULTANTS

Hashem Khaleel
BDO NATIONAL BROTHERS

Rami Khoury
FMI

Nabil A. Mushahwar
LAW OFFICES OF NABIL A. MUSHAHWAR

Michael F. Orfaly
PRICEWATERHOUSECOOPERS

Nazmi Oweideh
ATTORNEY-AT-LAW

Taysir S. Qutteineh
PALESTINIAN BANKING CORPORATION

Samir Sahhar
OFFICE OF SAMIR SAHHAR

Karim Shehadeh
ATTORNEY

Sami Shehadeh
ATTORNEY

Farouq Zaiter
PADICO

Maurice Ziadeh

Kosty Ziadeh
ZIADEH LAW OFFICE

YEMEN

Ali Sheikh Alamakdi
YEMPAC CARGO

Abdalla Al-Meqbeli
ABDALLA AL-MEQBELI & ASSOCIATES

Moh'd Ali Lajam
MIDDLE EAST SHIPPING CO. LTD.

Mohamed Taha Hamood Al-Hashimi
MOHAMED TAHA HAMOOD & CO.

ZAMBIA

Shaira Adamali
PRICEWATERHOUSECOOPERS

D. Bwalya
CORPUS GLOBE ADVOCATES

Chewe K. Bwalya
D. H. KEMP & CO.

Elias Chipimo
CORPUS GLOBE ADVOCATES

David Doyle
MANICA ZAMBIA

Abdul Dudhia

Robin Durairajah
CHIBESAKUNDA & CO.

Harriet Kapampa Kapekele
CORPUS GLOBE ADVOCATES

Pixie Kasonde-Yangailo
P.H. YANGAILO & CO.

Glenan Kasumpa
ZAMBIA BUSINESS FORUM

Jacob Lushinga
ZAMBIA INVESTMENT CENTER

Gibson Masumbu
ZAMBIA BUSINESS FORUM

Victor Mesquita
MANICA AFRICA

Jyoti Mistry
PRICEWATERHOUSECOOPERS

Henry Musonda
KIRAN & MUSONDA ASSOCIATES

Marjorie Grace Mwenda
M.G. JOHNSON-MWENDA & CO.

Danmore Nyanga
PRICEWATERHOUSECOOPERS

Solly Patel
CHRISTOPHER, RUSSELL COOK & CO.

Kanti Patel
CHRISTOPHER, RUSSELL COOK & CO.

Henry Sakalas
ZAMBIA PRIVATISATION AGENCY

ZIMBABWE

Mark Badenhorst
PRICEWATERHOUSECOOPERS

Richard Beattie
THE STONE BEATTIE STUDIO

Peter Cawood
PRICEWATERHOUSECOOPERS

Innocent Chagonda
ATHERSTONE & COOK

Augustine Chigudu

Simplisius Chihambakwe
CHIHAMBAKWE, MUTIZWA & PARTNERS

Lionel Chinyamutansira

Paul De Chalain
PRICEWATERHOUSECOOPERS

Paul Fraser
LOFTY & FRASER LEGAL PRACTITIONERS

Emma Fundira

Obert Chaurura Gutu
GUTU & CHIKOWERO

Harry Kantor
KANTOR & IMMERMAN

Engelhardt Kongoro

Erle Koomets
PRICEWATERHOUSECOOPERS

Rodrick Kusano

Peter Lloyd
GILL, GODLONTON & GERRANS

Manuel Lopes
PRICEWATERHOUSECOOPERS

Weston Makwara

Rose Mazula

Stenford Moyo
SCANLEN & HOLDERNESS

B.T. Mtetwa

John Nhavira

Pindie Nyandoro

Vanani Nyangulu
V.S. NYANGULU & ASSOCIATES

John Robertson

Malvern Rusike

Josephat Tshuma
WEBB, LOW & BARRY

Chris Venturas
BYRON VENTURAS & PARTNERS

Ralph Watungwa

Doing Business 2007
How to reform

STANDING ORDER FORM

Standing orders are available to institutional customers only.

If you or your organization would like to automatically receive each new edition of **Doing Business** as it is published, please check the box below, complete your address details, and mail or fax this order form to us. This will establish a standing order for your organization, and you will be invoiced each year upon publication. You may also e-mail books@worldbank.org requesting your standing order for **Doing Business**. At any time you can cancel the standing order by sending an e-mail to books@worldbank.org.

☐ I would like to automatically receive each new edition of *Doing Business*. I understand that I will be invoiced each year upon publication.

Name

Title

Organization

Address

City

State   Zip/ Postal code

Country

Phone

Fax

Email

By mail
World Bank Publications
P.O. Box 960, Herndon
VA 20172-0960, USA

Online
www.worldbank.org/publications

By fax
+1-703-661-1501

Questions?
E-mail us at books@worldbank.org

By phone
+1-703-661-1580 or 800-645-7247

Institutional customers in the U.S. only:
Please include purchase order.

Available for US customers only, international customers please contact your local distributor to establish a standing order.

Individuals interested receiving future editions of **Doing Business** may request to be added to our mailing list at books@worldbank.org.

Please indicate in your e-mail that you would like to be added to the **Doing Business** e-mail list.